49.95

MATHEMATICAL
METHODS
IN
ECONOMICS

HANDBOOK OF APPLICABLE MATHEMATICS

GUIDEBOOKS

1: **MATHEMATICAL METHODS IN SOCIAL SCIENCE**
David J. Bartholomew, *London School of Economics and Political Science*
2: **MATHEMATICAL METHODS IN MANAGEMENT**
Geoffrey Gregory, *Loughborough University of Technology*
3: **MATHEMATICAL METHODS IN MEDICINE**
Part I Statistical and Analytical Technique
Edited by David Ingram, *The Medical College of St Bartholomew's Hospital* and Ralph Bloch, *McMaster University, Ontario*
4: **MATHEMATICAL METHODS IN MEDICINE**
Part II Applications in Clinical Specialities
Edited by David Ingram, *The Medical College of St Bartholomew's Hospital* and Ralph Block, *McMaster University, Ontario*
5: **MATHEMATICAL METHODS IN ENGINEERING**
Edited by Glyn A.O. Davies, *Imperial College*
6: **MATHEMATICAL METHODS IN ECONOMICS**
Edited by Frederick van der Ploeg, *London School of Economics and Political Science*

CORE VOLUMES

Volume I: **ALGEBRA**
Edited by Walter Ledermann, *University of Sussex* and Steven Vajda, *University of Sussex*
Volume II: **PROBABILITY**
Emlyn Lloyd, *University of Lancaster*
Volume III: **NUMERICAL METHODS**
Edited by Robert F. Churchhouse, *University College Cardiff*
Volume IV: **ANALYSIS**
Edited by Walter Ledermann, *University of Sussex* and Steven Vajda, *University of Sussex*
Volume V: **COMBINATORICS AND GEOMETRY (PARTS A AND B)**
Edited by Walter Ledermann, *University of Sussex* and Steven Vajda, *University of Sussex*
Volume VI: **STATISTICS (PARTS A AND B)**
Edited by Emlyn Lloyd, *University of Lancaster*

MATHEMATICAL METHODS IN ECONOMICS

Edited by
FREDERICK VAN DER PLOEG

London School of Economics and Political Science
and
Darwin College, Cambridge

A Wiley–Interscience Publication

JOHN WILEY & SONS

Chichester · New York · Brisbane · Toronto · Singapore

Copyright © 1984 by John Wiley & Sons Ltd.

Library of Congress Cataloging in Publication Data:

Main entry under title:
Mathematical methods in economics.

   'A Wiley Interscience publication.'
   Guidebook 6 to Handbook of applicable mathematics.
   Includes bibliographical references and index.
   1. Economics, Mathematical.   I. Ploeg, Frederick
van der, 1956–.   II. Handbook of applicable
mathematics.
HB135.M366 1984   330′.01′51   84–2327
ISBN 0 471 90422 8

British Library Cataloguing in Publication Data:

Mathematical methods in economics.—(Handbook of
   applicable mathematics; guidebook 6)
   1. Economics, Mathematical
   I. Ploeg, Frederick van der   II. Series
   510′.2433   HB135

   ISBN 0 471 90422 8

Photosetting by Thomson Press (India) Ltd., New Delhi
and printed by Page Bros. (Norwich) Ltd.

Contributing Authors

Vani K. Borooah, University of Cambridge, Cambridge, U.K.
David Currie, Queen Mary College, London, U.K.
Wim Driehuis, University of Amsterdam, Amsterdam, Netherlands
Robert A. Evans, University of Cambridge, Cambridge, U.K.
John D. Hey, University of York, York, U.K.
S. M. Kanbur, University of Essex, Colchester, U.K.
Tony Lawson, University of Cambridge, Cambridge, U.K.
Paul Levine, Polytechnic of the South Bank, London, U.K.
David A. Livesey, University of Cambridge, Cambridge, U.K.
Ben Lockwood, Birkbeck College, London, U.K.
David M. G. Newbery, Churchill College, Cambridge, U.K. and World Bank, Washington D.C., U.S.A.
M. H. Pesaran, Trinity College, Cambridge, U.K.
Frederick van der Ploeg, London School of Economics and Political Science, London, U.K.
F. Punzo, UCLA, Los Angeles, U.S.A., and University of Siena, Italy
Frank R. Schupp, University of Illinois, Urbana-Champaign, U.S.A.
Sir Richard Stone, University of Cambridge, Cambridge, U.K.
Stephen Vajda, University of Sussex, Brighton, U.K.
K. Velupillai, European University, Florence, Italy
Martin R. Weale, University of Cambridge, Cambridge, U.K.
Claus Weddepohl, University of Amsterdam, Amsterdam, Netherlands

Contents

PART V: ECONOMIC METHODOLOGY

PART VI: OPTIMIZATION OVER SPACE AND TIME

Editorial Note

Mathematical skills and concepts are increasingly being used in a great variety of activities. Applications of mathematics range from intricate research projects to practical problems in commerce and industry.

Yet many people who are engaged in this type of work have no academic training in mathematics and, perhaps at a late stage of their careers, have neither the inclination nor the time to embark upon a systematic study of mathematics.

To meet the needs of these users of mathematics we have produced a series of texts or *guidebooks* with uniform title. One of these is *Mathematical Methods in Economics* (with similar books on Medicine, Engineering and so on). The purpose of this volume is to describe how mathematics is used as a tool in Economics and to illustrate it with examples from this field. The guidebooks do not, as a rule, contain expositions of mathematics *per se*. A reader who wishes to learn about a particular mathematics topic, or consolidate his knowledge, is invited to consult the *core volumes* of the *Handbook of Applicable Mathematics*; they bear the titles

    I Algebra
   II Probability
  III Numerical Methods
  IV Analysis
   V Combinatorics and Geometry (Parts A and B)
  VI Statistics (Parts A and B)

The core volumes are specifically designed to elaborate on the mathematical concepts presented in the guidebooks. The aim is to provide information readily, to help towards an understanding of mathematical ideas and to enable the reader to master techniques needed in applications. Thus the guidebooks are furnished with references to the core volumes. It is essential to have an efficient reference system at our disposal. This system is explained fully in the Introduction to each core volume; we repeat here the following points. The core volumes are denoted by the Roman numerals mentioned above. Each mathematical item belongs to one of the six categories, namely:

  (i) Definitions
 (ii) Theorems, propositions, lemmas and corollaries
(iii) Equations and other displayed formulae
(iv) Examples
 (v) Figures
(vi) Tables

A typical item is designated by a Roman numeral followed by three Arabic numerals a, b, c, where a refers to the chapter, b to the section and c to the individual item enumerated consecutively in each category. For example, 'IV Theorem 6.2.3' is the third theorem of section 2 in Chapter 6 of the core volume IV. We refer to equation 6.2.3 of Volume IV as IV (6.2.3), and section 6.2 of Volume IV as IV §6.2.

We trust that these guidebooks will contribute to a deeper appreciation of the mathematical methods available for elucidating and solving problems in all the various disciplines covered by the series.

Preface and Acknowledgements

This guidebook to the *Handbook of Applicable Mathematics* is meant for students of economics, students of other disciplines (e.g. mathematics, engineering, geography and management science) interested in economic problems, and professional economists. The objective of the book is to introduce the reader to a number of economic problems whose solutions have benefited from the use of mathematics. Whenever mathematical concepts are employed, the reader is helped by cross-references to suitable chapters in the six core volumes which explain the relevant mathematics. The guidebook is not a textbook of mathematics for economists, but serves much more to 'whet the appetite' of the reader to solve economic problems with the aid of mathematical techniques.

Inevitably the choice of economic 'case studies' is somewhat subjective. We have, however, tried to attain the twin objectives of illustrating the applicability of as many mathematical techniques as possible and of discussing as many relevant economic problems as possible. Consequently the material in this book refers to all six core volumes and discusses linear economics, macroeconomic behaviour, macroeconomic models, microeconomics, economic methodology, urban economics and the economics of oil.

Some contributors would like to make acknowledgements. David Currie and Paul Levine are grateful to the Social Science Research Council (Grant AR8029) and David Newbery is grateful to the *Economic Journal* for permission to include parts of previously published material and to Eric Maskin and Alistair Ulph for extensive discussions on the economics of oil.

The editor would like to thank Steven Vajda, who has patiently read the chapters in this book. Many chapters have benefited substantially from his constructive comments. The editor is also grateful to Walter Lederman for his encouragement and many comments on this book. Carol van der Ploeg has done a superb job of preparing the cross-references, which are essential to the success of this book. The unfailing help of these three people has improved this book considerably. Nevertheless, the editor takes full responsibility for any remaining errors or omissions.

Mathematical Methods in Economics
Edited by F. van der Ploeg
© 1984, John Wiley & Sons, Ltd.

1

Introduction

FREDERICK VAN DER PLOEG, *London School of Economics and Darwin College, Cambridge, UK*

The use of mathematics to solve economic problems has a long and respectable history (see Theocharis (1961) and Irving Fisher's bibliography to Cournot (1963)). Theocharis traces the first application as far back as the principle of reciprocation for exchange of goods developed by Aristotle in his *Nicomachean Ethics, Book V* (pp. 1131–1133). The better known work on the economics of smuggling and optimal tax evasion was developed in Italy as early as 1711 by Ceva and later on by Beccaria in 1764. This early work applied elementary analysis and is mainly of historical interest. Perhaps the first mathematical contribution of significant economic importance was the classic work by Bernoulli (1738), later extended by Laplace in 1812 and Poisson in 1837, on the application of probability theory to expected utility analysis for decision making under uncertainty (see Chapter 17). Bernoulli's insight was that maximizing the expected monetary value is unsatisfactory, since this presumes risk-neutrality. Instead he suggested to allow for risk-aversion by maximizing the expected utility of money, although the axiomatic foundation of this approach had to be completed by von Neumann and Morgenstern (1947) much later. A much less formal contribution was the *Tableau Economique* developed by Quesnay in 1758, which turned out to be of extreme importance in subsequent applications of linear algebra to national accounting and linear economic models (see Chapters 2, 3 and 4). Another important early contribution was the work by von Thünen (1826) on location theory, who found that a series of concentric zones, each devoted to a single agricultural product, would develop around a town in the middle of an isolated plain. His analysis relied on simple analysis and optimization theory to show that the relative distance at which crops are farmed depends upon relative transportation costs (see Chapter 19). A final example of mathematical contributions to particular economic problems is the classic work by Gauss in 1845 on actuarial methods, who used advanced probability theory and statistical methods in his analysis of pensions and insurance (see Chapter 18).

His well-known work on least squares regression has found wide applicability in applied macroeconomics (see Chapters 5 and 7).

However, the credit for developing in 1838 the first systematic mathematical treatise on a wide variety of microeconomic problems covering the theories of value and exchange, demand, monopoly, competition and social income (see Chapters 12 and 13) must go to the 'founding father' of mathematical economics, Antoine Augustin Cournot. It took almost forty years for Cournot's approach to gain recognition, which was mainly due to Jevons (1871) and Walras (1874). The methods initiated by Cournot used marginal analysis of the behaviour of the producer and the household and relied upon calculus, in particular the use of total and partial derivatives and Lagrange multipliers, to solve and characterize microeconomic problems. Walras (1874) was the first to define the concept of a competitive equilibrium of an economy (see Chapter 14) and discuss the issue of stability of market clearing, although the formal set-theoretic proof of existence of a competitive equilibrium using the modern theory of topology had to wait until the work of Arrow and Debreu (1954).

The above history of great economists and mathematicians makes clear that the use of mathematics in economics is both common and respectable and, indeed, this is reflected in the mathematical nature of most modern economics textbooks and journals. Since economics belongs to the social studies, it is often a daunting task for the prospective economist to master the necessary mathematics. This is perhaps best illustrated by the following quotation.

> ask yourself what advice you would have to give to a young man who steps into your office with the following surprisingly common story: I am interested in economic theory. I know little mathematics. And when I look at the journals, I am greatly troubled. Must I give up hopes of being a theorist? Must I learn mathematics? If so, how much? I am already past twenty-one; am I past redemption?... I think a better answer might go somewhat as follows: Some of the most distinguished economic theorists have known some degree of mathematics. Obviously you can become a great theorist without knowing mathematics. Yet it is fair to say that you will have to be that much more clever and brilliant. (Samuelson, 1952, pp. 64–65)

Samuelson quotes, in addition to the classical mathematical economists Cournot, Edgeworth, Walras and Pareto, other great economists such as Marshall, Wicksell, Wicksteed, Cassel and Malthus with intermediate mathematical training. Some would argue that the use of mathematics *alone* is of not much use in understanding economic problems, although it does provide an invaluable tool for formalizing intuitive insights into economics precisely:

> But I know I had a growing feeling in the later years of my work at the subject that a good mathematical theorem dealing with economic hypotheses was

very unlikely to be good economics: and I went more and more on the rules—(1) Use mathematics as a shorthand language, rather than as an engine of inquiry. (2) Keep to them till you have done. (3) Translate into English. (4) Then illustrate by examples that are important in real life. (5) Burn the mathematics. (6) If you can't succeed in 4, burn 3. This last I did often. (Letter from A. Marshall to A. L. Bowley, 27 February 1906, in Pigou, 1956).

Thus mathematics can be used as an essential aid to work out economic ideas in a rigorous and consistent manner, although the end product is best communicated in common-sense language for the ideas to gain acceptance. It should be borne in mind however that mathematical economics is not merely the gloss on verbal reasoning, since many important concepts in economics can *only* be dealt with in mathematics from the outset.

The objective of this volume on *Mathematical Methods in Economics* is to discuss a variety of economic topics from a mathematical perspective. It is clear that the contents of all chapters have benefited considerably from a mathematical analysis of the economic issues and the hope is that the reader will be stimulated to formulate his own economic problems in terms of a mathematical model and to derive meaningful economic results from it. The unique feature of this volume is that, whenever a mathematical method is applied, the reader is given a cross-reference to the appropriate section in one (or more) of the six cone volumes of the *Handbook of Applicable Mathematics*. This sets it apart from the more research-oriented Arrow and Intriligator (1981), since the present volume offers complete guidance on the employed mathematics whenever needed. One benefit of this approach is that the reader 'learns by doing' a wide variety of mathematical methods in the course of studying interesting economic problems.

The chapters in the volume may be used as tutorial reading in quantitative economics courses, since they typically offer a very up-to-date survey of the literature at the same time as paying ample attention to technical details. They should also provide stimulating reading for the professional economist wishing to improve his knowledge of quantitative approaches to the subject and the mathematician looking for new fields of application. Each chapter may be read independently of the others, although the reader would benefit from reading the other chapters in the same part of the volume.

The volume consists of six parts: disaggregated approaches to economics, macroeconomic behaviour, macroeconomic models, microeconomics, economic methodology and optimization over space and time.

Disaggregated approaches to economics (Part I) discusses the importance of accounting matrices in linear economic analysis and social demography and emphasizes the duality between price and quantity systems. This part makes extensive use of linear algebra (Vol. I, Chapters 6, 7 and 11) and some use of Markov chains (Vol. II, Chapter 19). Since the methods described in this part have great practical importance and apply to matrices of large dimensions, efficient numerical methods for solving systems of linear equations, matrix inversion and computation of eigenvalues are essential (Vol. III, Chapters 3 and 4).

Macroeconomic behaviour (Part II) is concerned with the specification and estimation of aggregate consumption, expectations, investment and employment. This part mainly uses least squares regression, hypothesis testing and other statistical methods such as the Kalman filter (Vol. VI, Chapters 5, 8 and 20) and probability theory (Vol. II, Chapters 1, 5–8, 11, 13, 16 and 19), although the derivation of the equations describing economic behaviour makes use of algebra (Vol. I, Chapters 14 and 15), numerical solution of nonlinear equations (Vol. III, Chapter 5) and elementary analysis (Vol. IV, Chapters 1, 3 and 5).

Macroeconomic models (Part III) deals with macroeconomic principles, such as comparative statics, comparative dynamics and the correspondence principle, the New Classical School, rational expectations in a dynamic open economy and various macro-dynamic explanations of economic growth and fluctuations. This part is mainly concerned with solving and analysing the properties of economic models. The general philosophy of mathematical modelling is outlined elsewhere (Vol. IV, Chapter 14). The simplest economic models are static and correspond in mathematical terms to systems of simultaneous nonlinear equations, which can be solved by iterative numerical methods (Vol. III, Chapter 5) and analysed by means of multivariate differential calculus (Vol. IV, Chapters 1–5) and linear algebra (Vol. I, Chapters 5–7 and 14). The disequilibrium paths of an economy are formulated as dynamic economic models and correspond to differential or difference equations (Vol. IV, Chapters 7 and 8). Of course, the implications of economic policy and economic 'laws' are not precisely known and the models are therefore probabilistic (Vol. II, Chapters 8–10, 13, 16–19 and 22, Vol. IV, Chapter 18). Once the model has been formulated and analysed, the next question is how to choose the economic policy instruments to maximize social welfare. This is done with the aid of optimization theory (Vol. IV, Chapters 15–17, Vol. III, Chapter 11).

Microeconomics (Part IV) commences with discussing the behaviour of the individual firm and household. The economist approaches this problem by assuming that the individual acts to pursue human wants (profits, utility, etc.) as best as possible given scarce resources (production possibilities, budget, etc.), which corresponds in mathematics to optimization under constraints (Vol. I, Chapter 11; Vol. IV, Chapter 15). In practice the actions of one firm may depend upon the actions of other firms, which is most conveniently analysed with the aid of game theory (Vol. I, Chapter 13). This part also pursues the question of whether the actions of all firms and households in the economy pursuing their own self-interest can be compatible. In other words, whether a system of prices exists that clears all markets. This question is answered with the aid of fixed point theorems and other methods in topology (Vol. V, Chapter 5).

This part concludes with a discussion of aggregation of individual preferences, which is essential for the formulation of a social welfare function. This is an interesting exercise, since it shows how economists use an axiomatic approach to demonstrate the intricacies of voting paradoxes (Vol. IV, Chapters 1–2).

Economic methodology (Part V) deals with three quantitative methods found useful in economics. Chapter 16 discusses the measurement of inequality and poverty, which is of immense practical relevance. It makes extensive use of linear algebra, probability theory (Vol. II, Chapters 8–10) and analysis (Vol. IV, Chapters 2–5, 10, 15 and 21). The next chapter discusses decision making under uncertainty, which is based upon the classic work by von Neumann and Morgenstern and uses probability theory and analysis. Chapter 18 discusses actuarial methods, which rely a great deal on probability theory, statistical methods and numerical methods.

Optimization over space and time (Part VI) discusses the problems of urban economics (space) and the economics of oil (time). These chapters rely on analysis, in particular dynamic optimization theory (Vol. IV, Chapters 12, 15–17). There is a similarity with the optimal control techniques advocated by systems engineers (Engineering Guidebook, Chapter 14). The main difference is, however, that humans, in contrast to mechanical components of machines, might anticipate future events and react accordingly. This invalidates the well-known principle of dynamic programming (Vol. IV, Chapter 16), so that backward deduction is no longer valid. This raises problems of governments cheating the agents in the economy, discussed in Chapter 20.

REFERENCES

Aristotle (1965). *Ethics* (translated), Penguin, Harmmondsworth.
Arrow, K. J. and Debreu, G. (1954). Existence of equilibrium for a competitive economy, *Econometrica*, **22**, pp. 265–290.
Arrow, K. J. and Intriligator, M. D. (1981). *Handbook of Mathematical Economics*, Vols. I, II and III, North-Holland, Amsterdam.
Beccaria, C. (1764). Tentativo analitico sui contrabbandi, *Estratto dal foglio periodico initolato: Il Caffé*, vol. I, Brescia.
Bernoulli, D. (1738). Specimen theoriae novae de mensura sortis, *Commentarii Academia Scientiarum Imperialis Petropolitanae*, vol. V, pp. 175–192.
Ceva, G. (1711). De re nummaria, quoad fieri potuit geometrice tractata, ad illustrissimos et excellentissimos dominos Praesidem Quaestoresque hujus arciduclais, *Caesaraei Magistratus Manthae*, Mantova.
Cournot, A. (1838). *Recherches sur les principes mathématiques de la théorie des richesses*, Hachette, Paris. Also translated: (1963). *The Mathematical Principles of the Theory of Wealth* (with I. Fisher's original notes), R. D. Irwin, Homewood, Illinois.
Jevons, W. S. (1871). *The Theory of Political Economy*, Macmillan, London.
Pigou, A. (ed.) (1956). *Memorials of Alfred Marshall*, Kelley & Millman, Inc., New York.
Quesnay, F. (1758). *Tableau Economique*, Versailles.
Samuelson, P. A. (1952). Economic theory and mathematics—an appraisal, *American Economic Review (Supplements)*, **42**, 2, 56–66.

Theocharis, R. D. (1961). *Early Developments in Mathematical Economics*, Macmillan, London.

Von Neumann, J. and Morgenstern, O. (1947). *Theory of Games and Economic Behaviour*, Princeton University Press.

Von Thünen J. H. (1826). *Der Isolierte Staat in Beziehung auf Nationalökonomie und Landwirtschaft*, Gustav Fischer, Stuttgart.

Walras, L. (1874). *Éléments d'économie politique pure*, Lausanne, Paris and Basle.

Part I

Disaggregated Approaches to Economics

Mathematical Models in Economics
Edited by F. van der Ploeg
© 1984, John Wiley & Sons, Ltd.

2

Accounting Matrices in Economics and Demography

RICHARD STONE, *University of Cambridge, Cambridge, UK*

2.1 INTRODUCTION

Accounting matrices are widely used in the social sciences because they provide a convenient way of presenting systems of flows and of relating these to the corresponding stocks. The most obvious area of application is economics, where transactions (flows) are customarily set out in accounts, and the corresponding assets and liabilities (stocks) are shown in balance sheets. In this case the unit of account is money, and by grouping transactors and suitably elaborating the system of accounts we can set up a matrix for a whole region, such as a national economy, or some division of it, such as its productive system [see I, §6.2].

The applications of accounting matrices are not confined to economics, however. Matrices with human beings as the unit of account can be used to relate stocks and flows of population in a country or in some division of it, such as its school system.

These two types of accounting matrix, the economic and the socio-demographic, are not of precisely the same form. In economics the main object of study is the productive process and its contribution to the material well-being and wealth of a country; in social demography it is the development of individuals in society from birth to death. In both cases we are interested in transformation, but the pace and nature of the transformation are different in each case.

For the great majority of products transformation is not only rapid, a matter of days or at most months, but leads to loss of identity, which can be equated to death: the metal, beeswax, paint, fuels etc. absorbed by the chemical industry become a tin of polish; similarly, the eggs, flour, sugar, water, gas etc. absorbed by a household become a cake. The transformations that take place in households are very difficult to measure, although attempts have been made to estimate their value; but those that take place in the productive system are recorded and can be arranged in a static matrix relating the inputs of the period to the outputs of the period. The inputs are of two kinds: intermediate (raw materials, fuels, semi-finished goods) and primary (labour and capital, the factors of production). The outputs fall into two groups: intermediate products, which are re-absorbed into current production; and final products, which flow out of the productive system and may either be purchased by domestic buyers for current consumption, or go to increase the country's accumulated stock of capital goods (assets), or be exported. Thus only a small part of a period's total output, the assets which flow into accumulation, survives in the country beyond the period of account. This is entered in a balance sheet which shows closing assets and liabilities and carries the net stock of assets into the succeeding period.

For human beings transformation is slow and does not lead to loss of identity: the baby who becomes a schoolboy, then a worker and finally an old-age pensioner is the same individual throughout. Furthermore, the number of individuals in a population who survive in the country from period to period far exceeds the number of those who die or emigrate. In demography we start with the numbers in the different states in the opening stock and end, after transitions between states, reductions from deaths and emigrations (leavers) and increases from births and immigrations (new entrants), with the numbers in the different states in the closing stock. This information can be arranged in a dynamic matrix relating the entries in the opening stock vector to to those in the closing stock vector.

In spite of their different form, economic and demographic matrices can be combined provided the same definitions and classifications are used in both.

2.2 ECONOMICS: THE PRODUCTIVE SYSTEM

Let us begin with the productive system of a closed economy in which each branch (industry) produces a single good or service (commodity). Further, let us assume that there is only one primary input, labour say, and one buyer of final output. And let us measure all flows in money rather than in physical units; thus inputs will appear as costs (money outgoings) and outputs as sources of revenue

Table 2.1 An economic input–output matrix

	Production: industries (commodities)	Final outputs	Totals
Production: industries (commodities)	**W**	**e**	**q**
Primary inputs	**y′**	**0**	μ
Totals	**q′**	μ	

(money incomings). This information can be arranged in an input–output matrix with inputs in the columns and outputs in the rows, as shown in Table 2.1.

In Table 2.1 the period of account is one year. The meaning of the symbols is as follows [see I, §6.2]:

$\mathbf{W} =$ a square matrix showing the flows of intermediate products within the productive system (inter-industry flows): thus w_{jk} represents the amount of industry j's output used as an input into current production by industry k.

$\mathbf{e} =$ a column vector showing final outputs, that is goods and services sold by industries to final buyers.

$\mathbf{q} =$ a column vector showing total outputs by industries, which are equal in value to total inputs into industries.

$\mathbf{y}' =$ a row vector showing the costs of primary inputs into industries, that is wages, salaries etc. paid to the factors of production.

$\mu =$ a scalar showing the total cost of primary inputs, which is equal to the total value of final outputs.

The basic relationships between the entries in Table 2.1 can be expressed in three equations, as follows.

The quantity equation. From the row for industries we see that

$$\mathbf{q} = \mathbf{Wi} + \mathbf{e} \qquad (2.2.1)$$

where $\mathbf{i}$ denotes the vector $(1, 1, \ldots, 1)'$ so that $\mathbf{Wi}$ represents the row sums of $\mathbf{W}$. Thus all output is either intermediate or final. From this we can form the usual input–output coefficient matrix, $\mathbf{A}$ say, defined as

$$\mathbf{A} = \mathbf{W}\hat{\mathbf{q}}^{-1}, \qquad (2.2.2)$$

where $\hat{\mathbf{q}}^{-1}$ denotes the inverse of a diagonal matrix $\text{diag}(\mathbf{q})$ [see I, §6.4 and (6.7.3)]. On substituting for $\mathbf{W}$ from (2.2.2) into (2.2.1) we obtain

$$\mathbf{q} = \mathbf{Aq} + \mathbf{e}$$
$$= (\mathbf{I} - \mathbf{A})^{-1}\mathbf{e}, \qquad (2.2.3)$$

which expresses total outputs in terms of final outputs premultiplied by the matrix multiplier $(\mathbf{I} - \mathbf{A})^{-1}$. Provided $\mathbf{A}$ remains constant or any changes in its elements can be estimated, (2.2.3) enables us to calculate $\mathbf{q}$ for a given $\mathbf{e}$. A generalization of this type of multiplier analysis will be found in section 2.3 below.

The price equation. With a common unit of measurement, money, the column for industries can be added up as well as the row. Thus

$$\mathbf{q} = \mathbf{W}'\mathbf{i} + \mathbf{y} \qquad (2.2.4)$$

and if the vector of primary inputs per unit of output in the different industries is denoted by **f**, then

$$\mathbf{f} = \hat{\mathbf{q}}^{-1}\mathbf{y}. \tag{2.2.5}$$

On substituting for **W** and **y** from (2.2.2) and (2.2.5) into (2.2.4) and premultiplying the result by $\hat{\mathbf{q}}^{-1}$, we obtain

$$\begin{aligned} \mathbf{i} &= \mathbf{A}'\mathbf{i} + \mathbf{f} \\ &= (\mathbf{I} - \mathbf{A}')^{-1}\mathbf{f} \\ &= \mathbf{p}, \end{aligned} \tag{2.2.6}$$

where **p** denotes the vector of product prices. Naturally, if we measure products in £s worth all prices will be 1.

A basic identity. By combining (2.2.3) and (2.2.6) we can see that

$$\begin{aligned} \mathbf{f}'\mathbf{q} &= \mathbf{p}'(\mathbf{I} - \mathbf{A})(\mathbf{I} - \mathbf{A})^{-1}\mathbf{e} \\ &= \mathbf{p}'\mathbf{e} \end{aligned} \tag{2.2.7}$$

or total primary input equals total final output.

So far we have assumed that each industry produces only its own characteristic commodity. In fact some industries have more than one characteristic commodity, and almost every industry produces, either as subsidiary products or as by-products, some of the commodities characteristic of other industries. To see what this implies we must elaborate Table 2.1 and replace it by Table 2.2.

In table 2.2, commodities are distinguished from industries and **W** is replaced by **U** and **V**. Thus:

U = a matrix of dimensions commodity × industry, termed the absorption matrix: each row of **U** shows the amounts of a given commodity absorbed by

Table 2.2 An elaborated version of Table 2.1

		Production		Final outputs	Totals
		Commodities	Industries		
Production	Commodities		U	e	q
	Industries	V			g
Primary inputs			y′		μ
Totals		q′	g′	μ	

the different industries; and each column shows the amounts of different commodities absorbed by a given industry.

$\mathbf{e}$ = a column vector with as many elements as there are commodities, showing final commodity outputs.

$\mathbf{q}$ = a column vector with as many elements as there are commodities, showing total commodity outputs.

$\mathbf{V}$ = a matrix of dimensions industry × commodity, termed the make matrix: each row of $\mathbf{V}$ shows the amounts of different commodities made by a given industry; and each column shows the amounts of a given commodity made by the different industries.

$\mathbf{g}$ = a column vector with as many elements as there are industries, showing the total outputs of industries = total inputs into industries.

$\mathbf{y}'$ = a row vector with as many elements as there are industries, showing the costs of primary inputs into industries.

μ = a scalar showing the total cost of primary inputs = the total value of final outputs.

In this table the third row and column are essentially the same as in Table 2.1, but this arrangement brings out the fact that final buyers buy commodities while income to the factors of production (the primary inputs) is paid out by industries.

In terms of Table 2.2, input–output analysis rests on six relationships, of which three are arithmetic identities and the other three are assumptions relating to the conditions of production.

The first relationship is

$$\mathbf{q} = \mathbf{Ui} + \mathbf{e}, \tag{2.2.8}$$

where $\mathbf{Ui}$ represents the row sums of $\mathbf{U}$. This is essentially the same as (2.2.1).

The second relationship is

$$\mathbf{q} = \mathbf{V}'\mathbf{i}, \tag{2.2.9}$$

that is to say, the total output of each commodity is equal to the sum of the amounts made in each of the industries.

The third relationship is

$$\mathbf{g} = \mathbf{Vi}, \tag{2.2.10}$$

that is to say, each industry's total output is equal to the sum of its outputs of each commodity.

The fourth relationship is

$$\mathbf{U} = \mathbf{B}\hat{\mathbf{g}}, \tag{2.2.11}$$

where $\mathbf{B}$ is a matrix of coefficients of dimensions commodity × industry and $\hat{\mathbf{g}} = \mathrm{diag}(\mathbf{g})$ [see I, (6.7.3)]. Thus it is assumed in (2.2.11) that intermediate inputs of commodities are proportional to the industry outputs into which they enter.

The fifth relationship is

$$\mathbf{V}' = \mathbf{C}\hat{\mathbf{g}}, \tag{2.2.12}$$

where $\mathbf{C}$ is a matrix of coefficients of the same dimensions as $\mathbf{B}$. Thus it is assumed in (2.2.12) that each industry makes commodities in its own fixed proportions.

The final relationship is

$$\mathbf{V} = \mathbf{D}\hat{\mathbf{q}}, \tag{2.2.13}$$

where $\mathbf{D}$ is a matrix of coefficients of dimensions industry × commodity. Thus it is assumed in (2.2.13) that commodities come in their own fixed proportions from the various industries.

In constructing an input–output table from the data of Table 2.2 we can make either of two limiting assumptions or we can mix them: we can assume either a commodity technology or an industry technology or some combination of the two.

The assumption of a commodity technology. This means that a commodity is assumed to have the same input structure whichever industry it is produced in. This can be expressed by combining (2.2.8), (2.2.9), (2.2.11) and (2.2.12). Thus we can write

$$\begin{aligned} \mathbf{q} &= \mathbf{U}\mathbf{i} + \mathbf{e} \\ &= \mathbf{B}\mathbf{g} + \mathbf{e} \\ &= \mathbf{B}\mathbf{C}^{-1}\mathbf{q} + \mathbf{e} \\ &= (\mathbf{I} - \mathbf{B}\mathbf{C}^{-1})^{-1}\mathbf{e} \end{aligned} \tag{2.2.14}$$

and

$$\begin{aligned} \mathbf{g} &= \mathbf{C}^{-1}(\mathbf{I} - \mathbf{B}\mathbf{C}^{-1})^{-1}\mathbf{e} \\ &= (\mathbf{I} - \mathbf{C}^{-1}\mathbf{B})^{-1}\mathbf{C}^{-1}\mathbf{e}. \end{aligned} \tag{2.2.15}$$

Thus, still denoting the input–output coefficient matrix by $\mathbf{A}$, we find that on this assumption: $\mathbf{A} = \mathbf{B}\mathbf{C}^{-1}$ for a commodity × commodity table; and $\mathbf{A} = \mathbf{C}^{-1}\mathbf{B}$ for an industry × industry table. It will be noticed that both (2.2.14) and (2.2.15) involve the matrix inverse $\mathbf{C}^{-1}$, so that the assumption of a commodity technology can only be used if the number of commodities is so defined as to be equal to the number of industries.

The assumption of an industry technology. This means that an industry is assumed to have the same input structure whatever its product mix. This can be expressed by combining (2.2.8), (2.2.10), (2.2.11) and (2.2.13). Thus we can write

$$\begin{aligned} \mathbf{q} &= \mathbf{U}\mathbf{i} + \mathbf{e} \\ &= \mathbf{B}\mathbf{g} + \mathbf{e} \\ &= \mathbf{B}\mathbf{D}\mathbf{q} + \mathbf{e} \\ &= (\mathbf{I} - \mathbf{B}\mathbf{D})^{-1}\mathbf{e} \end{aligned} \tag{2.2.16}$$

and

$$\mathbf{g} = \mathbf{D}(\mathbf{I} - \mathbf{BD})^{-1}\mathbf{e}$$
$$= (\mathbf{I} - \mathbf{DB})^{-1}\mathbf{De}. \qquad (2.2.17)$$

In this case we find that $\mathbf{A} = \mathbf{BD}$ for a commodity $\times$ commodity table and $\mathbf{A} = \mathbf{DB}$ for an industry $\times$ industry table.

Mixed technology assumptions. We can mix the limiting assumptions. Let us divide the make matrix, $\mathbf{V}$, into two parts so that [see I, §6.2 (ii)]

$$\mathbf{V} = \mathbf{V}_1 + \mathbf{V}_2, \qquad (2.2.18)$$

say, where the elements of $\mathbf{V}_1$ are outputs which it seems reasonable to treat on the assumption of a commodity technology; and those of $\mathbf{V}_2$ are to be treated on the assumption of an industry technology. Many subsidiary products are likely to come into $\mathbf{V}_1$ while by-products are likely to come into $\mathbf{V}_2$. We might assume that

$$\mathbf{g}_1 = \mathbf{V}_1\mathbf{i}$$
$$= \mathbf{C}_1^{-1}\mathbf{q}_1 \qquad (2.2.19)$$

and

$$\mathbf{g}_2 = \mathbf{V}_2\mathbf{i}$$
$$= \mathbf{D}_2\mathbf{q}, \qquad (2.2.20)$$

from which we can write

$$\mathbf{q}_2 = \mathbf{V}_2'\mathbf{i}$$
$$= \hat{\mathbf{q}}\mathbf{D}_2'\mathbf{i}$$
$$= \widehat{\mathbf{D}_2'\mathbf{i}}\mathbf{q}, \qquad (2.2.21)$$

where $\widehat{\mathbf{D}_2'\mathbf{i}}$ denotes a diagonal matrix formed from the vector $\mathbf{D}_2'\mathbf{i}$. We can combine these equations to give

$$\mathbf{g} = \mathbf{g}_1 + \mathbf{g}_2$$
$$= [\mathbf{C}_1^{-1}(\mathbf{I} - \widehat{\mathbf{D}_2'\mathbf{i}}) + \mathbf{D}_2]\mathbf{q}, \qquad (2.2.22)$$

which, when combined with the second row of (2.2.14) or (2.2.16), gives

$$\mathbf{q} = \mathbf{B}[\mathbf{C}_1^{-1}(\mathbf{I} - \widehat{\mathbf{D}_2'\mathbf{i}}) + \mathbf{D}_2]\mathbf{q} + \mathbf{e}$$
$$= \{\mathbf{I} - \mathbf{B}[\mathbf{C}_1^{-1}(\mathbf{I} - \widehat{\mathbf{D}_2'\mathbf{i}}) + \mathbf{D}_2]\}^{-1}\mathbf{e}$$
$$= (\mathbf{I} - \mathbf{BR})^{-1}\mathbf{e}, \qquad (2.2.23)$$

say. Since $\mathbf{g} = \mathbf{Rq}$, it follows that

$$\mathbf{g} = \mathbf{R}(\mathbf{I} - \mathbf{BR})^{-1}\mathbf{e}$$
$$= (\mathbf{I} - \mathbf{RB})^{-1}\mathbf{Re}. \qquad (2.2.24)$$

In this case the input–output coefficient matrix is: $\mathbf{A} = \mathbf{BR}$ for a commodity $\times$ commodity table; and $\mathbf{A} = \mathbf{RB}$ for an industry $\times$ industry table.

Alternatively, it might seem preferable to replace (2.2.19), (2.2.20) and (2.2.21) by

$$\mathbf{g}_1 = \mathbf{V}_1 \mathbf{i}$$
$$= \mathbf{D}_1 \mathbf{q}_1 \tag{2.2.25}$$

$$\mathbf{q}_2 = \mathbf{V}_2' \mathbf{i}$$
$$= \mathbf{C}_2 \mathbf{g} \tag{2.2.26}$$

and

$$\mathbf{g}_2 = \mathbf{V}_2 \mathbf{i}$$
$$= \hat{\mathbf{g}} \mathbf{C}_2' \mathbf{i}$$
$$= \widehat{\mathbf{C}_2' \mathbf{i}} \mathbf{g}. \tag{2.2.27}$$

Proceeding as before, we find that

$$\mathbf{q} = (\mathbf{I} - \mathbf{BS})^{-1} \mathbf{e} \tag{2.2.28}$$

and

$$\mathbf{g} = (\mathbf{I} - \mathbf{SB})^{-1} \mathbf{Se} \tag{2.2.29}$$

where

$$\mathbf{S} = (\mathbf{I} + \mathbf{D}_1 \mathbf{C}_2 - \widehat{\mathbf{C}_2' \mathbf{i}})^{-1} \mathbf{D}_1. \tag{2.2.30}$$

Some numerical examples of the results obtained with these different forms are given in UNSO (1968, pp. 42–45).

2.3. PRODUCTION AND CONSUMPTION: INDUSTRIES AND SECTORS

The type of analysis described in the last section can be applied to other parts of the economy. For instance, we can introduce consumers into the picture. In order to do this, the vector of final outputs, $\mathbf{e}$, must be disaggregated so as to distinguish between commodities sold to domestic buyers for consumption within the period of account and all other final outputs. Domestic consumption is subdivided by category of consumer, or sector (households, central government etc.), and becomes an endogenous part of the system. All other final outputs can at this stage be compressed into a single vector assumed to be given exogenously. At the same time the vector of primary input costs, $\mathbf{y}'$, is disaggregated into an

Table 2.3 An extension of Table 2.1

	Production: industries	Consumption: sectors	All other accounts	Totals
Production: industries	W	C	n	q
Consumption: sectors	Y	H	t	r
All other accounts	m'	s'	0	ρ
Totals	q'	r'	ρ	

endogenous matrix of factor-income payments to the domestic sectors supplemented by a vector containing all other costs incurred by industries. The extended system then looks as in Table 2.3. In this table, for simplicity, production is represented as in Table 2.1, without distinction between industries and commodities.

In Table 2.3:

$\mathbf{W}$ = a square matrix showing inter-industry flows of intermediate products.

$\mathbf{C}$ = a matrix of dimensions industry × sector, showing sales of consumption goods and services by the industries to the domestic sectors.

$\mathbf{n}$ = a column vector showing sales by the industries to the exogenous accounts (capital goods and exports).

$\mathbf{q}$ = a column vector showing total outputs by industries = total inputs into industries.

$\mathbf{y}$ = a matrix of dimensions sector × industry, showing payments of factor incomes to the domestic sectors plus payments of indirect taxes by the industries.

$\mathbf{H}$ = a square matrix showing inter-sectoral current transfers (gifts, benefits, taxes on income etc.).

$\mathbf{t}$ = a column vector showing incomings into the sectors from the exogenous accounts (mainly income from the rest of the world).

$\mathbf{r}$ = a column vector showing the total incomes = the total outlays of the sectors.

$\mathbf{m}'$ = a row vector showing outgoings from the industries to the exogenous accounts (provisions for the depreciation of fixed assets, purchases of imports and factor payments to the rest of the world).

$\mathbf{s}'$ = a row vector showing outgoings from the sectors to the exogenous accounts (mainly saving and transfers to the rest of the world).

ρ = a scalar showing the total incomings = the total outgoings of the exogenous accounts (domestic capital accounts and rest of the world accounts).

It can be seen from the definitions of $\mathbf{n}, \mathbf{t}, \mathbf{m}'$ and ρ that the assumption of a closed economy is now discarded and the system opened to recognize the existence of the rest of the world, which plays an important role in determining a country's economic behaviour.

From Table 2.3 we can construct four coefficient matrices for the endogenous parts of the system: $\mathbf{A}_{11} = \mathbf{W}\hat{\mathbf{q}}^{-1}$, $\mathbf{A}_{12} = \mathbf{C}\hat{\mathbf{r}}^{-1}$, $\mathbf{A}_{21} = \mathbf{Y}\hat{\mathbf{q}}^{-1}$ and $\mathbf{A}_{22} = \mathbf{H}\hat{\mathbf{r}}^{-1}$. (Section 2 of Chapter 3 gives a very simple example of this procedure.) These matrices can be arranged in the form [see I, §6.6]

$$\mathbf{A} = \begin{bmatrix} \mathbf{A}_{11} & \mathbf{A}_{12} \\ \mathbf{A}_{21} & \mathbf{A}_{22} \end{bmatrix}$$

$$= \begin{bmatrix} \mathbf{A}_{11} & \mathbf{0} \\ \mathbf{0} & \mathbf{A}_{22} \end{bmatrix} + \begin{bmatrix} \mathbf{0} & \mathbf{A}_{12} \\ \mathbf{A}_{21} & \mathbf{0} \end{bmatrix}$$

$$= \mathbf{B} + \mathbf{C}, \tag{2.3.1}$$

say. If we denote by $\mathbf{y}$ the vector of totals of the endogenous accounts, so that $\mathbf{y} = \{\mathbf{q} \quad \mathbf{r}\}$ [see I, (5.10.2)], and by $\mathbf{x}$ the vector of injections into these accounts from the exogeneous accounts, so that $\mathbf{x} = \{\mathbf{n} \quad \mathbf{t}\}$, and if we put $\mathbf{D} = (\mathbf{I} - \mathbf{B})^{-1}\mathbf{C}$, then

$$
\begin{aligned}
\mathbf{y} &= \mathbf{Ay} + \mathbf{x} \\
&= \mathbf{By} + \mathbf{Cy} + \mathbf{x} \\
&= \mathbf{Dy} + (\mathbf{I} - \mathbf{B})^{-1}\mathbf{x} \\
&= (\mathbf{I} - \mathbf{D})^{-1}(\mathbf{I} - \mathbf{B})^{-1}\mathbf{x} \\
&= (\mathbf{I} + \mathbf{D})(\mathbf{I} - \mathbf{D}^2)^{-1}(\mathbf{I} - \mathbf{B})^{-1}\mathbf{x} \\
&= \mathbf{M}_3 \mathbf{M}_2 \mathbf{M}_1 \mathbf{x} \\
&= \mathbf{Mx} \qquad\qquad\qquad\qquad\qquad\qquad (2.3.2)
\end{aligned}
$$

say. This generalization of the matrix multiplier appeared in Pyatt, Roe and associates (1977). An application to the British national accounts is given in Stone (1978).

If we write out in full the matrices in the sixth row of (2.3.2) we obtain the following expressions.

First [see I, §6.6]

$$
\mathbf{M}_1 = \begin{bmatrix} (\mathbf{I} - \mathbf{A}_{11})^{-1} & \mathbf{0} \\ \mathbf{0} & (\mathbf{I} - \mathbf{A}_{22})^{-1} \end{bmatrix}. \qquad (2.3.3)
$$

Thus the multiplier effects included in $\mathbf{M}_1$ arise from the repercussions of the initial injection within the group of accounts which it originally entered, and so may be said to measure the intra-group effects.

Second,

$$
\mathbf{M}_2 = \begin{bmatrix} \mathbf{I} - (\mathbf{I} - \mathbf{A}_{11})^{-1}\mathbf{A}_{12}(\mathbf{I} - \mathbf{A}_{22})^{-1}\mathbf{A}_{21} & \mathbf{0} \\ \mathbf{0} & \mathbf{I} - (\mathbf{I} - \mathbf{A}_{22})^{-1}\mathbf{A}_{21}(\mathbf{I} - \mathbf{A}_{11})^{-1}\mathbf{A}_{12} \end{bmatrix}
$$

$$
(2.3.4)
$$

Thus the multiplier effects included in $\mathbf{M}_2$ arise from the repercussions of the initial injection when it has completed a tour through both groups and returned to the one it originally entered, and so may be said to measure the inter-group effects.

Finally,

$$
\mathbf{M}_3 = \begin{bmatrix} \mathbf{I} & (\mathbf{I} - \mathbf{A}_{11})^{-1}\mathbf{A}_{12} \\ (\mathbf{I} - \mathbf{A}_{22})^{-1}\mathbf{A}_{21} & \mathbf{I} \end{bmatrix}. \qquad (2.3.5)
$$

Thus the multiplier effects included in $\mathbf{M}_3$ arise from the repercussions of the initial injection when it has completed a tour outside its original group without returning to it, and so may be said to measure the extra-group effects.

It is a simple matter to express $\mathbf{M}$ in terms of additive components, and for some purposes it is convenient to do so. Thus

$$\mathbf{M} = \mathbf{I} + (\mathbf{M}_1 - \mathbf{I}) + (\mathbf{M}_2 - \mathbf{I})\mathbf{M}_1 + (\mathbf{M}_3 - \mathbf{I})\mathbf{M}_2\mathbf{M}_1. \qquad (2.3.6)$$

In this expression we start in the first term with a matrix of injections, the unit matrix $\mathbf{I}$, and in the succeeding terms we add on the effects associated with $\mathbf{M}_1$, $\mathbf{M}_2$ and $\mathbf{M}_3$.

While the matrices described above are useful in gaining some insight into economic interdependence, their limitations will be apparent. In the first place all the relationships are linear. In the second place they are static and take no account of the time needed for effects to work themselves out. In the third place we have chosen, as is often done, to treat as exogenous certain parts of the system which are not altogether exogenous: current spending is likely to induce both new investment, which is part of the capital accounts, and exports, which are part of the rest of the world account. Finally, to conclude a list which is by no means complete, I have not distinguished between quantity changes and price changes: if it appears that food expenditure will rise by so much, there is nothing to tell us whether this means more food at the same prices or the same amount of food at higher prices. None of this is new. There is a limit to what we can hope to get out of even sophisticated multiplier analysis, and if we want to deal with the issues just raised we must build more complicated models.

2.4. NATIONAL ACCOUNTS AND BALANCE SHEETS

In Table 2.3 all transactions other than those relating to production and consumption were compressed into a single row-and-column pair. If this is disaggregated to distinguish between capital transactions and foreign transactions we obtain four sets of accounts relating respectively to production, consumption, accumulation and the rest of the world. These are the four national accounts, which show all the flows occurring in a country's economy within a given period. The capital accounts can then be complemented by revaluation

Table 2.4 A system of national accounts and balance sheets

	1	2	3	4	5	6	7
1. Opening stocks				A_{14}			
2. Production		T_{22}	T_{23}	T_{24}	T_{25}		
3. Consumption		T_{32}	T_{33}	T_{34}	T_{35}		
4. Accumulation	L_{41}		T_{43}	T_{44}	T_{45}	R_{46}	L_{47}
5. Rest of the world		T_{52}	T_{53}	T_{54}			
6. Revaluations				R_{64}			
7. Closing stocks				A_{74}			

accounts and balance sheets showing the opening and closing stocks of assets and liabilities. The complete system is shown in Table 2.4. In this table the inner square contains the national accounts and the outer entries represent the revaluation accounts and balance sheets. All the entries are matrices. The symbol **T** denotes a matrix of transactions, whose position in the system is indicated by suffixes; **A** denotes assets; **L** denotes liabilities; and **R** denotes revaluations.

In Table 2.4:

A_{14} = opening net stock of written down tangible assets (buildings, plant, machinery etc.) and financial assets (securities, cash etc.) held by the domestic sectors in this country and abroad.

T_{22} = inter-industry flows of domestic intermediate products.

T_{23} = sales of consumption goods and services to the domestic sectors.

T_{24} = sales of capital goods to the domestic sectors.

T_{25} = sales of all goods and services to the rest of the world (exports).

T_{32} = payments of factor incomes to the domestic sectors plus payments of indirect taxes (net of subsidies) plus provisions for depreciation.

T_{33} = Inter-sectoral current transfers

T_{34} = The negative of provisions for depreciation.

T_{35} = factor incomes and current transfers received by the domestic sectors from the rest of the world.

L_{41} = opening net worth (wealth) = opening gross assets less opening liabilities = opening net assets.

T_{43} = saving by the domestic sectors.

T_{44} = inter-sectoral lending and capital transfers.

T_{45} = net capital transfers from the rest of the world.

R_{46} = revaluations of net worth.

L_{47} = closing net worth = opening net worth plus new claims issued (net) plus revaluations = closing net assets.

T_{52} = purchases of goods and services from the rest of the world (imports) plus factor incomes paid abroad.

T_{53} = current transfers paid by the domestic sectors to the rest of the world.

T_{54} = net lending to the rest of the world.

R_{64} = revaluations of net assets.

A_{74} = closing net stock of assets = opening net stock plus new investment (net) plus revaluations = closing net worth.

It will be noticed that several of the entries in Table 2.4 are qualified as net: assets are net of liabilities, indirect taxes are net of subsidies and so on. This is inevitable in a table as aggregated as this one is. The degree of disaggregation needed to show explicitly the entries here netted out would be out of place in this chapter. However, Table 2.4 is based, with some variations, on the United Nations' System of National Accounts (SNA for short) and the reader who wishes to pursue the matter will find a full description in UNSO (1968, especially pp. 4–11 and 17–32).

In setting out their national accounts most market economies make use of the SNA or something like it. The centrally planned economies, on the other hand, use a different framework usually called the System of Balances of the National Economy or the Material Products System (MPS for short). The main difference between the two systems lies in the definition of production: in the MPS production is restricted to 'material products', which include a few services, whereas in the SNA it includes all services. Ignoring other, less important differences, the two systems can be compared by arranging the data in three accounts, one for the production of material products, one for the production of services and one for everything else. These three accounts can be brought together in a matrix, **P** say, as follows:

$$\mathbf{P} = \begin{bmatrix} P_{11} & P_{12} & P_{13} \\ P_{21} & P_{22} & P_{23} \\ P_{31} & P_{32} & P_{33} \end{bmatrix} \tag{2.4.1}$$

In this matrix the first row and column relate to material production. In the row we find the destinations of this output: P_{11} = material products absorbed in material production; P_{12} = material products absorbed in rendering services; and P_{13} = material products absorbed in everything else. In the column we find the corresponding costs: P_{11} = material products absorbed as intermediate inputs; P_{21} = services absorbed as intermediate inputs; and P_{31} = all other costs. Analogous explanations could be given for the entries in the second row and column, relating to services, and for those in the third row and column, relating to everything else.

Final output can be expressed for each system in terms of the entries in 2.4.1. Denoting final output (MPS) by α, we have

$$\alpha = P_{12} + P_{13} \tag{2.4.2}$$

and, denoting final output (SNA) by β, we have

$$\beta = P_{13} + P_{23}. \tag{2.4.3}$$

Since each row-and-column pair in (2.4.1) is an account which balances, it follows from the second row and column that

$$P_{23} - P_{12} = P_{32} - P_{21}. \tag{2.4.4}$$

Thus $\beta \gtreqless \alpha$ according as $P_{23} \gtreqless P_{12}$ or $P_{32} \gtreqless P_{21}$: that is to say, according as the input of services into everything else $\gtreqless$ the input of services into material production.

A description of the MPS is given in UNSO (1971) and a comparison of the conceptual relationships of the two systems in UNSO (1977). A numerical comparison is given in Stone (1970, XIII).

2.5. SOCIAL DEMOGRAPHY: THE STANDARD MATRIX

As was said in the introduction, economic and socio-demographic matrices are not of precisely the same form. The standard demographic stock-flow matrix is set out in Table 2.5.

In Table 2.5 the period of account is one year (year θ). The meaning of the symbols is as follows:

α = a scalar showing the number of babies born in our country during year θ who die in our country before the end of the year.

β = a scalar showing the number of babies born in our country during year θ who emigrate before the end of the year.

b = a column vector showing the number of babies born in our country during year θ who survive in our country to the end of the year.

Writing $\mathbf{i} = \{1, 1, 1, \ldots, 1\}$, then $\alpha + \beta + \mathbf{i}'\mathbf{b}$ denotes the total live births in our country during year θ.

δ = a scalar showing the number of immigrants into our country during year θ who die in our country before the end of the year.

γ = a scalar showing the number of immigrants into our country during year θ who emigrate before the end of the year.

f = a column vector showing the number of immigrants into our country during year θ who survive in our country to the end of the year.

The sum $\delta + \gamma + \mathbf{i}'\mathbf{f}$ denotes the total immigrants into our country in year θ.

$\mathbf{d}'$ = a row vector showing the deaths in our country during year θ of those who were present in it at the beginning of the year.

The sum $\alpha + \delta + \mathbf{d}'\mathbf{i}$ denotes the total deaths in our country in year θ.

$\mathbf{e}'$ = a row vector showing the emigrants from our country in year θ who were present in it at the beginning of the year.

The sum $\beta + \gamma + \mathbf{e}'\mathbf{i}$ denotes the total emigrants from our country in year θ.

Table 2.5 The standard demographic stock-flow matrix

State at new year θ / State at new year $\theta + 1$	Other world	Rest of this world	Our country: opening states	Closing stocks
Other world	α	δ	$\mathbf{d}'$	
Rest of this world	β	γ	$\mathbf{e}'$	
Our country: closing states	**b**	**f**	**S**	$\Lambda\mathbf{n}$
Opening stocks			$\mathbf{n}'$	

$\mathbf{S}$ = a square matrix showing the survivors in our country through year θ, classified by their opening states in the columns and their closing states in the rows.

$\mathbf{n'}$ = a row vector showing the opening stock in each state. It can be seen that $\mathbf{n} = \mathbf{d} + \mathbf{e} + \mathbf{S'i}$; in other words, the people present in our country at the beginning of year θ either die there or emigrate in the course of the year or survive there to the end of the year.

$\Lambda\mathbf{n}$ = a column vector showing the closing stock in each state. The symbol Λ denotes the shift operator defined by the relationship $\Lambda^{\tau}\mathbf{n}(\theta) = \mathbf{n}(\tau + \theta)$. It can be seen that $\Lambda\mathbf{n} = \mathbf{b} + \mathbf{f} + \mathbf{Si}$; in other words, the people present in our country at the end of year θ were either born in it or immigrated into it in the course of the year or were already present in it at the beginning of the year.

The flows in Table 2.5 can be classified according to whether or not the individuals they contain form part of the opening or of the closing stock. The people represented by α, β, γ and δ appear in neither; those represented by $\mathbf{d}$ and $\mathbf{e}$ appear in the opening but not in the closing stock; those represented by $\mathbf{b}$ and $\mathbf{f}$ appear in the closing but not in the opening stock; and those represented by $\mathbf{S}$ appear in both.

The framework provided by Table 2.5 can in principle accommodate any classification of the population by subdividing the single row and column for our country into as many rows and column as there are states we wish to distinguish. If the only transition we wish to record is ageing, the states may be either single years of age or age-groups. In the first case the non-zero elements in S will be confined to the leading subdiagonal [see I, (6.2.6)], since in a year every survivor will become a year older. In the second case there will be non-zero elements in both the diagonal and the leading subdiagonal. For instance, if our age-groups span five years, the first group in the opening stock will be aged 0 to 4; in year θ the children in the four younger ages will remain in that group and therefore appear in the diagonal; only the 4-year-olds will move out of it and will therefore appear in the subdiagonal, flowing into the closing stock as members of the second group, ages 5 to 9. If we add other classifications to age, relating say to learning, earning and 'non-active' states (infancy, retirement etc.), then the non-zero entries will appear in diagonal and subdiagonal blocks instead of single cells.

Table 2.5 is a slightly expanded version of the demographic matrix given in UNSO (1975, p. 42), which also gives numerical examples of most of the models described in the next three sections.

2.6. TWO BASIC IDENTITIES AND SOME SIMPLE MODELS

We can see from Table 2.5 that identities are given by the row and column for our country. From the row,

$$\Lambda\mathbf{n} = \mathbf{Si} + \mathbf{b} + \mathbf{f}, \qquad (2.6.1)$$

Table 2.6 A variant of Table 2.5

State at new year $\theta+1$ \\ State at new year θ	Elsewhere	Our country: opening states	Closing stocks
Elsewhere	α^*	$\mathbf{d}'$	
Our country: closing states	$\mathbf{b}^*$	$\mathbf{S}$	$\Lambda\mathbf{n}^*$
Opening stocks		$\mathbf{n}^*$	

and from the column, after transposition.

$$\mathbf{n} = \mathbf{S}'\mathbf{i} + \mathbf{d} + \mathbf{e}. \tag{2.6.2}$$

For most purposes it is desirable to treat migration as net immigration, that is to subtract $\mathbf{e}$ from both sides of each equation. This will ensure that we restrict ourselves to people who remain in our country until they die. Let us therefore rewrite Table 2.5 as Table 2.6, where $\alpha^* = \alpha + \delta - \beta$, $\mathbf{b}^* = \mathbf{b} + \mathbf{f} - \mathbf{e}$, $\mathbf{n}^* = \mathbf{n} - \mathbf{e}$ and $\Lambda\mathbf{n}^* = \mathbf{S}\mathbf{i} + \mathbf{b}^*$.

The forward quantity equation. From the row for our country in Table 2.6 we can see that

$$\begin{aligned}\Lambda\mathbf{n}^* &= \mathbf{S}\mathbf{i} + \mathbf{b}^* \\ &= \mathbf{C}\mathbf{n}^* + \mathbf{b}^*, \end{aligned} \tag{2.6.3}$$

where $\mathbf{C}$ denotes a matrix of outflow coefficients, usually termed transition proportions [see II, §19.3], defined as

$$\mathbf{C} = \mathbf{S}\hat{\mathbf{n}}^{*-1}, \tag{2.6.4}$$

where $\hat{\mathbf{n}}^* = \text{diag}(\mathbf{n}^*)$ [see I, (6.7.3)] and $\hat{\mathbf{n}}^{*-1}$ is its inverse [see I, §6.4].

If the population is in stationary equilibrium, then $\Lambda^\theta\mathbf{n}^* = \mathbf{n}^*$ and $\Lambda^\theta\mathbf{b}^* = \mathbf{b}^*$, in which case (2.6.3) takes the form

$$\begin{aligned}\mathbf{n}^* &= \mathbf{C}\mathbf{n}^* + \mathbf{b}^* \\ &= (\mathbf{I} - \mathbf{C})^{-1}\mathbf{b}^*, \end{aligned} \tag{2.6.5}$$

which expresses $\mathbf{n}^*$ as a matrix transform of $\mathbf{b}^*$. If $\mathbf{C}$ can be regarded as a matrix of probabilities and not merely a matrix of proportions, then the inverse $(\mathbf{I} - \mathbf{C})^{-1}$ can be interpreted as the fundamental matrix of an absorbing Markov chain [see II, Example 19.3.3].

Equation (2.6.5) is formally identical to (2.2.3), the quantity equation of an open input–output model of the productive system. This suggests that, as in economics, there is a corresponding cost equation.

The forward cost equation. The cost equation corresponding to (2.6.5) can be described as follows. Suppose that $\mathbf{n}^*$ relates to the population throughout the life span, say a century, and that some of its elements relate to educational states, such as attending primary school or studying science at a university as an undergraduate. Let $\mathbf{m}$ denote a vector, of the same type as $\mathbf{n}^*$, whose elements measure the educational costs incurred this year in respect of an individual in one of the states distinguished in $\mathbf{n}^*$; and let $\mathbf{k}$ denote a vector of total costs to be incurred on average in educating or completing the education of an individual now in one of the states of $\mathbf{n}^*$. Then

$$\mathbf{k} = \mathbf{m} + \mathbf{C}'\mathbf{m} + \mathbf{C}'^2\mathbf{m} + \cdots$$
$$= \mathbf{m} + \mathbf{C}'\mathbf{k}$$
$$= (\mathbf{I} - \mathbf{C}')^{-1}\mathbf{m}, \tag{2.6.6}$$

where C' is the transpose of $\mathbf{C}$ [see I, §6.5]

The identity corresponding to (2.2.7). By combining (2.6.5) and (2.6.6) we can see that

$$\mathbf{m}'\mathbf{n}^* = \mathbf{k}'(\mathbf{I} - \mathbf{C})(\mathbf{I} - \mathbf{C})^{-1}\mathbf{b}^*$$
$$= \mathbf{k}'\mathbf{b}^*, \tag{2.6.7}$$

that is, for a population in stationary equilibrium with constant educational unit costs, this year's expenditure on education, $\mathbf{m}'\mathbf{n}^*$, is equal to the future cost of educating this year's new entrants, $\mathbf{k}'\mathbf{b}^*$.

The backward model. The model based on the row for our country in Table 2.6 is forward-looking and is appropriate if the capacity of the system leaves people free to move as they wish. This is not always the case: the supply of places in some branches of an educational system may carry more weight than the demand for them in determining movements. In other words, the existence of vacancies is important. To model this situation we need to consider the column for our country in Table 2.6 and form a coefficient matrix of what may be termed admission proportions by dividing the elements in each row of $\mathbf{S}$ by the appropriate element in the closing stock vector. Thus, corresponding to (2.6.3) through (2.6.7), we can write

$$\mathbf{n}^* = \mathbf{S}'\mathbf{i} + \mathbf{d}$$
$$= \mathbf{G}'\Lambda\mathbf{n}^* + \mathbf{d}, \tag{2.6.8}$$

where

$$\mathbf{G}' = \mathbf{S}'\Lambda\hat{\mathbf{n}}^{*-1} \tag{2.6.9}$$

denotes the matrix of admission proportions. For a population in stationary equilibrium

$$\mathbf{n}^* = \mathbf{G}'\mathbf{n}^* + \mathbf{d}$$
$$= (\mathbf{I} - \mathbf{G}')^{-1}\mathbf{d} \tag{2.6.10}$$

so that this model is driven by leavers rather than by entrants. If we denote by **l** a vector each of whose elements represents the total educational costs incurred on average in reaching a given state, the, corresponding to (2.6.6), we have

$$\mathbf{l} = (\mathbf{I} - \mathbf{G})^{-1}\mathbf{m} \tag{2.6.11}$$

and, corresponding to (2.6.7), we have

$$\mathbf{m}'\mathbf{n}^* = \mathbf{l}'\mathbf{d}. \tag{2.6.12}$$

2.7. VARIANTS AND GENERALIZATIONS

Forecasting and models with changing coefficients. If the coefficients in any of the models described above remained constant through time, forecasts could be made from (2.6.3) by repeated applications of the lag operator Λ. Thus on the first application

$$\Lambda^2\mathbf{n}^* = \mathbf{C}\Lambda\mathbf{n}^* + \Lambda\mathbf{b}^*$$
$$= \mathbf{C}^2\mathbf{n}^* + \mathbf{C}\mathbf{b}^* + \Lambda\mathbf{b}^* \tag{2.7.1}$$

and in general

$$\Lambda^\tau\mathbf{n}^* = \mathbf{C}^\tau\mathbf{n}^* + \sum_{\theta=0}^{\tau-1} \mathbf{C}^\theta\Lambda^{\tau-\theta-1}\mathbf{b}^*, \tag{2.7.2}$$

which expresses the stock vector τ periods hence in terms of the present stock vector and the supposedly known new entry vectors from the present period through period $\tau - 1$.

It can safely be assumed, however, that some at any rate of the coefficients of **C** will change through time, and allowance must be made for this. If **C** changes, then (2.7.1) and (2.7.2) become

$$\Lambda^2\mathbf{n}^* = \Lambda\mathbf{C}\Lambda\mathbf{n}^* + \Lambda\mathbf{b}^*$$
$$= (\Lambda\mathbf{C}.\mathbf{C})\mathbf{n}^* + \Lambda\mathbf{C}\mathbf{b}^* + \Lambda\mathbf{b}^* \tag{2.7.3}$$

and

$$\Lambda^\tau\mathbf{n}^* = \prod_{\beta=0}^{\tau-1} \Lambda^\beta\mathbf{C}\mathbf{n}^* + \sum_{\theta=1}^{\tau-1} \left[\prod_{\beta=\tau-1}^{\tau-\theta} \Lambda^\beta\mathbf{C} \right]\Lambda^{\tau-\theta-1}\mathbf{b}^* + \Lambda^{\tau-1}\mathbf{b}^*$$
$$= \mathbf{C}(\tau)\mathbf{n}^* + \sum_{\theta=1}^{\tau-1} \Lambda^{\tau-\theta}\mathbf{C}(\theta)\Lambda^{\tau-\theta-1}\mathbf{b}^* + \Lambda^{\tau-1}\mathbf{b}^*, \tag{2.7.4}$$

where $\prod$ denotes the operation of forming a product and

$$\mathbf{C}(\theta) = \prod_{\beta=0}^{\theta-1} \Lambda^\beta\mathbf{C}. \tag{2.7.5}$$

Model with cost discounting. If ρ denotes the rate of interest, then $\sigma = 1/(1 + \rho)$

denotes the discount factor [see Chapter 18]; and if the states of **C** are separated by annual intervals it is easy to calculate the discounted streams of future costs corresponding to (2.6.6). Let $\tilde{\mathbf{k}}$ denote the vector of discounted accumulated costs and let $\tilde{\mathbf{C}} = \sigma\mathbf{C}$. Then (2.6.6) is replaced by

$$\tilde{\mathbf{k}} = (\mathbf{I} - \tilde{\mathbf{C}}')^{-1}\mathbf{m}$$
$$= \hat{\mathbf{s}}^{-1}(\mathbf{I} - \mathbf{C}')^{-1}\hat{\mathbf{s}}\mathbf{m}, \qquad (2.7.6)$$

where

$$\mathbf{s} = \{1, \ldots, 1, \sigma, \ldots, \sigma, \sigma^2, \ldots, \sigma^2, \sigma^3, \ldots\}. \qquad (2.7.7)$$

In (2.7.7) the powers of σ are repeated as many times as the number of states distinguished at successive years of age.

Models restricted to survivors. It is useful to be able to ignore deaths and concentrate on survivors so as to account fully for a part of life, say the ages 15 to 19. Let us define a matrix, **D** say, as

$$\mathbf{D} = \mathbf{S}(\hat{\mathbf{n}}^* - \hat{\mathbf{d}})^{-1}. \qquad (2.7.8)$$

Some care is needed in using this matrix since the definitions may be such that the column sums of **D** are all 1, so that $(\mathbf{I} - \mathbf{D})$ is singular and has no inverse [see I, Theorem 6.4.2]. This difficulty can be circumvented if age is one of the criteria of classification, as explained in Stone (1981, pp. 313–314).

Models with age-free matrices. In applying the models described so far it is an advantage if age, narrowly defined, is one of the criteria of classification, since each column of **C** then relates to a particular year of birth and the elements of **n*** are appropriate divisors. Social and demographic data, however, do not always come classified by year of birth and so we must do what we can with matrices in which the states, say stage of education and types of employment, are defined without reference to age. In this case each element in a column of **C** will span an age-range of varying and uncertain width: employees who move back into education will typically be young and those who move into retirement will typically be old, while the people remaining in the same job may span the whole working age-range. This means that we must adjust our data to what would have been observed had the population remained stationary over the past century. An example of how to make these adjustments is given in Stone (1972).

2.8. THE FUNDAMENTAL MATRIX AND THE LIFE TABLE

The elements of the fundamental matrix $(\mathbf{I} - \mathbf{C})^{-1}$ measure the probability of reaching the state indicated by the row if one starts from the state indicated by the column, as can readily be seen from a simple example. Consider a species that can live for four years at most, and a **C**-matrix in which the non-zero elements relate simply to the survival rates from one age to the next. Then

$$\mathbf{C} = \begin{bmatrix} 0 & 0 & 0 & 0 \\ C_{21} & 0 & 0 & 0 \\ 0 & C_{32} & 0 & 0 \\ 0 & 0 & C_{43} & 0 \end{bmatrix} \tag{2.8.1}$$

whence

$$(\mathbf{I} - \mathbf{C}) = \begin{bmatrix} 1 & 0 & 0 & 0 \\ -C_{21} & 1 & 0 & 0 \\ 0 & -C_{32} & 1 & 0 \\ 0 & 0 & -C_{43} & 1 \end{bmatrix} \tag{2.8.2}$$

and

$$(\mathbf{I} - \mathbf{C})^{-1} = \begin{bmatrix} 1 & 0 & 0 & 0 \\ C_{21} & 1 & 0 & 0 \\ C_{32}C_{21} & C_{32} & 1 & 0 \\ C_{43}C_{32}C_{21} & C_{43}C_{32} & C_{43} & 1 \end{bmatrix} \tag{2.8.3}$$

From (2.8.3) it can be seen that the elements in the columns of $(\mathbf{I} - \mathbf{C})^{-1}$ are the products of the survival rates through the states that have to be traversed in order to get from the column state to the row state. It is tempting to interpret these numbers as the expected times to be spent in different states by an individual entering the state indicated by the column. This would be correct if death always occurred at the end of a period. Since death may occur at any time, it would seem better to assume that it occurs on average in the middle of the period: people who die in a period are alive in it on average for half its length. We can allow for this by replacing $(\mathbf{I} - \mathbf{C})^{-1}$ by a matrix, $\mathbf{T}^*$ say, defined as

$$\mathbf{T}^* = \tfrac{1}{2}\tau(\mathbf{I} + \hat{\mathbf{c}})(\mathbf{I} - \mathbf{C})^{-1}, \tag{2.8.4}$$

in which $\mathbf{c} = \{C_{21}\ C_{32}\ C_{43}\ 0\}$ is a vector of survival rates, $\hat{\mathbf{c}} = \mathrm{diag}(\mathbf{c})$ and τ, which in this example is 1, allows for the possibility that the span of the age-group is different in length from the period for which the standard matrix is set up. It is not difficult to see that

$$\mathbf{i}'\mathbf{T}^* = \mathbf{i}'[(\mathbf{I} - \mathbf{C})^{-1} - \tfrac{1}{2}\tau], \tag{2.8.5}$$

so that the column sums of $\mathbf{T}^*$ are uniformly smaller than the corresponding column sums of $(\mathbf{I} - \mathbf{C})^{-1}$ by half an interval.

The properties of $\mathbf{T}^*$ can be summarized as follows.

First, the diagonal elements measure the average time to be spent in a state by those entering it.

Second, the ratio of an off-diagonal element to the diagonal element in the same row measures the probability of reaching the state represented by the row if one starts from the state represented by the column containing the off-diagonal element. This property is shared with $(\mathbf{I} - \mathbf{C})^{-1}$.

Third, the sum of the elements in a column measures the complete expectation of life of those entering the state represented by the column.

Fourth, with the help of a life table [see §18.3], the information provided by the preceding property makes it possible in an age-free matrix to calculate the average age at which each state is entered.

A numerical example illustrating these properties is given in Stone (1972; 1981, pp. 318–319).

2.9. RECONCILING PREFERENCES: A TOY MODEL

In any society, people have preferences about the jobs they would like to perform and about the commodities they would like to consume. If a rise in the price of a given labour input or a given commodity output leads to an increase in its supply and a reduction in the demand for it, a scheme for reconciling labour supplies and commodity demands can be set out as follows.

The parameters in such an adjustment process enter into three sets of equations. First, there are those relating to the technical conditions of production: the equations connecting inputs and outputs in each branch of productive activity. In what follows these take the form of an open, static Leontief system. Second, there are those relating to final demand, here restricted to private consumption: the equations connecting the amount of each commodity demanded with income and prices. In what follows these take the form of a linear expenditure system. Third, there are those relating to the supply of factors of production, here restricted to labour: the equations determining the supply of labour to each branch of production. In what follows these take the form of homogeneous linear functions [cf. I, (14.5.3)] of an exogenously given labour force and a set of relative wage rates, so designed that changes in these rates alter the distribution of the labour force without changing its total.

In order to calculate the equilibrium value of the variables, namely the price vector, $\mathbf{p}$, the wage vector, $\mathbf{w}$, the labour supply vector, $\mathbf{l}$, income, μ, the supply vector of final commodities, $\mathbf{e}_s$, and the demand vector, $\mathbf{e}_d$, we start with an arbitrary vector of commodity prices, $\mathbf{p} = \mathbf{i}$ say, and solve the following cycle of equations iteratively until $\mathbf{e}_s = \mathbf{e}_d$.

From the initial price vector we calculate a vector of wages from the usual input–output relationship

$$\mathbf{w} = \hat{\mathbf{f}}^{-1}(\mathbf{I} - \mathbf{A}')\mathbf{p} \tag{2.9.1}$$

where $\mathbf{A}$ denotes the input–output coefficient matrix for intermediate products and $\mathbf{f}$ denotes the input–output coefficient vector for labour. Quantities can be measured in physical units. In this system the vector $\mathbf{f}$ and the matrix $\mathbf{A}$ control the technical possibilities of production.

Next, we combine $\mathbf{w}$ with the exogenously given labour force, λ say, to give the labour supply vector from the relationship

$$\mathbf{l} = \mathbf{g}\lambda + (\mathbf{I} - \mathbf{g}\mathbf{i}')\hat{\mathbf{h}}(\mathbf{i}'\mathbf{w})^{-1}\mathbf{w} \tag{2.9.2}$$

where **g** and **h** are vectors of parameters and $\mathbf{i'g} = 1$. If **l** were not influenced by relative wages, then its elements would be fixed proportions of λ; but if $\mathbf{h} \neq \{0\ldots0\}$, then these constant shares are modified by relative wages, the elements of $(\mathbf{i'w})^{-1}\mathbf{w}$. In this system the vectors **g** and **h** control job preferences.

We are now in a position to calculate two new variables: income, μ, and the supply vector of final commodities, $\mathbf{e}_s$. The first is given by the definition

$$\mu = \mathbf{w'l} \qquad (2.9.3)$$

and the second comes from the usual input–output relationship

$$\mathbf{e}_s = (\mathbf{I} - \mathbf{A})\hat{\mathbf{f}}^{-1}\mathbf{l}, \qquad (2.9.4)$$

which measures the amount of each commodity that can be delivered to final demand with a given supply and allocation of labour.

This brings us to the demand vector of commodities for final consumption, $\mathbf{e}_d$, the only form of final demand in the system. This is determined by the equations of the linear expenditure system [see §13.10], namely

$$\mathbf{e}_d = \hat{\mathbf{p}}^{-1}[\mathbf{b}\mu + (\mathbf{I} - \mathbf{bi'})\hat{\mathbf{c}}\mathbf{p}], \qquad (2.9.5)$$

where **b** and **c** are vectors of parameters and $\mathbf{i'b} = 1$. By premultiplying this equation by $\mathbf{p'}$, it can readily be seen that $\mathbf{p'e}_d = \mu$. In this system the vectors **b** and **c** control commodity preferences.

At this stage we should not expect to find that $\mathbf{e}_d = \mathbf{e}_s$. We need, therefore, a systematic way of revising prices so that this equality is eventually reached. An obvious method is to raise prices where demand exceeds supply and to lower them where supply exceeds demand. We could calculate $\Delta\mathbf{p}$ from

$$\Delta\mathbf{p} = \gamma\hat{\mathbf{e}}_d^{-1}(\mathbf{e}_d - \mathbf{e}_s) \qquad (2.9.6)$$

where γ is a parameter. The next cycle of calculations will start with $\mathbf{p} + \Delta\mathbf{p}$ in place of **p**.

An example of this scheme applied to three branches of production is set out in Table 2.7. The data consist of the exogenously given labour force, $\lambda = 1$, and the following values of the parameters:

$$\mathbf{A} = \begin{bmatrix} 0 & 0.2 & 0.2 \\ 0.1 & 0 & 0.2 \\ 0.3 & 0.1 & 0 \end{bmatrix} \qquad (2.9.7)$$

$$\mathbf{f'} = \{0.2 \quad 0.3 \quad 0.4\} \qquad (2.9.8)$$

$$\mathbf{g'} = \{0.5 \quad 0.3 \quad 0.2\} \qquad (2.9.9)$$

$$\mathbf{h'} = \{0.1 \quad 0.2 \quad 0.3\} \qquad (2.9.10)$$

$$\mathbf{b'} = \{0.60 \quad 0.25 \quad 0.15\} \qquad (2.9.11)$$

$$\mathbf{c'} = \{0.01 \quad 0.04 \quad 0.10\} \qquad (2.9.12)$$

$$\gamma = 0.1. \qquad (2.9.13)$$

Table 2.7 Reconciling preferences: a constructed numerical example

Cycle	p	w	l	e_s	e_d
1	1.0000	3.0000	0.4549	1.9493	1.3868
	1.0000	2.3333	0.3149	0.7070	0.6137
	1.0000	1.5000	0.2302	−0.2117	0.4442
6	0.8358	1.0635	0.3973	1.6371	1.3533
	0.9211	1.9231	0.2875	0.6020	0.5479
	1.7699	3.5464	0.3153	0.0964	0.2586
11	0.7864	0.3532	0.3746	1.5142	1.4587
	0.9029	1.7904	0.2756	0.5599	0.5658
	2.0850	4.3677	0.3489	0.2182	0.2366
16	0.7776	0.2458	0.3714	1.4966	1.4828
	0.9091	1.8036	0.2759	0.5576	0.5649
	2.1250	4.4691	0.3527	0.2328	0.2347
21	0.7751	0.2240	0.3708	1.4934	1.4882
	0.9137	1.8191	0.2762	0.5588	0.5625
	2.1297	4.4798	0.3530	0.2342	0.2345
31	0.7736	0.2133	0.3706	1.4920	1.4910
	0.9170	1.8306	0.2765	0.5598	0.5606
	2.1309	4.4819	0.3530	0.2344	0.2344
41	0.7734	0.2113	0.3705	1.4918	1.4915
	0.9177	1.8330	0.2765	0.5601	0.5602
	2.1311	4.4822	0.3529	0.2344	0.2344
51	0.7733	0.2109	0.3705	1.4917	1.4917
	0.9178	1.8335	0.2766	0.5601	0.5601
	2.1311	4.4822	0.3529	0.2344	0.2344

In this example $e_d = e_s$ at the fifty-first cycle, after which none of the figures changes: equilibrium has been reached. The world is much more complicated than this, but this example formalizes the kind of adjustment process needed in modelling an adaptive, self-equilibrating system and it provides a starting point for the development of more realistic models. A more mathematical analysis of the properties of general equilibrium may be found in Chapter 14.

2.10. CONSTRUCTION OF ECONOMIC AND DEMOGRAPHIC ACCOUNTING MATRICES

There are two stages in the construction of economic and demographic matrices. The first consists of using available data to make as complete a set of direct estimates as possible; and the second consists of adjusting and completing the direct estimates so as to meet the constraints that hold between their true values. The data available are always in some degree inaccurate, inconsistent and incomplete, and it is therefore unsatisfactory to rely on the first stage and ignore the second.

Direct estimation. To construct a matrix of any complexity it will be necessary to combine information drawn from a variety of sources. When these are brought together it will be possible to see the inconsistencies and gaps that remain even after the most skilful use has been made of the data. For instance, in Britain official estimates of the national economic accounts are published every year in the Blue Books on *National Income and Expenditure* (UKCSO, 1952–), and the sources and methods used are described in UKCSO (1968). It is not difficult to set out this material so that the inconsistencies and gaps in the direct estimates are brought out explicitly.

The adjustment procedure. The adjustment of the initial estimates depends on the constraints to which the true elements are subject and on the relative accuracy attached to the data. In the present context the commonest forms of constraint are: components sum to totals, accounts balance, elements are single-valued. The accuracy of the data can rarely be measured but the compilers can usually form assessments of their reliability, and these can be used as a basis for variance estimates. The method consists of minimising the sum of squares of the adjustments which enable the constraints to be met, the squares being weighted by the reciprocals of the variances [see VI, §8.2.6]. It may happen that all the elements have been estimated directly and so all the constraints can be used to adjust them; or it may happen that there are some direct estimates missing and that the set of constraints can be divided into two subsets, the first of which is used to adjust the direct estimates and the second to supply the missing figures.

The adjustment procedure can be formalized as follows. Let $\mathbf{x}$, of type $v \times 1$, denote a vector of the true values of the unknowns which are subject to μ independent linear constraints given by

$$\mathbf{Gx} = \mathbf{h}, \tag{2.10.1}$$

which $\mathbf{G}$, the constraint matrix, is of type $\mu \times v$ and rank μ [see I, §5.6]; and $\mathbf{h}$, a vector of known constants, is of type $\mu \times 1$. Further, let $\mathbf{x}^*$ denote a vector of unbiased estimates of the elements of $\mathbf{x}$ [see VI, §3.3.2]; let $\mathbf{V}^*$, of order v and rank greater than μ, denote the variance matrix of the elements of $\mathbf{x}^*$ [see II, §13.3.1]; and assume that any constraints satisfied by $\mathbf{x}^*$ are linearly independent of (2.10.1) [see I, §5.3].

The best linear unbiased estimator, $\mathbf{x}^{**}$ say [see VI, §3.3.2], of $\mathbf{x}$ can be written as

$$\mathbf{x}^{**} = \mathbf{x}^* - \mathbf{F}(\mathbf{Gx}^* - \mathbf{h}), \tag{2.10.2}$$

where $\mathbf{F}$ denotes a matrix of type $v \times \mu$. The estimator $\mathbf{x}^{**}$ will satisfy (2.10.1) provided that

$$\mathbf{Gx}^{**} - \mathbf{h} = \mathbf{0}, \tag{2.10.3}$$

that is, from (2.10.2), provided that

$$(\mathbf{I} - \mathbf{GF})(\mathbf{Gx}^* - \mathbf{h}) = \mathbf{0} \tag{2.10.4}$$

for all values of $\mathbf{x}^*$, and this requires that

$$\mathbf{GF} = \mathbf{I}. \tag{2.10.5}$$

The variance matrix, $\mathbf{V}^{**}$, of $\mathbf{x}^{**}$ is

$$\mathbf{V}^{**} = (\mathbf{I} - \mathbf{FG})\mathbf{V}^*(\mathbf{I} - \mathbf{FG})' \tag{2.10.6}$$

and in order to obtain estimates of the elements of $\mathbf{x}^{**}$ with least variance we must minimize the diagonal elements of (2.10.6) subject to (2.10.5). From this it follows that $\mathbf{F}^*$, the estimator of $\mathbf{F}$, must satisfy the relationship

$$-\mathbf{V}^*\mathbf{G}' + \mathbf{F}^*\mathbf{GV}^*\mathbf{G}' - \mathbf{G}'\mathbf{L} = \mathbf{0}, \tag{2.10.7}$$

where $\mathbf{L}$ denotes a matrix, of order μ, of Lagrange multipliers [see IV, §15.1.4]. If we premultiply (2.10.7) by $\mathbf{G}$ we see that $\mathbf{GG}'\mathbf{L} = \mathbf{0}$ since $\mathbf{GF}^* = \mathbf{I}$. Hence $\mathbf{L} = \mathbf{0}$ since $\mathbf{GG}'$ is nonsingular. Consequently

$$\mathbf{F}^* = \mathbf{V}^*\mathbf{G}'(\mathbf{GV}^*\mathbf{G}')^{-1} \tag{2.10.8}$$

which can always be formed since $\mathbf{GV}^*\mathbf{G}'$ is also nonsingular [see I, Theorem 6.4.2]. From (2.10.2) and (2.10.8)

$$\mathbf{x}^{**} = \mathbf{x}^* - \mathbf{V}^*\mathbf{G}'(\mathbf{GV}^*\mathbf{G}')^{-1}(\mathbf{Gx}^* - \mathbf{h}), \tag{2.10.9}$$

from which we see that $\mathbf{V}^*$ need only be known up to a scalar multiplier which will cancel out. From (2.10.6) and (2.10.8)

$$\mathbf{V}^{**} = \mathbf{V}^* - \mathbf{V}^*\mathbf{G}'(\mathbf{GV}^*\mathbf{G}')^{-1}\mathbf{GV}^*. \tag{2.10.10}$$

This is one way of setting out the problem and its solution, but it is not the only way. As is pointed out by Byron (1978), equation (2.10.3) can be obtained by combining the first-order conditions for minimizing a constrained quadratic loss function [see VI, §19.1]. Thus, denoting the loss by ω, the function can be written as

$$\omega = \tfrac{1}{2}(\mathbf{x}^{**} - \mathbf{x}^*)'\mathbf{V}^{*-1}(\mathbf{x}^{**} - \mathbf{x}^*) + \mathbf{l}'(\mathbf{Gx}^{**} - \mathbf{h}), \tag{2.10.11}$$

where $\mathbf{l}$ denotes a vector of Lagrange multipliers. Writing $\mathbf{l}^*$ for the estimator of $\mathbf{l}$, the first-order conditions for a minimum of (2.10.11) are [cf. IV, §5.15]

$$\mathbf{l}^* = (\mathbf{GV}^*\mathbf{G}')^{-1}(\mathbf{Gx}^* - \mathbf{h}) \tag{2.10.12}$$

and

$$\mathbf{x}^{**} = \mathbf{x}^* - \mathbf{V}^*\mathbf{G}'\mathbf{l}^*. \tag{2.10.13}$$

Table 2.8 A version of the British national accounts with the errors shown explicitly: initial and finally adjusted estimates for 1969 (£ million)

Note: In each cell the upper (roman) figure is the initial estimate and the lower (italic) figure is the finally adjusted estimate.

Category	Account	1	2	3	4	5	6	7	D	8	9	10	11	12	13	E	Totals
Production	1. Britain		10109 *10117*	29233 *29286*			7997 *7999*			1297 *1316*	4167 *4320*	1414 *1414*	2286 *2286*				56503 *56738*
Production	2. Rest of the world	9930 *9922*															9930 *9922*
Income and outlay	3. Persons	31290 *31230*			35 *35*		3937 *3936*	341 *341*	3864 *3864*								39467 *39406*
Income and outlay	4. Companies	3815 *3798*						1161 *1164*	1619 *1619*								6595 *6581*
Income and outlay	5. Public corporations	445 *445*						15 *15*	80 *80*								540 *540*
Income and outlay	6. General government	7488 *7487*		7420 *7422*	1131 *1131*	610 *610*		203 *203*	176 *176*								17028 *17029*
Income and outlay	7. Rest of the world		−179 *−195*	416 *415*	458 *458*		554 *554*										1249 *1232*
	D. Dividends and interest n.e.s.			761 *761*	3306 *3306*	120 *120*	1552 *1552*										5739 *5739*
Capital transactions	8. Persons	812 *804*		1637 *1522*									186 *186*				2635 *2512*
Capital transactions	9. Companies	1553 *1532*			1665 *1651*								606 *606*				3824 *3789*
Capital transactions	10. Public corporations	1024 *1024*				−190 *−190*				6 *6*	14 *14*		50 *50*				904 *904*
Capital transactions	11. General government	496 *496*					2988 *2988*			577 *577*	48 *48*	0 *0*					4109 *4109*
Capital transactions	12. Rest of the world							−471 *−491*					0 *0*				−471 *−491*
	13. Net acquisitions of fin. assets									1810 *613*	−1407 *−593*	−514 *−510*	975 *981*	−864 *−491*			0 *0*
	E. Errors	−350 *0*								−1055 *0*	1002 *0*	4 *0*	6 *0*	393 *0*			0 *0*
	Totals	56503 *56738*	9930 *9922*	39467 *39406*	6595 *6581*	540 *540*	17028 *17029*	1249 *1232*	5739 *5739*	2635 *2512*	3824 *3789*	904 *904*	4109 *4109*	−471 *−491*	0 *0*	0 *0*	

Note. The noughts in cells 11.10 and 12.11 refer respectively to net capital transfers to general government from public corporations and net capital transfers abroad from general government. In 1969 these items happened to be zero but this is not always the case.

By substituting for l* from (2.10.12) into (2.10.13) we obtain (2.10.9).

The significance of this reformulation lies in the computational possibilities it opens up. Procedures based on the conjugate gradient algorithm can be used to solve the system of linear equations (2.10.12) [see III, §11.3 and IV, §15.9.7] and these turn out to be much more efficient, in terms both of time taken and of storage capacity in the computer, than the traditional methods of solving (2.10.9). Thus the decisive difficulty in carrying out the adjustment of very large matrices is removed.

A numerical example. An example of the initial (direct) and final (adjusted) estimates of a set of national accounts is given in Table 2.8. The initial estimates (upper figures in roman type) are taken from the 1980 *Blue Book*, UKCSO (1952–) and the final estimates (lower figures in italic type) are fully described in Stone (1982).

This version consists of fourteen accounts, the row-and-column pairs headed 1 to 13 and D, plus an explicit statement of discrepancies, the row and column headed E. For the directly measured items the variance estimates are based on the reliability ratings given in UKCSO (1968); and for the unmeasured items the estimates are equated to the sum of the variances of the remaining items in the account. All the entries in accounts 1, 5, 6, D, 10 and 11 are estimated directly. But in accounts 2, 3, 4, 7, 8, 9 and 12, entries 7.2, 8.3, 9.4, 12.7, E.8, E.9 and E.12 are residuals. The variances of 7.2, 8.3, 9.4, E.8 and E.9 are estimated as the sum of the remaining variances in accounts 2, 3, 4, 8 and 9. The constraints from accounts 1 to 6, D, and 8 to 11 can then be used to balance those accounts, and the remaining two constraints can be used to estimate 12.7 and 13.12 so as to balance accounts 7 and 12 and, consequently, 13.

Applications of this method of adjusting accounting matrices are comparatively new. Further examples and a discussion will be found in Byron (1978), Ploeg (1982) and Stone (1975, 1982).

2.11 REFERENCES

Byron, Ray P. (1978). The estimation of large social account matrices. *Journal of the Royal Statistical Society, Series A*, **141**, pt. 3, 359–367.

Ploeg, Frederick van der (1982). Reliability and the adjustment of sequences of large economic accounting matrices (with discussion). *Journal of the Royal Statistical Society, Series A*, **145**, pt. 2, 169–194.

Pyatt, Graham, ROE, Alan R. and associates (1977). *Social Accounting for Development Planning with special reference to Sri Lanka.* Cambridge University Press, London.

Stone, Richard (1970). A comparison of the SNA and the MPS, in *Mathematical Models of the Economy and Other Essays.* Chapman and Hall, London.

Stone, Richard (1972). The fundamental matrix of the active sequence, in *Input–Output Techniques* (eds. A. Bródy and A. P. Carter). North-Holland, Amsterdam.

Stone, Richard (1975). Direct and indirect constraints in the adjustment of observations, in *Nasjonalregnskap Modeller og Analyse* (essays in honour of Odd Aukrust). Statistisk Sentralbyrå, Oslo.

Stone, Richard (1978). The disaggregation of the household sector in the national accounts, Paper presented at the World Bank SAM Conference, Cambridge, 1978.

Stone, Richard (1981). The relationship of demographic accounts to national income and product accounts, in *social Accounting Systems: essays on the state of the art* (eds. F. Thomas Juster and Kenneth C. Land). Academic Press, New York.

Stone, Richard (1982). Balancing the national accounts: Britain, 1969–1979, Paper presented at the Ivor Pearce Conference, Southampton, Jan. 1982, to be published in *Demand, Trade and Equilibrium*. Macmillan, Basingstoke.

UKCSO (UK, Central Statistical Office) (1952–). *National Income and Expenditure.* HMSO, London, annually since 1952.

UKCSO (UK, Central Statistical Office) (1968). *National Accounts Statistics: Sources and Methods.* HMSO, London.

UNSO (UN, Statistical Office) (1968). *A System of National Accounts,* Studies in Methods, series F, no. 2, rev. 3. United Nations, New York.

UNSO (UN, Statistical Office) (1971). *Basic Principles of the System of Balances of the National Economy,* Studies in Methods, series F, no. 17. United Nations, New York.

UNSO (UN, Statistical Office) (1975). *Towards a System of Social and Demographic Statistics,* Studies in Methods, series F, no. 18. United Nations, New York.

UNSO (UN, Statistical Office) (1977). *Comparisons of the System of National Accounts and the System of Balances of the National Economy: Part one, conceptual relationships,* Studies in Methods, series F, no. 20. United Nations, New York.

Mathematical Methods in Economics
Edited by F. van der Ploeg
© 1984, John Wiley & Sons, Ltd.

3

Linear Economic Models

M ARTIN R. W EALE, *University of Cambridge, Cambridge, U K*

3.1 INTRODUCTION

The modelling of an interdependent system such as an economy with distinct industries or institutional sectors, or if needed of a system of distinct nations can be a problem of considerable complexity. For any solution of the model must take account of 'feedback' effects. The demand for cars is likely to affect the output of the steel industry, or the level of spending in North America is likely to affect the demand there for imports from Europe and thus require extra output from Europe. But this higher output in Europe may mean that more people are employed in Europe and they therefore want to buy more imports from America.

The accounting structure used by National Accountants to show the inter-dependence of the transactions within the economy (UN, 1968) can also be used to provide a simple linear framework in order to model the behaviour of the economy. The advantages of adopting a linear specification lie in the fact that it is possible to solve linear models analytically and to derive properties of the solution in a simple manner. In so far as an economy is in fact only approximately linear such a model will only provide an approximation to the actual path of the economy. This chapter considers static linear models of closed economies used by economists, showing how they relate to an underlying accounting framework, and demonstrates extensions needed to incorporate problems of capital accumulation and thereby provides an extension of the discussion in sections 2–4 of Chapter 2. The techniques introduced are also used to analyse a model of two countries linked by international trade.

The chapter also takes the opportunity to discuss and apply various mathematical properties of matrices, such as matrix diagonalization [see I, §7.4], Solow conditions, Hawkins–Simon's conditions, Frobenius theorems [see I, §7.11], the properties of stochastic matrices [see II, §19.3] and linear programming [see I, Chapter 11].

3.2. THE KEYNESIAN MODEL

This model provides perhaps the simplest example of a linear model. Its origins can be found in Kahn (1931) and Keynes (1936) and its structure led to quantification by Tinbergen (1937) as a basis for modelling. The model is designed to show how changes in the level of spending generate changes in the level of income which lead to further changes in spending. Total spending consists either of consumption or investment. The model considers production in aggregate and therefore nets out inputs used in the production of their own or other industries' output; industrial activity may be considered as generating a single 'composite good'. All output must either be consumed or invested and the production of one unit of output generates an equal amount of income. Since it is impossible for a closed economy to create net financial assets (foreign investment and foreign disinvestment are impossible) total income must equal total expenditure and therefore total saving must equal total investment. The model differs from previous models of savings and investment behaviour in the mechanism whereby investment and saving are brought into equality.

In the Keynesian system consumption (C) is regarded as a linear function of national income gross of depreciation (Y) and saving (S) is equal to that part of income which is not consumed

$$S = Y - C.$$

Investment (I) is regarded as exogenous to the system being determined by variables such as the rate of interest and the optimism of entrepreneurs rather than the current level of income or output and since income equals expenditure, this yields

$$Y = C + I.$$

This and the previous equation imply between them that

$$S = I,$$

an identity which does not imply that planned saving is necessarily equal to planned investment but does imply that other variables in the system must adjust so that actual saving equals actual investment.

Consider now the effects of an exogenous increase in investment in such an economy of an amount ΔI. For the reasons explained above this must lead to an equal increase in income of ΔI. This extra income is of course paid out as wages and profit. Assuming that a constant fraction, c, of income is consumed, that is that the ratio C/Y is constant and independent of Y [cf. §5.2], implies, in this example, that consumption rises immediately by $c\Delta I$. The extra consumption of course requires extra output of an equal amount and this new output generates a further increment to income of $c\Delta I$. The process continues for further rounds—of this next increment to income an amount $c^2\Delta I$ is consumed and so the process continues. The total increment to income is given as

$$\Delta Y = (1 + c + c^2 + c^3 + \ldots)\Delta I,$$

where the expression in brackets represents the sum to infinity of a geometric progression [see IV, Example 1.7.3]. It is clear that if $c > 1$ the economy will be wildly unstable any movement in investment or even any investment would imply an infinite movement in output and income, because each increment to income generates a further larger increment to income and no expansion of income is capable of generating enough savings to fund the investment. If $c < 1$ the expression can be solved by subtracting $c\Delta Y$ or its equivalent in terms of the investment increment from both sides of the equation. For this yields simply

$$(1 - c)\Delta Y = \Delta I$$

or

$$\Delta Y = \Delta I/(1 - c)$$

This change in income of course generates consumption of $c\Delta Y$ and therefore saving of $(1 - c)\Delta Y$; the solution yields once again that saving is equal to investment. Exactly the same technique can of course be used to determine the level of income associated with a given level of, rather than change in, investment.

Such a model is of course only useful in a situation where output is determined by the level of demand and not by physical constraints. If capacity is fully utilized an increase in investment cannot lead to a multiplied increase in output. Under such circumstances equilibrium would be maintained by an adjustment in prices restraining consumers' income. This process is described by Keynes (1940), and provides an important example of the way in which linearity may only be a realistic assumption in some circumstances and for variables within some ranges.

Although this model is vary straightforward, casting it in an accounting matrix [cf. §2.3] provides an example of a more general technique. The economy has just one production account generating a 'composite' good. Only the consolidated income/expenditure decisions of the nation are shown. There is no split between institutional sectors such as households and firms or between different types of income such as wages and profit. Since the economy is closed and the sectors are not distinguished there are no financial balances and no transactions with the rest of the world [see §2.4].

In the matrix shown in Table 3.1 the identities outlined above are expressed in the fact that the total of the ith row must equal the total of the ith column. In the production account we see that output is the sum of consumption and investment; the second account shows that income is either consumed or saved. In this simple consolidated set of accounts the third account is trivial but in a more complex structure where different industries were identified it would express the fact that aggregate consumption equalled the total value of the output of the distinct industries supplied to consumption. The fourth account expresses the fact that all savings must be invested since there are no net financial balances,

Table 3.1 An accounting matrix for a simple Keynesian economy

		Produc-tion	Income/Outlay National Income	Income/Outlay Consump-tion	Accumulation Saving	Accumulation Invest-ment	Totals
Produc-tion				C		I	Y
Income–Outlay	National income	Y					Y
	Consump-tion	C					C
Accumu-lation	Saving		S				S
	Invest-ment				I		I
	Totals	Y	Y	C	S	I	

and the fifth is, in this case, trivial for the same reasons as the third.

If each column of the matrix is divided by its column total we obtain a matrix of propensities to spend, showing the fraction of the receipts of each type of account going to each type of expenditure. In this simple framework only national income is 'spent' in more than one way, going partly to consumption and partly to saving, but in a more disaggregate model the income generated in production would be divided between wages, profit and indirect taxes, and consumption would go on the products of several distinct industries.

The average expenditure propensities in the simple Keynesian System, obtained by dividing each account item by the relevant column total, are:

	Produc-tion	National Income	Consump-tion	Saving	Invest-ment
Production			1		1
National income	1				
Consumption		c			
Saving		$1-c$			
Investment				1	

where $C = cY$ and $S = (1 - c)Y$ as before.

The matrix of propensities is partitioned [see I, §6.6] into propensities relating to endogeneous and exogeneous accounts respectively, and the row totals shown in the previous matrix may be partitioned as a vector in the same way, yield

	Endogenous accounts	Exogenous accounts	Row totals
Endogenous accounts	$\mathbf{A}_{11}$	$\mathbf{A}_{12}$	$\mathbf{z}_1$
Exogenous accounts	$\mathbf{A}_{21}$	$\mathbf{A}_{22}$	$\mathbf{z}_2$

where $\mathbf{A}_{11}$ and $\mathbf{A}_{22}$ are square matrices which are assumed to have distinct eigenvalues [see I, §7.1].

In this example $\mathbf{A}_{11}$ is 4×4 and $\mathbf{A}_{22}$ is 1×1 (in fact $\mathbf{A}_{22} = 0$), since investment is the only exogenous account. In a more complex model government and export demand could also be treated as exogenous. In this framework the vector of total receipts of the endogenous accounts from the exogenous accounts is $\mathbf{A}_{12}\mathbf{z}_2$ and the vector of receipts to each endogenous account from spending by endogenous accounts is $\mathbf{A}_{11}\mathbf{z}_1$ [see I, §6.2(vi)]. But this must equal total receipts and total payments by the endogenous accounts and therefore

$$\mathbf{z}_1 = \mathbf{A}_{11}\mathbf{z}_1 + \mathbf{A}_{12}\mathbf{z}_2.$$

The process explained whereby exogenous investment leads to income which leads to further demand and thus to further income can be applied equally to the interdependent system modelled here. Exogenous payments are allocated as receipts to the endogenous accounts (and they may be transfer payments of state pensions for example, as well as demand for goods). The income of these endogenous accounts is raised and they therefore increase their payments. Some of the payments leak to exogenous accounts—in this example paying for investment goods, while others re-enter as income to endogenous accounts, and this new income generates both further leakages and further payments to the endogenous accounts.

The full process is again represented as the sum of a geometric progression with matrix coefficients

$$\mathbf{z}_1 = (\mathbf{I} + \mathbf{A}_{11} + \mathbf{A}_{11}^2 + \mathbf{A}_{11}^3 + \ldots)\mathbf{A}_{12}\mathbf{z}_2.$$

If $\mathbf{A}_{11}$ has the (distinct) eigenvalues $\lambda_1, \ldots, \lambda_4$ then there exists a non-singular matrix $\mathbf{P}$ and a diagonal matrix $\mathbf{\Lambda} = \text{diag}(\lambda_1, \ldots, \lambda_4)$ such that

$$\mathbf{P}^{-1}\mathbf{A}_{11}^n\mathbf{P} = \mathbf{\Lambda}^n$$

for all powers of $\mathbf{A}_{11}$ [see I, Theorem 7.4.2], so that

$$\mathbf{z}_1 = \mathbf{P}(\mathbf{I} + \mathbf{\Lambda} + \mathbf{\Lambda}^2 + \cdots)\mathbf{P}^{-1}\mathbf{A}_{12}\mathbf{Z}_2.$$

But since $\lambda = \mathrm{diag}(\lambda_1, \ldots, \lambda_4)$ this series will converge if the series $1 + \lambda_i + \lambda_i^2 + \lambda_i^3 + \cdots$ converges for all λ_i. This will be true if and only if $|\lambda_i| < 1$ for all i [see IV, Example 1.7.2], and under these circumstances the infinite series of diagonal matrices above will sum to a diagonal matrix $(\mathbf{I} - \mathbf{\Lambda})^{-1}$ with non-zero elements $1/(1 - \lambda_i)$, applying the solution to each element individually. Now

$$\mathbf{I} - \mathbf{\Lambda} = \mathbf{P}(\mathbf{I} - \mathbf{A}_{11})\mathbf{P}^{-1},$$

so by [I, (6.4.4)]

$$(\mathbf{I} - \mathbf{\Lambda})^{-1} = \mathbf{P}^{-1}(\mathbf{I} - \mathbf{A}_{11})^{-1}\mathbf{P},$$

and since

$$\mathbf{z}_1 = \mathbf{P}(\mathbf{I} - \mathbf{\Lambda})^{-1}\mathbf{P}^{-1}\mathbf{A}_{12}\mathbf{z}_2$$

we have

$$\mathbf{z}_1 = (\mathbf{I} - \mathbf{A}_{11})^{-1}\mathbf{A}_{12}\mathbf{z}_2.$$

The matrix $(\mathbf{I} - \mathbf{A}_{11})^{-1}$ is known as a *multiplier matrix*. It shows how the effects of exogenous receipts by some or all of the endogenous accounts are multiplied throughout the system. The condition that the largest eigenvalue (the *Frobenius root*) of $\mathbf{A}_{11}$ should be less than 1 may be somewhat complex. Solow (1952) proved the following which is a special case of [I, Proposition 7.3.14]:

If $\mathbf{A}$ is a nonnegative indecomposable matrix none of whose column sums is greater than one and at least one of whose column sums is less than one, then all the eigenvalues of $\mathbf{A}$ have modulus less than one and the infinite series $\mathbf{I} + \mathbf{A} + \mathbf{A}^2 + \cdots$ will converge.

If $\mathbf{A}$ is decomposable [see I, Definition 7.11.1] then $\mathbf{I} + \mathbf{A} + \mathbf{A}^2 + \cdots$ converges if the Solov restriction holds for each of its indecomposable diagonal submatrices, in these cases $\mathbf{A}$ is called a *Solow matrix*. Note that Solow's theorem may also be formulated in terms of an equivalent condition on the rows, since transposition does not affect eigenvalues [see I, Proposition 7.2.4].

In this example $\mathbf{A}_{11}$ has one of the four column sums zero and none greater than 1, and the matrix is not decomposable. Thus the multiplier matrix exists and indeed, since

$$\mathbf{I} - \mathbf{A}_{11} = \begin{pmatrix} 1 & 0 & -1 & 0 \\ -1 & 1 & 0 & 0 \\ 0 & -c & 1 & 0 \\ 0 & c-1 & 0 & 1 \end{pmatrix},$$

we have [see I, (6.12.1)]

$$(\mathbf{I} - \mathbf{A}_{11})^{-1} = \begin{pmatrix} \dfrac{1}{1-c} & \dfrac{c}{1-c} & \dfrac{1}{1-c} & 0 \\[2ex] \dfrac{1}{1-c} & \dfrac{1}{1-c} & \dfrac{1}{1-c} & 0 \\[2ex] \dfrac{c}{1-c} & \dfrac{c}{1-c} & \dfrac{1}{1-c} & 0 \\[2ex] 1 & 1 & 1 & 1 \end{pmatrix}.$$

Looking at the elements of this multiplier matrix we see the effect on the total income of each account of one unit of exogenous income to each account. Thus one unit of extra investment generates one unit of exogenous income to production and raises production and national income (which are equal) by $1/(1-c)$ (the result derived in the earlier case). Consumption rises by $c/(1-c)$ and savings by 1. Income and output adjust so that enough savings are generated to pay for investment. One unit of exogenous national income has a smaller effect on output since a part of it is saved and does not generate demand for real output. One unit of exogenous consumption has the same effects on output as exogenous investment (it can be thought of as government consumption), but leads to a higher increment in consumption. One unit of exogenous savings has no effect except a unit addition to saving since savings leak out of the system immediately and no component of saving is paid to any of the endogenous accounts.

3.3. INPUT–OUTPUT MODELS

The previous example showed how a linear model based on a set of accounts could be constructed for a complete economy. The structure of production was not disaggregated in that simple example but, from the algebraic exposition it was clear how such a model could be extended to show both production and the institutional side of the economy in greater detail [see §2.3]. This section looks at the tradition of input–output modelling, which focuses on the production side of the economy and devotes less attention to the determinants of final demand [see §2.2]. Input–output models originally developed by Leontief (1936) relate a given structure of final demand (as opposed to intermediate demand for the output of one industry as an input to itself or another industry) to gross output. The dual of the system can be seen as naturally representing a system of relative prices. [see §3.4]. Both the system and its dual are simply modified to cover the case where the incremental inputs needed to provide marginal output differ from the average input mix per unit of output. The dual of this system provides a set of relative prices calculated on the assumption that prices are set equal to marginal rather than average cost. Finally the models are extended to show the effects of subsistence wages and capital accumulation in such disaggregate economies.

3.3.1. The simple input–output system

This system can again best be considered from the standpoint of an accounting matrix. Each industry produces only one good, if this simplifying assumption were not made goods and industries would have to be distinguished see Table 2.2), and the output of each industry is supplied as inputs to other industries or goes to meet final demand. The difference between the value of the material inputs consumed and the value of an industry's output is the value it adds in the productive process. This value added, which goes to pay wages and yields profits, will in practice normally be positive but it is possible that there may be demand for the output of industries whose operation *subtracts* value.

The full set of accounts appears as in Table 2.1 and yields

$$\mathbf{q} = \mathbf{Aq} + \mathbf{e} = (\mathbf{I} - \mathbf{A})^{-1}\mathbf{e}, \tag{3.3.1}$$

where $\mathbf{q}$ and $\mathbf{e}$ denote the output vector and the vector of final demands, and $\mathbf{A}$ denotes the input–output coefficient matrix. The vector of value added per unit of output is given by

$$\mathbf{f} = \hat{\mathbf{q}}^{-1}\mathbf{y}, \tag{3.3.2}$$

where $\mathbf{y}$ denotes the vector of costs of primary inputs into industries. It is seen that, in order to meet a vector of final demand $\mathbf{e}$, material inputs $\mathbf{Ae}$ are needed and value $\mathbf{f'e}$ is added. These inputs require further inputs of $\mathbf{A}^2\mathbf{e}$ and generate additional value added of $\mathbf{f'Ae}$. Following through the process total output is given as $\mathbf{q} = (\mathbf{I} + \mathbf{A} + \mathbf{A}^2 + \cdots)\mathbf{e}$ and this generates value added of $\mathbf{f'q}$. Provided $\mathbf{A}$ satisfies the eigenvalue condition of the previous section $\mathbf{q} = (\mathbf{I} - \mathbf{A})^{-1}\mathbf{e}$ and the total value added is $z = \mathbf{f'}(\mathbf{I} - \mathbf{A})^{-1}\mathbf{e}$. But $\mathbf{f'} = \mathbf{i'}(\mathbf{I} - \mathbf{A})$ where $\mathbf{i'} = (1, 1, 1, 1)$ and therefore

$$z = \mathbf{i'}(\mathbf{I} - \mathbf{A})(\mathbf{I} - \mathbf{A})^{-1}\mathbf{e} = \mathbf{i'e}$$

proving that in the solution to this model, total value added equals total final demand [cf. Equation (2.2.7)].

Provided each industry adds value, a vector of positive gross output will also be associated with a positive vector of final demand. Under these circumstances $\mathbf{A}$ will be a Solow matrix: Solow (1952) proved also that if $\mathbf{A}$ satisfies his conditions all the elements of $(\mathbf{I} - \mathbf{A})^{-1}$ will be positive and therefore a positive vector of final demand must also imply a positive vector of gross output.

But if some industries subtract value under what circumstances is the economy as a whole still capable of meeting positive final demand for all goods? Clearly if some key industry, whose output is needed as input to other industries, subtracts value, then it may be that the economy as a whole is incapable of meeting positive final demand. Or alternatively a positive final demand would only be met in the impossible situation of negative gross output.

Although the Solow conditions may be sufficient for the economy to be productive they are not necessary. It may be possible to meet a positive vector of final demand with positive gross output even though some industries subtract value. Hawkins and Simon (1949) investigated necessary conditions for an economy as a whole to be productive (a productive economy being one that meets positive final demand). If the economy is represented by an input–output coefficient matrix, **A**, derived as in the example above, then the following theorem holds.

THEOREM 3.3.1. *An economy will be productive if and only if all the principle minors of the matrice* $(I - A)$ *are positive.*

Algebraically this may be expressed as

$$1 - a_{ii} > 0 \quad \begin{vmatrix} 1 - a_{ii} & -a_{ij} \\ -a_{ji} & 1 - a_{jj} \end{vmatrix} > 0 \quad \begin{vmatrix} 1 - a_{ii} & -a_{ij} & -a_{ik} \\ -a_{ji} & 1 - a_{jj} & -a_{jk} \\ -a_{ki} & -a_{kj} & 1 - a_{kk} \end{vmatrix} > 0 | (I - A) | > 0$$

$\forall i \neq j \neq k$ [see I, §7.3 and §7.11]
Metzler (1945) presents an alternative condition expressed in the following:

THEOREM 3.3.2. *The following two conditions are equivalent:*
  (1) *The largest eigenvalue of* **A** *is less than 1.*
  (2) *All the principle minors of* **A** *are positive.*

For a proof of this see for example Woods (1978). The meaning may be seen most clearly from the condition $1 - a_{ii} > 0$. If an industry needs more than one unit of its own output as an input to produce one unit of output clearly that industry will not be capable of meeting positive final demand from positive output. The subsequent conditions apply this same principle taking account of indirect inputs embodied in the output of other industries. If industry i produces a major input into industry j and industry j produces a major input into industry i then although each industry on its own may use little 'own input' there is a large amount of indirect own input and this can equally imply that some industries are incapable of meeting positive final demand from positive gross output. This problem may apply equally to indirect inputs routed through other intermediate inputs. The condition that all principle minors be positive takes account of all possible combinations of industries and ensures that, for no industry can direct or indirect inputs exceed output. A consequence of the Hawkins–Simon conditions is, as with the Solow conditions, that $[I - A]^{-1}$ is positive definite [see I, §9.2].

Classic input–output analysis assumes a fixed technology. In the presence of local economies or diseconomies of scale it will be the case that marginal input requirements differ from average requirements. This problem is, however, solved in exactly the same way. For a marginal input–output table can, at least notionally be constructed as the difference between two standard input–output tables produced on the same price base. It will also satisfy the constraints that each row total equals each column total and, dividing by column totals the marginal coefficients can be obtained. Pyatt and Round (1979) show the effects of replacing average by marginal coefficients in a linear disaggregate model of the Sri Lanka economy, although in a slightly different context.

Let $\mathbf{M}$ represent the matrix of marginal coefficients, and $\mathbf{e}$ and $\mathbf{q}$ be defined as before. Now the accounting constraint together with the assumption about marginal input technology implies that

$$\Delta = \mathbf{M}\Delta\mathbf{q} + \Delta\mathbf{e}.$$

Again $\mathbf{I} - \mathbf{M}$ must satisfy the Hawkins–Simon conditions for a positive increment to gross output to be associated with a positive increment to final demand. The full relation between gross output and final demand is of course

$$\mathbf{q} = \mathbf{q}_0 + (\mathbf{I} - \mathbf{M})^{-1}(\mathbf{e} - \mathbf{e}_0),$$

where $\mathbf{e}_0$ and $\mathbf{q}_0$ represent the level of final demand and gross output about which the marginal multipliers are calculated. One consequence of the use of marginal relationships is non-homogeneity. Multiplying final demand by some matrix does not normally multiply gross output by that matrix (unless $\mathbf{e}_0, \mathbf{q}_0 = \mathbf{0}$).

3.3.2. Expanded reproduction

The simple input–output system is a static system. If an expanding system is considered some of the output which, in the previous casewent to meet final demand, must be added to the inputs required in the expanding system. One must put aside an amount $g\mathbf{Aq}$ in order to meet the increased demands, where g is the rate of growth of the economy. Thus the multiplier equation becomes

$$\mathbf{q} = (\mathbf{I} - \mathbf{A})^{-1}(\mathbf{e} + g\mathbf{Aq})$$

so that

$$\mathbf{e} = (\mathbf{I} - (1 + g)\mathbf{A})\mathbf{q}.$$

The *maximum sustainable rate of growth* is that growth in an economy which re-invests all its net output and does not supply any final demand. In this case $\mathbf{e} = \mathbf{0}$ implying that $|(\mathbf{I} - (1 + g)\mathbf{A})| = 0$ as $\mathbf{q} \neq 0$ [see I, Definition 6.4.2]. Thus the rate of growth is given by $\lambda = (1 + g)^{-1}$, that is

$$g = \lambda^{-1} - 1,$$

where λ is an eigenvalue of $\mathbf{A}$ [see I, Theorem 7.2.3]. The problem of which eigenvalue gives the maximum sustainable rate of growth is solved using the following theorem of Frobenius [see I, Theorem 7.11.1]:

THEOREM No. 3.3.3. *If* $\mathbf{A}$ *is nonnegative and indecomposable then the largest eigenvalue* λ^* *of* $\mathbf{A}$ *is the only positive eigenvalue of* $\mathbf{A}$ *and the associated eigenvector is the only positive eigenvector of* $\mathbf{A}$.

Only this eigenvalue will be associated with an economically feasible maximum growth rate (see Woods, 1978, p. 23). Barker (1971) found a value of 25% p.a. for the economy.

In the marginal case where returns to scale are only asymptotically constant the solution is more complex and less neat. In the long run the solution associated with the largest root of the matrix of marginal coefficients dominates.

3.4. PRICE SYSTEMS

Since the system of matrices relates inputs to outputs and expresses the technology of production in terms of the inputs per unit of output, it may also be used to relate costs to prices; the price of one unit of output will equal the total costs involved in its production. Thus, for industry 1 in a 2-good case

$$p_1 = a_{11}p_1 + a_{21}p_2 + w_1 f_1,$$

where p_i is the price of output of industry i and
   w_i is the price of value-added per unit of output.

In the case considered above where $\mathbf{A}$ and $\mathbf{f}$ represent coefficients in terms of value rather than physical units the prices of goods and of value added can be considered as base-weighted index numbers.

In vector form we have [cf. Equation (2.2.6)], provided $\mathbf{A}$ satisfies the same conditions as before,

$$\mathbf{p}' = \mathbf{p}'\mathbf{A} + \hat{\mathbf{w}}\mathbf{f}$$

or

$$\mathbf{p}' = \hat{\mathbf{w}}\mathbf{f}(\mathbf{I} - \mathbf{A})^{-1},$$

where $\hat{\mathbf{w}}$ is a diagonalization of the vector $\mathbf{w}$. Just as in the quantity case it was possible to derive the solution as the sum of an infinite series representing the 'inputs required to produce inputs' and so on, so here we have the cost of the inputs used in producing the inputs. In the simple case where the price index of value added is the same for all industries, one has all prices depending on direct and indirect factor inputs and if labour is the only factor input prices will then be dependent on the value of labour input—the labour theory of value will hold sway.

If $\mathbf{A}$ is replaced by the matrix of marginal coefficients $\mathbf{M}$, we instead obtain the variation in price arising from a change in variable costs

$$\Delta \mathbf{p}' = \Delta \hat{\mathbf{w}} \mathbf{f} (\mathbf{I} - \mathbf{M})^{-1}.$$

If pricing is carried out on a marginal cost basis this, rather than the differential of the previous (average cost), price equation will show the effects of a change in the price of factor inputs on the prices of output.

So far a system in which there are no profits, or in which profits and wages are not distinguished in the value added vector has been considered. However, one may express profit as a mark-up on prices so that the price equation becomes instead

$$\mathbf{p}' = \mathbf{p}'\mathbf{A} + \pi \mathbf{p}'\mathbf{A} + \hat{\mathbf{w}}^* \mathbf{f}^{*\prime},$$

where π is a proportional mark-up applied to all prices and $\mathbf{w}^*$ and $\mathbf{f}$ now refer only to a wage index and labour input/unit output (as a fraction in base-period prices).

In this system described by Sraffa (1960),

$$\mathbf{p}' = \hat{\mathbf{w}}^* \mathbf{f}^{*\prime} (\mathbf{I} - (1 + \pi)\mathbf{A})^{-1}$$

and the maximum mark-up possible is given as a solution to

$$\mathbf{p}'(\mathbf{I} - (1 + \pi)\mathbf{A}) = 0$$

since the wage cannot be negative.

As in Section 3.3.2, solutions to this system are given if $1/(1 + \pi)$ is an eigenvalue of $\mathbf{A}$, and the only eigenvalue yielding positive prices is that eigenvalue corresponding to the Frobenius root. The situation corresponds exactly to the earlier case where the maximum feasible growth rate was analysed. The economic meaning is clear: in one situation all the net output of the economy is reinvested; in the other all the value added is appropriated as a mark-up leaving none left for wages; but value added equals net output and the ratio of value added to gross output must equal the ratio of net to gross output. Further since in the first case all industries expand at the same rate while in the second the mark-up is the same in all industries the two ratios must be equal. Unfortunately, although the approach used in modelling quantities extends naturally to model the institutional side of the economy no clear interpretation can be given to the solution of the dual problem.

3.5. A SUBSISTENCE WAGE AND FIXED CAPITAL

The above discussion has looked at the maximum profit share or the maximum rate of growth attainable on the assumption that the whole of output can be accumulated, which, because of the gross domestic product identity is equivalent to the assumption that wages can be driven down to zero in the dual problem. The modifications required to remove this are relatively straightforward. For we can assume that a vector **l** of labour inputs is associated with a vector of unit outputs, and that one unit of labour requires for its subsistence a vector of goods **c**. The goods required to sustain the labour producing output **q** are therefore given as **cl′q** (**c**, **l** and **q** are all n-dimensional column vectors) and the equation showing commodity balances is

$$\mathbf{q} = \mathbf{Aq} + \mathbf{cl'q} + \mathbf{e} \quad \text{in the static case,}$$

where **e** is now the vector of surplus available after meeting the subsistence wage rather than the vector of final demand. The Hawkins–Simon conditions now have to apply to $\mathbf{I} - (\mathbf{A} + \mathbf{cl'})$ rather than $\mathbf{I} - \mathbf{A}$ for the system to be capable of generating a positive surplus in each industry.

In the case of an expanding economy enough surplus output must be retained to accumulate not only extra material inputs, but also to pay a subsistence wage to the expanding labour force; thus in the case of accumulation the system becomes

$$\mathbf{q} = \mathbf{Aq} + \mathbf{cl'q} + g(\mathbf{Aq} + \mathbf{cl'q}) + \mathbf{e}$$

and the maximum rate of growth (at which $\mathbf{e} = \mathbf{0}$) is given from the largest eigenvalue of

$$\mathbf{A} + \mathbf{cl'}.$$

THEOREM 3.5.1. *If A is an indecomposable matrix and* $\mathbf{A} - \mathbf{B}$ *is nonnegative with no element of* **B** *negative, then the Frobenius root of A is greater than that of* **B**. [See Woods, 1978, p. 23, for proof, and I, §7.11].

It is therefore clear that, since **cl′** is positive, the payment of a subsistence wage must reduce the maximum feasible growth rate.

In the system above final demand was split into an endogenous component (the subsistence wage) and an exogenous component. In the same way the value added can be split into wages and surplus. The wage component must, by definition, at the ruling prices, be adequate to buy the goods required for subsistence and therefore the surplus will, as a consequence of the fact that accounting balances hold for all other rows and columns in the system, buy the exogenous component. Since it was only this exogenous component which could be accumulated in the expanding economy and it is this exogenous component bought by profit (which is now earned on all capital, material inputs and wage goods) one would expect the duality between the maximum rate of growth and the maximum rate of profit to continue to hold.

In this system the subsistence wage is equal to **p′c** since it buys the goods in the subsistence basket **c**, and the accounting balance of the price equation is therefore given as

$$\mathbf{p'} = \mathbf{p'A} + \mathbf{p'cl'} + \mathbf{f},$$

where **f** represents the surplus per unit of output. If the surplus is expressed as a mark-up, π, on inputs of goods and labour one obtains

$$\mathbf{p}' = \mathbf{p}'(1 + \pi)(\mathbf{A} + \mathbf{cl}')$$

and the maximum mark-up is again given as the solution to the system

$$\mathbf{p}'(\mathbf{I} - (1 + \pi)(\mathbf{A} + \mathbf{cl}')) = \mathbf{0}.$$

The duality between this and the maximum growth rate problem is clear and again the result that any increase in the subsistence wage must unambiguously reduce the maximum mark-up is obtained.

The previous examples have assumed that no fixed capital is involved in the productive process. Accumulation is only necessary to add to the stock of material inputs and the wages fund. On the other hand most macroeconomic models focus on capital as though it is entirely fixed, which is more nearly true. An extension of the previous examples to consider both fixed and circulating capital requires a slightly different presentation of accumulation but preserves the dual nature of the quantity and price models seen so far.

Suppose that in order to produce a vector $\mathbf{q}$ of output, a vector $\mathbf{Vq}$ of capital goods is required. This includes not only fixed equipment such as buildings and machinery, but also the stock of inputs needed to run the process and the basket of wage goods needed to pay labour. Fixed capital is assumed to be not used up, and the stocks of inputs and wage goods are regenerated in the productive process. Further a vector $\mathbf{k}$ of these capital goods requires a combination of $\mathbf{Kk}$ output goods. $\mathbf{K}$ is a classification converter which shows for example the inputs of steel and engineering goods needed to produce one unit of 'plant and machinery' or the inputs needed to make one 'wage good' or one 'input' mix for each industry. The commodity balance equation is now

$$\mathbf{q} = \mathbf{Aq} + \mathbf{cl}'\mathbf{q} + g\mathbf{KVq} + \mathbf{e},$$

where the first two terms represent the fact that circulating capital must be replaced and the third shows the output goods which must be accumulated in order to allow the various types of capital to grow at rate g.

Again the system will be capable of meeting a positive demand for surplus and growing at rate g if $(\mathbf{I} - \mathbf{A} - \mathbf{cl}' - g\mathbf{KV})$ satisfies the Hawkins–Simon conditions. Since $g\mathbf{KV}$ and $\mathbf{I} - \mathbf{A} - \mathbf{cl}'$ are positive, this matrix must also satisfy these conditions. The maximum rate of growth is given as g satisfying

$$|\mathbf{I} - \mathbf{A} - \mathbf{cl}' - g\mathbf{KV}| = 0$$

but

$$(\mathbf{I} - \mathbf{A} - \mathbf{cl}' - g\mathbf{KV}) = (\mathbf{I} - g\mathbf{KV}(\mathbf{I} - \mathbf{A} - \mathbf{cl}')^{-1})(\mathbf{I} - \mathbf{A} - \mathbf{cl}').$$

Since only the term $\mathbf{I} - g\mathbf{KV}(\mathbf{I} - \mathbf{A} - \mathbf{cl})^{-1}$ is variable in $\mathbf{g}$, only it need be considered. The Frobenius root of $\mathbf{KV}(\mathbf{I} - \mathbf{A} - \mathbf{cl})^{-1}$ clearly leads to the solution and is the only root associated with an entirely positive eigenvector [see Theorem 3.3.3]. This in turn is required to yield an entirely positive vector of gross outputs, since $\mathbf{I} - \mathbf{A} - \mathbf{cl}'$ satisfies the Hawkins–Simon conditions. By exact analogy with the previous examples, and for the same economic reasons, it will be seen that this maximum rate of growth is also the rate or profit measured as a return on capital associated with the given subsistence wage and positive prices.

3.6. A TRADE MODEL AND FINANCIAL BALANCES

The previous sections have showed how a variety of basic linear economic models can be cast in an accounting matrix so that their solution can be helpfully expressed as the inversion of a matrix of coefficients derived from the accounting matrix. The Keynesian model focused on the expenditure decision while the input–output models analysed production and devoted little attention to the determinants of demand. A full model may of course disaggregate both. This section applies a simple disaggregation of both to a linear model of two-country trade. Under these circumstances trade flows become intermediate rather than final demand. Indeed if one considers each country in the same way as an industry in the input–output table the analogy is clear. Imports are an intermediate input used in the production process and exports by one country can be considered as meeting intermediate demand in the other. This approach to modelling the international economy was first developed by Metzler (1950) and has subsequently been applied by others such as Thorbecke and Field (1974). Machlup (1943) also considered the analysis of multipliers in economies facing foreign trade.

As in the case of a model of the domestic economy the degree of consolidation depends on the issue the modeller wishes to highlight. Here a simple model with two countries trading with one another is considered. The institutional sectors within the two countries are not distinguished, the model can be considered as a simple two-country version of the Keynesian model. The accounting matrix has the form shown in Table 3.2. In this matrix M_{12} shows imports by country 2 from country 1 while M_{21} shows imports by country 1 from country 2. Otherwise variables have the same meaning as in the Keynesian model considered earlier, the indices indicating the countries to which they refer. B_i indicates the financial saving of country i. Since the system as a whole cannot acquire net financial assets $B_1 + B_2 = 0$. One can consider investment and the financial accounts as exogenous so that saving is a leakage from the system and the economies are driven by investment in the two countries. Dividing by column totals the following coefficient matrix is obtained for a consolidated system

$$\begin{pmatrix} 0 & m_{12} & 0 & 0 & 1 & 0 & 0 & 0 \\ m_{21} & 0 & 0 & 0 & 0 & 1 & 0 & 0 \\ 1-m_{21} & 0 & 0 & 0 & 0 & 0 & 0 & 0 \\ 0 & 1-m_{12} & 0 & 0 & 0 & 0 & 0 & 0 \\ 0 & 0 & c_1 & 0 & 0 & 0 & 0 & 0 \\ 0 & 0 & 0 & c_2 & 0 & 0 & 0 & 0 \\ 0 & 0 & 1-c_2 & 0 & 0 & 0 & 0 & 0 \\ 0 & 0 & 0 & 1-c_2 & 0 & 0 & 0 & 0 \end{pmatrix},$$

Table 3.2

		Production 1	Production 2	National income 1	National income 2	Consumption 1	Consumption 2	Saving 1	Saving 2	Investment 1	Investment 2	NAFA	Total
Production	1		M_{12}			C_1				I_1			Z_1
	2	M_{21}					C_2				I_2		Z_2
National income	1	Y_1											Y_1
	2		Y_2										Y_2
Consumption	1			C_1									C_1
	2				C_2								C_2
Saving	1			S_1									S_1
	2				S_2								S_2
Investment	1							I_1					I_1
	2								I_2				I_2
NAFA								B_1	B_2				0
Total		Z_1	Z_2	Y_1	Y_2	C_1	C_2	S_1	S_2	I_1	I_2	0	

where c_i represents the propensity to consume from national income in region i and m_{ij} is the fraction of final demand or gross output (national income plus imports) spent on imports. The more usual propensity to import from income is given as $m_{ij}/(1 - m_{ij})$. Again saving generates no income for the endogenous accounts; it all leaks away into the capital account. Provided both the propensities to import and to consume are less than 1 this matrix is a Solow matrix and therefore the model derived from it can be solved with positive values for demand and income in both countries. Looking only at the effects of exogenous final demand for brevity, the following submatrix of the full multiplier matrix is derived

$$\mathbf{A}^* = \frac{1}{\Delta} \begin{pmatrix} 1 - c_2(1 - m_{12}) & m_{12} \\ m_{21} & 1 - c_1(1 - m_{21}) \end{pmatrix},$$

where $\Delta = (1 - c_2(1 - m_{12}))(1 - c_1(1 - m_{21})) - m_{12}m_{21}$.

This shows the vector of gross output derived from a vector of exogenous final demand such as investment, as

$$\begin{pmatrix} Z_1 \\ Z_2 \end{pmatrix} = \mathbf{A}^* \begin{pmatrix} I_1 \\ I_2 \end{pmatrix}.$$

Provided the propensities to import and consume are less than 1 domestic investment has a larger effect on the home than the foreign country, for

$$1 - c_j(1 - m_{ij}) > m_{ij}, \, i, j = 1, 2 \text{ and } i \neq j$$

so that

$$1 - c_j > m_{ij}(1 - c_j) \text{ and } m_{ij} < 1 \text{ provided } c_j < 1.$$

This result provides a specific example of the proposition that, in an input–output system which satisfies the Hawkins–Simons conditions an increase in the demand for one good, with no other changes, leads to a larger increase of the output of that good than of any other good (see Woods, 1978, p. 55). In this model the goods are of course replaced by countries.

Financial balances

Although trade multiplier models usually focus on the international transmission of changes in demand, the system described above can be used to determine the financial balances arising from given levels of exogenous demand in each country. Goodwin (1980) provides a numerical example of this. Taking another submatrix of the full multiplier matrix, to show the savings generated by investment in each country, the savings multiplier is

$$\mathbf{S} = \frac{1}{\Delta} \begin{pmatrix} (1 - c_1)(1 - m_{21})[1 - c_2(1 - m_{12})] & (1 - c_1)(1 - m_{21})m_{12} \\ (1 - c_2)(1 - m_{12})m_{21} & (1 - c_2)(1 - m_{12})[1 - c_1(1 - m_{21})] \end{pmatrix}$$

where the saving vector $\begin{pmatrix} S_1 \\ S_2 \end{pmatrix}$ is related to the investment vector

$$\begin{pmatrix} I_1 \\ I_2 \end{pmatrix} \text{ as } \begin{pmatrix} S_1 \\ S_2 \end{pmatrix} = S \begin{pmatrix} I_1 \\ I_2 \end{pmatrix}.$$

Now total saving $S_1 + S_2$ must equal total real investment $I_1 + I_2$ although they need not be equal in either of the countries (one can borrow from the other). But this condition implies that each column sum of the matrix S must be 1, for if $i' = (1, 1)$ then

$$i' \begin{pmatrix} I_1 \\ I_2 \end{pmatrix} = i'S \begin{pmatrix} I_1 \\ I_2 \end{pmatrix} \Rightarrow i'S = i'$$

since this holds for any investment vector. A non-negative matrix whose column sums are all 1 is known as a stochastic matrix, from probability theory [cf. I, Example 7.11.2]. It may be proved that the Frobenius root of a stochastic matrix is 1 [see Woods, 1978, p. 51, and I, Proposition 7.13.4]. This condition implies that the level of investment in each country, such that no borrowing is taking place, is positive. For the vector of financial balances $\begin{pmatrix} B_1 \\ B_2 \end{pmatrix}$ is derived as savings less investment.

$$\begin{pmatrix} B_1 \\ B_2 \end{pmatrix} = (S - I) \begin{pmatrix} I_1 \\ I_2 \end{pmatrix}$$

but if

$$\begin{pmatrix} B_1 \\ B_2 \end{pmatrix} = \begin{pmatrix} 0 \\ 0 \end{pmatrix}$$

then $\begin{pmatrix} I_1 \\ I_2 \end{pmatrix}$ is the eigenvector of S associated with the Frobenius root and is therefore positive. [see I, Theorem 7.11.1]. In this example the eigenvector is a multiple of

$$\begin{pmatrix} (1 - c_1)(1 - m_{21})m_{12} \\ (1 - c_2)(1 - m_{12})m_{21} \end{pmatrix}$$

and it is clear that, if the propensities to consume and import are less than 1, this vector is positive.

In a more general framework full account must be taken of capital transfers before financial balances can be calculated. If some sectors in an economy save but do not invest or pay capital transfers then it will no longer be possible to calculate a positive vector of exogenous investment such that all financial balances are zero. For example, if households only spend a part of their income then any positive level of income will lead to household saving; if they do not invest or pay substantial transfers they can only save in financial assets. But this implies that another sector must spend more than it receives. In many economies the Government sector fulfils this role of 'mopping up' private saving: private investment is itself too low.

3.7. CONCLUSIONS

This chapter has illustrated through a variety of examples the application of and analytical properties of linear models. The problems in deriving the data needed to construct such matrices and their empirical application in developing countries are described in sources such as Pyatt and Roe (1977) while the analytical properties of linear models are considered further by, for example, Woods (1978) and Murata (1977).

The systems extend naturally to full dynamic frameworks in which, for example, the behaviour of accounts considered here as exogenous may in fact be determined by the history of the system. If investment is cumulated into a capital stock and itself depends on the level of output and the existing capital stock, then a model of the Hicks–Samuelson (1939) accelerator type will be derived. The simple steady growth models considered here will be seen as a special case of these more general models. Cumulation of real capital is not the only cause of dynamic motion in such a model. If an institutional sector or a country is borrowing it will have to pay interest on its cumulated debt, and the lenders will receive interest on their financial assets. Thus the historical path as well as the current level of exogenous demand will influence the outcome.

The application of such linear models cannot be considered to be restricted by doubts about the linearity of real economies. They provide powerful tools to analyse the behaviour of economies and the structural simplicity they offer can be regarded as compensating adequately for the approximation of linearity.

3.8. REFERENCES

Barker, T. S. (1971). A maximum sustainable growth rate for the British economy. *Review of Economic Studies*, **38**, 369–376.

Goodwin, R. M. (1980). World trade multipliers. *Journal of Post-Keynesian Economics*.

Hawkins, D., and Simon, H. A. (1949). Note: Some conditions of macroeconomic stability. *Econometrica*, **17**, 245–248.

Hicks, J. R. (1950). *A Contribution to the Theory of the Trade Cycle*. Oxford University Press, London.

Kahn, R. F. (1931). The relation of home investment to unemployment. *Economic Journal*, **41**.

Keynes, J. M. (1936). *The General Theory of Employment, Interest and Money*. Harcourt, New York.

Keynes, J. M. (1940). *How to Pay for the War*. Macmillan, London.

Leontief, W. (1936). Quantitative input and output relations in the economic system of the United States. *Review of Economics and Statistics*.

Machlup, F. (1943). *International Trade and the National Income Multiplier*. Blakiston, Philadelphia.

Metzler, L. A. (1945). Stability of multiple markets: the Hicks conditions. *Econometrica*, **13**, 277–292.

Metzler, L. A. (1950). A multiple-region theory of income and trade. *Econometrica*, **18**, 329–354.

Murata, Y. (1977). *Mathematics for Stability and Optimisation of Economic Systems.* Academic Press, London.

Pyatt, F. G., and Roe, A. R. (1977). *Social Accounting for Development Planning with Special Reference to Sri Lanka.* Cambridge University Press, London.

Pyatt, F. G., and Round, J. (1979). Accounting and fixed price multipliers in a social accounting matrix. *Economic Journal*, **89**.

Samuelson, P. A. (1939). Interactions between the multiplier analysis and the principle of acceleration. *Review of Economics and Statistics*, **21**, 75–78.

Solow, R. M. (1952). On the structure of linear models. *Econometrica*, **20**, 29–46.

Sraffa, P. (1960). *Production of Commodities by Means of Commodities.* Cambridge University Press, London.

Thorbecke, E., and Field, A. J. (1974). A ten-region model of world trade. *International Trade and Finance* (ed. Sellekaerts). Macmillan, London.

Tinbergen, J. (1937). *An Econometric Approach to Business Cycle Problems.* Herman & Cie.

UNSO (United Nations) (1968). *A System of National Accounts*, Studies in Methods, series F, no. 2, rev. 3. United Nations, New York.

Woods, J. E. (1978). *Mathematical Economics.* Longman, London.

Mathematical Methods in Economics
Edited by F. van der Ploeg
© 1984, John Wiley & Sons, Ltd.

4

Multisectoral Models and Joint Production

Lionello F. Punzo, *Institute of Economics, Siena* * and Kumaraswamy Velupillai, *European University Institute, Florence, Italy*

4.1. INTRODUCTION

This chapter continues the theme of linear economic models, adopted in Chapters 2 and 3, and pays particular attention to joint production and a modern treatment of Sraffa's (1960) classic work *Production of commodities by means of commodities*. We start with a review of some relevant mathematics. Consider the mapping $f(x, \lambda)$ where $f: \Delta x Z \rightarrow Y$, where Δ is an open set in a Banach space [see IV, §§11.2, 11.6], Z, Y are Banach spaces and f and its first Frechet derivatives [see IV, Definition 19.5.5] are continuous [see IV, §5.3]. In the study of

$$f(x, \lambda) = 0, \lambda \in \Delta, x \in Z;$$ (4.1.1)

a solution of (4.1.1) is given by $(x, \lambda) \in \Delta x Z$ such that (4.1.1) is satisfied. Let $M \subset \Delta x Z$ denote the set of solutions of (4.1.1) and, $\forall \lambda \in \Delta$, put:

$$M_\lambda = \{x \in X : (x, \lambda) \in M\}.$$ (4.1.2)

It has not been sufficiently well recognized that a study of the dependence of the set M_λ on λ can be a unifying analytical framework for important problems in economics, whether static or dynamic, whether within an optimizing system or not. The study of the structure of zeros of (4.1.1) via (4.1.2) by interpreting Δ as a parameter set together with appropriate equivalence relations in open subsets of Z leads, as special cases, to classic results in *comparative statics* in economic

This chapter is dedicated to Richard M. Goodwin in honour of his 70th birthday. Many of the tools and concepts we have employed were first introduced to economists by R. M. Goodwin. In particular, the Perron–Frobenius theorem, now so familiar, was first brought to the attention of the economics community by him in his celebrated discussion with John Chipman in the pages of the *Economic Journal*.

*Visiting Professor, *Department of Economics, UCLA, Los Angeles, USA*

analysis [see also Chapter 8]. On the other hand, when **f** is restricted to be a vector field with suitable equivalence relations [see I, §§5.2, 1.3.3], the analysis of the above equation(s) includes, as special cases, problems in economic dynamics. An example of the former is the nonlinear eigenvalue problem arising, naturally, in Joint Production Systems. Almost all nonlinear *macrodynamic* formulations in economics can be subsumed as examples of the latter (cf. Chapter 11 of the present volume).

Taking a particular realization of (4.1.1) and (4.1.2) as $\mathbf{Ax} \in \lambda \mathbf{Bx}$, we can approach the study of joint production and multisectoral models in economics — and their associated balanced growth paths, implied labour values and the resulting nonsubstitution results — as *generalized eigenvalue problems* and problems in the applications of so-called *generalized theorems of the alternative*. It will be clear, then, that the above membership relation when replaced by (in)equality relations results in applications of Perron–Frobenius type theorems [see I, Theorem 7.11.1] and theorems of the alternative [see V, §4.2.3], and hence can easily be interpreted in terms of well-known formulations of linear multisectoral models of single product economic systems. In this chapter we attempt to present a particular unifying analysis of classic economic problems encountered in the economic theories of growth, value and distribution in terms of mathematical theorems of the above type.

The mathematical formalizations of problems of joint production and multisectoral models in the economics of growth, value and distribution have been determined largely by two sets of issues. On the one hand the extent to which so-called intrinsic joint production, for example of the wool–mutton or iron–coke variety, has been emphasized, has determined, as in mainstream neoclassical theory (cf. Marshall, 1920; Edgeworth, 1881; Jevons, 1871; Samuelson, 1966; Kuga, 1973; Chapter 12), the production function approach. The emphasis on the problems of intrinsic joint production, and hence its formalization in terms of production functions, *implied* accounting concepts emphasising stock-flow dimensions (particularly in the case of durable capital goods). On the other hand, where the causality ran the other way round, that is from the needs of the *accounting and political arithmeticians* [see Chapter 2], it was natural that only flow concepts were emphasized — again, in the particular case of durable goods. The accountant and the political arithmetician had to solve a valuation problem determined by a (periodic) time interval that did not necessarily coincide with the physically determined length of, in particular, durable capital goods. It was therefore not possible to ignore the fact that there were classes of goods that appeared and re-appeared for several of the actuarial and fiscal time periods. The analytical device of considering durable (or fixed) capital goods lasting more than one time period as many different goods appeared as an almost natural solution to this valuation problem. The result was that flow concepts dominated the scheme. Sraffa (1960) and von Neumann (1937) (and their pre-neoclassical predecessors) developed this line of analysis to an outstanding degree of perfection in relation to theories of growth, value and distribution. A third approach, to some extent a hybrid of the above two, resulted from the so-called

Austrian or Neo-Austrian models where accounting relations and intrinsic joint production jointly determined the formalization (cf. in particular Hicks, 1956, 1973) and, thus, stock and flow concepts were equally emphasized. The necessity of an analytical scheme, capable of handling the intricacies of durable capital goods and the complexities of joint production, in one unified format, led, almost naturally, to generalizations of Böhm–Bawerk's ideas of input and output flows characterized as distributions. The distributions, as such, characterized the flows and the moments defined measures of the stock concepts of the production process.

In addition to the *economic rationale* that led to the three different approaches we have outlined above, there are, at least three other inter-related issues that have dominated the mathematical and economic formalization of problems in multisectoral and joint production models. Briefly, they relate to, in mathematical terms, problems of:

(a) homogeneous *vs* inhomogeneous systems [see I, §§5.9, 5.10];
(b) mathematical relations in terms of inequalities as against in terms of equalities [see IV, Chapter 21];
(c) the representations of linear operators as matrices with square *vs* rectangular dimensions [see I, §5.11].

Economically, the above problems translate respectively to (a) so-called closed *vs* open economic systems, (b) whether choice of technique is explicitly considered or not and, finally, (c) whether there is equality between the number of processes and of commodities. Though we treat both homogeneous and inhomogeneous systems, that is closed and open multisectoral models, we have not been as catholic with regard to cases (b) and (c). We have, in the case of (b) and (c) chosen to concentrate on representing economic relations in production in terms of equalities with the associated linear operator given by a square matrix. One major, mathematical, reason is the following: we have relied on a few simple mathematical tools, well known and extensively utilized in economics, to demonstrate most of the important economic propositions. More specifically, we have relied on the *topological* method of theorems of the alternative and the *algebraic* methods of Perron–Frobenius theorems. Thus, a unified methodological and conceptual presentation becomes feasible if the formalization of the economic models is in terms of equalities and square matrices. It seems to us that the study of the structure of zeros of mappings have a generic feature which is increasingly evident in several branches of modelling.

There are other, strictly economic and accounting reasons for choosing to represent relations in terms of inequalities and rectangular matrices. Indeed, a controversy over this issue has, not very long ago, even enlivened the pages of leading economic journals. It is not clear, however, whether the controversy resulted in any light being shed on the advantages of any one choice. At any rate, these issues are brought to the foreground immediately in *any* problem involving joint production. We ourselves, are, therefore, compelled to discuss, however briefly, these problems as soon as we consider joint production.

In our analysis of production in multisectoral models of the economy we take as the prototype the second of the above three approaches for illustrating the applicability of mathematical methods in elucidating problems in the theory of economic growth, value and distribution. Thus, in section 4.2 after formalizing the concept of production in multisectoral models we go on to consider the *special case* of single product industries from the value and quantity aspects. In section 4.3 the general case of multiple product industries or joint production in multisectoral models is analysed. In section 4.4, first the concept of joint production is utilized to analyse the problem of the choice of the economic life time of durable capital goods; and, secondly some discussion of the nonsubstitution theorem in a generalized form is presented. Finally, in a concluding section some directions and hints for explorations along the lines developed at the beginning of this introduction are discussed.

4.2. LINEAR MULTISECTORAL MODELS WITHOUT JOINT PRODUCTION

4.2.1. Simple no joint production systems (NJPS)

From a mathematical point of view, the NJPS is a special 'limiting' case in a class of models: a proper interpretation of its mathematical properties and their consequences for the analysis of growth and distribution, is given in section 4.3 below. Economically, it is interpreted as a *model of industries*. Each industry is represented by a triple $(\mathbf{a}^j, \mathbf{e}^j, l_j)$, where $\mathbf{a}^j$ is a column vector of inputs of material goods, $\mathbf{e}^j$ is a column of outputs where only one entry is assumed to be non-zero and finally l_j is the labour input coefficient (the amount of labour required to produce one unit of the jth good) [see I, §6.2]. There is therefore a strict symmetry between 'industries', identified with the production processes, and goods produced.

It is such a symmetry that is lost in the *general joint production* model (JPS), where a process $(\mathbf{a}^j, \mathbf{b}^j, l_j)$ *may* produce a positive amount of more than one good. From a purely theoretical point of view, this latter framework therefore must be considered as more general.

In capital theory, the NJP model is interpreted as a model of circulating capital, in the sense that only capital goods lasting one period of production are allowed. More precisely, it is assumed that the economic and technological lifetimes of all capital goods are equal to one another and to a common length of time, say the normalized 'year', see Sraffa (1960). On the contrary the JP model is interpreted as the model where the presence of fixed capital goods is allowed for. The jth capital good, installed in the kth process of production, is characterized by a *technological parameter* T_k^j representing the maximal length of time, as a multiple of some basic period, for which the capital good may be used, and by a new *economic variable* t^j, the *economic lifetime* for which, taking into account the other economic variables, it is *profitable* to use it. The problem of choosing the optimal economic lifetime is one of choice of techniques [cf. Chapter 7], a technique now being defined as a mixture of feasible lifetimes for the set of capital goods. From this point of view, the NJP model is again to be seen as a simplified framework where no such choice is considered.

Let us start with Sraffa's (1960) example of 'an extremely simple society' producing just enough to maintain itself and where the necessary commodities are produced by separate industries:

$$240 \text{ gr of wheat} \oplus 12 \text{ t iron} \oplus 18 \text{ pigs} \ominus 450 \text{ gr wheat}$$
$$90 \text{ gr of wheat} \oplus 6 \text{ t iron} \oplus 12 \text{ pigs} \ominus 21 \text{ t iron}$$
$$120 \text{ gr of wheat} \oplus 3 \text{ t iron} \oplus 30 \text{ pigs} \ominus 60 \text{ pigs}$$

Let $\mathbf{Q}$ be the diagonal matrix of gross output, and let $\mathbf{M}$ be the matrix of flows on the left of the above relations. Then, the assumption on the system state can be written as

$$\mathbf{M}'\mathbf{i} = \mathbf{Q}\mathbf{i} \qquad (4.2.1)$$

where $\mathbf{i}$ is the unit sum vector, $\mathbf{i} = (1, 1, \ldots, 1)$, and $\mathbf{M}'$ denotes the transpose of $\mathbf{M}$.

It is then supposed that these produced commodities are exchanged at the annual market which leads Sraffa to make the assertion that:

> There is a unique set of exchange values which, if adopted by the market, restores the original distribution of the products and makes it possible for the process to be repeated; such values spring directly from the methods of production. (Sraffa, 1960, p. 3)

We have here two formal propositions: (a) there is a unique set of exchange values, and (b) these values spring directly from the methods of production. Introducing the prices of the commodities as unknowns, the above example may be rewritten in matrix form [see I, §5.10] as

$$\mathbf{p}\mathbf{T} = \mathbf{p} \qquad (4.2.2)$$

where $\mathbf{T}$ is the input–output matrix, $\mathbf{T} = \mathbf{Q}^{-1}\mathbf{M}'$ [see Chapter 2 and 3, §§3 and 4] and $\mathbf{p}$ is the row-vector of unknown exchange values. The coefficient t_{ij} represents the *share* of the output of the ith good that is being employed in the production of the jth commodity.

Propositions (a) and (b) above can now be stated as: (a)' there is a unique price such that (4.2.2) is satisfied and (b)' this unique vector $\mathbf{p}$ depends on the matrix of technological input–output coefficients $\mathbf{T}$.

At this point some assumptions are introduced [see I, §7.11] in order to solve (4.2.2):

A.1: $\mathbf{T}$ is a nonnegative square matrix
A.2: $\mathbf{T}$ is characterized by the fact that for each row, the sum of the coefficients along the row, is equal to unity
A.3: $\mathbf{T}$ is indecomposable

Note that A.1 derives from the very nature of the input–output coefficients, t_{ij}. A.2 instead comes from the assumption that the system is a closed system, with no inflows or outflows of goods (so that all means of production are produced within the system itself), *and* from the balance relation defining the 'self-reproducing' state of the system. A.3 comes from the idea of focusing on the set of 'basic' goods only, that is the set of goods that are used and produced by themselves. Formally, then, Sraffa's proposition can be summarized in the statement:

THEOREM 4.2.1. *Given* **T** *and A.1, A.2 and A.3, there exists a price vector which is positive and unique up to a scale factor.*

We note that this theorem has been proved also by Gale (1960) for Remak's model of equilibrium in an exchange economy and for a formally analogous model of international trade. Sraffa's matrix shares with Remak's (and the matrix of incomes in international trade) the fact that, not only is it nonnegative, but it can be so transformed also such that column sums are all equal to unity. Matrices of this sort are usually called stochastic, transition or, in Gale's terminology, exchange matrices [see II, §19.3].

Proof. We first prove the existence of a semi-positive price vector without assuming indecomposability of **T**. Then we assume an indecomposable **T** and prove that the semi-positive price vector is in fact a unique set of positive relative prices. From (4.2.2) we have

$$\mathbf{p}(\mathbf{I} - \mathbf{T}) = \mathbf{0} \tag{4.2.3}$$

By a theorem of the alternative (cf. Gale, 1960, pp. 42–49), a variant of a separating hyperplane theorem [IV, §15.2.3] or Farkas Lemma [IV, §15.2.5], we know that (4.2.2) has no solution $\mathbf{p} \geqslant 0$ only if there exists a vector $\mathbf{x}$ such that

$$(\mathbf{I} - \mathbf{T})\mathbf{x} > \mathbf{0}, \tag{4.2.4}$$

or

$$x_i > \sum_{j=1}^{n} t_{ij} x_j, \quad \forall i = 1, 2, \dots, n. \tag{4.2.5}$$

Let $v = \underset{i}{\text{Min}}\, x_i$, say $v = x_1$ without loss of generality. Sum the vectors $\mathbf{t}^j = (t_{ij}, \dots, t_{kj})'$ to give

$$\sum_{j=1}^{n} t_{ij} = 1, \quad \forall i = 1, 2, \dots, n. \tag{4.2.6}$$

Multiply (4.2.6) by x_1 and subtract from (4.2.5)

$$x_i - x_1 > \sum_{j=1}^{n} t_{ij}(x_j - x_1) = \sum_{j=2}^{n} t_{ij}(x_j - x_1), \forall i$$

and, in particular, $\sum_{j=2}^{n} t_{1j}(x_j - x_1) < 0$. But this is impossible because both $(x_j - x_1)$ and t_{1j} are nonnegative, $\forall j$. Thus no such vector $\mathbf{x}$ exists, that is

$$\exists \text{ a semi-positive vector } \mathbf{p} \, s.t \, \mathbf{pT} = \mathbf{p}.$$

Now let $\mathbf{T}$ be indecomposable. Assume that the price vector $\mathbf{p}$ is not positive. This means that there exists $p_j = 0$ for some submatrix of $\mathbf{T}$ and $p_i > 0$, $\forall i$ in the complement. Call the submatrix for which the prices are positive $\mathbf{M}$ and its complement $\mathbf{M'}$. Then, for all indices $i \in \mathbf{M'}$, we have

$$\mathbf{p}t^i = p_i = 0 = \sum_{j \in \mathbf{M}} t_{ji} p_j$$

and, therefore, $t_{ji} = 0, j \in \mathbf{M}, i \in \mathbf{M'}$. This means that $\mathbf{M}$ is independent of the rest of $\mathbf{T}$. But, by assumption, $\mathbf{T}$ is indecomposable. Hence $\mathbf{M} = \mathbf{T}$ or $p_j > 0$, $\forall j = 1, 2, \ldots, n$, that is $\mathbf{p} > 0$.

Finally, to prove uniqueness, let $\mathbf{p}, \mathbf{p'}$ be linearly independent solution vectors. Let $\lambda = \underset{i}{\text{Min}} \, (p_i/p_i')$ and assume $\lambda = p_1/p_1'$. Then, as both $\mathbf{p}, \mathbf{p'} > \mathbf{0}, \mathbf{p}^* = \mathbf{p} - \lambda \mathbf{p'}$ is a nonnegative vector. As any linear combination of independent solutions to homogeneous equations is a solution itself, $\mathbf{p}^*$ has to be a solution too, $\mathbf{p}^* \mathbf{T} = \mathbf{p}^*$, but $\mathbf{p}^* \not> \mathbf{0}$ by hypothesis. [In fact $p_1^* = 0$.] Therefore, in $\mathbf{p}^* [\mathbf{I} - \mathbf{T}] = \mathbf{0}, \mathbf{p}^* = \mathbf{0}$ or $\mathbf{p} = \lambda \mathbf{p'}$, that is they differ only by a scalar factor, and the theorem is proved. $\qquad \Box$

As a realization of a multisectoral model, the above system is very simple in a number of ways:

(i) from the point of view of its structure, it is not 'complete' at least in the sense that there is no production to be decided upon, for production has already taken place 'yesterday';
(ii) there is no surplus and therefore no positive rate of profit, nor
(iii) a positive rate of growth;
(iv) finally, each sector is assumed to produce only one commodity (no joint production).

To go further into multisectoral modelling in terms of relaxing the above limitations, we have: (i) to construct a quantity system; (ii) to allow for the possibility of a positive rate of profit and/or of growth; finally, (iii) to allow for joint production. We will proceed to this by steps.

The quantity system corresponding to system (4.2.2) takes the form (cf. Chapters 2 and 3)

$$\mathbf{Ax} = \mathbf{x}, \tag{4.2.7}$$

where $\mathbf{A}$ is formally the same as matrix $\mathbf{T}$, operating in the price system, but with a crucial difference. As long as we are interested in the properties of (4.2.2) from the point of view of the existence, positiveness and uniqueness of the set of 'exchange values', we need no assumptions on the technology, for example on the returns to scale, involved. The only technological assumption is that *the system is closed*. The problem involved in matrix equation (4.2.7) is different. We now want to determine a set of activity levels **x** such that for each commodity the balance relation (4.2.7) is satisfied. The quantity system (4.2.7) involves a set of true unknowns, so that it is logically different from (4.2.2) which instead states an assumption.

Duality of the quantity and the price systems is obtained only if we show that matrix **A** and matrix **T** collect the same coefficients. This means that $t_{ij} = \Delta^i a_{ij}$, where $\Delta^i > 0$, is a scalar. Coefficients a_{ij} are defined in the usual way (each a_{ij} represents the amount of the ith good that is technologically required to produce one unit of commodity j). This implies the assumption that the technique represented by $(\mathbf{A}, \mathbf{I})$ is linear and with constant production coefficients. In other words, coefficients a_{ij} *do not* change with the level of the output. Note that (4.2.6) implies that outputs, instead of being measured by their natural units (tons, pairs, etc.), *were normalized to one*. This represents a mere change of units, while (4.2.7), implies a *law of returns*. By introducing this law, the structure of our system is enriched. We can now not only find out the equilibrium 'exchange values' but also determine *equilibrium levels of production*. Note also that, if we 'complete' the price system with quantity equations of the type (4.2.7), and in the latter accept the assumption on the returns to scale, matrices **T** and **A** are one and the same thing, so that (4.2.2) *and* (4.2.7) *are 'dual' systems*. The data of a closed system of production characterized by constant returns to scale (in the form of constant production coefficients) will be summarized by the couple $(\mathbf{A}, \mathbf{I})$, that is by a set of $2n$ vectors with n entries (in $\mathbb{R}^n$ [see I, Example 5.2.2]).

The existence proof we need is the following:

THEOREM 4.2.2. *Dual systems* (4.2.2) *and* (4.2.7) *have nonnegative solutions* **x** *and* **p** *such as to satisfy the condition*

$$\mathbf{pIx} > 0$$

under identical assumptions.

The last qualification allows us to interpret the theorem in the following way. If one of the above systems has a nonnegative solution, then the other has it also. Moreover, any economically meaningful solution must imply that a positive value of the output is produced. We frame it in this way for we want to take advantage of the theorem of the alternative we have used before.

Let us introduce the following assumptions on matrix **A** [see I, §7.11] as we did on **T**:

A.1′: **A** is nonnegative square
A.2′: each row in **A** sums up to unity
A.3′: **A** is indecomposable

A.1' needs no explanation; A.3' states that there are only basic goods (cf. Sraffa (1960)), and is made for convenience (we will come back to the decomposable case in a different context). Once A.2' is justified, we can rely on Theorem 4.2.1 to assert at least the existence of $\mathbf{p}'$ and draw the implications. (A dual proof along the same line would complete the reasoning in the opposite direction: conditions ensuring the existence of $\mathbf{x}$ will ensure the existence of $\mathbf{p}$). This is easily done by noting that, if condition A.2' is satisfied, the system is capable of a self-reproducing state (the one corresponding to the vector $\mathbf{x} = (1, 1, \ldots, 1)'$ or any scalar multiple of it).

Under the above assumptions, it has already been proved that there is a positive vector $\mathbf{p}$, which moreoever is unique up to scalar multiplication. We have to prove that this implies that (i) there exists a nonnegative $\mathbf{x}$ solving (4.2.7), and (ii) that for any such $\mathbf{x}$, $\mathbf{p}I\mathbf{x}$ is positive.

Proof

(i) That (4.2.7) has a semi-positive solution, implies that the set $X = \{\mathbf{x} | (\mathbf{I} - \mathbf{A})\mathbf{x} > 0\}$ is empty. Geometrically this means that the cone intersections $\Delta(\mathbf{I} - \mathbf{A}) \cap \mathbb{R}^n_+$ and $\Delta(\mathbf{A} - \mathbf{I}) \cap \mathbb{R}^n_+$ are both empty. Therefore, the cone spanned by column vectors in $(\mathbf{I} - \mathbf{A})$ is really a k-dimensional linear subspace in $\mathbb{R}^n$. In other words, the equation

$$(\mathbf{I} - \mathbf{A})\mathbf{z} = 0$$

has at least one non-zero, nonnegative solution $\mathbf{z}$.
(ii) As the solution to (4.2.7) is strictly positive, $\mathbf{p}I\mathbf{z} > 0$ for all $z \geqslant 0$ solving equation (4.2.7). $\quad\square$

A completely parallel reasoning will show that under the above assumptions, the vector $\mathbf{x}$ solving (4.2.7) is itself positive and unique up to a scalar multiple (these latter two properties are a result of A.3').

Assumption A.2' is in a sense too particular, since we can make a more general statement with a minimum of assumptions:

THEOREM 4.2.3

(i) *Assume that matrix A satisfies A.1' and the following condition replacing A.2':*

A.4 *there exists a positive vector x such that* $A\mathbf{x} = \mathbf{x}$,
then there is a semi-positive price vector $\mathbf{p}$ *satisfying the dual equation* $\mathbf{p}A = \mathbf{p}$.

(ii) *vice versa, assume that together with A.1', the following condition is satisfied*

A.5 *there exists a positive price vector such that* $\mathbf{p}A = \mathbf{p}$,
then there is a semi-positive solution to the quantity equation $A\mathbf{x} = \mathbf{x}$.

Note that we know that, under indecomposability, both the price and the quantity vectors are strictly positive and unique, in the sense defined. The weaker formulation we are using would serve as a bridge to the so-called complementary slackness conditions of a formulation in terms of linear programming.

In the formulation above, the properties of the dual systems are linked together very closely, and have an economic interpretation: in the formulation (i), the statement says that, if the system is capable of reproducing itself running all activities (A.4), then there is a set of semi-positive prices that satisfy the zero profit condition of competitive markets; in the formulation (ii) vice versa, it says that, if there is a set of competitive, zero-profit prices, then the system admits of a self-reproducing state.

We see that in both cases, given the semi-positivity of one of the vectors and the positivity of the other, we always obtain solutions $(\mathbf{x}, \mathbf{p})$ that also satisfy the condition $\mathbf{p}\mathbf{I}\mathbf{x} > 0$.

Theorem 4.2.3 will be used in the following section to study the existence of nonnegative solutions for a number of more general closed models, before introducing an alternative approach based on the well-known Perron–Frobenius theorem [see I, Theorem 7.11.1].

4.2.2. More general closed models of production

(i) Consider the following input matrix

$$\hat{\mathbf{A}} = (\mathbf{A} + h\mathbf{c}\mathbf{l}), \tag{4.2.8}$$

where h is a scalar indicating a (given) level of real wages in terms of standard wage basket $\mathbf{c}$, $\mathbf{A}$ is the technological matrix, and for any given h, $\mathbf{c}\mathbf{l}$ is a dyadic matrix of consumption goods for labour. Matrix $\hat{\mathbf{A}}$ is called *Morishima's augmented matrix* of inputs (cf. Morishima, 1971; Brody, 1970). The dual systems of equations are now

$$\mathbf{p}\hat{\mathbf{A}} = \mathbf{p} \qquad \mathbf{p} \geqslant 0 \tag{4.2.9}$$

and

$$\hat{\mathbf{A}}\mathbf{x} = \mathbf{x} \qquad \mathbf{x} \geqslant 0, \tag{4.2.10}$$

where the data is the matrix $\hat{\mathbf{A}}$ and the unknowns are the relative prices and activity levels, $\mathbf{p}$ and $\mathbf{x}$. The matrix $\hat{\mathbf{A}}$ is really a *matrix of functions of the scalar h*, $\hat{\mathbf{A}}(h)$, but for any given value of h, it is a matrix of constant coefficients, and we will consider it as such now.

THEOREM 4.2.4. *For matrix $\hat{\mathbf{A}}$ evaluated at a given $\bar{h}$, and corresponding dual systems, existence of nonnegative economic solutions is established via assumptions A.1', A.3' and the dual characterization established in Theorem 4.2.3.*

(ii) We re-define the coefficients of our matrix: the best known way is due to Leontief (1941). Matrix $\mathbf{A}$ is made up of n columns and n rows, so that neither labour nor consumption have been explicitly incorporated. The simple model describes flows of commodities in a sort of automatized economy. We now 'augment' $\mathbf{A}$ by one column and one row [see I, §5.10], so as to obtain a matrix $\mathbf{A}^*$ of order $n + 1$, where the last column is made up of n coefficients of consumption by each worker plus a zero at the $n + 1$ entry (i.e. $\mathbf{c} = (c_1,\ldots,c_n,0)$). The $(n + 1)$th column describes in this way the 'wage rate' in real terms as a consumption basket. The $(n + 1)$th row, instead is made up of n labour input coefficients (i.e. $\mathbf{a}_{n+1} = (l_1,\ldots,l_n,0)$). The price vector is now given by the row-vector $\hat{\mathbf{p}} = (p_1, p_2,\ldots, p_n, w)$, where w stands for the nominal wage rate. The activity level vector is now given by $\hat{\mathbf{x}} = (x_1, x_2,\ldots, x_n, L)'$, where L stands for the level of employment. With this interpretation the price system $\hat{\mathbf{p}}\mathbf{A}^* = \hat{\mathbf{p}}$ may be split into

$$\mathbf{p}\mathbf{A} + w\mathbf{a}_{n+1} = \mathbf{p} \quad \text{and} \quad \mathbf{pc} = w. \tag{4.2.11}$$

The dual system is now $\mathbf{A}^*\hat{\mathbf{x}} = \hat{\mathbf{x}}$ or

$$\mathbf{A}\mathbf{x} + L\mathbf{c} = \mathbf{x} \quad \text{and} \quad \mathbf{a}_n + 1 = L. \tag{4.2.12}$$

We can now use the fact that, if Equations (4.2.11) and (4.2.12) have non-zero solutions, they determine only relative prices and relative activity levels, $\hat{\mathbf{p}}$ and $\hat{\mathbf{x}}$. We can therefore fix a normalization rule for both of them by setting $w = 1$ and $L = 1$, which is the Leontief closed model. It is obvious that $\mathbf{A}$ can be obtained as a particular case of either $\hat{\mathbf{A}}$ or of $\mathbf{A}^*$—Theorem 4.2.4 then applies here as well.

4.2.3. Perron–Frobenius theorems and an application

We have, thus far, considered the solution to homogeneous equations associated with matrices $\mathbf{A}$, $\mathbf{A}^*$ and $\hat{\mathbf{A}}$ from a purely topological point of view. In the language of topology, a solution vector like $\mathbf{p}$ or $\mathbf{x}$ is a fixed point of a linear map, but there is also an algebraic approach to the above set of problems characterized by a set of theorems associated with the names of Perron and Frobenius. Consider (4.2.2) and (4.2.7). From an economic point of view, we are interested primarily in non-zero, and, if possible, nonnegative solutions. If there is one such solution $\mathbf{x}$ (or $\mathbf{p}$), it is called an eigenvector (or characteristic vector) of the matrix $\mathbf{A}$ [see I, §7.1]. If there is more than one vector $\mathbf{x}$ (respectively $\mathbf{p}$) solving equation 4.2.2 (respectively 4.2.7), the set of such solutions span a space in $\mathbb{R}^n$ [see I, §5.5] called the *eigenspace*.

Let us now consider a more general system

$$\mathbf{p}(\mathbf{I} - (1 + r)\mathbf{A}) = 0$$

and

$$(\mathbf{I} - (1 + g)\mathbf{A})\mathbf{x} = 0,$$

where g is the rate of growth and r is the uniform rate of profit. The above form a dual system *only if* we consider the golden rule rate of growth, $g = r$. Set $\beta = 1/(1 + g)$ and $\rho = 1/(1 + r)$ and we obtain

$$\mathbf{p}(\rho\mathbf{I} - \mathbf{A}) = \mathbf{0} \qquad (4.2.13)$$

$$(\mathbf{I}\beta - \mathbf{A})\mathbf{x} = \mathbf{0}. \qquad (4.2.14)$$

The value system (4.2.13) and the quantity system (4.2.14) unless connected via some choice-theoretic paradigm, are solved independently. Parametrizing equation (4.2.13) and (4.2.14) in terms of ρ and β, it is clear that (4.2.2) and (4.2.7) are special cases of the above for $\rho = \beta = 1$. However, we wish to consider the problem when ρ and β instead of being parameters are unknowns. There are non-trivial solutions if and only if β and ρ are eigenvalues of $\mathbf{A}$ [see I, §7.2]. But, the solutions, to make economic sense, must not only be non-zero but also nonnegative. Considering for simplicity, only the quantity side, we can apply the Perron–Frobenius theorem [see I, Theorem 7.11.1]. Note that the eigenvalues of $\mathbf{A}$ and $\mathbf{A}'$ are the same [see I, §7.2], so that (4.2.13) also has solutions that are positive and unique in the sense defined by the theorem.

THEOREM 4.2.5. *Equations (4.2.13), (4.2.14) for an indecomposable matrix have positive solutions $\hat{\mathbf{p}}, \hat{\mathbf{x}}$ if and only if we set $\beta = \rho = \hat{\beta}$, where $\hat{\beta}$ is the maximal eigenvalue of $\mathbf{A}$.*

COROLLARY. *The solution vectors $(\hat{\mathbf{p}}, \hat{\mathbf{x}})$ satisfy the requirement $\hat{\mathbf{p}}\mathbf{I}\hat{\mathbf{x}} > 0$.*

By using the Perron–Frobenius theorem, we may establish an existence result for equations (4.2.2)–(4.2.7) and (4.2.9)–(4.2.10).

THEOREM 4.2.6. *Let $\mathbf{A}$ (or $\hat{\mathbf{A}}, \mathbf{A}^*$) be indecomposable. Then the equations have positive solutions $\mathbf{p}$ and $\mathbf{x}$, each unique up to a scale factor, if and only if the maximal eigenvalue of $\mathbf{A}$ (or $\hat{\mathbf{A}}, \mathbf{A}^*$) is equal to one.*

There is a version of the Perron–Frobenius theorem for *general decomposable matrices*, but the results are for obvious reasons weaker. Among other things, we obtain that the maximal eigenvalue is just nonnegative, the associated eigenvector is simply nonnegative and the maximal root can appear more than once so that there is a whole space of eigenvectors associated with it [see IV, §15.2.2]. The condition that the eigenvalue be equal to one is only a part of a more complex sufficient condition to ensure the nonnegativeness of the solution (e.g. Berman and Plemmons, 1979).

Associated with the above homogeneous equations, are the resolvent equations for the 'open systems'

$$(1 + g)\mathbf{A}\mathbf{x} + \mathbf{c} = \mathbf{x} \qquad (4.2.15)$$

$$(1 + r)\mathbf{p}\mathbf{A} + w\mathbf{l} = \mathbf{p} \qquad (4.2.16)$$

whose solutions are

$$\mathbf{x} = [\mathbf{I} - (1+g)\mathbf{A}]^{-1}\mathbf{c}$$
$$\mathbf{p} = w\mathbf{l}[\mathbf{I} - (1+r)\mathbf{A}]^{-1}$$

where the inverse matrices $[\mathbf{I} - (1+r)\mathbf{A}]^{-1}$ and $[\mathbf{I} - (1+g)\mathbf{A}]^{-1}$ are the resolvents. If the resolvents exist, the solutions are uniquely determined. If the resolvents are nonnegative, the solutions, being obtained by multiplying the inverses by nonnegative vectors $\mathbf{c}$, $w\mathbf{l}$, will also be nonnegative; precisely results anologous to those we have previously obtained via theorems of the alternative. We now state two results, the first one rather trivial.

(i) The resolvent exists if and only if the reciprocal of the scalars $(1+g)$ and $(1+r)$ are not eigenvalues of $\mathbf{A}$ [see I, Theorem 7.2.3].
(ii) Let $\hat\beta$ be the maximal eigenvalue of matrix $\mathbf{A}$. By Perron–Frobenius [see I, Theorem 7.11.1] it is nonnegative; then, for any scalar μ larger than $\hat\beta$, the matrix $(\mu\mathbf{I} - \mathbf{A})$ has a nonnegative inverse (Debreu and Herstein, 1953).
(iii) If $\mathbf{A}$ is indecomposable, then $(\mu\mathbf{I} - \mathbf{A})^{-1}$ is positive.

Now, interpreting $\mu = 1/(1+g)$ and $\hat\beta = 1/(1+g_{max})$ (and likewise for the rates of profit), the two results establish that there are unique nonnegative solutions to equations (4.2.15), (4.2.16) only for all those values of the rate of growth and/or of the rate of profit that are less than the maximal rates obtained by solving the homogeneous systems (4.2.13), (4.2.14). Finally, are these values of the rates of profit and growth, for which nonnegative price and quantity solutions exist, nonnegative themselves? This is so only if the maximal rates r_{max} and g_{max} are positive themselves, that is if the Perron–Frobenius root, $\hat\beta$, is strictly less than one. This means that the matrix $\mathbf{A}$ is *productive* (Nikaido, 1970), that is there is a nonnegative vector of activity levels $\mathbf{x}$ such that $(\mathbf{I} - \mathbf{A})\mathbf{x}$ is semi-positive. This implies that the system $(\mathbf{A}, \mathbf{I})$ can produce a surplus of at least one good. There are various equivalent formulations of the conditions ensuring that a matrix like $\mathbf{A}$ is productive, and the best known goes under the name of Hawkins–Simon (e.g. Chapter 3).

We may summarize the above discussion in the following statement: solutions of the inhomogeneous systems (4.2.15), (4.2.16) are uniquely determined and as nonnegative corresponding to nonnegative rates of profit and of growth whenever the system represented by input matrix $\mathbf{A}$ and output matrix $\mathbf{I}$ are productive.

To enrich the economic content of the immediately preceding discussion and as an unusual exercise in the usefulness of the Perron–Frobenius theorem we now use these results and concepts in deriving the linear wage–profit curve (cf. Sraffa, 1960). For the above open (inhomogeneous) systems (4.2.15), (4.2.16), in addition to the earlier assumptions, assume also that $\mathbf{A}$ has n *distinct eigenvalues*. Then, there exists a similarity transformation $\mathbf{H}^{-1}\mathbf{AH} = \Lambda$, where Λ is a diagonal matrix made up of the n distinct eigenvalues (λ_i) and the columns of $\mathbf{H}$ are made up of the eigenvectors corresponding to each of the distinct eigenvalues [see I, Theorem 7.4.2]. Now, define $\mathbf{p}^d\mathbf{H} = \mathbf{p}$, $\mathbf{l}^d\mathbf{H} = \mathbf{l}$, $\mathbf{H}^{-1}\mathbf{x}^d = \mathbf{x}$ and $\mathbf{H}^{-1}\mathbf{c}^d = \mathbf{c}$. Then (4.2.15) and (4.2.16) can be rewritten as

$$\mathbf{p}^d[\mathbf{I} - (1 + r)\mathbf{\Lambda}] = w\mathbf{l}^d \tag{4.2.17}$$

and

$$[\mathbf{I} - (1 + g)\mathbf{\Lambda}]\mathbf{x}^d = \mathbf{c}^d \tag{4.2.18}$$

[see I, (6.7.4)]. Note, that out of the original n commodities, n new *composite commodities* have been formed. Corresponding to this set of composite commodities, we have a totally decoupled system. However, to the n eigenvalues λ_i, there corresponds only one positive eigenvector (by Perron–Frobenius) and this vector defines Sraffa's multipliers that will reduce the 'actual' system to a Standard System (Sraffa, 1960, pp. 24–28). In the decoupled system each of the composite commodities are 'standard commodities'—but only the one corresponding to the maximum eigenvalue can refer to Sraffa's 'standard system'. Now, define unit labour cost, $\gamma_i = wl_i^d/p_i^d$, and unit consumption, $\delta_i = c_i^d/x_i^d$. Then, (4.2.18) and (4.2.17) can be written as

$$1 = \lambda_i + \delta_i + g\lambda_i, \tag{4.2.19}$$

i.e. materials + consumption + investment, and

$$1 = \lambda_i + \gamma_i + r\lambda_i, \tag{4.2.20}$$

i.e. materials + wages + profits. Resubstituting γ_i and redefining the composite good which corresponds to the dominant eigenvalue λ^* to be the numeraire, one obtains from (4.2.20)

$$1 = \lambda_i^* + wl_i^d + r\lambda_i^*. \tag{4.2.21}$$

When the units are chosen so that: when $r = 0$, $w^* = 1$ and when $w = 0$, $r^* = 1$, that is $w^* = wl_i^d/(1 - \lambda_i^*)$ and $r^* = r\lambda_i^*/(1 - \lambda_i^*)$, we get $r^* = 1 - w^*$. This is similar to Sraffa's famous linear relation between the distributive variables $r = (1 - w)r_{max}$ except that we have redefined units so that r_{max} is always unity. The dual consumption-growth curve can be derived in a similar way.

From the gross output equation (4.2.19) we can see that one unit of gross product needs λ_i units of itself and, therefore, $l_i^d\lambda_i$ units of labour—and so on. Thus the total direct and indirect labour content in one unit of output will be given by [see IV, Example 1.7.3]

$$l_i^d(1 + \lambda_i + \lambda_i^2 + \cdots) = \frac{l_i^d}{1 - \lambda_i} \tag{4.2.22}$$

Now, the importance of the 'productivity' assumption (in another form also known as the Hawkins–Simon conditions) becomes evident. The maximal eigenvalue of a productive matrix $\mathbf{A}$ is less than one, so that for all eigenvalues the inequality $0 < |\lambda_i| < 1$ holds, which makes (4.2.22) meaningful. From (4.2.20) we have

$$p_i^d = \frac{wl_i^d}{1 - \lambda_i} + \frac{r}{r_{max}} \qquad (4.2.23)$$

Clearly prices are not simple multiples of labour values, although prices are *proportional* to labour values when $r = 0$.

As a final *corollary* to the Perron–Frobenius theorem, we have the following very useful result [see IV, §5.1] for rates of growth and of profit *less* than the maximal ones, the resolvents are not only nonnegative but such that each coefficient is a continuous non-decreasing function of the rates g, r. This result is strengthened if the matrix **A** is indecomposable [see I, §7.11] for then the coefficients are strictly increasing functions (of the exogenously given g, r). This result is very useful in comparative statics, that is, when we compare price and/or quantity solutions corresponding to different levels of the rate of profit and/or the rate of growth. As the price vector is obtained by multiplying the resolvent to the left by the labour input vector times the wage rate, the price vector is a vector of increasing functions of the rate of profit, once the nominal wage rate is given: in a different, more 'classical' jargon, if we take the wage rate as numeraire, i.e. if we set $w = 1$, then 'labour commanded prices' $\hat{\mathbf{p}} = \mathbf{p}/w$ all increase, though at different relative speeds, if the rate of profit increases. Likewise, if the vector of final demand is positive and/or the matrix **A** is indecomposable, any increase of the exogenously given rate of growth g will require an increase in at least one entry of the solution vector **x** of equation (4.2.15).

We may briefly compare the results obtained so far. By appealing to one of the theorems of the alternative, we have given a simple prototype of an existence proof for nonnegative solutions to our dual systems of linear equations. This proof establishes certain local properties as the rate of profit and the rate of growth are treated as given parameters. The Perron–Frobenius theorems and their corollaries, instead, allow us not only to establish analogous existence results, under conditions that lend themselves to an easy economic interpretation, but also to treat such solutions as vectors of functions of r and/or g. We can make use of this important information to derive two central tools for the modern theory of growth and distribution.

Let us specify the wage rate in terms of a bundle of goods in fixed proportions, that is the nonnegative vector **c**. For any given set of prices, the scalar $(\mathbf{pc})^{-1}$ is an index of the real wage rate. As a consequence of the preceding corollary, this index is a function of the rate of profit treated as exogenous, and the first derivative of the price vector is positive, if we introduce the natural assumption of a positive labour input vector. Thus the real wage rate $(\mathbf{p}(r)\mathbf{c})^{-1}$ in terms of any predetermined **c**, is a decreasing function of the rate of profit, via $\mathbf{p}(r)$. This allows us to draw the real wage rate/rate of profit curve associated with the given technique, as a strictly decreasing curve. The envelope of the set of curves associated with all available techniques is the so-called Wage–Profit Frontier of the given technology.

On the other hand, let **c** be a representative consumption basket. Given the rate of growth, how many of these baskets are left available to each member of society? This will depend on the amount of labour that has to be spent to produce one such basket as net consumption: that is, on 'labour productivity' in terms of net output above the assigned accumulation rate. Given this, to obtain the vector **c**, the amount $\mathbf{lx}^C$ of labour has to be expended. Therefore, the number of baskets per capita will be equal to $(\mathbf{lx}^C)^{-1}$. Remembering that, for *given* **c**, $(\mathbf{lx}^C)^{-1}$ is a function of g via $\mathbf{x}^C(g)$, we obtain that the level of consumption per capita is a decreasing function of the rate of growth. By repeated calculation of $(\mathbf{lx}^C(g))^{-1}$ for different values of g, *with* **x** *constrained to range over a given technique*, we derive the Consumption–Investment curve of a given technique. The envelope of the curves for all available techniques is the C–I Frontier of the technology. An analogous result holds if we assume, following Marx and von Neumann, that the wage rate is advanced by capitalists before the production process takes place (see Morishima, 1973).

4.3 GENERAL JOINT PRODUCTION SYSTEMS

We have so far generalized our basic production model in various directions, but the structure of a non-joint production model was retained. We now remove this last restriction introducing the joint production model in its full generality. The output matrix is, therefore, a matrix **B**, which if diagonal gives the NJPS as a special case. Dimensions are kept the same, so that *both output and input matrices A, B are square of order n*. We will start with the open system while the closed one is discussed in the last section of the chapter from the point of view of a generalized Perron–Frobenius problem.

The quantity- and a price-systems are represented by

$$\mathbf{Bx} = (1+g)\mathbf{Ax} + \mathbf{c} \tag{4.3.1}$$

and

$$\mathbf{pB} = (1+r)pA + w\mathbf{l}, \tag{4.3.2}$$

where the following

A.1* **A** and **B** are nonnegative square matrices
A.2* there exists a positive vector $\mathbf{x} : (\mathbf{B} - A)\mathbf{x} \geqslant 0$
A.3* the labour-input vector is positive

are assumed. To simplify notation let us introduce the symbols $\mathbf{M}(r) = (\mathbf{B} - (1+r)A)$ and $\mathbf{M}(g) = (\mathbf{B} - (1+g)A)$, where $\mathbf{M}(r)$ and $\mathbf{M}(g)$ are matrices parameterized by r and g. Likewise, $\mathbf{M}^{-1}(\cdot)$ stands for the inverse (or resolvent) matrix, when it is defined (and $\mathbf{M}^{-1,j}(\cdot)$ is its jth column). On the basis of these

assumptions one has been able to establish a number of remarkable results for the
NJPS. Firstly, A.2* implies that 1 is not an eigenvalue of matrix $\mathbf{A}$, and therefore,
rank $(\mathbf{I} - \mathbf{A}) = n$ and the net-output matrix is invertible. Secondly, as A.2* implies
that the Perron–Frobenius root of $\mathbf{A}$ is less than one, $(\mathbf{I} - (1 + r)\mathbf{A})$ and
$(\mathbf{I} - (1 + g)\mathbf{A})$ are nonnegatively invertible for all r, $g : 0 \leqslant r, g < r_{max}$, g_{max}.
So, on the basis of A.2* only we could get solutions in $\mathbf{x}$ and $\mathbf{p}$ which are unique
and moreover nonnegative for a closed interval of values for the rate of profit and
the rate of growth including zero.

Here, A.2* also implies that 1 is not a root of the equation $\det(\beta\mathbf{B} - \mathbf{A}) = 0$ (it is
not a generalized eigenvalue of $\mathbf{A}$ versus $\mathbf{B}$ [see §4.4] so that rank $(\mathbf{B} - \mathbf{A})$ is equal
to n and the inverse of the net-output matrix exists. However, we do not have
the same closed interval as before, which can be seen by transforming
$\det(\beta\mathbf{B} - \mathbf{A}) = \det(\beta\mathbf{I} - \mathbf{B}^{-1}\mathbf{A})$, if $\det \mathbf{B} \neq 0$, or $\det(\beta\mathbf{B} - \mathbf{A}) = \det(\beta\mathbf{A}^{-1}\mathbf{B} - \mathbf{I})$ if $\det$
$\mathbf{A} \neq 0$ and noticing that the matrix $\mathbf{B}^{-1}\mathbf{A}$ (matrix $\mathbf{A}^{-1}\mathbf{B}$, respectively), is *not* in
general nonnegative and therefore has complex eigenvalues. $\mathbf{M}(r)$ and $\mathbf{M}(g)$ are
invertible for all scalars r and g such that $(1 + r)^{-1}$ and $(1 + g)^{-1}$ are not roots of the
characteristic equation: *for this set of scalars*, formal solutions to (4.3.1) and (4.3.2)
can be found via the resolvent equations

$$\hat{\mathbf{p}} = \mathbf{l}\mathbf{M}^{-1}(r), \quad \hat{\mathbf{p}} = p/w \tag{4.3.3}$$

$$\mathbf{x} = \mathbf{M}^{-1}(g)\mathbf{c} \tag{4.3.4}$$

for any given $\mathbf{l}, \mathbf{c}$. Solutions $\mathbf{x}$ and $\hat{\mathbf{p}}$ are, just like in the NJPS, uniquely determined
via the resolvents, but, the above assumptions are not sufficient to establish that
they are also nonnegative.

However, both equations (4.3.3) and (4.3.4) have nonnegative solutions if and
only if the vector of final demand *and* the vector of labour-input coefficients
satisfy, at the given values of the parameters, the following independent
conditions (Manara, 1968):

(i) $\mathbf{l} \in \Delta\mathbf{M}(r)$, where $\Delta[\mathbf{M}(r)] = \{\mathbf{y} \in \mathbf{R}^n | \mathbf{y} = \hat{\mathbf{p}}\mathbf{M}(r), \hat{\mathbf{p}} \geq 0\}$
(ii) $\mathbf{c} \in \Delta\mathbf{M}(g)$, where $\Delta[\mathbf{M}(g)] = \{\mathbf{z} \in \mathbf{R}^n | \mathbf{z} = \mathbf{M}(g)\mathbf{x}, \mathbf{x} \geq 0\}$

$\Delta[\mathbf{M}(r)]$ and $\Delta[\mathbf{M}(g)]$ are convex polyhedral cones spanned by matrices $\mathbf{M}'(r)$
and $\mathbf{M}(g)$; if $r = g = \lambda$, λ a common scalar, the matrices are the transpose of each
other so that $\Delta[\mathbf{M}(r)]$ is spanned by the rows and $\Delta[\mathbf{M}(g)]$ by the columns of the
same matrix $\Delta\mathbf{M}(\lambda)$.

In the NJPS, the assumption that the technique is productive implies that the
whole nonnegative orthant is contained in the net output cone spanned by $\mathbf{M}(g)$
for all $g : 0 \leqslant g < g_{max}$ where $g_{max} = 1 - \hat{\beta}/\hat{\beta}$, $\hat{\beta}$ the Perron–Frobenius root of $\mathbf{A}$
(while for $g = g_{max}$, $\mathbf{M}(g)$ spans a $k - 1$ linear subspace such that the nonnegative
orthant lies completely on one side of it). Therefore, condition (ii) is naturally
satisfied by all nonnegative vectors $\mathbf{c}$. On the other hand, productiveness implies

also that there is a nonnegative vector $\mathbf{p} : \mathbf{pM}(r) > \mathbf{0}$ for all $r : 0 \leqslant r < r_{max} = g_{max}$.
In other words, the nonnegative orthant is included in the cone spanned by $\mathbf{M}(r)$,
$0 \leqslant r < r_{max}$ (and, again, for $r = r_{max}$, $\mathbf{pM}(r_{max})$ spans a hyperplane through the
origin supporting the nonnegative orthant). Therefore, condition (i) is naturally
satisfied by all nonnegative vectors $\mathbf{l}$. This relation of cone inclusion is the
topological meaning of the nonnegative invertibility of both $\mathbf{M}(r)$ and $\mathbf{M}(g)$.

In the joint production model, the above conditions place additional
requirements upon sets of data (vector $\mathbf{c}$ and net output matrix $\mathbf{M}(g)$, vector $\mathbf{l}$ and
matrix $\mathbf{M}(r)$). To illustrate why negative solutions may arise, let us assume for the
moment, that the rate of growth and the rate of profit are equal to each other (say
λ). We can thus use only one cone, $\Delta[\mathbf{M}(\lambda)]$, and the solutions to the quantity
system will lie on an affine subspace on the cone (in general, a hyperplane) while
the corresponding price solutions will be a (cone of) vector(s) normal to that affine
subspace. Joint Production assumption A.2* (the technique is productive),
merely implies that the intersection between $\Delta[\mathbf{M}(\lambda)]$ and the interior of the
nonnegative orthant is non-empty, but does *not* necessarily imply that the whole
nonnegative orthant is included in $\Delta[\mathbf{M}(\lambda)]$.

To emphasize the contrast with NJPS, Figure 4.1 represents a situation that
can typically arise only in the Joint Production model, with a cone of net-output
spanned by $\mathbf{M}(\lambda)$ lying in the interior of the nonnegative orthant. Now, as long as
the given vector of final demand $\mathbf{c}$ belongs to the interior of $\Delta[\mathbf{M}(\lambda)]$, it can be
produced by using both processes with positive activity levels, while if it is
collinear either with $\mathbf{M}^1(\lambda)$ or with $\mathbf{M}^2(\lambda)$, only one process is run and the other
stays idle (i.e. it fetches a zero activity level). However, goods cannot be produced
excatly in proportions like $\mathbf{c}'$ or $\mathbf{c}''$ that lie *outside* $\Delta[\mathbf{M}(\lambda)]$ as one of them would
be overproduced. Proportions like $\mathbf{c}'$, $\mathbf{c}''$ could be obtained only 'notionally' by
giving one of the two process a negative activity level. (see Sraffa, 1960, p. 43).

To give a geometrical interpretation to part (i) of the condition; consider the
equation on the cone

$$\hat{\mathbf{p}}\mathbf{M}(\lambda)\mathbf{x} = \bar{\mathbf{K}}. \qquad (4.3.5)$$

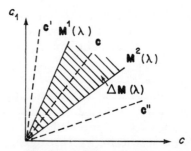

Figure 4.1: Joint production

Vector $\hat{\mathbf{p}} = \mathbf{l}\mathbf{M}^{-1}(\lambda)$ is the outward direction coefficient vector, normal to the transformation hyperplane $\mathbf{M}(\lambda)\mathbf{x}$. In $\mathbb{R}^2$, the equation of the hyperplane is

$$\bar{K} = \hat{p}_1 c_1 + \hat{p}_2 c_2 = \mathbf{l}\mathbf{M}^{-1,1}(\lambda) + \mathbf{l}\mathbf{M}^{-1,2}(\lambda)c_2 \qquad (4.3.6)$$

whence the slope

$$dc_1/dc_2 = -(\hat{p}_2(\lambda)/\hat{p}_1(\lambda)) = -(\mathbf{l}\mathbf{M}^{-1,2}(\lambda))/\mathbf{l}\mathbf{M}^{-1,1}(\lambda). \qquad (4.3.7)$$

In the NJPS, input coefficients a_{ij} are usually standardized with reference to unit gross outputs. However, here this cannot be done (unless the output matrix is diagonal), and we may assume that entries in $(\mathbf{A}, \mathbf{B})$ are (input and output) coefficients per unit of labour input (i.e. the labour vector is the unit sum vector $\mathbf{i}$). In this way, each vector $\mathbf{M}^j(\lambda)$, $j = 1$, 2, represents the net output, above accumulation at the given rate $\lambda = g$, produced by a unit of labour in the jth process. Expression (4.3.7) becomes

$$dc_1/dc_2 = -(\mathbf{i}\mathbf{M}^{-1,2}(\lambda)/\mathbf{i}\mathbf{M}^{-1,1}(\lambda)). \qquad (4.3.8)$$

A negative slope of the transformation curve implies that both prices $\hat{\mathbf{p}}_1$, $\hat{\mathbf{p}}_2$ are positive. However, in the JPS the slope may well be positive and, therefore, the rate of transformation between goods 1, 2 may be positive as in the following example. In Figure 4.2 any vector of final demand such as $\mathbf{c}$ can technically be produced with nonnegative (in fact, positive) activity levels and no overproduction would appear. Therefore, corresponding to the set of vectors $\mathbf{c}$ belonging to $\Delta[\mathbf{M}(\lambda)]$ (a cone itself), Equation (4.3.5) would have nonnegative $\mathbf{x}$ solutions. However, the net output vectors $\mathbf{M}^1(\lambda)$ and $\mathbf{M}^2(\lambda)$ satisfy $\mathbf{M}^1(\lambda) > \mathbf{M}^2(\lambda)$, and the hyperplane connecting them (the transformation curve over $\Delta[\mathbf{M}(\lambda)]$) has a positive slope, so that the direction coefficient vector $\mathbf{p}(\lambda)$ contains entries with opposite signs. The use of process $\mathbf{M}^2(\lambda)$ implies a sort of 'inefficiency' in the allocation of labour among the available processes, and this is indirectly revealed by the appearance of a partly negative price solution in the dual system (4.3.4).

Within the algebraic approach we have consistently used so far, we may only find certain sufficient conditions to obtain nonnegative solutions and provide for

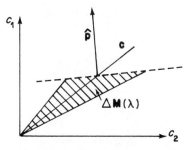

Figure 4.2: Inefficiency in the allocation of labour

them an economic justification. However, the major justification for this approach comes from the fact that we obtain a full characterization of the NJPS as the special JPS where all such conditions are naturally satisfied.

Taken together, (i) and (ii) ensure that the x solutions corresponding to a given rate of growth and the price solutions corresponding to a rate of profit are nonnegative. They do not impose the so called golden rule, i.e. they do not require equality between r and g, which we are assuming for simplicity. There are many such conditions, but we briefly discuss only the most important of them. Keeping the assumption of a rate of growth equal to the rate of profit, it can be shown, as a special case, that solutions are simultaneously nonnegative for both (4.3.4) and (4.3.5) *only if* the net output matrix $\mathbf{M}(\lambda)$, corresponding to a given rate of growth, satisfies the requirement.

A.4* there exists a vector $\mathbf{x} > \mathbf{0} : \mathbf{M}(\lambda)x \geqslant 0$ *and* if $\mathbf{M}(\lambda)$ is a *Z-matrix*, i.e. a matrix with the pattern $M_{ij}(\lambda) \leqslant 0, i \neq j$

Note that A.4* generalizes the notion of productiveness as stated by A.2*: a system is said to be productive at λ, if $\mathbf{M}(\lambda)$ satisfies the first half of A.4* (and obviously, it is productive in the usual sense if A.4* is satisfied for $\lambda = 0$). If $\mathbf{M}(\lambda)$ is a productive Z-matrix (more technically, a P-matrix, see Berman and Plemmons (1979)), it is nonnegatively invertible and, therefore, both prices and quantities, corresponding to λ, are unique and nonnegative for all vectors l and c. The NJPS is the typical, though not the only, representative of joint production systems whose net output matrices are Z-matrices. The important difference, however, is that, for NJPS, $\mathbf{M}(\lambda)$ is a Z-matrix for all λs between zero and a maximal rate, $r_{max} = g_{max}$, while this is not in general true for JPS. In this case, $\mathbf{M}(\lambda)$ may happen to be a Z-matrix at some given positive $\bar{\lambda}$, and thus it will stay so for $\lambda > \bar{\lambda}$, *without* this implying that it is a Z-matrix for all $\lambda : 0 \leqslant \lambda < \bar{\lambda}$.

At this point, it should be emphasized that both conditions (i)–(ii) and the condition that $\mathbf{M}(\lambda)$ be a productive Z-matrix share the property that, even if either is satisfied, it still would hold only locally, i.e. for the given rate of profit (equal to the rate of growth, by hypothesis). (This is why they are stated with reference to given values of the parameters). Moreover, if the latter condition holds, conditions (i) and (ii) are satisfied automatically, but *not* vice versa. The only way to avoid this problem would require assuming that the net output matrix is a productive Z-matrix already at $\lambda = 0$. However, nothing new would be gained, since the JPS would behave just like the NJPS, and they could not be distinguished. The price equation could be put into the form:

$$\mathbf{p} = r\mathbf{p}\mathbf{A}(\mathbf{B} - \mathbf{A})^{-1} + w\mathbf{l}(\mathbf{B} - \mathbf{A})^{-1} = r\mathbf{p}\mathbf{F} + w\mathbf{l}, \mathbf{F} = A(\mathbf{B} - \mathbf{A})^{-1},$$

where $\mathbf{F}$ and $\hat{\mathbf{l}}$ are nonnegative when $(\mathbf{B} - \mathbf{A}) = \mathbf{M}(0)$ is a productive Z-matrix. Therefore, prices are positive for all $r : 0 \leqslant r < r_{max}$ with r_{max} equal to the reciprocal of the Perron–Frobenius root of $\mathbf{F}$. Analogous manipulations of the quantity system yield a nonnegative matrix $\mathbf{K} = \mathbf{M}(0)^{-1}\mathbf{A}$, as the vertically integrated capital matrix (see Pasinetti, 1973) for this reason, the x-solutions are positive and unique in a closed interval of g, $[0, g_{max})$.

We have assumed so far that $r = g$. To complete the list of difficulties arising in an equation approach to general JPS, we now consider briefly the case where the two rates are allowed to differ (and, obviously, $r \geqslant g$). Then, the net output matrix $\mathbf{M}(r)$ may even be a productive Z-matrix at some given $r = \bar{r}$ (so that, the corresponding prices are positive), while $\mathbf{M}(g)$ is not, for $g \neq \bar{r}$ (hence, the quantity solutions may turn out to be partly negative), unless we are prepared to assume that condition (ii) is also satisfied. This again is not the case with NJPS, where $\mathbf{M}(r)$ and $\mathbf{M}(g)$ are, naturally, Z-matrices already at r, $g = 0$. This allowed us to solve, independently, quantity and price systems. In the JPS, the assumption of a golden rule balanced growth is *sufficient* to ensure that, whenever $\mathbf{M}(r)$ is a Z-matrix, so is $\mathbf{M}(g)$, and that the x- and $\hat{\mathbf{p}}$-solutions to the dual systems of equations are both nonnegative.

One important outcome of the preceding discussion is that it makes clear how in JPS, and in NJPS as a *special case*, the existence and uniqueness of nonnegative solutions are determined by the properties of the net output matrix, and *not* by the individual properties of the $\mathbf{A}$, $\mathbf{B}$. The NJPS is 'simpler' just because certain properties of the input matrix are carried over to the net output matrix. The JPS, instead, forces us to discuss the existence and uniqueness of nonnegative solutions by analysing the relations between all our data: namely, the input/output matrices, on one side, and the labour and final demand vectors, on the other.

Our discussion (and examples) of negative solutions can easily be interpreted in terms of the two neoclassical rules of pricing and choice of techniques. The rule of free goods is violated if the quantity system yields some negative activity levels; on the other hand, the *rule of efficiency* is violated if the price system yields a semi-negative solution. In the neoclassical approach, only techniques whose associated vectors $(\mathbf{x}, \mathbf{p})$ satisfy these two rules are *entitled* to represent a competitive equilibrium. That is a situation where goods in excess supply become free goods and processes yielding less than the uniform rate of profit are discarded.

Again the contrast between JPS and NJPS is sharp. In the NJPS, if a technique is productive, any vector of final demand can be produced exactly in the required proportions. Supply can always be made to match demand and, for equilibrium, no good must fetch a zero price. On the other hand, as sectors are so specialized that they produce a positive net quantity of at most one good, no-two vectors can be such that $\mathbf{M}^i(\lambda) > \mathbf{M}^j(\lambda)$ implying a positive slope of the transformation curve. This means that there are no choices between alternative activities, so that the only choice is between to produce or not (and if to produce, in what amounts) and the question of efficiency does not arise.

The above neo-classical rules can only be introduced as complementary slackness conditions for the two sets of dual inequalities that should replace the above quantity and price equations. In other words, instead of an algebraic approach, as we could use for the NJPS, JPS requires a more clear topological approach and a choice theoretical framework. In fact the interest of JPS lies in that it enriches the simple structure of the linear production model by introducing the salient feature of the general equilibrium model, essentially nonlinear in nature, that is the interdependence between technological choices and patterns of demand. The equation approach, therefore, is not adequate to determine competitive equilibrium solutions for a general joint production model. It fails whenever at least one of the very general conditions discussed in this section is not satisfied. Actually, we have in general to expect either nonnegative activity levels (or prices) coupled with semi-negative prices (or activity levels, respectively), or even two semi-negative solution vectors. They are both nonnegative only by fluke. However, a semi-negative solution in the activity levels has a different economic implication from a (partly) negative solution for prices. In fact, in the former case, the given technique would violate the condition of equilibrium between demand and supply. In the latter, it would violate the postulate of profit maximization on the part of producers. If we do not care about the determination of general equilibrium positions, but are rather interested in whether a technique could or could not be considered as part of their choice set by producers, it is only the condition that prices are nonnegative that is relevant. (No technique showing semi-negative prices at the ruling rate of profit can belong to the producers' choice set). This would only be a sort of partial analysis focussing on 'observable' as opposed to 'equilibrium'. techniques. This point of view is properly Sraffa's (the so called 'production prices approach'), whereas the general equilibrium viewpoint is von Neumann's. The algebraic approach is seen to provide a clear characterization of the set of technological choices open to maximizing producers.

We have briefly illustrated where partly negative prices arise, by means of a two good–two processes example, as the case where a process, by employing the same amount of labour, produces a larger net output of all goods than the other process. The 2×2 example is a lucky one for direct vector comparison is possible; but unfortunately, vectors cannot be directly compared in the $n \times n$ case and we have to consider linear combinations of them in comparing net outputs. A linear combination, with positive weights, of processes taken from a given $(\mathbf{A}, \mathbf{B}, \mathbf{i})$ is called a *subsystem* (obviously, $(\mathbf{A}, \mathbf{B}, \mathbf{i})$ itself forms a sybsystem). The following definition borrows the terminology from game theory: *a technique is dominated at a given rate of profit $\bar{r}$, if it contains a subset of processes, which, taken as a subsystem, could produce a larger net output, above $g = \bar{r}$, of at least one good, using the same amount of labour.*

The definition emphasizes that the quantity system corresponding to the golden rule rate of growth, $g = \bar{r}$, is only being used here as an auxiliary construction without implying any proper duality relation with the price system.

However, the concept of domination, being related with the (auxiliary) quantity side, looks independent from the valuation side and even prior to it. It can be ascertained before determining prices. Nevertheless, the presence of prices that are not all positive, signals that some processes not only are unnecessary, but should be discarded for a correct choice of the technique. This is formalized in the following theorem:

THEOREM 4.3.1. *Prices corresponding to dominated techniques are not all positive.*

Proof In order to make use of a theorem of the alternative, first, we construct an (augmented) net output matrix, $\bar{\mathbf{M}}(\lambda) = \mathbf{M}(\lambda) - \mathbf{c}\mathbf{i}$, where $\mathbf{c}$ is a predetermined wage basket (and the wage rate is $w = \mathbf{p}\mathbf{c}$). Assume $\lambda \neq (1 - \beta)/\beta$, where β is a root of det $(\beta\mathbf{B} - \mathbf{A})$. Assume that there is a non-trivial solution $\hat{\mathbf{x}}$ for $\hat{\mathbf{M}}(\lambda)\mathbf{x} = \mathbf{0}$ such that $\mathbf{i}\hat{\mathbf{x}} = \bar{K}$ (total employment). Whenever $(\mathbf{A}, \mathbf{B}, \mathbf{i})$ is dominated, there is a subset of processes $j \in J \subset N = 1, 2, \ldots, n$, such that for a vector $\mathbf{x}^{(j)} : x_j > 0, j$ in J, and $x_k = 0$ otherwise, the following inequality is satisfied $\hat{\mathbf{M}}(\lambda)\mathbf{x}^{(j)} \geqslant \hat{\mathbf{M}}(\lambda)\hat{\mathbf{x}}$ with $\mathbf{x}^{(j)} : \mathbf{i}\mathbf{x}^{(j)} = \bar{K}$. Therefore, there is a solution to the inequality: $\hat{\mathbf{M}}(\lambda)\mathbf{x} \geqslant \mathbf{0}$, and, by a theorem of the alternative, there is *no positive* left vector $\mathbf{p}$, such that $\mathbf{p}\hat{\mathbf{M}}(\lambda) = \mathbf{0}$. $\qquad\square$

The proof of the preceding theorem looks a bit artificial for it specifies the wage basket. Nevertheless, it can be done for any composition of the wage basket, provided consumption of the workers is not a function of the price vector. Therefore, no loss of generality is involved in assuming, as we did, a particular composition of the wage basket. Unfortunately, we have only established that, whenever a technique is dominated, its prices are *not all positive*. They can be a zero vector, a semi-positive vector or a vector with *some* negative entries. (Owning to the assumption that the system is productive, prices cannot all be negative.) In the first case, the solution is trivial, and therefore, economically uninteresting. In the second, some goods are free goods, and the slope of the transformation curve is zero or infinity; the last case we saw to be associated with the phenomenon of negative prices. The following characterization of dominated techniques (i.e. techniques with a transformation curve of a negative slope in the direction of at least one good):

THEOREM 4.3.2. *Whenever the price vector corresponding to a given value of the rate of profit λ, contains some negative entries the auxiliary quantity system can produce no smaller net output by using less labour.*

Proof. We use a fundamental theorem of the alternative, namely the so-called Farkas lemma. We need not transform the original system into an homogeneous one, hence we use matrix $\mathbf{M}(\lambda)$ [and *not* $\hat{\mathbf{M}}(\lambda)$]. Then, the theorem assumes that there is no nonnegative solution vector to the equation $\hat{\mathbf{p}}\mathbf{M}(\lambda) = \mathbf{i}$. Therefore, there is a solution to the inequalities $\mathbf{M}(\lambda)\mathbf{z} \geqslant \mathbf{0}$ and $\mathbf{iz} < \mathbf{0}$. We interpret $\mathbf{z}$ as the vector of subsystem multipliers in the following way. Assume that there is a *nonnegative solution* $\mathbf{x}^0$ to $\mathbf{M}(\lambda)\mathbf{x}^0 = \mathbf{c}^0, \mathbf{c}^0 \neq \mathbf{0}$ such that total employment is $\mathbf{ix}^0 = \bar{K}$. Now increase $\mathbf{c}^0$ to $\mathbf{c}^0 + \mathbf{e}_i$, where $\mathbf{e}_i' = (0, \ldots, 1, \ldots, 0)$. Then, as $\mathbf{c}^0 \neq \mathbf{0}$, $\mathbf{M}(\lambda)$ is invertible, and there is a solution $\hat{\mathbf{x}}$ to $\mathbf{M}(\lambda)\mathbf{x} = \mathbf{c}^0 + \mathbf{e}_i$, whence, by linearity,

$$\hat{\mathbf{x}} = \mathbf{M}^{-1}(\lambda)\mathbf{c}^0 + \mathbf{M}^{-1}(\lambda)\mathbf{e}_i$$

and, letting $\mathbf{z} = \hat{\mathbf{x}} - \mathbf{x}^0, \mathbf{M}^{-1}(\lambda)\mathbf{z} = \mathbf{e}_i$. We may repeat the exercise for each good to obtain the set of multiplier vectors

$$S = \{\mathbf{z} \in \mathbb{R}^n \,|\, \mathbf{M}(\lambda)\mathbf{z} = \mathbf{e}_i, \ i = 1, 2, \ldots, n\}.$$

Then, there is at least one $\mathbf{z} \in S$, such that $\mathbf{M}(\lambda)\mathbf{z} \geqslant \mathbf{0}$ *and* $\mathbf{iz} < 0$, or $\mathbf{i}(\hat{\mathbf{x}} - \mathbf{x}^0) = \mathbf{i}\hat{\mathbf{x}} < \mathbf{ix}^0 = \bar{K}$ □

Corollary: *If, at some $r = \bar{r}$, $\hat{p}_i(\bar{r}) < 0$, then the net output of the ith commodity, above $g = \bar{r}$, could be increased whilst saving labour.*

Proof. let $\Delta\mathbf{c}_i' = (0, \ldots, c_i, 0, \ldots, 0)$, with $c_i > 0$. Then,

$$\mathbf{M}(\lambda)\mathbf{z} = \Delta\mathbf{c}_i \Leftrightarrow \mathbf{z} = \mathbf{M}^{-1}(\lambda)\Delta\mathbf{c}_i.$$

Multiplying both sides by the labour input vector $\mathbf{i}$:

$$\mathbf{iz} = \mathbf{iM}^{-1}(\lambda)\Delta\mathbf{c}_i = \hat{p}_i(\lambda)c_i.$$

But $\hat{\mathbf{p}}_i(\bar{r}) = \mathbf{iM}^{-1}(\lambda)$ is negative, therefore

$$\mathbf{iz} = \mathbf{i}(\hat{\mathbf{x}} - \mathbf{x}^0) < 0 \ \text{ or } \ \mathbf{i}\hat{\mathbf{x}} < \mathbf{ix}^0 = \bar{K}.$$ □

It is apparent that the condition for a technique to have all positive prices is that it is not dominated. On the other hand, the choice set that will be considered by maximizing producers is the set of non-dominated techniques. Finally, the definition makes it clear that domination is a property depending on the value of the parameter λ. Techniques dominated at a given value of r, need not be so at a different value of the rate of profit (a 'truth' that came out of the debate in capital theory, and re-appears in the debate on negative labour values corresponding to positive production prices, (Morishima and Steedman, 1976; Wolfstetter, 1976).

Finally, a generalization of the concept of non-dominated technique to allow for rectangular matrices, is at the basis of the generalized Non-Substitution theorem we discuss in section 4.5 below. Only non-dominated techniques can hold the Non-Substitution property. Before doing this, we will show that, notwithstanding all the difficulties it runs into in the general JPS, the equation approach has some justification when applied to fixed capital (as by Sraffa, 1960, and Hicks, 1973).

4.4. FIXED CAPITAL AS JOINT PRODUCT AND THE NON-SUBSTITUTION THEOREM

4.4.1. The fixed capital case

Both in Von Neumann and in Sraffa, Joint Production is introduced not only to deal with the 'classical case' of mutton–wool type, but also as a *method* to deal with problems related with the use of fixed capital goods. For example, assume that there is only one machine or plant and only one output (say, 'steel'). In production, the machine at different stages of wear and tear is combined with, possibly, steel as input, and labour, to produce some output. Let us take the following *simple profile* of the technological processes:

$$M_0 \oplus steel \oplus labour \ominus steel \oplus M_1$$
$$M_1 \oplus steel \oplus labour \ominus steel \oplus M_2$$
$$M_2 \oplus steel \oplus labour \ominus steel$$

(and we note that it is a non-homogeneous system). From the point of view of the 'plant', this is installed new at time zero, M_0, and yields a flow of steel at times 1, 2, 3. Vintage machines are M_1, M_2 which appear both on the output side, next to steel, as improper products, and on the input side as inputs to produce some more steel, till they die out completely, $M_3 = 0$. We may therefore split the general output sub-matrix **B** representing the above profile of the working life of the machine into a matrix of outputs as finished goods (in our case, only steel), indicated by $\mathbf{B}^*$, and a matrix of the machine as output, $\mathbf{M}_1$. Likewise, we split the general input sub-matrix **A** into the matrix of material inputs currently used as circulating capital $\mathbf{A}^*$ and the matrix $\mathbf{M}_0$ representing the machine coefficients as inputs. Obviously, $\mathbf{A} = \mathbf{A}^* + \mathbf{M}_0$ and $\mathbf{B} = \mathbf{B}^* + \mathbf{M}_1$. Likewise, labour coefficients have a time index, that is coefficient l_t refers to the process using the plant at the tth stage of wear and tear. For our simple example, therefore, the matrices will have the following pattern, if we call b_i and a_j output or input of steel

$$\mathbf{B}^* = \begin{pmatrix} b_1, & b_2,\ldots, & b_T \\ 0 & & 0 \\ \vdots & & \vdots \\ 0 \cdots & \cdots \cdots 0 \end{pmatrix} \quad \text{and} \quad \mathbf{M}_1 = \begin{pmatrix} 0 \cdots \cdots 0 & & 0 \\ 0 \cdots \cdots 0 \cdots \cdots 0 \\ M_1 & 0 & \vdots \\ \vdots & \ddots & \vdots \\ 0 \cdots \cdots & \ddots & \vdots \\ 0 \cdots \cdots & M_{T-1} & 0 \end{pmatrix}$$

Under the hypothesis that the machine dies out completely at time T. Similarly.

$$\mathbf{A}^* = \begin{pmatrix} a_0, & a_1,\ldots, & a_{T-1} \\ 0 \cdots & \cdots \cdots 0 \\ \vdots & & \vdots \\ 0 \cdots & \cdots \cdots 0 \end{pmatrix}, \quad \mathbf{M}_0 = \begin{pmatrix} 0 \cdots \cdots \cdots \cdots 0 \\ M_0 & & 0 \\ 0 & M_1 & \vdots \\ \vdots & & \ddots & \vdots \\ 0 \cdots \cdots \cdots & M_{T-1} \end{pmatrix}$$

and $l = (l_0, l_1, \ldots, l_{T-1})$. We can now produce 'vertically integrated profiles'. The machine has a maximal lifetime T and we have the alternative of running it for any number of periods t not exceeding T. Each length t represents an economic lifetime as conceptually different from the physical/technological lifetime which we take as a datum. The choice as to which of them is the most profitable, depends on the 'ruling rate of profit' we take as given in the open system. Obviously, we have to make flows of inputs and flows of outputs, appearing at different stages, comformable by discounting. This can be done by constructing vertically integrated matrices $\hat{A}(\bar{r})$ and $\hat{B}(\bar{r})$ and vector $\hat{l}(\bar{r})$, where each column of the matrix $\hat{A}(\bar{r})$ is characterized by a given time index, say t, and represents the set of coefficients of inputs over a lifetime equal to t, properly discounted to $t = 0$ (that is to the stage where the new machine is installed). In other words, each column of $\hat{A}(\bar{r})$, is a column of entries of the type

$$\sum_{\tau=1}^{t} a_\tau (1 + r)^{-(\tau-1)}, \text{ for each good } i = 1, 2, \ldots, n$$

for a fixed t. These are vertically integrated coefficients as they represent discounted streams of inputs applied to production. In a similar way, we construct matrix $\hat{B}(\bar{r})$ of discounted streams of outputs over alternative feasible lifetimes of the machine or plant, and the corresponding vector of labour coefficients $\hat{l}(\bar{r})$.

Example 4.4.1. $t = 2$ yields

$$p_1 a_{11}(1 + r) + M_0(1 + r) + l_1 w = p_1 b_1 + p_2 M_1$$
$$p_2 M_1(1 + r) + p_1 a_{12}(1 + r) + l_2 w = p_1 b_2.$$

To discount, multiply the second row by $(1 + r)^{-2}$ and the first by $(1 + r)^{-1}$:

$$p_1 a_{11} + M_0 + l_1 w(1 + r)^{-1} = p_1 b_1 (1 + r)^{-1} + p_2 M_1 (1 + r)^{-1}$$
$$p_2 a_{12}(1 + r)^{-1} + p_2 M_1(1 + r)^{-1} + l_2 w(1 + r)^{-2} = p_1 b_2 (1 + r)^{-2}$$

Summing up, we obtain

$$p_1(a_{11} + a_{12}(1 + r)^{-1}) + M_0 + w(l_1(1 + r)^{-1} + l_2(1 + r)^{-2})$$
$$= p_1(b_1(1 + r)^{-1} + b_2(1 + r)^{-2}).$$

Now $(a_{11} + a_{12}(1 + r)^{-1})$ is the vertically integrated input coefficient (of the first good) referred to a lifetime $t = 2$, $(b_1(1 + r)^{-1} + b_2(1 + r)^{-2})$ is the corresponding output coefficient, and finally, $(l_1(1 + r)^{-1} + l_2(1 + r)^{-2})$ is the labour input coefficient.

In this process of vertically integrating, vintage machines, once appearing as outputs as well as inputs, cancel out, under the assumption that vintage capital goods are fully employed so that the output coefficient at time t is equal to the input coefficient at time $t + 1$. In this way, the net output matrix contains only new goods (machines, circulating capital goods and final goods) and is a z-matrix, because $B(r)$ is diagonal. If it is also productive in the sense of A.4*, prices of final goods are positive (see Schefold).

In the simple examples above, there are three crucial assumptions. (i) There is no intrinsic joint production, (ii) the fixed capital good is not transferable once it has been installed and (iii) for any feasible economic lifetime $t \leqslant T$, the old machine appearing as last by-product has a zero coefficient. Under these assumptions, we obtain as many new unknowns, i.e. prices as '*accounting values*' of the $t - 1$ machines at different stages of wear and tear, as new equations. As long as we accept the assumptions above, for any choice of feasible lifetime of the set of machines, we have square input and output submatrices of final and old capital goods. However, we note that the above description can accommodate any behaviour of the efficiency of the plant or machine (see Böhm–Bawerk, 1889; Hicks, 1973; and Sraffa, 1960).

Rectangular matrices appear as soon as we allow the machine, once it has become old, to move from the production of one good to the production of another. That is, only one good is produced at any one time by the machine as in (i) but the good varies according to the age of the machine. Consider the following example:

$$M_0 \oplus a_0 \oplus wl_0 \ominus b \oplus M_1$$
$$M_1 \oplus a_1 \oplus wl_1 \ominus b \oplus M_2$$
$$M_2 \oplus a_2 \oplus wl_2 \ominus c$$

The machine M_0 lasts three periods and may produce in the first two periods good b while at stage 2 it may 'migrate' into the production of c. We have three equations, while the unknowns are p_0, p_1, p_2, p_b, p_c and w, with the rate of profit as given. If we take the wage rate as numeraire and assume that in the rest of the system there is an equation where the price p_0 may be determined, we still are left with four unknowns or one too many. In other words, the system becomes rectangular with the number of columns (i.e. price equations) smaller than the number of unknowns. The system is *under-determined* on the price side but would be *over-determined* on the quantity side. This can also be seen by performing the vertical integration over the lifetime of the machine, $T = 3$. We obtain the equation

$$p_0 M_0 + p_b(a_0 + a_1(1+r)^{-1} + a_2(1+r)^{-2} + w(l_0 + l_1(1+r)^{-1} + l_2(1+r)^{-2}$$
$$= p_b b((1+r)^{-1} + (1+r)^{-2}) + p_c c(1+r)^{-3}),$$

where we have reduced the number of unknowns as ageing capital goods disappear in the process of vertical integration but, after assuming that $w = 1$ and that p_0 has an equation of its own, we still have at least two unknowns, p_b and p_c and one single equation to determine them.

This shows that, if capital goods are transferable over their lifetimes, and we consider their profile over a sufficient length of time as to allow them to produce different goods a kind of intrinsic joint production arises. In this case the 'classical' 'algebraic' method of counting the (number of independent) equations fails to attain the objective of proving the existence of a mathematical solution and even if it does succeed, it is in general inadequate to prove that the mathematical solution satisfies also the economic criterion of being nonnegative. This was the method of General Equilibrium analysis till the contributions of Wald and von Neumann in the 1930s. The inadequacy is even more obvious for systems of nonlinear equations. Modern theory uses fixed point theorems (see Chapter 14) as well as other topological and algebraic methods.

4.4.2. Notes on the Non-Substitution theorem

One approach that we have not been able to develop, but which plays an important role in the treatment of open multisectoral models, is based on the theory of extrema of linear functionals on convex sets. It is not logically independent from our development of the simplest applications of a theorem of the alternative, nor from the Perron–Frobenius treatment, but just a different point of view based on the theory of functions and generalizations of classical results on the extrema of functions in analysis [see IV, Chapter 5]. We could have done without referring to it, but it provides the quickest link with linear programming [see I, Chapter 11] and its use becomes particularly important as we come to the discussion of the so-called Non-Substitution theorem.

Associated with linear production models is the Non-Substitution theorem, originally established by Arrow, Samuelson, Georgescu-Roegen and others. All these seminal papers appear in a volume edited by T. Koopmans (1951). In the standard version, originally proved for a NJP-system $(\mathbf{A}, \mathbf{I}, \mathbf{l})$, the theorem states that, under certain assumptions, there is one set of activities or processes, as many as the number of products to be produced for final and intermediate uses, that will be 'efficient' irrespective of the *composition* of 'demand'. Associated with this technique there is a unique positive price vector, which will clear markets and satisfy the competitive condition of zero profits. The theorem has been extended to allow for a positive rate of profit, equal throughout all industrial sectors, and re-named the *dynamic* Non-Substitution theorem' (Samuelson, 1961). Such a Non-Substitution result is very useful as it simplifies calculations for general equilibrium models where a linear productive structure is incorporated and is important in exercises in comparative statics. The assumptions required to obtain this useful result are:

(i) there is only one 'primary factor of production', usually labour;
(ii) no joint production of the 'intrinsic type' and the obvious assumption we already introduced in §4.2 of constant returns to scale; and
(iii) the technology is productive.

Joint production of the intrinsic type has to be excluded, both at a given point of time *and* at different stages of life of capital goods. The model of fixed capital goods not transferable during their lifetimes satisfies the conditions for the Non-

Substitution theorem, which is a result hinted at by Samuelson (1961) and proved later by Mirrlees (1969). Stiglitz (1970) (under some additional assumptions on the efficiency patterns of the capital goods) and finally, in full generality, by Bliss (1975). However we want to arrive at this simple Non-Substitution result starting from the general Joint Production case.

In §4.3, we derived the transformation curve as the curve describing for a given open model $(\mathbf{A}, \mathbf{B}, \mathbf{l})$ the set of net outputs that can be obtained with the technique subject to the constraint of the availability of labour. No restriction was placed there on the gross output vector arising as a result of the productive activity: we allowed for 'intrinsic' joint production. The matrix $(\mathbf{B} - (1 + \bar{g})\mathbf{A})$ spans a cone in $\mathbb{R}^n$ [see IV, §15.2.4], representing the set of net output bundles that can be made available above the material requirements to expand the system at balanced growth rate $\bar{g}$. The constraint set by the total availability of the non-reproducible resource 'labour' sets a bound to the levels of the final uses that can be satisfied. The transformation curve is *piecewise linear*, with a finite number of kinks, due to the assumption of a linear, constant coefficient structure of the production relations. The rate of transformation between any two goods is therefore constant over whole ranges of net output compositions, as in the example below (see Figure 4.3) where the transformation curve is a broken line. Over any given range portion of this broken line, prices are uniquely determined. Therefore, as long as the vector of final uses is restricted to vary only within a given range, one and *the same price vector* implicit in the technique will be able to clear the markets.

The Non-Substitution theorem deals with 'efficiency'. If the technique is efficient, then there is no need to change it when $\mathbf{c}$ changes. In other words, if the technique is efficient in producing a given vector of final demand, it will also be efficient in producing any other vector 'close enough' not to fall out of its own cone of net output. The same price vector, (if it was a competitive 'equilibrium' for the original vector $\mathbf{c}$) would still be an equilibrium for a number of alternative configurations. Let $(\mathbf{A}, \mathbf{B}, \mathbf{l})$ again be a *technique*, where a competitive set of prices

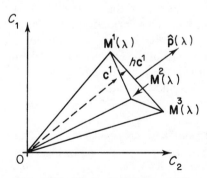

Figure 4.3: Non-substitution with intrinsic joint production: $[M^2(\lambda), M^3(\lambda)]$ is the efficient technique, (as $h > 1$)

associated with $(\mathbf{A}, \mathbf{B}, \mathbf{l})$ is a nonnegative vector $\mathbf{p}$ such as to ensure a uniform rate of profit, say $\bar{r}$. By definition, for $\mathbf{p}$ the following equation is satisfied:

$$\mathbf{p}(\mathbf{B} - (1 + \bar{r})\mathbf{A}) = w\mathbf{l} \qquad (4.4.1)$$

where we may choose $w = 1$ for the sake of simplicity. Assume now that for $(\mathbf{A}, \mathbf{B}, \mathbf{l})$ at the rate of growth $\bar{g}$, the given vector of final demand $\mathbf{c}$ is being met, i.e.

$$(\mathbf{B} - (1 + \bar{g})\mathbf{A})\mathbf{x} = \mathbf{c} \qquad (4.4.2)$$

with nonnegative vector $\mathbf{x}$. Finally, assume that for price vector $\mathbf{p}$,

$$\mathbf{p}(\mathbf{B}' - (1 + \bar{r})\mathbf{A}') \leqq w\mathbf{l}' \qquad (4.4.3)$$

at the same rate of profit and for all other available techniques $(\mathbf{A}', \mathbf{B}', \mathbf{l}')$. This implies that technique $(\mathbf{A}, \mathbf{B}, \mathbf{l})$ is a competitive equilibrium technique. If we now assume that the set of net output vectors, above $\bar{g}$, producible by techniques $(\mathbf{A}', \mathbf{B}', \mathbf{l}')$ may also be produced by $(\mathbf{A}, \mathbf{B}, \mathbf{l})$ then the same $(\mathbf{A}, \mathbf{B}, \mathbf{l})$ is a competitive equilibrium technique for any vector $\mathbf{c}$ in this set. (This is a simplified version of Johansen's (1972) General Non-Substitution theorem). The importance of the theorem lies in that it does not require the Non-Substitution property to hold for all compositions of final demand but only for a subset.

It is clear that the above problem can be interpreted in terms of linear programming. Technique $(\mathbf{A}, \mathbf{B}, \mathbf{l})$ is formed by the set of K activities that fetch positive activity levels in the optimal vector $\hat{\mathbf{x}}$ for the linear program min $\mathbf{lx}$ s.t. $(\hat{\mathbf{B}} - (1 + g)\mathbf{A})\mathbf{x} \geqslant \mathbf{c}$ and $\mathbf{x} \geqslant \mathbf{0}$ while the price vector $\mathbf{p}$ is the shadow price vector solving the dual program [see **I**, §11.2] max $\mathbf{pc}$ s.t. $\mathbf{p}(\hat{\mathbf{B}} - (1 + r)\hat{A} \leqq w\mathbf{l}$ for $\bar{r} = g$, and rectangular matrices $\hat{B}$ and $\hat{A}$ are formed by augmenting B with B', and A with A' respectively.

In other words, matrices $(\mathbf{A}, \mathbf{B})$ form a basic solution for the primal programme. This solution may or may not be degenerate according as to whether the number of activities in $(\mathbf{A}, \mathbf{B})$, i.e. the number of columns k is less than or equal to the number of goods n. It can be proved that if the solution is a *basic non-degenerate one*, then except for flukes, the transformation curve has pieces that are flat, that is pieces where the rates of transformation are constant, and therefore prices are determined independently from the composition of the final demand (provided the latter does not vary to the point of 'falling out' of the range on which the technique is optimal). A sufficient condition for this can be stated.

THEOREM 4.4.1. *If technique* $(\mathbf{A}, \mathbf{B})$ *and* $\mathbf{l}$ *has a 'competitive equilibrium' price vector, satisfying* (4.4.1)–(4.4.3) *corresponding to a final demand vector* $\mathbf{c}$ *that belongs to the interior of the cone* $\Delta(\mathbf{B} - (1 + \bar{g})\mathbf{A})$, *then there is a whole set of vectors* $\{\mathbf{c}'\}$ *for which that same technique represents an optimal solution.*

All cases where fixed capital goods are transferable over their lifetimes between the production of various goods fall under this theorem. The vertically integrated input and output matrices referred to profiles where the capital good is transferred, do show more than one positive output entry being positive and therefore are assimilated to the Johansen case.

On the other hand, the theorem (with its local validity) shows that the original, much stronger, version springs from a peculiar property of NJP techniques. If they are productive, (i.e., if the feasible region defined by the constraints to the primal programme is non-empty), they are able to produce not just a set of final vectors, c, but final goods in any desired proportions. The whole non-negative orthant (and not just a portion of it) is contained in the net output cone of a NJP technique, so that it is efficient for the production of any other vector c. In the wording used before, the transformation curve associated with the technique has no kinks and is a *hyperplane* over the nonnegative orthant with a unique outward direction vector representing competitive prices.

When fixed capital goods are non-transferable, we know that the output matrix $\hat{\mathbf{B}}(r)$ is a matrix of coefficients where for each capital good there are streams of a single homogeneous good running. Joint production over lifetime is by assumption banned and the vertically integrated net output matrix $[\hat{\mathbf{B}}(r) - (1 + r)\hat{\mathbf{A}}(r)]$, if at all productive, *contains the nonnegative orthant*. Therefore, if a particular choice of lifetimes is efficient for a given bundle of goods c, that same choice will also be efficient for any alternative bundle (Bliss's Dynamic Non-Substitution theorem).

4.4.3. Generalized Perron–Frobenius theorems

We have shown by means of very simple examples how theorems of the alternative (and separation theorems [see IV, §15.2.3]) are useful tools to prove the existence of nonnegative solutions. We have dealt briefly with a related result, the Non-Substitution theorem, stating that, under certain conditions, in an open system of production equilibrium prices can be determined independently from final demand. This property is held by a particular choice of processes belonging to the set of techniques with which nonnegative prices are associated. From this point of view, the Non-Substitution theorem is an optimization result linked both with the theory of (mathematical) programming, and with the general body of existence results.

By taking as a prototype a version of Johansen's theorem (1972), our treatment should have made clear that the really crucial assumptions for the Non-Substitution theorem to hold, are a linear structure of production relations and the existence of a unique primary factor. On the contrary, the assumption of no-joint production can be disposed of if we are satisfied with local results. Our statement on dominancy provides a necessary condition for a general joint production system to have the Non-Substitution property for only techniques satisfying that condition may represent a competitive equilibrium. This links together two results whose derivation we have sketched.

As an alternative approach, we have been analysing the properties of the characteristic equation associated with the input matrix $\mathbf{A}$. A mathematical result we found very useful in this context, the Perron–Frobenius theorem, states certain properties of the set of eigenvalues of the nonnegative matrix $\mathbf{A}$, and of the corresponding left- and right-eigenvectors, $\hat{\mathbf{p}}$ and $\hat{\mathbf{x}}$, respectively [see I, Theorem 7.11.1]. These results allow us to establish readily under which conditions general homogeneous systems like $\mathbf{x} = (1 + g_{max})\,\mathbf{A}\mathbf{x}$ and $\mathbf{p} = (1 + r_{max})\mathbf{p}\mathbf{A}$ have a nonnegative solution in r_{max}, g_{max}, $\mathbf{x}$ and $\hat{p}$. The triple $(r_{max} = g_{max}, \hat{\mathbf{x}}, \hat{\mathbf{p}})$ represents a Golden rule balanced growth path. This existence result, originally associated with the name of John von Neumann (1937), is obtained via a mathematical approach of an algebraic, and not of topological, nature. Von Neumann's proof deals with a more general structure, where output matrix $\mathbf{I}$ is replaced by $\mathbf{B}$ allowing for Joint production and matrices are rectangular, and makes use of the mini-max theorem in the theory of games and the earliest version of what came to be known as Kukatani's Fixed Point theorem [see V, §5.6].

We then have shown the relevance of the above theorem in diagonalizing an open system $(\mathbf{A}, \mathbf{I}, \mathbf{l})$, a procedure first introduced by R. M. Goodwin (1976). The PF theorem ensures that at least one of the eigensectors (or diagonal sectors) is real. Closing the loop, we have briefly shown the relevance of a corollary of the theorem for establishing the existence of nonnegative solutions still for the open system and in deriving their behaviours as the parameter (r and/or g) changes. The discussion of the roots of the characteristic polynomial [see I, §7.3] seems to provide a more homogeneous and unifying approach to a variety of problems associated with the linear multisectoral models. This provides a good motivation for looking for generalizations of the Perron–Frobenius theorem. This can be done essentially in three directions:

  (i) relaxing the assumption that $\mathbf{A}$ is square, i.e. have a system whose coefficients are the rectangular matrices $(\mathbf{A}, \mathbf{I})$ by taking $\mathbf{B}$ as a matrix of output without joint production;
 (ii) we may keep the square dimension and introduce only the general joint production matrix $\mathbf{B}$;
(iii) finally, we may consider (as the most general case) a system of both joint production and rectangular dimensions.

With the approach we have applied consistently throughout this chapter, the hypothesis under (iii) would imply treating system in the von Neumann format with equations rather than inequalities. By introducing appropriate conditions on the matrices, this *may be done*, and, for purposes of calculating the balanced growth path, *it is done* (see for instance Thompson and Weil, 1971). The trouble is that, usually, a rectangular dimensions renders one of the above dual problems solvable while the other becomes trivial, so that proper duality is lost. Therefore, the equation approach as applied to solving a von Neumann model both in price-rate of profit *and*, simultaneously, in quantity-rate of growth, seems not very fruitful. (For a full explanation of the analytical reasons, that are rooted in the basic theory of vector spaces, see Mangasarian (1971), and Punzo (1980).)

We have seen that, for the class of models where the only phenomenon allowed of joint production is of non-tranferable fixed capital goods, the format of the matrices is naturally square (for any choice of lifetimes of the fixed capital goods, there are as many equations as unknowns). Therefore, the need for assuming rectangular matrices really only arises with transferable fixed capital goods *and* with joint production of the intrinsic type. It is in these two (important) cases that we have no analytical justification, in principle, for taking square matrices, for there is no longer correspondence between processes and products. (Nevertheless, a non-analytical justification can be found in Marshall (1920, Book V, Chapter 6) and Sraffa (1960, p. 43, footnote).) However, we gain something very important from assuming square matrices. In fact, it can be formally proved that, in this case, the systems.

$$\mathbf{Ax} = \beta \mathbf{Bx}$$

and

$$\mathbf{pA} = \beta \mathbf{pB}$$

may be solved for the same scalar β. Here we can only state one simple result that may be obtained (for a more comprehensive discussion, the reader is invited to consult the references).

THEOREM 4.4.2 (*Generalized Perron–Frobenius theorem*) : *Assume there exists a square matrix* $\mathbf{X}$ *such that either* $\mathbf{A} = \mathbf{BX}$, *or* $\mathbf{B} = \mathbf{AX}$. *Let in the first case the rank of* $\mathbf{B}$ *be equal to n and in the second case the rank of* $\mathbf{A}$ *be n* [see I, §5.6]. *Then*

(i) *the set of eigenvalues of* $\mathbf{X}$ (*i.e. the spectrum of* $\mathbf{X}$) *is also the spectrum of* $\mathbf{A}$ *versus* $\mathbf{B}$, (*i.e. the roots satisfying the generalized determinantal eqn.* $|\mathbf{A} - \lambda \mathbf{B}| = 0$), *or of* $\mathbf{B}$ *versus* $\mathbf{A}$, *respectively.*
(ii) *Let* $\mathbf{X}$ *be a nonnegative matrix. Then, it has a maximal nonnegative eigenvalue* β *and correspondingly nonnegative left and right eigenvectors. These triples solve the dual homogeneous equations for the system* $(\mathbf{A}, \mathbf{B})$.

This statement makes clear that, in order to obtain a generalized result of the Perron–Frobenius type, the two sets of (input and output) proportions must not be independent. In fact, they are required to be related by a third nonnegative matrix $\mathbf{X}$ so that either the cone of input proportions is included in the cone of output proportions or vice versa. For the NJPS this is always satisfied.

In the terminology introduced by Hicks (1965), the two cases considered in the statement above are named 'simple backward' and 'simple forward narrowing' respectively. In either case, the generalized eigensolution $(\hat{\beta}, \hat{\mathbf{x}}, \hat{\mathbf{p}})$ represents a balanced growth path with full utilization of produced goods. For details and a number of other applications to linear models, see Punzo (1978, 1980).

4.5 CONCLUDING REMARKS

In a chapter which aims to *survey* an exciting but controversial area of economics it is not possible to go into all details. In particular, important results relating to control, stability and identification of linear economic systems have been completely omitted (see, however, Chapter 8). We have nowhere introduced the concept of the *state space* in our discussions [see IV, §7.11.3]. It is, nevertheless, implicit in the particular way in which we have, following von Neumann and Sraffa, dealt with the problem of fixed capital in joint production systems. Recent advances in linear (and nonlinear) systems theory enable one to dispense with the somewhat restrictive assumption (that we have employed) of representing linear operators as *square* matrices [see IV. Example 19.1.4]. Luenberger's elegant results on the theory of observers (cf. Velupillai, 1979) and Kalman's development of the theory of filtering, controllability and observability are, of course, highly relevant in *any* theory of *linear* models (see Engineering).

It is possible that a chapter on multisectoral models and joint production could have been better unified in terms of the tools and concepts of systems theory. In economics, in particular, there is a strong case to be made for such an approach, not least because of the obvious possibilities to consider problems in the theory of economic policy also as special cases. If such a unifying framework, based on a formal system theoretic paradigm, is used, some of the controversy, surrounding problems in the theory of growth, value and distribution could perhaps be defused.

Finally, important developments in game theory [I, Chapter 13], also of relevance to linear models with joint production, have also been omitted. We have, here, in mind Shapley values in particular. It is possible that, here too, the system theoretic paradigm may act as the ultimate unifying concept.

4.6 REFERENCES

Abraham-Frois, G. and Berrebi. E. (1979). *Theory of Value, Prices and Distribution.* Cambridge University Press, Cambridge.

Arrow, K. J. (1951). Alternative proof of the substitution theorem for Leontief models in the general case, in Koopmans (1951).

Berman, A., and Plemmons, R. J. (1979). *Nonnegative Matrices in the Mathematical Sciences.* Academic Press, New York.

Bliss, C. J. (1975). *Capital Theory and the Distribution of Income.* North-Holland, Amsterdam.

Bohm-Bawerk, E. von (1889). *Positive Theorie des Kapitals,* as vol. 2 of *Capital and Interest* (1959), Librarian Press, Illinois.

Brody, A. (1970). *Prices, Proportions and Planning.* North-Holland, Amsterdam.

Bruno, M. (1968). Fundamental duality relations in the pure theory of capital and growth, *Review of Economic Studies,* **XXXVI** (1) 105, 39–53.

Burmeister, E. and Kuga, K. (1970). The factor price frontier, duality and joint production, in *Review of Economic Studies*, **XXXVII**, (1) 1109, 11–19.

Debreu, G. and Herstein, I. N. (1953). Non-negative square matrices, *Econometrica*, **21**, 4, 597–607.

Edgeworth, F. Y. (1881). *Mathematical Physics*. Kelley Reprint (1957), New York.

Fujimoto, T. (1975). Duality and the uniqueness of growth equilibrium. *International Economic Review*, **16**, no. 3.

Gale D. (1960). *The Theory of Linear Economic Models*. McGraw-Hill, New York.

Gantmacher, F. R. (1960). *The Theory of Matrices*, vols 1 and 2. Chelsea, New York.

Georgescu-Roegen, N. (1951). Some properties of a generalized Leontief model, in Koopmans (1951).

Goodwin, R. M. (1976). Use of normalised general co-ordinates in linear value and distribution theory, in Polenske and Skolka (eds), *Advances in Input–Output Analysis*. Ballinger Publishing Co., Cambridge, Mass.

Hicks, J. (1956). Methods of dynamic analysis, in 25 *Essays in honour of E. Lindahl*. Ekonomisk Tidskrift, Stockholm.

Hicks, J. (1965). *Capital and Growth*. Clarendon Press, Oxford.

Hicks, J. (1973). *Capital and Time*. Clarendon Press, Oxford.

Jevons, W. S. (1871). *The Theory of Political Economy*. Kelley Reprint (1957), New York.

Johansen, L. (1972). Simple and general nonsubstitution theorems for input–output models. *Journal of Economic Theory*, **5**, no. 3.

Koopmans, T. C. (ed.) (1951). *Activity Analysis of Production and Allocation*. John Wiley & Sons, New York.

Koopmans, T. C. (1951). Alternative proof of the substitution theorem for Leontief models in the case of three industries', in Koopmans (1951).

Kuga, K. (1973). More about joint production. *International Economic Review*, **14**, no. 1.

Leontief, W. W. (1941). *The Structure of the American Economy* 1919–1929. Harvard University Press, Cambridge, Mass.

Manara, C. F. (1968). Il modello di Sraffa per la produzione congiunta di merci a mezzo di merci. *l'Industria*, no. 1.

Mangasarian, O. (1971). The generalized Perron–Frobenius theorem. *Journal of Mathematical Analysis and Applications*, no. 36.

Marshall, A. (1920). *Principles of Economics* (8th edn). Macmillan, London.

Mirrlees, J. A. (1969). The dynamic non-substitution theorem, in *Review of Economic Studies*, **XXXVI**, (1), 105, 67–76.

Morishima, M. (1971). Consumption–investment frontier, wage-profit frontier and the von Neumann equilibrium, in G. Bruckmann and W. Weber (eds), *Contributions to the von Neumann Growth Model, Zeitschrift für Nationalökonomie*, Supplementum 1. Springer Verlag, New York.

Morishima, M. (1973). *Marx's Economics: A Dual Theory of Value and Growth*. Cambridge University Press, Cambridge.

Morishima, M. (1974). Marx in the light of modern economic theory, *Econometrica*, **42**, 4, 611–632.

Morishima M. (1976). Marx from a von Neumann viewpoint, in M. Brown, K. Sato and P. Zarembka (eds), *Essays in Modern Capital Theory*. North-Holland, Amsterdam.

Morishima, M. (1976). Positive profit with negative surplus-value. A comment. *Economic Journal*, **86**, 599–603.

Neumann, J. Von (1937). Über ein ökonomisches Gleichungssystem und eine Verall-gemeinerung des Brouwerischen Fixpunktsatzes. *Ergebnisse Math. Kolloquiums*, no. 8 (English translation, *Review of Economic Studies*, (1945–46)).

Nikaido, H. (1970). *Introduction to Sets and Mappings in Modern Economics*. North-Holland, Amsterdam.

Pasinetti, L. L. (1973). The notion of vertical integration in economic analysis, *Metroeconomica*. **XXV**, Gennaio-Aprile 1973, Fascicolo 1, 1–29.

Pasinetti, L. L. (1976). *Lectures in the Theory of Production*. Macmillan, London.

Punzo, L. F. (1978). Labour values in single product- and joint product-systems. *Economic Notes*, **7**, no. 1.

Punzo, L. F. (1980). Economic applications of a generalized Perron–Frobenius problem. *Economic Notes*, **9**, no. 3.

Remak, R. (1929). Kann die Volkswirtschaftslehre eine exakte Wissenschaft werden? *Jahrbücher für Nationalökonomie und Statistik*, Band III, Folge Band 76.

Samuelson, P. A. (1951). Abstract of a theorem concerning substitution in open Leontief models, in Koopmans (1951).

Samuelson, P. A. (1961). A new theorem on non-substitution, in H. Hegelend (ed.), *Money, Growth and Methodology, and Other Essays in Economics*, Essays in honour of J. Akermann. CWK Gleerup, Lund.

Samuelson, P. A. (1966). The fundamental singularity theorem for non-joint production. *International Economic Review*, **7** no. 10.

Schefold. B. (1971). *Piero Sraffa Theorie der Kuppelproduktion, des Kapitals und der Rente*. Private printing, Basel.

Schefold, B. (1977). Fixed Capital as a Joint Product. *Jahrbücher für Nationalökonomie und Statistik*.

Schefold, B. (1980). von Neumann and Sraffa: Mathematical equivalence and conceptual difference. *Economic Journal*, **90**. No. 357, 140–156.

Sraffa, P. (1960). *Production of Commodities by Means of Commodities* Cambridge University Press, Cambridge.

Stiglitz, J. E. (1970). Non-substitution theorems with durable capital goods. *Review of Economic Studies*, **37**, 4, 112, 543–553.

Thompson, G. L. and Weil, R. L. (1971). Von Neumann solutions are generalized eigensystems, in G. Bruckman and W. Weber (eds), *Contributions to the von Neumann Growth Model*. Springer Verlag, New York.

Velupillai K. (1979). Application of observers and Kalman filtering techniques to dynamic input–output economies, in J. M. L. Janssen, I. F. Pau, A. Straszak (eds), *Models and Decision Making in National Economies*. North-Holland, Amsterdam.

Wolfstetter, E. (1976). Positive profits with negative surplus-value: A comment. *Economic Journal*, **86**, 864–872.

Part II

Macroeconomic Behaviour

Mathematical Methods in Economics
Edited by F. van der Ploeg
© 1984 John Wiley & Sons, Ltd.

5

The Aggregate Consumption Function

ROBERT A. EVANS, *University of Cambridge, Cambridge, UK*

5.1 INTRODUCTION

The consumption function describes the relationship between consumers' expenditure on goods and services and the factors that are assumed to influence this expenditure. Since its chief purpose is to act as an instrument of macroeconomic forecasting and analysis, it is usually defined at the level of the economy as a whole, as a relation between aggregate variables. But in order to formulate a satisfactory macroeconomic function there is a need to theorize or speculate about the factors that influence the spending and saving of individuals, so that much of the discussion that follows concerns theories about the behaviour of 'representative' or idealized individuals. The literature on the consumption function is vast and we will do no more here than survey briefly some of the main developments that have occurred, beginning with Keynes's *General Theory* (1936), which first introduced the concept.

5.2. KEYNES AND THE KEYNESIAN CONSUMPTION FUNCTION

For Keynes the importance of aggregate consumption behaviour lay in the potential it implied for instability in a market economy in which savings and investment decisions are taken by different people, the former by individuals and the latter by firms. In the pre-Keynesian theory the equality between aggregate savings and aggregate investment which is necessary for 'equilibrium' was brought about by a movement in the rate of interest, savings being an increasing and investment a decreasing function of the latter. Keynes felt, however, that changes in interest rates, at least in the short run, had a complex and uncertain effect on savings and that the principal variable affecting the latter was current income. Savings and investment therefore equalized, in Keynes's theory, by changes in aggregate income and, hence, in output and employment. An autonomous fall in investment, for example, causes a multiplied fall in income the size of which depends on the relation between income and savings (or, equivalently, consumption). In elementary texts this is often formalized in an income–expenditure model of a simple economy with no government or foreign trade consisting of two equations [cf. Chapter 3]:

$$y_t = c_t + a_t \quad \text{aggregate supply function,} \tag{5.2.1}$$

$$c_t = a + by_t \quad \text{aggregate consumption function.} \tag{5.2.2}$$

Equation (5.2.1) relates the output or income of the economy in period t, y_t, to the two components of demand, households' consumption demand, c_t, and autonomous spending, a_t, which in this simple model is the same as firms' investment spending. Equation (5.2.2) is a 'Keynesian' linear consumption function in which a and b are constants and $0 < b < 1$. The parameter b is called the marginal propensity to consume out of current income (m.p.c.). Eliminating c_t and differentiating with respect to a_t [see IV, §3.2] gives $dy_t/da_t = 1/(1 - b)$ so that the size of the response of output to autonomous disturbances (the degree of instability) depends on the m.p.c. If b is substantially greater than zero it follows that, when government activity is introduced into the model, an active policy of counter-cyclical government spending can have a powerful effect on demand and employment. On the other hand, there were, in Keynes's view, some forces making for stability: in particular, the 'fundamental psychological law, upon which we are entitled to depend with great confidence both *a priori* from our knowledge of human nature and from the detailed facts of experience...that men are disposed, as a rule and on the average, to increase their consumption as their income increases, but not by as much as the increase in their income' (Keynes, 1936, p. 96). That is, $b < 1$. This is partly because the urge to accumulate only reveals itself when a certain level of material comfort has been achieved, but also, in the short run, because of the persistence of habitual consumption patterns in the face of changes in income. The fact that $b < 1$ implies that the economy may settle at an equilibrium at less than full employment of resources (in the absence of increased investment) because consumers will spend less than the aggregate supply price when employment increases, making such employment unprofitable. Keynes also suggested that the proportion of income spent would decrease with income, that is $d(c/y)/dy = -a/y^2 < 0$, so that $a > 0$ and the income elasticity of consumption satisfies $(dc/dy)(y/c) < 1$.

Despite the impression given by many studies of consumer behaviour, Keynes never advocated the 'Keynesian' consumption function (5.2.2). He neither suggested that the relationship was linear nor that its parameters were stable. As well as stressing the factor, mentioned above, of habit persistence, which implies a higher long-run than short-run m.p.c., he provided a catalogue of 'subjective' and 'objective' factors capable of altering this propensity. The foremr set of factors he supposed to alter only gradually over long periods but some of the latter, including fiscal policy, unexpected changes in the value of wealth and large changes in the interest rate, might, he felt, have a noticeable effect even in ordinary circumstances. Certainly it is hard to see how the simple linear relationship (5.2.2) with $a > 0$ and $0 < b < 1$ can make any sense as a stable relationship as opposed to a local approximation either for whole economies or for individual households because the positive intercept implies negative saving (borrowing or consuming wealth) at low income levels. As Modigliani (1975) points out, this implies that the USA, for example, must have had negative saving in all years before some break-even point, which raises the question of how accumulation could have taken place at all. Similarly, while some of the permanently poor may be able to borrow for a period, they will not, in our society, be able to do so on the average.

Doubts about the simple linear consumption function were confirmed by post-war empirical evidence. It was found that regressions of this form [see VI, §6.5.1] fitted to pre-war aggregate time-series data, while giving a good fit and yielding parameter estimates agreeing with those suggested by Keynes, consistently under-predicted consumption in the immediate post-war period. Although budget studies (regression fitted to observations on a sample of households at a single period) found a significant positive intercept and a m.p.c. less than unity, Kuznets (1942) and Goldsmith (1955) found, using US data, that the aggregate consumption–income ratio was constant over a long period of time despite rising income. A number of modifications were suggested in the late nineteen-forties and early nineteen-fifties to reconcile these conflicting findings. Duesenberry (1949) argued that consumption is a function not of absolute but of relative income. For example those households with high income relative either to the average or to their own past experience will have a low average propensity to consume (a.p.c.), which accounts for the results of the budget studies, but as average income increases, the a.p.c. remains unchanged. This can be formulated in two ways. Denoting the consumption and income of the ith household at time t by c_{it} and y_{it} respectively, we have, in non-stochastic form,

$$c_{it}/y_{it} = a_0 + a_1 \bar{y}_t/y_{it}, a_1 > 0,$$

where the mean income across the sample is given by $\bar{y}_t = \sum_{i=1}^{n} y_{it}/n$ [see II, §8.1]. Since

$$c_{it} = a_0 y_{it} + a_1 \bar{y}_t,$$

a regression on a sample of households at time t will yield a positive intercept $a_1 \bar{y}_t$ and m.p.c. a_0. Summing over i,

$$\sum_{i=1}^{n} c_{it} = (a_0 + a_1) \sum_{i=1}^{n} y_{it}$$

so that a time series aggregate regression [see VI, §18.2] will yield a m.p.c. greater than a_0 and an elasticity of consumption equal to unity (implying a constant share of consumption in income). Alternatively, consumption may depend on the household's own past experience, giving, in aggregate,

$$c_t = b_0 + b_1 y_t + b_2 y_t^0,$$

where

$$y_t^0 = \max(y_{t-j}), j \geq 1$$

It was a simple step from here to Brown's (1952) formulation in which past consumption replaces past income and its effect is allowed to be symmetrical:

$$c_t = b_0 + b_1 y_t + b_2 c_{t-1}, 0 < b_2 < 1 \qquad (5.2.3)$$

In this simple 'habit persistence' model the short-run m.p.c., b_1, is less than the long-run m.p.c. given by setting $c_t = c_{t-1}$, that is the long-run m.p.c. equals $b_1/(1 - b_2)$, so that it can explain the conflict between aggregate time-series and budget studies. This, as mentioned above, was part of Keynes's original hypothesis. Equation (5.2.3) is undoubtedly an improvement on the simple linear function (5.2.2) but if it is intended as a universal description of the consumption process rather than as a local linear approximation it is open to some of the criticisms made above and like all the theories mentioned so far it provides no explanation of why consumers should choose one level of consumption and saving rather than another. Two theories, similar but not identical, attempted in the nineteen-fifties to provide such an explanation on the basis of the neoclassical theory of intertemporal choice first developed by Fisher (1907, 1930). These theories, the life-cycle hypothesis of Modigliani and Brumberg (1955), and the permanent income hypothesis of Friedman (1957) have formed the basis of most of the subsequent empirical work on the consumption function.

5.3. THE LIFE-CYCLE HYPOTHESIS

5.3.1. Theory

The fact that budget studies revealed that households with low incomes have negative savings aroused the suspicion that this group contains some who are only temporarily poor. The obvious corollary is that the upper income brackets contain some who are temporarily rich. It is clear that in an economy in which nobody inherits wealth saving over the whole lifetime of an individual must be zero and his lifetime m.p.c. = a.p.c. = 1. This suggests that saving serves merely to redistribute the stream of income receipts to accord with the desired intertemporal pattern of consumption—thus a typical person may have negative saving when young (on the security of future earnings) and again after retirement (living off past savings). These are the essential ideas of the life-cycle hypothesis (LCH).

The level of an individual's consumption in any period then depends on that individual's total lifetime resources, including expected future income as well as current income and assets (wealth), and on the desired pattern of consumption over time which will be a function of family circumstances, relative preference for present and future consumption, and so on. The standard neoclassical way of analysing this is to postulate that each individual attempts to maximize an intertemporal utility, or preference, function subject to a lifetime budget constraint [see IV, Chapter 16]. The solution to this dynamic programming problem is a consumption function exactly analogous to a Marshallian demand function. Consider the two-period case for an individual with consumption at constant prices denoted by c_t, employment income at constant prices y_t and assets at current value A_t, where assets are measured at the end of the discrete period. If interest is paid on assets at the beginning of period t at rate r_t and the price of the consumption good is p_t, we have the following stock-flow relations:

$$A_1 = A_0(1 + r_1) + p_1 y_1 - p_1 c_1$$
$$A_2 = A_1(1 + r_2) + p_2 y_2 - p_2 c_2.$$

If we make the simplifying assumption that there are no bequests, that is $A_2 = 0$, then

$$p_2 c_2/(1 + r_2) + p_1 c_1 = A_0(1 + r_1) + p_1 y_1 + p_2 y_2/(1 + r_2)$$

which is the lifetime budget constraint. The economic interpretation of this equation is that the discounted present value of lifetime consumption equals the present value of lifetime resources [see I, §15.1.1]. This can be rewritten as

$$p_2^* c_2 + p_1 c_1 = A_0(1 + r_1) + p_1 y_1 + p_2^* y_2,$$

where $p_2^* = p_2/(1 + r_2)$ is the discounted second period price. The extension of this constraint to L periods, L being the remaining length of life of the consumer, is

$$\sum_{t=1}^{L} p_t^* c_t = A_0(1 + r_1) + \sum_{t=1}^{L} p_t^* y_t \tag{5.3.1}$$

where $p_t^* = p_t/(1 + r_t)(1 + r_{t-1})\ldots(1 + r_2)$, $t = 2, \ldots, L$ and $p_1^* = p_1$. The consumer's problem as conceived by the LCH is to maximize a utility function of the form

$$U = U(c_1, c_2, \ldots, c_L)$$

subject to the budget constraint. In a strict neoclassical analysis, the arguments of the function should also include labour supply, making income and expected income dependent on the maximizing process but it is often assumed that working hours are fixed for all periods. Of course, at the time the decision is made all variables dated time 2 and later are unknown and have to be replaced by their anticipated values, introducing difficult problems of uncertainty which will not be discussed here [see Chapter 17]. Clearly the theory so far is too general to yield firm predictions as the form of the utility function and the process of formation of expectations have to be formulated more precisely. Two assumptions about $U(\mathbf{c})$

that are often made are that it is strictly additive and not indexed on time, that is

$$U = \sum_{t=1}^{L} [u^*(c_t)/(1 + \delta)^{t-1}],$$

where δ, the rate of time preference, represents the degree of the consumer's 'impatience'. The additivity assumption, which has been described as implying that 'the marginal rate of substitution between lunch and dinner is independent of the amount of breakfast' (Dixit, 1976), is rather strong but is not strictly necessary to the argument. Maximizing U subject to the lifetime constraint leads to a function relating planned consumption in each period to expected lifetime resources and expected future discounted prices:

$$c_{t1} = g(W_1, p_1^*, p_2^*, \ldots, p_L^*), \qquad (5.3.2)$$

where c_{t1} is the consumption planned in period 1 for period t and W_1 is perceived lifetime resources in period 1, given by

$$W_1 = A_0(1 + r_1) + \sum_{t=2}^{L} p_t^* {}_1 y_t^e + p_1 y_1. \qquad (5.3.3)$$

where ${}_1 y_t^e$ represents the expectation of income at t formed in period 1, and, for convenience, p_t^* now represents expected discounted price. The planned consumption for the current period, c_{11}, is presumably realized, although we discuss in section 4.6 Deaton's (1977) disequilibrium model in which consumers do not buy the 'equilibrium' planned amount because they mistake real for relative price changes. Planned consumption for future periods will not in general be realized because consumers have the opportunity in each period to replan their consumption path in the light of new information relevant to the future and, perhaps, in response to past 'mistakes' revealed, for example, in an undesired accumulation of assets. If consumers do not need to correct past 'errors' and if they make optimal use of all presently available information then the difference between successive plans should be random; if not, that is if these revisions are systematically related to earlier information, then they would already have been taken account of in the earlier plan. This is the idea behind Hall's (1977) rational expectations theory, which is discussed in the next section. If the desired consumption path is given by a linear difference equation, the implication is that actual consumption will follow a random walk [see II, §18.3]

$$c_t = a_0 + a_1 c_{t-1} + v_t,$$

where v is a random regression disturbance. The linearity of the relationship would follow, for example, from an additive quadratic utility function where

$$u^*(c_t) = -(1/2)(\bar{c} - c_t)^2,$$

in which $\bar{c}$ is called the 'bliss' or saturation level of consumption. The Lagrangian is then given by

$$L = -(1/2) \sum_{t=1}^{L} [(\bar{c} - c_t)^2/(1 + \delta)^{t-1}]$$

$$+ \lambda \left[\sum_{t=1}^{L} p_t^* c_t - A_0(1 + r_1) - \sum_{t=1}^{L} p_{t-1}^* y_t^e \right].$$

where λ is a Lagrange multiplier [see IV, §15.1.4]. Taking partial derivatives with respect to c_t and c_{t-1} (assuming they exist [see IV, §5.3]) and equating them to zero gives

$$\delta L/\delta c_t = (\bar{c} - c_t)/(1 + \delta)^{t-1} + \lambda p_t^* = 0$$

$$\delta L/\delta c_{t-1} = (\bar{c} - c_{t-1})/(1 + \delta)^{t-2} + \lambda p_{t-1}^* = 0.$$

Eliminating λ:

$$c_t - \bar{c} = (p_t^*/p_{t-1}^*)(1 + \delta)(c_{t-1} - \bar{c}).$$

Now define r_t^*, the real interest rate, as the difference between the nominal rate of interest, r_t, and the rate of inflation, π_t, that is

$$r_t^* = r_t - \pi_t \quad \text{and} \quad \pi_t = (p_t - p_{t-1})/p_{t-1}.$$

Then $(p_t^*/p_{t-1}^*) = (p_t/p_{t-1})/(1 + r_t) = (1 + \pi_t)/(1 + r_t)$. For small π_t we can use the Taylor series approximation $(1 + \pi_t) \simeq 1/(1 - \pi_t)$ [see IV, §3.6] so that, for small r_t, $(p_t^*/p_{t-1}^*) \simeq 1/(1 + r_t^*)$. The optimum consumption path can then be written, if r_t^* is assumed constant,

$$c_t = \alpha_0 + \alpha_1 c_{t-1},$$

where

$$\alpha_0 = \bar{c}(r^* - \delta)/(1 + r^*), \quad \alpha_1 = (1 + \delta)/(1 + r^*).$$

Thus, if $r^* < \delta$ (implies $\alpha_1 > 1$) and $c_{t-1} < \bar{c}$, consumption will grow through time. This solution applies only if W_1 is large enough to ensure nonnegative c.

If the consumption path implies by the life-cycle optimization exercise involves borrowing at any point, there may be institutional constraints preventing the consumption from taking place, for example if lending institutions do not accept the borrower's assessment of future earning prospects. Such liquidity constraints will mean that a 'second-best' solution is adopted. In aggregate this may make no difference to the amount of consumption since a constrained individual who correctly predicted future income will spend correspondingly more in later life when he is no longer constrained. Aggregating across age-groups should therefore cancel out such effects in a stationary economy although in a growing economy this will not be true because the forced saving of the young (prevention of negative saving) will be greater than the corresponding extra spending of the old, each generation having larger lifetime resources than the preceding one.

5.3.2. Evidence

Even if one makes the clearly unrealistic assumption that all consumers have a single specific form of utility function the LCH is very hard to test. Apart from the emphasis it places on unobservable expectations, the changing age structure of the population and the changing distributions of wealth, income and expected income across age groups will all affect its predictions. One way of dealing with such problems is Tobin and Dolde's (1972) method. They construct a simplified schematic model of the US household sector with appropriate parameters for the age distribution of households, for the profile of income across ages and so on, observe the effect of different forms of liquidity constraint, taxes, etc., on the aggregate saving predicted by the model, and see whether the outcome of the simulations can account, in an approximate way, for the actual aggregate characteristics of the US economy. They conclude that it can, a result which may be regarded as evidence in favour of the theory, but of course simple data consistency cannot be regarded as a very powerful test. Certainly this form of simulation, as opposed to statistical modelling, seems a promising method of analysing the question. The classic aggregate econometric study of the LCH is by Ando and Modigliani (1963). In order to make the theory manageable they assumed that the intertemporal utility function was homothetic. This means that it can be expressed in the form $U(\mathbf{c}) = h[g(\mathbf{c})]$ (see Lau, 1969) where h is monotonically increasing [see IV, §2.7] and g is homogeneous of degree one [cf. I, (14.15.3)]. Monotonicity of h implies that a vector $\mathbf{c}$ maximizing g also maximizes U, so that the first-order conditions for the constrained maximization [see IV, §5.15] can be written

$$(\delta g[\mathbf{c}']/\delta c_i)/(\delta g[\mathbf{c}']/\delta c_j) = p_i^*/p_j^* \quad i,j = 1,\ldots,L.$$

Since $g(\theta\mathbf{c}) = \theta g(\mathbf{c})$ for all $\theta > 0$,

$$(\delta g[\theta\mathbf{c}]/\delta c_i)/(\delta g[\theta\mathbf{c}]/\delta c_j) = (\delta g[\mathbf{c}]/\delta c_i)/(\delta g[\mathbf{c}]/\delta c_j),$$

which implies that any scalar multiple of $\mathbf{c}'$ also satisfies the first-order conditions, for given relative intertemporal prices. If preference sets are strictly convex these solutions will be unique and the desired distribution of consumption between different time periods will be independent of the level of lifetime resources. A given increase in assets, for example, will increase planned consumption by the same amount in each period. This means that the consumption function takes the form

$$c_t = kW_t$$

where k depends on present and expected future real interest rates, assumed by Ando and Modigliani to be constant for all periods. They further simplified the model by postulating that expected future discounted real labour income is proportional to current real labour income, y_t, an alternative assumption being that it depended on the rate of unemployment. Their stochastic model was, therefore,

$$p_t c_t = a_0 + a_1 p_t y_t + a_2 A_{t-1} + u_t,$$ (5.3.4)

$$1 > a_1 > a_2 > 0$$

in which a_0 is expected to be zero, and u_t is a random disturbance term. This equation is an aggregate relationship so that its parameters are weighted averages of the parameters of individual functions such as (5.3.2). If it can be assumed that these latter functions differ only in that the parameters depend on the age of the individual then a_1 and a_2 will be constant through time if certain aggregation restrictions are satisfied. One sufficient set quoted by Ando and Modigliani is the constancy in time of (i) the parameters of the function for each age group, (ii) the age structure of the population and (iii) the relative distribution of income, expected income and net worth (assets) over the age groups. Ando and Modigliani estimated the parameters a_0, a_1 and a_2 using US annual data on p_t, c_t, y_t and A_t for 1929–1959, omitting the war years. The ordinary least squares (OLS) method of estimation, that is choosing that point in the parameter space which yields the least sum of squares of estimated disturbance terms, $\sum_{t=1}^{n} \tilde{u}_t^2$, n being the number of observations, [see VI, §12.1] gave the result

$$p_t c_t = 8.1 + 0.75 p_t y_t + 0.042 A_{t-1} + \tilde{u}_t$$ (5.3.5)

$$(1.0) \quad (0.05) \quad\quad (0.009)$$

$$R^2 = 0.998 \quad\quad DW = 1.26,$$

where the figures in brackets are the estimated standard errors of the parameter estimates, R^2 is the multiple correlation coefficient [see VI, §12.1.1] and DW is the Durbin–Watson statistic (see below). It is noticeable that the hypothesis that $a_0 = 0$ is rejected in this model, which suggests the presence of 'money illusion'. By the Gauss–Markov theorem [see VI, §8.2.3], the OLS estimator has minimum variance in the class of linear unbiased estimators if the probability distribution of the disturbance terms obeys the classical assumptions:

(i) $$E(u_i) = 0$$

(ii) $$E(u_i^2) = \sigma^2$$

(iii) $$E(u_i u_j) = 0, \; i \neq j$$

and, (iv), that the disturbances are independent of the regressors, income and net worth. Furthermore, by an application of the Rao–Blackwell theorem [see VI, §3.4.3] the OLS estimates can be shown to have minimum variance in the class of all unbiased estimators if, in addition, to (i)–(iv), the distribution of the disturbance terms is normal (see Silvey, 1975). Unfortunately, as is the case with most time-series of economic data, the disturbance terms are likely to be serially correlated [see VI, §§18.7–18.9], so that assumption (iii) above is probably unwarranted. This is suggested by the low value of the sample DW statistic, which is defined as

$$DW = \sum_{t=2}^{n} (\tilde{u}_t - \tilde{u}_{t-1})^2 / \sum_{t=1}^{n} \tilde{u}_t^2.$$

Since $DW \simeq 2(1 - \rho)$ where ρ (in this example about 0.37) is the coefficient of correlation between $\tilde{u}_t$ and $\tilde{u}_{t-1}$, a value of DW substantially below 2 probably indicates positive first-order serial correlation of the disturbance terms, that is

$$u_t = \alpha u_{t-1} + v_t, \tag{5.3.6}$$

where v_t is serially uncorrelated. If this is the case, the OLS estimates given above will be inefficient in the sense that their variances may be much larger than the best that can be achieved by linear unbiased estimators while the quoted standard errors of the estimates will be biased and may seriously underestimate the true standard errors. If the form of the departure from classical assumptions is known, more efficient estimates can be obtained either by the method of maximum likelihood or by some form of weighted least squares. The latter involves minimizing a weighted sum of squared residuals (estimated disturbances) where the weight attached to a particular disturbance corresponds to its 'chance of being small'. Consider the model (5.3.4), where u_t follows the first-order process given in Equation (5.3.6). Applying a 'quasi-differencing' transformation gives

$$p_t c_t - \alpha p_{t-1} c_{t-1} = a_0(1 - \alpha) + a_1(p_t y_t - \alpha p_{t-1} y_{t-1}) + a_2(A_{t-1} - \alpha A_{t-2}) + v_t,$$

in which v_t now obeys the classical assumptions, so that OLS method can be applied. If

$$\tilde{\mathbf{v}} = (\tilde{v}_2, \tilde{v}_3, \ldots, \tilde{v}_n), \tilde{\mathbf{u}} = (\tilde{u}_1, \tilde{u}_2, \ldots, \tilde{u}_n) \text{ and } \tilde{\mathbf{u}}^* = (\tilde{u}_2 - \alpha\tilde{u}_1, \tilde{u}_3 - \alpha\tilde{u}_2, \ldots, \tilde{u}_n - \alpha\tilde{u}_{n-1})$$

then $\sum_{t=2}^{n} \tilde{v}_t^2 = \tilde{\mathbf{v}}'\tilde{\mathbf{v}} = \tilde{\mathbf{u}}^*\tilde{\mathbf{u}}^* = \tilde{\mathbf{u}}'\mathbf{S}\tilde{\mathbf{u}}$ where $\mathbf{S}$ is the $n \times n$ matrix

$$\mathbf{S} = \begin{bmatrix} \alpha^2 & -\alpha & 0 & . & . & . & 0 \\ -\alpha & 1+\alpha^2 & -\alpha & 0 & . & . & 0 \\ 0 & -\alpha & 1+\alpha^2 & -\alpha & 0 & . & 0 \\ 0 & 0 & -\alpha & 1+\alpha^2 & -\alpha & . & 0 \\ . & & & . & & & . \\ 0 & . & . & . & . & 1+\alpha^2 & -\alpha \\ 0 & . & . & . & . & -\alpha & 1 \end{bmatrix}$$

Therefore the quasi-differencing method is equivalent to using the weighted least squares method with the weighting matrix $\mathbf{S}$ [see VI, §8.2.6].

Ando and Modigliani, however, differenced their model to eliminate the serial correlation of the disturbances, in effect assuming $\alpha = 1$. This gave the result:

$$\Delta p_t c_t = 0.52 \Delta p_t y_t + 0.072 \Delta A_{t-1} + \tilde{v}_t$$

$$(0.11) \qquad\quad (0.018)$$

$$R^2 = 0.929 \quad DW = 1.85$$

where Δ is the first difference operator. The DW statistic is now sufficiently close to 2 to suggest that the disturbances in this transformed model are independent of each other. On the assumption that $v_t \sim \tilde{N}(0, \sigma^2)$, it can be shown that $\hat{a}_i \sim \tilde{N}(a_i, \tilde{\sigma}_{a_i}^2)$ where $\tilde{a}_i$, $\tilde{\sigma}_{a_i}$, $i = 1, \ldots, k$ are respectively the OLS estimates of the slope parameters and the standard errors of the estimates, k being the number of regressors including the constant. Therefore $\hat{a}_i / \tilde{\sigma}_{\tilde{a}_i}$ follows a t-distribution with $n - k$ degrees of freedom under the null hypothesis $H_0 : a_i = 0$ [see VI, §5.8.2]. In the equation above the marginal propensity to consume out of assets is significantly different from zero since $\tilde{a}_2 / \tilde{\sigma}_{\tilde{a}_2} = 0.072/0.018 = 4$, while the 5% critical value of the t-distribution with 24 degrees of freedom is 2.06 [see VI, §4.5.1]. The equation therefore verifies an important implication of the LCH. Significant wealth effects on consumption have often been discovered in subsequent studies, but usually with smaller magnitude.

5.4. THE PERMANENT INCOME HYPOTHESIS AND RATIONAL EXPECTATIONS

The main alternative theory advanced in the nineteen-fifties was Friedman's permanent income hypothesis (PIH). Like the LCH, it is based on the neoclassical theory of intertemporal choice and, like Ando and Modigliani, Friedman made the assumption of a homothetic utility function, so that consumption is again proportional to lifetime resources with the constant of proportionality depending on current and expected real interest rates. The main differences between the theories are that, first, Friedman ignores the influence of assets, and, second, he uses the approximation that the consumer's length of life is infinite. One definition of permanent income, y^P, is that maximum amount which the consumer can spend in each period for the indefinite future, given his future income. Since this can be expressed, for constant interest rate r, as rW_1 where W_1 is lifetime resources in period 1 as defined in (5.3.3), this should include earnings on accumulated savings (assets) but in practice most empirical formulations have ignored the influence of changes in assets. Friedman's version of the consumption function was

$$c_t^P = k(r^*)y_t^P, \tag{5.4.1}$$

where c_t^P is 'permanent' or planned consumption and the constant k depends as before on the particular form of the utility function as well as on real interest rates. Since $\delta c_t^P / \delta y_t^P = c_t^P / y_t^P = k$, the long-run m.p.c. (k) is equal to the a.p.c. and the income elasticity of consumption (permanent) is equal to one, in contrast to the prediction of the simple 'Keynesian' linear function. On the basis of this theory Friedman was able to offer an explanation of the empirical results mentioned earlier, that the m.p.c. estimated from a 'Keynesian' function subsequently underpredicted consumption and that cross-section (budget) and time-series estimates of the function were apparently incompatible. The essential point is that the properties of the 'Keynesian' function are statistical illusions resulting from the fact that observed consumption and income do not correspond to the relevant permanent concepts. Observable consumption c and income y are defined by the relations

$$c = c^P + c^T$$
$$y = y^P + y^T,$$

where c^T, y^T are 'transitory' consumption and income respectively. In order to give these definitions operational content Friedman makes the further statistical assumptions [see II, §9.8] that

(i)　　　　　　　　　　　　$\text{cov}(y^P, y^T) = 0$

(ii)　　　　　　　　　　　　$\text{cov}(c^P, c^T) = 0$

(iii)　　　　　　　　　　　　$\text{cov}(y^T, c^T) = 0$

(iv)　　　　　　　　　　　　$E(y^T) = E(c^T) = 0.$

The third of these assumptions is clearly very strong—it implies that unexpected windfalls in income (bequests, for example) are not spent on non-durable goods and services. The effect of the first assumption is to ensure that in this model, in contrast to that of Ando and Modigliani, expectations of future real income are highly inelastic to current income. Given these assumptions, it follows that an ordinary least squares regression of c on y will tend to underestimate k. To show this, consider the cross-section regression

$$c_i = a_0 + a_1 y_i + v_i$$

where subscript i refers to the ith household, $i = 1, \ldots, n$, and v_i is a stochastic disturbance term obeying the classical assumptions [see §5.3.2 above]. The ordinary least squares estimate of a_1, which, under these circumstances, is efficient and unbiased [see VI, §3.3.2], is

$$\tilde{a}_1 = \sum_{i=1}^{n} (c_i - \bar{c})(y_i - \bar{y}) / \sum_{i=1}^{n} (y_i - \bar{y})^2.$$

Given the definitions of c and y, the 'true' consumption function (5.4.1) and the assumptions (i)–(iv), this implies that

$$\text{plim } \tilde{a}_1 = k[\text{var}(y_i^p)/\text{var}(y_i)] \leqslant k$$

since

$$\text{var}(y_i) = \text{var}(y_i^p) + \text{var}(y_i^T).$$

Plim (or probability limit) of a sequence $\tilde{a}_n$ of estimators of a, n being the sample size, is defined as follows. Plim $\tilde{a}_n = a$ if, for arbitrarily small positive real numbers ε and η, a sample size n_0 exists such that

$$\Pr[|\tilde{a}_n - a| < \varepsilon] > 1 - \eta \quad \text{for all } n > n_0,$$

in which case $\tilde{a}_n$ is called a consistent sequence. Hence $\tilde{a}_1$ will underestimate the m.p.c. in large samples to the extent that the variance of permanent income is less than that of observed income. Therefore cross-section regressions using data from groups of households who have large fluctuations in their transitory income—such as farmers and self-employed businessmen—will produce a smaller slope coefficient than corresponding regressions for those with small transitory income fluctuations, even if they have the same k, a prediction consistent with the available evidence (although, once again, other models would predict the same result). The income elasticity of consumption will be underestimated by the same factor as k since this elasticity, estimated at the sample means, is

$$\tilde{\eta} = (\mathrm{d}c_i/\mathrm{d}y_i)(\bar{y}/\bar{c}) = \tilde{a}_1(\bar{y}/\bar{c}).$$

On the other hand the a.p.c. $\bar{c}/\bar{y}$ is a consistent estimator of k since

$$\mathrm{plim}\,(\bar{c}/\bar{y}) = \left[\mathrm{plim}\,(1/n)\sum_{i=1}^{n}c_i\right]\Bigg/\left[\mathrm{plim}\,(1/n)\sum_{i=1}^{n}y_i\right]$$

$$= \left[\mathrm{plim}\,(1/n)\sum_{i=1}^{n}ky_i^{\mathrm{p}}\right]\Bigg/\left[\mathrm{plim}\,(1/n)\sum_{i=1}^{n}y_i\right]$$

$$= k.$$

Thus plim $\tilde{\eta} = [\mathrm{var}\,(y_i^{\mathrm{p}})/\mathrm{var}\,(y_i)]$ while the 'true' value of η is unity. Cross-section and time-series evidence on observed consumption and income is reconciled because while the former underestimates the m.p.c., Kuznets's and Goldsmith's time-series averages give a consistent estimate of it.

Clearly a major problem with the PIH is that y^{p} is an unobservable quantity so that the hypothesis cannot be properly tested unless permanent income is precisely specified. This means postulating a mechanism by which consumers predict future incomes (the same applies, of course, to the LCH). Following Cagan (1958), Friedman suggested an adaptive expectations scheme, given in discrete time form by

$$y_t^{\mathrm{P}} - y_{t-1}^{\mathrm{P}} = (1-\lambda)(y_t - y_{t-1}^{\mathrm{P}}), \quad 0 \leqslant \lambda \leqslant 1,$$

which implies that perceived permanent income is a weighted average of current observed income and lagged permanent income. Successive substitution for y_{t-1}, y_{t-2} etc. solves the first-order difference equation and gives

$$y_t^{\mathrm{P}} = (1-\lambda)\sum_{j=0}^{\infty}\lambda^j y_{t-j} \tag{5.4.2}$$

so that y_t^{p} is perceived by consumers as a weighted average of past incomes, the weights declining geometrically. Friedman himself truncated this series (adjusted to allow for a trend in income) after 17 terms and estimated λ by a search procedure in the regression

$$c_t = \alpha + ky_t^{\mathrm{P}} + v_t, \tag{5.4.3}$$

where the disturbance term v_t represents transitory consumption. He found α, as expected, to be not significantly different from zero while his estimate of k was 0.88, close to the observed a.p.c., again as expected.

It is, however, more convenient to estimate this form of infinite distributed lag using Koyck's (1954) transformation. Equation (5.4.2) can be written as

$$y_t^P = (1 - \lambda) \sum_{j=0}^{\infty} \lambda^j L^j y_t,$$

where L is the lag operator defined by $L^j y_t = y_{t-j}$. It follows that $y_t^P = [(1 - \lambda)/(1 - \lambda L)]y_t$, so that substituting in (5.4.3) gives (suppressing the constant)

$$c_t = [k(1 - \lambda)/(1 - \lambda L)]y_t + v_t, \tag{5.4.4}$$

which implies

$$c_t = k(1 - \lambda)y_t + \lambda c_{t-1} + v_t - \lambda v_{t-1}.$$

Comparing this with Equation (5.2.3), we can see that Friedman's time-series model is almost indistinguishable from Brown's habit persistence model—the only means of choosing between them, if the habit persistence model does not insist on a positive intercept, being by the error process. Friedman's model predicts a first order moving average process if the original error v is serially uncorrelated.

If certain modifications are made to this theory it becomes identical to the LCH. Friedman's infinite life assumption is not crucial: the essential results are unchanged if it is dropped. In addition, permanent income can be redefined to include the influence of assets. Suppose, for simplicity, that permanent income is defined to be constant over the life-cycle as the maximum possible steady consumption stream. Then, with the infinite life approximation,

$$(1 + r^*)A_{t-1} + \sum_{j=0}^{\infty} [(_t y_{t+j}^e - y_t^p)(1 + r^*)^{-j}] = 0,$$

where $_t y_{t+j}^e$ represents the expectation of income at time $t + j$ formed at time t. This simply equates current assets plus present value of expected income to the present value of the permanent income stream (as perceived at time t). Then, using

$$\sum_{j=0}^{\infty} (1 + r^*)^{-j} = (1 + r^*)/r^*,$$

$$y_t^P = r^*A_{t-1} + [r^*/(1 + r^*)] \sum_{j=0}^{\infty} {}_t y_{t+j}^e (1 + r^*)^{-j} \tag{5.4.5}$$

with the same notation as before. The third difference between Friedman and the LCH theorists is the former's adaptive expectations mechanism, which does not predict income particularly well. One reason for this may be the unlikely assumption of a constant adjustment coefficient λ. This limitation of model (5.4.2) is highlighted elsewhere in this volume [Chapter 6] where an attempt is made to overcome it.

The response of some theorists to this suggested weakness of model (5.4.2) has been to adopt a very different expectations theory, the rational expectations hypothesis (REH). Sometimes this hypothesis is presented merely as the assumption that people make in some sense 'optimal' use of information available to them in forming their 'mathematical' expectations. In this form the hypothesis is entirely without novelty, being the implicit assumption in most previous analyses. Under the definition of the REH, of course, it proves possible to determine a stochastic income generating equation so that the simple adaptive expectations model above becomes rational if it is assumed that the stochastic equation represents the information available to consumers [see Chapter 6, this volume].

The stronger and more novel version of the REH is that consumers form expectations as if they were in possession of all relevant information. In other words people are assumed to form expectations of future income on the basis of some 'true' stochastic process. Two ways have been suggested of testing this theory, both of which derive from an implication of the RE-PIH which was first pointed out by Hall (1977). This is that, since revisions of permanent income take place only in response to new information, these revisions, and hence deviations of consumption from the previous planned path, will be independent of all previously available information. This can be seen by differencing Equation (5.4.5):

$$\Delta y_t^p = r^* \Delta A_{t-1} + [r^*/(1+r^*)] \sum_{j=0}^{\infty} [{}_t y_{t+j}^e - {}_{t-1} y_{t+j-1}^e](1+r^*)^{-j}$$

$$(5.4.6)$$

where Δ is the first difference operator defined by $\Delta y_t = y_t - y_{t-1}$ [see III, §1.4]. The expression in square brackets can be split into two parts: the change in expectations, given by ${}_t y_{t+j}^e - {}_{t-1} y_{t+j}^e$ and the expectation at time $t-1$ of the change in income, given by ${}_{t-1}\Delta y_{t+j}^e$. Since ${}_{t-1}\Delta y_t^{Pe} = 0$ and since ${}_{t-1}\Delta A_{t-1}^e = \Delta A_{t-1}$ if the consumer's spending and saving plans are fulfilled, we have, on taking expectations at time $t-1$,

$$\Delta A_{t-1} = [-1/(1+r^*)] \sum_{j=0}^{\infty} {}_{t-1}\Delta y_{t+j}^e (1+r^*)^{-j}$$

which states that households arrange their saving (change in assets) in such a way that the value of permanent income is expected to be constant over the lifetime. Substituting in (5.4.6):

$$\Delta y_t^p = [r^*/(1+r^*)] \sum_{j=0}^{\infty} ({}_t y_{t+j}^e - {}_{t-1} y_{t+j}^e)(1+r^*)^{-j}. \qquad (5.4.7)$$

Therefore, for constant expected real interest rate r^*, the change in permanent income and therefore, through (5.4.1), in the planned consumption path depends on information relevant to future income which was unknown at time $t-1$.

Hall's method of testing this is to postulate that the planned consumption path is given by a linear difference equation [see §5.3] so that the actual consumption path obeys a first order Markov process [see II, Chapter 19] such as

$$c_t = \lambda c_{t-1} + v_t \tag{5.4.8}$$

where v_t represents the influence of unanticipated income changes and is therefore independent of all information dated $t-1$ and earlier, that is $_{t-1}v_t^e = 0$. The parameter λ will depend on the subjective rate of time preference and the (constant) real interest rate r^* (see the discussion of Hall's theory in section 5.3.1). Hall used quarterly aggregate US data on per capita consumption and income to test for the joint significance in (5.4.8) of consumption dated $t-2$ and earlier and income dated $t-1$ and earlier. In most cases he finds that these lagged variables do not add significantly to the prediction of current consumption. On the other hand, leaving aside the considerable aggregation assumptions involved, subsequent studies using other data have rejected the random walk hypothesis (see, for example, Davidson and Hendry, 1981).

The alternative method of testing the RE-PIH involves supposing that households forecast future income using a linear regression of income on various current and lagged exogenous variables. The change in permanent income, and therefore in the consumption path, then becomes a function of the current value of the stochastic disturbance in this regression. A simple version of this, for example, might have income as a function of its own past values. For a second-order process this can be written

$$\Delta y_t = \alpha_1 y_{t-1} + \alpha_2 y_{t-2} + u_t \tag{5.4.9}$$
$$E(u_t) = 0, \; E(u_t u_s) = 0, \; t \neq s.$$

By successive substitution for lagged values of y, Δy_t can be expressed as an infinite order moving average of the innovations in the income process:

$$\Delta y_t = \sum_{i=0}^{\infty} b_i u_{t-i}$$

The household is supposed to observe the innovation in the current period (the relevant new information) and use it to change its prediction of future income:

$$_t\Delta y_{t+i}^e - _{t-1}\Delta y_{t+i}^e = b_i u_t,$$

which implies that

$$\sum_{j=0}^{t} {}_t\Delta y_{t+j}^e - \sum_{j=0}^{i} {}_{t-1}\Delta y_{t+j}^e = \sum_{j=0}^{i} b_j u_t \; .$$

Since $\sum_{j=0}^{i} \Delta y_{t+j} = y_{t+i} - y_{t-1}$,

$$_t y_{t+i}^e - _{t-1} y_{t+i}^e = \sum_{j=0}^{i} b_j u_t,$$

so that, substituting this expression into (5.4.7),

$$\Delta y_t^P = [r^*/(1 + r^*)] \sum_{i=0}^{\infty} \sum_{j=0}^{i} b_j u_t (1 + r^*)^{-i}.$$

Therefore $\Delta y_t^P = b' u_t$, where

$$b' = [r^*/(1 + r^*)] \sum_{i=0}^{\infty} \sum_{j=0}^{i} b_j (1 + r^*)^{-i}$$

$$= [r^*/(1 + r^*)] \left[b_0 \sum_{i=0}^{\infty} (1 + r^*)^{-i} + b_1 \sum_{i=1}^{\infty} (1 + r^*)^{-i} + \right.$$

$$\left. \cdots + b_n \sum_{i=n}^{\infty} (1 + r^*)^{-i} + \cdots \right].$$

Since

$$\sum_{i=n}^{\infty} (1 + r^*)^{-i} = \sum_{i=0}^{\infty} (1 + r^*)^{-i} - \sum_{i=0}^{n-1} (1 + r^*)^{-i}$$

$$= [(1 + r^*)/r^*] - [1 - (1 + r^*)^{-n}]/[1 - (1 + r^*)^{-1}]$$

$$= [(1 + r^*)/r^*][(1 + r^*)^{-n}],$$

$$b' = \sum_{i=0}^{\infty} b_i (1 + r^*)^{-i}.$$

Substituting in (5.4.3) for Δy_t^P,

$$\Delta c_t = kb' u_t + v_t - v_{t-1}$$

$$= kb' y_t - kb'(\alpha_1 + 1) y_{t-1} - kb' \alpha_2 y_{t-2} + \bar{v}_t, \qquad (5.4.10)$$

where $\bar{v}_t = v_t - v_{t-1}$.

This formulation can be tested against a general distributed lag consumption function such as

$$c_t = a_0 + a_1 c_{t-1} + a_2 y_t + a_3 y_{t-1} + a_4 y_{t-2} + v_t.$$

Equations (5.4.10) and (5.4.9) involve imposing the following restrictions on the parameters of this function:

$$a_0 = 0; \; a_1 = 1; \; a_3 = -a_2(\alpha_1 + 1); \; a_4 = -a_2 \alpha_2,$$

so that, given some assumption about the probability distribution characterizing the error process, such as normality of v_t [see II, §11.4], a likelihood ratio test [see VI, §5.5] can be used to decide whether these restrictions are valid. In general this type of procedure has not lent much support to the RE-PIH (see Sargent, 1977, and Bilson, 1980). This is hardly surprising in view of the extraordinary amount of information and sophistication consumers are assumed to possess. It seems extremely unlikely that most people have such a well-defined mathematical expectation of future income, as Keynes remarked in the General Theory. After mentioning changes in expectations of the relation between the present and the future level of income as one factor affecting the propensity to consume out of present income, he discounted its practical importance, saying 'it is a matter about which there is, as a rule, too much uncertainty for it to exert much influence' (Keynes, 1936, p. 95).

5.5. RECENT ECONOMETRIC FORMULATIONS: THE ERROR CORRECTION MECHANISM

If it is accepted that expectations of future changes in real interest rates are too uncertain to have much noticeable effect on consumption and that expectations of future real income, while no doubt important, are highly responsive, in the aggregate, to current real income the most plausible model of aggregate consumption, given a constant price level, is

$$c_t = a_0 + a_1 y_t + a_2 A_{t-1} + v_t \qquad (5.5.1)$$

$$a_2 < a_1, 0 < a_1, a_2 < 1.$$

As we have seen in the last section, this is essentially the same as Ando and Modigliani's (1963) model and is therefore consistent, if a number of restrictions are made, with the strict life-cycle theory. It can just as easily, of course, be interpreted as a simple representation of Keynes's theory. Its relation to the habit persistence theory can be seen on differencing and substituting for assets using the identity

$$A_{t-1} - A_{t-2} = y_{t-1} - c_{t-1}.$$

(Since we are assuming a constant price level, there are no capital gains or losses on assets and the change in assets is given simply by saving.) This gives

$$c_t = a_1 y_t + (a_2 - a_1) y_{t-1} + (1 - a_2) c_{t-1} + v_t - v_{t-1},$$

which might explain why Brown's model [Equation (5.2.3)] was consistent with the data. Since the income terms can be written as $a_2 y_t + (a_1 - a_2)\Delta y_t$, they could be interpreted as representing income expectations. In fact all of the empirical models discussed in the previous sections, including RE, can be represented as different distributed lag formulations in consumption and income. A recent important study, by Davidson, Hendry, Srba and Yeo (1978), henceforth DHSY, provides an original approach to modelling this dynamic relationship. Their argument is that income and consumption tend towards an equilibrium relationship with each other. Because of the influence of habits and so forth the adjustment is not instantaneous but follows some unknown lag process. In order to disentangle the short-run dynamics from the long-run equilibrium, they suggest imposing the theoretical long-run solution on the model and choosing whichever dynamic process consistent with this fits the data best. The equilibrium requirement is simply that consumption has unit income elasticity, that is $c_t = k y_t$, as follows from both the permanent income and the LCH hypotheses. In logarithms [see IV, §2.11], $\ln c_t = k^* + \ln y_t$. The dynamic adjustment process can then be expressed in the most general terms as

$$A(L) \ln c_t = k^* + B(L) \ln y_t + v_t,$$

where $A(L)$ and $B(L)$ are polynomials in the lag operator L and v_t is white noise. In its simplest form:

$$\ln c_t = k^* + a_1 \ln y_t + a_2 \ln y_{t-1} + a_3 \ln c_{t-1} + v_t$$

Imposing the requirement of long-run proportionality of consumption to income (that is, proportionality in steady state, when c_t and y_t are growing at the same constant rate through time) involves imposing the restriction $a_1 + a_2 + a_3 = 1$. This can be seen by differencing and setting $\Delta \ln c_t = \Delta \ln c_{t-1} = \Delta \ln y_t = \Delta \ln y_{t-1}$ (since $\Delta \ln z_t = \ln [z_t/z_{t-1}] \simeq [z_t - z_{t-1}]/z_{t-1}$, the proportional growth rate, by the Taylor-series approximation $\ln [1 + x] \simeq x$) [see IV, Example 3.6.3]. The restriction implies that

$$\Delta \ln c_t = k^* + a_1 \Delta \ln y_t + (a_3 - 1) \ln (c/y)_{t-1} + v_t.$$

This equation can be interpreted as an 'error correction' mechanism, with the response of consumption to changes in income being mediated by the consumption-income ratio in the previous period in such a way that the process tends towards the 'target' proportionality. Estimating this type of model on UK quarterly data for the period 1958(i) to 1970(iv) yielded the preferred specification (ignoring a dummy variable)

$$\Delta_4 \ln c_t = a_1 \Delta_4 \ln y_t - a_2 \Delta_1 \Delta_4 \ln y_t - (1 - a_3) \ln (c/y)_{t-4}, \qquad (5.5.2)$$

where Δ_4 represents the change over the corresponding quarter a year earlier. The structure of the lags is validated in the sense that the model cannot be rejected against a model in which $\ln c_t$ is regressed, without coefficient restrictions, on $\ln c_{t-1}$, $\ln c_{t-2} \ldots \ln c_{t-5}$ and on $\ln y_t \ldots \ln y_{t-5}$. The equation also fits the data extremely well and has the important advantage that it can account, supposing it to be true, for the particular results of a number of earlier econometric formulations. On the other hand DHSY discovered that it failed a forecast test for the period 1971(i)–1975(iv).

The standard way of testing for instability in an econometric relationship is by the analysis-of-covariance test [see VI, §10.1.7] known to econometricians as the Chow test (see Chow, 1960). Consider the linear regression model

$$y_1 = X_1 b_1 + v_1$$
$$y_2 = X_2 b_2 + v_2,$$

where y_1 and y_2 are $(n_1 \times 1)$ and $(n_2 \times 1)$ vectors respectively of observations on the dependent variable, X_1 and X_2 are respectively $(n_1 \times k)$ and $(n_2 \times k)$ matrices of observations on k exogenous variables, $\mathbf{b}_1$ and $\mathbf{b}_2$ are $(k \times 1)$ vectors of regression parameters and $\mathbf{v}_1$ and $\mathbf{v}_2$ are respectively $(n_1 \times 1)$ and $(n_2 \times 1)$ vectors of random disturbances, with mean $\mathbf{0}$ and covariance matrices $\sigma_1^2 \mathbf{I}_{n_1}$ and $\sigma_2^2 \mathbf{I}_{n_2}$, $\mathbf{I}_n$ being the $n \times n$ identity matrix [see I, (6.2.7)]. Estimating a combined regression on all $n_1 \times n_2$ observations amounts to imposing the k restrictions $\mathbf{b}_1 = \mathbf{b}_2$. The Chow test is based on the following statistic, which, if $\sigma_1^2 = \sigma_2^2 = \sigma^2$, has an F-distribution with k and $(n_1 - k) + (n_2 - k)$ degrees of freedom under the null hypothesis that $\mathbf{b}_1 = \mathbf{b}_2$ [see VI, §5.8.6].

$$F(k, n_1 + n_2 - 2k)$$
$$= \frac{[(\mathbf{y}_1 - \mathbf{X}_1 \tilde{\mathbf{b}})'(\mathbf{y}_1 - \mathbf{X}_1 \tilde{\mathbf{b}}) + (\mathbf{y}_2 - \mathbf{X}_2 \tilde{\mathbf{b}})'(\mathbf{y}_2 - \mathbf{X}_2 \tilde{\mathbf{b}}) - (\tilde{\mathbf{v}}_1'\tilde{\mathbf{v}}_1 + \tilde{\mathbf{v}}_2'\tilde{\mathbf{v}}_2)]/k}{(\tilde{\mathbf{v}}_1'\tilde{\mathbf{v}}_1 + \tilde{\mathbf{v}}_2'\tilde{\mathbf{v}}_2)/(n_1 + n_2 - 2k)}$$

in which, as before, tildes denote estimated values and $\tilde{\mathbf{b}}$ represents the vector of parameters estimated from the combined regression. The numerator is, apart from the term involving degrees of freedom, the difference between the constrained and unconstrained sums of squares of residuals and the denominator is the unconstrained sum.

A related test, also given by Chow, compares the sum of squares of the forecast errors with the sample variance of the regression on the first n_1 observations, where the vector of forecast errors is given by $\mathbf{f} = (\mathbf{y}_2 - \mathbf{X}_2 \tilde{\mathbf{b}}_1)$. The covariance matrix of $\mathbf{f}$ [see II, §13.3.1] is $[\mathbf{I} + \mathbf{X}_2(\mathbf{X}_1'\mathbf{X}_1)^{-1}\mathbf{X}_2']\sigma^2$, and the ratio

$$F(n_2, n_1 - k) = \mathbf{f}'[\mathbf{I} + \mathbf{X}_2(\mathbf{X}_1'\mathbf{X}_1)\mathbf{X}_2']\mathbf{f}/n_2 \tilde{\sigma}_1^2$$

has an F-distribution with n_2 and $n_1 - k$ degrees of freedom. DHSY employed a variant of this test, using the statistic

$$z(n_2) = \sum_{t=1}^{n_2} (f_t/\tilde{\sigma}_1^2)^2$$

which, if the parameters are stable, tends to a χ^2 distribution with n_2 degrees of freedom as n_1 tends to infinity [see VI, §2.5.4]. In Equation (5.5.2), $Z(20) = 130$, compared with a critical value at the 5% level of 31.4, so that the equation was rejected on the grounds that its parameters are not stable.

5.6. THE EFFECT OF INFLATION ON AGGREGATE CONSUMPTION

In fact all traditional econometric models seriously overpredicted consumption in the nineteen-seventies in the UK because, as in most other industrial countries, there was an unprecedented rise in the proportion saved out of aggregate income (the saving ratio). Since this phenomenon coincided with a marked increase in the rate of inflation, a number of studies examined the possible relations between these variables. One of these studies, by Deaton (1977), provided DHSY with a means of modifying their model, Deaton had suggested that savings will increase if prices rise by more than consumers anticipate because a consumer who lacks information about all relevant prices simultaneously will think that a general inflation is simply a relative increase in the price of the good under consideration and will therefore buy less of it. Of course, when the mistake is subsequently discovered, it will be corrected although by then there may be more unanticipated inflation. Deaton's disequilibrium model can be set out as follows. Suppose that a consumer's demand for commodity i, denoted by q_i, is a function of the anticipated price vector $\mathbf{p}^*$, observed price p_i and anticipated consumption c^* [cf. Chapter 11]

$$q_i = f_i(p_1^*, \ldots, p_{i-1}^*, p_i, p_{i+1}^*, \ldots, p_n^*, c^*).$$

By a first-order Taylor series expansion [see IV, §3.6]

$$q_i \simeq f_i(\mathbf{p}^*, c^*) + (p_i - p_i^*)\delta f_i / \delta p_i$$

If $f_i(\mathbf{p}^*, c^*) = q_i^*$ and the price elasticity of good i, $e_{ii} \simeq (\delta f_i / \delta p_i)(p_i / q_i^*)$, this can be written, on multiplying by p_i, rearranging and summing over all goods and all consumers, as

$$c = \mathbf{p}'\mathbf{q} \simeq c^* + \sum_i q_i^*(1 + e_{ii})(p_i - p_i^*).$$

If the share of spending on the ith good in total spending is given by $W_i^* = (p_i^* q_i^*)/c^*$

$$\ln c \simeq \ln c^* + \ln \left[1 + \sum_i W_i^*(1 + e_{ii})(p_i - p_i^*)/p_i^* \right],$$

and, using the Taylor-series approximation $\ln(1 + x) \simeq x$:

$$\ln c \simeq \ln c^* + \sum_i W_i^*(1 + e_{ii})(\ln p_i - \ln p_i^*).$$

If P is an appropriately defined weighted index of prices, we can write

$$\ln c \simeq \ln c^* + (1 + \phi)(\ln P - \ln P^*),$$

where $\phi = \sum_i W_i^* e_{ii}$. This can be converted to an equation in the saving ratio using the same approximation as above

$$(s/y) \simeq -\ln\left[\{y - (y - c)\}/y \right] = \ln y - \ln c.$$

In other words $(s/y) \simeq (s^*/y^*) + [\ln(y/P) - \ln(y^*/P^*)] - \phi(\ln P - \ln P^*)$ where y^* is the anticipated current price value of income. This means that the saving ratio will differ from the anticipated saving ratio because of unanticipated real income (cf. Friedman's 'transitory' income) and of unexpected price changes. In principle this model can be applied to any model of equilibrium saving behaviour; Deaton himself used Friedman's PIH in his empirical work. Therefore

$$s^*/y^* = 1 - k,$$

since y^* in effect is permanent income. Consumers are supposed by the model to adapt to their mistakes so that the change in the desired saving ratio is proportional to the current mistake:

$$\Delta(s^*/y^*)_t = \sigma[(1-k) - (s/y)_t].$$

In order to make this model operational anticipated real income and prices have to be known. Deaton's solution is to postulate the following expectations mechanisms for the rate of growth of real income, ρ, and of prices, π:

$$\rho^e = \beta\rho + (1-\beta)\rho^0, \quad 0 \leqslant \beta \leqslant 1$$
$$\pi^e = \pi^0.$$

Where β, π^0 and ρ^0 are constants, so that, in particular, expected inflation is supposed to be constant. Combining these elements yields the model

$$(s/y)_t = a_0 + a_1\rho_t + a_2\pi_t + a_3(s/y)_{t-1} + v_t. \tag{5.6.1}$$

On both US and UK data this gives a significant value for the 'unanticipated' inflation parameter a_2, a result which does not depend only on the experience of the nineteen-seventies in which (s/y) and π happened to have a common upward trend. On the other hand, since it is inflation rather than unanticipated inflation which is doing the work, it is doubtful that Deaton's disequilibrium effect is really responsible for the relative empirical success of the model. Since the saving ratio in most advanced countries has shown a secular trend increase, its movements are unlikely to be well explained by any variable representing errors in expectations.

DHSY adapted their model, (5.5.2), to take account of the Deaton effect by adding to it the terms $\Delta_4 \ln P_t$ and $\Delta_1\Delta_4 \ln P_t$. Since, if π_t is small, $\ln(P_t/P_{t-1}) = \ln(1 + \pi_t) \simeq \pi_t$ the first of these terms represents the annual inflation rate and the second represents the quarterly change in this rate. The first term is significant and, as predicted by Deaton's theory, both have negative sign. The modified equation also passes the forecast test since $Z(20) = 21.8$ while the 5% critical value of the χ^2 distribution with 20 degrees of freedom is 31.4. On statistical grounds, therefore, it is a remarkably successful model.

On the other hand, with the inflation terms introduced in this way the model no longer gives a plausible general representation of the consumption–income relationship. In deterministic form, the model is

$$\Delta_4 \ln c_t = a_1\Delta_4 \ln y_t + a_2\Delta_1\Delta_4 \ln y_t + a_3 \ln(c/y)_{t-4}$$
$$+ a_4\Delta_4 \ln P_t + a_5\Delta_1\Delta_4 \ln P_t,$$
$$0 < a_1 < 1; a_3, a_4, a_5 < 0.$$

In long-run steady state with constant growth rate ρ of real income and consumption and constant inflation rate π, that is $\Delta_4 \ln y_t = \Delta_4 \ln c_t = \rho$,

$$\Delta_4 \ln P_t = \pi \quad \text{and} \quad \Delta_1\Delta_4 \ln y_t = \Delta_1\Delta_4 \ln P_t = 0,$$

the constant of proportionality, k, of consumption to income is

$$k = \exp\left[\{(1 - a_1)\rho - a_4\pi\}/a_3\right],$$

which implies that

$$\lim(c/y) = 0.$$

For values of π and ρ close to actual UK experience in the nineteen-sixties such as $\pi = 0.05$ and $\rho = 0.02$ the long-run saving ratio $1 - k$ is given as 0.16 which is not far from the actual average value, but for very high steady rates of inflation the model is clearly not appropriate. (The positive relationship between the aggregate saving ratio and the rate of growth of real income is in keeping, incidentally, with the life-cycle hypothesis by a similar argument to that mentioned at the end of section 5.3.1 in relation to liquidity constraints.) In view of the observational similarity between the effects of lagged income and consumption and the effects of assets, it is likely that the DHSY formulation is approximating a dynamic inter-relationship between assets, inflation and consumption. Consider a version, expressed in constant price terms, of Ando and Modigliani's aggregate life-cycle model, Equation (5.3.4),

$$c_t = a_0 + a_1 y_t + a_2 A_{t-1}/p_t + v_t,$$
$$0 < a_1, a_2 < 1; a_1 > a_2.$$

Multiplying by p_t, taking first differences and substituting for assets using the stock–flow relation (again ignoring capital gains and losses)

$$A_{t-1} - A_{t-2} = p_{t-1}y_{t-1} - p_{t-1}c_{t-1}$$

gives

$$p_t c_t - p_{t-1}c_{t-1} = a_0(p_t - p_{t-1}) + a_1(p_t y_t - p_{t-1}y_{t-1})$$
$$+ a_2(p_{t-1}y_{t-1} - p_{t-1}c_{t-1}) + v_t^*.$$

Dividing by p_t and rearranging,

$$c_t - c_{t-1}/(1 + \pi_t) = a_0[\pi_t/(1 + \pi_t)] + a_1 y_t + (a_2 - a_1)y_{t-1}/(1 + \pi_t)$$
$$- a_2 c_{t-1}/(1 + \pi_t) + \varepsilon_t, \qquad (5.6.2)$$

where $\varepsilon_t = v_t - (v_{t-1})/(1 + \pi_t)$. Thus the effect of inflation on consumption and saving can be explained by consumers valuing their assets A_{t-1}, given by their past saving decisions, at current prices p_t. To the extent that prices rise more rapidly, their perception of the value of their wealth falls and so therefore does consumption. In order to compare this formulation with those of Deaton and DHSY, rewrite (5.6.2) in terms of the saving ratio:

$$(s/y)_t = (1 - a_1)(1 - \theta_t) - a_0[\pi_t/(1 + \pi_t)y_t] + (1 - a_2)\theta_t(s/y)_{t-1} + \bar{v}_t,$$
$$(5.6.3)$$

where θ_t is the inverse of the rate of growth of money income:

$$\theta_t = 1/(1 + \rho_t)(1 + \pi_t)$$

and $\bar{v}_t = -v_t/y_t$. Since $\theta_t \simeq 1 - \rho_t - \pi_t$, we can take a linear approximation to the above function:

$$(s/y)_t \simeq (1 - a_1)\rho_t + (1 - a_1 - (a_0/y_t))\pi_t + (1 - a_2)(1 - \rho_t - \pi_t)(s/y)_{t-1}$$

which, for low rates of real income growth and inflation, is close to Deaton's equation (5.6.1).

Furthermore, if we again use the approximations

$$(s/y) \simeq \ln y - \ln c = -\ln(c/y)$$
$$\Delta_4 \ln y_t \simeq \rho_t \quad \text{and} \quad \Delta_4 \ln p_t \simeq \pi_t,$$

the deterministic part of Equation (5.6.1) can be written, in quarterly terms,

$$\ln(c/y)_t = -a_0 - a_1\Delta_4 \ln y_t - a_2\Delta_4 \ln p_t + a_3 \ln(c/y)_{t-4}.$$

Therefore

$$\Delta_4 \ln c_t = -a_0 - (a_1 - 1)\Delta_4 \ln y_t - a_2\Delta_4 \ln p_t + (a_3 - 1)\ln(c/y)_{t-4},$$

which is a close approximation to DHSY's formulation. Both Deaton's and DHSY's models can, therefore, be regarded as linear approximations to the inflation-adjusted life-cycle model. We have already shown that the DHSY formulation gives an unbounded saving ratio as inflation increases (the same is true of Deaton's formulation). The life-cycle model (5.6.3), on the other hand, gives a more plausible result:

$$\lim(s/y)_t = (1 - a_1) - a_0/y_t$$

for a given steady-state value of ρ. Since a_0 is positive and less than y_t (it can be interpreted as the minimum level of consumption) and since a_1, the m.p.c. out of current income, is substantially greater than zero, the upper bound of the saving ratio is well below unity. (5.6.3) can therefore be regarded as a more plausible general model of aggregate consumption under conditions of inflation than either of the other two models. The model is developed and empirically tested in Pesaran and Evans (1984): on annual data for 1953–1981 it performs better than the best alternative models, including annual versions of (5.6.1) and (5.6.2), the best estimate of a_1 being 0.55 and of a_2 0.047. In order to estimate these parameters accurately it is necessary to adapt the model to take account of gains and losses on capital assets (stocks and bonds) both in the stock–flow relation defining the change in the value of assets and directly as an element in current income. The latter element is extremely significant, bearing out Keynes's observation that windfall changes in capital assets may alter the m.p.c. and that the chief influence of interest rates on consumption is likely to operate through the revaluation of existing bonds.

5.7. CONCLUDING REMARKS

As this chapter is itself a summary of the literature, no overall summary will be presented here. Instead we mention but one point which seems to emerge. Despite the fact that the consumption function is often regarded as the shining example of scientific progression in economics, it is clear that in their essentials most of the theoretical (that is economic) developments were anticipated by Keynes and indeed incorporated into his own theory. Instead the major developments lie more in the realm of mathematics or modelling. The simple linear form (Equation 5.2.2)—which was, of course, a gross simplification of Keynes's views—has been replaced by forms reflecting greater technical sophistication. Thus whether the historical record is one of progress in economic understanding seems, at best, an open issue.

We conclude with a short comment on further reading. The best book on consumer behaviour is Deaton and Muellbauer (1980), to which section 5.3 in particular owes a great deal, and Theil (1971) is a useful text on econometric theory. These and other references are given below.

5.8. REFERENCES

Ando, A. and Modigliani, F. (1963). The 'life-cycle' hypothesis of saving: aggregate implications and tests. *American Economic Review*, **53**, 55–84.

Bilson, J. F. O. (1980). The rational expectations approach to the consumption function. *European Economic Review*, **13**, 273–299.

Brown, T. M. (1952). Habit persistence and lags in consumer behaviour. *Econometrica*, **20**, 355–371.

Cagan, P. (1958). Monetary dynamics of hyperinflation, in M. Friedman (ed.), *Studies in the Quantity Theory of Money*. Chicago University Press, Chicago.

Chow, G. C. (1960). Tests of equality between sets of coefficients in two linear regressions. *Econometrica*, **28**, 591–605.

Davidson, J. E. H. and Hendry, D. F. (1981). Interpreting econometric evidence: The behaviour of consumers' expenditure in the UK. *European Economic Review*, **16**, 177–192.

Davidson, J. E. H., Hendry, D. F., Srba, F. and Yeo, S. (1978). Econometric modelling of the aggregate time-series relationship between consumers' expenditure and income in the United Kingdom. *Economic Journal*, **88**, 661–692.

Deaton, A. S. (1977). Involuntary saving through unanticipated inflation. *American Economic Review*, **67**, 899–910.

Deaton, A. S. and Muellbauer, J. (1980). *Economics and Consumer Behaviour*. Cambridge University Press, Cambridge.

Dixit, A. K. (1976). *Optimization in Economic Theory*. Oxford University Press, Oxford.

Duesenberry, J. S. (1949). *Income, Saving, and the Theory of Consumer Behavior*, Harvard University Press, Cambridge, Mass.

Fisher, I. (1907) *The Rate of Interest: Its Nature, Determination and Relation to Economic Phenomena*. Macmillan, New York.

Fisher, I. (1930). *The Theory of Interest*. Yale University Press, New Haven, Conn.

Friedman, M. (1957). *A Theory of the Consumption Function*. Princeton University Press, Princeton, N.J.

Goldsmith, R. W. (1955). *A Study of Saving in the United States, I.* Princeton University Press, Princeton, N.J.

Hall, R. E. (1977). Stochastic implications of the life-cycle—permanent income hypothesis: theory and evidence. *Journal of Political Economy*, **86**, 971–987.

Keynes, J. M. (1936). *The General Theory of Employment, Interest and Money.* Macmillan, London.

Koyck, L. M. (1954). *Distributed Lags and Investment Analysis*, North-Holland, Amsterdam.

Kuznets, S. (1942). *Uses of National Income in Peace and War.* National Bureau of Economic Research, Occasional Paper No. 6.

Lau, L. J. (1969). Duality and structure of utility functions. *Journal of Economic Theory*, **1**, 374–396.

Modigliani, F. (1975). The life-cycle hypothesis of saving twenty years later, in M. Parkin and A. R. Nobay (eds.), *Contemporary Issues in Economics.* Manchester University Press, Manchester.

Modigliani, F. and Brumberg, R. (1955). Utility analysis and the consumption function: an interpretation of cross-section data, in K. K. Kurihara (ed.), *Post-Keynesian Economics.* George Allen and Unwin, London.

Pesaran, M. H. and Evans, R. A. (1984). Inflation, capital gains and UK personal savings, 1953–1981, *Economic Journal*, **94**, 237–257.

Sargent, T. J. (1977). Rational expectations, econometric exogeneity, and consumption. *Journal of Political Economy*, **86**, 673–700.

Silvey, S. D. (1975). *Statistical Inference.* Chapman and Hall, London.

Theil, H. (1971). *Principles of Econometrics.* John Wiley, New York.

Tobin, J., and Dolde, W. (1972). *Wealth, Liquidity and Consumption.* Yale: Cowles Foundation Paper No. 360.

Mathematical Methods in Economics
Edited by F. van der Ploeg
© 1984, John Wiley & Sons, Ltd.

6

Generalized Adaptive Expectations

TONY LAWSON, *University of Cambridge, Cambridge, UK*

6.1. INTRODUCTION

A common assumption in studies of the determinants of community spending habits is that consumers make a distinction between income they expect to continue and income they believe to be purely transitory. The theoretical basis for this distinction is normally attributed to Friedman's Permanent Income Hypothesis, PIH [see §5.4]. Although the PIH in most essential respects can be found in Keynes's General Theory, Permanent Income, which is usually equated to expected income, cannot be observed directly, and this fact poses a problem for empirical study. The impasse is usually resolved, and Friedman himself adopted this strategy, by assuming that expectations are formed adaptively, via a mechanism similar to the following:

$$_t y_{t+1}^e = {}_{t-1}y_t^e + \lambda(y_t - {}_{t-1}y_t^e), 0 < \lambda < 1; \lambda \text{ constant.} \qquad (6.1.1)$$

Here $_t y_{t+1}^e$ is the expectation of disposable income at time $t + 1$, y_{t+1}, with the expectation formed and held at time t. If consumption at $t + 1$, denoted C_{t+1}, is a linear function of $_t y_{t+1}^e$, say $C_{t+1} = a + b_t y_{t+1}^e$ then it follows that $C_{t+1} - (1 - \lambda)C_t = \lambda(a + by_t)$ is a linear function of y_t. With the aid of Equation (6.1.1) the unobservable expectations term can therefore be eliminated from the consumption equation.

Equation (6.1.1) is frequently criticized, especially by proponents of the rational expectations hypothesis (REH). According to the rational expectations hypothesis people form expectations as if they know the process which will ultimately generate the actual outcomes. See Muth (1961) for the defining article, and see, for example, B. M. Friedman (1979), Shiller (1978) and Chapter 9 for useful discussions. The criticism arise from two limiting characteristics it possesses. The first is the property that when the variable y_t reveals a trend, expectations generated by model (6.1.1) are *certain* to be inaccurate. This can be most easily seen by rewriting the model in the following form:

$$_t y^e_{t+1} - {_{t-1}} y^e_t = \lambda(y_t - {_{t-1}} y^e_t), \quad 0 < \lambda < 1. \tag{6.1.2}$$

If y_t is trended then for expectations also to be so the left-hand side of (6.1.2) must be different from zero, in which case the right-hand side must also be different from zero, thus constraining $_{t-1} y^e_t$ from being equal to y_t. (This form of criticism of model (6.1.1) is made, for example, in Barro and Fischer, 1976, p. 155; Minford, 1980, p. 10 and M. Friedman, 1957, p. 27).

A second more fundamental limitation concerns the assumed constancy of the adjustment coefficient λ in (6.1.1). Critics suggest that λ will be closer to unity at times of greater uncertainty when people are assumed to attach greater weight to actual observations when deriving forecasts. Moreover, it is typically argued that this inflexibility of (6.1.1) prevents the consistent or 'valid' econometric testing of the core 'monetarist' assumption, the natural rate hypothesis. (The earliest development of this argument is in Lucas (1972), but see also M. Friedman, (1957, p. 26), Minford (1980, p. 10) or Sargent and Wallace (1975).)

A perusal of Friedman's book *A Theory of the Consumption Function* (1957) reveals that not only did Friedman assume that, in order to form expectations, people subdivide income in the suggested manner, but that he also accepts this subdivision as a realistic characterization of the income generating process. People, in forming expectations, are then assumed to act as optimal predictors. Several authors (for example Lucas (1976) or Sargent (1977)) have made this point, arguing that Friedman's model essentially equates subjective and objective probability distributions. This hypothesis is, of course, the theory of Rational Expectations.

Clearly there is a problem inherent in this discussion: proponents of the REH tend to criticize Equation (6.1.1) when proposing the adoption of the REH whilst Friedman seems to imply that (6.1.1) is consistent with the REH. A main intention of this chapter is therefore to clarify this issue.

In section 6.2 the REH is applied to the PIH to see if Equation (6.1.1) can be so derived. As we shall see this can only be achieved under a very restrictive assumption.

Relaxing this particular assumption in section 6.3 it is found that in order to maintain consistency with both the REH and the PIH, it is *not* necessary to abandon the assumption that expectations are adaptive. Instead, through the application of Bayes Theorem [see II, §16.4], a generalized adaptive expectations hypothesis is derived which is consistent with both the PIH and the REH and which is also immune to the criticisms of Equation (6.1.1) discussed above.

6.2. A PERMANENT INCOME HYPOTHESIS

For most people nominal income does not change significantly from one year to the next. At least the change is not sufficiently large that people estimate the income they will receive in the second year entirely independently of what they received in the first year. Instead people usually estimate the *change* in income that will occur. At the bargaining table, for example, wage demands and offers are conducted in terms of absolute or percentage increases, rather than in terms of wage and salary *levels*.

Of course a 10% rise in earnings may not result in disposable nominal income in the second period being calculated as 110% of the level achieved in the first period. It will almost definitely be the case that part of the first period's income included transient (that is non-'permanent') windfall gains or losses, due perhaps to temporary tax changes or bequests from relatives. This latter amount will clearly be deducted before the 110%—new level—is calculated.

This view of the income generating process can be formalized as:

$$y_t = S_t + \pi_{t-1}, \tag{6.2.1}$$

where π_{t-1} is 'permanent' income at time $t-1$, or equivalently that part of disposable income received at $t-1$ that is expected to continue, and S_t is the new 'shock' or addition to disposable income at time t. The latter component is 'new' in the sense that it represents an element that was not considered to have been received at $t-1$. (It is not the same as the numerical increase (or change) in income at time t over that received at $t-1$.) This new component will, in turn, comprise a permanent component which, without loss of generality, we denote by $\beta_t S_t$ and a transitory component which we denote by $(1 - \beta_t)S_t$.

We can thus rewrite the income generating process represented by (6.2.1) as

$$y_t = \pi_t + (1 - \beta_t)S_t \tag{6.2.2}$$

$$\pi_t = \pi_{t-1} + \beta_t S_t. \tag{6.2.3}$$

Historically, nominal income has tended to increase year after year, so that the shocks S_t have been, and will be expected to be, positive. To simplify the exposition, however, we shall *initially* assume zero growth in disposable income, so that the shocks are assumed to be independently distributed with zero mean. We shall relax this assumption in due course.

The REH requires that stochastic terms be set at their expected values (which are assumed to exist). Thus in this situation:

$$_{t-1}S_t^e = 0. \tag{6.2.4}$$

Applying the REH to Equation (6.2.1) we discover that:

$$_{t-1}y_t^e = \pi_{t-1} \tag{6.2.5}$$

and

$$_ty_{t+1}^e = \pi_t. \tag{6.2.6}$$

A little manipulation of Equations (6.2.1) to (6.2.6) now produces the following adaptive mechanism:

$$_ty_{t+1}^e = {}_{t-1}y_t^e + \beta_t(y_t - {}_{t-1}y_t^e) \tag{6.2.7}$$

If we refer back to Equation (6.1.1) we can see it is consistent with the REH only if the adjustment coefficient β_t in Equation (6.2.7) is a constant λ in every period. In other words, it is correct to use (6.1.1) in a rational expectations framework (assuming zero growth) *only* under the rather unrealistic assumption that a *constant* proportion of the shock in each period has a lasting or permanent effect. Thus Friedman's use of a mechanism similar to Equation (6.1.1) seems to be inconsistent with the rest of his analysis. [Friedman in fact includes a constant, non-zero, growth term in his adaptive hypothesis, but this does not alter the above conclusion. For if we write the constant growth term as g, then:

$$S_t = g + r_t,$$

say, where $_{t-1}r_t^e = 0$ and so $_{t-1}S_t^e = g$. If β_t is now the proportion of r_t that is permanent, then we can write:

$$\pi_t = \pi_{t-1} + g + \beta_t r_t.$$

Manipulation of these equations and (6.2.1) now produces the following adaptive mechanism:

$$_t y_{t+1}^e = {}_{t-1}y_t^e + \beta_t(y_t - {}_{t-1}y_t^e) + g$$

so that a constant coefficient of adjustment implies the same unrealistic restriction for β_t as in the case with no trend (above). (Moreover the constancy of g is itself restrictive, and this assumption will be relaxed in section 6.3.3.)]

6.3. A GENERALIZED ADAPTIVE EXPECTATIONS HYPOTHESIS

6.3.1. Real income

Before we generalize the above procedure by dropping the constancy restriction on β_t, a further caveat must be filled in, which, so far, has been ignored in order to facilitate ease of exposition. Following Keynes's analysis of consumer spending in the General Theory, most economists, including Friedman, have assumed that people estimate their income in quantity terms. In other words instead of assuming that people derive expectations of nominal income, as in section 6.2, it is assumed that they attempt to gauge their permanent disposable *real* income.

If we now assume that y denotes disposable real income rather than nominal income, the analysis outlined so far remains largely unchanged. Using π_t to denote the permanent component of *real* income, and so forth, we shall still derive the updating mechanism described by Equation (6.2.6). There is, however, an important difficulty. In any inflationary period it will be difficult to discern which part of the shock, or real income change, is permanent and which is transitory even after y_t has been observed. If prices for similar goods differ from shop to shop, or if a prices and incomes policy is in force, or if the taxation system is frequently changing, then the observation y_t may be particularly 'noisy' in the sense that it will be difficult to identify what element is transitory. An observation y_t coupled with a 'posterior' estimate of $\pi_{t-1}(\pi_{t-1}$ is no longer observable) does provide an estimate of the shock S_t, but the permanent and transitory components will certainly be independently distributed and unobservable.

For simplicity (and lacking contrary evidence) we assume that all such shocks and disturbances are distributed independently [see II, Definition 6.6.1] and Normally [see II, §11.4], so that we can write:

$$S_t = \varepsilon_t + u_t \tag{6.3.1}$$

$$\varepsilon_t \sim IN(0; W_t) \tag{6.3.2}$$

$$u_t \sim IN(0; R_t), \tag{6.3.3}$$

where u_t is the permanent component of the new shock, and ε_t is the transient part. The reformulated income generating process can be written:

$$y_t = \pi_t + \varepsilon_t \tag{6.3.4}$$

$$\pi_t = \pi_{t-1} + u_t \tag{6.3.5}$$

so that Equations (6.3.1) to (6.3.5) now describe the permanent income hypothesis. However, unlike the hypothesis adopted in section 6.2, no specific relationship between the transient and permanent components, that is ε_t and u_t, is assumed. Instead, as noted above, they are taken to be independently distributed.

6.3.2. Combining rational expectations and the PIH

We now apply the REH to Equations (6.3.1) to (6.3.3) and examine how in this situation expectations adjust to previous prediction errors.

Writing the density function of π_t at $t-1$ as [see II, §11.4]

$$N(_{t-1}\pi_t^e, \Sigma_t) \tag{6.3.6}$$

and applying Bayes Theorem [see II, §16.4] it can be shown that the posterior (mean) estimate of π_t, derived after observing y_t, is given by (for example Lawson, 1980, p. 316):

$$_t\pi_t^e = {}_{t-1}\pi_t^e + \beta_t(y_t - {}_{t-1}\pi_t^e), \tag{6.3.7}$$

where

$$\beta_t = \frac{\Sigma_t}{W_t + \Sigma_t} \tag{6.3.8}$$

and where the variance of the posterior estimate is given by:

$$\sigma_t = \Sigma_t - \frac{(\Sigma_t)^2}{W_t + \Sigma_t}. \tag{6.3.9}$$

Notice that $_t\pi_t^e$ is the revised estimate of π_t, determined after y_t has been observed. The estimate forms the basis for predicting future outcomes. It can be seen from (6.3.5) by taking expectations (conditional on all information available up to $t-1$) on both sides of Equation (6.3.5) that

$$_t\pi_{t+1}^e = {}_t\pi_t^e \tag{6.3.10}$$

so that

$$_t\pi_{t+1}^e = {}_{t-1}\pi_t^e + \beta_t(y_t - {}_{t-1}\pi_t^e), \tag{6.3.11}$$

where $0 < \beta_t < 1$ and the variance of the estimate $_t\pi_{t+1}^e$ is given by:

$$\Sigma_{t+1} = \sigma_t + R_t. \tag{6.3.12}$$

Equation (6.3.11) shows that the period ahead prediction $_t\pi_{t+1}^e$ is a convex combination of the last prediction $_{t-1}\pi_t^e$ and of the observation y_t itself. The weights attached to $_{t-1}\pi_t^e$ and y_t (($1 - \beta_t$) and β_t respectively), depend on the degree of belief attached to the prior $_{t-1}\pi_t^e$, and on the degree of belief attached to the possibility that y_t is free of noise. This can be seen from Equation (6.3.8). Some numerical examples illustrating how the size of the adjustment coefficient, β_t, will vary in differing circumstances is provided in Lawson (1980). (Notice that the size of this coefficient is important for determining the magnitude of the Keynesian multiplier. The marginal propensity to consume will be large if the change in current income induces a significant adjustment in expected income. Friedman merely assumes that the change in permanent income induced by a change in income is very small, taking the adjustment coefficient to be small. The above approach imposes no such restriction.)

We have thus derived the adaptive expectations mechanism that is consistent with the PIH and with the REH, under the assumption that the income series exhibits no trend.

6.3.3. An incremental growth term

Historically, of course, real personal disposable income has tended to rise, although not at a constant rate. We now replace the assumption of no growth in income, with the more realistic specification that the growth rate, g_t, follows a random walk process. Maintaining the assumption that shocks and disturbances are independently and Normally distributed we can now write the PIH as:

$$y_t = \pi_t + \varepsilon_t \qquad\qquad \varepsilon_t \sim N(0; W_t) \tag{6.3.13}$$

$$\pi_t = \pi_{t-1} + g_t + u_t \qquad\qquad u_t \sim N(0; R_t) \tag{6.3.14}$$

$$g_t = g_{t-1} + v_t \qquad\qquad v_t \sim N(0; Z_t). \tag{6.3.15}$$

Transforming to matrix notation [see I, §6.2] we define

$$\mathbf{P}_t = \begin{pmatrix} \pi_t \\ g_t \end{pmatrix} \qquad \alpha_t = \begin{pmatrix} u_t \\ v_t \end{pmatrix}$$

$$\alpha_t \sim N\begin{pmatrix} 0 \\ 0 \end{pmatrix}; \mathbf{F}_t \end{pmatrix} \text{ so that } \mathbf{F}_t = \begin{pmatrix} R_t & 0 \\ 0 & Z_t \end{pmatrix}.$$

Let

$$\mathbf{S}_1 = \begin{pmatrix} 1 & 1 \\ 0 & 1 \end{pmatrix} \quad \mathbf{S}_2 = \begin{pmatrix} 1 & 1 \\ 0 & 1 \end{pmatrix} \quad \mathbf{X} = (1 \quad 0)$$

so that Equations (6.3.13) to (6.3.15) may be written as

$$y_t = \mathbf{X}\mathbf{P}_t + \varepsilon_t \qquad\qquad \varepsilon_t \sim N(0; W_t) \qquad\qquad (6.3.16)$$

$$\mathbf{P}_t = \mathbf{S}_1 \mathbf{P}_{t-1} + \mathbf{S}_2 \alpha \qquad \alpha_t \sim N(0; \mathbf{F}_t) \qquad\qquad (6.3.17)$$

where (6.3.16) denotes the observation equation and (6.3.13) denotes the state equation.

If the expectations of $\mathbf{P}_t$ held at $t-1$ is $_{t-1}\mathbf{P}_t^e$, with variance Σ_t [see II, §13.3.1], then the posterior, or updated, estimate of $\mathbf{P}_t$, following the observation of y_t, is $_t\mathbf{P}_t^e$ where (for proof see Graybill (1961), Theorem 3.10, p. 63):

$$_t\mathbf{P}_t^e = {}_{t-1}\mathbf{P}_t^e + \beta_t(y_t - \mathbf{X}_{t-1}\mathbf{P}_t^e) \qquad\qquad (6.3.18)$$

The adjustment coefficient is given by:

$$\beta_t = {}_{t-1}\Sigma_t \mathbf{X}'(\mathbf{X}_{t-1}\Sigma_t\mathbf{X}' + W_t)^{-1}; \qquad\qquad (6.3.19)$$

and variance of the estimate is:

$$_t\Sigma_t = {}_{t-1}\Sigma_t \mathbf{X}'(\mathbf{X}_{t-1}\Sigma_t\mathbf{X}' + W_t)^{-1}\mathbf{X}_{t-1}\Sigma_t. \qquad\qquad (6.3.20)$$

It follows from (6.3.17) that

$$_t\mathbf{P}_{t+1}^e = \mathbf{S}_{1t}\mathbf{P}_t^e \qquad\qquad (6.3.21)$$

and that the variance of this forecast is given by:

$$_t\Sigma_{t+1} = \mathbf{S}_{1t}\Sigma_t\mathbf{S}_1' + \mathbf{S}_2\mathbf{F}_2\mathbf{S}_2'. \qquad\qquad (6.3.22)$$

Thus an adaptive expectations mechanism consistent with the PIH and the REH has been derived.

As they stand Equations (6.3.16) and (6.3.17) are expressed in what control engineers call 'state space form'. The recursive algorithm displayed in Equations (6.3.8) to (6.3.22) is known as the Kalman Filter (Kalman, 1960) [see VI, Chapter 20]. An interesting discussion of Kalman Filtering Methods and their usefulness for economics can be found in Athans (1974).

Once we have decided how to determine the initial values of the different error variance terms and of the components of $\mathbf{P}_0$ and Σ_0, a permanent income series consistent with the REH can now be generated using these adaptive formulae. This is a procedure which takes some space to describe, and is dealt with in Harrison and Stevens (1971) and Lawson (1980).

6.4 OTHER APPLICATIONS

This chapter has considered adaptive expectations models in the restricted context of consumers forecasting their real disposable income, although, of course, the field of application is much wider.

Amongst the earliest contributors to use a model similar to the simple adaptive mechanism of Equation (6.1.1) were Brown (1959), Magee (1958) and Winters (1961) in the context of short-term forecasting of sales, and primarily inventory control. Other early and perhaps better-known studies include Cagan's (1958) study of demand for cash balances during hyperinflation and Nerlove's (1958) study of agriculture supply. Over the last twenty years the simple adaptive mechanism has been used in perhaps most areas of applied economics and is undoubtedly the most common expectations hypothesis adopted in empirical work.

Recent studies, however, have begun to use models similar to the more generalized hypothesis formulated in this chapter. Examples include Beath (1979) who uses the model to forecast unit labour costs and Harrison and Stevens (1971) who have proposed the model, with its Kalman filter interpretation, as a device for forecasting short-term demand in marketing studies.

6.5. CONCLUDING REMARKS

In conclusion, a generalized adaptive mechanism has been derived that is consistent with both rational expectations and the permanent income hypothesis. That such a mechanism exists is of interest if only because the proponents of the rational expectations hypothesis, when discussing the virtues of assuming rationality, frequently set up adaptive expectations as the straw person to be knocked down. The tools used for generating optimal expectations were basically Bayes Theorem and the Kalman filter.

6.6. REFERENCES

Athans, M. (1974). The importance of Kalman filtering methods for economic systems. *Annals of Economic and Social Measurement*, 3(1), 49 and 64.
Beath, J. (1979). Target profits, cost expectations and the incidence of the corporate income tax. *Review of Economic Studies*, no. 144, 513–526.
Barro, R. J. and Fischer, S. (1976). Recent developments in monetary theory. *Journal of Monetary Economics*, 2, 133–167.
Brown, R. G. (1959). *Statistical Forecasting for Inventory Control*. McGraw-Hill, New York.

Cagan, P. (1958). Monetary dynamics of hyperinflation, in M. Friedman (ed.), *Studies in the Quantity Theory of Money*, Chicago University Press, Chicago.

Friedman, B. M. (1979). Optimal expectations and the extreme information assumptions of 'rational expectations' macromodels. *Journal of Monetary Economics*, **5**, 23–41.

Friedman, M. (1957). *A Theory of the Consumption Function*. Princeton University Press, Princeton, N.J.

Friedman, M. (1973). 'Unemployment versus inflation'. Institute of Economic Affairs, London.

Graybill, F. A. (1961). *An Introduction to Linear Statistical Methods*, Vol. 1. McGraw-Hill, New York.

Harrison, P. J. and Stevens, C. F. (1971). Short-term forecasting. *Operations Research Quarterly*, **22**(4), 341–364.

Kalman R. E. (1960). A new approach to linear filtering and prediction problems, *Journal of Basic Engineering*, Transactions ASME, series D, **83**, 33–45.

Keynes, J. M. (1973). The general theory of employment, interest and money, in *Collected Writings*, Vol. VII. Macmillan, London.

Lawson, T. (1980). Adaptive expectations and uncertainty, *Review of Economic Studies*, pp. 305–320.

Lucas, R. E. (1972). Econometric testing of the natural rate hypothesis, in *The Econometrics of Price Determination Conference*, edited by O. Eckstein. Federal Reserve Board, Washington.

Lucas, R. E. (1976). Econometric policy evaluation: A critique. *Journal of Monetary Economics*, Supplement.

Magee, J. F. (1958). *Production Planning and Inventory Control*. McGraw-Hill, New York.

Minford, P. (1980). The nature and purpose of UK macroeconomic models. *Three Banks Review*, March, pp. 3, 26.

Muth, J. F. (1961). Rational expectations and the theory of price movements. *Econometrica*, **24**, 315–375.

Nerlove, M. (1958). *The Dynamics of Supply : Estimation of Farmer's Response to Price*. Johns Hopkins Press, Baltimore.

Sargent, T. J. and Wallace, N. (1975). 'Rational' expectations, the optimal monetary instrument, and the optimal money supply rule. *Journal of Political Economy*, **83**, 241 and 254.

Sargent, R. J. (1977). Observations on improper methods of simulating and teaching Friedman's time series consumption model. *International Economic Review*, **18**, 445–462.

Shiller, R. J. (1978). Rational expectations and the dynamic structure of macroeconomic models. *Journal of Monetary Economics*, **4**, 91 and 96.

Winters, P. R. (1961). Forecasting sales by exponentially weighted moving averages. *Management Science*, **6**, 324–342.

Mathematical Methods in Economics
Edited by F. van der Ploeg
© 1984, John Wiley & Sons, Ltd.

7

Macroeconomic Investment and Employment Functions

WIM DRIEHUIS, *University of Amsterdam, Amsterdam, Netherlands*

7.1. INTRODUCTION

At any given time each firm has to make a decision about the quantity of capital and/or labour it wants to use. These decisions are taken to realize certain objectives in the near or the remote future. This decision making process has its internal and external data: the given circumstances at a point in time. The production technology of a firm is the most important example of an internal datum. The price formation process on the markets for inputs and outputs on which the firm operates is an example of an external datum.

If the future could be exactly known, the individual firm could always find a set of production inputs in terms of capital and labour which would guarantee an optimal realization of the firm's objective at every moment in time [see Chapter 12]. Although this would not necessarily imply such an optimal result for *all* firms at the same time (Harrod, 1939), we concentrate here on the situation that the future is not known. Firms' decisions are taken with respect to the installation of stocks of capital and labour of a certain kind which can render flows of services during the time that they are used in the production process, but it is by no means sure that these flows contribute to the production of *profitable* outputs.

Two approaches can be distinguished in the literature with respect to the study of demand for production inputs, viz. the eclectic approach and the production function approach. The former was popular before the war and thereafter till the beginning of the nineteen-sixties. This approach will be discussed in section 7.3. The production function approach, which has been developed thereafter, is the subject of section 7.4. But first section 7.2 will deal with the problem of timelags. Aspects of statistical estimation of investment and employment functions are not considered in this chapter (see, however, Dhrymes, 1981, and Rowley and Trivedi, 1975).

7.2. LAGS IN ECONOMIC BEHAVIOUR

Since all the models developed for the explanation of demand for capital and labour make an extensive use of all kinds of lags we anticipate our survey by a short comment on lags. Lags are the timeshape of all kind of reactions. According to Koyck (1954) they arise from *objective* and *subjective* causes, the objective causes being divided into technological and institutional ones.

Technological lags are mainly related to physical restrictions in production (and consumption). They imply planning lags, production lags, delivery lags and so on. Institutional lags arise from laws or customs. Subjective reasons for lags are related to psychological inertia, expectations, desires, habits etc. Usually objective lags lengthen subjective lags. Whatever the exact reasons for lags, they all imply that desired adjustments do not take place immediately.

The analysis of reasons why economic reactions may be spread over time has been especially developed for the behaviour of the individual economic agent. It will be clear that, whatever the reason of a lag, it may consist of one, or more, definite periods of time. In general we may say that the lag in the reaction of an individual economic subject will have a determinate length: either the length of a *single* lag or the length of a *distributed* lag, viz. when the reaction is not instantaneous but is distributed over a period of time. It seems reasonable that when dealing with the reactions of a collection of individual agents the reaction of the aggregate will be spread over a longer period of time, unless individual lags completely cancel out. This may be due to the fact that for different individuals single lags are not identical and because there are differences in the starting point of reaction. So, the distributed lags one expects when analysing reactions on an aggregated level, may be caused by aggregation of several single lags or by a combination of different single and distributed lags.

Another classification of lags that can be made relates to the distinction between *finite* and *infinite* lags. Single lags are by definition finite, but distributed lags may be of a finite or an infinite character. By a finite lag we mean a scheme in which past signals are translated within a fixed period of time, whereas with infinite lag structures the adjustment proceeds during an infinite number of periods.

In the literature on the formalization of distributed lags the rational distributed lag functions are frequently used. A distributed lag function is defined by:

$$y_t = p_0 x_t + p_1 x_{t-1} + p_2 x_{t-2} + \cdots, \qquad (7.2.1)$$

where y_t and x_t are values of dependent and independent variables at time t and the coefficients $\{p_j\}$ are unknown parameters. We impose the restriction that the series p_j converges. Thus, without loss of generality, we may assume that

$$\sum_{j=0}^{\infty} p_j = 1.$$

This restriction implies that a finite change in the value of the independent variable which persists indefinitely will result in a finite change in the dependent variable. According to Jorgenson (1966) distributed lag functions may be called rational when the sequence p_j of coefficients has a rational generating function.

Let the generating function of the sequence p_j be represented by $P(L)$, where L denotes the lag operator defined as $L^n x_t = x_{t-n}$

$$P(L) = p_0 + p_1 L + p_2 L^2 + \cdots \tag{7.2.2}$$

If this function is rational, we may write $P(L) = G(L)/H(L)$ where $G(L)$ and $H(L)$ are polynomials in [see I, §14.9]

$$G(L) = g_0 + g_1 L + g_2 L^2 + \cdots + g_m L^m \tag{7.2.3}$$

$$H(L) = h_0 + h_1 L + h_2 L^2 + \cdots + h_n L^n. \tag{7.2.4}$$

Under the restriction that these polynomials have no root in common, a rational distributed lag function may be represented by the ratio of two polynomials. A distributed lag function can be written as:

$$y_t = \alpha P(L)x_t = \alpha[p_0 + p_1 L + p_2 L^2 + \cdots]x_t. \tag{7.2.5}$$

Alternatively, if $P(L)$ is rational, this relationship may also be formulated as

$$y_t = \alpha P(L)x_t = \alpha \frac{G(L)}{H(L)} x_t, \tag{7.2.6}$$

where $G(L)$ and $H(L)$ are polynomials in the lag operator (L). This general formulation of a distributed lag of the variable x_t on y_t includes a number of different distributed lag models. If we take, for instance, $G(L) = \gamma_0 + \gamma_1 L + \cdots + \gamma_m L^m$ and $H(L) = 1$ a finite distributed lag is obtained of the form:

$$y_t = \alpha[\gamma_0 x_t + \gamma_1 x_{t-1} + \cdots + \gamma_m x_{t-m}] = \alpha \sum_{i=0}^{m} \gamma_i x_{t-i}. \tag{7.2.7}$$

The γs, or reaction coefficients, give the response of the variable y to a shock in the variable x over m periods earlier. The immediate, or short run, response is described by γ_0 and the total, or long run, response is $\sum_0^m \gamma_i$. If the γ_i's are all positive, γ_i may be regarded as the weight given to the lag of length i. The average lag may then be calculated as $\sum(i\gamma_i)/\sum\gamma_i$.

An example of an infinite distributed lag arising from the general equation (7.2.6) is the geometrically distributed lag function used by Koyck (1954). In this case we take $G(L) = 1 - \lambda$ and $H(L) = 1 - \lambda L$ so that

$$y_t = \lambda y_{t-1} + \alpha(1 - \lambda)x_t. \tag{7.2.8}$$

This gives rise to the Koyck transformation of the form

$$y_t = \alpha \sum_{i=0}^{\infty} (1 - \lambda)\lambda^i x_{t-i}, \quad 0 < \lambda < 1. \tag{7.2.9}$$

A more general infinite distributed lag function is the Pascal distribution (Solow, 1960), which is defined by $G(L) = (1 - \lambda)^r$ and $H(L) = (1 - \lambda L)^r$. The final form of this distributed lag function, for $r = 2$, is

$$y_t = \alpha(1 - \lambda)^2 x_t + 2\lambda y_{t-1} - \lambda^2 y_{t-2}. \qquad (7.2.10)$$

An attractive property of this lag function is that the influence of x on y_t can first rise and then decline. This and other properties of rational distributed lag functions are formulated by Jorgenson (1966) and discussed in some detail by Griliches (1967). For aspects of statistical estimation see Dhrymes (1981).

So far the existence of distributed lags was postulated. Cagan (1956) and Nerlove (1958) have developed hypotheses on economic behaviour which yield specifications like equation (7.2.8).

According to Cagan's hypothesis—*the adaptive expectations hypothesis* (also see Chapter 6)—expectations of a variable (x^e) are revised in proportion to the error associated with the previous level of expectations, thus:

$$x_t^e - x_{t-1}^e = (1 - \lambda)(x_{t-1} - x_{t-1}^e), \qquad 0 < \lambda < 1. \qquad (7.2.11)$$

Substitution of this hypothesis in a relationship of the type (where an error term is omitted)

$$y_t = \beta_0 + \beta_1 x_t^e \qquad (7.2.12)$$

yields after the Koyck transformation

$$y_t = \lambda y_{t-1} + \beta 1(1 - \lambda)x_{t-1} + \beta_0(1 - \lambda). \qquad (7.2.13)$$

Nerlove formulated a model, *the partial adjustment model*, in which a desired level of y_t, say y_t^d, depends on the current value of an exogenous variable x_t:

$$y_t^d = \beta_0 + \beta_1 x_t \qquad (7.2.14)$$

but only some fixed fraction of the desired adjustment is accomplished within a particular period of time, that is

$$y_t - y_{t-1} = (1 - \lambda)(y_t^d - y_{t-1}), \qquad 0 < \lambda < 1, \qquad (7.2.15)$$

hence

$$y_t = \lambda y_{t-1} + \beta_1(1 - \lambda)x_t + \beta_0(1 - \lambda) \qquad (7.2.16)$$

The partial adjustment equations (7.2.14) and (7.2.15) are frequently used in demand for capital and labour models to be discussed in the following paragraphs.

A problem we have neglected up to now is whether, if more than one independent variable is included in the estimating equation, all these variables have identical lag distributions or not. In our view, there are no *a priori* reasons for the time shape of different independent variables to be of similar form and length, that is for lags to be *uniform*. Neither through theoretical reasoning nor empirically are we able to reach conclusions which could support such a phenomenon. Some variables have only technological lags, others have lags mainly arising from psychological inertia and still others are a mixture of adaptive and expectation lags. It is for these reasons that one might cast some doubts on the economic meaning of equations involving uniform lags for all explanatory variables.

When a uniform time pattern of reaction for each of the explanatory variables is postulated above, or is derived from either the Cagan or Nerlove hypothesis, an equation usually takes on the form

$$y_t = \lambda y_{t-1} + \alpha_1(1 - \lambda)x_t + \alpha_2(1 - \lambda)w_t + \alpha_3(1 - \lambda)z_t + (1 - \lambda)\alpha_0, \quad (7.2.17)$$

where y_t is the dependent variable and x_t, w_t and z_t are three independent variables with an identical lag distribution, its form being dependent on the value of λ. Sometimes high values for λ are found (0.7, 0.8 or 0.9), especially when the series y_t has a strong trend and y_t and y_{t-1} are highly correlated. The reason is that the the impact of the other explanatory variables, particularly if one is working with variables with a strong rising or declining trend, is considerably reduced. As a consequence such models are weak in explaining turning points.

It will be clear that similar difficulties may arise when for each independent variable an adjustment pattern of the Pascal type is chosen. It is true that in that case the reaction first increases and then declines, which may be sometimes more realistic than the geometrically declining curves of the Koyck type, but it seems just as unrealistic to postulate identical humped curves of adjustment for *each* explanatory variable. In addition, as Griliches (1967) has pointed out, the use of the Pascal distributed lag requires the fulfilment of a number of rather stringent conditions, otherwise one will arrive at unacceptable results.

Apart from the fact that lag distributions are assumed to be uniform for all explanatory variables, the question has been raised whether it is realistic to accept that they are *fixed*. The answer is obviously no. To solve this problem several 'solutions' have been suggested (Helliwell, 1976).

We deal here with the matter by presenting a general specification, which will be used in the following paragraphs. This specification assumes that a desired variable x_t^d is a function of n variables y_t, each having its own lag structure:

$$x_t^d = \sum_{k=1}^{n} \alpha_k \left\{ \frac{G(L)_k}{H(L)_k} \right\} y_{kt}. \quad (7.2.18)$$

Furthermore the actual value of x is related to its desired value through an unknown lag function $G(L)_i/H(L)_i$ plus a number of additional variables (z_j) influencing the adjustment process itself, each of such additional variables having its own lag structure:

$$x_t = \frac{G(L)_0}{H(L)_0} x_t^d + \sum_{j=1}^{m} \beta_j \left\{ \frac{G(L)}{H(L)} \right\}_{j+n} z_{jt}. \quad (7.2.19)$$

This leads to the specification:

$$x_t = \frac{G(L)_0}{H(L)_0} \sum_{k=1}^{n} \alpha_k \left\{ \frac{G(L)_k}{H(L)_k} \right\} y_{kt} + \sum_{j=1}^{m} \beta_j \left\{ \frac{G(L)_{j+n}}{H(L)_{j+n}} \right\} z_{jt}. \qquad (7.2.20)$$

In the following paragraphs we will frequently use these general lag specifications in order to avoid too much detail on this point. A term $G(L)/H(L)$ with a suffix may therefore denote *any* lag structure in the specifications which follow. Furthermore the lag structures are numbered *per* model under discussion.

A flexible method, also frequently used in demand for capital and labour functions, for estimating different distributed lags for different explanatory variables is the method developed by Almon (1965). This method assumes the weights of the lag distribution to be coefficients of Lagrange polynomials. The degree and length of the polynomial determines the lag scheme. After varying both these parameters the distribution yielding the highest coefficient of determination is accepted, provided that the regression coefficients have the right sign and are significant. The data series used in applied economics are typically short and therefore the number of degrees of freedom is small, which explains the popularity of Almon's method. Applied to one independent variable and provided a limited number of variations with the degree of the polynomial are made, one can obtain acceptable results within a reasonable time. Things become more difficult when the Almon procedure is applied to more than one independent variable because a considerable amount of combination is then possible and a considerable number of iterations with both the degree and length of several polynomials has to be made.

7.3. THE ECLECTIC APPROACH

7.3.1. General characteristics

The *first* approach in investigating the demand for capital goods and labour by firms is the so-called *eclectic approach*. This approach can be characterized by the following assumptions and procedures:

— the analysis is mainly, but not exclusively, on a macroeconomic level without a strong reference to specific formal microeconomic theory;
— no reference is made to a specific production technology; sometimes input substitution is allowed for, sometimes complementarity between production factors is assumed;
— mostly no specific clarification is given about the production goals of firms;
— the structure of input and output markets is usually not explicitly specified;
— technical progress is autonomous, neutral and disembodied;
— there is no sharp distinction between desired and actual values of variables; the analysis is mostly directly orientated towards the explanation of *observed* investment and employment figures;

— the possible inter-relatedness of demand for inputs is not taken into account; the demand for capital goods and labour is treated independently.

7.3.2. Three types of investment theories

Throughout this chapter we will use the definition: gross investment, I is equal to investment for expansion, I_e, plus investment for replacement, I_r. The latter are in the studies under discussion often assumed to be identical to depreciation. Among the theories with respect to private investment (excluding residential construction and inventory formation) three types can be distinguished, viz. theories emphasizing the role of

(1) profits
(2) the rate of interest
(3) output or changes in output

Before going into some details we quote Tinbergen (1939, pp. 10, 12, 13), one of the founders of modern econometries, who has succinctly summarized the idea behind the eclectic method in general.

> The method essentially starts with *a priori* considerations about what explanatory variables are to be included. This choice must be based on economic theory or common sense. If *a priori* knowledge regarding the lags to be taken is available, these may be specified also. In many cases, for example, reactions are so quick that only lags of zero length are acceptable. If no such *a priori* knowledge is available, lags may be tried according to some principles as coefficients—i.e. by finding what lags give the highest correlation... In order to test the accuracy of results, *statistical tests of significance* must be applied.... Apart from purely statistical tests, there are *economic tests* of the significance of the coefficient. The most important one is that of their algebraic sign, which in most cases the economist knows on *a priori* grounds.

Profit theories

Examples of profit theories of private investment can be found in the pioneering works of Tinbergen (1936, 1939) and Kalecki (1943).

Tinbergen postulated and estimated in 1936 one of the first econometric models, the annual model for the Netherlands economy. It contained an investment function of the following type (a dot over a variable indicates a relative rate of change), which we write in a general distributed lag form

$$\dot{I} + \dot{p}_i = i\left[\frac{G(L)}{H(L)}\dot{Z}, t\right], \qquad i_1 > 0, \qquad i_2 > 0, \qquad (7.3.1)$$

where $I(i)$ = gross investment in constant (current) prices,

p_i = price of investment

Z = profits in current prices,

t = time trend.

Tinbergen's explanation (1936, p. 55) is as follows:

> The volume of total sales (domestic production + imports) of production equipment changes mainly as a result of changes in the profit expectations, the latter (at least as far as their systematic part is concerned) are assumed to be parallel to the actual profits realized. In this equation a total lag of one year has been assumed, which can be interpreted as the sum of a psychological waiting period, a technical preparation period and a technical execution period.

He continues (1936, p. 56):

> In analyzing the influence of the rate of interest on short-term loans, we find, by means of a statistical investigation carried out in the same way as for the other equations, that such an influence is very slight. This is a consequence of the relatively slight share which this type of interest cost represents in total investment costs. The same is found with regard to the rate of interest for long-term loans.... Finally, we might think of the funds that are absorbed by the enterprises through the issuing of shares.... High share prices, however, are always present when profits are high: there is a very strong parallelism between both these two variables. Therefore the influence of the rate of interest on the volume of investments cannot be separated from the influence of profits already mentioned.

Furthermore Tinbergen adds a trend term as to explain the impact of slow technical and structural changes.

In a subsequent study (Tinbergen, 1939) a more refined investment function is postulated and estimated by least squares regression for the United States, the United Kingdom and Germany [see VI. §8.2]. The theory is fundamentally the same as in his 1936 study. The specification used is of the type

$$\dot{I} + \dot{p}_i = i\left[\frac{G(L)}{H(L)}\{\dot{Z}_m, \dot{r}_s, \dot{p}_i, (\dot{p} - \beta\dot{p}_L)\}, t\right], i_1 > 0, i_2 < 0, i_3 < 0, i_4 < 0, i_5 70$$

(7.3.2)

where Z_m = profits in manufacturing industries (current prices)

r_s = share yield

$(p - \beta p_L)$ = margin between output goods price and wage rate (with β being the weight of labour costs in total costs) as an indication of profit expectations

As has been said, profits are the most important variable in the explanation of investment. The influence of the other variables was weak, as measured by the *t*-ratios [see VI, §5.8.2], if a correct sign could be found.

Perhaps by way of curiosity it should be noted that Tinbergen's 1939 specification could be almost identically found in different versions of the so called annual model of the Central Planning Bureau for the Netherlands economy. In its latest version the investment function, which was in use till 1973 (see Verdoorn *et al.*, 1971) reads:

$$\dot{I}_t + \dot{p}_i = 0.45\dot{Z}_{dt-1} + 0.70\dot{M}_{bt} - 7.89\dot{u}_t + 0.63\dot{p}_{it} + 0.97, \qquad (7.3.3)$$

where (new variables only) Z_d = profits after taxes, M_b = deposits with banks, as a measure of general liquidity, u = a curvilinear transformation of the unemployment rate, as a measure of overcapacity.

Note that in addition to internal funds also external funds have been used as an explanatory variable, as well as the degree of over-capacity. This type of specification is also in line with Kalecki's work. However, in his investment function variables are defined in real terms.

Using again a general lag specification, his investment function (Kalecki, 1943) can be written as (depreciation is included in constant term).

$$I = I\left[\frac{G(L)_1}{H(L)_1}\{(S/p_i, \Delta(Z_d/p_i), \Delta K^*\}\delta\right], I_1 > 0, I_2 > 0, I_3 < 0, I_4 > 0, \qquad (7.3.4)$$

where (new variables only) S = current gross savings by firms, K^* = stock of fixed capital (volume), δ = rate of technical progress.

In Kalecki's view investment decisions are closely related to the internal accumulation of capital, that is to gross savings of firms. Similar to Tinbergen a variable representing profit expectations is also included, viz. by the change in real disposable profits. Furthermore a new dynamic element is introduced by considering the negative impact of the net increment of the capital stock. The idea behind this was that if new enterprises enter the markets investment plans of established firms become less profitable. Kalecki also pays explicit attention to investment for replacement which is assumed to be a fraction of the capital stock.

A Kaleckian type of investment function has been estimated by Klein (1951) for the United States with pre-war data. One of his result reads:

$$I_{et} = 0.48(Z_t/p_{it}) + 0.33(Z_{t-1}/p_{it-1}) - 0.11 K^*_{t-1} + 10.1,$$
$$(0.10) \qquad\qquad (0.10) \qquad\qquad (0.03) \qquad\qquad\qquad (7.3.5)$$

where the figures in parentheses denote asymptotic standard errors (see Klein, 1951, p. 75).

Finally, we should mention that economic policy measures can mainly have, according to the theories mentioned, an impact on private fixed investment through influencing the internal and external financing conditions of firms. These policies may take the form of fiscal policy (tax reduction, investment allowances), monetary policy (influencing the amount of liquidity) and incomes policy (influencing profits).

Interest rate theories

The interest rate approach was essentially developed by Keynes (1936). In the words of the *General Theory* (p. 135):

> When a man buys an investment or capital asset, he purchases the right to the series of prospective returns, which he expects to obtain from selling its output, after deduction the running expenses of obtaining that output, during the life of the asset. This series of annuities it is convenient to call the *prospective* yield of the investment.
>
> Over against the prospective yield of the investment we have the *supply price* of the capital asset, meaning by this, not the market-price at which an asset of the type in question can be actually purchased in the market, but the price which would just induce a manufacturer to produce an additional unit of such assets, i.e. what is sometimes called its *replacement cost*. The relation between the prospective yield of a capital asset and its supply price of replacement cost, i.e. the relation between the prospective yield of one more unit of that type of capital and the cost of producing that unit, furnishes us with the *marginal efficiency of capital* of that type. More precisely, I define the marginal efficiency of capital as being equal to that rate of discount which would make the present value of the series of given by the returns expected from the capital asset during its life just equal to its supply price.

When X represents the supply price of capital Keynes's theory of the marginal efficiency of capital can be written as

$$r_i = \left\{ r \left| \frac{a_1}{(1+r)^1} + \frac{a_2}{(1+r)^2} + \cdots + \frac{a_n}{(1+r)^n} - X = 0 \right. \right\}, \qquad (7.3.6)$$

where $a_1, a_2, \ldots, a_n$ represent an expected stream of net future returns associated with the given investment project. The marginal efficiency of capital is represented by r_i, which is the internal rate of discount for which an investment project just is profitable, and is usually found with some iterative algorithm [see III, Chapter 5].

All investment projects for which the internal rate of return exceeds the market rate of interest will be undertaken $(r_i > r)$. In this way we find the aggregate investment demand-schedule, which relates investment to the market rate of interest for a given aggregate marginal efficiency of capital.

$$I = I\left[\frac{G(L)}{H(L)} r \right], \quad (I_1 < 0). \qquad (7.3.7)$$

It should be noted that this demand function is, according to Keynes, not a stable one. Because: 'If there is an increased investment in any given type of capital during any period of time, the marginal efficiency of the type of capital will diminish as the investment in it is increased, partly because the prospective yield will fall as the supply of that type of capital is increased, and partly because, as a rule, pressure on the facilities for producing that type of capital will cause its supply price to increase' (p. 136). But the marginal efficiency of capital in not only fluctuating with the rate of capital accumulation, it is also strongly dependent on the *state of long-term expectations* with respect to the prospective yield on investment. These expectations are partly based on existing facts which can be assessed for the future with more or less confidence, such as those related to '(..) future changes in the type and quantity of the stock of capital-assets and in the tastes of the consumer, the strength of effective demand from time to time during the life of the investment under consideration, and the changes in the wage-unit in terms of money which may occur during its life' (p. 147). But the state of long-term expectations also depends on the *state of confidence*, on psychological factors. This state of the investor's mind has also become known as the *animal spirits* of the entrepreneur.

It should be noted that the internal rate of return approach to investment decisions need not be consistent with the maximization of the present value of the firm [see also §7.4 and Alchian, 1955, and Hirschleifer, (1970)].

Note also that difficulties may arise because the Keynesian investment function is in fact a polynomial of degree n with n roots, where n is the number of periods. Suppose there is a three-period cash flow. Equation (7.3.5) then reduces to

$$\frac{a_1}{(1+r)} + \frac{a_2}{(1+r)^2} - X = 0. \tag{7.3.8}$$

Cross-multiplying yields

$$-X(1+r)^2 + a_1(1+r) + a_2 = 0, \tag{7.3.9}$$

which has two roots. As long as these roots are negative or imaginary [see I, §2.7] they can be ignored, but more than one positive root makes the investment decision indeterminate (Lorie and Savage, 1955). However, the macroeconomic use of the Keynesian investment function ignores this problem (compare the reswitching of techniques issue in the capital debate).

From an empirical point of view it is essential whether the marginal efficiency of capital is stable enough to find a relationship between investment and the market rate of interest. Empirical studies by Tinbergen (1939), Klein (1951) and many others have shown that Equation (7.3.5) as such is not an adequate explanation of private fixed business investment. Keynes warned about this. He believed that '... it seems likely that the fluctuations in the market estimation of the marginal efficiency of different types of capital ... will be too great to be offset by any practicable changes in the rate of interest' (p. 164).

Finally, it will be clear that in the type of investment function as in (7.3.7) private capital accumulation can mainly be influenced through monetary policy.

Output theories

The third type of eclectic investment model is the accelerator model. The original idea is due to Aftalion (1911) and Clark (1917). In its naive form the acceleration principle states a fixed relationship between the capital stock (K^*) and capacity output (y^*) through a fixed capital coefficient (κ), that is

$$K^* = \kappa y^*, \qquad (\kappa > 0). \tag{7.3.10}$$

Taking first differences yields the following specification for investment for expansion (I_e)

$$I_e = \Delta K^* = \kappa \Delta y^*. \tag{7.3.11}$$

Adding a simple specification for investment for replacement (i_r) and taking into account unknown lags for decisions, financing, etc., we have

$$I = I_e + I_r = \kappa \frac{G(L)_1}{H(L)_1} \Delta y^* + \delta K^* \tag{7.3.12}$$

Since $K^* = \kappa y^*$ we may also write gross investment as a function of capacity output alone

$$I = \kappa \frac{G(L)_1}{H(L)_1} \Delta y^* + \delta \kappa y^*. \tag{7.3.13}$$

A variant of this model is the so-called flexible accelerator model developed by Goodwin (1951), Chenery (1952) and Koyck (1954). In their models investment for expansion is related to the discrepancy between the desired capital stock and the actual capital stock in the preceding period. Adding again investment for replacement and including a general lag structure, we have

$$I = \frac{G(L)_1}{H(L)_1} (K^{*d} - LK^*) + \delta LK^*, \tag{7.3.14}$$

where K^{*d} is the desired capital stock. According to the studies of the authors mentioned we may write the desired capital stock as a proportion of expected output, which is represented as a distributed lag of output

$$K^{*d} = \kappa y^e = \kappa \frac{G(L)_2}{H(L)_2} y. \tag{7.3.15}$$

Substitution in Equation (7.3.12) yields:

$$I = \frac{G(L)_1}{H(L)_1} \left\{ \kappa \frac{G(L)_2}{H(L)_2} y - LK^* \right\} + \delta LK^*. \tag{7.3.16}$$

In this specification existing over-capacity has its influence on investment because the desired capital stock is related to *actual* output, instead of capacity output. In this way one of the objections against the naive acceleration model, viz. the lack of impact of over-capacity, can be overcome. Note that economic policy measures can only influence private investment through their impact on output. There is no possibility in this specification to model the direct impact of tax policies, monetary policies, etc. Empirical results with this type of investment function can be found in Chenery (1952) and Koyck (1954), Meyer and Kuh (1957) and Jorgenson and Siebert (1968). The latter compare profit, interest rate and accelerator studies with the so-called neoclassical investment function which is discussed in section 7.43.

Synthesis

Several attempts have been undertaken to find a synthesis between the three eclectic approaches. The reasoning is roughly as follows. The output theories emphasize the need for new capital goods, because they relate the desired capital stock to the actual capital stock. This type of theory emphasizes determinants of the need for new capital goods. The two other theories emphasize the determinants of the degree to which these needs can be realized. Profit theories mainly bring to the attention that internal funds are necessary to finance investment plans. Furthermore they emphasize that in addition to the technical desire to increase the capital stock also profit expectations play a part in taking the investment decision. Finally, interest rate theories consider the cost of external financing.

The results of attempts to estimate hybrid demand for capital goods functions show a new class of eclectic functions, in which profits, interest rates and output (changes) occur (see Meyer and Kuh, 1958; Kuh, 1963; and Eisner, 1965). These studies also show that the impact of explanatory variables need not be constant over time. In periods of capital scarcity, profit and interest rates form the limiting factors in the investment decision, rather than expected output. On the other hand when interest rates are low and profit margins are relatively large there is no reason to invest when idle capacity is in existence and output expectations are weak.

7.3.3. Employment theories

The eclectic approach with respect to labour demand is extremely simple. Employment (E) is a positive function of production and labour-saving technical progress, which is supposed to be autonomous (Tinbergen, 1936):

$$E = E(y, t), \quad E_1 > 0, E_2 < 0. \tag{7.3.17}$$

Keynes postulated an employment function with aggregate demand as the main explanatory variable. However, he defined aggregate demand in terms of wage units, therefore his employment function can be written as

$$E = E\left(v, \frac{P_E}{P}\right), \, E_1 > 0, \quad E_2 < 0, \tag{7.3.18}$$

where v is total aggregate demand in volume terms. It should be noted that Keynes also considered the *composition* of demand as relevant for employment (Keynes, 1936, p. 286). 'For the way in which we suppose the increase in aggregate demand to be distributed between different commodities may considerably influence the volume of employment.

The Keynesian type of employment function has been estimated for the United States by Klein (1951) in the form of an equation for the real wage sum:

$$P_{E_t}E_t/p_t = 0.44y_t + 0.15y_{t-1} + 0.13(t - 1931) + 1.50. \tag{7.3.19}$$
$$\phantom{P_{E_t}E_t/p_t = {}}(0.03) \quad (0.04) \qquad (0.03)$$

Verdoorn *et al.* (1971) has estimated a Keynesian employment function for the Netherlands in which aggregate demand is a weighted average of the main macro-economic expenditure items, the weights representing the labour intensity of the respective expenditures.

The employment functions considered can be characterized as short-run functions, because of the weak specification of lags and the lack of a capacity (capital stock) variable. Employment is dominated by variations in output (or aggregate demand). A negative trend term represents the long-run growth of labour productivity, but a positive trend term represents the increasing power of labour unions after 1931 on the wage sum. Output coefficients are usually below unity because of labour hoarding. Although labour is a variable input factor in the short run its downward adjustment to output changes is incomplete, because (see Oi, 1962; Hubbard, 1968):

(1) a minimum number of workers is necessary to operate the plant and equipment, and to produce output at all;
(2) a minimum amount of labour is required to perform the routine clerical and secretarial functions;
(3) a minimum amount of labour is required for supervision;
(4) large amounts of training and reorientation may be required to adjust a worker to a new organization and new equipment;
(5) contractual agreements relating to the duration of employment may limit the reduction in employment;
(6) laying off workers and later hiring additional workers is a costly procedure.

Finally, it is mainly through output that economic policy measures can have an impact on employment. In the short run (real) wages have too small an impact on employment to be an important channel through which policy can have a significant influence. Of course this conclusion may change when a longer decision period of the firm is considered.

7.4. THE PRODUCTION FUNCTION APPROACH

7.4.1. General characteristics

The *second* approach to investigating the demand for capital goods and labour by firms is the production function approach. This approach is usually characterized by the following assumptions and procedures:

— a microeconomic foundation of the behaviour of firms, leading to specific demand for input functions which are applied on a macro or sectoral level by analogy, that is without explicitly considering an aggregation procedure;
— a well-behaved production function, which allows smooth substitution between production inputs with a constant elasticity of substitution between − 1 and zero [see §12.5];
— an optimizing behaviour of firms in the context of either maximization of profits or the minimization of production costs, the optimization period being one or more periods [see Chapter 12];
— perfect competition in markets for both products and production inputs [see §12.10 and Chapter 14];
— technical progress is autonomous, neutral and disembodied;
— actual values of variables are represented as functions of desired values of variables, which are determined by the optimizing behaviour of firms under the constraint of the production function;

7.4.2. General specifications

In the following we distinguish four cases with respect to the goal of the individual firm, viz. profit maximization and cost minimization, each in the one-period and multi-period case. In the first case the firm's output is not given, but subject to decisions. Input and output prices are determined on the market. In the second case output is fixed and no assumptions have to be made about the product market in which the firm operates.

Suppose the firm is maximizing its profits for one period ahead and the technology is given by

$$y^* = y/q_y = f(E/q_E, K/q_K) = f(E^*, K^*), \qquad (7.4.1)$$

where $E^* =$ stock of (homogeneous) labour (jobs)

$K =$ utilized capital services
$q_y =$ utilization rate of capacity

q_E = utilization rate of jobs (1-unemployment rate)

q_K = utilization rate of capital stock

and time subscripts have been omitted for convenience.

The variables have been chosen in such a way that the service flows of capital and labour are proportional to their stocks when these are fully utilized. It should be noted that the production function is often used in an inconsistent way, viz. by using actual output, actual employment and the *fully utilized* capital stock. In the following we start from Equation (7.4.1) which implies that K^* will be used instead of K. If one prefers to use specifications in terms of employment and output, rather than jobs (potential employment) and capacity output, then the relevant utilization rates should be taken into account.

Maximization of profits under perfect competition yields that the marginal products of labour and capital equal their real prices. These conditions may be inverted by the implicit function theorem [see IV, §5.13] to give the factor demand and supply functions [see Chapter 12]. In such a one-period profit maximization model under perfect competition, changes in real factor prices, which are exogenous to the firm, lead, via an instantaneous adjustment, to optimum levels of output and factor inputs. It is therefore only through influencing factor prices that economic policy can have an impact on the capital stock and employment in this case. In practice, however, markets may not be competitive and production functions may have increasing returns to scale, which is incompatible with profit maximization under perfect competition (Brechling, 1975). Chapter 12 also discusses an alternative approach, based upon cost minimization, which does not suffer from these disadvantages.

Turning now to the more-period optimization models we will add, as usual in the literature, some new elements, viz. firms pay taxes and are assumed to maximize the present value of the net cash flow. Net cash flow, R, is defined as

$$R = py^* - p_i I - p_E E^* - T \tag{7.4.2}$$

where (new variables only) T is profit taxes. The present discounted value of the net cash flow (V) at time $t = 0$ can be written as

$$V = \int_0^\infty e^{-rt} R(t) \, dt, \tag{7.4.3}$$

where the rate of interest, r, proxies the best alternative return the firm can obtain. This should be maximized subject to the constraint of the production function (7.4.1) and the equation

$$I = \frac{dK^*}{dt} + \delta K^*. \tag{7.4.4}$$

To do so we form the Lagrangian expression [see IV, §15.1.4 and §17.4.2]

$$G = \int_0^\infty [e^{-rt} R + \lambda_0 \{ f(E^*, K^*) - y^* \} + \lambda_1 (\dot{K}^* - I + \delta K^*)] \, dt$$

The first order conditions for a maximum of the present value of the firm are

$$\frac{\partial G}{\partial y^*} = e^{-rt}p - \lambda_0 = 0$$

$$\frac{\partial G}{\partial E^*} = -e^{-rt}p_E + \lambda_0 \frac{\partial f}{\partial E^*} = 0$$

$$\frac{\partial G}{\partial I} = -e^{-rt}p_i - \lambda_1 = 0$$

$$\frac{\partial G}{\partial K^*} - \frac{d}{dt}\frac{\partial G}{\partial (d\dot{K}^*/dt)} = \lambda_0 \frac{\partial f}{\partial K^*} + \delta\lambda_1 - \frac{d}{dt}\lambda_1 = 0.$$

From these equations we can derive the marginal productivity conditions

$$\frac{\partial y^*}{\partial E^*} = \frac{p_E}{p} \qquad (7.4.5)$$

$$\frac{\partial y^*}{\partial K^*} = \frac{p_i(\delta + r - \dot{p}_i)}{p} = \frac{p_K}{p}. \qquad (7.4.6)$$

The main difference between the one-period and the multi-period maximization of profits under perfect competition lies in the specification of the user cost of capital, p_K, which now consists of the real price of capital goods, the interest rate, the depreciation rate and the rate of change in the price of capital goods. From the marginal productivity condition and the production function, employment and investment functions can be derived similar to those in the one period maximization case.

An element not specified so far is the production function, (for details see Ferguson, 1971). A general form is the constant elasticity of substitution (CES) production function

$$y^* = A[\theta K^{*-\psi} + (1 - \theta)E^{*-\psi}]^{-1/\psi}, \quad 0 < \theta < 1; \gamma > 0; \infty \geqslant \psi > -1, \quad (7.4.7)$$

where A = scale factor

θ = distribution parameter

ψ = substitution parameter $\left(1 - \dfrac{1}{\tau}\right)$

τ = elasticity of substitution $\left(\dfrac{d \ln K^*/E^*}{d \ln p_E/p_K}\right)$.

The CES production function reduces to the Cobb–Douglas production function for $\tau = 1$

$$y^* = AK^{*\theta}E^{*(1-\theta)} \qquad (7.4.8)$$

and to the Leontief (fixed proportions) production function for $\tau = 0$

$$y^* = A \min(K^*, E^*). \qquad (7.4.9)$$

All production functions can, of course, also be specified for y, E and K that is taking into account the respective utilization rates. Unfortunately, the use of the production function in formulating investment and employment functions is often inconsistent. Actual output (y) is frequently related to actual employment (E) and the fully utilized capital stock (K^*), instead of the utilized capital stock (K).

We should realize that the foregoing production functions are all based on the assumption that production factors are homogeneous. Instead we may consider the capital stock and the amount of labour as made up of units of different vintages, according to the year that they were taken into use in the past. New technology then enters into the production process through new vintages of capital and/or labour and new machines and additional labour are more productive than machines and labour already in use. Technical progress is now called embodied, contrary to the situation where it is disembodied and added to the production functions mentioned applying equally to all units of capital and labour in use (compare for instance with equation (7.4.16)). When there is no bias of technical progress in the direction of increasing production per unit of capital or per unit of labour it is called neutral. Technical progress is called capital-augmenting when an increasing output is produced with a given labour input and a capital input that is becoming more productive over time. Similarly, we also have labour-augmenting technical progress, when labour input is becoming more productive with a given capital stock. An example of a vintage CES production function with two types of technical progress is the following variation on Equation (7.4.7):

$$y^*_{(\tau,\tau)} = A[\theta\{(1+\chi)^\tau I^*_{(\tau,\tau)}\}^{-\psi} + (1-\theta)\{(1+\mu)^\tau E^*_{(\tau,\tau)}\}^{-\psi}]^{-1/\psi} \quad (7.4.10)$$

where $y^*_{(\tau,\tau)}$ = capacity output of vintage τ in period τ
$\quad\quad E^*_{(\tau,\tau)}$ = jobs of vintage τ in period τ
$\quad\quad I_{(\tau,\tau)}$ = gross investment of vintage τ in period τ
$\quad\quad \chi$ = rate of embodied capital-augmenting technical progress
$\quad\quad \mu$ = rate of embodied labour-augmenting technical progress.

In relation to the foregoing argument with respect to the vintage production function a distinction has been made concerning the degree of substitutability between factors of production. In a putty–putty technology substitution is always and completely possible irrespective whether capital goods are new or already in operation. When substitution is only possible for new equipment but not for old ones, we speak of the putty–clay case. Both cases are possible in the case of Cobb–Douglas, CES or other production functions which allow substitution. The clay–clay situation, where neither *exante* nor *expost* substitution is possible, is of course only relevant when a fixed properties production function (such as Equation (4.7.9)) is assumed.

7.4.3. Specific investment functions

A well-known investment function is the one developed by Jorgenson (1963, 1965). He uses a Cobb–Douglas production function with diminishing returns to scale in a multi-period profit maximization model.

In his studies he specifies the tax variable in (7.4.2) as

$$T = w[py - p_E E - p_i\{g\delta + mr - n\dot{p_i}\}]K \qquad (2.4.11)$$

where w is the rate of taxation of net income and g, m and n represent the proportions of depreciation, cost of capital and capital loss which may be charged against revenue less outlays on current account. This leads to the following definition for the user cost of capital

$$p_K = p_i\left[\left\{\frac{1-wq}{1-w}\right\}\delta + \left\{\frac{1-wm}{1-w}\right\}r - \left\{\frac{1-wn}{1-w}\right\}\dot{p_i}\right]. \qquad (7.4.12)$$

From the marginal productivity condition (7.4.6) and the assumed production function, it follows that the *optimal* or *desired* capital stock, say K^{*d}, can be represented by

$$K^{*d} = \alpha\frac{py}{p_K}. \qquad (7.4.13)$$

Jorgenson then postulates that investment for expansion is related to the discrepancy between the desired and existing capital stock in the previous period. Under certain conditions regarding the distribution of completions of initial investment projects over time, investment for expansion is a distributed lag function of first differences in the desired capital stock (Jorgenson, 1965)

$$I_e = \frac{G(L)_1}{H(L)_1}(1 - L)K^{*d} \qquad (7.4.14)$$

If we add for replacement investment $I_{rt} = \delta K^*_{t-1}$ we find:

$$I = I_e + I_r = \frac{G(L)_1}{H(L)_1}\alpha(1 - L)\frac{py}{p_K} + \delta LK^*. \qquad (7.4.15)$$

Note that we have not written y^*, but y in agreement with Jorgenson's specification, which is therefore based on an inconsistent use of the production function. This problem could be solved by a proper introduction of the degree of capacity utilization.

Jorgenson's investment function is an example of the flexible accelerator approach. Note that in addition to the change in output also the *change* in the real user cost of capital plays a part, among which a *change* in the rate of interest, which is in contrast to the Keynesian specification of the impact of the interest rate on investment. Jorgenson's function is called the neoclassical investment function because there will be no investment for expansion in equilibrium, that is when $K^{*d} = K^*$. When not in equilibrium, policy measures can influence investment through their impact on output and via the user cost of capital, which also includes relevant tax variables.

Contrary to most of the eclectic theories the neoclassical investment function has been estimated with quarterly data for the United States (and later on for many other countries) in order to find the appropriate lags. Jorgenson estimates his function with restricted lag distributions. This econometric work has been subject to criticism. Since then many attempts have been undertaken with alternative specifications (see Rowley and Trivedi, 1975).

Other comments on this neoclassical investment function relate to the neglect of adjustment costs. In the model under discussion it is assumed that firms can adjust the stocks of capital and labour costlessly. This seems not realistic (Eisner and Strotz, 1963). Attempts have therefore been undertaken to incorporate adjustment costs into the neoclassical theory of investment behaviour. A distinction is made in internal and external adjustment costs. External adjustment costs arise because of market circumstances, while internal adjustment costs are related to the adjustment of capital and/or labour within the firm. For external adjustment costs, see Brechling (1975), while internal adjustments costs are for instance discussed in Lucas (1967), Gould (1968) and Treadway (1969, 1970 and 1971). Brechling (1975) shows that several functions may be specified to represent the relationship between adjustment costs and the size of the adjustment. This specification is important for the extent to which adjustment costs create additional lags in the adjustment of capital and labour and therefore involve particular time paths for net investment (and net hiring of labour) not being derived in an ad hoc manner from the comparative static levels of K^* (and E^*). It can be shown, assuming a multi-period cost minimization approach, that even 'perverse' effects of the wage rate and user cost of capital on demand for production factors are possible in the short run (Brechling 1975).

Other qualifications with respect to the neoclassical investment function relate to the fact that investment for replacement is not a constant share of the capital stock. The alternative theory says that, although there may be a long-run constantness of replacement investment to the capital stock, these investment expenditures may very well show cyclical variations in the short run caused by factors similar to those for investment for expansion such as changes in output, relative factor prices etc. (see Feldstein and Foot, 1971, Eisner, 1972, Driehuis, 1972, Feldstein, 1974, Feldstein and Rothschild, 1974, and Nickell, 1975).

Other comments refer to the fact that the adjustment of capital stock is not independent of adjustments with respect to the stock of labour (e.g. Nadiri and Rosen, 1973). In fact this approach assumes that labour costs also play a part in the investment decision. It is therefore in the logic that in this case we start from the cost minimization behaviour of firms instead of the profit maximization approach.

Moreover the putty–putty character of the neoclassical investment function has been criticized. Authors, who prefer a vintage approach are, for instance, Bischoff (1968) and King (1972). The latter estimates a vintage investment model for the UK based on a putty–clay variant of the Cobb–Douglas production function.

Finally, it has been suggested that the production function approach is unnecessarily restrictive to a number of factors which influence investment-decision making under uncertainty. Duesenberry (1958) emphasizes in this respect financial considerations. In Driehuis (1972) an attempt has been undertaken to arrive at a synthesis between the production function approach and the eclectic approach, which pays ample attention to financial factors. He starts from

$$y^* = A e^{\omega t}(E^* h)^\alpha (K^* d)^\beta \qquad (7.4.16)$$

where A is a scale factor, ω is the rate of disembodied technical progress, h is labour time and d is machine time. On the basis of the theory of the foregoing section we have:

$$\frac{E^*}{K^*} = \frac{\alpha}{\beta} \frac{p_K (1 + 1/e_K)}{p_E (1 + 1/e_E)}, \qquad (7.4.17)$$

where e_E and e_K denote the price elasticities of the supply of labour and of capital. After rewriting this equation, interpreting K^{*d} as the desired capital stock, introducing unknown lags and using (7.4.16), we find, for $h = d$,

$$\ln K^{*d} = \frac{1}{\alpha + \beta} \frac{G(L)_2}{H(L)_2} \ln y^* - \frac{\alpha}{\alpha + \beta} \frac{G(L)_3}{H(L)_3} \ln \frac{p_K}{p_E}$$
$$- \frac{\alpha}{\alpha + \beta} \ln \left(\frac{1 + 1/e_K}{1 + 1/e_E} \right) - \ln h - \frac{\omega}{\alpha + \beta} t$$
$$- \frac{\alpha}{\alpha + \beta} \ln \frac{\alpha}{\beta} - \frac{1}{\alpha + \beta} \ln A. \qquad (7.4.18)$$

Note that both output and relative factor prices now have a separate unknown lag structure with respect to the desired capital stock.

Several steps have to be undertaken before this specification is manageable in empirical research. First of all, we can split up the capacity variable in actual output and the rate of capacity utilization (see (7.4.1)). Secondly, assumptions have to be made with respect to the supply elasticities of capital and labour. One possibility is to assume that they are identical. Another possibility is to assume that they are constant and a third possibility is to hypothesize that they vary with the respective utilization rates. Then we have, for example,

$$(1 + 1/e_E) = q_E^{-\xi_1} c_1 \qquad (7.4.19)$$

$$(1 + 1/e_K) = q_K^{-\xi_2} c_2. \qquad (7.4.20)$$

If it is furthermore assumed that

$$\ln q_K = \xi \ln q_E + c_3;$$ (7.4.21)

we can also write

$$\ln q_y = \alpha \ln q_E + \beta \ln q_K = (\alpha + \beta \xi) \ln q_E + \beta c_3.$$ (7.4.22)

Taking these amendments into account, (7.4.18) can be rewritten as

$$\ln K^{*d} = \frac{1}{\alpha + \beta} \frac{G(L)_2}{H(L)_2} \ln y^* - \frac{\alpha}{\alpha + \beta} \frac{G(L)_3}{H(L)_3} \ln \frac{p_K}{p_E}$$

$$+ \zeta \frac{G(L)_4}{H(L)_4} \ln q_E - \ln h - \frac{\omega}{\alpha + \beta} t + b,$$ (7.4.23)

where b represents a constant term.

Approximating the flexible accelerator function in log-linear form we have, using $K^* = K_0^* \exp(\varepsilon_1 t)$, where K_0 is the capital stock in a base year,

$$\ln I_e = \frac{G(L)_1}{H(L)_1} \{ \ln K^{*d} - L \ln(K^{*d}) \} + \varepsilon_1 t + \ln K_0^* + \ln(1 - K_0^{*-\varepsilon_1}).$$ (7.4.24)

Completely reasoning within the production function approach would yield a log-linear investment function when (7.4.23) is substituted into (7.4.24). But this seems unnecessarily restrictive, since in many studies it has been observed that the adjustment of investment to a change in the desired capital stock is influenced by the rate of capacity utilization (see Koyck, 1954; Chenery, 1952; Hickman, 1957; Greenberg, 1964; Junankar, 1970; Taubinan and Wilkinson, 1970; and Smith, 1969). Similarly, disposable real profits may play a part in the adjustment process as an indication of internal financing opportunities as well as the rate of interest, or the relative amount of money in society (M/py) as an indicator of the availability of external funds.

Therefore we can write, amending (7.4.24),

$$\ln I_e = \varepsilon_2 \frac{G(L)_5}{H(L)_5} \ln \frac{M}{yp} + \varepsilon_3 \frac{G(L)_6}{H(L)_6} \ln \frac{Z_d}{p_i} + \varepsilon_4 \frac{G(L)_4}{H(L)_4} \ln q_E$$

$$+ \frac{G(L)_1}{H(L)_1} \Delta \ln K^{*d} + \varepsilon_1 t + b'.$$ (7.4.25)

Alternatively, the real rate of interest can be used instead of the liquidity ratio. Substitution of (7.4.23) in (7.4.25) now yields the final investment function which should be completed by an appropriate specification for replacement investment. This function has been successfully estimated with quarterly data for the Netherlands (Driehuis, 1972).

7.4.4. Specific employment functions

One category of employment functions concentrates on the *short-run* (for a survey of short-run employment functions, see Hazledine (1981)). Three types of costs associated with labour input are distinguished, viz. wage costs, employment costs such as payroll, hiring, training and lay-off costs and hours costs due to overtime work. Wage and payroll costs are related to the *level* of employment, while other labour costs are mainly a function of the *change* of employment. In the instantaneous-hours-cost-minimizing-theory (Killingsworth, 1970) the firm selects its labour input in terms of the desired amount of man hours which minimizes total labour costs subject to a production function in which the capital stock does *not* play a role, owing to the short-run assumption,

All types of costs are part of total labour costs (C_E). These costs can be ultimately (see Killingsworth) specified in terms of workers and hours alone:

$$C_E = C(E,h). \tag{7.4.26}$$

Rewriting the production function, for example a Cobb–Douglas one, in such a way that the hours variable is a function of output and workers (assuming that hours and workers have the same output elasticity) yields:

$$\ln h = \frac{1}{\alpha}\ln A - \frac{1}{\alpha}\ln E + \frac{1}{\alpha}\ln y - \frac{\omega t}{\alpha}. \tag{7.4.27}$$

The cost function can then be minimized and solved for the optimal level of employment (E^d). By means of an adjustment function, which we here present in a general distributed lag form, it is then found that actual employment is a function of output, and disembodied technical progress, t,

$$\ln E = \frac{G(L)_1}{H(L)_1}\{\ln y, t\}. \tag{7.4.28}$$

In empirical specifications for the UK and Australia (see Brechling, 1965; Ball and St. Cyr, 1966; Smyth and Ireland, 1967) employment is explained by one-period lagged employment, several unlagged and lagged output terms and a trend term. Since the coefficient of the lagged employment term is usually high, one might wonder what these equations in fact explain. Finally, it should be mentioned that more sophisticated short-run employment specifications are used by Fair (1969) who simultaneously explains employment and hours worked.

Long-run theories with respect to employment can be found in the category of cost-minimization-over-time theories. Nadiri (1968) arrives in this way at the following employment function

$$\ln E = -\tau\ln\left(\frac{\theta}{1-\theta}\right) + \tau\ln\left(\frac{p_K}{p_E}\right) + \log K, \tag{7.4.29}$$

where p_K is defined similar to (7.4.12) and $\sigma(=1/1+\tau)$ and θ are parameters of the CES production function (7.4.7). Using again a general distributed lag function he estimates (7.4.29) for the United States with quarterly data.

An example of the multi-period profit maximizing approach is found in

Dhrymes (1969), where he starts from a CES production function and imperfect competition on the markets for labour and capital. From the marginal productivity condition and considering the supply elasticities for capital and labour as time invariant, he arrives at the following specification for desired labour input

$$
\ln E^{d} = -\frac{\psi}{1+\psi}\ln A - \frac{1}{1+\psi}\frac{G(L)_3}{H(L)_3}\ln\left(\frac{p_E}{p}\right)
$$

$$
+ \frac{G(L)_2}{H(L)_2}\ln y + \frac{1}{1+\psi}\ln(1-\theta). \tag{7.4.30}
$$

Dhrymes wishes to explore the dependence of employment on the *time profile* of the capital stock, because he expects the marginal productivity of labour to depend on the vintages of capital in operation. He formalizes this relationship by making the parameter $(1-\theta)$ dependent on a weighted sum of investment outlays. This weighting average can be represented in a general way by

$$
\frac{1}{1+\psi}\ln(1-\theta) = \frac{G(L)_4}{H(L)_4}\ln I. \tag{7.4.31}
$$

When furthermore desired employment is written as a general distributed lag function $\ln E = \{G(L)_1/H(L)_1\}\ln E^d$, we arrive at

$$
\ln E = \frac{G(L)_1}{H(L)_1}\frac{G(L)_2}{H(L)_2}\ln y - \frac{1}{1-\beta}\frac{G(L)_1}{H(L)_1}\frac{G(L)_3}{H(L)_3}\ln(p_E/p)
$$

$$
+ \frac{G(L)_1}{H(L)_1}\frac{G(L)_4}{H(L)_4}\ln I - \frac{\psi}{1+\psi}\ln A \tag{7.4.32}
$$

which is estimated with annual figures for two-digit US industries.

The view, expressed in Dhrymes's employment function viz. that subsequent vintages of capital need less labour, because of technical progress, has been the subject of a lot of empirical research in the nineteen-seventies, especially in a number of European countries. We refer to the seminal study of Den Hartog and Tjan (1976) for the Netherlands. Similar research has been undertaken for France (Benassy *et al.*, 1975, and Germany (Gorzig, 1976)). Den Hartog and Tjan assume a clay–clay vintage production technology which does not allow for *direct* substitution between labour and capital. Production capacity is determined by installed capital goods, the relationship being regulated for each capital vintage by a capital–output ratio which is fixed for every vintage and for all time (Equation (7.4.33)). The jobs (or employment at full capacity utilization) created by installed capacity decrease by a constant percentage when the capital goods are of a younger vintage (Equation (7.4.34)). Technical progress is thus of the labour-augmenting type embodied in new vintages of capital. Both equations involve the impact of hours. The respective functions read

$$y_t^* = \sum_{\tau=v}^{t} y_{t,\tau}^* = \frac{1}{\kappa} d_t^{\delta_1} \sum_{\tau=v}^{t} \Omega_{t-\tau} I_{t,\tau} \qquad (7.4.33)$$

$$E_t^* = \sum_{\tau=v}^{t} E_{t,\tau}^* = h_t^{-\delta_2} \frac{1}{\phi} \sum_{\tau=v}^{t} y_{t,\tau}^* e^{-\mu\tau}. \qquad (7.4.34)$$

$\Omega_{t-\tau}$ represents the survival fraction of capital after $(t-\tau)$ years, κ is the capital–output ratio, ϕ is the level of labour productivity of a vintage of capital in a certain base year and μ is the rate of labour-augmenting technical progress.

Although direct substitution between capital and labour is impossible for each vintage, the capital–labour ratio can change through scrapping of the oldest capital goods in use and replacing it by new capital goods with a higher labour productivity. This process of obsolescence of capital is governed by technical and economic factors. Technical obsolescence is introduced by a survival scheme with a maximum lifetime of 45 years. Economic obsolescence is determined by the firm's comparison of marginal costs (here: wage costs only) and marginal revenue per vintage. The minimal condition for keeping a vintage of capital installed in year v in operation in year t is

$$y_{t,v}^* p_t = E_{t,v}^* p_{Et}, \qquad \text{if} \qquad t-v \leqslant 45, \qquad (7.4.35)$$

where v is the year of installation of the oldest capital vintage in operation. Substitution of (7.4.33) in (7.4.35) for $\tau = v$ yields

$$v = \frac{1}{\mu} \{\ln(p_E/p) - \delta_2 \ln h - \ln \phi\}. \qquad (7.4.36)$$

In order to arrive at a demand for labour function one needs a relationship between potential employment (E^*) and actual labour demand. Two situations are distinguished by the authors, viz.

— a situation in which labour supply is less than the number of jobs, $N \leqslant E^*$,
— a situation in which $N \geqslant E^*$.

In the first case employment will partially be determined by the number of jobs, but mainly by labour supply (less frictional unemployment u_0). This is formalized as

$$E = \eta E^* + (1-\eta)(N - u_0). \qquad (7.4.37)$$

The second possibility is formalized as

$$E = \beta q_y E^* + (1-\beta)E^* \qquad (7.4.38)$$

in which case the employment function becomes

$$E_t = [\beta q_{y_t} + (1 - \beta)]\frac{1}{\kappa\phi}h_t^{\delta_1 - \delta_2}\sum_{\tau = v_t}^{t}\Omega_{t-\tau}I_{\tau,\tau}e^{-\mu\tau} \qquad (7.4.39)$$

for $h_t = d_t$.

This equation has been iteratively estimated with annual data for the whole enterprise sector of the Netherlands. Many estimating problems have to be solved, among which the pinpointing of several coefficients, but it is outside the scope of this survey to deal with them in detail. Numerous data problems have to be solved too, in particular with respect to the investment data for the pre-war period.

The study of Den Hartog and Tjan has been the subject of much criticism. This criticism was related to both empirical and theoretical aspects of the study (a survey of the debate is given in Driehuis, 1979).

What concerns us here are the following points:

— since statistical series on production capacity and its labour requirements were lacking the authors had to resort to an extensive trial and error method to select a set of coefficients that gave the best adjustment of potential to actual employment;
— the model was estimated for the whole enterprise sector, instead of for those sectors where the use of capital is important for the production process, that is the manufacturing and capital intensive services industries;
— rather than using a scrapping condition as represented in (7.4.36), which is based on the assumption of perfect competition, it would be appropriate to use a replacement condition for capital in a situation of imperfect competition;
— it would be relevant to introduce more types of technical progress.

These remarks have led to an alternative specification of the clay–clay vintage model discussed above. First of all it can be shown (Driehuis *et al.*, 1979) that under certain conditions (7.4.33) and (7.4.34) can be written in relative first differences. In this way a number of estimation problems can be avoided. The production function can then be formulated as

$$\dot{y}^* = \frac{1}{\kappa}(ld^{\delta_1}) + \theta dA + \delta_1\dot{d} - \pi + \varepsilon, \qquad (7.4.40)$$

where π represents the trend of economic and technical obsolescence of the capital stock, A is the economic lifetime of the oldest vintage in use, l is the gross investment ratio and ε is disembodied capital augmenting technical progress.

The function for potential employment (= jobs) then becomes

$$\dot{E}^* = \dot{y}^* + \psi dA - \delta_2\dot{h} - \mu - \chi, \qquad (7.4.41)$$

where χ represents disembodied labour augmenting technical progress. When it is furthermore adopted that

$$\dot{E} = \frac{G(L)_1}{H(L)_1} \dot{E}^d \tag{7.4.42}$$

and

$$\dot{E}^d = \dot{E}^* + \beta(\dot{y} - \dot{y}^*) \tag{7.4.43}$$

(where β represents the labour hoarding effects discussed earlier), we arrive at the following employment function in relative first differences [see III, §1.4]

$$\dot{E} = \frac{G(L)_1}{H(L)_1} \left[\left\{ \beta \frac{G(L)_2}{H(L)_2} \dot{y} + \frac{1-\beta}{\kappa} \frac{G(L)_3}{H(L)_3} (ld^{\delta_1}) + \{(1-\beta)(\theta + \psi)\} \right. \right.$$

$$\left. \cdot \frac{G(L)_4}{H(L)_4} dA + \{(1-\beta)(\delta_1 - \delta_2)\} \frac{G(L)_5}{H(L)_5} \dot{h} - (1-\beta)(\pi - \varepsilon + \mu + \chi) \right\} \left. \vphantom{\frac{G(L)_2}{H(L)_2}} \right]. \tag{7.4.44}$$

For the derivation of the lifetime variable we have to introduce a replacement condition for capital. This condition can be formulated as: capital of a given vintage is used as long as its operation cost of producing a unit of output with that vintage is less than the marginal cost of producing that unit of output with capital of the most recent vintage (Malcomson, 1975). This can be formulated as

$$\frac{p_{E_t} E_{t,v}^*}{y_{t,v}^*} = \frac{p_{E_t} E_{t,t}^* + p_{K_t} I_{t,t}}{y_{t,t}^*}, \tag{7.4.45}$$

or in continuous form

$$p_E \left\{ \frac{1}{\phi} e^{-\mu v} e^{-\chi t} - \frac{1}{\phi} e^{-\mu t} e^{-\chi t} \right\} h^{-\delta_2} = \kappa h^{-\delta_1} p_K e^{-\varepsilon t}. \tag{7.4.46}$$

After differentiation [see IV, §3.2] we find

$$dA = \frac{1}{1+C} \left\{ \frac{-(\dot{p}_E - \dot{p}_K) - (\delta_1 - \delta_2)\dot{h} + \chi - \varepsilon}{\mu} + 1 \right\}, \tag{7.4.47}$$

where C is the ratio between the cost of labour and capital per unit of output of the newest vintage. This ratio is equal to

$$C = \frac{p_E \dfrac{1}{\phi} e^{-(\mu + \chi)t} h^{\delta_2}}{\kappa p_k h^{\delta_1} e^{-\varepsilon t}}. \tag{7.4.48}$$

Once C_t is assessed for a certain base year it can be used for calculating different sets of dA for different values of μ, χ and ε (which are not completely independent of each other). Alternative series dA can then be used for the estimation of (7.4.44). This has been successful for the capital using sector (manufacturing and capital intensive services) in the Netherlands. Alternatively, (7.4.47) can be substituted into Equation (7.4.44) for a direct estimation for the employment function. (See Driehuis (1981) for such a procedure for the United Kingdom capital-using sector.) It should be noted that we have not taken into account here the possibility that p_K is dependent on dA (see Driehuis *et al.*, 1979).

Finally, we mention the most recent development in estimating employment functions, that is the estimation of putty–clay employment functions. For instance, Kuipers and Van Zon (1982), starting from (7.4.10), have successfully estimated such functions for the Netherlands.

7.5. CONCLUDING REMARKS

From a historical point of view the production function approach to macroeconomic investment and employment functions has replaced the eclectic approach. But in the course of time it became clear that the production function approach was too rigorous and too static, although attractive for purposes of analytical consistency, to provide an acceptable explanation of firm's demand for labour and capital goods in the aggregate. Influences emphasized in the eclectic approach could not be missed in understanding the factor demand behaviour of the firm. Nevertheless economists cannot be very proud of their attempts to explain and forecast this behaviour, especially not when investment is concerned. Obviously, there are still many deficiencies in the specifications which are developed. In our view the most important deficiencies relate to assumptions with respect to the homogeneity of both capital and labour, the neglect of adjustment costs, the ad hoc way in which lags and financial variables are included and the ignorance of the role of risk and uncertainty. One of the main tasks for us is undoubtedly to integrate available microeconomic theory which considers these deficiencies into better empirical macroeconomic investment and employment functions (see Nickell, 1978).

7.6. REFERENCES

Aftalion, A. (1911). Les Trois Notions de la productivité et les revenues. *Revue d'Economie Politique*.
Alchian, A. A. (1955). The rate of interest, Fisher's rate of return over costs and Keynes' internal rate of return. *American Economic Review*, 938–943.
Almon, S. (1965). The distributed lag between capital appropriations and expenditures. *Econometrica*, **33**, 178–196.
Ball, R. J. and St. Cyr, E. B. A. (1966). Short-term employment functions in british manufacturing industry. *Review of Economic Studies*, **33**, 179–207.
Benassy, J. P., Fouquet, D. and Malgrange, P. (1975). Estimation d'une fonction de production à générations de capital. *Annales de l'Insee*, no. 19, 3–53.
Bischoff, C. W. (1968). Lags in fiscal and monetary impacts on investment in producers' durable equipment. *Cowles Foundation Discussion Paper no. 250*, Yale University.
Brechling, F. P. R. (1965). The relationship between output and employment in British manufacturing industries. *Review of Economic Studies*, **32**, 187–216.

Brechling, F. (1975). *Investment and Employment Decisions.* Manchester University Press Manchester.

Cagan, P. (1956). The monetary dynamics of hyperinflation, in Friedman (ed.), *Studies in the Quantitative Theory of Money.* Chicago University Press, Chicago.

Chenery, H. B. (1952). Overcapacity and the acceleration principle. *Econometrica,* **20,** 1–28.

Clark, J. M. (1917). Business acceleration and the law of demand. *Journal of Political Economy,* **25,** 217–235.

Den Hartog, H. and Tjan, H. S. (1976). Investment, wages, prices and demand for labour. *De Economist,* 124, 32–55.

Dhrymes, P. J. (1969). A model of short-run labor adjustment, Ch. 5 of *The Brookings Model: Some Further Results.* North-Holland, Amsterdam.

Dhrymes, P. J. (1981). *Distributed Lags.* North-Holland, Amsterdam.

Driehuis, W. (1972). *Fluctuations and Growth in a Near Full Employment Economy.* Rotterdam University Press, Rotterdam.

Driehuis, W. (1979). An analysis of the impact of demand and cost factors on employment. *De Economist,* 127, 255–286.

Driehuis, W. (1981), Employment and technical progress in open economies, in Z. Hornstein *et al.* (eds.) *The Economics of the Labour Market.* HMSO, London.

Driehuis, W., Heineken, K. A. and De Savornin Lohman, A. F. (1979). De Werkgelegenheid in Kapitaal gebruikende Bedrijfstakken, in J. J. Klant *et al., Samenleving en Onderzoek.* Stenfert Kroese, Leiden.

Duesenberry, J. A. (1958). *Business Cycles and Economic Growth.* McGraw Hill, New York.

Eisner, R. (1965). Realization of investment anticipations, in *Brookings Quarterly Econometric Model of the United States,* edited by J. S. Duesenberry, et al., North-Holland, Amsterdam.

Eisner, R. (1972). Components of capital expenditure: Replacement and maximization versus expansion. *Review of Economics and Statistics,* pp. 297–305.

Eisner, R. and Strotz, R. H. (1963). Determinants of business investment, in Commission on Money and Credit, *Impacts of Monetary Policy.* Prentice-Hall, Englewood Cliffs, N.J., pp. 59–337.

Fiar, R. (1969). *The Short-run Demand for Workers and Hours.* North-Holland, Amsterdam.

Feldstein, M. S. (1974). Tax incentives, stabilization policy and the proportional replacement hypothesis: Some negative conclusions. *Southern Economic Journal,* **7,** 544–552.

Feldstein, M. S. and Rothschild M. (1974). Towards an economic theory of replacement investment. *Econometrica,* **42,** 393–423.

Feldstein, M. S. and Foot, D. K. (1971). The other half of gross investment: replacement and modernization expenditures. *Review of Economics and Statistics,* pp. 49–58.

Ferguson, C. E. (1971). *The Neoclassical Theory of Production and Distribution.* Cambridge University Press, London.

Goodwin, R. M. (1951). The non-linear accelerator and the persistance of business cycles. *Econometrica,* **19,** 1–17.

Görzig, B. (1976). Results of a vintage-capital model for the Federal Republic of Germany. *Empirical Economics,* **1,** 153–166.

Gould, J. P. (1968). Adjustment costs in the theory of investment of the firm. *Review of Economic Studies,* pp. 47–56.

Greenberg, E. (1964). A stock adjustment investment model. *Econometrica,* **32,** 339–357.

Griliches, Z. (1967). Distributed lags: A survey. *Econometrica,* **35,** no. 1, pp. 16–49.

Harrod, R. (1939). An essay in dynamic theory. *Economic Journal*, **49**, 14–33.
Hazledine, T. (1981). Employment functions and the demand for labour in the short-run, in Z. Hornstein *et al.* (eds.), *The Economics of the Labour Market*, HMSO, London.
Helliwell, J. F. (ed.) (1976). *Aggregate Investment*. Penguin Modern Economic Readings, Harmondsworth.
Hickman, B. (1957). Capacity utilization and the acceleration principle, in *Problems of Capital Formation*. Studies in Income and Wealth, Vol. 19, Princeton University Press, Princeton, N. J.
Hirschleifer, J. (1970). *Investment, Interest and Capital*. Prentice-Hall, Englewood Cliffs, N.J.
Hubbard, N. S. (1968). Short-run changes in labour productivity in United States manufacturing 1954–1959. *Yale Economic Essays*, **8**, 59–133.
Jorgenson, D. W. (1963). Capital theory and investment behavior. *American Economic Review*, pp. 247–259.
Jorgenson, D. W. (1965). Anticipations and investment behavior, in Duesenberry *et al.* (eds.), *The Brookings Quarterly Econometric Model of the United States*. North-Holland, Amsterdam.
Jorgenson, D. W. (1966). Rational distributed lag functions. *Econometrica*, **34**, 135–149.
Jorgenson, D. W. and Siebert, C. D. (1968). A comparison of alternative theories of corporate investment behavior. *American Economic Review*, pp. 681–712.
Junankar, P. N. (1970). The relationship between investment and spare capacity in the United Kingdom, 1957–1966. *Econometrica*, **37**, 277–292.
Kalecki, M. (1943). *Studies in Economic Dynamics*. Allen & Unwin, London.
Keynes, J. M. (1936). *The General Theory of Employment, Interest and Money*. Macmillan, London.
Killingsworth, M. R. (1970). A critical survey of neoclassical models of labour. *Bulletin Oxford University Institute of Economics and Statistics*, **32**, 133–165.
Klein, L. R. (1951). *Economic Fluctuations in the United States, 1921–1941*. Cowles Commission Monograph, no. 11, Wiley, New York.
Koyck, L. M. (1954). *Distributed Lags and Investment Analysis*. North-Holland, Amsterdam.
King, M. A. (1972). Taxation and investment incentives in a vintage investment model. *Journal of Public Economics*, **1**, 121–147.
Kuh, E. (1963). *Capital Stock Growth: A Micro Econometric Approach*. North-Holland, Amsterdam.
Kuipers, S. K. and van Zon, A. H. (1982). Output and employment growth in the Netherlands in the postwar period: A putty–clay approach. *De Economist*, **130**, 38–70.
Lorie, J. H. and Savage, L. J. (1955). Three problems in rationing capital. *Journal of Business*.
Lucas, R. E. (1967). Adjustment costs and the theory of supply, *Journal of Political Economy*, **75**, 321–334.
Malcomson, J. M. (1975). Replacement and the rental value of capital equipment subject to obsolescence. *Journal of Economic Theory*, **19**, 24–53.
Meyer, J. and E. Kuh, (1957). *The Investment Decision*. Cambridge University Press, London.
Nadiri, M. I. (1968). The effects of relative prices and capacity on the demand for labour in the U.S. manufacturing sector. *Review of Economic Studies*, July, pp. 273–288.
Nadiri, M. I. and Rosen, S. (1973). *A Disequilibrium Model of Demand for Factors of Production*. National Bureau of Economic Research, New York.
Nerlove, M. (1958). *The Dynamics of Supply: Estimation of Farmers' Response to Price*, Johns Hopkins Press, Baltimore.

Nickell, S. J. (1975). A closer look at replacement investment. *Journal of Economic Theory*, **10**, 54–88.

Nickell, S. J. (1978). *The Investment Decisions of Firms*, Cambridge University Press, Cambridge.

Oi, W. (1962). Labour as a Quasi-fixed factor. *Journal of Political Economy*, **70**, 538–555.

Rowley, J. C. R. and Trivedi, P. K. (1975). *Econometrics of Investment*. Wiley, London.

Smith, K. R. (1969). The effects of uncertainty on monopoly price, capital stock and utilization of capital. *Journal of Economic Theory*, **1**, 48–59.

Smyth, D. J. and Ireland, N. J. (1967). Short-term employment functions in Australian manufacturing. *Review of Economics and Statistics*, **49**, 537–544.

Solow, R. M. (1960). On a family of lag distributions. *Econometrica*, **28**, 2, 399–406.

Taubinan, P. and Wilkinson, M. (1970). User cost, capacity utilization and investment theory. *International Economic Review*, **11**, 209–215.

Tinbergen, J. (1936). An economic policy for 1936, in L. H. Klaassen, *et al.* (eds.), *Jan Tinbergen Selected Papers* (translation of the original 1936 article). North-Holland, Amsterdam (1959), pp. 228–239.

Tinbergen, J. (1939). *Statistical Testing of Business Cycle Theories*, Part 1. A Method and its Application to Investment Activity. League of Nations, Geneva.

Treadway, A. B. (1969). On rational entrepreneural behavior and the demand for investment. *Review of Economic Studies*, **36**, 227–239.

Treadway, A. B. (1970). Adjustment costs and variable inputs in the theory of the competitive firm, *Journal of Economic Theory*, **2**, 329–347.

Treadway, A. B. (1971). On the multivariate flexible accelerator. *Econometrica*, **39**, 845–856.

Verdoorn, P. J., Post, J. J. and Goslinga, S. S. (1971). Het Jaarmodel 1969-C, in *Centraal Economisch Plan*, Den Haag.

Part III

Macroeconomic Models

Mathematical Methods in Economics
Edited by F. van der Ploeg
© 1984, John Wiley & Sons, Ltd.

8

Macroeconomic Theory and Policy

F. R. SHUPP, *University of Illinois, Urbana-Champaign USA*

8.1. INTRODUCTION

Macroeconomic analysis is a massive and complex subject, and much of that subject is amenable to mathematical analysis. Consequently any chapter length treatment of the relationship between macroeconomics and mathematics must necessarily be selective and illustrative. The particular selections and illustrations presented in this chapter are loosely tied together by two theorems, the neutrality argument and the correspondence principle. The neutrality argument, which serves to integrate the first half of this study, is a theorem in economics. Mathematics are used to illustrate and define the conditions under which it can be correctly employed. On the other hand, the correspondence principle, which serves to integrate the second half of the paper, is essentially a theorem in mathematics. This mathematical argument provides the basis for theorizing about the consequences of economic behaviour. Mathematics is thus seen to play two distinct roles in macroeconomics: to prove and refine theorems developed on some *a priori* basis and to suggest new theorems in economics and new designs for economic policy.

There is a second important consideration which distinguishes the two halves of this chapter. Section 8.2 deals with comparative statics and section 8.3 with comparative dynamics. While it is self-evident that all real economies are dynamic, much of the existing macroeconomics literature has been usefully developed in terms of comparative statics. Consequently, both forms of analysis are used in this review. On average, the mathematics used in the dynamic analysis is somewhat more demanding than that used in the static analysis. In all instances, however, the mathematics employed and the models specified are kept as simple as possible. Generalizations and rigour are sacrificed for accessibility and intuition. This approach is compensated for by frequent references to more sophisticated studies of the materials analysed. In addition, four book-length studies offering both a more comprehensive and more rigorous survey of the use of mathematics in macroeconomics can be recommended. These are authored by Gapinski (1982), Nagatani (1981), Sargent (1979), and Turnovsky (1977).

8.2. COMPARATIVE STATICS AND THE NEUTRALITY ARGUMENT

It has been stated repeatedly during recent years that macroeconomics is in a state of disarray or, put more kindly, in a state of ferment. Yet the questions of the early nineteen-eighties are very similar to those of the early nineteen-thirties. These questions can be summarized as follows: (i) in the near short run is the market clearing process characterized primarily by a price adjustment mechanism or a quantity adjustment mechanism? (ii) in the near short run does the quantity of money effect real quantities or simply prices? (iii) in the near short run is the assumption of perfect foresight or rational expectations a plausible working hypothesis? These are essentially the same questions that set Keynes against Walras, and which today distinguish the neo-Keynesian from the neo-Walrasian.

The differences between the neo-Walrasian and the neo-Keynesian can also be conveniently summarized in terms of the Friedman–Lucas *neutrality argument*. Put baldly this argument states that growth in aggregate real output is essentially independent of (that is neutral with respect to) monetary and also fiscal policy. Neo-Walrasians accept this argument and neo-Keynesians reject it.

It seems appropriate therefore to begin this review of the use of mathematics in macroeconomics with two simple models, one representing an extreme neo-Walrasian perspective and the other representing an extreme neo-Keynesian position. These two models have a common *demand side* structure which is derived from the familiar Hicksian IS–LM framework.[1] The two models have differing *supply side* structures, however. The neo-Walrasian supply side is derived from a Lucas type supply function, while the neo-Keynesian supply side is derived from an expectation augmented Phillips Curve. A novel formulation of the latter serves to clarify the traditional arguments.

8.2.1. The demand side model

As noted immediately above the demand side of the representative neo-Walrasian and neo-Keynesian models is common and is given by the familiar IS–LM arguments. In this framework, the demand for real output can be modelled by

$$X = X^{\alpha} R^{\bar{\beta}} E^{\gamma}, \quad \alpha \geqslant 0, \bar{\beta} \leqslant 0, \gamma \geqslant 0, \tag{8.2.1}$$

where X, R, and E denote respectively the levels of real output, real interest rate, and real autonomous expenditure. The parameters α, $\bar{\beta}$ and γ denote the respective output elasticities.

Assume further that the *natural* or Walrasian equilibrium is defined by

$X^* \equiv X^{*\alpha} R^{*\bar{\beta}} E^{*\gamma}$. It follows from totally differentiating both (8.2.1) and this definition with respect to time [see IV, §3.1], dividing through by X and X^* respectively, and subtracting that

$$x - x^* \simeq \alpha(x - x^*) + \bar{\beta}(r - r^*) + \gamma(e - e^*).$$

Approximating this result in discrete (rather than continuous) time yields

$$x = x^* + \beta(R - R^*) + v, \qquad \beta \leqslant 0, \tag{8.2.2}$$

where x and x^* denote respectively the prevailing and natural growth rates of real output defined by $x \equiv \dot{X}/X$ and $x^* \equiv \dot{X}^*/X^*$, where r and r^* denote respectively the prevailing and natural growth rates of the real interest rate defined by $r \equiv \dot{R}/R$ and $r^* \equiv \dot{R}^*/R^* = 0$, and where v denotes the expenditure disturbance defined by $v \equiv \gamma(e - e^*)/(1 - \alpha)$, with e, in turn, defined by $e \equiv \dot{E}/E$. The parameter β is defined by $\beta \equiv \bar{\beta}/(1 - \alpha)R^*$, with the lagged real interest rate given by $R_{-1} = R^*$. It follows from (8.2.2) that the growth of aggregate real output equals the natural growth rate adjusted for both real interest rate considerations and any real expenditure disturbance.

Similarly beginning with the assumption that the demand for real balances is given by

$$M/P = X^{\delta} I^{\bar{\varepsilon}}, \qquad \delta \geqslant 0, \bar{\varepsilon} \leqslant 0, \tag{8.2.3}$$

where M, P, and I denote respectively the nominal money stock, price level, and nominal interest rate, and where δ and $\bar{\varepsilon}$ are the respective elasticities, it follows, as above, by totally differentiating and discretizing that

$$m - p = \delta x + \varepsilon(I - I^*), \qquad \varepsilon \leqslant 0, \tag{8.2.4}$$

where m, p, and x denote respectively the growth rates of the money stock, price level, and real income, where I^* denotes the natural or Walrasian nominal interest rate, and where ε denotes the interest rate elasticity defined by $\varepsilon \equiv \bar{\varepsilon}/I^*$. The standard interpretation of (8.2.4) is that growth in transaction and asset demand for real balances is related both to growth in real national income and to changes in the nominal interest rate.

Finally it is assumed that the Wicksellian interest rate relationship is valid, so that the nominal interest rate equals the real interest rate plus the expected rate of inflation. This is given by

$$I = R + p^e, \tag{8.2.5}$$

where p^e denotes the expected rate of inflation.

If the *preceding* period is characterized by a Walrasian equilibrium and an expected rate of inflation $p^{e*} = \phi$, it follows from substituting (8.2.5) into (8.2.4), solving this for $R - R^*$, and substituting this result into (8.2.2) that growth in aggregate real demand can be given by

$$x = \Lambda\{x^* + (\beta/\varepsilon)(m - p) - \beta p^e + \beta\phi + v\}, \tag{8.2.6}$$

where $\Lambda \equiv \varepsilon/(\beta\delta + \varepsilon) > 0$, because the price elasticities β and ε are negative and the income elasticity δ is positive.

8.2.2. The supply side

As noted above, two distinct supply relationships are posited, one illustrative of the neo-Walrasian framework and the other representative of the neo-Keynesian viewpoint. There is, of course, no single neo-Walrasian or single neo-Keynesian supply side theory or model. The models presented are extreme or polar versions of these two viewpoints. This is particularly true of the neo-Keynesian model outlined below. The chosen specifications have the advantage however, that they highlight the different roles that prices play in the two systems. In the neo-Walrasian model transient deviations from the natural or Walrasian equilibrium output generate changes in relative prices which return the output to the natural or equilibrium level (rate). Deviations from this natural level occur only in response to unanticipated changes in (relative) prices. In the neo-Keynesian model, on the other hand, transient deviations from the natural output level produce only changes in nominal prices. Relative prices remain fixed. As a consequence, there is no mechanism for returning the economy to the natural or Walrasian equilibrium level.

The neo-Walrasian supply side

The neo-Walrasian supply side relationship is given by

$$x = x^* + \lambda(p - p^e), \qquad \lambda \geqslant 0, \tag{8.2.7}$$

where λ denotes the supply elasticity. There are two rather distinct interpretations of this neo-Walrasian relationship, which might appropriately be identified as Walrasian and Lucasian. The Walrasian interpretation states that growth in output is equal to the Walrasian or natural growth rate whenever the Walrasian relative price obtains. Furthermore any transient shift in the relative price which increases profits induces a faster growth rate of output. This interpretation requires that the expected price p^e be viewed as a proxy for increases in factor costs, particularly labour and capital costs. To the extent that these factor costs are contracted ahead on the basis of prices which are expected to prevail, p^e is a reasonable proxy for factor cost increases. The output price increase p, however, is assumed to respond to both anticipated and unanticipated changes in demand, and therefore it can readily differ from the factor cost increase proxied by p^e. The deviation between p and p^e reflects a non-Walrasian profit level, and it is this difference which induces either more or less output growth than the Walrasian or natural rate x^*.

The second interpretation of the supply side relationship given by (8.2.7) above does not rely on any explicit change in the relative price of input and output.

Instead Lucas argues that output is adjusted around the natural rate whenever the nominal price (increase) differs from the expected price (increase). This difference occurs because agents can not always correctly infer what part of any price increase reflects an increase in the demand for the good under question and what part reflects a general price increase. In Lucas's (1976) own words

> Though simple, equation [(8.2.7)] captures the main features of the expectational or 'natural rate' view of aggregate supply. The supply of goods x is viewed as following a trend path x^* which is not dependent on nominal price movements. Deviations from this path are induced whenever the nominal price p deviates from the level that was expected to prevail on the basis of past information. These deviations occur because agents are obliged to infer current general price movements on the basis of incomplete information.

In this quotation the variables p and x represent the logarithm of the price and output rather than growth rates of these same variables as assumed in this study. This difference, however, is unimportant to the subsequent analysis.

The Walrasian interpretation of this supply side relationship can be applied equally to the labour market. In this case

$$n = n^* + \lambda_1(w - w^e), \qquad \lambda_1 \geqslant 0, \tag{8.2.8}$$

where n and w denote respectively the growth rates in employment and money wages. In this case the argument w^e is regarded as a proxy for the expected price increase p^e. The interpretation of (8.2.8) is thus immediate. Growth in employment will equal the Walrasian or natural rate unless the offered money wage increase differs from the expected price increase.

If (8.2.8) is assumed to be stable in the sense that it is invertible ($\lambda_1 \neq 0$), it can be rewritten as

$$w = w^e(\text{or } p^e) + (n - n^*)/\lambda_1. \tag{8.2.8'}$$

In case (8.2.8) is a nonlinear function, stability and invertibility are guaranteed when the conditions of the implicit function theorem are satisfied [see IV, §5.12]. Combining this expression with the appropriate expression of Okun's Law,[2] that is with $U = U^* - \mu_1(n - n^*)$, yields the standard expectations-augmented Phillips Curve relationship given by

$$w = p^e - (U - U^*)/\mu_1\lambda_1, \qquad \mu_1 \geqslant 0. \tag{8.2.9}$$

The rearrangement of the neo-Walrasian labour supply relationship (8.2.8) into a standard Phillips Curve (8.2.8') can be quite misleading. Mathematically the two expressions are identical; economically they are not. In (8.2.8) a prior increase in the expected real wage induces the work force to supply more labour. In (8.2.8') a prior increase in the demand for labour leads to an increase in the real wage. It follows therefore that the assumption of a stable relationship is an important assumption and should be made only after a most careful consideration.[3]

The neo-Keynesian supply side

A closer examination of the standard Phillips relation given by (8.2.9) reveals that this specification is itself inconsistent with the neo-Keynesian argument that relative prices (in this case the expected real wage) do *not* respond to transient or cyclical changes in excess demand. A Phillips Curve specification which *is* consistent with this neo-Keynesian fixed real wage argument is given instead by

$$w = p^e \equiv p^e|(U = U^*) - (U^e - U^*)/\mu_2\lambda_2, \qquad \mu_2 \geqslant 0, \lambda_2 \geqslant 0. \qquad (8.2.10)$$

The distinguishing feature of this novel specification of the Phillips relationship is the *conditional expectation term*, $p^e|(U = U^*)$ [see II §8.9 and Chapter 16]. This conditional expectation is defined as the inflation rate that would be expected in the absence of any labour market pressure, that is the expected rate of inflation if the unemployment rate were equal to the natural unemployment rate. It is perhaps instructive to note that all agents expect the unconditional inflation rate p^e as defined in (8.2.10) and not the conditional rate. The latter is simply the base from which the former is calculated. As shown below the primary determinants of this base or conditional expected rate of inflation are (i) the historical rate of inflation and (ii) the equilibrium growth rate of the money stock.[4]

The neo-Keynesian supply side specification given by (8.2.10) is consistent with both Phillips's observation and neoclassical disequilibrium theory that *money wages* respond to excess demand in the labour market. The reason for this behaviour are several. First, in a tight labour market, the firm is likely to grant a money wage increase simply to remain competitive, especially with respect to experienced workers. Second, when the labour market is tight, output sales are usually good. As a consequence, the typical firm is less likely to resist employee demands for wage increases, because it realizes that it can raise its product price to offset the increased wage cost. Third, the individual employee (or union leader) recognizes that a tight aggregate labour market typically implies higher costs and therefore higher prices. Consequently, he bargains for a money wage increase to preserve both his real purchasing power and his relative wage position. The foresight attributed to both employee and employer in these three arguments is rather substantial. However, this attribution is quite consistent with the rational expectation analysis used below.

While money wages respond to transient excess demand in the labour market, it is clear from (8.2.10) that (expected) real wages do not. In this neo-Keynesian specification, the expected real wage always equals the Walrasian real wage even when the labour market is not in equilibrium, that is even when $U \neq U^*$.[5]

This neo-Keynesian model also assumes that product prices are determined by adding a mark-up to wage and other factor costs. It is further assumed that this mark-up is invariant with respect to transient or cyclical excess demand.[6] This implies that $p = w$. One rationale for this mark-up strategy is that it is designed to maximize long-run profits by preserving the relative price structure at a level which precludes entry or loss of market share.

If prices are marked up to cover wage increases and if, in addition, the relevant specifications of Okun's Law applies, that is if $U = U^* - \mu_2(x - x^*)$, it follows directly from (8.2.10) that the neo-Keynesian supply side relationship can be given by

$$p = p^e|(x = x^*) + \lambda_2(x - x^*). \tag{8.2.11}$$

In summary, the natural growth rate x^* (or the natural unemployment rate U^*) is the Walrasian or long-run equilibrium rate in both the neo-Walrasian and neo-Keynesian models. In the neo-Walrasian model it is a natural rate because even transient deviations from this rate precipitate changes in relative prices which induce a return to this natural rate. By contrast in the neo-Keynesian model transient deviations from the natural rate give rise only to nominal price changes. In particular, reductions in the unemployment rate below the natural rate lead to increases in the money wage rate which, in turn, induce similar increases in the general price level. In this neo-Keynesian scheme the natural unemployment rate U^* is perhaps more accurately characterized as the non-accelerating inflationary rate of unemployment. The acronym NAIRU is sometimes used when this interpretation is intended.

8.2.3. The complete model and rational expectations

The neo-Walrasian model is thus given by the demand side equation (8.2.6) and the supply side equation (8.2.7), while the neo-Keynesian model is expressed by the demand side equation (8.2.6) and the supply side equation (8.2.11). As shown immediately below this neo-Walrasian model is consistent with the Friedman–Lucas neutrality argument, which is the principal basis of the non interventionist posture of most monetarists. The neo-Keynesian model is not. In the neo-Keynesian model defined above both monetary and fiscal policy are capable of influencing aggregate real output.

In deriving his neutrality result Friedman (1968) employs the adaptive expectation (inflation) hypothesis. Lucas (1976), on the other hand, employs the rational expectation hypothesis first suggested by Muth (1961). Because the validity of the neutrality argument can be most easily and rigorously demonstrated with the rational expectation hypothesis, this hypothesis is employed below.

The neo-Walrasian equilibrium

The solution to the neo-Walrasian model can be found by first combining (8.2.6) and (8.2.7) and solving respectively for x and p [see I, §5.8]. This yields

$$x = \frac{\Lambda}{\Gamma}\left\{\left(1 + \frac{\beta}{\varepsilon\lambda}\right)x^* + \frac{\beta}{\varepsilon}m - \left(\beta + \frac{\beta}{\varepsilon}\right)p^e + \beta\phi + v\right\} \qquad (8.2.12)$$

and

$$p = \frac{1}{\lambda\Gamma}\left\{(\Lambda - 1)x^* + \frac{\beta}{\varepsilon}\Lambda m + (\lambda - \beta\Lambda)p^e + \beta\Lambda\phi + \Lambda v\right\}, \qquad (8.2.13)$$

where $\Gamma \equiv (1 + \beta\Lambda/\varepsilon\lambda) > 0$, because the supply elasticity λ is positive and the demand elasticities β and ε are negative.

It is evident from these two reduced form equations that the real growth rate x and the inflation rate p are both functions of the money growth rate m and the expected inflation rate p^e. The money growth rate is assumed to be determined exogenously by the relevant authorities. However, the expected inflation rate is determined endogenously. In forming these inflation expectations it is further assumed that all agents act rationally in the sense that they fully understand the actual inflation process and make the best possible use of any available information. It follows therefore from (8.2.13) that

$$p^e \equiv E(p|I) = E\left[\frac{1}{\lambda\Gamma}\left\{(\Lambda - 1)x^* + \frac{\beta}{\varepsilon}\Lambda m + (\lambda - \beta\Lambda)p^e + \beta\Lambda\phi + \Lambda v\right\}\right], \qquad (8.2.14)$$

which after taking expectations and simplifying [see II, Chapter 8] yields

$$p^e = -\left(\frac{\delta}{1+\varepsilon}\right)x^* + \frac{1}{1+\varepsilon}m^e + \frac{\varepsilon}{1+\varepsilon}\phi, \qquad (8.2.14')$$

where m^e denotes the expected money growth rate, and where the available information I is assumed to include in addition to m^e, the natural real growth rate x^* and the previous period inflation rate ϕ. It does not include any real disturbance v.

Substituting (8.2.14') into (8.2.12) and (8.2.13) yields respectively after some simplification

$$x = x^* + \frac{\beta}{\varepsilon}\frac{\Lambda}{\Gamma}(m - m^e) + \frac{\Lambda}{\Gamma}v, \qquad (8.2.15)$$

and

$$p = -\frac{\delta}{1+\varepsilon}x^* + \frac{1}{1+\varepsilon}m + \frac{\varepsilon}{1+\varepsilon}\phi + \frac{\Lambda}{\lambda\Gamma}v. \qquad (8.2.16)$$

It follows immediately from these two equations that the neutrality argument holds for the neo-Walrasian model. From (8.2.16) it is evident that any increase in the money growth rate causes an increase in the inflation rate. However, it is equally obvious from (8.2.15) that only an *unanticipated* increase in the money growth rate, (that is $m \neq m^e$) causes an increase in the growth rate of aggregate real output. Monetary policy is effective in influencing real output only if the authorities have superior information which leads to a money growth rate different from that expected by the community, or if for some other reason the authorities pursue a policy which differs from that expected. In short, to be effective monetary policy must surprise the economic community.

In this model *anticipated fiscal policy* is similarly ineffective in influencing aggregate real output. It may, of course, change the composition of that output. However, *unanticipated* fiscal policy as well as any unanticipated private sector disturbance, both of which are measured by v, do affect the rate of output growth as can be seen from (8.2.15).

The mechanism (following the Walrasian interpretation of the model) which produces these two results is easily explained. Consider first the case of *anticipated* inflationary shocks deriving from either monetary or fiscal policy. Since the inflation induced by these policies is fully anticipated, factor costs covered by forward contracts rise as rapidly as output prices do. This precludes any increase in profits which, in turn, implies the absence of any incentive to produce more than the natural or equilibrium output. Furthermore these same anticipated inflationary shocks give rise to both higher nominal interest rates and higher prices. However, since the real interest rate remains unchanged, real demand growth continues at the natural rate.

However, when inflationary disturbances are *unanticipated*, product prices rise relative to factor costs and this induces an increase in supply. At the same time unanticipated money increases produce both a higher nominal and a lower real interest rate. The latter induces an increase in real demand. In this instance both demand and supply adjust with the resulting equilibrium governed by the value of the respective elasticities.

The neo-Keynesian equilibrium

The solution to the neo-Keynesian model is found by combining the demand side equation (8.2.6) with the supply side equation (8.2.11) and solving for x and p. This yields respectively

$$x = \frac{\Lambda}{\Gamma}\left\{\frac{\varepsilon\lambda + \beta}{\varepsilon\lambda}x^* + \frac{\beta}{\varepsilon}m - \frac{\beta}{\varepsilon}p^e|(\cdot) - \beta p^e + \beta\phi + v\right\} \qquad (8.2.17)$$

and

$$p = \frac{1}{\lambda\Gamma}\left\{(\Lambda - 1)x^* + \frac{\beta}{\varepsilon}\Lambda m - \beta\Lambda p^e + \lambda p^e|(\cdot) + \beta\Lambda\phi + \Lambda v\right\}. \qquad (8.2.18)$$

As with the neo-Walrasian model it is evident that the real growth rate x and the inflation rate p are both functions of money growth m and the expected inflation. However, in this case both the conditional expectation $p^e|(\cdot)$ and the unconditional expectation p^e are involved.

Assuming rational expectations the unconditional expected rate of inflation is defined by $p^e \equiv E(p|I)$ and the conditional expected rate of inflation is defined by

$p^e|(\cdot) \equiv E(p|I, x = x^*)$ [see II, §8.1 and §8.9]. This *conditional* expected inflation rate represents the *core or underlying rate of inflation* which depends on the past inflation rate ϕ, equilibrium money growth $m^*(x = x^*)$, and equilibrium real growth x^*. The *unconditional* expected rate of inflation, on the other hand, *is the sum of the expected core rate and the expected shock rate of inflation*. The latter is related to expected aggregate excess demand which, in turn, is related to the expected (actual) money growth. Given these definitions it follows from equation (8.2.18) that in the neo-Keynesian model:

$$p^e = -\left(\frac{\delta}{1+\varepsilon}\right)x^* + \frac{1}{1+\varepsilon}m^e + \frac{\varepsilon}{1+\varepsilon}\phi + \frac{1}{(1+\varepsilon)\Gamma}\Delta m \qquad (8.2.19)$$

and

$$p^e|(\cdot) = -\left(\frac{\delta}{1+\varepsilon}\right)x^* + \frac{1}{1+\varepsilon}m^e + \frac{\varepsilon}{1+\varepsilon}\phi + \frac{\Upsilon}{(1+\varepsilon)\Gamma}\Delta m, \qquad (8.2.20)$$

where $\Delta m \equiv m^*(x = x^*) - m^e$, and $\Upsilon \equiv (\lambda\Gamma + \beta\Lambda)/\lambda > 0$ because $\lambda, \beta > 0$.

Substituting these expectation results back into (8.2.17) and (8.2.18) respectively yields the reduced form neo-Keynesian results

$$x = x^* + \frac{\beta}{\varepsilon}\frac{\Lambda}{\Gamma}(m - m^e) + \frac{\Lambda}{\Gamma}v - \frac{\beta}{\varepsilon}\frac{\Lambda}{\Gamma}\Delta m, \qquad (8.2.21)$$

and

$$p = \frac{\delta}{1+\varepsilon}x^* + \frac{1}{1+\varepsilon}m + \frac{\varepsilon}{1+\varepsilon}\phi + \frac{\Lambda}{\lambda\Gamma}v + \frac{1}{(1+\varepsilon)\Gamma}\Delta m. \qquad (8.2.22)$$

It is immediately evident from (8.2.22) that any increase in the money growth rate (whether anticipated or not) raises the rate of inflation. The more interesting conclusion follows from (8.2.21). The presence of the final term in that equation implies that, in general, money growth also affects the growth rate of real output. This represents a denial of the *neutrality argument* for the neo-Keynesian model. Note that if money growth is anticipated, that is if $m = m^e$, the influence of monetary behaviour on real output growth is completely expressed by the final or deviation term of (8.2.21). It follows that monetary policy is neutral only if this deviation Δm is zero. Since the deviation is defined by $\Delta m \equiv m^*(x = x^*) - m^e$ this condition is satisfied only when the expected money growth m^e equals the money growth required to generate the natural rate of output growth, $m^*(x = x^*)$. However, this result (that is $\Delta m = 0$) implies that if and when the monetary authority anticipates any disturbance, it employs, and is known to employ, a sufficiently vigorous policy to completely offset this disturbance. But such a response is unlikely because it is non-optimal whenever there are either direct costs (e.g. the disruption of the money market) or indirect costs (e.g. induced inflation) associated with this use of policy. In any event, in the neo-Keynesian case the natural rate solution obtains in response to vigorous intervention by the authorities rather than automatically through the market as in the neo-

Walrasian model. The neutrality argument is thus seen to be invalid in the neo-Keynesian model.

A careful comparison of the neo-Keynesian solutions (8.2.21) and (8.2.22) with the corresponding neo-Walrasian solutions (8.2.15) and (8.2.16) reveals the following additional insights:

(i) the neo-Keynesian quantity response (output multiplier) to an unanticipated disturbance (either real or monetary) is larger than the corresponding neo-Walrasian response

(ii) the neo-Keynesian inflation response to a given disturbance (either real or monetary) is smaller than the corresponding neo-Walrasian response.

Conclusions (i) and (ii) also follow from the presence of the deviation term in the neo-Keynesian equations and its absence in the neo-Walrasian equations. In particular it follows from (8.2.15) that the neo-Walrasian output multiplier $(dx/dv)_W$ is given by

$$\left(\frac{dx}{dv}\right)_W = \frac{\partial x}{\partial v} = \frac{\Lambda}{\Gamma} > 0$$

[see IV, §5.2]. Similarly it follows from (8.2.21) that the neo-Keynesian output multiplier $(dx/dv)_K$ is given by

$$\left(\frac{dx}{dv}\right)_K = \frac{\partial x}{\partial v} + \frac{\partial x}{\partial \Delta m} \cdot \frac{\partial \Delta m}{\partial v}.$$

Assuming as above that $m = m^e$ it follows that $\partial x/\partial \Delta m \simeq \partial x/\partial m^* = -\beta \Lambda/\varepsilon \Gamma < 0$ and that $\partial \Delta m/\partial v \simeq \partial m^*/\partial v = -\varepsilon/\beta < 0$. It follows directly that $(dx/dv)_W < (dx/dv)_K$, that is conclusion (i) holds. Conclusion (ii) can be demonstrated in the same way starting with Equations (8.2.16) and (8.2.22).

An intuitive explanation of conclusions (i) and (ii) is straightforward. Real output is less responsive to both real and monetary disturbances in the neo-Walrasian scheme than in the neo-Keynesian one because in the former these disturbances generate a shift in relative prices which tends to offset the original disturbance and return the economy to the Walrasian or natural equilibrium. In the neo-Keynesian model the only quantity moderating shift in relative prices is the induced change in the real interest rate. Inflation, on the other hand, is more responsive to real or monetary disturbances in the neo-Walrasian model than the neo-Keynesian model. This follows because the neo-Walrasian worker intensifies his real wage claims (and therefore his money wage claim) in response to an inflationary disturbance and moderates his claims in response to a deflationary disturbance. His neo-Keynesian counterpart, on the other hand, presses the same real wage claim irrespective of the real or monetary disturbance. A similar story applies to capital and profit claims.

8.2.4. Neo-Walrasian–Neo-Keynesian synthesis

The distinguishing feature of the two models outlined above is the behaviour of *relative prices*. In the neo-Walrasian model relative prices are perfectly flexible. In the neo-Keynesian model they are perfectly inflexible. There are two obvious approaches to reconciling these differences. The first assumes that the separate models are both valid, although each is valid only within a restricted domain. This approach might be labelled the *time–space synthesis*. The second approach assumes that neither of the above models is valid, but that some third model in which relative prices adjust only with a pronounced lag is the only legitimate framework. This approach might be labelled the *lagged-adjustment synthesis*.

The time–space synthesis

As noted immediately above a synthesis of these two competing models can be realized by arguing that the behaviour implied by the neo-Walrasian model is appropriate to one time and/or place and that the behaviour implied by the neo-Keynesian model is appropriate to another time and/or place. There are two variants of this synthesis: one which stresses the time dimension and one which stresses the spatial dimension.

The synthesis which stresses time is the older. Put simply this synthesis suggests that when the conomy is functioning in the neighbourhood of the natural or Walrasian equilibrium, the neo-Walrasian model is operative. However, when the economy is functioning somewhat below this level, the neo-Keynesian model is operative. An equally important part of this synthesis is the further argument that the coefficients of the separate models are related to 'the phase of the cycle'. For the moment, at least, this cycle oriented synthesis, which is frequently associated with Tobin (1980) has receded into the background.

A more recent synthesis stresses the spatial or rather sectoral dimension. In this synthesis it is argued that some sectors of the economy are characterized by neo-Walrasian behaviour, while at the same time other sectors are characterized by neo-Keynesian behavior. These respective divisions or markets are labelled flexprice and fixprice by Hicks (1974) and auction and customer by Okun (1981). Attempts to offer a simple macro model which combines these two market structures have been proposed by Ackley (1959), by Okun (1981), and by Schlagenhauf and Shupp (1978). One of the attractions of this synthesis is that it allows for the construction of a plausible stagflation argument.

The reasons some markets respond in a fixprice manner and others in a flexprice manner are numerous, complex, and not yet fully understood, but in general pricing behaviour appears to be determined by the organization of the market and the technology of production. More particularly flexprice markets are characterized by (i) large stocks held by middlemen or speculators, (ii) a short-run pricing perspective, (iii) high rent and low labour intensities, and (iv) a supply response which faithfully reflects prevailing relative prices. On the other hand, fixprice markets are characterized by (i) producer-sellers, (ii) a longer-run pricing or profit maximizing perspective, and (iii) relatively high labour intensities. Agriculture and commodity markets are representative of flexprice behaviour, while motor-car and steel markets are representative of fixprice behaviour.

A version of this fixprice–flexprice model which is based on the Schlagenhauf and Shupp study cited above is given by

$$q_A^D = q_A^* + \beta_1(R - R^*) + \beta_2(p_A - p_C) + v_1, \quad \beta_1 \leqslant 0, \beta_2 \leqslant 0 \tag{8.2.23}$$

$$q_A^S = q_A^* + \lambda_3(p_A - p_A^e) + v_2, \quad \lambda_3 \geqslant 0 \tag{8.2.24}$$

$$x = x^* + \beta(R - R^*) + \rho(q_A^S - q_A^*) + v_3, \quad \beta \leqslant 0, \rho \geqslant 0 \tag{8.2.25}$$

$$w = p^e|(x = x^*) + \lambda_2(x - x^*), \quad \lambda_2 \geqslant 0 \tag{8.2.26}$$

$$p_C = \theta_1 p_A + \theta_2 p_C + \theta_3 w, \quad \theta_1 \geqslant 0, \quad \theta_2 \geqslant 0, \theta_3 \geqslant 0, \sum_{j=1}^{3} \theta_j = 1 \tag{8.2.27}$$

$$p = \pi p_A + (1 - \pi)p_C, \quad 0 \leqslant \pi \leqslant 1 \tag{8.2.28}$$

$$m = p + \delta x + \varepsilon(I - I^*) \tag{8.2.29}$$

and

$$R = I - p^e, \tag{8.2.30}$$

where the subscripts A and C denote respectively the flexprice or auction market and the fixprice or customer market, and where the θ_j denote the factor cost shares of the auction good, customer good and labour respectively. These shares must sum to one. The parameter π denotes the output share of the auction good, the β_j and λ_j denote the relevant demand and supply elasticities, and the v_j denote the relevant disturbances. The variables q_A^D, q_A^S, and q_A^* denote respectively demand growth, supply growth, and natural growth rates of the flexprice good.

The *flexprice* sector is given by Equations (8.2.23) and (8.2.24). These equations correspond to the neo-Walrasian model given by Equations (8.2.2) and (8.2.7). The demand relation (8.2.23) has been modified to include a relative price term. The *fixprice* sector is defined by Equations (8.2.25)–(8.2.28). These equations correspond to the neo-Keynesian model given by Equations (8.2.2) and (8.2.11). Equation (8.2.25) includes the term $\rho(q_A^S - q_A^*)$ which corrects for the fact that flexprice sector disturbances and responses differ from those which occur in the fixprice sector and which are incorporated in the remaining terms of this equation. In this equation ρ is the flexprice sector's share of total output. The set (8.2.26–8.2.28) replaces (8.2.11) in which the implicit mark-up relation is $p = w$. The mark-up relationship appropriate to the posited flexprice–fixprice economy is given by (8.2.27) and the necessary price index by (8.2.28). The money market equations (8.2.29) and (8.2.30) are identical to Equations (8.2.4) and (8.2.5) above

The Lagged adjustment synthesis

A very different synthesis of the neo-Walrasian and neo-Keynesian models derives from the argument that the latter is appropriate to the very short run and the former to the very long run. It is presumed therefore that there exists an intermediate run period in which either price expectations or relative prices are sticky. The term *temporary equilibrium* is often associated with the former (that is sticky price expectations) while the term *disequilibrium* is sometimes associated with the latter.

The *temporary equilibrium* argument is clearly the more neo-Walrasian. Relative prices adjust rather promptly to short-run market forces but price expectations which also constitute an important decision argument adjust more slowly. This analysis is associated with the work of Hicks (1939) and of Arrow and Hahn (1971). Price (inflation) expectations are revised only when the initial expectations prove to be wrong, that is when the market clearing prices prove to be different from those anticipated. In this scenario, prices adjust more rapidly than do price expectations. The comparative static framework employed above is ill-equipped to accommodate this development. What is required is a framework which provides for non-uniform lagged responses of prices and price expectations.

One popular macroeconomic application of this temporary equilibrium argument which incorporates a specific lag structure for price expectations is the adaptive expectation hypothesis employed by Friedman (1968). In the Friedman framework prices adjust promptly to excess demand but expectations adjust more slowly and only in response to past price behaviour. This adaptive expectation hypothesis can be given by either

$$\frac{dp^e}{dt} = \tau_1(p_t - p_t^e), \quad \tau_1 \geqslant 0, \tag{8.2.31}$$

or

$$p_{t+1}^e = p_t^e + \tau_2(p_t - p_t^e) \quad \tau_2 \geqslant 0. \tag{8.2.32}$$

It is easy to show that the latter is equivalent to

$$p_{t+1}^e = \tau_2[p_t + (1 - \tau_2)p_{t-1} + (1 - \tau_2)^2 p_{t-2} + \cdots], \tag{8.2.32'}$$

where τ denotes the adaptation coefficient which governs the speed of adjustment. In this Friedman model the neutrality argument holds only in the long run when inflationary expectations catch up with the rate of inflation.

In the *disequilibrium* model, on the other hand, it is relative prices (not price expectations) which are assumed to adapt only slowly to excess demand considerations. Two of the most familiar studies dealing with this subject are by Fischer (1977) and by Phelps and Taylor (1977).[7] The models in these two papers assume that nominal wages are set for a number of periods in advance, while nominal prices are determined each period in response to current excess demand conditions. This wage stickiness derives from forward contracting which is typically justified in terms of transaction or information (search) costs.

In a simple model in which individual contracts are made for both the current period and the succeeding one and in which there are overlapping contracts, average wage behaviour is given by

$$w_t = \psi p_t^e + (1 - \psi)p_{t-1}^e + [\psi(x_t - x_t^*) + (1 - \psi)(x_{t-1} - x_{t-1}^*)]/\lambda, \quad (8.2.33)$$

where ψ denotes the fraction of contracts negotiated in period t and $1 - \psi$ the fraction settled in period $t - 1$.

The wage behaviour exhibited by Equation (8.2.33) can also be derived starting from negotiated wage settlements in which relative wages constitute an important argument. If, for example, the peer labour group has settled in period $t - 1$ on the basis of the expected inflation and labour market conditions prevailing at that time, then $(1 - \psi)$ can be interpreted as the weight given to this relativities argument, and ψ as the weight given to the standard Phillips Curve argument implicit in (8.2.7) or (8.2.9).

Assume further, as above, that demand is governed by (8.2.6). It follows directly from (8.2.6) and (8.2.33) that

$$x_t = \frac{\Lambda}{\Gamma} \left\{ \left(1 + \frac{\beta\psi}{\varepsilon\lambda} \right) x_t^* + \frac{\beta}{\varepsilon} m_t - \left(\beta + \frac{\beta\psi}{\varepsilon} \right) p_t^e + \beta\phi_t + v_t \right.$$
$$\left. + \frac{\beta}{\varepsilon}(1 - \psi)[p_{t-1}^e - (x_{t-1} - x_{t-1}^*)] \right\}. \quad (8.2.34)$$

Unlike in its counterpart equation (8.2.12) discussed above, in this relationship output growth x_t is a function of both p_t^e and p_{t-1}^e. Moreover, only the expected inflation rate p_t^e is a function of current policy. Consequently policy, even if fully anticipated, can influence the growth rate of real output x_t.

The intuitive explanation of this result is straightforward. For example, a fully anticipated expansionary monetary policy will raise both the inflation rate and the expected inflation rate. Wage settlements made in the current year will also reflect the higher rate of inflation. However, those contracted in the previous year will not. Consequently price increases will exceed *average* wage increases. This raises the profit rate which induces suppliers to increase output beyond the natural rate of increase. Again in this situation the *neutrality argument* is invalid.

8.3. COMPARATIVE DYNAMICS AND THE CORRESPONDENCE PRINCIPLE

The analysis in the first half of this chapter is a comparative static analysis—an *ex ante–ex post* equilibrium analysis. However, the concern of this chapter— short-term macroeconomics—is also properly the dynamic behaviour which connects these two equilibria. There is, of course, some sort of correspondence between the static analysis treated above and the dynamic analysis outlined below. This relationship is summarized by Samuelson's (1947) correspondence principle, one form of which can be stated informally as

> It is possible to infer the effects of certain parameter shifts in a dynamic model from the corresponding static model only if the dynamic model is itself inherently stable.[8]

It is this form of the correspondence principle which serves to both motivate and integrate the second half of this survey.

8.3.1. Static and dynamic multipliers

A reduced form single equation specification of the two basic models discussed in section 8.2 above is given by

$$X = X^\alpha M^\eta E^\gamma, \quad \alpha, \eta, \gamma \geqslant 0, \tag{8.3.1}$$

where X, M and E are respectively the levels of income (output), money, and autonomous expenditure and where α, η, and γ are the relevant output elasticities. In the neo-Walrasian version of the model the elasticity η is zero when changes in the money stock are anticipated. It is non-zero if the change is only partially anticipated. In the neo-Keynesian model η is non-zero in either event, but smaller when the change in the money stock is partially or fully anticipated.

The model given by (8.3.1) can be rewritten in percentage change or growth form as

$$x = \frac{\gamma e + \eta m}{1 - \alpha}, \tag{8.3.2}$$

where $x \equiv \dot{X}/X$, $m \equiv \dot{M}/M$ and $e \equiv \dot{E}/E$, or, expressing the model in terms of deviations from Walrasian equilibrium growth, as

$$x = x^* + \frac{\eta(m - m^*)}{1 - \alpha} + v, \tag{8.3.3}$$

where x^*, m^* and e^* are the natural or Walrasian equilibrium growth rates and where the real disturbance v is defined by $v \equiv \gamma(e - e^*)/1 - \alpha$.

In either of the above specifications the expenditure and money multipliers are given respectively by

$$\frac{\partial x}{\partial e} = \frac{\gamma}{1 - \alpha} \text{ and } \frac{\partial x}{\partial m} = \frac{\eta}{1 - \alpha}. \tag{8.3.4}$$

Since the aggregate output function is expressed in growth terms, these comparative static multipliers are expressed in terms of the income elasticity rather than in terms of the more familiar income propensity to spend. It is immediately evident that the multipliers are nonnegative and finite as long as this elasticity is strictly less than one.

A *dynamic* formulation (using a difference equation structure) of this same model is given by [see I, §14.12]

$$x_t = \alpha x_{t-1} + \eta m_t + \gamma e_t. \tag{8.3.5}$$

The most common rationale for the dynamic framework given immediately above is some form of the permanent income hypothesis of consumption and investment. This dynamic framework however is also consistent with any number of other consumption and investment hypotheses; in particular, it is consistent with Keynes's absolute income hypothesis when this hypothesis is coupled with a common Keynesian argument that supply follows demand with a one period lag. The same lag arguments are also appropriate to a Walrasian world.

The solution to the difference equation (8.3.5) is given by

$$x_t = \alpha^t x_0 + \alpha^{t-1}(\eta m_1 + \gamma e_1) + \alpha^{t-2}(\eta m_2 + \gamma e_2) + \cdots + (\eta m_t + \gamma e_t), \tag{8.3.6}$$

[see I, §14.13] from which it follows that the impact, second period, and $(n+1)$th period multipliers are given respectively by

$$\frac{\partial x_t}{\partial m_t} = \eta, \quad \frac{\partial x_{t+1}}{\partial m_t} = \alpha\eta, \quad \text{and} \quad \frac{\partial x_{t+n}}{\partial m_t} = \alpha^n\eta.$$

It is evident from this construction that the *cumulative multiplier*, $\partial \bar{x}_n/\partial m_1$ defined as the effect over n periods of the change in the money growth rate in period 1 is given by [see IV, Example 1.2.6]

$$\frac{\partial \bar{x}_n}{\partial m_1} = \eta(1 + \alpha + \alpha^2 + \cdots + \alpha^{n-1}) = \frac{\eta(1 - \alpha^n)}{1 - \alpha}. \tag{8.3.7}$$

Furthermore, if a constant level of money expenditure growth is sustained indefinitely, it follows that (8.3.6) can be rewritten as

$$x_t = \alpha^t x_0 + \frac{1 - \alpha^{t-1}}{1 - \alpha}(\eta\bar{m} + \gamma\bar{e}). \tag{8.3.6'}$$

It is immediately apparent from this that the *steady-state multiplier* $\partial x_n/\partial \bar{m}$ defined as the multiplied impact in period n of a sustained change in money growth is given by

$$\frac{\partial x_n}{\partial \bar{m}} = \eta\frac{(1 - \alpha^n)}{1 - \alpha}. \tag{8.3.8}$$

It is also apparent from comparing (8.3.7) and (8.3.8) that these two quite different multipliers (the cumulative response over n periods to a change in money growth in period one, and the nth period response to a sustained change in money growth covering n periods) are numerically the same. Furthermore if the dynamic system is stable, that is if $-1 < \alpha < 1$, the limits of these two dynamic money multipliers (the cumulative multiplier $\partial \bar{x}_n / \partial m_1$ and the steady-state multiplier $\partial x_n / \partial \bar{m}$) *correspond* exactly to the comparative static money multiplier $\partial x / \partial m$ given in (8.3.4), that is [see IV, §1.2]

$$\operatorname*{Lim}_{n \to \infty} \partial \bar{x}_n / \partial m_1 = \operatorname*{Lim}_{n \to \infty} \partial x_n / \partial \bar{m} = \partial x / \partial m = \frac{\eta}{1 - \alpha}. \tag{8.3.9}$$

Similarly the limits of the cumulative and steady-state dynamic *expenditure* multipliers correspond to the comparative static expenditure multiplier and are given by

$$\operatorname*{Lim}_{n \to \infty} \partial \bar{x}_n / \partial e_1 = \operatorname*{Lim}_{n \to \infty} \partial x_n / \partial \bar{e} = \partial x / \partial e = \frac{\gamma}{1 - \alpha}. \tag{8.3.10}$$

Analogous results obtain for simultaneous equation systems [see I, §5.8]. The matrix counterpart of the comparative static model given by (8.3.2) is

$$\mathbf{x} = (\mathbf{I} - \mathbf{A})^{-1} (\mathbf{Bu} + \mathbf{Ce}), \tag{8.3.11}$$

where, for example, $\mathbf{x}' = (x, p)$, $\mathbf{u}' = (m, g)$ and g denotes the rate of growth of government expenditure. From (8.3.11) it follows that the matrix multipliers are

$$\frac{\partial \mathbf{x}}{\partial \mathbf{u}} = (\mathbf{I} - \mathbf{A})^{-1} \mathbf{B} \quad \text{and} \quad \frac{\partial \mathbf{x}}{\partial \mathbf{e}} = (\mathbf{I} - \mathbf{A})^{-1} \mathbf{C}. \tag{8.3.12}$$

Similarly the matrix counterpart to the dynamic model given by (8.3.5) is

$$\mathbf{x}_t = \mathbf{A} \mathbf{x}_{t-1} + \mathbf{B} \mathbf{u}_t + \mathbf{C} \mathbf{e}_t, \tag{8.3.13}$$

from which it follows that for sustained levels of $\bar{\mathbf{u}}$ and $\bar{\mathbf{e}}$ that

$$\mathbf{x}_t = \mathbf{A}^t \mathbf{x}_0 + (\mathbf{I} - \mathbf{A})^{-1} (\mathbf{I} - \mathbf{A}^{t-1}) (\mathbf{B} \bar{\mathbf{u}} + \mathbf{C} \bar{\mathbf{e}}). \tag{8.3.14}$$

Again assuming stability, that is that $\mathbf{A}^t \to 0$ as $t \to \infty$, it follows that the limits of the steady-state policy and disturbance multipliers are given respectively by

$$\operatorname*{Lim}_{n \to \infty} \frac{\partial \mathbf{x}_n}{\partial \bar{\mathbf{u}}} = (\mathbf{I} - \mathbf{A})^{-1} \mathbf{B}, \quad \text{and} \quad \operatorname*{Lim}_{n \to \infty} \frac{\partial \mathbf{x}_n}{\partial \bar{\mathbf{e}}} = (\mathbf{I} - \mathbf{A})^{-1} \mathbf{C}. \tag{8.3.15}$$

The exact *correspondence* between the static multipliers and the limits of the dynamic multipliers follows from (8.3.12) and (8.3.15).

A second illustration of the correspondence principle involves an explicit optimizing framework [see IV, §15.1]. Assume that the policy maker wishes to maximize a welfare function given by

$$W = \tfrac{1}{2} x^2 - \tfrac{1}{2} r m^2, \quad r \geqslant 0 \tag{8.3.16}$$

Subject to

$$x = \alpha x + \eta m + \gamma e,$$

where r is a subjective weight such that rm/x defines the policy maker's estimate of the rate of substitution between growth in real output and growth in the money stock. The latter can be viewed as a proxy for inflation.

Given the static setting the optimal money growth $m^\dagger$ and optimal real growth $x^\dagger$ can be readily calculated using ordinary differential calculus [see IV, §3.5] (assuming that the relevant second order conditions hold) as

$$m^\dagger = \frac{-\eta\gamma e}{\eta^2 - r(1-\alpha)^2},$$

(8.3.17)

and

$$x^\dagger = \frac{r(1-\alpha)\gamma e}{\eta^2 - r(1-\alpha)^2}.$$

(8.3.18)

The dynamic formulation of this same problem is given by

$$\text{Max } W \equiv \sum_{t=1}^{T} \tfrac{1}{2}x_{t-1}^2 - \tfrac{1}{2}rm_t^2$$

(8.3.19)

Subject to

$$x_t = \alpha x_{t-1} + \eta m_t + \gamma e_t,$$

where T is the length of the planning horizon.

The problem can be solved using either dynamic programming [see IV, Chapter 16] or the Pontryagin maximum principle [see Engineering Guide, §14.11]. If the latter technique is employed, the relevant Hamiltonian is given by

$$H_t \equiv \tfrac{1}{2}x_{t-1}^2 - \tfrac{1}{2}rm_t^2 + \lambda_t(\alpha x_{t-1} + \eta m_t + \gamma e_t),$$

(8.3.20)

where λ_t is the Euler–Lagrange multiplier [see IV, §17.4]. The solution to (8.3.20) requires maximizing the Hamiltonian and simultaneously satisfying the two canonical equations defined by $x_t \equiv \partial H/\partial \lambda_t$ and $\lambda_{t-1} \equiv \partial H/\partial x_{t-1}$. These conditions are given by

(i) $\qquad\qquad\qquad \partial H/\partial m_t = -rm_t + \eta\lambda_t = 0^9$

(ii) $\qquad\qquad\qquad x_t \equiv \dfrac{\partial H}{\partial \lambda_t} = \alpha x_{t-1} + \eta m_t + \gamma e_t$ (8.3.21)

(iii) $\qquad\qquad\qquad \lambda_{t-1} \equiv \dfrac{\partial H}{\partial x_{t-1}} = x_{t-1} + \alpha\lambda_t$

It is evident from (8.3.21) that the policy rule given by $m_t = (\eta/r)\lambda_t$ is a time variant one because λ_t varies according to (8.3.21iii). However, if a *steady-state* solution exists, then that solution is characterized by $\lambda_t = \lambda_{t-1}$ and $x_t = x_{t-1}$, which implies that

$$m_t^\dagger = \frac{-\eta\gamma e_t}{\eta^2 - r(1-\alpha)^2},$$

(8.3.22)

and

$$x_t^\dagger = \frac{r(1 - \alpha)\gamma e_t}{\eta^2 - r(1 - \alpha)^2}. \tag{8.3.23}$$

It follows from the essential equivalence of Equations (8.3.17) and (8.3.22), and of (8.3.18) and (8.3.23) respectively that the optimal static and the optimal dynamic steady-state behaviour is the same. More particularly the comparative static and the dynamic steady-state expenditure multipliers correspond exactly and are given by

$$\frac{\partial x^\dagger}{\partial e} = \frac{\partial x_t^\dagger}{\partial e_t} = \frac{r(1 - \alpha)\gamma}{\eta^2 - r(1 - \alpha)^2}.\,^{10} \tag{8.3.24}$$

Analogous results obtain for optimizing systems based on simultaneous equation models. The matrix counterpart to the comparative static model given by (8.3.16) above is itself given by

$$\text{Min } W = \tfrac{1}{2}\mathbf{x}'\mathbf{Q}\mathbf{x} + \tfrac{1}{2}\mathbf{u}'\mathbf{R}\mathbf{u} \tag{8.3.25}$$

subject to

$$\mathbf{x} = \mathbf{A}\mathbf{x} + \mathbf{B}\mathbf{u} + \mathbf{C}\mathbf{e},$$

where $\mathbf{Q}$ and $\mathbf{R}$ are positive definite weighting matrices [see I, §9.2].

The optimal state vector $\mathbf{x}^\dagger$ can be obtained using the ordinary differential calculus and is given by

$$\mathbf{x}^\dagger = [\mathbf{B}'\mathbf{Q}\mathbf{B} - (\mathbf{I} - \mathbf{A})'\mathbf{R}(\mathbf{I} - \mathbf{A})]^{-1}(\mathbf{I} - \mathbf{A})'\mathbf{R}\mathbf{C}\mathbf{e} \tag{8.3.26}$$

Similarly the related dynamic model is given by

$$\text{Min } W = \sum_{t=1}^{T} \tfrac{1}{2}\mathbf{x}_t'\mathbf{Q}\mathbf{x}_t + \tfrac{1}{2}\mathbf{u}_t'\mathbf{R}\mathbf{u}_t \tag{8.3.27}$$

subject to

$$\mathbf{x}_t = \mathbf{A}\mathbf{x}_{t-1} + \mathbf{B}\mathbf{u}_t + \mathbf{C}\mathbf{e}_t.$$

As above the maximum principle can be employed to find optimal policy rules. The *steady-state* optimal solution to (8.3.27) is given by

$$\mathbf{x}_t^\dagger = [\mathbf{B}'\mathbf{Q}\mathbf{B} - (\mathbf{I} - \mathbf{A})'\mathbf{R}(\mathbf{I} - \mathbf{A})]^{-1}(\mathbf{I} - \mathbf{A})'\mathbf{R}\mathbf{C}\mathbf{e}_t. \tag{8.3.28}$$

Since (8.3.26) and (8.3.28) are essentially the same, their respective matrix multipliers must also correspond. Again, in this instance, the correspondence principle applies only in the presence of a steady-state solution.

These multiplier examples of the correspondence principle illustrate its inherent usefulness and also its inherent weakness. The principle can be used to infer steady-state dynamic properties of a relatively complex model from its comparative static solution. This is a very attractive property—particularly when dealing with rational expectation models. This application, however, requires a prior knowledge that the system is stable. The primary weakness of the principle is that it provides almost no information about the equally important transient behaviour of the system. A corollary of this observation is that policy measures based on the comparative static or steady-state properties of an economic model are quite likely to be suboptimal and can even be counterproductive.

8.3.2. Controllability

As indicated above, both the neo-Walrasian and the neo-Keynesian model of section 8.2 can be given by the matrix equation

$$\mathbf{x} = \mathbf{A}\mathbf{x} + \mathbf{B}\mathbf{u} + \mathbf{C}\mathbf{e}, \tag{8.3.29}$$

where $\mathbf{x}' = (x, p)$ and $\mathbf{u} = m$.

Suppose further that the policy maker has identified target values of real growth and inflation denoted by x^+ and p^+ respectively, and wishes to know whether these targets can be achieved with the single policy instrument m. Formally this question is equivalent to asking whether there exists a vector $\mathbf{u}$ which satisfies

$$\mathbf{x}^+ = \mathbf{x} = (\mathbf{I} - \mathbf{A})^{-1}(\mathbf{B}\mathbf{u} + \mathbf{C}\mathbf{e}), \tag{8.3.30}$$

or equivalently

$$\mathbf{D}\mathbf{u} = \mathbf{k}, \tag{8.3.30'}$$

where $\mathbf{D} \equiv (\mathbf{I} - \mathbf{A})^{-1}\mathbf{B}$, and $\mathbf{k} \equiv \mathbf{x}^+ - (\mathbf{I} - \mathbf{A})^{-1}\mathbf{C}\mathbf{e}$.

As is well known the system given by (8.3.30') has a non-trivial solution and therefore is said to be controllable if and only if the rank of $\mathbf{D}$ equals the rank of $(\mathbf{D}, \mathbf{k})$ [see I, §5.6 and Engineering Guide, §14.10]. In this particular application it is obvious that the rank of $\mathbf{D}$ is constrained by the number of policy instruments n. Also since the matrix $\mathbf{D}, \mathbf{k}$ contains the target column, its rank can not exceed the number of target variables m. Consequently the rank argument implies that the number of policy instruments n must at least equal the number of target variables m if a solution is to exist. This existence or controllability argument for the comparative static case was first enunciated by Tinbergen (1952). In this particular illustration the controllability requirement is not met. The rank of $\mathbf{D}$ is one while the rank of $\mathbf{D}, \mathbf{k}$ is two, that is only one policy instrument, money growth, is available to meet two targets, real output growth and the inflation rate.

As noted above, dynamic versions of neo-Walrasian and neo-Keynesian models can be given by

$$\mathbf{x}_t = \mathbf{A}\mathbf{x}_{t-1} + \mathbf{B}\mathbf{u}_t + \mathbf{C}\mathbf{e}_t, \tag{8.3.31}$$

which has a solution form

$$\mathbf{x}_t = \mathbf{A}^t\mathbf{x}_0 + \mathbf{A}^{t-1}(\mathbf{B}\mathbf{u}_1 + \mathbf{C}\mathbf{e}_1) + \mathbf{A}^{t-2}(\mathbf{B}\mathbf{u}_2 + \mathbf{C}\mathbf{e}_2) + \cdots + \mathbf{A}^{t-n}(\mathbf{B}\mathbf{u}_n + \mathbf{C}\mathbf{e}_n). \tag{8.3.32}$$

One-period controllability, that is achieving the target vector $\mathbf{x}^+$ in period 1, thus requires a solution to

$$\mathbf{x}_1^+ = \mathbf{x}_1 = \mathbf{A}\mathbf{x}_0 + \mathbf{B}\mathbf{u}_1 + \mathbf{C}\mathbf{e}_1 \qquad (8.3.33)$$

or

$$(\mathbf{x}^+ - \mathbf{A}\mathbf{x}_0 - \mathbf{C}\mathbf{e}_1) = \mathbf{k} = \mathbf{B}\mathbf{u}_1.$$

But, as above, (8.3.33) has a non-trivial solution $\mathbf{u}$ only if the rank of $\mathbf{B}$ equals the rank of $\mathbf{B}, \mathbf{k}$. Since the rank of $\mathbf{B}, \mathbf{k}$ is equal to the number of target variables m and the rank of $\mathbf{B}$ is constrained by the number of policy variables n, this one-period controllability corresponds to the comparative static criterion.

The same approach can be used to show that the criterion for two-period and more generally N-period controllability, that is achieving the target variables every second or Nth period, are given respectively by

$$\text{rank}\,[\mathbf{AB} \quad \mathbf{B}] \geqslant m, \text{ and} \qquad (8.3.34)$$

$$\text{rank}\,[\mathbf{A}^{N-1}\mathbf{B} \quad \mathbf{A}^{N-2}\mathbf{B} \quad \ldots \quad \mathbf{AB} \quad \mathbf{B}] \geqslant m,$$

where $[\mathbf{AB} \quad \mathbf{B}]$ is the matrix $\mathbf{AB}$ augmented with the matrix $\mathbf{B}$ [see I, §5.10].

Since the rank of $\mathbf{B}$ is n, the rank of $(\mathbf{AB} \quad \mathbf{B})$ could easily be $2n$. This apparent relaxation of the rule that the number of policy instruments must at least equal the number of target variables is easily explained. When a two-period planning horizon is considered, each policy instrument is used twice and therefore counts as two instruments. The above result, however, is somewhat deceptive since targets are met only after two periods and every second period thereafter. If all targets are to be achieved in each period, the Tinbergen requirement must be retained.

Perfect controllability can also be shown in the context of a long-run steady-state target. The long-run steady-state solution to (8.3.31) above is given by (8.3.14). Given the assumed inherent (asymptotic) stability of the system, that is $\mathbf{A}^t \to 0$ as $t \to \infty$, it follows that

$$(\mathbf{I} - \mathbf{A})^{-1}\mathbf{B}\bar{\mathbf{u}} = (\mathbf{x}^+ - \mathbf{A}^t\mathbf{x}_0 - (\mathbf{I} - \mathbf{A})^{-1}\mathbf{C}\bar{\mathbf{e}}) \equiv \mathbf{k}. \qquad (8.3.35)$$

Controllability thus requires that the rank of $[(\mathbf{I} - \mathbf{A})^{-1}\mathbf{B}]$ equal the rank of $[(\mathbf{I} - \mathbf{A})^{-1}\mathbf{B}, \mathbf{k}]$. This result is identical to the comparative static condition. The correspondence principle is thus seen to apply to questions of controllability. A more complete discussion of controllability is found in Aoki and Canzoneri (1979).

8.3.3. The assignment problem

Even if a system or model is perfectly controllable it is unlikely that policies will be pursued with sufficient vigour to achieve each target in each period. The logic of this claim is straightforward. Perfect controllability requires the use of as many policy instruments as there are target variables. Optimizing requires balancing the costs of employing these policy instruments against the benefits of improved target performance. Consequently only if the instrument costs are near zero will these instruments be used intensively enough to meet all targets in every period.

The more conventional approach to policy making is to employ simple ad hoc rules. Hopefully these rules imply at least asymptotic controllability; this guarantees that once the target is achieved it is maintained. The relevant test therefore is an asymptotic stability test.

Consider again the model employed above but in this instance with the autonomous term set to zero. This yields

$$x_t = Ax_{t-1} + Bu_t, \tag{8.3.13'}$$

Assume furthermore that policy behaviour is governed by the linear control rule

$$u_t = Gx_{t-1}. \tag{8.3.36}$$

If the elements of x_t and u_t are interpreted as deviations from targeted values of the state and policy variables respectively, this rule implies that discretionary policy intensity is proportional to the relevant target gaps.

Substituting (8.3.36) into (8.3.13') yields

$$x_t = (A + BG)x_{t-1}, \tag{8.3.37}$$

which has the solution

$$x_t = (A + BG)^t x_0. \tag{8.3.38}$$

It is evident from this construction that the system is stable if and only if all the characteristic roots of $A + BG$ lie within the unit circle. However since the authorities select both the sign and magnitude of the elements of G, they can ensure that this condition is always in fact met. It is possible that meeting this condition implies a large g_{ij}. In this event the rule loses much of its intuitive appeal since this implies the extravagant use of the ith policy measure.

The policy rule given by (8.3.36) contains the implicit assumption that all or most of the elements of G are non-zero, that is there is the assumption that the response of *each* instrument is related to the attainment of each and every target. Mundell (1962) has argued that, in practice, particular policy instruments are often *assigned to* (or paired with) particular targets or objectives, and that the change in the intensity of any policy response is often related to the assigned target gap. This implies a policy rule given by

$$\frac{du}{dt} = Gx_t, \tag{8.3.39}$$

where the matrix G is diagonal. Mundell has shown that if this rule is observed, and that if, in addition, policy instruments are always assigned to those targets with which they have a *comparative advantage*, asymptotic stability is guaranteed.

The sufficiency of the *comparative advantage* criterion can be readily demonstrated. Recall the chain rule

$$\frac{d\mathbf{x}}{dt} = \frac{d\mathbf{x}}{d\mathbf{u}} \cdot \frac{d\mathbf{u}}{dt}, \tag{8.3.40}$$

and that from the matrix analogue of (8.3.7) that the asymptotic cumulative matrix multiplier $\partial \mathbf{x}_n / \partial \mathbf{u}_1$ is given by

$$\frac{\partial \bar{\mathbf{x}}_n}{\partial \mathbf{u}_1} = (\mathbf{I} - \mathbf{A})^{-1}\mathbf{B}. \tag{8.3.41}$$

Invoking the correspondence principle and substituting (8.3.41) and (8.3.39) into (8.3.40) yields

$$\frac{d\mathbf{x}}{dt} = \mathbf{HG}\mathbf{x}_t, \tag{8.3.42}$$

where $\mathbf{H} \equiv (\mathbf{I} - \mathbf{A})^{-1}\mathbf{B}$.

If only two targets and two instruments are involved, the matrix $\mathbf{HG}$ is of the form

$$\mathbf{HG} \equiv \begin{pmatrix} h_{11}g_{11} & h_{12}g_{22} \\ h_{21}g_{11} & h_{22}g_{22} \end{pmatrix}$$

Since (8.3.42) is a differential equation, stability requires that the real roots of the eigenvalues of $\mathbf{HG}$ be negative [see IV, Theorem 7.9.5]. A necessary and sufficient condition for this is that the trace of $\mathbf{HG}$ be negative and the determinant of $\mathbf{HG}$ be positive [see I, §7.3], or that (i) $h_{11}g_{11} + h_{22}g_{22} < 0$ and (ii) $h_{11}h_{22}g_{11}g_{22} - h_{12}h_{21}g_{11}g_{22} > 0$. Condition (i) holds if g_{11} and g_{22} are chosen to have the opposite sign to h_{11} and h_{22} respectively. Given that condition (i) holds by construction, condition (ii) is satisfied whenever $|h_{11}| \cdot |h_{22}| > |h_{12}| \cdot |h_{21}|$. This last condition implies comparative advantage, which is typically defined as $|h_{11}|/|h_{21}| > |h_{12}|/|h_{22}|$. In other words a stable assignment is attained, when each instrument is assigned to that target for which it has a relative advantage in effecting.

It should be noted that the comparative advantage criterion is expressed in terms of the cumulative (or steady-state) multipliers h_{ij} rather than the impact multipliers b_{ij}. It is therefore possible for an asymptotically stable assignment to generate perverse initial movements. For a more comprehensive treatment of the assignment argument the reader should consult Gapinski (1982) or Livesey (1980).

In his original article Mundell assigned monetary policy to the external payments gap and fiscal policy to the employment gap. More recently Wanniski (1975) has suggested assigning monetary policy to the inflation gap and fiscal policy to the employment gap. In a period of stagflation this implies a restrictive monetary policy and an expansionary fiscal policy. Even if this unusual assignment accords with the comparative advantage requirement and therefore implies asymptotic stability, there is, as we have seen above, no guarantee that the impact or short-run behaviour will not be perverse.

8.3.4. Lyapunov stability and optimal policy rules

One of the attractions of the ad hoc policy rule given by (8.3.36) and analysed above is that it is simple and intuitive. Yet as noted earlier ensuring stability can entail employing a matrix $\mathbf{G}$ containing an arbitrarily large element(s). This eventuality would render the rule unattractive since it implies a potentially massive use of some policy measure. A second approach to policy design is to replace these ad hoc rules with derived optimal rules in which instrument volatility is penalized.

Consider again the system given by (8.3.13′) and a criterion function given by (8.3.27) where, as above, $\mathbf{Q}$ and $\mathbf{R}$ are positive definite and where $\mathbf{x}_t$ and $\mathbf{u}_t$ represent deviations from the targeted values of the state and policy vectors respectively. The maximum principle can be used to show that under these conditions the optimal policy rule is given by

$$\mathbf{u}_t = \mathbf{G}_t \mathbf{x}_{t-1},\qquad(8.3.43)$$

where

$$\mathbf{G}_t = -(\mathbf{R} + \mathbf{B}'\mathbf{K}_t\mathbf{B})^{-1}\mathbf{B}'\mathbf{K}_t\mathbf{A},\qquad(8.3.44)$$

and where

$$\mathbf{K}_{t-1} = \mathbf{Q} + \mathbf{G}_t'\mathbf{R}\mathbf{G}_t + (\mathbf{A} + \mathbf{B}'\mathbf{G}_t)'\mathbf{K}_t(\mathbf{A} + \mathbf{B}'\mathbf{G}_t).^{[11]}\qquad(8.3.45)$$

Note that the optimal policy rule given by (8.3.43) differs from the ad hoc rule given by (8.3.36) in that the policy coefficient matrix $\mathbf{G}_t$ is time varying in the former and time invariant in the latter.

Substituting (8.3.43) into (8.3.13′) yields

$$\mathbf{x}_t = (\mathbf{A} + \mathbf{B}\mathbf{G}_t)\mathbf{x}_{t-1}.\qquad(8.3.46)$$

Given the indicated time varying $\mathbf{G}_t$, the direct test of stability employed above is inappropriate. The Lyapunov indirect test can, however, be used in this situation [IV, §7.11.5]. The relevant Lyapunov theorem states that a difference equation system is stable around $\mathbf{x}^*$ if a distance measure V exists such that

(i)	$V(\mathbf{x}) = 0$	for $\mathbf{x} = \mathbf{x}^*$
(ii)	$V(\mathbf{x}) > 0$	for $\mathbf{x} \neq \mathbf{x}^*$
(iii)	$V(\mathbf{x}) \to \infty$	for $\mathbf{x} \to \infty$
(iv)	$V(\mathbf{x}_t) - V(\mathbf{x}_{t-1}) < 0.$	

To test the stability of (8.3.46) above, define the distance function as

$$V_t \equiv \mathbf{x}_t'\mathbf{K}_t\mathbf{x}_t.\qquad(8.3.47)$$

If follows from (8.3.45) that $\mathbf{K}_t$ is positive definite because $\mathbf{Q}$ and $\mathbf{R}$ are [see I, §9.2]. This implies that (8.3.47) fulfils conditions (i), (ii) and (iii) outlined immediately above.

It also follows from this definition of V_t that

$$V_t - V_{t-1} = \mathbf{x}_t'\mathbf{K}_t\mathbf{x}_t - \mathbf{x}_{t-1}'\mathbf{K}_{t-1}\mathbf{x}_{t-1} \qquad (8.3.48)$$

Substituting (8.3.45) and (8.3.46) into (8.3.48) and rearranging yields

$$V_t - V_{t-1} = \mathbf{x}_{t-1}'(-\mathbf{Q} - \mathbf{G}_t'\mathbf{R}\mathbf{G}_t)\mathbf{x}_{t-1}. \qquad (8.3.49)$$

Since $\mathbf{Q}$ and $\mathbf{R}$ are both positive definite, the matrix $(-\mathbf{Q} - \mathbf{G}_t'\mathbf{R}\mathbf{G}_t)$ is negative definite, and therefore (8.3.49) satisfies condition (iv). All the conditions for stability are thus fulfilled, and it follows that the system is asymptotically controllable when the optimal policy rule given by (8.3.43) and (8.3.44) is employed. Because the criterion function (8.3.27) penalizes all deviations of the policy variables from their target level, instrument stability is also guaranteed. For a more rigorous direct test see Aoki (1976).

8.3.5. Income and price stability

To this point the test of inherent stability has been used only to validate the application of the correspondence principle. It is obvious, however, that stability plays a far more basic and fundamental role in economics than this. If an economic system is not inherently stable, its very life is threatened. In this section both a simple income and a simple price model are examined for stability. The latter is shown to be only marginally stable.

Assume that the relevant system can be modelled by (8.3.13). In this event inherent stability requires that $\mathbf{A}^t \to 0$ as $t \to \infty$. As noted above either the direct (characteristic root) test or the indirect (Lyapunov) test can be employed to determine whether or not this condition is satisfied. The direct test is used below.

Consider the aggregate real output model examined above and given by (8.3.5). This has the solution (8.3.6). If, in addition $m_t = \bar{m}$ and $e_t = \bar{e}$ for all t, (8.3.6) reduces to (8.3.6′).

The direct test of stability requires only that $-1 < \alpha < 1$, in which case it follows that

$$x_t \to \frac{\eta\bar{m} + \gamma\bar{e}}{1 - \alpha} \quad \text{as} \quad t \to \infty. \qquad (8.3.50)$$

Recall that in this model the parameter α is the income elasticity of expenditure. Since some income is saved and some taxed, the expenditure elasticity is always less than one (and more than zero), and therefore, the system given by (8.3.5) is inherently stable.

The situation is less clear for the analogous inflation model. Assume that the expectation augmented Phillips relationship is given by

$$w_t = \xi p_t^e + \kappa(x_t - x_t^*), \quad \xi > 0, \kappa > 0 \tag{8.3.51}$$

that the expectation formation equation is given by

$$p_t^e = \zeta p_{t-1}, \quad \zeta > 0 \tag{8.3.52}$$

and that the mark-up relationship is given by

$$p_t = w_t, \tag{8.3.53}$$

with w_t, p_t, p_t^e and x_t defined as above. It follows from (8.3.51) to (8.3.53) that the inflation rate p_t is given by

$$p_t = \xi\zeta p_{t-1} + \kappa(x_t - x_t^*), \tag{8.3.54}$$

which has the solution

$$p_t = (\xi\zeta)^t p_0 + (\xi\zeta)^{t-1}\kappa(x_1 - x_1^*) + (\xi\zeta)^{t-2}\kappa(x_2 - x_2^*) + \cdots + \kappa(x_t - x_t^*). \tag{8.3.55}$$

In this situation inherent stability requires that $-1 < \xi\zeta < 1$, or that either ξ or ζ or both are less than one. However, if wage increases fully compensate for expected inflation and if inflationary expectations fully reflect past inflation, both ξ and ζ equal one. This implies that $\xi\zeta = 1$ and that the system is only *razor edge* stable. In this case it follows from (8.3.55) that in the absence of any excess demand disturbances, that is in a situation in which $x_t = x_t^*$, the initial inflation rate p_0 is sustained indefinitely.

This same phenomenon characterizes the well-known *wage-price spiral*. Assume that the mark-up equation is rewritten as

$$p_t = w_{t-1}. \tag{8.3.53'}$$

In this case the inflation model is given by

$$\begin{pmatrix} w_t \\ p_t \end{pmatrix} = \begin{pmatrix} 0 & \xi\zeta \\ 1 & 0 \end{pmatrix} \begin{pmatrix} w_{t-1} \\ p_{t-1} \end{pmatrix} + \begin{pmatrix} \kappa(x_t - x_t^*) \\ 0 \end{pmatrix}. \tag{8.3.56}$$

Again if $\xi\zeta = 1$ it follows that, in the absence of any excess demand pressure, the initial level of wage and price inflation is sustained. The same essential argument also holds for the more general flexprice–fixprice model given by Equations (8.2.23) to (8.2.30). A dynamic version of the pricing sector of that model can be represented by (8.3.13), where $\mathbf{x}_t' = (p_{At}, p_{Ct}, w_t)$.

In this model the $\mathbf{A}$ matrix is a *stochastic matrix* [see I, Example 7.11.2], and therefore $\mathbf{A}^t$ converges to another probability matrix [see II, §19.3]. This implies that, in the absence of any disturbance, the initial inflation vector is *sustained* in some modified form rather than *damped*. This result obtains because, as above, it is assumed that wage increases and returns-to-capital fully compensate for expected inflation, that expected inflation fully reflects past inflation, that all factor costs are fully marked up, and that output demand is homogeneous of degree zero. Consequently there is no leakage comparable to the tax and saving leakage of the expenditure model.

The contrast between the *self-sustaining* inflation structure and the *damped* expenditure (output) structure is important. Indeed this difference is perhaps the major single reason why some economists are today more concerned with the inflation problem than with the employment (output) problem.

8.4. CONCLUDING REMARKS

As noted in the introduction, this survey is intuitive rather than rigorous, and the coverage is selective rather than comprehensive. Furthermore the models outlined above are extraordinarily simple. For example, no distinction is made between consumption and investment demand, or between private and public expenditure. Nor is any explicit allowance made for capital accumulation or technical progress. Instead, the Walrasian growth rate, to which the models of section 8.2 are anchored, is given exogenously. Another serious omission is the absence of any discussion of uncertainty or of international transactions.

Nonetheless the simple reduced form models developed above are useful in distinguishing between neo-Walrasian and neo-Keynesian behaviour, between static and dynamic conclusions, between output stability and price stability. Mathematical reasoning and modelling is useful in each of these areas because it enforces a consistency in terms of assumptions as well as in terms of consequences. Moreover, for more comprehensive models, especially those involving complex feedbacks and/or rational expectations, the mathematical approach appears to be the only feasible one.

All this notwithstanding, certain precautions must be observed when applying mathematics to macroeconomic analysis. Two come to mind immediately. First, simple and elegant mathematical models have an aesthetic appeal which often blinds the user to the models' shortcomings. Many macroeconomic phenomena are messy and can not be modelled both elegantly and accurately. This should always be kept in mind. Secondly, a mathematical statement typically implies that the posited relationship is *stable* in the sense of being invertible (including reversing the direction of causation). Not all macroeconomic relationships are stable in this sense. Consequently, each relationship should be examined in this context before it is included in a larger model.

8.5. NOTES

1. As Hahn (1980) has pointed out the IS–LM model is not a pure Walrasian construction since aggregate income is an important argument in this framework. Nonetheless both neo-Walrasian (monetarists) and neo-Keynesians have accepted it as an appropriate demand side statement.

2. Okun's Law can be derived by taking a Taylor series approximation of, for example, a Cobb–Douglas production function in which capital is held fixed in the short run.

3. Addressing this question of stable relationships and the related issue of causality remains an important research concern in macroeconomics. The interpretation of the money market equation (8.2.4) is just as controversial as the interpretation of the labour market equations (8.2.8) and (8.2.9). One school led by Sims (1980) believes these questions of interpretation can be resolved empirically.

4. In a more comprehensive framework such as the flexprice–fixprice model outlined below, the conditional rate of inflation may also be dependent on sectoral excess demand.

5. It follows of course that the Walrasian equilibrium condition given by

$$\partial Q/\partial N = W^*/P^* = -(\partial V/\partial N)/(\partial V/\partial Q),$$

where $\partial Q/\partial N$ is the marginal product of labour, W^*/P^* is the Walrasian real wage, and $(\partial V/\partial N)/(\partial V/\partial Q)$ is the marginal rate of substitution between the consumption of output and the supply of labour, may be satisfied only in the long run. In the short run this condition may be violated as the market clears to the short side. Keynes's own position regarding the posited cyclically invariant real wage is somewhat ambiguous in the *General Theory*. However, in a later clarifying article published in the *Economic Journal* (Keynes, 1939) his support is unequivocal.

6. The assumption that the size of the mark-up does not vary over the cycle does not imply that the same size mark-up is applied in all industries. The magnitude of the mark-up is often explained by limit pricing behaviour in which the price is set as high as possible without attracting any new firm into the industry. The limit price and therefore the size of the mark-up, is dependent on existing barriers-to-entry which are, in turn, related to economies-of-scale in production, distribution, and finance.

7. The term 'disequilibrium' is more typically associated with the studies of Barro and Grossman (1976), Malinvaud (1976) and Grandmont (1974). In these studies, relative prices are rigid as in the neo-Keynesian model above, rather than merely sticky as in the two studies cited.

8. The converse of this proposition, i.e. that unless certain restrictions are imposed on the underlying dynamic behaviour, it is not always possible to infer the actual effects of shifts in certain parameters from a comparative static analysis, is emphasized by some economists including Dernburg and Dernburg (1969) and Hansen (1970).

9. Equation (8.3.21i) is a necessary condition only for an interior maximum. It is often convenient to formulate the criterion function in deviation form, in which case all deviations (from, for example, the natural rates) are penalized. Since the criterion function is to be minimized and since all criterion function coefficients are positive, the necessary condition is also a sufficient one.

10. The optimizing multipliers given by (8.3.24) are smaller than their non-optimizing multipliers given by (8.3.10) because the former include an offsetting policy response while the latter do not. An increase in the direct cost of the policy reduces this offsetting action and therefore increases the size of the multiplier. This can be seen by differentiating (8.3.24) which yields

$$\frac{\partial\left(\dfrac{\partial x}{\partial e}\right)}{\partial r} = \frac{\eta^2(1-\alpha)e}{[n^2 - r(1-\alpha)^2]^2} > 0.$$

11. This is a standard result which can be found in Aoki (1976), Chow (1975), and Kendrick (1981).

8.6. REFERENCES

Ackley, G. (1959). Administered prices and the inflationary process. *American Economic Review*, **49**, 419–430.

Aoki, M. (1976). *Optimal control and system theory in dynamic economic analysis*. North-Holland, Amsterdam.

Aoki, M. and Canzoneri, M. (1979). Sufficient conditions for control of target variables and assignment of instruments in dynamic macroeconomic models. *International Economic Review*, **20**, 605–616.

Arrow, K. J. and Hahn, F. (1971). *General competitive analysis*. Holden-Day, San Francisco.

Barro, R. J. and Grossman, H. I. (1976). *Money, employment and inflation*. Cambridge University Press, Cambridge.

Chow, G. C. (1975). *Analysis and control of dynamic economic systems*. Wiley, New York.

Dernburg, T. F. and Dernburg, J. D. (1969). *Macroeconomic analysis*. Addison-Wesley, Reading, Mass.

Fischer, S. (1977). Long term contracts, rational expectations, and the optimal money supply rule. *Journal Political Economy*, **85**, 191–205.

Friedman, M. (1968). The role of monetary policy. *American Economic Review*, **58**, 1–17.

Gapinski, J. H. (1982). *Macroeconomic theory, statics, dynamics, and policy*. McGraw-Hill, New York.

Grandmont, J. (1974). On the short run equilibrium in a monetary economy, in J. Dreze (ed.), *Allocation under uncertainty, equilibrium, and optimality*. Wiley, New York.

Hahn, F. (1980). Monetarism and economic theory. *Economica*, **47**, 1–17.

Hansen, B. (1970). *A survey of general equilibrium systems*. McGraw-Hill, New York.

Hicks, J. R. (1939). *Value and capital*. Oxford University Press, London.

Hicks, J. R. (1974). *The crises in Keynesian economics*. Basic Books, New York.

Kendrick, D. A. (1981). *Stochastic control for economic models*. McGraw-Hill, New York.

Keynes, J. M. (1939). Relative movement of real wages and output. *Economic Journal*, **49**, 34–51.

Livesey, D. A. (1980). The uncertain foundations of fiscal policy, in G. A. Hughes and G. M. Heal (eds.), *Public policy and the tax system*. Allen & Unwin, London.

Lucas, R. E. (1976). Econometric policy evaluation: a critique, in K. Brunner and A. Meltzer (eds.), *The Phillips curve and labor markets*. North-Holland, Amsterdam.

Malinvaud, E. (1976). *The theory of unemployment reconsidered*. Blackwell, Oxford.

Mundell, R. A. (1962). The appropriate use of monetary and fiscal policy. *IMF Staff Papers*, **9**, 70–79.

Muth, J. F. (1961). Rational expectations and the theory of price movements, *Econometrica*, **29**, 315–335.

Nagatani, K. (1981). *Macroeconomic dynamics*. Cambridge University Press, Cambridge.

Okun, A. M. (1981). *Prices and quantities*. Brookings, Washington.

Phelps, E. S. and Taylor, J. G. (1977). Stabilizing powers of monetary policy under rational expectations. *Journal Political Economy*, **85**, 163–189.

Samuelson, P. A. (1947). *Foundations of economic analysis*. Harvard University Press, Cambridge, Mass.

Sargent, T. A. (1979). *Macroeconomic theory*. Academic, New York.

Schlagenhauf, D. and Shupp, F. R. (1978). Wage-price controls in a fixprice-flexprice model. *Annals Economic and Social Measurement*, **6**, 501–516.

Sims, C. A. (1980). Macroeconomics and reality. *Econometrica*, **48**, 1–48.

Tinbergen, J. (1952). *On the theory of economic policy*. North-Holland, Amsterdam.

Tobin, J. (1980). *Asset accumulation and economic activity*. Blackwell, Oxford.

Turnovsky, S. J. (1977). *Macroeconomic analysis and stabilization policy*. Cambridge University Press, Cambridge.

Wanniski, J. (1975). The Mundell–Laffer hypothesis—a new view of the world. *Public Interest*, **39**, 31–46.

Mathematical Methods in Economics
Edited by F. van der Ploeg
© 1984, John Wiley & Sons, Ltd.

9

The New Classical Macroeconomics: A Critical Exposition

M. H. PESARAN, *Trinity College, Cambridge, U.K.*

9.1. INTRODUCTION

The hallmark of the new classical macroeconomics is undoubtedly its 'policy neutrality' proposition which, broadly speaking, states that macroeconomic policy is at best innocuous and at worst de-stabilizing. Put more precisely the new classical school maintains that attempts at systematic changes in monetary policy will be ineffective with respect to real economic variables, and non-systematic policy changes that have real effects are undesirable since they increase the variability of the economic system around its full information equilibrium path. On the basis of this policy neutrality proposition the new classical economists see no rationale in the Keynesian-type macroeconomic policy interventions and argue that such interventions in market forces can only have harmful effects in the form of accelerating inflation and rising interest rates. The belief that market economies are self-regulating and hence self-curing is not, however, new and has its roots in the writings of the classical economists. The major claim of the new classical economics is that the policy neutrality proposition holds even in an uncertain economic environment. The present chapter is devoted to a critical exposition of the basic premises that lie behind this fundamental policy neutrality proposition. Such a critical appraisal is needed particularly now that the new classical policy prescriptions have acquired political prominence in government circles on both sides of the Atlantic.

The exposition starts with a description of the two basic building blocks of the new classical macroeconomic models, namely the 'natural rate hypothesis' and the 'rational expectations hypothesis'. We then consider the consequences of incorporating these two hypotheses within a simple IS–LM framework and show how under linearity and additive disturbances the policy neutrality proposition follows. Throughout, the limitations of the new classical framework and the extreme nature of its assumptions, in particular with respect to the learning process that must underline the formation of rational expectations, will be emphasized.

9.2. THE NATURAL RATE HYPOTHESIS

The natural rate hypothesis is a theory of aggregate supply which is founded on intertemporal substitution of work and leisure and postulates that economic agents with exogenously given tastes, technology and endowments base their supply decisions on perceived current and future wages and prices. Formalization of this theory has been attempted in the literature by a number of authors notably, Friedman (1968), Phelps (1970), Lucas and Rapping (1969), Lucas (1972a, 1973), Barro (1976) and Fischer (1977a), each basing their formulation on different theoretical grounds.

Friedman develops his 'natural rate of unemployment' hypothesis by extending the Wicksellian theory of the 'natural' rate of interest to the analysis of the labour market. The essence of the hypothesis is that the actual rate of unemployment can deviate from its natural rate only to the extent that price changes are unanticipated. When price changes are fully anticipated the actual rate of unemployment will become equal to the 'natural rate of unemployment' defined by Friedman (1968, p. 8) to be

> ...the level that would be ground out by the Walrasian system of general equilibrium equations, provided there is imbedded in them the actual structural characteristics of the labor and commodity markets, including market imperfections, stochastic variability in demands and supplies, the cost of gathering information about job vacancies and labour availabilities, the costs of mobility, and so on.

Friedman's rationale for the existence of a stable relationship between the deviation of the rate of unemployment from its natural level and unanticipated changes in prices is based on an assumed asymmetry in the response of demand and supply of labour to actual and expected real wages. The source of this asymmetry is Friedman's casual empiricism that product prices typically respond faster to an anticipated rise in nominal demand than do wages.

Alternatively, Friedman's natural rate hypothesis (NRH) can be derived from an expected inflation augmented Phillips Curve. While the original Phillips Curve postulates a stable relation between the rate of change of money wages and the rate of unemployment, the inflation augmented Phillips Curve refers to a spectrum of Phillips Curves each corresponding to a different expected rate of inflation. According to this modification of the Phillips Curve the formation of money wages is described by the following equation:

$$\dot{W}_t = \lambda \, {}_{t-1}\Pi_t^e + f(U_t), \quad f'(U_t) < 0, \quad \lambda > 0 \qquad (9.2.1)$$

where $\dot{W}_t = (W_t - W_{t-1})/W_{t-1}$, represents the rate change of money wages, $_{t-1}\Pi_t^e$ the expected rate of price changes formed at time $t-1$, U_t the actual rate of unemployment, and $f(U_t)$ the short-run Phillips Curve, postulated to have a negative slope. For each expected rate of inflation there exists a unique inverse relationship between the rate of change of money wages and the rate of unemployment. But when inflation expectations are formed endogenously, an attempt to exploit the short-run trade-off between unemployment and inflation causes a revision of inflation expectations and therefore alters the trade-off itself. Whether there will be a long-run trade-off between inflation and unemployment crucially depends on the magnitude of the reaction coefficient λ and the precise way that $_{t-1}\Pi_t^e$ is formed. We shall discuss the problem of the formation of inflation expectations in the next section. In order to see how the NRH can be derived from (9.2.1) it is analytically more convenient to approximate $\dot{W}_t$ and $_{t-1}\Pi_t^e$ by $w_t - w_{t-1}$ and $_{t-1}p_t^e - p_{t-1}$ respectively where w_t and p_t represent the logarithms of the money wage rate and the price level, in that order [see IV, §2.11]. Specifically we use a first order Taylor series expansion [see IV, §3.6] to approximate $w_t - w_{t-1} = \ln(W_t/W_{t-1}) \cong (W_t - W_{t-1})/W_{t-1} = \dot{W}_t$; and similarly $_{t-1}p_t^e - p_{t-1} = \ln(_{t-1}P_t^e/P_{t-1}) \cong (_{t-1}P_t^e - P_{t-1})/P_{t-1} = _{t-1}\Pi_t^e$. As a result (9.2.1) can also be written as

$$w_t - w_{t-1} = \lambda(_{t-1}p_t^e - p_{t-1}) + f(U_t), \qquad (9.2.2)$$

Now according to Friedman's hypothesis when price changes are fully anticipated the equilibrium real wage will be determined by the demand and supply of labour within a Walrasian general equilibrium framework and the rate of unemployment associated with this equilibrium real wage will be the natural rate of unemployment. Therefore consistent with the traditional perfect foresight neoclassical theory, the change in the real wage rate becomes a function of excess demand and in equilibrium there will be a unique relation between the natural rate of unemployment ($\bar{U}_t$) and the change in the equilibrium real wage rate. The form of this relation is dependent on the prevailing market structures, stochastic variations in demand and supply, the costs of mobility, etc. (See the quotation from Friedman above.) Approximating the rate of change of real wages by $(w_t - p_t) - (w_{t-1} - p_{t-1})$, so that

$$(w_t - w_{t-1}) - (p_t - p_{t-1}) = f(\bar{U}_t). \qquad (9.2.3)$$

Using this relation to eliminate the rate of change of money wages from (9.2.2) we obtain

$$f(U_t) - f(\bar{U}_t) = \lambda(p_t - _{t-1}p_t^e) + (1 - \lambda)(p_t - p_{t-1}).$$

Notice that $p_t - _{t-1}p_t^e = (p_t - p_{t-1}) - (_{t-1}p_t^e - p_{t-1}) = \Pi_t - _{t-1}\Pi_t^e$, and the above relation can be written equivalently as

$$f(U_t) - f(\bar{U}_t) = \lambda(\Pi_t - _{t-1}\Pi_t^e) + (1 - \lambda)\Pi_t. \qquad (9.2.4)$$

It is now clear that even when inflation is perfectly anticipated (that is $\Pi_t = {}_{t-1}\Pi_t^e$), a lower rate of unemployment can still be traded off for a higher rate of inflation so long as $\lambda < 1$. It is only when $\lambda = 1$ that the natural rate hypothesis follows from (9.2.2) and (9.2.3). Although whether $\lambda = 1$ at first appears to be an empirical issue, due to the presence of ${}_{t-1}\Pi_t^e$ in (9.2.4) the estimation of λ is inextricably linked to the problem of how price expectations are formed in the labour and the product markets. In the absence of direct reliable observations on price expectations it seems unlikely that the choice of a value for λ can be settled on purely empirical grounds. (For example witness the empirical studies of the inflation augmented Phillips Curve by Perry (1966), Solow (1969) and Gordon (1971), and the subsequent critique of this type of studies by Lucas (1972b).) The interpretation of λ is not without ambiguity either. The neoclassical economists have usually interpreted $\lambda = 1$ to represent the absence of money illusion. But this is not the only possible interpretation. Parameter λ can equally well be interpreted as a measure of workers' ability to transmit inflationary expectations into an increase in money wages.

Bearing in mind these difficulties and ambiguities regarding the estimation and interpretation of the parameter λ we now proceed to derive the NRH from (9.2.4). Setting $\lambda = 1$, a formal representation for the NRH can be written as

$$f(U_t) - f(\bar{U}_t) = \Pi_t - {}_{t-1}\Pi_t^e.$$

Equivalently using a well-known empirical relationship between the rate of unemployment and output (the so-called Okun's Law), the NRH can also be written down in terms of real output. In particular if we set $f(U_t) = \alpha^{-1} y_t (\alpha > 0)$ we get what is usually referred to as the Lucas aggregate supply function. That is

$$y_t - \bar{y}_t = \alpha(\Pi_t - {}_{t-1}\Pi_t^e) + \varepsilon_{t1}, \tag{9.2.5}$$

where y_t represents the logarithm of real output and ε_{t1} is a zero mean serially independent disturbance term added to the relation to capture supply shocks. The natural level of output $\bar{y}_t$ is generally left unspecified. But in empirical studies $\bar{y}_t$ is invariably replaced by a linear trend with little theoretical rationale.

Alternative derivations of (9.2.5) based directly on a neoclassical model with incomplete information have been proposed by Lucas and Rapping (1969), Phelps (1970), Lucas (1972a, 1973) and Barro (1976). In their paper Lucas and Rapping obtained the aggregate supply function from a two-period consumer decision model in which consumers are assumed to be confronted with the choice between current and future consumption of goods and leisure. They consider a 'representative' household faced with the problem of determining its current and future supply of labour and consumption such that its utility $U(C_t, C_{t+1}, L_t, L_{t+1})$ is maximized subject to the two-period budget constraint ($U_1, U_2 > 0$; U_3, $U_4 < 0$),

$$A_t + W_t L_t + \frac{W_{t+1} L_{t+1}}{1 + r_t} \geqslant P_t C_t + \frac{P_{t+1} C_{t+1}}{1 + r_t},$$

where C_t and C_{t+1} are current and future consumption, L_t and L_{t+1} are current and future labour supply; P_t and P_{t+1} are the current and future levels of consumer prices; W_t and W_{t+1} are the current and future levels of nominal wages; A_t is the initial nominal non-human assets of the household and r_t is the nominal rate of interest. The solution of this constrained maximization problem is straightforward [see IV, Chapter 15] and assuming it is unique may be written as zero-degree homogeneous functions of current and future prices and money wages (discounted to their current values) and the initial non-human asset [see §12.3]. In the case of current labour supply function one obtains

$$L_t = F\left(A_t, W_t, \frac{W_{t+1}}{1+r_t}, P_t, \frac{P_{t+1}}{1+r_t} \right). \qquad (9.2.6)$$

As it is clear the derivation assumes future wages and prices are known at the time L_t is determined which is unsatisfactory. A different and more plausible formulation of the Lucas–Rapping model that does not assume known future wages and prices is, however, attempted by Sargent (1979, Chapter XVI) who considers a *quadratic* form for the utility function but instead of taking future wages and prices to be known assumes that the representative household knows the stochastic processes that generate them. A closed-form solution to the problem for a *general* specification of the utility function and *unknown* future money wages and prices does not seem to be possible. To give an operational meaning to the above labour supply function, Lucas and Rapping simply suggest replacing W_{t+1} and P_{t+1} in (9.2.6) by their expectations formed at time t. On the basis of this intertemporal substitution framework Lucas (1972a) in his paper on econometric testing of the natural rate hypothesis specifies the following version of the aggregate supply function:

$$y_t - \bar{y}_t = \alpha(p_t - {}_t p^e_{t+1}) + \varepsilon_{t1}, \quad \alpha > 0, \qquad (9.2.5')$$

where ${}_t p^e_{t+1}$ denotes the expectation of p_{t+1} formed at time t. As will be shown later on, despite their apparent similarities the above two formulations of the NRH (that is (9.2.5) and (9.2.5′)) have different policy implications under the rational expectations hypothesis (REH).

The theoretical framework adopted by Lucas (1973), and subsequently extended by Barro (1976), is based on Phelps's island economy parable and the uncertainty arises not because of the problem of intertemporal choice but owing to the lack of full *current* information. Barro and Lucas consider an economy where suppliers of a single commodity are located in a large number of perfectly competitive markets that are physically separated from one another. Individual suppliers are assumed to know the prices ruling in their own local market but not the general price level in the economy as a whole. In each period demand is distributed randomly over markets. The commodity is assumed to be non-durable and no trading is allowed across markets. The markets are differentiated from one another only with respect to the size of their specific demand shocks.

Starting from the assumption that supply in each market is determined by relative prices as perceived by agents, Lucas then shows that the aggregate supply (averaged over all markets) is governed by a relation such as (9.2.5) where output is directly related to the gap between the average price level and the agents' expectation of the price level. (Lucas (1973) also introduces a one-period lagged value of $y_t - \bar{y}_t$ in his supply function but does not provide any theoretical rationale for it. However, see Sargent (1979, Chapter XVI).) According to this derivation of the NRH, the slope of the aggregate supply curve (that is α) is not constant and varies inversely with the variance of the monetary growth rate.

9.3. ADAPTIVE EXPECTATIONS AND THE RATIONAL EXPECTATIONS HYPOTHESIS

None of the above formulations of the aggregate supply function are, however, complete without a theory that sets out clearly how price changes are decomposed into their anticipated and unanticipated components. This requires a theory of expectations formations. Up until the early 1970s most studies of inflation and unemployment relied rather heavily on adaptive or extrapolative schemes for the determination of price expectations. In its most general form the hypothesis of adaptive expectations states that in any one-period expectations are revised (linearly) in the light of past errors of expectations. In its simplest form it can be written as

$$\Pi_t^e - \Pi_{t-1}^e = \theta(\Pi_{t-1} - \Pi_{t-1}^e), \tag{9.3.1}$$

where Π_{t-i}^e stand for expectations of Π_{t-i} formed at time $t - i - 1$. The size of the adjustment is determined by the coefficient θ assumed to lie in the range $0 < \theta \leqslant 1$. A high θ means a rapid rate of adjustment.

One important feature of the adaptive mechanism is the fact that it can be written as an infinite distributed lag function of past prices with suitable restrictions on its coefficients. Using the one-period lag operator $L(L\Pi_t = \Pi_{t-1})$ equation (9.3.1) may be written as

$$\{1 - (1 - \theta)L\}\Pi_t^e = \theta\Pi_{t-1},$$

and since $0 < \theta \leqslant 1$, the inversion of the linear lag operator function on Π_t^e yields

$$\Pi_t^e = \theta\{1 - (1 - \theta)L\}^{-1}\Pi_{t-1}$$

or

$$= \theta \sum_{i=1}^{\infty} (1 - \theta)^{i-1}\Pi_{t-i} \tag{9.3.1'}$$

Therefore, the adaptive expectation hypothesis can also be viewed as a special case of a more general hypothesis that postulates

$$\Pi_t^e = \sum_{i=1}^{\infty} \delta_i \Pi_{t-i}, \quad \delta_i \geqslant 0 \tag{9.3.2}$$

with the weights δ_i restricted to follow a geometrically declining sequence with the weights also restricted to add up to unity. A comparison of (9.3.1) and (9.3.2) reveals that $\delta_i = \theta(1-\theta)^{i-1}$ with $\sum_{i=1}^{\infty} \delta_i = 1$. Clearly, less restrictive patterns for δ_i are possible. But the restriction $\sum \delta_i = 1$ is essential for the identification of λ in (9.2.4).

The adaptive expectations hypothesis whether in its simple form (9.3.1) or the general distributed lag form (9.3.2) is, however, subject to two major objections. Firstly in periods when the rate of inflation is accelerating expectations of the inflation rate formed according to the adaptive hypothesis will systematically underestimate the actual rate of inflation. This undesirable property can be illustrated by means of the following simple example. Suppose the actual rate of inflation is accelerating at a constant rate ρ. That is

$$\Pi_t = \Pi_0(1+\rho)^t, \quad \rho > 0.$$

Using this expression in (9.3.1') gives

$$\Pi_t^e = \Pi_0 \theta \sum_{i=1}^{\infty} (1-\theta)^{i-1}(1+\rho)^{t-i}$$

which can be simplified [see IV, Example 1.7.3 with $x = (1-\theta)/(1+\rho)$] to

$$(\Pi_t^e/\Pi_t) - 1 = -\rho/(\rho+\theta).$$

Since by assumption θ and ρ are positive it follows that $\Pi_t^e < \Pi_t$ for all t, which establishes that when inflation is accelerating Π_t^e will be systematically below the actual rate of inflation. This example also shows that when inflation is decelerating the inflation expectations will be systematically above the actual rate of inflation (assuming θ is large enough to ensure that $\theta + \rho > 0$).

The second objection to the adaptive expectations hypothesis or the general extrapolative formulation (9.3.2) is more fundamental and concerns the limited information set upon which the adaptive expectations are based. The adaptive hypothesis ignores relevant information that may be available to economic agents other than past rates of inflation. Obvious examples of such relevant pieces of information are the size of current wage settlements and announced changes in government policy.

These objections to the adaptive expectations hypothesis have led the new classical macroeconomists to Muth's conception of 'rational' expectations which is at the other extreme to the adaptive expectations and postulates that economic agents form their expectations on the basis of the *true* model of the economy and a correct understanding of the government policy rules. Muth's own definition of what he means by rational expectations is given in the widely quoted statement that 'expectations, since they are informed predictions of future events, are essentially the same as the predictions of the relevant economic theory' (see Muth, 1961, p. 316). The choice of the economic theory for formation of expectations is, however, of crucial importance. Expectations formed by economic agents will be only full rational if the economic theory chosen by agents happens to be the true one. In the case of fully rational expectations the subjective probability distributions held by economic agents will be the same as the objective probability distributions of the relevant variables conditional on the 'true' model of the economy. But there is no reason to believe that subjective expectations formed on the basis of mis-specified models would be the same as their corresponding objective mathematical expectations.

Under the rational expectations hypothesis the logarithm of price expectations will be formed according to

$$_{t-1}p_t^e = E(p_t|\Omega_{t-1}), \tag{9.3.3}$$

where Ω_t represents the information set available to economic agents at time t and E denotes the mathematical expectations operator. The information set Ω_t contains data on the past history of all the variables that enter the economic model and the government policy rules. Initially, it is assumed that the mathematical expectations are taken under the true model of the economy. The case where expectations are formed on the basis of a mis-specified model will be discussed later.

Rational expectations (when formed on the basis of the true model) possess two fundamental properties that are crucial for the validity of the policy ineffectiveness proposition of the new classical school. Firstly expectation errors conditioned on the available information set will have zero means [see II, §8.9], and secondly they will be uncorrelated with the values of all the variables in the information set and therefore with their own past [see II, §9.8]. The proof is quite straightforward. Denoting the error of rational expectations of p_t by ξ_t, one has

$$E(\xi_t|\Omega_{t-1}) = E\{[p_t - E(p_t|\Omega_{t-1})]|\Omega_{t-1}\}$$
$$= E(p_t|\Omega_{t-1}) - E(p_t|\Omega_{t-1}) = 0.$$

The proof of the second property also follows immediately from the fact that for $i \geqslant 1$

$$E(\xi_t\xi_{t-i}|\Omega_{t-i}) = \xi_{t-i}E(\xi_t|\Omega_{t-i}).$$

The first property is usually referred to as the unbiasedness property. These two properties, however, do not hold if expectations are formed on the basis of a mis-specified model or a correct model structure but with incorrect parameter values.

A simple example would help clarify some of these points. Consider the aggregate supply function (9.2.5) and following Lucas (1972b) suppose the aggregate demand function is given by

$$y_t + p_t = x_t, \tag{9.3.4}$$

where x_t, the logarithm of nominal income is viewed as a policy variable. Eliminating y_t from (9.3.4) and (9.2.5) yields (recall that $\Pi_t = p_t - p_{t-1}$ and

$$_{t-1}\Pi_t^e = {}_{t-1}p_t^e - p_{t-1}).$$

$$p_t = \mu \, _{t-1}p_t^e + (1-\mu)\omega_t, \quad 0 \leqslant \mu < 1, \tag{9.3.5}$$

where $\mu = \alpha/(1+\alpha)$ and $\omega_t = x_t - \bar{y}_t - \varepsilon_{t1}$. Under REH, $_{t-1}p_t^e = E(p_t|\Omega_{t-1})$. In this example $\Omega_t = (p_t, x_t, y_t, \bar{y}_t; p_{t-1}, x_{t-1}, y_{t-1}, \bar{y}_{t-1}, \ldots)$ and mathematical expectations are taken assuming relations (9.2.5) and (9.3.4) provide a true characterization of the process generating output and prices. Replacing $_{t-1}p_t^e$ in (9.3.5) by $E(p_t|\Omega_{t-1})$, a solution for $E(p_t|\Omega_{t-1})$ can be obtained by taking expectations of both sides of (9.3.5) conditional on Ω_{t-1} [see II, Chapter 16]. The result is easily seen to be

$$_{t-1}p_t^e = E(p_t|\Omega_{t-1}) = E(\omega_t|\Omega_{t-1}).$$

In effect the problem of expectations formation of p_t is replaced by the problem of forming rational expectations of ω_t. To solve this latter problem the economic agents also need to know how the three components of ω_t (that is ε_{t1}, $\bar{y}_t$ and x_t) are generated. In view of the NRH, ε_{t1} are assumed to be serially independent with zero means and $\bar{y}_t$ are treated as exogenously determined. For x_t the following simple autoregressive policy rule is usually adopted

$$x_t = \delta x_{t-1} + \eta_t, \tag{9.3.6}$$

where $\{\eta_t\}$ represents a serially independent sequence with zero mean and a constant variance. Given these assumptions and choosing a linear specification for $\bar{y}_t (= a_0 + a_1 t)$ one obtains the following expressions for the components of ω_t

$$E(\varepsilon_{t1}|\Omega_{t-1}) = 0$$
$$E(\bar{y}_t|\Omega_{t-1}) = a_0 + a_1 t$$
$$E(x_t|\Omega_{t-1}) = \delta x_{t-1}.$$

Therefore expectations of p_t formed rationally at time t will be

$$_{t-1}p_t^e = E(p_t|\Omega_{t-1}) = \delta x_{t-1} - a_0 - a_1 t. \tag{9.3.7}$$

Using this result in (9.3.5), the RE solution of p_t follows as

$$p_t = (1-\mu)x_t + \mu\delta x_{t-1} - a_0 - a_1 t - (1-\mu)\varepsilon_{t1} \tag{9.3.8}$$

The expectations errors of p_t or the inflation rate can now be obtained by subtracting (9.3.7) from (9.3.8). That is

$$\xi_t = p_t - {}_{t-1}p_t^e = (1-\mu)(x_t - \delta x_{t-1}) - (1-\mu)\varepsilon_{t1}, \tag{9.3.9}$$

or upon using (9.3.6)

$$\xi_t = (1-\mu)(\eta_t - \varepsilon_{t1}), \tag{9.3.10}$$

which exhibits both of the two major properties of the rational expectations hypothesis, namely that ξ_t have zero means and are uncorrelated with their past.

Suppose now agents know the structure of the model but do not know the true value of δ for the policy rule (9.3.6). Instead they form their expectations of p_t using an incorrect value for δ, say $\bar{\delta}$. In this case (9.3.10) will no longer be valid and the error of price expectations will be given by

$$\xi_t = (1 - \mu)(\delta - \bar{\delta})x_{t-1} + (1 - \mu)(\eta_t - \varepsilon_{t1}).$$

It is now clear that ξ_t will no longer have zero (conditional) means and systematic errors of expectations can not be ruled out. Specifically $E(\xi_t|\Omega_{t-1}) = (1 - \mu)(\delta - \bar{\delta})x_{t-1}$ which can markedly differ from zero so long as $\bar{\delta} \neq \delta$. Whether agents are capable of learning the true value of δ from their past errors of forecasting p_t is an open issue and crucially depends on the type of *a priori* knowledge one is prepared to assume agents have about the way the economy actually functions. How agents are supposed to acquire the knowledge required by the rational expectations hypothesis is not made clear in the literature of the new classical school. Authors such as Cyert and De Groot (1974), Taylor (1975), Blanchard (1976), Friedman (1979), Bray (1982) and Blume and Easley (1982) who have concerned themselves with the learning process that must underlie agent's expectations have confined their studies to specific problems. The results of these studies broadly suggest that a 'rational' learning process, in the sense that agents' expectations eventually converge to the rational expectations solution, will be possible only when agents know the 'true' model of the economy but are uncertain about the 'true' parameter values of that model. In the more relevant case that agents have no *a priori* knowledge of the way the economy functions and therefore attempt to learn on the basis of possibly mis-specified models the outcome of the learning process is far from certain. In fact, as is shown by Blume and Easley (1982) even when one of the models considered by agents in their learning process happens to the 'true' one, there is no guarantee that the learning process would not get stuck at an incorrect model. The fact that agents may base their decisions on expectations formed from a mis-specified model also poses an additional problem. The actual outcomes will not be invariant to agents' perceived view of the economy. As a result, in their attempt to learn, agents have to constantly disentangle the effect that their own perception of reality has upon the outcomes from the results that would have followed if a different model had been true.

9.4. THE NON-UNIQUENESS PROBLEM

Another difficulty that surrounds the application of the rational expectations hypothesis is the existence of the multiplicity of rational expectations solutions when the model under consideration contains expectations of *future* variables. A simple but important example of such a model is given by (9.2.5′), which is the version of the NRH derived from the principles of intertemporal substitution. Combining (9.2.5′) with the simple aggregate demand function (9.3.4) and assuming expectations are formed rationally the following expectational equation in p_t can be obtained

$$p_t = \mu E(p_{t+1}|\Omega_t) + (1 - \mu)\omega_t. \tag{9.4.1}$$

Except for the term involving expectations this equation is exactly the same as (9.3.5) and μ and ω_t are defined as before. The solution of this equation is not straightforward and a number of different approaches and solutions have been proposed in the literature, for example by Sargent and Wallace (1973), Shiller (1978), Blanchard (1978), Taylor (1977), Pesaran (1981) and Gourieroux *et al.* (1982).

One method of solution which is originally due to Muth (1961) and has been used by Taylor (1977) and Blanchard (1978) involves first writing p_t as a linear distributed lag function of past and future expected values of ω_t conditional on Ω_t and then determining the unknown coefficients of the linear function such that p_t is a solution of (9.4.1). This method is known in the literature as the 'method of undetermined coefficients'. Although this solution procedure has proved useful in the literature it does not necessarily reveal all the solutions of (9.4.1).

An alternative procedure due to Sargent and Wallace (1973) is to solve for p_t recursively in terms of future expected values of ω_t and a terminal expected price variable conditioned on the information set Ω_t. This method which is similar to the familiar method of solving difference equations [see I, §14.13] is known as the 'forward recursive substitution method'. The application of this solution method to (9.4.1) proceeds along the following lines. Rewriting (9.4.1) for $t + 1$ and then taking expectations conditional on Ω_t yields

$$E(p_{t+1}|\Omega_t) = \mu E[E(p_{t+2}|\Omega_{t+1})|\Omega_t] + (1 - \mu)E(\omega_{t+1}|\Omega_t).$$

However, since Ω_t is contained within Ω_{t+1} using known results [see II, Chapter 16] on conditional expectations (for a simple proof see footnote 2 on page 6 of Shiller's article)

$$E[E(p_{t+2}|\Omega_{t+1})|\Omega_t] = E(p_{t+2}|\Omega_t),$$

and

$$E(p_{t+1}|\Omega_t) = \mu E(p_{t+2}|\Omega_t) + (1 - \mu)E(\omega_{t+1}|\Omega_t).$$

Substituting this result for $E(p_{t+1}|\Omega_t)$ in (9.4.1) now yields

$$p_t = \mu^2 E(p_{t+2}|\Omega_t) + (1 - \mu)[\omega_t + \mu E(\omega_{t+1}|\Omega_t)].$$

Repeating the above process for $t + 2, t + 3, \ldots$ and recursively using the results to eliminate $E(p_{t+2}|\Omega_t)$, $E(p_{t+3}|\Omega_t)$ and so on we finally obtain

$$p_t = \mu^N E(p_{t+N}|\Omega_t) + (1 - \mu) \sum_{i=0}^{N-1} \mu^i E(\omega_{t+i}|\Omega_t). \tag{9.4.2}$$

This expression for p_t can only be regarded as a solution of (9.4.1) if the terminal conditional price expectation $E(p_{t+N}|\Omega_t)$ is known for some $N > 0$. In effect this is like starting from a known point in the future and then working backwards to the present. Generally, this is not a satisfactory procedure. In the present case that $\mu = \alpha/(1 + \alpha) < 1$ the expression $\mu^N E(p_{t+N}|\Omega_t)$ can be ignored if one assumes that prices will grow slowly enough so that $\mu^N E(p_{t+N}|\Omega_t)$ approaches zero as N tends to infinity. This condition is often referred to as the 'transversality condition'. The assumption that prices will not explode too fast in the future may or may not be appropriate. What is important, however, is to note that a unique rational expectations solution of (9.4.1) is not possible unless some *a priori* assumption concerning the *future* movement of prices is made.

The nature of multiplicity of solutions of (9.4.1) can be more fully demonstrated by noting that when p_t is a solution of (9.4.1) so will $\tilde{p}_t = p_t + \mu^{-t} A_t$, where A_t is a martingale process. The theory of martingales and sub-martingales has been discussed in some detail in Doob (1953). A process A_t is said to be a martingale with respect to Ω_t if $E(A_t|\Omega_{t-1}) = A_{t-1}$ [see IV, §18.2.2]. A random walk is a simple example of such a process [see II, §18.3]. Setting δ in (9.3.6) equal to unity and taking conditional expectations $E(x_t|\Omega_{t-1}) = x_{t-1}$. Therefore for $\delta = 1$, x_t is an example of a martingale process. Starting with the first expression in the right-hand side of (9.4.1) we have

$$\mu E(\tilde{p}_{t+1}|\Omega_t) = \mu E(p_{t+1} + \mu^{-t-1} A_{t+1}|\Omega_t),$$
$$= \mu E(p_{t+1}|\Omega_t) + \mu^{-t} E(A_{t+1}|\Omega_t),$$

and since A_t is a martingale then

$$\mu E(\tilde{p}_{t+1}|\Omega_t) = \mu E(p_{t+1}|\Omega_t) + \mu^{-t} A_t.$$

But since p_t is a solution of (9.4.1) it follows that

$$\mu E(\tilde{p}_{t+1}|\Omega_t) = p_t - (1 - \mu)\omega_t + \mu^{-t} A_t,$$
$$= \tilde{p}_t - (1 - \mu)\omega_t.$$

Thus

$$\tilde{p}_t = \mu E(\tilde{p}_{t+1}|\Omega_t) + (1 - \mu)\omega_t,$$

which establishes that $\tilde{p}_t$ will also be a solution of (9.4.1). In fact for any particular solution p_t the general solution of (9.4.1) can be written as $p_t + \mu^{-t} A_t$. Notice that unlike the case of solving ordinary difference equations, the knowledge of past history of prices and output does not enable us to identify the martingale process A_t. Some knowledge of future prices would be needed. Assuming $\mu^N E(p_{t+N}|\Omega_t)$ vanishes as N approaches infinity and recalling that $0 \leqslant \mu < 1$ ensures that the only solution of (9.4.1) which does not explode too fast (relative to μ^{-N} as $N \to \infty$) is given by

$$p_t = (1 - \mu) \sum_{i=0}^{\infty} \mu^i E(\omega_{t+i}|\Omega_t), \tag{9.4.3}$$

where, as before, $\omega_t = x_t - \bar{y}_t - \varepsilon_{t1}$. Again assuming x_t is governed by (9.3.6) and that $E(\bar{y}_{t+i}|\Omega_t) = a_0 + a_1(t+i)$, one has

$$E(\omega_t|\Omega_t) = x_t - a_0 - a_1 t - \varepsilon_{t1},$$
$$E(\omega_{t+i}|\Omega_t) = \delta^i x_t - a_0 - a_1(t+i), \quad \text{for } i \geqslant 1.$$

Substituting these results in (9.4.3) and calculating the infinite series involved assuming $|\delta\mu| < 1$ [see IV, §1.7], we obtain

$$p_t = \left(\frac{1-\mu}{1-\delta\mu}\right)x_t - a_0 - a_1 t - \left(\frac{a_1\mu}{1-\mu}\right) - (1-\mu)\varepsilon_{t1}. \tag{9.4.4}$$

It is a simple exercise to show that the above expression for p_t is in fact a solution of (9.4.1). As argued before this solution is not unique as $\tilde{p}_t = p_t + \mu^{-t}A_t$, where A_t is a martingale process, gives a family of solutions.

9.5. NEW CLASSICAL POLICY NEUTRALITY PROPOSITION

We are now in a position to show how and under what conditions the natural rate hypothesis when combined with the rational expectations hypothesis can lead to the new classical 'policy neutrality' (or ineffectiveness) proposition. But first a clear description of what is meant by a 'policy change' in the new classical framework is needed. Consider the simple aggregate demand equation (9.3.4) where x_t, the log of the aggregate nominal income, is viewed as a policy variable. A change in policy can be defined in two ways. Either by a change in the level of x_t made once and for all, or by a sustained change in x_t through a systematic shift in the feedback policy rule given for example by (9.3.6). The new classical policy analysis focuses on the latter notion of a policy change and crucially depends on the assumption that government policy can be described and formalized in terms of a policy rule. Strictly speaking, the policy neutrality proposition states that the choice among alternative policy feedback rules (in the case of (9.3.6) represented by different values of δ) is irrelevant for the probability distribution of the deviation of output from its 'natural' level. Note firstly that this proposition is primarily applicable to analysis of the effects of alternative steady-state policy rules on the long-run steady-state equilibrium values of the economic variables. (On this aspect of new classical policy analysis see Buiter (1980).) Secondly, even if the policy neutrality proposition as stated above is correct it does not necessarily mean that macroeconomic policy will have no effect on the full information level of output. As is shown by Fischer (1979a, 1979b) and Begg (1980), and also acknowledged by McCallum (1979) both monetary and fiscal policies have real effects on $\bar{y}_t$ even under perfect foresight. The case that $\bar{y}_t$ is also unaffected by a systematic change in policy is usually referred to as the 'superneutrality' or 'strong neutrality' property that even the most avowed advocates of the new classical macroeconomics would not endorse (for example, see Begg, 1982, pp. 143–150). Here we do not concern ourselves with the superneutrality proposition.

To see under what type of conditions the policy neutrality proposition is likely to hold, first consider the version of the NRH given by (9.2.5) together with the log-linear aggregate demand function (9.3.4) and assume that expectations are formed rationally in Muth's sense. Later, the effect of relaxing some of these assumptions for the validity of the neutrality proposition are analysed. Suppose that at time $t = T$ a change in policy is brought into effect by altering the parameter of the policy rule (9.3.6), thus shifting it to $x_t = \tilde{\delta} x_{t-1} + \eta_t$ for $t \geqslant T$. The consequences of this policy change for $y_t - \bar{y}_t$ can be worked out from the rational expectations solution for p_t given by (9.3.8). Substituting this result in (9.3.4) yields

$$y_t - \bar{y}_t = \mu(x_t - \delta x_{t-1}) + (1 - \mu)\varepsilon_{t1}. \tag{9.5.1}$$

Noting that after the policy change the value of x_t is given by $\tilde{\delta} x_{t-1} + \eta_t$ and its substitution in (9.5.1) gives

$$y_t - \bar{y}_t = \mu(\tilde{\delta} - \delta)x_{t-1} + \mu\eta_t + (1 - \mu)\varepsilon_{t1}.$$

However, if the policy change is sustained long enough, under the REH it is *assumed* that agents eventually learn about the true value of the new policy parameter and $\tilde{\delta} - \delta$ approaches zero. In such a circumstance the term involving the systematic part of the policy vanishes from the above relation and one gets

$$y_t - \bar{y}_t = \mu\eta_t + (1 + \mu)\varepsilon_{t1}.$$

Therefore, it immediately follows that in full rational expectations equilibrium the probability distribution of $y_t - \bar{y}_t$ is independent of the policy parameter δ. That is, systematic changes in policy will have no lasting impact upon the deviation of output from its natural level.

The policy neutrality proposition holds even if (9.2.5) is generalized to include lagged values of $y_t - \bar{y}_t$ or that the aggregate demand equation (9.3.4) is replaced by a log-linear IS–LM equation system [cf. Chapter 8] with additive disturbances. Such a model has been analysed in some detail by Sargent (1973), Sargent and Wallace (1975) and McCallum (1978). A simple version of the Sargent and Wallace model can be written as

$$y_t - \bar{y}_t = \alpha[p_t - E(p_t|\Omega_{t-1})] + \sum_{i=1}^{n} \lambda_i(y_{t-i} - \bar{y}_{t-i}) + \varepsilon_{t1}, \tag{9.5.2}$$

$$y_t = \beta_0\{r_t - E(p_{t+1} - p_t|\Omega_{t-1})\} + \beta_1 g_t + \varepsilon_{t2}, \tag{9.5.3}$$

$$m_t - p_t = \gamma_0 y_t + \gamma_1 r_t + \varepsilon_{t3}, \tag{9.5.4}$$

where, as before, Ω_t is the available data set at time t defined as $\Omega_t = (z_t, z_{t-1}, z_{t-2}, \ldots)$, and $z_t' = (y_t, p_t, r_t, m_t, g_t)$. The expected signs of the parameters are: $\alpha > 0$, $\beta_0 < 0$, $\beta_1 > 0$, $\gamma_0 > 0$, and $\gamma_1 < 0$.

Equation (9.5.2) is a straightforward generalization of (9.2.5) which allows for the observed persistent pattern in output. Equation (9.5.3) is a standard specification of the IS curve which relates aggregate real demand to real expected rate of interest and the logarithm of the real government expenditure (g_t). The equilibrium condition for the money market (the so-called LM curve) is given by (9.5.4). The variables r_t and m_t represent the nominal rate of interest and the logarithm of the money supply respectively. The disturbance terms ε_{ti} are assumed to be serially and contemporaneously independent random variables with zero means and constant variances. (The relaxation of the assumption of serial independence of ε_{ti} does not alter the basic conclusions regarding the policy neutrality proposition.)

Suppose now the monetary and fiscal policy are formulated according to the following general linear feedback rules:

$$m_t = \sum_{i=1}^{n_1} \phi_i' z_{t-i} + \varepsilon_{tm}, \qquad (9.5.5)$$

$$g_t = \sum_{i=1}^{n_2} \psi_i' z_{t-i} + \varepsilon_{tg}, \qquad (9.5.6)$$

where ϕ_i and ψ_i are vectors of policy parameters, and the random variables ε_{tm} and ε_{tg} represent the unsystematic components of monetary and fiscal policies respectively. As before only changes in ϕ_i and ψ_i will be viewed as a policy change.

Because of the presence of future expected values of p_t in the IS curve an explicit solution of the above model is rather complicated and is subject to the ambiguities of the non-uniqueness problem discussed in the previous section. However, in the present case where all expectations are taken conditional on Ω_{t-1} it is possible to solve for $y_t - \bar{y}_t$ without first solving for the price expectations. The method which is explained in more detail in Pesaran (1982, appendix) involves taking mathematical expectations of relations (9.5.2)–(9.5.4) and then subtracting the resultant expressions from the corresponding equations in (9.5.2)–(9.5.4). The resulting system of equations would only contain *unanticipated* components of the endogenous and exogenous variables. Noting that since by assumption $E(\bar{y}_t | \Omega_{t-1}) = \bar{y}_t$, the conditional expectations of (9.5.2)–(9.5.4) with respect to the information set Ω_{t-1} will be

$$E(y_t | \Omega_{t-1}) - \bar{y}_t = \sum_{i=1}^{n} \lambda_i (y_{t-i} - \bar{y}_{t-i}), \qquad (9.5.7)$$

$$E(y_t | \Omega_{t-1}) = \beta_0 \{ E(r_t | \Omega_{t-1}) - E(p_{t+1} - p_t | \Omega_{t-1}) \} + \beta_1 E(g_t | \Omega_{t-1}), \qquad (9.5.8)$$

$$E(m_t | \Omega_{t-1}) - E(p_t | \Omega_{t-1}) = \gamma_0 E(y_t | \Omega_{t-1}) + \gamma_1 E(r_t | \Omega_{t-1}), \qquad (9.5.9)$$

Subtracting relations (9.5.7)–(9.5.9) from (9.5.2)–(9.5.4) respectively and using the operator ∇ to represent transformation of a variable into its unanticipated value defined for example by $\nabla p_t = p_t - E(p_t | \Omega_{t-1})$ or $\nabla r_t = r_t - E(r_t | \Omega_{t-1})$, one has

$$\nabla y_t = \alpha \nabla p_t + \varepsilon_{t1},$$

$$\nabla y_t = \beta_0 \nabla r_t + \beta_1 \nabla g_t + \varepsilon_{t2},$$

$$\nabla m_t - \nabla p_t = \gamma_0 \nabla y_t + \gamma_1 \nabla r_t + \varepsilon_{t3}.$$

Assuming $\beta_0 + \alpha(\beta_0\gamma_0 + \gamma_1) \neq 0$ and solving for ∇y_t yields [see I, §5.8]

$$\nabla y_t = f_1 \nabla m_t + f_2 \nabla g_t + v_t, \qquad (9.5.10)$$

where $f_1 > 0$ and $f_2 > 0$ are given by

$$f_1 = \alpha\beta_0/D, f_2 = \alpha\beta_1\gamma_1/D,$$
$$D = \beta_0 + \alpha(\beta_0\gamma_0 + \gamma_1) < 0,$$

and

$$v_t = (\beta_0\varepsilon_{t1} + \alpha\gamma_1\varepsilon_{t2} - \alpha\beta_0\varepsilon_{t3})/D,$$

Using (9.5.7) to eliminate $E(y_t|\Omega_{t-1})$ from (9.5.10) one finally obtains

$$y_t - \bar{y}_t = \sum_{i=1}^{n} \lambda_i(y_{t-i} - \bar{y}_{t-i}) + f_1\nabla m_t + f_2\nabla g_t + v_t. \qquad (9.5.11)$$

Under the rationality hypothesis and assuming that agents are capable of fully discovering the policy changes, the policy rules (9.5.5) and (9.5.6) imply that

$$\nabla m_t = m_t - E(m_t|\Omega_{t-1}) = \varepsilon_{tm},$$
$$\nabla g_t = g_t - E(g_t|\Omega_{t-1}) = \varepsilon_{tg}.$$

Substituting these results in (9.5.11) yields

$$y_t - \bar{y}_t = \sum_{i=1}^{n} \lambda_i(y_{t-i} - \bar{y}_{t-i}) + f_1\varepsilon_{tm} + f_2\varepsilon_{tg} + v_t,$$

which establishes that the probability distribution of $y_t - \bar{y}_t$ in conditions of full rational expectations equilibrium is independent of the policy parameter ϕ_i and ψ_i. The result is not sensitive to specification of a real balance effect or inclusion of lagged values of z_t in the IS–LM equations.

9.6. CASES OF POLICY NON-NEUTRALITY

Although the policy neutrality proposition seems to be quite robust to changes in specification of the IS–LM system, slight modifications of the aggregate supply function or the policy rule can result in its breakdown even if the two pillars of the new classical macroeconomics are upheld. Here we concentrate on three such cases. To simplify our exposition we confine our analysis to the simple aggregate demand equation given by (9.3.4).

(i) Suppose that in place of (9.3.6) the feedback policy rule is specified to contain a multiplicative random component. That is

$$x_t = \delta\eta_t x_{t-1}, \qquad (9.3.6')$$

where η_t are now assumed to be distributed independently of x_t with unit means and constant variances. The multiplicative disturbance term in (9.3.6') can arise either under a random coefficient specification of the policy rule or when economic agents' information concerning the parameter(s) of the policy rule is uncertain. Notice, however, that this multiplicative specification of the policy rule does not alter the systematic component of the policy. We still have $E(x_t|\Omega_{t-1}) = \delta x_{t-1} E(\eta_t|\Omega_{t-1}) = \delta x_{t-'1}$. Therefore, the relevant expression for $y_t - \bar{y}_t$ will still be given by relation (9.5.1). The departure from the neutrality proposition arises when (9.3.6') is used to eliminate x_t from (9.5.1). This gives

$$y_t - \bar{y}_t = \mu\delta(\eta_t - 1)x_{t-1} + (1 - \mu)\varepsilon_{t1}.$$

It is evident from this result that the probability distribution of $y_t - \bar{y}_t$ is no longer independent of the systematic part of the policy rule. Although the conditional means of $y_t - \bar{y}_t$ cannot be influenced by policy changes [that is $E(y_t - \bar{y}_t|\Omega_{t-1}) = 0$], there will be scope for pure stabilization policy *vis-à-vis* the variance of $y_t - \bar{y}_t$. This example clearly demonstrates the importance of policy rules with only additive disturbances for the validity of the policy neutrality proposition. The issue of multiplicative disturbances and their implications for the policy neutrality proposition has also been discussed by Snower (1981).

(ii) The neutrality proposition also breaks down if instead of (9.2.5) the version of the NRH derived from the principles of intertemporal substitution is adopted as the aggregate supply function. This version of the NRH which is due to Lucas is given by (9.2.5'). The solution of (9.2.5') when combined with (9.3.4) has already been discussed in section 9.4. Relation (9.4.4) gives the rational expectation solution of p_t, which if used in (9.3.4) yields:

$$y_t - \bar{y}_t = \frac{\mu(1 - \delta)}{1 - \delta\mu}x_t + \frac{a_1\mu}{1 - \mu} + (1 - \mu)\varepsilon_{t1}.$$

It is therefore evident that in this case the conditional means as well as the conditional variances of $y_t - \bar{y}_t$ are dependent on the policy parameter δ, and the policy neutrality proposition no longer holds. (This non-neutrality result has also been pointed out by Beenstock (1980, pp. 174–175)). This non-neutrality result is valid irrespective of whether the additive or multiplicative versions of the policy rule is considered.

(iii) A third example of policy non-neutrality follows if the (stochastic) market clearing assumption of the new classical school is relaxed. Following Buiter (1980) suppose that the actual price level p_t does not adjust to its market clearing (or equilibrium) value instantaneously but adjusts to it with a lag characterized by the following simple partial adjustment mechanism

$$p_t - p_{t-1} = \phi(p_t^* - p_{t-1}), \quad (0 < \phi \leqslant 1), \tag{9.6.1}$$

where p_t^* represents the equilibrium value of p_t and parameter ϕ the adjustment coefficient. A high value of ϕ implies a fast rate of adjustment of p_t to p_t^*. The market clearing assumption corresponds to the value of $\phi = 1$. To focus on the relevance of the market clearing assumption for the neutrality proposition we confine our analysis to the version of the NRH given by (9.2.5). With p_t at its equilibrium market clearing value (p_t^*), relation (9.2.5) becomes

$$y_t - \bar{y}_t = \alpha(p_t^* - {}_{t-1}p_t^e) + \varepsilon_{t1}. \tag{9.6.2}$$

Using (9.6.1) to eliminate p_t^* from the above relation yields

$$y_t - \bar{y}_t = \alpha(p_t - {}_{t-1}p_t^e) + \alpha(\phi^{-1} - 1)(p_t - p_{t-1}) + \varepsilon_{t1},$$

which is in the same format as an expectation augmented Phillips Curve. Now with the help of (9.3.8) and (9.3.9) and assuming that agents are fully aware of authorities' policy rule (9.3.6), the above relation can also be written as (using $\alpha(1 - \mu) = \mu$)

$$y_t - \bar{y}_t = (\mu/\phi)(\eta_t - \varepsilon_{t1}) + (\alpha/\phi)(1 - \phi)(\delta x_{t-1} - \bar{y}_t - p_{t-1}).$$

This result establishes that even under the NR/RE hypothesis there will be scope for an activist macroeconomic policy so long as markets do not clear instantaneously (i.e. $\phi < 1$). However, see McCallum (1978) for specifications of price level stickiness which do not invalidate the policy neutrality proposition.

Other plausible modifications of the aggregate supply function have also been suggested by Fischer (1977b) and Phelps and Taylor (1977) which lead to the breakdown of the neutrality proposition. Fischer, while accepting the REH and the NRH, derived the latter on the assumption that wages are set according to nominal wage contracts for two or more periods in advance. In such a multi-period wage contract set-up, the non-neutrality of monetary policy follows because the policy rule can take account of disturbances (unknown at the time the contracts are signed) which occur after wage contracts come into effect even if monetary or fiscal policies are fully anticipated. Similar results follow for multi-period price setting arrangements whereby prices are set in advance of the period in which they are supposed to apply. The introduction of nonlinearities in the aggregate supply function or the IS–LM equations can also invalidate the neutrality proposition.

9.7. CONCLUDING REMARKS

As we have seen, the relevance of the new classical macroeconomics and the policy neutrality proposition to actual policy debates is rather limited. Even the most ardent adherents of the new classical school do not deny that fully anticipated monetary and fiscal policies have a lasting impact upon the 'natural' or capacity levels of real output. As a result the emphasis of the policy neutrality debate has shifted to the issue of the desirability and feasibility of pure stabilization policies aimed at reducing the variability of output around its natural level. Our account of the circumstances under which macroeconomic policy can be non-neutral clearly suggests the extent to which there is scope for stabilization policies even within the new classical framework. Purely theoretical considerations are unlikely to resolve the present controversy over the role of stabilization policies. Unfortunately, owing to the ambiguities that surround the empirical tests of the NR/RE hypothesis and the 'observational equivalence' of new classical models with and without the policy neutrality property, empirical studies are unlikely to be decisive either. (On this point see for example Sargent (1976), McCallum (1979) and Pesaran (1982).) This unsatisfactory state of affairs is partly due to the inherently non-refutable nature of the REH when direct reliable observations on price expectations are not available. The REH should be regarded as one of many possible models of expectations formations and not as the only plausible one that exists. Its popular appeal stems from the often-repeated but deceptive argument that any process of expectations formations which are not 'rational' will be consistently wrong and 'sensible' economic agents will ultimately abandon such schemes in favour of the REH. It is, however, important to note that the abandonment of a false expectations formations mechanism, although essential for the existence of a 'rational' learning process, does not necessarily ensure that agents will be led to the 'true' model of the economy. (This issue has been discussed by the author in some detail elsewhere; see Pesaran (1984).) When agents' learning process fails to converge to the rational expectations solutions, the effectiveness of macro-economic stabilization policies does not rest on the authorities' ability to 'fool all of the people all of the time'. People, no matter how sensible they are, may still end up fooling themselves all of the time if they form their expectations on the basis of a false model but behave as if they knew the true model of the economy. Outside 'the tranquillity of a long-run steady state' the policy neutrality proposition of the new classical school must remain a theoretical curiosity.

9.8. REFERENCES

Barro, R. J. (1976). Rational expectations and the role of monetary policy. *Journal of Monetary Economics*, **2**, 1–32.

Beenstock, M. (1980). *A neoclassical analysis of macroeconomic policy*. Cambridge University Press, Cambridge.

Begg, D. K. H. (1980). Rational expectations and the non-neutrality of systematic monetary policy. *Review of Economic Studies*, **47**, 293–303.

Begg, D. K. H. (1982). *The rational expectations revolution in macroeconomics*. Philip Allan, Oxford.

Blanchard, O. (1976). The non-transition to rational expectations. Massachusetts Institute of Technology, mimeo.

Blanchard, O. J. (1978). Backward and forward solutions for economics with rational expectations. Discussion Paper 627, Harvard University, Cambridge, Mass.

Blume, L. E., and Easley, D. (1982). Learning to be rational. *Journal of Economic Theory*, **26**, 340–351.

Bray, M. (1982). Learning, estimation, and the stability of rational expectations. *Journal of Economic Theory*, **26**, 318–339.

Buiter, W. H. (1980). The macroeconomics of Dr. Pangloss: a critical survey of the new classical macroeconomics. *Economic Journal*, **90**, 34–50.

214   *9. The New Classical Macroeconomics: A Critical Exposition*

Cyert, R. M. and De Groot, M. H. (1974). Rational expectations and Bayesian analysis. *Journal of Political Economy*, **82**, 521–536.

Doob, J. L. (1953). *Stochastic processes.* Wiley, New York.

Fischer, S. (1977a). Wage indexation, and macroeconomic stability, in Brunner, K. and A. H. Meltzer (eds.), *Stabilization of the domestic and international economy.* North-Holland, Amsterdam.

Fischer, S. (1977b). Long term contracts, rational expectations and the optimum money supply rule. *Journal of Political Economy*, **85**, 191–206.

Fischer, S. (1979a). Anticipations and the non-neutrality of money. *Journal of Political Economy*, **87**, 225–252.

Fischer, S. (1979b). Capital accumulation on the transition path in a monetary optimising economy. *Econometrica*, **47**, 1433–1440.

Friedman, B. M. (1979). Optimal expectations and the extreme informational assumptions of rational expectations macromodels, *Journal of Monetary Economics*, **5**, 23–41.

Friedman, M. (1968). The role of monetary policy. *American Economic Review*, **58**, 1–17.

Gordon, R. J. (1971). Inflation in recession and recovery. *Brookings Papers on Economic Activity*, pp. 105–166.

Gourieroux, C., Laffont, J. J. and Monfort, A. (1982). Rational expectations in dynamic linear models: analysis of the solutions. *Econometrica*, **50**, 409–425.

Lucas, R. E. (1972a). Expectations and the neutrality of money. *Journal of Economic Theory*, **4**, 103–124.

Lucas, R. E. (1972b). Econometric testing of the natural rate hypothesis, in Eckstein, O. (ed.), *The Econometrics of Price Determination Conference*, Board of Governors, Federal Reserve System, Washington, D.C.

Lucas, R. E. (1973). Some international evidence on output-inflation trade-offs. *American Economic Review*, **63**, 326–334.

Lucas, R. E., and Rapping, L. A. (1969). Real wages, employment and inflation. *Journal of Political Economy*, **77**, 721–754.

McCallum, B. T. (1978). Price level adjustments and the rational expectations approach to macroeconomic stabilization policy. *Journal of Money, Credit and Banking*, **10**, 418–436.

McCallum, B. T. (1979). The current state of the policy-ineffectiveness debate. *American Economic Review*, (papers and proceedings), **69**, 240–245.

Muth, J. F. (1961). Rational expectations and the theory of price movements. *Econometrica*, **29**, 315–335.

Perry, G. L. (1966). *Unemployment money wage rates and inflation*, MIT Press, Cambridge, Mass.

Pesaran, M. H. (1981). Identification of rational expectations models. *Journal of Econometrics*, **16**, 375–398.

Pesaran, M. H. (1982). A critique of the proposed tests of the natural rate-rational expectations hypothesis. *Economic Journal*, **92**, 529–554.

Pesaran, M. H. (1984). Expectations formations and macroeconometric modelling, in Malgrange, P. and P.-A. Muet (eds.), *Contemporary Macroeconomic Modelling*, Basil Blackwell, Oxford.

Phelps, E. S. (1970). Introduction: the new microeconomics in employment and inflation theory, in Phelps *et al.* (eds.), *Microeconomic foundations of employment and inflation theory.* Macmillan, London.

Phelps, E. S., and Taylor, J. B. (1977). Stabilizing powers of monetary policy under rational expectations. *Journal of Political Economy*, **85**, pp. 163–190.

Sargent, T. J. (1973). Rational expectations, the real rate of interest and the natural rate of unemployment. *Brookings Papers on Economic Activity*, pp. 429–472.

Sargent, T. J. (1976). The observational equivalence of natural and unnatural rate theories of macroeconomics. *Journal of Political Economy*, **84**, 631–640.

Sargent, T. J. (1979). *Macroeconomic Theory*, Academic Press, New York.

Sargent, T. J. and Wallace, N. (1973). Rational expectations and the dynamics of hyperinflation. *International Economic Review*, **14**, 328–350.

Sargent, T. J. and Wallace, N. (1975). Rational expectations, the optimal monetary instrument and the optimal money supply rule. *Journal of Political Economy*, **83**, 241–254.

Shiller, R. J. (1978). Rational expectations and the dynamic structure of macroeconomic models: a critical review. *Journal of Monetary Economics*, **4**, 1–44.

Snower, D. J. (1981). Rational expectations, stochastic coefficients and monetary stabilization policy. *Birkbeck College Discussion Paper*, No. 95.

Solow, R. M. (1969). *Price expectations and the behaviour of the price level.* Manchester University Press, Manchester.

Taylor, J. B. (1975). Monetary policy during a transition to rational expectations. *Journal of Political Economy*, **83**, 1009–1021.

Taylor, J. (1977). Conditions for unique solutions in stochastic macroeconomic models with rational expectations. *Econometrica*, **45**, 1377–1386.

Mathematical Methods in Economics
Edited by F. van der Ploeg
© 1984, John Wiley & Sons, Ltd.

10

Stochastic Macroeconomic Policy Simulations for a Small Open Economy

DAVID CURRIE, *Queen Mary College, University of London, UK*
and
PAUL LEVINE, *Polytechnic of the South Bank, London, UK*

10.1. INTRODUCTION

The object of this chapter is to present a model of a small open economy, within which we can examine questions of policy evaluation, focusing particularly on the interactions between fiscal policy, monetary policy and the exchange rate. Controversy in recent macroeconomic policy debates has centred on these issues, and the literature dealing with these issues is vast. (No attempt is made to survey this literature here. A representative set of theories and views is provided by the essays in Eltis and Sinclair (1981).) This controversy continues unabated, in large part because of the complexities of open economy macroeconomics. In particular, springing from these economic complexities, modelling of the exchange rate under a floating (whether pure or managed) regime has tended to be technically deficient.

In what follows, we assume that agents in the foreign exchange market are sufficiently astute that arbitrage and speculative behaviour eliminates all systematic opportunities for profitable gain. This leads us to assume that foreign exchange operators form their expectations rationally and to treat the exchange rate as a free or jump variable. (We explain these terms later.) An important part of this chapter is concerned to show how a complex stochastic dynamic model of the kind that is set out here may be solved. Although we apply the method of solution to our specific open economy model, it is more general and may be applied to a wide class of dynamic stochastic rational expectations models. It is, therefore, of general interest.

Earlier approaches to modelling the exchange rate were deficient in one of two respects. One approach (to be found, for instance, in the main macroeconometric forecasting models developed by HM Treasury, the London Business School and the National Institute in the UK or by the Wharton Project in the USA) was to model the exchange rate via ad hoc relationships, which implied continuing and systematic arbitrage and speculative opportunities for gain. The difficulty with this is that it is plausible that agents in the foreign exchange market will come to perceive these opportunities for gain, and base speculative or arbitrage decisions on them. But this action will tend to eliminate these opportunities for gain and simultaneously alter the behaviour of the exchange rate. Relationships of the ad hoc type are, therefore, unlikely to be stable over time, and will be unreliable in forecasting or policy evaluation.

The other approach has been to assume rational expectations, but in the context of rather simple models where the solution under this assumption is relatively tractable. (The seminal article in this area is Dornbusch (1976).) The simplicity of these models precludes examination of the dynamic wealth interactions arising from the financing of the government budget and the current account of the balance of payments, and possible dynamics in aggregate demand, asset demand and wage/price relationships, all of which we can allow for in the analysis which follows.

Despite the added complexity and realism of the model analysed here, some continuing simplications are made for expositional simplicity. We assume perfect capital mobility between countries, despite the substantial body of evidence that systematic deviations from perfect mobility, due probably to risk aversion, can be observed. We ignore interest payments in the government budget and current account of the balance of payments, despite the undoubted endogeneity of these payments. We also ignore the accumulation of real capital and its consequences on the supply of the economy and on the demand side via expenditure and asset demand functions. Incorporating these effects is not intrinsically difficult, but doing so leads to a model which is rather intractable for expositional purposes.

The structure of the chapter is as follows. Section 10.2 sets out our basic model of a small open economy. Section 10.3 discusses types of policy rules, focusing particularly on regimes of monetary targets, exchange rate targets, nominal income targets and price level targets. Section 10.4 then presents the complete dynamic model, including policy rules. Section 10.5 presents the general solution method for dynamic stochastic models under rational expectations, while section 10.6 gives a simple example of the method derived from the exchange rate target regime. Section 10.7 presents some analysis of the stability of the complete system. Section 10.8 presents the simulation results and draws policy conclusions with observations about current directions of research work in this area and section 10.9 presents suggestions for further reading.

10.2. A SHORT-RUN MODEL OF A SMALL OPEN ECONOMY

In this chapter we analyse a small open economy. By small, it is meant that domestic developments have negligible impact on the rest of the world, which may therefore be treated as exogenously given. As a first stage in the development of the full analysis we set out a more limited and fairly standard model similar to well-known textbook models of a small open economy (e.g. Turnovsky, 1977, Chapter 10, 11 and 12).

10.2.1. The output market

Product market equilibrium is given by

$$Y = C(Y - S(Y) - T, V) + I(r - \pi, Y) + G + X(Q) - QZ(Q, Y);$$
$$0 < C_1 < 1, C_2 > 0, I_1 < 0, I_2 > 0, X_1 > 0, Z_1 < 0, Z_2 > 0 \qquad (10.2.1)$$

where

Y = real output
C = real private consumption
I = real private investment
G = real government expenditure
X = real exports (independent of Y for a small economy)
Z = real imports
$S(Y)$ = component of real taxes (fully indexed for inflation) varying with income
T = autonomous real taxes
V = real private wealth
r = nominal rate of interest
π = expected rate of inflation
Q = P^*E/P_d is the competitiveness of domestically produced goods where P^*, E and P_d denote the foreign price level, the exchange rate defined as the price of foreign exchange in terms of domestic currency and the price of domestically produced goods respectively.

Subscript i denotes a partial derivative with respect to argument i of the relevant function.

We note that $Y, C, I, G, X, Z, S(Y)$ and T are nominal levels deflated by the price of domestically produced goods P_d. V is nominal wealth deflated by the price level for final expenditure P. $S(Y)$ captures the dependence of taxes on the level of activity in the economy. We may treat as fiscal instruments T (the autonomous part of taxes), and the schedule $S(\ )$, as reflected, for example, in the marginal tax rate $S'(Y)$.

10.2.2. The wage-price sector

The price level for all final expenditure is given by

$$P = P_d^{1-\theta}(P^*E)^\theta, 0 < \theta < 1, \qquad (10.2.2)$$

where θ is the direct import content of final expenditure. Taking logarithms of (10.2.2) and differentiating [see IV, §2.11 and §3.1], we obtain

$$\dot{p} = (1 - \theta)\dot{p}_d + \theta(\dot{p}^* + \dot{e}), \tag{10.2.3}$$

where $\dot{x} = (d/dt)(\ln X) = (1/X)(dX/dt)$. Equation (10.2.3) expresses the overall rate of inflation in terms of its domestic and imported components. We obtain $\dot{p}_d$, the rate of inflation of the price of domestically produced goods, from the following wage-price system:

$$\dot{w} = f(Y) + \dot{p}^e; f' > 0 \tag{10.2.4}$$

$$\dot{p}_d = g(Y) + b_1(\dot{p}^* + \dot{e})^e$$
$$+ (1 - b_1)(c_1\dot{w} + (1 - c_1)(\dot{p}^* + \dot{e})^e); g' > 0, 0 < b_1 < 1, 0 < c_1 < 1 \tag{10.2.5}$$

where W is the wage rate, $w = \ln W$ and the superscript e denotes expectations (i.e. $\pi = \dot{p}^e$ in (10.2.1)). Equation (10.2.4) is an expectations augmented Phillips Curve with the level of output Y as a proxy for the demand for labour (as implied by Okun's Law) [see Chapter 8]. In (10.2.5), Y is a proxy for demand on the product market, b_1 reflects the competitive effects of foreign prices on domestic price decisions and $(1 - b_1)$ reflects the cost element in which c_1 is the weight of wages and $(1 - c_1)$ is the weight of imported inputs.

Taking expectations of (10.2.3) and combining with (10.2.4) and (10.2.5) we obtain

$$\dot{p}_d = h(Y) + \beta_2(\dot{p}^* + \dot{e})^e + (1 - \beta_2)\dot{p}_d^e, \qquad h' > 0, \tag{10.2.6}$$

where $h(Y) = g(Y) + (1 - b_1)c_1 f(Y)$ and $\beta_2 = 1 - (1 - b_1)(1 - \theta)c_1$.

In a steady state inflationary equilibrium, expectations are fulfilled and $\dot{e} = \dot{p} - \dot{p}^*$. Then $\dot{p} = \dot{p}_d = \dot{p}^* + \dot{e}$ at the 'natural' level of output defined as that Y for which $h(Y) = 0$; this is a straightforward implication of the assumed homogeneity of degree one in price levels of Equations (10.2.2)–(10.2.5).

10.2.3. The monetary sector

Equilibrium in the monetary sector requires

$$M = PL(Y, r, V), \quad L_1 > 0, L_2 < 0, L_3 > 0, \tag{10.2.7}$$

where M is the nominal money stock and L denotes the real demand for money.

We further note that $M = D + F$ where D is the domestic component of the nominal money stock and F is the volume of foreign reserves.

10.2.4. The government budget constraint and wealth accumulation

A simple form of the government budget constraint, ignoring interest payments on government bonds, is

$$\dot{D} + \frac{1}{r}\dot{A} = P(G - S(Y) - T) \tag{10.2.8}$$

where A denotes the number of bonds assumed to be perpetuities paying a coupon at a rate of one domestic current unit per period and hence trading at a market valuation of $\int_0^\infty \exp(-rt)\mathrm{d}t = 1/r$ [see IV, §4.2].

The net real wealth of the private sector is given by

$$V = \left(M + \frac{A^D}{r} + \frac{\tilde{A}}{r^*} + K \right)\Big/ P \qquad (10.2.9)$$

where A^D, $\tilde{A}$ are the number of government and foreign bonds respectively held by domestic residents, r^* is the foreign rate of interest and K is the value of domestic private capital stock. (Here we assume foreign bonds are denominated in domestic currency terms. Otherwise the term for foreign bonds in (10.2.9) becomes $\tilde{A}e/r^*$, and $\dot{e}$ enters (10.2.10) below.) Then differentiating (10.2.9) we obtain

$$\dot{V} = \left(\dot{D} + \dot{F} + \frac{\dot{A}}{r} + \frac{\dot{\tilde{A}}}{r^*} - \frac{\dot{A}^F}{r} + \dot{K} - V\dot{P} \right)\Big/ P \qquad (10.2.10)$$

where A^F are government bonds held by foreigners and therefore $A = A^D + A^F$. In (10.2.10) $\dot{F}$ is the balance of payments given by

$$\dot{F} = P(X(Q) - QZ(Q, Y)) + \frac{\dot{A}^F}{r} - \frac{\dot{\tilde{A}}}{r^*} \qquad (10.2.11)$$

since $\dot{A}^F/r - \dot{\tilde{A}}/r^*$ is the net inflow of money capital. In the following, we ignore the effects of the accumulation of capital, and so assume that $\dot{K} = 0$. Then, combining (10.2.8), (10.2.10), and (10.2.11) gives

$$\dot{V} = G - S(Y) - T + X(Q) - QZ(Q, Y) - V\dot{p}, \qquad (10.2.12)$$

since $\dot{p} = (\mathrm{d}/\mathrm{d}t)(\ln P) = \dot{P}/P$.

10.2.5. Expected exchange rate changes and perfect capital mobility

We assume perfect capital mobility so that domestic and foreign bonds are perfect substitutes. It follows that their expected rates of return in terms of a common currency must be equal. Thus an interest rate differential in favour of the home currency must be offset by an expected exchange rate depreciation, that is

$$\dot{e}^e = r - r^*. \qquad (10.2.13)$$

Equation (10.2.13) should *not* be interpreted as saying that a rise in domestic interest rates, r, causes the expectation that exchange rates will depreciate, the opposite of economic intuition. Rather as we note in section 10.6, a rise in r causes an appreciation of the exchange rate, to the point where it is *subsequently* expected to depreciate.

10.2.6. Summary of short-run model

The model up to this stage can be summarized by the following relationships:

$$Y = Y(Q, r - \dot{p}^e, V, G, T); \quad Y_1 > 0, Y_2 < 0, Y_3 > 0, Y_4 > 0, Y_5 < 0 \qquad (10.2.14)$$

(which is (10.2.1) solved for Y with the aid of the implicit function theorem)

$$M = PL(Y, r, V); \quad L_1 > 0, L_2 < 0, L_3 > 0. \qquad (10.2.7')$$

$$\dot{p} = (1 - \theta)\dot{p}_d + \theta(\dot{p}^* + \dot{e}). \qquad (10.2.3')$$

$$\dot{p}_d = h(Y) + \beta_2(\dot{p}^* + \dot{e})^e + (1 - \beta_2)\dot{p}_d^e; \, h' > 0. \qquad (10.2.6')$$

$$\dot{V} = G - S(Y) - T + X(Q) - QZ(Q, Y) - V\dot{p}; \quad X_1 > 0, Z_1 < 0, Z_2 > 0. \quad (10.2.12')$$

$$\dot{e}^e = r - r^*. \qquad (10.2.13')$$

From $Q = P^*E/P_d$ we have

$$\dot{e} = \dot{q} + \dot{p}_d - \dot{p}^*. \qquad (10.2.15)$$

Noting that $\dot{q}$ and $\dot{p}$ are the proportional rates of change of Q and P respectively, and $\dot{V}$ is the rate of change of V, Equations (10.2.14), (10.2.7'), (10.2.3'), (10.2.6'), (10.2.12'), (10.2.13') and (10.2.15') give us seven equations in seven endogenous variables, $\dot{e}, \dot{q}, \dot{p}, \dot{V}, \dot{p}_d$, Y, and r with the expectational variables, $\dot{p}^e, \dot{p}_d^e, \dot{e}^e, \dot{p}^{*e}$ as yet exogenous alongside the government policy variables M, G, $S(.)$ and T and the world variables r^* and $\dot{p}^* \cdot P_d$ and V are variables predetermined in the short run but determined over time by the dynamic equations (10.2.6') and (10.2.12'). The determination of e, and hence p and Q, is described in section 10.6.

10.2.7. Long-run equilibrium

Here we examine the long-run equilibrium of the system, and consider its response to two exogenous disturbances. For simplicity, we focus on a non-inflationary non-growth equilibrium with a similar equilibrium for the rest of the world. This requires that the policy target, whether for the money supply, exchange rate, price level or nominal income, should be a constant.

In long-run equilibrium, $\dot{e} = \dot{p} = \dot{p}_d = \dot{p}^* = \dot{V} = 0$ and expectations are fulfilled. Then the model reduces to:

$$Y = Y(Q, r, V, G, T). \qquad (10.2.16)$$

$$M = PL(Y, r, V). \qquad (10.2.17)$$

$$h(Y) = 0. \qquad (10.2.18)$$

$$G - T - S(Y) + X(Q) - QZ(Q, Y) = 0. \qquad (10.2.19)$$

$$r = r^*. \qquad (10.2.20)$$

The assumption of perfect capital mobility may appear not to require long-run current account balance, permitting governments to borrow indefinitely internationally. But perfect capital mobility would necessarily break down were governments to do so. Perfect capital mobility is best regarded as an approximation that may be valid so long as governments maintain current account equilibrium in the long run. Accordingly, we require that in the long run:

$$X(Q) - QZ(Q, Y) = 0. \tag{10.2.21}$$

(10.2.20) and (10.2.21) imply $\dot{A}^F - \dot{A} = 0$ in (10.2.11). It also ensures that fiscal policy is in balance at the long run equilibrium level of output $\bar{Y}$ given by (10.2.18), so that $\bar{G} - \bar{T} - S(\bar{Y}) = 0$ (where long-run equilibrium values are denoted by a bar). (10.2.20) implies $\bar{r} = r^*$, so that domestic interest rates are at their world level. Long-run competitiveness is given from (10.2.21) as the solution $\bar{Q}$ to $X(\bar{Q}) - \bar{Q}Z(\bar{Q}, \bar{Y}) = 0$. $\bar{V}$ may then be found from (10.2.16); while (10.2.17) gives the real money supply $\bar{M}/\bar{P}$, which for given $\bar{M}$ implies $\bar{P}$. Our long-run model can, therefore, be straightforwardly solved in a sequential manner. (This is *not* true of the short-run model.) We now consider some comparative static results for the long-run equilibrium.

We consider two disturbances: a permanent rise in the export function, say to $X(Q) + \tilde{X}$; and a permanent fall in aggregate supply, represented by a shift of $h(Y)$ to $h(Y) + \tilde{h}$. (This shock might arise, for example, from increased wage pushfulness.) We consider these shifts separately, all other relationships being held constant and assume that fiscal adjustments take the form of a change in government expenditure. (Similar results obtain if taxes alter instead.) Then we may obtain from (10.2.1) and (10.2.17)–(10.2.21) that

$$\frac{\partial \bar{Y}}{\partial \tilde{X}} = 0 \qquad\qquad \frac{\partial \bar{Y}}{\partial \tilde{h}} = -h_1^{-1} < 0$$

$$\frac{\partial \bar{Q}}{\partial \tilde{X}} = -(X_1 - QZ_1 - Z)^{-1} < 0 \qquad \frac{\partial \bar{Q}}{\partial \tilde{h}} = -h_1^{-1}QZ_2(X_1 - QZ_1 - Z)^{-1} < 0$$

$$\frac{\partial \bar{r}}{\partial \tilde{X}} = 0 \qquad\qquad \frac{\partial \bar{r}}{\partial \tilde{h}} = 0$$

$$\frac{\partial \bar{G}}{\partial \tilde{X}} = 0 \qquad\qquad \frac{\partial \bar{G}}{\partial \tilde{h}} = -S_1 h_1^{-1} < 0$$

$$\frac{\partial \bar{V}}{\partial \tilde{X}} = 0 \qquad\qquad \frac{\partial \bar{V}}{\partial \tilde{h}} = -C_2^{-1}h_1^{-1}[(1 - C_1)(1 - S_1) - I_2] < 0$$

$$\frac{\partial(\bar{M}/\bar{P})}{\partial \tilde{X}} = 0 \qquad\qquad \frac{\partial(\bar{M}/\bar{P})}{\partial \tilde{h}} = -h_1^{-1}[L_1 + L_3 C_2^{-1}((1 - C_1)$$
$$\cdot (1 - S_1) - I_2)] < 0$$

$$\tag{10.2.22}$$

In signing these long-run effects, we have assumed that the Marshall–Lerner condition $(X_1 - QZ_1 - Z > 0)$ is satisfied, so that a devaluation improves the current account of the balance of payments. (Empirical evidence suggests that this is generally the case.) In addition, we assume that $(1 - C_1)(1 - S_1) > I_2$, which holds if the accelerator effect on investment is not too large. It can be shown that this assumption is required for the multiplier process to be stable under a policy of balancing the government budget, and hence is necessary to make sense of the results for the $\tilde{h}$ disturbance.

To interpret these results, consider the effect of a fall in exports, so that X is negative. Then real competitiveness must increase to maintain current account balance. No fiscal adjustment is then required, and output, interest rates, real wealth and the real money supply then remain unchanged in the long run. Under the alternative disturbance of a fall in capacity output (so that $\tilde{h}$ is positive), real competitiveness must fall to maintain current account balance. In addition, the fall in output requires a more contractionary fiscal stance in the long run. The fall in government spending and competitiveness both lower aggregate demand. But private savings are likely to cushion the fall, so that aggregate demand will not decline to the new lower level of $\bar{Y}$ unless $\bar{V}$ falls. (This may result, for example, from a period of budget surpluses in the transition.) A fall in both income and real wealth implies an associated decline in real money balances.

The above comparative statics analysis deals exclusively with real variables. To determine nominal variables, we must specify which policy regime is in force. We consider four regimes: targets for the money supply, exchange rate, price level or nominal income. We assume (following our later analysis) that a price level target is formulated in terms of the final expenditure price index, P (though it is not difficult to rework the analysis on the assumption that p_d is the relevant target variable). Similarly for nominal income targets, we assume that PY is targeted.

From the definition of Q, with P^* constant, and from (10.2.2), we have:

$$\frac{\partial \bar{Q}}{\partial u} = \bar{Q}\left(\frac{1}{\bar{E}}\frac{\partial \bar{E}}{\partial u} - \frac{1}{\bar{P}_d}\frac{\partial \bar{P}_d}{\partial u}\right)$$

$$\frac{1}{\bar{P}}\frac{\partial \bar{P}}{\partial u} = \frac{(1 - \theta)}{\bar{P}_d}\frac{\partial \bar{P}_d}{\partial u} + \frac{\theta}{\bar{E}}\frac{\partial \bar{E}}{\partial u}$$

for any disturbance u. Rearranging, we may obtain:

$$\frac{1}{\bar{P}_d}\frac{\partial \bar{P}_d}{\partial u} = \frac{1}{\bar{P}}\frac{\partial \bar{P}}{\partial u} - \frac{\theta}{\bar{Q}}\frac{\partial \bar{Q}}{\partial u} \tag{10.2.23}$$

$$\frac{1}{\bar{E}}\frac{\partial \bar{E}}{\partial u} = \frac{(1 - \theta)}{\bar{Q}}\frac{\partial \bar{Q}}{\partial u} + \frac{1}{\bar{P}}\frac{\partial \bar{P}}{\partial u}. \tag{10.2.24}$$

Now consider the case where $u = \tilde{X}$. Since real money balances $\bar{M}/\bar{P}$ and real income $\bar{Y}$ are unaffected by this disturbance, monetary targets, price level targets and nominal income targets all imply $\partial \bar{P}/\partial \tilde{X} = 0$. Since $\partial \bar{Q}/\partial \tilde{X} < 0$, it follows from (10.2.23) and (10.2.24) that $\partial \bar{E}/\partial \tilde{X} < 0$, $\partial \bar{P}_d/\partial \tilde{X} > 0$. For these policies, the increase in competitiveness resulting from a fall in exports occurs via a depreciation of the exchange rate. Since this raises the price of the imported goods component entering the overall price index, the price, P_d, of domestically produced goods must fall.

Matters are somewhat different for an exchange rate target regime. With $\bar{E}$ fixed, $\partial \bar{Q}/\partial \tilde{X} < 0$ implies $\partial \bar{P}/\partial \tilde{X} > 0$, and hence $\partial \bar{P}_d/\partial X > 0$, using (10.2.23) and (10.2.24). In the face of a fall in exports, $\bar{Q}$ can rise only through a fall in $\bar{P}$. Since $\bar{P}$ falls, with $\bar{E}P^*$ constant, the fall in $\bar{P}_d$ must be greater than for the other regimes. Exchange rate targets are, therefore, likely to impose a longer period of deflation relative to the other regimes.

Now consider the alternative shock, $\tilde{h}$, bringing about a fall in equilibrium output $\bar{Y}$. For this case, each of the four regimes has distinct effects. Under monetary targets,

$$\frac{1}{\bar{P}} \frac{\partial \bar{P}}{\partial \tilde{h}} = -\frac{\bar{P}}{\bar{M}} \frac{\partial(\bar{M}/\bar{P})}{\partial \tilde{h}} > 0$$

so that the price level, $\bar{P}$, rises. Since $\partial \bar{Q}/\partial \tilde{h} < 0$, $\partial \bar{P}_d/\partial \tilde{h} > 0$ from (10.2.23). Thus the fall in real money balances occurs via a rise in the general price level, associated also with a rise in its domestic component. But from (10.2.24) $\partial \bar{E}/\partial \tilde{h}$ is ambiguous, depending on whether the fall in competitiveness resulting from the rise in P_d falls short of, or exceeds, the required fall in competitiveness, any shortfall being made up by an appreciation of the exchange rate.

Under exchange rate targets, $\bar{E}$ is constant, so $\partial \bar{Q}/\partial \tilde{h} < 0$ implies $\partial \bar{P}/\partial \tilde{h} > 0$, from (10.2.24) the required loss in competitiveness occurring via a rise in both $\bar{P}$ and $\bar{P}_d$. Under price level targets, $\bar{P}$ is constant, and $\partial \bar{Q}/\partial \tilde{h} < 0$ implies $\partial \bar{P}_d/\partial \tilde{h} > 0$ from (10.2.23). (Note, however, that the rise in the domestic price component is less than that under exchange rate targets.) Also $\partial \bar{E}/\partial \tilde{h} < 0$, so that an appreciation of the exchange rate occurs. Under nominal income targets, $\bar{P}\bar{Y}$ is constant, while $\partial \bar{Y}/\partial \tilde{h} < 0$, so that $\partial \bar{P}/\partial \tilde{h} > 0$, and hence from (10.2.23) $\partial \bar{P}_d/\partial h > 0$. But from (10.2.24) $\partial \bar{E}/\partial \tilde{h}$ is ambiguous, since the loss of competitiveness induced by the rise in prices may exceed or fall short of the required loss in competitiveness, the difference being made up by an exchange rate adjustment.

The foregoing illustrates that the impact of exogenous disturbances depends on the nature of the disturbance and the policy regime in force. It also emphasizes the fact that policy, notably fiscal policy, is heavily constrained in the context of a small open economy, at least as long as a stable price level (or, more generally, a given inflation target) remains a policy objective.

10.2.8. Linearization of the model

For the subsequent analysis it is convenient to linearize the model in the vicinity of the long-run equilibrium. For variable X with long-run equilibrium value $\bar{X}$ let us denote $\log X/\bar{X}$ by x. Then (10.2.14), (10.2.6′), (10.2.7′) and (10.2.12′) can be expressed in log-linear form as

$$y = \alpha_1 q - \alpha_2(r - \dot{p}^e) + \alpha_3 v + \alpha_4 g - \alpha_5 t, \tag{10.2.25}$$

$$\dot{p}_d = \beta_1 y + \beta_2(\dot{p}^* + \dot{e})^e + (1 - \beta_2)\dot{p}_d^e, \tag{10.2.26}$$

$$m = \gamma_1 y - \gamma_2 r + p + \gamma_3 v, \tag{10.2.27}$$

$$\dot{v} = \phi_0 g - \phi_1 y + \phi_2 q - \phi_3 t - p, \tag{10.2.28}$$

where all parameters are positive, all variables except the interest rate are in log form and r has been redefined so that $\bar{r} = 0$ (that is r is the deviation from its long-run equilibrium value). In (10.2.28) we have that

$$\phi_0 = \frac{\bar{G}}{\bar{V}}; \; \phi_3 = \frac{\bar{I}}{\bar{V}} \tag{10.2.29}$$

and

$$\phi_1 = \frac{1}{\bar{V}}\left(\frac{\partial S}{\partial y} + \frac{\partial(QZ)}{\partial y}\right) \simeq \frac{\bar{Y}}{\bar{V}}\left(\frac{\partial S}{\partial Y} + \frac{\partial(QZ)}{\partial Y}\right), \tag{10.2.30}$$

since $X \simeq \bar{X}(1 + x)$ for small x. In (10.2.30.) $\partial S/\partial Y$ and $\partial(QZ)/\partial Y$ are the marginal taxation rate and the marginal propensity to import at $Y = \bar{Y}$ respectively. The parameter ϕ_2 is given by

$$\phi_2 = \frac{1}{\bar{V}}\left(\frac{\partial X}{\partial q} - \frac{\partial}{\partial q}(QZ)\right), \tag{10.2.31}$$

where the term in brackets is the response of the balance of payments to a change in competitiveness. If M, G and T are exogenous government policy variables, then $g = t = m = 0$.

10.3. POLICY RULES

The specification of fiscal instruments in the model is relatively straightforward. Government spending, G, may be treated as an instrument. Autonomous taxes, T, and the tax schedule $S(.)$, may be considered as instruments. Since we work in terms of a linearized model, we confine attention to T, rather than $S(.)$, since changes in the latter modify the coefficients, α_i, of Equation (10.2.25).

It is fairly common to treat the money supply as the monetary instrument. The problem with this approach is that the government does not usually control the money supply directly, as is illustrated by the failure of governments to attain their explicitly formulated and publicly announced targets for the money supply. A more realistic formulation is to treat the money supply as demand determined at given levels of interest rates, and to permit the monetary authorities to adjust short-term interest rates (over which they have a very great influence) to attain monetary targets or other policy objectives. Thus the rate of interest, not the money supply, is treated as the monetary instrument. Thus the instruments of policy are G, T and r.

It will be noted that the exchange rate is *not* an instrument, though the authorities can seek to influence it indirectly through their choice of G, T and r. (In this, it resembles the money supply.) We exclude the possibility that the authorities could use direct intervention in the foreign exchange market to control the exchange rate. The feasible size of such intervention is small relative to the volume of privately controlled mobile money capital, and this assumption appears to conform most realistically to the impracticability of control through this route. (Formally the assumption of perfect capital mobility implies that an infinite volume of funds would be required by the authorities to influence the exchange rate.)

The government may use its instruments to try to influence those final objectives (e.g. real output, y and/or the price level, p) with which it is concerned. The problem it faces is how to determine the appropriate time path for its instruments and the way in which instruments should be varied in response to fluctuations in the final objectives.

This problem may be tackled by dynamic programming [see IV, Chapter 16] or optimal control theory [see Engineering, Chapter 14]. A loss function is set up [see VI, §19.1], expressing the penalties attached to movements in final objectives away from their desired level, as well as the costs associated with movements in instruments. The optimal time path for instruments is then derived as the solution to the problem of minimizing the loss function.

This optimization problem is complex. But, in the context of our model with rational expectations, a further complication arises. When the authorities adopt the optimal rule, the dynamics and behaviour of the system will alter. (This is precisely the purpose of the policy.) But agents will take this into account in forming their expectations. Thus in contrast to physical systems in the context of which optimal control methods were developed, the behaviour of the system will alter as control is applied. This point, known as the Lucas critique of conventional econometric models (see Lucas, 1976) greatly complicates the task of formulating optimal policy (though it does not render it impossible).

One response to this complexity, combined with uncertainty about model specification, has been to propose the pursuit of intermediate targets; that is, variables which are not final objectives in their own right, but are felt to be sufficiently important in influencing key final objectives. Thus monetary targets have been advocated as desirable in maintaining stability in the price level, at least in the longer run. Exchange rate targets have also been proposed in this regard. (See Artis and Currie, 1981.)

In the following, we assume that the authorities pursue either final objectives or intermediate targets by means of rather simple policy response functions. Thus, we might envisage that interest rates are moved from their long-run level to the extent that intermediate and final objectives deviate from their desired level. For example, we might have

$$r - \hat{r} = \delta[\chi_1(m - \hat{m}) + \chi_2(e - \hat{e}) + \chi_3(p - \hat{p}) + \chi_4(y - \hat{y})] \qquad (10.3.1)$$

where $\hat{x}$ denotes the level of x desired by the authorities. Pursuit of a money supply target alone would be captured by $\chi_1 = 1$, $\chi_i = 0(i \neq 1)$. An exchange rate target regime or price level target regime can be modelled by $\chi_2 = 1$ or $\chi_3 = 1$, setting other coefficients to zero. A nominal income target (as advocated, for example, by Meade (1982)) is modelled by setting $\chi_3 = \chi_4 = 1$, $\chi_1 = \chi_2 = 0$. Intermediate regimes may be obtained by linear combinations of these parameter values.

In what follows, we assume that instruments are adjusted only gradually according to a lagged adjustment version of (10.3.1). Such sluggishness in response may well reflect costs associated with, or constraints on, the adjustment of instruments.

Similar adjustment rules may be specified for the fiscal variables G and T. However, in what follows, we assume that G and T are not varied. This amounts to assuming that fiscal policy is set appropriately for longer-run equilibrium, and then automatic fiscal stabilizers are allowed to operate as output and hence the fiscal deficit. (Recall that the tax schedule $S(.)$ is fixed, so that the level of taxes is endogenous, rising when the economy is expanding but falling in slump.) Thus, we will examine the effectiveness of monetary, exchange rate, price level and nominal income targets in combination with automatic fiscal stabilizers. It is of interest to note that the combination of automatic fiscal stabilizers with monetary targets is one often advocated by monetarists.

10.4. THE COMPLETE CONTINUOUS-TIME DYNAMIC MODEL

In the short-run model of Section 2, the expectational variables $\dot{p}^e$, $\dot{p}^e_d$, $\dot{e}^e$, $\dot{p}^{*e}$ were left as exogenously determined. The model can be closed by assuming that expectations are formulated by some learning process such as adaptive learning (e.g. Turnovsky, 1977, Chapter 12). However, we shall pursue the route of *rational expectations*; that is, we assume that economic agents know and use the model to formulate their expectations (see Chapter 9).

A second development of the model will be the inclusion of stochastic exogenous disturbances in the instantaneous equilibrium relationships. These will consist of a demand disturbance, e_1, in the output equation (10.2.25) which will capture, for instance, changes in savings or investment patterns; a supply disturbance, e_2, in the domestic inflation equation (10.2.26); a money demand disturbance, e_3, in (10.2.27); a disturbance, e_4, in (10.3.1) to capture policy errors and a wealth disturbance, e_7, in (10.2.28) which could arise, for example, from changes in capital stock. The exogenous world variables r^* and p^* can also be treated as stochastic disturbances and we write $e_5 = r^*$, $e_6 = p^*$.

A third development relates to the instantaneous equilibrium relationships in the output, wage-price and monetary sectors. We shall assume that these sectors adjust sluggishly at a rate proportional to the gap between actual and instantaneous equilibrium values. If we write the instantaneous equilibrium relationships (10.2.25)–(10.2.27) in the form $x_i = f_i(\mathbf{x})$ where $\mathbf{x}$ denotes the vector of endogenous variables, then the adjustment process for variable i can be written

$$\dot{x}_i = \psi_i(f_i(\mathbf{x}) - x_i), \quad \psi_i > 0 \tag{10.4.1}$$

where ψ_i is a constant indicating the speed at which x_i adjusts. (Thus the mean lag for x_i keeping x_j fixed, $j \neq i$, is given by

$$\frac{\int_0^\infty \tau \bar{x}_i(\tau) \, d\tau}{\int_0^\infty \bar{x}_i(\tau) \, d\tau} = \psi_i^{-1}$$

from (10.4.1) and integration by parts [see IV, §4.3] where $\bar{x}_i = x_i - f_i(\mathbf{x})$.)

Similarly, we assume that the policy instrument r adjusts slowly to its desired policy response. In other words, (10.3.1) now becomes a long-run response for an adjustment process.

$$\frac{dr}{dt} = \delta_2[\delta_1(\chi_1 m + \chi_2 e + \chi_3 p + \chi_4 y) - r] \tag{10.4.2}$$

where the desired values are for simplicity equal to zero (note that variables are measured as deviations from their long-run equilibrium), for the moment the stochastic disturbance is ignored and δ_2 has the same interpretation as ψ_i in (10.4.1)

Finally, competitiveness affects the accumulation of wealth indirectly through its effect on the balance of payments (see (10.2.10) and (10.2.1)). We assume that this effect occurs with a lag so that q in (10.2.25) and (10.2.28) is replaced with a competitiveness effect q_z where

$$\dot{q}_z = \psi(q - q_z). \tag{10.4.3}$$

With these changes the full dynamic model in log-linear form becomes in the case of one policy instrument, the interest rate, and treating fiscal variables q and t as given:

$$dy = \psi_1[\alpha_1 q - \alpha_2(r - \dot{p}^e) + \alpha_3 v - y + e_1] \, dt, \tag{10.4.4}$$

$$d\dot{p}_d = \psi_2[\beta_1 y + \beta_2(\dot{e}_6 + \dot{e})^e + (1 - \beta_2)\dot{p}_d^e - \dot{p}_d + e_2] \, dt, \tag{10.4.5}$$

$$dm = \psi_3[\gamma_1 y - \gamma_2 r + p + \gamma_3 v - m + e_3] \, dt, \tag{10.4.6}$$

$$dq_z = \psi_4(q - q_z) \, dt, \tag{10.4.7}$$

$$dv = [-\phi_1 y + \phi_2 q_z + e_7] \, dt - dp, \tag{10.4.8}$$

$$dr = \delta_2[\delta_1(\chi_1 m + \chi_2 e + \chi_3 p + \chi_4 y) - r + e_4] \, dt, \tag{10.4.9}$$

$$de^e = (r - e_5)\,dt, \tag{10.4.10}$$

where $e_5 = r^*$, $e_6 = p^*$, $q = p^* + e - p_d$ and $\dot{p} = (1 - \theta)\dot{p}_d + \theta(\dot{p}^* + \dot{e})$.

The reason for not writing the dynamic relationships in the form of a normal differential equation will become clear when we consider the dynamics of the stochastic disturbances below. But first the exchange rate relationship (10.4.10) requires further explanation. Unlike the output, wage-price and monetary sectors, which adjust slowly, the international capital market is assumed to adjust instantly in a world of perfect capital mobility. The exchange rate is a 'free variable' which can make discrete jumps in response to disturbances or changes in exogenous variables and policy rules so as to maintain equality between its expected rate of depreciation and the differential between domestic and foreign interest rates. Since e can make discrete jumps $\dot{e}^e$ must be interpreted as a right-hand side time derivative. The economic interpretation of this assumption is that all systematic opportunities for super-profitable trade in the foreign exchange market are eliminated by arbitrage or speculative behaviour.

The stochastic disturbances e_i are assumed to follow a first order autoregressive process. This can best be understood by first considering the more familiar discrete time case

$$e_{it+1} = \rho e_{it} + \varepsilon_{it+1}; \qquad t = 0, 1, 2, \ldots, \tag{10.4.11}$$

where $|\rho| < 1$ and ε_{it} is normally and independently distributed of past values with zero mean and constant variance σ_u^2. Now introduce a stochastic process (to become the Wiener process in continuous time [see II, Chapter 22 and IV, §18.1.3]) defined by $u_{it} = \sum_{\tau=0}^{t} \varepsilon_{it}$ so that $\varepsilon_{it+1} = u_{it+1} - u_{it}$. If we then replace the time interval of unity in (10.4.11) with a time interval h we obtain the continuous time analogue of (10.4.11) as the limit as $h \to 0$ of

$$e_i(t + h) - e_i(t) = -h^{-1}(1 - \rho(h))he_i(t) + u_i(t + h) - u_i(t), \tag{10.4.12}$$

where $u_i(t + h) - u_i(t) = \delta u_i$ is a normally and independently distributed disturbance with constant variance occurring at intervals of h [see II, §11.4 and IV, §18.1.3]. Letting $h \to 0$ in (10.4.12.) we arrive at

$$de_i = -\mu_i e_i dt + du_i, \tag{10.4.13}$$

where $\mu_i = \lim_{h \to 0} h^{-1}(1 - \rho(h))$ is positive and assumed to exist. Var(du_i) (where du_i is the limit of δu_i as $h \to 0$) can be found by noting that

$$\sigma^2 = \text{Var}\,(\varepsilon_i(t + 1)) = \text{Var}\,(u_i(t + 1) - u_i(t))$$
$$= \text{Var}\,(u_i(t + 1) - u_i(t + 1 - h) + u_i(t + 1 - h) - u_i(t + 1 - 2h) + \cdots$$
$$+ u_i(t + h) - u_i(t))$$
$$= h^{-1}\,\text{Var}\,(\delta u_i) \tag{10.4.14}$$

since there are h^{-1} divisions and δu_i is independently distributed with constant variance. We conclude that on letting $h \to 0$

$$du_i \sim \text{NID}(0, \sigma^2 dt) \tag{10.4.15}$$

that is, du_i is normally and independently distributed with a zero mean and constant variance $\sigma^2 dt$ [see II, §11.4].

Note that $u_i(t)$ is not differentiable with respect to time [see IV, §18.3]. For suppose that $u_i(t)$ is differentiable (in the mean square sense) [see IV, §18.3]. Then

$$\lim_{h \to 0} E \frac{(u_i(t+h) - u_i(t)}{h} - u_i'(t))^2 = 0 \tag{10.4.16}$$

must hold (Hoel *et al.*, 1972, p. 138). Since $E(u_i(t+h) - u_i(t)) = 0$ the condition becomes

$$\lim_{h \to 0} \text{Var} \frac{(\delta u_i)}{h} = E(u_i'(t))^2. \tag{10.4.17}$$

However, $\text{Var}(h^{-1} \delta u_i) = h^{-2} \text{Var}(\delta u_i) = \sigma^2 / h$ from (10.4.14) so that the limit in (10.4.17) does not exist.

The dynamic relationship (10.4.13) for e_i, $i = 1, \ldots, 7$ completes the specification of the model. The expected values of $\dot{p}^e$ and $\dot{p}_d^e$ appearing on the right-hand side of (10.4.4) and (10.4.5) can be replaced by $\dot{p}$ and p_d since with rational expectations the forecast error will depend only on the stochastic disturbances $d\mathbf{u} = (du_1, \ldots, du_7)'$ and, as we have seen, this is of order $dt^{1/2}$. Hence, replacing $\dot{p}^e$ and $\dot{p}_d^e$ with $\dot{p}$ and p_d amounts to ignoring terms of order $dt^{3/2}$, which is legitimate.

In what follows we restrict ourselves to the use of interest rates in the pursuit of a money supply level target, exchange rate target, price level target or nominal output target or some combination of those. In addition, we have the dynamic identity that

$$dp^d = \dot{p}_d dt. \tag{10.4.18}$$

We may then write (10.4.4)–(10.4.10), (10.4.13) and (10.4.18) as

$$\begin{bmatrix} d\mathbf{z} \\ d\mathbf{e}^e \end{bmatrix} = A \begin{bmatrix} \mathbf{z} \\ e \end{bmatrix} dt + d\mathbf{w} \tag{10.4.19}$$

where

$$\mathbf{z} = (\bar{y} \ \dot{p}_d \ p_d \ m \ r \ q_z \ v \ \mathbf{e})'$$
$$\mathbf{e} = (e_1, \ldots, e_7)'$$
$$d\mathbf{w} = (0 \ 0 \ 0 \ 0 \ 0 \ 0 \ -\theta \ du_6 \ du_1, \ldots, du_7 \ 0)'$$

and A is given in (10.4.20). Since $d\mathbf{w}/dt$ does not exist, we cannot divide (10.4.19) by dt to obtain a normal differential equation.

$$\mathbf{A} = \left[\begin{array}{ccccccc|cccc|ccc}
-\psi_1 & \alpha_2(1-\theta)\psi_1 & -\psi_1\alpha_1 & 0 & -\psi_1(1-\theta)\alpha_2 & 0 & \psi_1\alpha_3 & \psi_1 & 0 & 0 & 0 & -\psi_1\alpha_2\theta & \delta & \psi_1\alpha_1 \\
\psi_2\beta_1 & -\psi_2\beta_2 & 0 & 0 & \psi_2\beta_2 & 0 & 0 & 0 & \psi_2 & 0 & 0 & -\psi_2\beta_2 & -\psi_2\beta_2\mu_6 & 0 \\
0 & 1 & 0 & 0 & 0 & 0 & 0 & 0 & 0 & \psi_3 & 0 & 0 & 0 & 0 \\
\psi_3\gamma_1 & 0 & \psi_3(1-\theta) & -\psi_3 & -\psi_3\gamma_2 & 0 & \psi_3\gamma_3 & 0 & 0 & 0 & 0 & 0 & \psi_3\theta & \psi_3\theta \\
\delta_2\delta_1\chi_4 & 0 & \delta_2\delta_1(1-\theta)\chi_3 & \delta_2\delta_1\chi_1 & -\delta_2 & 0 & 0 & 0 & 0 & \delta_2 & 0 & 0 & 0 & \delta_2\delta_1(\chi_2+\theta\chi_3) \\
0 & 0 & -\psi_4 & 0 & 0 & -\psi_4 & 0 & 0 & 0 & 0 & 0 & 0 & \psi_4 & \psi_4 \\
-\phi_1 & -(1-\theta) & 0 & 0 & -\theta & \phi_2 & 0 & 0 & 0 & 0 & 0 & \theta & \theta\mu_6 & 0 \\
\hline
\multicolumn{7}{c|}{\mathbf{0}} & \multicolumn{4}{c|}{} & \multicolumn{3}{c}{} \\
 & & & & & & & \multicolumn{4}{c|}{\mathbf{D}} & 0 & 0 & 0 \\
 & & & & & & & \multicolumn{4}{c|}{} & 0 & -1 & 0 \\
\end{array}\right] \tag{10.4.20}$$

where $\delta = \alpha_1\psi_1 - \psi_1\alpha_2\theta\mu_6$ and $\mathbf{D}$ is a 7×7 diagonal matrix with ith element $-\mu_i$.

10.5. THE SOLUTION OF DYNAMIC STOCHASTIC MODELS UNDER RATIONAL EXPECTATIONS

The model summarized by (10.4.18) can be generalized to allow for any number of free variables without undue complication. We consider then the model

$$\begin{bmatrix} d\mathbf{z} \\ d\mathbf{x}^e \end{bmatrix} = \mathbf{A} \begin{bmatrix} \mathbf{z} \\ \mathbf{x} \end{bmatrix} dt + \begin{bmatrix} d\mathbf{w}^1 \\ d\mathbf{w}^2 \end{bmatrix}, \tag{10.5.1}$$

where $\mathbf{z}(t)$ is an $(n-m) \times 1$ vector of variables predetermined at time t; $\mathbf{x}(t)$ is an $m \times 1$ vector of 'free' or non-predetermined variables; $\mathbf{A}$ is an $n \times n$ matrix and $\text{cov}(d\mathbf{w}) = \mathbf{\Sigma} dt$ where $\mathbf{\Sigma}$ is an $n \times n$ covariance matrix [see II, §13.3.1]. The significance and meaning of the terms predetermined and non-predetermined should become clear as the solution procedure unfolds.

Assume that $\mathbf{A}$ has distinct eigenvalues and therefore is diagonalizable with $\mathbf{\Lambda}$ the diagonal matrix of eigenvalues of $\mathbf{A}$ and $\mathbf{M}$ the associated matrix of eigenvectors [see I, §7.4]. Then $\mathbf{M}\mathbf{A} = \mathbf{\Lambda}\mathbf{M}$ which on partitioning $\mathbf{\Lambda}$, $\mathbf{M}$ and $\mathbf{A}$ conformably [see I, §6.6] we write as

$$\begin{bmatrix} \mathbf{M}_{11} & \mathbf{M}_{12} \\ \mathbf{M}_{21} & \mathbf{M}_{22} \end{bmatrix} \begin{bmatrix} \mathbf{A}_{11} & \mathbf{A}_{12} \\ \mathbf{A}_{21} & \mathbf{A}_{22} \end{bmatrix} = \begin{bmatrix} \mathbf{\Lambda}_1 & 0 \\ 0 & \mathbf{\Lambda}_2 \end{bmatrix} \begin{bmatrix} \mathbf{M}_{11} & \mathbf{M}_{12} \\ \mathbf{M}_{21} & \mathbf{M}_{22} \end{bmatrix}, \tag{10.5.2}$$

where $\mathbf{\Lambda}_1$ is the $(n-\bar{m}) \times (n-\bar{m})$ diagonal matrix of eigenvalues with negative real parts and $\mathbf{\Lambda}_2$ is the $\bar{m} \times \bar{m}$ diagonal matrix of eigenvalues with positive real parts. We shall assume that $\bar{m} = m$ which Blanchard and Kahn (1980) have shown to be a necessary condition for a non-explosive solution to (10.5.1) to exist.

Define

$$\mathbf{y} = \begin{bmatrix} \mathbf{y}^1 \\ \mathbf{y}^2 \end{bmatrix} = \mathbf{M} \begin{bmatrix} \mathbf{z} \\ \mathbf{x} \end{bmatrix}. \tag{10.5.3}$$

Then from (10.5.1) and (10.5.2) we have

$$\begin{aligned} d\mathbf{y} &= \mathbf{M} \begin{bmatrix} d\mathbf{z} \\ d\mathbf{x} \end{bmatrix} \\ &= \mathbf{M} \begin{bmatrix} d\mathbf{z} \\ d\mathbf{x}^e \end{bmatrix} + \begin{bmatrix} 0 \\ d\mathbf{x} - d\mathbf{x}^e \end{bmatrix} \\ &= \mathbf{M}\mathbf{A} \begin{bmatrix} \mathbf{z} \\ \mathbf{x} \end{bmatrix} dt + d\mathbf{w} + \begin{bmatrix} 0 \\ d\mathbf{x} - d\mathbf{x}^e \end{bmatrix} \\ &= \mathbf{\Lambda}\mathbf{y}dt + 0(d\mathbf{w}) \end{aligned} \tag{10.5.4}$$

since the forecast error $d\mathbf{x} - d\mathbf{x}^e$ is $0(d\mathbf{w})$.

Focusing on the last $n-m$ elements of (10.5.4) we have that

$$dy_i = \lambda_i y_i \, dt + 0(\sqrt{dt}), \quad i = n-m+1, \ldots, n \tag{10.5.5}$$

since $dw = 0(\sqrt{dt})$. In (10.5.5) $\text{Re}(\lambda_i) > 0$ and it follows that the only non-explosive solution as $dt \to 0$ is $y_i = 0$, $i = n - m + 1, \ldots, n$; that is, $\mathbf{y}^2 = \mathbf{0}$. Hence from (10.5.3)

$$\mathbf{y}^2 = \mathbf{M}_{21}\mathbf{z} + \mathbf{M}_{22}\mathbf{x} = \mathbf{0}. \tag{10.5.6}$$

Assuming $\mathbf{M}_{22}$ is non-singular [see I, §6.4] we then arrive at

$$\mathbf{x} = \mathbf{M}_{22}^{-1}\mathbf{M}_{21}\mathbf{z}. \tag{10.5.7}$$

Substituting (10.5.7) into (10.5.1), $\mathbf{z}$ is then obtained as a solution to the stochastic differential equation

$$d\mathbf{z} = (\mathbf{A}_{11} - \mathbf{A}_{12}\mathbf{M}_{22}^{-1}\mathbf{M}_{21})\mathbf{z}\,dt + d\mathbf{w}^1. \tag{10.5.8}$$

The importance of the distinction between predetermined and non-predetermined variables can now be seen. Suppose that the economy is initially in a non-equilibrium state $\begin{bmatrix} \mathbf{z}(0) \\ \mathbf{x}(0) \end{bmatrix}$. The free variables must jump to the point $\mathbf{x}(0) = -\mathbf{M}_{22}^{-1}\mathbf{M}_{21}\mathbf{z}(0)$ to be on a stable trajectory given by (10.5.7) and in that sense they are not predetermined at $t = 0$.

If we put $\mathbf{B} = \mathbf{A}_{11} - \mathbf{A}_{12}\mathbf{M}_{22}^{-1}\mathbf{M}_{21}$ then the mean trajectory $\mathbf{z}^e$ is the solution to

$$d\mathbf{z}^e = \mathbf{B}\mathbf{z}^e\,dt \tag{10.5.9}$$

on taking expectations of (10.5.8) at time $t = 0$. The solution is

$$\mathbf{z}^e = \exp(\mathbf{B}t)\mathbf{z}^e(0) \tag{10.5.10}$$

where $\exp(\mathbf{B}t) = \sum_{r=0}^{\infty} \mathbf{B}^r t^r / r!$ and $\mathbf{z}^e(0) = \mathbf{z}(0)$ because $\mathbf{z}(0)$ is observed at $t = 0$. The full solution of (10.5.8) can be shown (Chow, 1979; Hoel *et al.* 1972) to be

$$\mathbf{z}(t) = \mathbf{z}^e + \int_0^t \exp\{\mathbf{A}(t - s)\}\,d\mathbf{w}^1(s), \tag{10.5.11}$$

where the integral in (10.5.11) is defined by

$$\int_a^b f(s)d\mathbf{w}^1 = f(b)\mathbf{w}^1(b) - f(a)\mathbf{w}^1(a) - \int_a^b \frac{df}{ds}\mathbf{w}^1(s)\,ds \tag{10.5.12}$$

(Note that although $\mathbf{w}^1(t)$ is not differentiable it is *continuous* so that the integral in (10.5.12) exists). From (10.5.11) we can see that $E(\mathbf{z}(t)\,d\mathbf{w}^{1'}(t)) = \mathbf{0}$ (a zero matrix) since $E(d\mathbf{w}^1(t)) = E(d\mathbf{w}^1(s)d\mathbf{w}^{1'}(t)) = 0$ for $s < t$ by the properties of $d\mathbf{w}$ already discussed.

Finally the covariance properties of the system [see II, §9.6] can be obtained as follows. Define

$$\text{cov}\begin{bmatrix} \mathbf{z} \\ \mathbf{x} \end{bmatrix} = \begin{bmatrix} \mathbf{Z} & \mathbf{Y} \\ \mathbf{Y}^T & \mathbf{X} \end{bmatrix}. \tag{10.5.13}$$

Then from (10.5.8) defining $\tilde{z} = z - z^e$ and $\tilde{x}$ similarly, we have

$$
\begin{aligned}
\mathbf{Y} &= E(\tilde{z}\tilde{x}') \\
&= -E(\tilde{z}\tilde{z}')(\mathbf{M}_{22}^{-1}\mathbf{M}_{21})' \\
&= -\mathbf{Z}(\mathbf{M}_{22}^{-1}\mathbf{M}_{21})'
\end{aligned}
\tag{10.5.14}
$$

and

$$
\begin{aligned}
\mathbf{X} &= E(\tilde{x}\tilde{x}') \\
&= \mathbf{M}_{22}^{-1}\mathbf{M}_{21}\mathbf{Z}(\mathbf{M}_{22}^{-1}\mathbf{M}_{21})',
\end{aligned}
\tag{10.5.15}
$$

using $\mathbf{Z} = E(\tilde{z}\tilde{z}')$. Following Chow (1979) we differentiate Z to obtain

$$
\begin{aligned}
\delta\mathbf{Z} &= E((\tilde{z} + \delta\tilde{z})(\tilde{z} + \delta\tilde{z})) - E(\tilde{z}\tilde{z}') \\
&= E(\tilde{z}\delta\tilde{z}' + \delta\tilde{z}'\tilde{z}) + E(\delta\tilde{z}\delta\tilde{z}').
\end{aligned}
\tag{10.5.16}
$$

From (10.5.8), $\delta\tilde{z} = \mathbf{B}\tilde{z}\delta t + \delta w^1$ so that (10.5.16) becomes

$$
\begin{aligned}
\delta\mathbf{Z} &= E(\tilde{z}\tilde{z}\mathbf{B}'\delta t + \tilde{z}\delta w^{1'} + \mathbf{B}\tilde{z}z'\delta t + \delta w^1 z' + \mathbf{B}\tilde{z}\tilde{z}\mathbf{B}'\delta t^2 + \\
&\quad \mathbf{B}z\delta w^{1'}\delta t + \delta w^1 z'\mathbf{B}'\delta t + \delta w^1\delta w^{1'}) \\
&= (\mathbf{Z}\mathbf{B}' + \mathbf{B}\mathbf{Z})\delta t + \mathbf{B}\mathbf{Z}\mathbf{B}'\delta t^2 + \Sigma_1\delta t,
\end{aligned}
\tag{10.5.17}
$$

where we have used the independence of z and dw^1 arising out of (10.5.11) and we have put $\operatorname{cov}(\delta w^1) = \Sigma_1\delta t$. On letting $\delta t \to 0$ (10.5.17) becomes

$$
\frac{d\mathbf{Z}}{dt} = \mathbf{Z}\mathbf{B}' + \mathbf{B}\mathbf{Z} + \Sigma_1
\tag{10.5.18}
$$

Equation (10.5.18) provides a method of finding the asymptotic covariance matrix $\mathbf{Z}^*$ in the long run steady state when $d\mathbf{Z}/dt = 0$. Putting $\mathbf{Z} = \mathbf{Z}^*$ and $d\mathbf{Z}^*/dt = 0$ in (10.5.18) gives

$$
\mathbf{Z}^*\mathbf{B}' + \mathbf{B}\mathbf{Z}^* + \Sigma_1 = 0
\tag{10.5.19}
$$

If we write $z^* = (z_{11}z_{12}\ldots z_{1n}z_{21}z_{22}\ldots z_{2n}\ldots z_{n1}\ldots z_{nn})$ where $\mathbf{Z}^* = [z_{ij}]$ and similarly define σ in terms of the elements of Σ, then (10.5.19) may be rewritten as

$$
(\mathbf{B} \times \mathbf{I} + \mathbf{I} \times \mathbf{B})z^* = \sigma
\tag{10.5.20}
$$

where $\mathbf{B} \times \mathbf{I}$ and $\mathbf{I} \times \mathbf{B}$ are Kronecker products [see I, §6.15] (see, for example, Johnston, 1968). It can be shown that the matrix on the left-hand side of (10.5.20) is non-singular (Currie and Levine, 1982) and we may therefore obtain the solution to $\mathbf{Z}^*$ in terms of z^* given by

$$
z^* = (\mathbf{B} \times \mathbf{I} + \mathbf{I} \times \mathbf{B})^{-1}\sigma.
\tag{10.5.21}
$$

10.6. A SIMPLE EXAMPLE OF THE SOLUTION PROCEDURE

The case of an *exchange rate target* regime where the disturbances de_4 and de_5 are 'white noise' processes provides a convenient illustration of the solution procedure described in section 10.5. In this case in (10.4.9) and (10.4.13), $\chi_2 = 1$, $\chi_i = 0, i = 2$ and $\mu_4 \neq \mu_5 = 0$. Then from (10.4.19) where z_r consists of the elements of z minus the element r. From (10.6.1) we can see that the pair of variables (r, e) satisfy the following independent subsystem

$$\begin{bmatrix} dr \\ de^e \end{bmatrix} = \begin{bmatrix} -\delta_2 & \delta_1\delta_2 \\ 1 & 0 \end{bmatrix} \begin{bmatrix} r \\ e \end{bmatrix} dt + \begin{bmatrix} du_4 \\ du_5 \end{bmatrix}. \tag{10.6.1}$$

The subsystem (10.6.2) provides us with a simple demonstration of the solution procedure with

$$\mathbf{A} = \begin{bmatrix} -\delta_2 & \delta_1\delta_2 \\ 1 & 0 \end{bmatrix}.$$

The eigenvalues of $\mathbf{A}$ are given by the characteristic equation [see I, §7.3]

$$\det \begin{bmatrix} -\delta_2 - \lambda & \delta_1\delta_2 \\ 1 & -\lambda \end{bmatrix} = 0,$$

which gives the quadratic equation

$$\lambda^2 + \delta_2\lambda - \delta_1\delta_2 = 0. \tag{10.6.2}$$

The roots of (10.6.3) are $\lambda_1, \lambda_2 = (-\delta_2 \pm \sqrt{\delta_2^2 + 4\delta_1\delta_2})/2$ say $\lambda_1 > 0$ and $\lambda_2 < 0$ [see I, §14.5]. The left-eigenvector corresponding to the eigenvector λ_1, $[m_{21}m_{22}]$ in the notation of section 10.5, is given by

$$[m_{21}m_{22}] \begin{bmatrix} -\delta_2 - \lambda & \delta_1\delta_2 \\ 1 & -\lambda_2 \end{bmatrix} = 0 \tag{10.6.3}$$

which gives

$$\frac{m_{22}}{m_{21}} = \delta_2 + \lambda_1 = \frac{\delta_1\delta_2}{\lambda_1} = \theta_1, \tag{10.6.4}$$

say. Similarly

$$\frac{m_{12}}{m_{11}} = \delta_2 + \lambda_2 = \frac{\delta_1\delta_2}{\lambda_2} = -\theta_2, \tag{10.6.5}$$

say, where $\theta_i > 0$ in (10.6.4) and (10.6.5). It follows that we may take

$$\mathbf{M} = \begin{bmatrix} 1 & -\theta_2 \\ 1 & \theta_1 \end{bmatrix} \tag{10.6.6}$$

with $\mathbf{M}_{22}^{-1} = m_{22}^{-1} = \theta_1^{-1}$ and $m_{21} = \mathbf{M}_{21} = 1$ in the notation of section 10.5. The stable trajectory (10.5.7) becomes in this simple case

$$e = -\theta_1^{-1}r \tag{10.6.7}$$

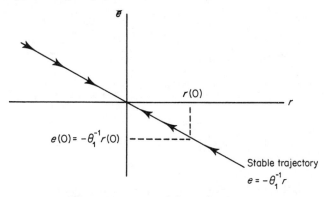

Figure 10.1: Jump of the exchange rate

and the stochastic differential equation (10.5.8) in the predetermined variables is

$$dr = -\delta_2(1 + \theta_1^{-1}\delta_1)r\,dt + du_4. \qquad (10.6.8)$$

The mean or expected trajectory for r is then given by

$$\dot{r}^e = -kr^e, \qquad (10.6.9)$$

where $k = \delta_2(1 + \theta_1^{-1}\delta_1)$ which has a solution [see IV, §7.1]

$$r^e(t) = r(0)e^{-kt}. \qquad (10.6.10)$$

We note that expectations in (10.6.9) and (10.6.10) are formed at $t = 0$, where $r^e(0) = r(0)$ because $r(0)$ is observed. From (10.6.7) and (10.6.10) it follows that

$$e^e(t) = -\theta_1^{-1}r(0)e^{-kt} \qquad (10.6.11)$$

Figure 10.1 shows the stable trajectory and the discrete jump of the exchange rate following a decline in the long-run equilibrium value of r. This could arise, for instance, if the foreign interest rate falls. Then the interest rate will be above its long-run value that is $r(0) > 0$. The exchange rate will then instantaneously *appreciate* to $e(0) = -\theta_1^{-1}r(0)$ before *depreciating* along its stable trajectory to its long-run equilibrium. The corresponding mean trajectories are shown in Figure 6.2 by continuous lines.

Turning to the stochastic properties of the system, (10.5.19) becomes simply

$$-2kZ^* + \Sigma_1 = 0,$$

where Z^* is the asymptotic variance of r, $\text{var}^*(r)$ say, and $\text{var}(du_4) = \Sigma_1\,dt$. It follows that

$$\text{var}^*(r) = (2k)^{-1}\Sigma_1 \qquad (10.6.12)$$

and from (10.5.14) and (10.5.15) that

$$\text{cov}^*(e,r) = -\theta_1^{-1}\,\text{var}^*(r) \qquad (10.6.13)$$

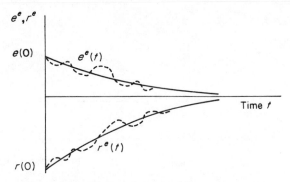

Figure 10.2: Time trajectory of the exchange rate

$$\text{var*}(e) = \theta_1^{-1} \text{var*}(r). \tag{10.6.14}$$

Summarizing,

$$\text{cov*}\begin{bmatrix} r \\ e \end{bmatrix} = (2k)^{-1}\Sigma_1 \begin{bmatrix} 1 & -\theta_1^{-1} \\ -\theta_1^{-1} & \theta_1^{-2} \end{bmatrix}. \tag{10.6.15}$$

Since $\theta_1 = 2\delta_1\delta_2/(-\delta_2 + \sqrt{\delta_2^2 + 4\delta_1\delta_2})$, for the central values discussed in section 8 of $\delta_1 = 4$, $\delta_2 = 1$ we have that $\theta_1 = 2.56$. This implies from (10.6.15) that the long-run volatility of the exchange rate captured by var*(e) is much less than that of the interest rate. Also from (10.6.15) we see that variations in the exchange rate and the interest rate about their mean trajectory are inversely related. These conclusions are illustrated in Figure 10.2 by typical random trajectories shown as dotted lines.

10.7. THE STABILITY OF THE COMPLETE MODEL

We recall from section 10.5 that a necessary condition for a non-explosive solution to the general form (10.5.1) to exist is that the number of stable eigenvalues equals the number of free or non-predetermined variables. From the solution procedure itself we find that the only other condition is that the matrix M_{22} is non-singular. This we shall assume, so that the former condition is also sufficient.

Returning to the full model of (10.4.19) the characteristic equation may be written as

$$\det\begin{bmatrix} \tilde{A} - \lambda I & \tilde{B} \\ 0 & D - \lambda I \end{bmatrix} = 0, \tag{10.7.1}$$

where

$$
\tilde{A} = \begin{bmatrix}
-\psi_1 & \psi_1\alpha_2(1-\theta) & -\psi_1\alpha_1 & 0 & 0 & \psi_1\alpha_3 & -\psi_1\alpha_2(1-\theta) & \psi_1\alpha_1 \\
\psi_2\beta_1 & -\psi_2\beta_2 & 0 & 0 & 0 & 0 & \psi_2\beta_2 & 0 \\
0 & 1 & 0 & 0 & 0 & 0 & 0 & 0 \\
\psi_3\gamma_1 & 0 & \psi_3(1-\theta) & -\psi_3 & 0 & \psi_3\gamma_3 & -\psi_3\gamma_2 & \psi_3\theta \\
0 & 0 & -\psi_4 & 0 & -\psi_4 & 0 & 0 & \psi_4 \\
-\theta_1 & -(1-\theta) & 0 & 0 & \phi_2 & 0 & -\theta & 0 \\
\delta_2\delta_1\chi_4 & 0 & \delta_2\delta_1(1-\theta)\chi_3 & \delta_2\delta_1\chi_1 & 0 & 0 & -\delta_2 & \delta_2\delta_1\chi_2 \\
0 & 0 & 0 & 0 & 0 & 0 & 1 & 0
\end{bmatrix}
$$

$$(10.7.2)$$

and **D** is as in (10.4.20). The matrix $\tilde{B}$ is irrelevant as far as the eigenvalues and stability are concerned because the roots of (10.7.1) are simply the eigenvalues of **A** plus those of **D**. The eigenvalues of **D** are, of course, $\{-\mu_i\}$, $i = 1, 7$.

In the case of an exchange rate target regime ($\chi_2 = 1$, $\chi_i = 0$, $i \neq 2$) the characteristic equation for $\tilde{A}$ decomposes into the subsystem examined in section 10.6, namely

$$
\det\begin{bmatrix}
-\delta_2 - \lambda & \delta_1\delta_2 \\
1 & -\lambda
\end{bmatrix} = 0
\tag{10.7.3}
$$

and

$$
\det\begin{bmatrix}
-\psi_1 - \lambda & \psi_1\alpha_2(1-\theta) & -\psi_1\alpha_1 & 0 & 0 & \psi_1\alpha_3 \\
\psi_2\beta_1 & -\psi_2\beta_2 - \lambda & 0 & 0 & 0 & 0 \\
0 & 1 & -\lambda & 0 & 0 & 0 \\
\psi_3\gamma_1 & 0 & \psi_3(1-\theta) & -\psi_3 - \lambda & 0 & \psi_3\gamma_3 \\
0 & 0 & -\psi_4 & 0 & -\psi_4 - \lambda & 0 \\
-\phi_1 & -(1-\theta) & 0 & 0 & \phi_2 & -\lambda
\end{bmatrix} = 0
$$

$$(10.7.4)$$

Since one of the roots of (10.7.3) is positive and one is negative, as we have seen in section 10.6, it follows that the system is stable if and only if the six roots of (10.7.4) all have negative real parts. Since $(-\psi_3 - \lambda)$ is a factor one of these roots is $\lambda = -\psi_3$. This leaves a characteristic equation of degree 5 which may be tested for stable roots using the Routh–Hurwitz condition [see IV, §7.4.1].

The application of the Routh–Hurwitz test to a fifth degree characteristic equation is very tedious to perform analytically. It is convenient to consider a slightly simpler model in which $q = q_z$, that is the lag in the effect of competitiveness on the balance of payments is ignored. Then the fifth row and column in (10.7.2) go out and the sixth row is replaced with $[-\phi_1 \;\; -(1-\theta) \;\; -\phi_2 \;\; 0 \;\; 0 \;\; -\theta \;\; \phi_2]$. After taking out the factor $(-\psi_3 - \lambda)$ we are then left with the characteristic equation

$$\det \begin{bmatrix} -\psi_1 - \lambda & \psi_1\alpha_2(1-\theta) & -\psi_1\alpha_1 & \psi_1\alpha_3 \\ \psi_2\beta_1 & -\psi_2\beta_2 - \lambda & 0 & 0 \\ 0 & 1 & -\lambda & 0 \\ -\phi_1 & -(1-\theta) & -\phi_2 & -\lambda \end{bmatrix} = 0.$$

On expanding the determinant we arrive at

$$a_0\lambda^4 + a_1\lambda^3 + a_2\lambda^2 + a_3\lambda + a_4 = 0 \tag{10.7.5}$$

where

$$a_0 = 1$$
$$a_1 = \psi_1 + \psi_2\beta_2$$
$$a_2 = \psi_1\alpha_3\phi_1 + \psi_1\psi_2\beta_2 - \psi_1\psi_2\beta_1\alpha_2(1-\theta)$$
$$a_3 = \psi_1\psi_2(\alpha_3[\beta_1(1-\theta) + \phi_1\beta_2] + \alpha_1\beta_1)$$
$$a_4 = \psi_1\psi_2\alpha_3\beta_1\phi_2.$$

By the Routh–Hurwitz condition the roots of (10.7.5) are all stable if and only if

$$a_0 > 0, \; a_1 > 0, \; \begin{vmatrix} a_1 & a_3 \\ a_0 & a_2 \end{vmatrix} > 0, \; \begin{vmatrix} a_1 & a_3 & 0 \\ a_0 & a_2 & a_4 \\ 0 & a_1 & a_3 \end{vmatrix} > 0,$$

$$\begin{vmatrix} a_1 & a_3 & 0 & 0 \\ a_0 & a_2 & a_4 & 0 \\ 0 & a_1 & a_3 & 0 \\ 0 & a_0 & a_2 & a_4 \end{vmatrix} > 0. \tag{10.7.6}$$

Since a_0, a_1, a_4, $a_3 > 0$, on expanding the third and fourth order determinants, (10.7.6) reduces to the following necessary and sufficient condition:

$$a_3 \begin{vmatrix} a_1 & a_3 \\ a_0 & a_2 \end{vmatrix} > a_1^2 a_4. \tag{10.7.7}$$

Substituting for a_i from (10.7.5) and following lengthy algebra the condition becomes

$$B\psi_1^2 + C(\psi_1^2\psi_2 + \psi_1^2\psi_2^2) - D\psi_1\psi_2 - E\psi_2^2 > 0 \tag{10.7.8}$$

where

$$A = \alpha_3[\beta_1(1-\theta) + \phi_2\beta_2] + \alpha_1\beta_1$$
$$B = A\alpha_3\phi_1 - \alpha_3\beta_1\phi_2$$
$$C = \beta_2[1 - \alpha_2(1-\theta)]$$
$$D = A[\alpha_3\beta_1(1-\theta) + \alpha_1\beta_1] + 2\beta_1\beta_2\phi_2$$
$$E = \beta_2^2\alpha_3\beta_1\phi_2.$$

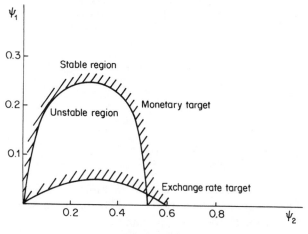

Figure 10.3:

For the central values of the parameters given in section 10.8 we have: $A = 1.1$, $B = 1.4, C = 0.6, D = 0.4, E = 0.01$. Hence the last term in (10.7.8) is negligible and the condition can be written approximately as

$$\psi_1 > \frac{\psi_2(D - C\psi_2)}{B + C\psi_2}. \tag{10.7.9}$$

The stable region in (ψ_1, ψ_2) space is shown in Figure 10.3 for central values of the other parameters. The comparable region for the case of a monetary target regime obtained numerically is also shown.

We conclude that for all but implausibly low values of ψ_1 the exchange rate target regime is always stable. For ψ_1 below 0.3 (that is with a mean lag of over three years) the monetary target regime is by contrast unstable for a range of low to medium values of ψ_2. That is to say if the output market adjusts slowly and the inflation rate somewhat sluggishly then the monetary target rule leads to unstability. However, for the combinations of parameter values drawn up in section 10.8 (considered to cover all plausible cases) this does not happen.

10.8. SIMULATION RESULTS AND POLICY CONSEQUENCES

To carry out simulations of our model, we must specify plausible parameter values. Our chosen set is presented in Table 10.1. Given the uncertainty deriving from the large confidence intervals of empirical studies, the sometimes contradictory results of different studies, and the dangers of structural change or specification bias, it would be unwise to rely too heavily on any given set of parameter values. Accordingly, our procedure is to specify a central set of parameter values, and then to examine the consequences of parameter variation

Table 10.1 Parameter values

ψ_1	0.5	θ	0.2
ψ_2	0.5	δ_1	4.0
ψ_3	0.5	δ_2	1.0
ψ_4	0.5	γ_1	1.0
α_1	0.3	γ_2	1.0
α_2	0.1	γ_3	1.0
α_3	1.0	ϕ_1	1.3
β_1	0.3	ϕ_2	0.1
β_2	0.55	$\mu_i(1 \leqslant i \leqslant 7)$	0.5

around these central values. The central, parameter values constitute our judgement of a 'consensus' drawn from a wide literature of econometric work. (See Currie (1981) for a discussion of some of these values.) Unfortunately, limitations of space prevent us from discussing all the variations in detail. Instead, we discuss the main results for the central parameter set (shown in Table 10.1), and then indicate in the text certain consequences of parameter variation.

Most of the parameters of the model listed in Table 10.1 contain an implicit time dimension. (Thus, for example, α_1 is the relationship between a dimensionless relative price and the flow of goods per unit period.) In considering the parameter values, it is therefore necessary to specify the unit time period in question. (Note that, because we work in continuous time, this is not given to us naturally.) It is convenient to work in terms of a period of one year.

The first important point is that the model has the unique saddle-point property for the specified parameter set under all four policy regimes (that is the number of roots with positive real part is just equal to the number of free variables, namely one in our case). Moreover, this remains true for relatively wide variations in parameter values from their specified values. Thus the system is formally stable, and this property is quite robust to parameter variations.

This is a striking result, particularly for the regime of monetary targets. It is a well-known result in the literature that monetary targets coupled with automatic fiscal stabilizers can be destabilizing. (See, for example, Blinder and Solow (1973), Curie (1976), Christ (1979). For a survey of much of this literature, see Currie (1978).) This arises because of the need to finance variations in the budget deficit by bond issues or retirements if the monetary targets are to be adhered to, but this gives rise to marked volatility in interest rates because of the wealth effect on money demand. This variation can feed through to output and hence, because of automatic fiscal stabilizers, to the budget, requiring additional variation in bond issues. If this feedback is large enough cumulative destabilization can result.

This instability would arise in our model if it were closed to international trade and capital movements. It would also arise if we were to model the world economy as the interaction of a set of n such models. But it does *not* arise when we analyse our model in isolation, treating the rest of the world as exogenously given.

For in this case, the exchange rate can move to stabilize the system, and this movement may occur if foreign exchange operators act in a sufficiently far-sighted manner.

This highlights an important point about policy formulation and evaluation at the international level. An appraisal of the combination of monetary targets and automatic fiscal stabilizers for the small open economy in the context of our model would lead to the conclusion that such a regime is stable. This conclusion might lead to its adoption (though other considerations, such as volatility, would also be relevant). But if it is appropriate for one small country to adopt it, so it will be for others. Yet if all countries adopt it, the regime may well be destabilizing. Socially informed policy formulation would consider the properties of a regime both for the single country and when generally adopted. But individual governments may have little incentive to consider the consequences of the regime being generally applied. In effect, there is in this case an external diseconomy in policy formulation at the international level.

Although instability in the usual sense does not arise, a rather different phenomenon, which we may term 'structural instability' does arise. (We use this term in its general sense that a small perturbation in parameter values could dramatically change the properties of the model.) This may be most simply illustrated in terms of Figure 10.1. Consider what happens as the stable trajectory becomes more steeply negative in slope. For any given disturbance to r, say $r(0)$, the required jump of e, to $e(0)$, becomes larger, tending to $-\infty$ as the stable trajectory tends to the vertical. If the stable trajectory could pass through the vertical, the required jump of e would change sign from negative to positive, passing through $-\infty$ and $+\infty$.

For this simple example of section 10.6, this change of sign cannot occur, since θ_1 is necessarily positive (see (10.6.4)). In more complex models, however it may occur when, in the parameter space, the system is in the neighbourhood of points where $|\mathbf{M}_{22}| = 0$. We have already noted that $|\mathbf{M}_{22}| \neq 0$ is a necessary condition for a solution. $|\mathbf{M}_{22}| = 0$ will be highly improbable, since the set of points where this occurs has measure zero. But $|\mathbf{M}_{22}|$ might be close to zero, so that $\mathbf{M}_{22}$ is nearly singular [see I, §6.12]. In such a position, a small parameter change might suffice to change the sign of $|\mathbf{M}_{22}|$, leading to a dramatic, discontinuous change in the jump responses of the free variables to the predetermined variables. In such neighbourhoods, the system would exhibit structural instability. A policy which places the system close to a point where $|\mathbf{M}_{22}| = 0$ is to be avoided, because the consequent behaviour of the system is unpredictable. Moreover, given such unpredictability, the stabilizing behaviour of forward-looking expectations implicit in our solution procedure appears less than plausible.

This problem arises for two of our policy regimes. For monetary targets and price level targets, $|\mathbf{M}_{22}|$ is close to zero for the specified parameter set. A consequence is that the jumps implied by the solution procedure are very large. More importantly, they can become very much larger and change sign for small

Table 10.2 Asymptotic standard deviations of output and inflation under alternative policy regimes

Disturbance variable / Regime	Aggregate demand		Aggregate supply		Money demand		Policy error		Foreign interest rates		Foreign prices		Government budget	
	Output	Inflation	Output	Inflation	Output	Inflation	Output	Inflation	Output	Inflation	Output	Inflation	Output	Inflation
Monetary targets	2.145	0.878	7.159	1.166	2.302	0.423	0.440	0.101	1.617	0.336	0.978	0.156	1.453	0.415
Exchange rate targets	1.062	0.210	2.236	1.786	0.0	0.0	0.063	0.037	0.188	0.132	0.325	0.231	0.828	0.239
Price targets	1.188	0.057	15.050	0.436	0.0	0.0	2.271	0.039	12.157	0.121	2.030	0.060	0.844	0.039
Nominal income targets	1.370	0.542	3.825	0.806	0.0	0.0	0.423	0.089	0.745	0.226	0.478	0.109	0.980	0.362

shifts in parameter values. Neither policy is likely to be robust in behaviour. The other two regimes are robust in this respect, $|M_{22}|$ becoming close to zero only for extreme and implausible parameter sets.

With these points concerning stability in mind, we may turn to consider the asymptotic standard deviations of output and inflation under alternative policy regimes and different disturbances, as presented in Table 10.2. The seven disturbances considered result in variation in both output and inflation under all policy regimes, with the exception that money demand shocks have no influence unless monetary targets are pursued.

A comparison of the regimes shows that a monetary target regime is entirely dominated by a regime of nominal income targets, in the sense that nominal income targets result in smaller variation in *both* output and inflation in the face of *all* types of disturbance. Exchange rate targets also perform well in relation to monetary targets. Monetary targets perform better only in stabilizing inflation in that face of supply shocks. Even here, the cost in output variation is high, and monetary targets would be preferred only if policy makers have an objective function in which inflation fluctuations are penalized with a weight more than four times that on output fluctuations.

This poor performance, together with the lack of robustness considered above, suggests that monetary targets are unlikely to be satisfactory as a policy regime in terms of output and inflation stabilization.

The comparison of the remaining three regimes for the central values is rather ambiguous. Exchange rate targets out-perform price level targets and nominal income targets in the face of policy errors; this is because the response of the exchange rate to errors is very fast, thereby eliciting a faster correction response. Exchange rate targets also out-perform nominal income targets in the face of shocks to aggregate demand, foreign interest rates and budget disturbances. For disturbances where the comparison is ambiguous (shocks to aggregate supply, and to foreign prices), exchange rate targets give better output stabilization relative to nominal income targets, at the expense of greater inflation variation. But since the gain in output stability is small relative to the loss in terms of inflation variability, it would require a low weight for inflation (if only 0.75 or less for supply shocks and 0.40 or less for foreign price shocks) for exchange rate targets to be superior.

With the exception of policy errors, a price level target gives greater inflation stability than exchange rate targets for the central values, but at the expense of greater output variability. In some cases, namely budget disturbances and aggregate demand shocks, the extra output variability is small relative to the reduction in inflation variability. In others, namely aggregate supply shocks, foreign interest rate and price level shocks, the opposite is true. But the susceptibility of price level targets to structural stability, discussed above, makes these comparisons less significant, and suggests that price level targets may be an unrobust policy regime.

To summarize, therefore, monetary targets and price level targets exhibit unrobust properties resulting from structural instability. This problem does not arise with exchange rate targets or nominal income targets. Exchange rate targets are likely to out-perform nominal income targets unless aggregate supply or foreign price disturbances dominate *and* inflation variation is not given a low weight relative to output variation.

These results are, of course, illustrative of a method of analysis, rather than representing definitive results about policy comparisons. The following represent limitations of the analysis, made necessary for ease of exposition and by limits of space.

1. The analysis is limited to the case of a small open economy where the rest of the world is treated as exogenous (though providing sources of stochastic disturbance to the model, e.g. through foreign interest rates). Different results might be obtained were we to consider these policies adopted by all countries simultaneously, so that feedbacks become important. This suggests the need for policy evaluation in interdependent economies.

2. We have assumed that fiscal policy reacts passively, with automatic fiscal stabilizers being allowed to operate fully. A different fiscal rule (e.g. a **PSBR** target, implying procyclical fiscal policy) might well avoid the structural instability associated with monetary or price level targets, though perhaps only at the expense of inappropriately timed fiscal responses to cyclical fluctuations. Use of the fiscal instruments is clearly called for, and requires analysis. But the complexities of the several instrument case probably requires analysis by optimal control methods if it is to be tractable. Optimal stochastic control with rational expectations is currently an active area of research.

3. Although parameter values were varied widely (though not discussed here), we cannot be sure that monetary targets, for example, will not perform rather better for policy parameters or rules outside the range examined here. A more comprehensive search over alternatives, or alternatively the use of optimal control methods, can be used to examine this possibility.

4. The model analysed here has a number of simplifications noted in the introduction, and should therefore be regarded mainly as illustrative. However, the methods may readily be applied to estimated rational expectations models. The estimation of complete rational expectations macromodels represents an important area of current research effort, though there are formidable problems of estimation in this area. (See Lucas and Sargent (1981) and Begg (1982).)

5. A further area of current research interests is the examination of the robustness of policies to alternative expectations schema. While the assumption of rational

expectations is theoretically and empirically appealing (see Begg (1982)), confidence in the efficacy of policy rules would be enhanced were they to perform well under alternative assumptions, such as adaptive expectations.

These extensions offer exciting and fertile lines of research activity that are generating important advances in knowledge. But the techniques of analysis presented in this chapter are important in understanding these more advanced issues. In addition, they have highlighted an important finding about policy design. Just as for a closed economy, the combination of monetary targets with automatic fiscal stabilizers will be a destabilizing policy for the small open economy, contrary to much monetarist analysis. Alternative policy designs that appear fairly robust include targeting of either the exchange rate or nominal income in conjunction with fiscal stabilizers.

10.9. SUGGESTIONS FOR FURTHER READING

For further reading in the area of international macroeconomics and monetary economics, the reader can usefully refer to Aoki (1981), Chacholiades (1978), Dornbusch (1980), Jones and Kenen (1982), and Turnovsky (1977). Issues of simulation and control in continuous time models are addressed in Chow (1981) and Davis (1977). Readers interested in the estimation of econometric models in continuous time may refer to Bergstrom (1976), Gandolfo *et al.* (1981), and Wymer (1972). Rational expectations and its implications for macromodelling are addressed in Begg (1981) and Lucas and Sargent (1981).

10.10. REFERENCES

Aoki, M. (1981). *Dynamic Analysis of Open Economies*. Academic Press, New York.

Artis, M. J. and Currie, D. A. (1981). Monetary targets and the exchange rate. A case for conditional targets, in Eltis, W. A. and Sinclair, P. J. N. (eds.), *The Money Supply and the Exchange Rate*. Oxford University Press, Oxford.

Begg, D. K. H. (1982). *The Rational Expectations Revolution in Macroeconomics*. Philip Allen, Deddington, Oxon.

Bergstrom, A. R. (ed.) (1976). *Statistical Inference in Continuous Time Economic Models*, North-Holland, Amsterdam.

Blanchard, O. J. and Kahn, C. M. (1980). The solution of linear difference models under rational expectations. *Econometrica*, **48**, 1305–1309.

Blinder, A. S. and Solow, R. M. (1973). Does fiscal policy matter? *Journal of Public Economics*, **2**, 319–337.

Chacholiades, M. (1978). *International Monetary Theory and Policy*. McGraw-Hill, New York.

Chow, G. D. (1979). Optimal control of stochastic differential equation system. *Journal of Economic Dynamics and Control*, **1**, 143–175.

Chow, G. C. (1981). *Econometric Analysis by Control Methods*. Wiley, New York.

Christ, C. F. (1979). On fiscal and monetary policies and the government budget restraint. *American Economic Review*, **69**, 526–538.

Currie, D. A. (1976). Optimal stabilization policies and the government budget constraint. *Economica*, **43**, 159–167.

Currie, D. A. (1978). Macroeconomic policy and government financing: A survey of recent developments, in Artis, M. J. and Nobay, A. R. (eds.), *Studies in Contemporary Economic Analysis*, Vol. 1. Croom Helm, London.

Currie, D. A. (1981). Monetary overshooting and the exchange rate. Queen Mary College, Department of Economics Discussion Paper No. 71.

Currie, D. A. and Levine, P. L. (1982). A solution technique for discrete and continuous time stochastic dynamic models under rational expectations with full and partial information sets. Queen Mary College, Programme of Research into Small Macromodels, Research Paper No. 1

Davis, M. H. A. (1977). *Linear Estimation and Stochastic Control*. Chapman & Hall, London.

Dornbusch, R. (1976). Expectations and exchange rate dynamics. *Journal of Political Economy*, **84**, 1161–1176.

Dornbusch, R. (1980). *Open Economy Macroeconomics*. Basic Books, New York.

Eltis, W. A. and Sinclair, P. J. N. (eds.) (1981). *The Money Supply and the Exchange Rate*. Oxford University Press, Oxford.

Gandolfo, G. *et al.* (1981). *Qualitative Analysis and Econometric Estimation of Continuous Time Dynamic Models*. North-Holland, Amsterdam.

Hoel, P. G., Port, S. C. and Stone, C. J. (1972). *Introduction to Stochastic Processes*. Houghton Mifflin, New York.

Johnston, J. (1968). *Econometric Methods*. McGraw-Hill, New York.

Jones, R. W. and Kenen, P. B. (eds.) (1982). *Handbook of International Economics*. North-Holland, Amsterdam.

Lucas, R. E. (1976). Econometric policy evaluation. A critique. *Journal of Monetary Economics* (Supplement), Carnegie–Rochester Conference Series, Vol. 1.

Lucas, R. E. and Sargent, T. J. (eds.) (1981). *Rational Expectations and Econometric Practice*. Allen & Unwin, London.

Meade, J. (1982). *Stagflation*, Vol. 1, *Wage Fixing*. Allen & Unwin, London.

Turnovsky, S. J. (1977). *Macroeconomic Analysis and Stabilisation Policy*. Cambridge University Press, Cambridge.

Wymer, C. R. (1972). Econometric estimation of stochastic differential equation systems. *Econometrica*, **40**, 565–577. Reprinted in Bergstrom (1976).

Mathematical Methods in Economics
Edited by F. van der Ploeg
© 1984, John Wiley & Sons, Ltd.

11

Macro-Dynamic Theories of Economic Growth and Fluctuations

FREDERICK VAN DER PLOEG, *London School of Economics and Darwin College, Cambridge, U.K.*

11.1. INTRODUCTION

Most of the attention in the literature on economic fluctuations has focused on the utilization of capacity over the business cycle and not much has been said about oscillations in the distribution of income. This is perhaps not surprising as unemployment was often ascribed to a lack of effective demand and this was also the main factor in business cycle studies. Furthermore business cycle theories were easy to model with the aid of simple linear differential equations. The disadvantage of these models is that fixed prices and a constant distribution of income are assumed, so that classical unemployment due to a too high cost of labour could not be analysed. Part of the reason for this lack of interest in modelling the distribution of income may be that this would cause nonlinearities in the differential equations, which is a relatively unknown feature in macroeconomics. The purpose of this chapter is to analyze unemployment, the utilization of capacity and the distribution of income by discussing the dynamic implications of the class struggle, the business cycle and economic growth.

The taxonomy of theories of cyclical growth given in Table 11.1 may be of some use in explaining the manner in which a large variety of macro-dynamic economic theories will be discussed. This also allows a demonstration of the wide applicability of ordinary differential equations (and optimization theory) in macroeconomics.

The Harrod–Domar conditions for attaining a warranted equilibrium (type I theory) are discussed in section 11.2 and suggest the post-Keynesian, neoclassical and Malthusian approaches to dynamic equilibrium and the possibility of permanent disequilibrium. The post-Keynesian approach gives rise to the predator–prey model of symbiosis and perpetual conflict and is discussed in section 11.3. It corresponds to the well-known Volterra–Lotka model [see IV,

Table 11.1 Taxonomy of conventional theories of cyclical growth

Class of theory	Section	Distribution of income	Substitution between factor inputs	Employment	Utilization of capacity	Economic growth	Mathematical model
I. Warranted and natural growth: Harrod (1948), Domar (1957)	11.2					V	n.a.
II. Post-Keynesian class struggle: Kalecki (1939), Kaldor (1956), Robinson (1956), Goodwin (1967)	11.3	V		V		V	Volterra–Lotka system [see IV, §7.11.4]
III. Neo-classical growth: Solow (1956), Swan (1956), Meade (1963)	11.4		V			V	Bernoulli's equation [see IV, §7.10.2]
IV. Profitability and un-employment: based on Kaldor (1957), Kennedy (1964), Samuelson (1965), Arrow (1962)	11.5	V	V	V		V	Structural form nonlinear O.D.E.s [see IV, §7.11]
V. Trade cycle: Kalecki (1935), Samuelson (1939), Kaldor (1940), Hicks (1950), Goodwin (1951), Phillips (1954), Duesenberry (1958)	11.6			V	V		Linear (mixed), Raleigh's, van der Pol's and Liénard's ODE
VI. General case: Phillips (1961), Bergstrom (1967), Malinvaud (1980)	11.7	V	V	V	V	V	Nonlinear O.D.E.s [see IV, §7.11]

A 'V' denotes that the variable is endogenously determined, whereas a blank denotes that the variable is assigned a constant value in the model.

§7.11.4] and focuses on the share of labour and the employment rate in a growing economy with strict complementarity between factor inputs. The section analyses the effects of a number of structural perturbations on the dynamic properties of the class struggle with the aid of Lyapunov's indirect stability test and the Routh–Hurwitz stability criterion [see IV, §7.11.5]. In section 11.5 possibilities for substitution are introduced in the extended model of the class struggle and this gives rise to three nonlinear differential equations. The extended model (type IV) contains the pure neoclassical theory of economic growth (type III) and the perpetual class struggle (type II) as special cases. The chapter explains how these and other intermediate cases are conveniently characterized when the eigenvalues are displayed on Argand's diagram [see I, §2.7.2] as a function of the speed of neoclassical recruiting and firing activities. The main advantage of the type IV model is the ability to analyse the inherent contradictions as well as the process of industrialization from a labour-intensive to a capital-intensive economy. These points are highlighted in a numerical simulation diagram.

A discussion of the multiplier–accelerator approach to the business cycle (type V theory) may be found in section 11.6. These theories concentrate on effective demand and ignore prices, so that they reduce to a number of simple linear differential equations. However, frustration of planned investment leads to nonlinear differential equations and limit cycles. The section also takes the opportunity to use control theory to derive a number of well-known stabilization policies. A full-scale theory of effective demand, the class struggle and economic growth (type VI) is formulated in section 11.7. The chapter argues that the standard form of the type VI economy is unstable, unless compensating effects are operating. For example the introduction of money illusion, adaptive expectations, labour hoarding, expected profitability, substitution or monetary factors may return the economy towards its dynamic equilibrium. This section also takes the opportunity to discuss *structural form* models.

A rather different view of economic fluctuations is provided by the political business cycle discussed in section 11.8, which blames myopic governments for causing economic instability. It uses probability theory to explain government popularity and dynamic programming to derive the vote-winning policy.

11.2. WARRANTED AND NATURAL RATES OF ECONOMIC GROWTH

Assume that the demand for products, consisting of goods for consumption (C) and gross investment (I) purposes, is immediately produced and therefore ignore stockbuilding. The receipts of production (Q) provide for net income (Y), in the form of wages ($W.E$) and profits (Π), and for depreciation (D). Net income is either spent on consumption goods (C) or saved (S). The accumulation of net investment ($I - D$) equals savings (S) and gives rise to the stock of physical assets of real wealth (K). The above may be summarized by the system of national

Table 11.2 A system of national accounts

Incomings	Outgoings 1	2	3	Totals
1. Production		C	I	Q
2. Income and outlay	$W.E + \Pi$			Y
3. Accumulation	D	S		I
Totals	Q	Y	I	

accounts presented in Table 11.2 and the balance sheet identity $\dot{K} = S = I - D$ [cf. Chapter 2].

The accounts may be closed with a number of behavioural relationships. The decision to consume follows from the consumption function [cf. Chapter 5]

$$C = (1 - \sigma)Q + \gamma K, \quad \gamma > 0 \tag{11.2.1}$$

where γ captures the real-balance effect. An alternative interpretation of the consumption decision is that the nation saves at a speed γ in order to close the gap between desired and actual wealth, where the ratio of desired wealth to gross income equals σ/γ. This alternative interpretation is highlighted by the savings function

$$S = Q - C = \gamma \left[\left(\frac{\sigma}{\gamma} \right) Q - K \right] \tag{11.2.1'}$$

Depreciation is a fixed proportion (δ) of the capital stock. Since in this simple model the capital stock equals wealth, $D = \delta K$. The production possibilities are characterized by the capital–output ratio, say $\alpha = K/Q$, and the rate of labour-augmenting technical progress, say $\omega = \dot{Q}/Q - \dot{E}/E$. There is only one good in this economy, which is like jelly. The produced good is therefore used for both consumption and investment purposes. The supply of labour, L, is exogenous. For example, a fixed proportion of the population. The population grows exponentially at the rate η. Thus $\dot{L}/L = \eta$.

These assumptions combined with the accounts and balance sheets imply that the warranted and actual rates of economic growth (supportable by machinery) are given by

$$g^w = \frac{\dot{K}}{K} = \frac{\sigma}{\alpha} - \gamma - \delta, \quad g^a = g^w - \dot{\alpha}/\alpha, \tag{11.2.2}$$

since $\dot{K}/K = S/K = (Q - C - D)/K = (\sigma/\alpha) - \gamma - \delta$ and $\dot{Q}/Q = \dot{K}/K - \dot{\alpha}/\alpha$, and the natural rate of growth (supportable by the supply of labour) is given by

$$g^n = \frac{\dot{Q}}{Q} - \left(\frac{\dot{E}}{E} - \frac{\dot{L}}{L} \right) = \omega + \eta \tag{11.2.3}$$

assuming that the employment rate (E/L) is fixed.

The warranted rate of growth increases when the propensity to save is raised and when the wealth effect, speed of depreciation or capital–output ratio are reduced, since these factors tend to increase accumulation and raise the output that can be produced with existing capacity. The natural rate of growth assumes full employment and is due to growth in labour productivity or population. For an economy to be in long-run balanced growth, the warranted rate must equal the natural rate. The variables in the dynamic equilibrium follow three types of trajectories: capital, output and demand grow at the rate $g^* = g^w = g^n$, demand and supply of labour per head are constant and real wages and productivity grow at the rate ω^*. There are three mechanisms for achieving balanced growth based on adjustment in η, α and ω or σ, respectively.

The first is based on the Malthusian notion of letting population growth depend positively on income, so that an excess of the warranted over the natural rate is removed by a population explosion. The second approach relies on neoclassical substitution between capital and labour, which depends on the relative profitability of the factors of production, to adjust the warranted in line with the natural rate (type III theory). Since it is difficult to separate a change in capital intensity from technical progress, the adjustment occurs in both α and ω. In view of the observed constancy of the capital–output ratio, the lack of substantial evidence for profit-maximizing behaviour and problems of aggregation, some have cast doubt on the validity of this second approach (e.g. Kaldor, 1956). The third approach assumes strict complementarity between factor inputs, and instead argues that changes in the distribution of the national income ensure equalization of the warranted and natural rates of growth (type II theory). Thus when the natural rate is below the warranted rate a change in the distribution of income in favour of wages will partially remedy this deficiency by virtue of a lower aggregate propensity to save. Similarly, a rise in the share of profits in value added increases investment and the warranted rate. The third approach will be referred to as the post-Keynesian, Cambridge or predator–prey approach. The dynamic implications of the latter two approaches are discussed in sections 11.3–11.5.

There is an alternative to the supply-oriented equilibrium approaches discussed above. This relies on a demand-oriented explanation of permanent unemployment and has been coined the 'Bastard Golden Age' (Kahn, 1959), since $g^a \lessgtr g^n$ always holds. In this case flexibility in the degree of capacity utilization enables adjustment of the trend to the natural rate (type V theory). This latter theory contains the well-known Keynesian theory of effective demand as a special case.

11.3. POST-KEYNESIAN DESCRIPTIONS OF CLASS CONFLICT

11.3.1. The basic model of perpetual conflict

Assume strict complementarity between capital and labour, that is $\alpha = \bar{\alpha}$ is fixed, and Kaldor's (1957) technical progress function

$$\omega = \frac{\dot{Q}}{Q} - \frac{\dot{E}}{E} = \phi\left(\frac{\dot{K}}{K} - \frac{\dot{E}}{E}\right), \quad \phi(0) > 0, \ \phi' > 0, \ \phi'' < 0, \qquad (11.3.1)$$

where E denotes the number of workers employed. Concavity of $\phi(\cdot)$ [see IV, §15.2.6] implies that the most profitable ideas are used first. The above implies endogenous technical progress, since the productivity of labour rises as the machinery available to workers is increased. Observe that a fixed $\alpha = K/Q$ implies $\omega = \phi(\dot{K}/K - \dot{Q}/Q + \dot{Q}/Q - \dot{E}/E) = \phi(\omega)$, so that the rates of labour-augmenting technical progress and natural growth are given by the fixed points ω^* and $\omega^* + \eta$ respectively. The warranted rate reduces to $(\sigma/\bar{\alpha} - \delta - \gamma)$ and depends on the distribution of income, hence consider the differential savings hypothesis

$$\sigma Q = \sigma_1(\Pi + D) + \sigma_2 W \cdot E, \quad 0 \leqslant \sigma_2 < \sigma_1 \leqslant 1, \tag{11.3.2}$$

where capitalists typically save more of their income than workers. Strictly speaking one can only refer to capitalists and workers when workers consume all their wages ($\sigma_2 = 0$), unless one assumes that each individual is both capitalist and worker. The separation between ownership and management in capitalist economies implies that retained earnings in corporations depend on profits earned rather than on who owns what proportion of the capital stock, which may be interpreted as a justification for the above assumption. On the other hand one could argue that management cannot implement savings against the will of shareholders indefinitely, since retention leads to stock appreciation and workers can consume the capital gains by selling shares (cf. Pasinetti, 1962).

The degree of imbalance in growth is best represented by the growth in the employment rate, that is (using $\dot{\alpha}/\alpha = 0$)

$$\frac{\dot{\varepsilon}}{\varepsilon} = g^w - g^n = \frac{[\sigma_1(1-\theta) + \sigma_2\theta]}{\bar{\alpha}} - \gamma - \delta - \omega^* - \eta = -h(\theta), \tag{11.3.3}$$

where $\varepsilon = E/L$ and $\theta = W \cdot E/Q$. The growth in real wages (W) depends on the bargaining strength of workers, proxied by the level of excess demand for labour, and is determined by the real (linearized) Phillips Curve

$$\frac{\dot{W}}{W} = \mu_1\varepsilon - \mu_2, \quad \mu_1, \mu_2 > 0. \tag{11.3.4}$$

The growth in the share of wages in the net national income, θ, may then be written as

$$\frac{\dot{\theta}}{\theta} = \frac{\dot{W}}{W} + \frac{\dot{E}}{E} - \frac{\dot{Q}}{Q} = \mu_1\varepsilon - \mu_2 - \omega^* = g(\varepsilon) \tag{11.3.5}$$

Equations (11.3.3) and (11.3.5) correspond to two nonlinear differential equations,

$$\dot{\varepsilon} = -\varepsilon h(\theta), \quad h' = (\sigma_1 - \sigma_2)/\bar{\alpha} \geqslant 0, \tag{11.3.6}$$

and

$$\dot{\theta} = \theta g(\varepsilon), \quad g' = \mu_1 \geqslant 0, \tag{11.3.7}$$

which describe the development of the economy over time in terms of the two dimensionless variables, ε and θ, only. They may be regarded as a post-Keynesian disequilibrium version of the Harrod–Domar conditions for balanced growth. The appropriate distribution of income, θ^*, ensures $g^w = g^n$, or a stationary employment rate, and is therefore given by

$$\theta^* = \frac{\sigma_1 - \bar{\alpha}(\gamma + \delta + \omega^* + \eta)}{\sigma_1 - \sigma_2} \qquad (11.3.8)$$

so that increases in technical progress, population growth, the real balance effect or the degree of differential savings depress the equilibrium share of labour and increase the return on capital. Feasibility of the long-run distribution of the net product is defined as $0 \leqslant \theta^* \leqslant 1$ and is ensured when the inequality $\sigma_2 \leqslant \bar{\alpha}(\gamma + \delta + \omega^* + \eta) \leqslant \sigma_1$ holds. The balanced rate of employment, ε^*, ensures a constant distribution of income and equals $(\omega^* + \mu_2)/\mu_1$, so that technical progress and low bargaining flexibility raise the equilibrium rate of employment.

The dynamic equilibrium is only attained when $\varepsilon = \varepsilon^*$ and $\theta = \theta^*$ are simultaneously achieved. The eigenvalues of the Jacobian matrix (evaluated at the equilibrium) of the state space system (11.3.6)–(11.3.7), that is [see IV, (5.12.2)]

$$\mathbf{J} = \begin{pmatrix} 0 & -\varepsilon^*(\sigma_1 - \sigma_2)/\bar{\alpha} \\ \theta^*\mu_1 & 0 \end{pmatrix} \qquad (11.3.9)$$

follow from the characteristic polynomial [see I, §7.3]

$$\lambda^2 - \mathrm{tr}(\mathbf{J})\lambda + \det(\mathbf{J}) = 0. \qquad (11.3.10)$$

They are therefore a conjugate pair of imaginary roots of the form

$$\lambda_{1,2} = \pm \sqrt{\mu_1 \left(\frac{\sigma_1 - \sigma_2}{\bar{\alpha}} \right) \theta^* \varepsilon^*}. \qquad (11.3.11)$$

Since the roots are imaginary the phase trajectory is described by either a focus or a centre [see IV, 7.11.12 and 7.11.13] and nothing can be said about local stability. Consider therefore the separable positive-definite Lyapunov function

$$V(\varepsilon, \theta) = \int_{\varepsilon^*}^{\varepsilon} \frac{g(z)}{z} \, dz + \int_{\theta^*}^{\theta} \frac{h(z)}{z} \, dz \qquad (11.3.12)$$

and note that its time derivative, that is

$$\dot{V} = \frac{g(\varepsilon)}{\varepsilon} \dot{\varepsilon} + \frac{h(\theta)}{\theta} \dot{\theta} = -g(\varepsilon)h(\theta) + h(\theta)g(\varepsilon) \qquad (11.3.13)$$

vanishes. The minimum value of $V(\cdot)$ is zero and attained at the equilibrium and, as $\dot{V} = 0$, this therefore establishes the existence of a conservative system whose solution, in terms of integral curves, follows from solving the algebraic equation

$$V(\varepsilon, \theta) = \mu_1 \left[\varepsilon - \varepsilon^* - \varepsilon^* \ln\left(\frac{\varepsilon}{\varepsilon^*}\right) \right]$$

$$+ \frac{\sigma_1 - \sigma_2}{\alpha} \left[\theta - \theta^* - \theta^* \ln\left(\frac{\theta}{\theta^*}\right) \right] = \text{constant}. \qquad (11.3.14)$$

for different values of the constant.

In fact the system (11.3.6)–(11.3.7) is a version of the well-known Volterra–Lotka model [see IV, §7.11.4] and is therefore not asymptotically stable, structurally unstable and follows closed trajectories around the equilibrium (Andronov *et al.*, 1973).

An alternative to the Lyapunov approach for finding the family of closed trajectories for (ε, θ) is to eliminate time by dividing Equations (11.3.6) and (11.3.7), that is to integrate the differential equation

$$d\varepsilon/d\theta = - \{\varepsilon h(\theta)\}/\{\theta g(\varepsilon)\} \qquad (11.3.15)$$

by the method of separation of variables [see IV, §8.2]. The resulting phase curves are the same as the ones given by Equation (11.3.14). An illustration of these results is given by the solid curves of the phase diagram given in Figure 11.1. The economy perpetually oscillates around the equilibrium, so that θ^* and ε^* are never simultaneously achieved. When the share of labour is at its highest, profitability is lowest and the reserve army of workers increases most rapidly. This reduces bargaining strength and causes a shift in the distribution of income in favour of profits. The depression stops when the reserve army is largest and the

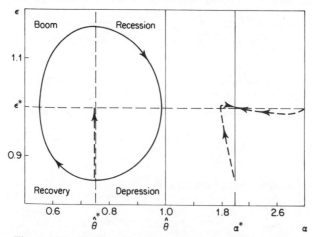

Figure 11.1: Simulations of a post-Keynesian description of the class struggle and a generalized neoclassical model of economic growth

return on capital increases most rapidly, so that the recovery sets in. When profitability is at its nadir the boom sets in with fast growth in employment. The too rigorous expansion carries the seeds of its own destruction by destroying the reserve army of workers and strengthening labour's bargaining power. At the end of the recession a new cycle of conflict commences.

This perpetual cycle highlights the symbiotic contradictions of capitalism, for the livelihood of each class in society depends on the existence of the other class and at the same time workers and capitalists fight for their share in the national income. The time it takes to traverse a complete cycle of conflict, say T, is approximately given by $T = 2\pi i/\lambda_{1,2}$. The accuracy of this formula may be verified by comparing T with the value obtained in a numerical simulation: the relative error for Figure 11.1 is only -0.48%. For a given share of labour and employment the length of the cycle decreases when the slope of the bargaining equation or the output–capital ratio rises and savings become more differentiated. Typical lengths vary from 6 to 25 years (cf. Atkinson, 1969).

11.3.2. Structural perturbations in wage formation

The conservative system (11.3.6)–(11.3.7) is structurally unstable, which implies that small perturbations in the economic structure can dramatically alter the qualitative nature of the trajectories of perpetual conflict (cf. Freedman and Waltman, 1975). Some perturbations relating to wage formation may be considered.

Consider therefore extending the competitive wage formation equation used above with non-competitive elements as follows

$$\frac{\dot{W}}{W} + \frac{\dot{P}}{P} = \mu_1 \varepsilon - \mu_2 + \mu_3 \frac{\dot{\varepsilon}}{\varepsilon} + \mu_4 \dot{p}^e, \quad \mu_i > 0, \tag{11.3.4'}$$

where the dependent variable is now percentage growth in nominal wages, $p^e = \ln P^e$ and $\dot{p}^e = \dot{P}^e/P^e$ denotes the expected rate of price inflation. Two explanations for the parameters μ_3 and μ_4 may be found. The first hypothesis says that trade unions desire and attain nominal earnings equal to a mark-up (v) on the anticipated cost of living, $W = vP^e$, where a high mark-up indicates the bargaining strength of workers or the ability (and willingness) of firms to pay when economic conditions, proxied by ε, are favourable. This hypothesis implies $\dot{W}/W = \dot{v}/v + \dot{p}^e$, so that $\mu_1 = \mu_2 = 0$, $\mu_4 = 1$ and μ_3 should be interpreted as the elasticity of v with respect to ε ($\mu_3 = d\log v/d\log \varepsilon$). The second hypothesis is based on rational trade union action to preserve membership and avoid redundancies, that is a monopolistic union maximizes a utility function in terms of real wages and employment, say $U = (1 - \beta)\log(W \cdot P/P^e) + \beta \ln \varepsilon$, subject to how *it* believes the economy functions, say $\varepsilon = f(W \cdot P/P^e)$. The first order conditions of optimality follow from differentiating U with respect to W (using the chain rule [see IV, §5.4])

$$dU/dW = (1 - \beta)(P^e/WP)(P/P^e) + (\beta/f)f'(P/P^e) = 0$$

and lead to the following policy rule for perceived real wages

$$(W \cdot P)/P^e = -\varepsilon(1 - \beta)/(\beta f').$$ (11.3.16)

In a classical world trade unions may be expected to believe $f' < 0$, so that when unemployment is high workers are prepared to *rationally* sacrifice earnings in order to produce more jobs. In this case $\mu_1 = 0$, $\mu_2 = -\dot{f}'/f'$ and $\mu_3 = \mu_4 = 1$. In practice the economy has both competitive and non-competitive elements in wage formation, so that the wage equation (11.3.4') is an average of (11.3.4) and the non-competitive formulations discussed above.

The economy is now defined by the state space equations (11.3.6) and

$$\dot{\theta} = \theta\{g(\varepsilon) - \mu_3 h(\theta) + \mu_4 \dot{p}^e - \dot{p}\}.$$ (11.3.7')

Concentrate first on fear of redundancies only, that is assume perfect anticipation and compensation for increases in the cost of living ($\mu_4 = 1$, $\dot{p}^e = \dot{p}$). Using the same Lyapunov function it can be shown that $\dot{V} = -\mu_3(\dot{\varepsilon}/\varepsilon)^2 < 0$ for $(\varepsilon, \theta) \neq (\varepsilon^*, \theta^*)$, so that the steady state of the system is now asymptotically stable. Thus loops in wage formation eventually eliminate perpetual conflict, because a high share of labour reduces the demand for employment and workers anticipate that, in this case, excessive wage claims could threaten jobs.

Now ignore fear of redundancies ($\mu_3 = 0$) and assume perfect anticipation of the inflation rate ($\dot{p}^e = \dot{p}$), but assume incomplete compensation for increases in the costs of living ($\mu_4 < 1$). This perturbation requires a theory of inflation. Two very different theories, although with similar dynamic implications, will be considered. The first embodies the post-Keynesian idea of producers setting prices to attain a desired share of profits in value added, say Δ, so that the desired price (P^d) equals the product of the mark-up factor $(1 - \Delta)^{-1}$ and unit labour costs ($W \cdot PE/Q$). The rate of cost-push inflation is then deduced from the exponential lag $\dot{P} = (P^d - P)/\tau_p$, so that (using $p = \ln P$)

$$\dot{p}^e = \frac{\dot{P}}{P} = \frac{1}{\tau_p}\left(\frac{P^d}{P} - 1\right) = \frac{1}{\tau_p}\left(\frac{\theta}{1 - \Delta} - 1\right), \quad \tau_p > 0,$$ (11.3.17)

where τ_p is the average time between marking up. When there is conflict and workers manage to reduce the share of profits below the aspired share, firms recover their share by raising prices and inflation results. The second theory is based on Fischer's quantity theory. This postulates that the real demand for cash balances is proportional to transactions (Q), ignores speculative components of the demand for money and equates nominal demand to the nominal supply of money, say M^s. Under these assumptions M^s is proportional to ($P \cdot Q$) and therefore the quantity rate of demand-pull inflation is given by

$$\dot{p}^m = m^s(t) - \frac{\dot{Q}}{Q} = m^s(t) - \{-h(\theta) + \omega^* + \eta\}, \tag{11.3.17'}$$

where $m^s(t) = \dot{M}^s/M^s$ is the exogenous growth in the supply of money. These two theories are complementary, since $\dot{p} = \text{Min}(\dot{p}^c, \dot{p}^m)$ and inflation is therefore cost-push determined unless there is an insufficient growth in the supply of money to finance the inflated transactions (cf. Rowthorn, 1977). The Jacobian (evaluated at the equilibrium) of the system (11.3.6)–(11.3.7') with (11.3.17) or (11.3.17') under the assumptions $\dot{p}^e = \dot{p}$ and $\mu_3 = 0$ is given by

$$\mathbf{J}' = \mathbf{J} + \theta^*(\mu_4 - 1)\bar{\lambda}\begin{pmatrix} 0 & 0 \\ 0 & 1 \end{pmatrix} \tag{11.3.9'}$$

and gives rise (using (11.3.10)) to the characteristic polynomial

$$\lambda^2 + \theta^*(1 - \mu_4)\bar{\lambda}\lambda + \lambda_1\lambda_2 = 0, \tag{11.3.18}$$

where $\bar{\lambda} = (\tau_p(1 - \Delta))^{-1}$ for the cost-push and $\bar{\lambda} = (\sigma_1 - \sigma_2)/\bar{\alpha}$ for the monetary theory of inflation ($\bar{\lambda} = \partial\dot{p}/\partial\theta$). The Routh–Hurwitz criterion predicts that the economy is locally stable when $\det \mathbf{J}' > 0$ and trace $\mathbf{J}' < 0$. The economy is therefore locally stable under money illusion ($\mu_4 < 1$), but explodes under over-compensation for increases in the cost of living ($\mu_4 > 1$). Examination of the discriminant in the expression for λ shows that the predator–prey cycle of perpetual conflict is replaced by monotonic decline (stable node) when

$$\mu_4 < 1 - \frac{2}{\bar{\lambda}}\sqrt{\lambda_1\lambda_2} \tag{11.3.19}$$

and by oscillations (stable or unstable spiral) otherwise. An example of elimination of conflict (node) occurs when firms revise prices immediately ($\tau_p \simeq 0$) and workers suffer from money illusion ($\mu_4 < 1$), but this is paid for by excessive inflation ($p \to \infty$).

When inflation expectations are not perfect, one may assume in addition adaptive expectations of the form

$$\frac{d}{dt}(\dot{p}^e) = \frac{1}{\tau_e}(\dot{p} - \dot{p}^e), \quad \tau_e > 0, \tag{11.3.20}$$

where τ_e is the adjustment coefficient. The economy is now described by three differential equations: (11.3.6), (11.3.7') and (11.3.20). Application of the Routh–Hurwitz condition to the Jacobian of the system, that is

$$\mathbf{J}'' = \left(\begin{array}{c|c} \mathbf{J} - \theta^*\bar{\lambda}\begin{pmatrix} 0 & 0 \\ 0 & 1 \end{pmatrix} & \begin{array}{c} 0 \\ \theta^*\mu_4 \end{array} \\ \hline 0 \qquad \bar{\lambda}/\tau_e & -1/\tau_e \end{array}\right) \tag{11.3.9''}$$

demands trace $(\mathbf{J}'') < 0$, $\det(\mathbf{J}'') < 0$ and $\{\det(\mathbf{J}'') - \operatorname{trace}(\mathbf{J}'')M\} > 0$, where M denotes the sum of the second order principal minors, for local stability. Using this result it can be shown that local stability holds under adaptive expectations as long as the lag in catching up with actual prices is long enough, that is if

$$\mu_4 < 1 + \left[\frac{\lambda_1 \lambda_2 \tau_e^2}{\tau_e \bar{\lambda} + 1} \right]. \tag{11.3.21}$$

Many other structural perturbations are considered by economists. A very important one is profit-maximizing behaviour of firms discussed in section 11.5, but first the famous neoclassical growth model needs to be reviewed.

11.4. NEOCLASSICAL VERSIONS OF ECONOMIC GROWTH

The essential feature of section 11.3 was complementarity between factors of production (fixed α), but the neoclassical model rejects this hypothesis by allowing firms to substitute machinery for workers. Thus firms choose the level of factor inputs to maximize gross profits, $\Pi^g = Q - W \cdot E$. This requires an explanation of Q in the form of a production function. A Cobb–Douglas production function with disembodied labour-augmenting technical progress and constant returns to scale (see Chapter 12) may be obtained by integrating a linearized version of Kaldor's technical progress function, say

$$\frac{\dot{Q}}{Q} - \frac{\dot{E}}{E} = \omega = \omega_1 + \omega_2 \left(\frac{\dot{K}}{K} - \frac{\dot{E}}{E} \right),$$

that is

$$Q = dK^{\omega_2} \bar{E}^{1-\omega_2}, \quad \frac{\dot{E}}{E} = \frac{\dot{E}}{\bar{E}} - \omega^*, \quad \omega^* = \frac{\omega_1}{1 - \omega_2} \tag{11.4.1}$$

where the constant d depends on initial conditions and $\bar{E}$ denotes the number of efficiency units of employed labour, $\bar{E} = E \exp(\omega^* t)$. Simple differentiation of Π^g with respect to E yields the stationarity condition $(\partial Q / \partial E) = W$, so that the best strategy is to recruit labour and scrap machinery until the marginal productivity of workers equals the real wage. (This policy defines a maximum, since concavity of the production function ensures $\Pi^{g''} = Q'' < 0$ as can easily be verified). Such a policy ensures that the share of labour in the gross national product (θ) is fixed at $1 - \omega_2$, because $\partial Q / \partial E = (1 - \omega_2)Q/E = W$. This allows one to write the neoclassical model in terms of the two simultaneous differential equations

$$\dot{\varepsilon} = [g^a - g^n]\varepsilon = \left[\frac{\sigma}{\alpha} - \gamma - \delta - \frac{1}{1-\omega_2} \frac{\dot{\alpha}}{\alpha} - \omega^* - \eta \right] \varepsilon \tag{11.4.2}$$

and

$$\dot{\alpha} = \left[\frac{1-\omega_2}{\omega_2} (\mu_1 \varepsilon - \mu_2 - \omega^*) \right] \alpha, \tag{11.4.3}$$

where the aggregate propensity to save (σ) and θ are fixed. The second equation implies that excess demand for labour never increases the share of labour, since any increase in real wages is immediately compensated for by an increase in productivity due to a higher capital intensity.

Most of the neoclassical literature assumes immediate clearing of the labour market ($\mu_1 = \infty$), which implies equalization of warranted and natural growth rates and $\varepsilon = \varepsilon^*$. This implies $\dot{\varepsilon}/\varepsilon = 0$ and reduces (11.4.2) to a linear differential equation in terms of α, that is $\dot{\alpha} = (1 - \omega_2)\sigma + \lambda_3\alpha$, whose solution is given by

$$\alpha = \alpha^* + (\alpha_0 - \alpha^*)\exp(\lambda_3 t), \qquad (11.4.4)$$

where the eigenvalue and equilibrium capital–output ratio are given by $\lambda_3 = -(1 - \omega_2)(\gamma + \delta + \omega^* + \eta)$ and $\alpha^* = \sigma/(\gamma + \delta + \omega^* + \eta)$. Incidentally one could formulate the neoclassical model in terms of $\bar{r} = K/\bar{E}$, that is $\dot{\bar{r}} + (\gamma + \delta + \omega^* + \eta)\bar{r} = \sigma d\bar{r}^{\omega_2}$, which is a Bernoulli-type differential equation [see IV, §7.10.2] and after the appropriate transformation yields the same solution. The model is stable and converges monotonically to the balanced growth trajectory from any initial state, α_0, since λ_3 is a negative real characteristic root. Adjustment in neoclassical models may take many decades, especially in slow-growing economies, although the wealth effect, γ, tends to speed up adjustment. The monotonic adjustment of the neoclassical model is in sharp contrast to the knife-edge properties of the neo-Keynesian economy without substitution. It is due to the profit-maximizing behaviour of firms.

Applications of the Routh–Hurwitz criterion to the generalized neoclassical model (11.4.2)–(11.4.3) with finite μ_1, which allows for departures from full employment, proves local stability. An illustrative numerical simulation of the system (11.4.2)–(11.4.3) is also drawn in Figure 11.1. The recovery for an initially too high capital–output (unemployment) ratio is monotonic, requires about 40 years to settle down within 5% of the equilibrium and causes transient reductions in the employment (capital–output) ratio. The simulation should be compared with the post-Keynesian simulation, where equilibrium is never achieved due to conflict over the distribution of income.

11.5. PROFITABILITY AND UNEMPLOYMENT IN A GROWING ECONOMY

11.5.1. Gradual adjustment of the capital intensity or optimal choice of technique

In this section the features of perpetual conflict and neoclassical growth are gathered in a hybrid model by having an accommodating capital–output ratio as well as a flexible income distribution. There are two ways of achieving this. The first approach assumes that the neoclassical adjustment of the capital intensity (measured by α or $\bar{r}$) to its optimal level may take some time, hence let

$$\dot{\alpha} = \xi(\alpha^d - \alpha) = \left[\xi\left(\left(\frac{\theta}{1-\omega_2} \right)^{\frac{1-\omega_2}{\omega_2}} - 1 \right) \right] \alpha = \psi(\theta)\alpha, \quad \psi' > 0, \quad (11.5.1)$$

where ξ is the speed of recruiting and firing (scrapping) activities and α^d is the capital–output ratio which ensures $\partial Q/\partial E = W$. This approach is not entirely satisfactory, since it is based on the integration of a *linearized* technical progress function. This implies that no distinction was made between changes in capital intensity and technical progress, so that some of the essential properties of the process of innovation were ignored. The nonlinear nature of $\phi(\cdot)$ allows for the possibility of increasing returns to scale, although there are decreasing opportunities for learning ($\phi'' < 0$). One interpretation of $\phi(\cdot)$ is that investment benefits productivity mainly because it provides opportunities for learning new methods, innovation and exploitation of previously unused inventions. Maximization of profits may be unrealistic and in any case a nonlinear $\phi(\cdot)$ is not easy to integrate into a production function. The second approach is therefore based on firms maximizing the reduction in unit costs subject to the invention possibility frontier, proxied by $\phi(\cdot)$. Thus assuming firms do not anticipate changes in the real wage or the real cost of capital, say ρ, firms maximize

$$UCR = -\frac{d}{dt}\left(\frac{WE + \rho K}{Q} \right) = -\left\{ W\left(\frac{\dot{E}}{Q} \right) + \rho\dot{\alpha} + \dot{W}\frac{E}{Q} + \dot{\rho}\alpha \right\} \simeq \omega\theta - \dot{\alpha}\rho \quad (11.5.2)$$

subject to $\omega = \phi(\dot{\alpha}/\alpha + \omega)$. When in the medium-term ρ equals the gross profit rate $(1-\theta)/\alpha$, the UCR becomes $\phi(\dot{r}/r) - (1-\theta)\dot{r}/r$, where $r = K/E$. The optimal solution for the best choice of technique is obtained by differentiating UCR with respect to the change in technology $\dot{r}/r$, which gives $\phi' = 1 - \theta$. This leads to $\dot{r}/r = (\phi')^{-1}(1-\theta)$, $\omega = \phi\{(\phi')^{-1}(1-\theta)\}$ and

$$\dot{\alpha} = [(\phi')^{-1}(1-\theta) - \omega]\alpha = \psi(\theta)\alpha, \quad (11.5.1)$$

where in this case $\psi' = -(1-\phi')((\phi')^{-1})'$. The above defines a maximal UCR, because $UCR'' = \phi'' < 0$, and ensures firms operate where the gradient of the technical progress function equals the gross profit rate. Since $\phi'' < 0$, $\psi' > 0$ as long as $\phi' < 1$ (which is likely, especially near the equilibrium). Hence high costs of labour induce the implementation of labour-saving innovations.

Although both approaches put a rather different interpretation on $\psi(\cdot)$ they imply the same investment specification

$$\frac{I}{K} = \frac{\dot{Q}}{Q} + \delta + \psi(\theta) \quad (11.5.3)$$

so that the accelerator driven by growth in demand ($\dot{Q}/Q$), replacement of existing machinery and the relative costs of labour (Ricardo effect) are the main determinants of gross investment (in relation to existing machinery). The corresponding growth in the demand for employment may be approximated by the first order Taylor series expansion [see IV, §5.8] $\omega = \phi(\omega^*) + \phi'(\omega + \dot{\alpha}/\alpha) - \omega^*)$ or

$$\frac{\dot{E}}{E} = \frac{\dot{Q}}{Q} - \frac{\phi'}{1 - \phi'}\psi(\theta) - \omega^*, \qquad (11.5.4)$$

which is exact for the first approach with $\phi' = \omega_2$, so that workers are fired when demand for products diminishes, the share of labour is too high or labour-augmenting technical progress increases. Thus a too high real wage must be compensated for by an increased productivity of labour, which may be achieved by additional investment and shedding of labour. It is the lack of profitability and not the lack of aggregate demand (see section 11.6) which causes unemployment, since a too high cost of labour causes too little savings (section 11.3) as well as a shift of the capital intensity in favour of machinery (section 11.4). Observe that the special cases $\beta = \infty$ and maximizing UCR subject to a *linear* $\phi(\cdot)$ degenerate to the neoclassical model, whereas the special case $\beta = 0$ corresponds to the post-Keynesian model.

11.5.2. Analysis of the hybrid model of cyclical growth

The hybrid model consists of the three nonlinear differential equations (11.4.2), (11.5.1) or (11.5.1′), and

$$\dot{\theta} = [\mu_1\varepsilon - \mu_2 - \phi\{(\phi')^{-1}(1 - \theta)\}]\theta \qquad (11.5.5)$$

in terms of the state space variables ε, α and θ. The equilibrium of the new system is defined by $\varepsilon^* = (\omega^* + \mu_2)/\mu_1$, $\theta^* = 1 - \phi'(\omega^*)$, α^* is as before and ω^* is the fixed point of $\phi(\cdot)$. The Jacobian matrix evaluated at the equilibrium, say $\hat{\mathbf{J}}$, of this system can be written in the form

$$\hat{\mathbf{J}} = \begin{pmatrix} 0 & -\dfrac{\sigma_1 - \sigma_2}{\alpha^*}\varepsilon^* & -(\gamma + \delta + \omega^* + \eta)\dfrac{\varepsilon^*}{\alpha^*} \\ \mu_1\theta^* & 0 & 0 \\ 0 & 0 & 0 \end{pmatrix} - \xi\begin{pmatrix} 0 & \dfrac{\varepsilon^*}{\phi'\theta^*} & 0 \\ 0 & 1 & 0 \\ 0 & -\dfrac{\alpha^*}{\phi'} & 0 \end{pmatrix}$$

$$(11.5.6)$$

where $\phi' = \omega_2$ in the first approach and $\xi = \phi'z\theta^*$, $z = -((\phi')^{-1})' > 0$, in the second approach. It can be shown after some algebraic manipulations that the characteristic polynomial of the matrix $\hat{\mathbf{J}}$ [see IV, §7.3] is given by

$$1 + \frac{\xi(\lambda - \lambda_4)(\lambda - \lambda_5)}{\lambda(\lambda - \lambda_1)(\lambda - \lambda_2)} = 0, \qquad (11.5.7)$$

where λ_1, λ_2 are the eigenvalues of the post-Keynesian model (11.3.6)–(11.3.7) and λ_4, λ_5 are the eigenvalues of the neoclassical model (11.4.2)–(11.4.3). The Routh–Hurwitz criterion requires det $(\hat{\mathbf{J}})$, trace $(\hat{\mathbf{J}}) < 0$ and $\{\det(\hat{\mathbf{J}}) + \text{trace}(\hat{\mathbf{J}})\hat{\mathbf{J}}_{12}\hat{\mathbf{J}}_{21}\} > 0$ for local stability. The first two conditions are always satisfied and the third condition is satisfied when the inequality $(1 - \theta^*)\alpha^* z > \sigma_2$ holds. Therefore under the classical savings hypothesis ($\sigma_2 = 0$) firms can always ensure dissipation of the class struggle by either tending towards the optimal capital intensity or by choosing the cost-minimizing direction of technological progress. However, there is no reason why workers should accept technical change implemented by capitalists. Intensification of the class struggle can occur when workers gain control over the means of production by allocating a large part of wages for accumulation purposes, since a too high σ_2 causes instability. This possibility for escalation of conflict increases when wages form a greater part of the national product. A related weapon of workers is to demand pecuniary compensation for having to operate more advanced machinery. Such action is likely to be successful, since firms are more able to grant wage increases when productivity is increased. It can be shown that adding the term $\mu_5\omega$ to the wage-formation equation is, according to the Routh–Hurwitz criterion, de-stabilizing. Indeed when workers get full compensation for productivity increases ($\mu_5 = 1$) and firms introduce cost-minimizing technology the model is always unstable and class conflict escalates. The proofs of these last results are left as an exercise for the reader.

The above characteristic polynomial may be used to derive a root-locus

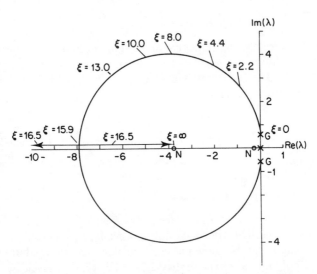

Figure 11.2: The root lucus for a model of damped conflict with the speed of recruiting and firing activities (ξ) as gain parameter

diagram (Evans, 1948; Aoki, 1976) with ξ as the gain parameter (see Figure 11.2). The root-locus diagram is extremely useful for analysing parametric stability [see Engineering, §§14.5, 14.7], since it shows the position of the eigenvalues of an economy in the complex plane as ξ varies from 0 to ∞. In economics it allows one to position radically different theories in the same diagram. The present model locates the post-Keynesian model of perpetual conflict at the poles $\lambda_{1,2}$ on the imaginary axis, where the locus starts with $\xi = 0$, and locates the neoclassical model of monotonic growth at the zeros $\lambda_{4,5}$ on the negative real axis, where the locus ends up with $\xi = \infty$. Intermediate cases are characterized by finite ξ and the diagram suggests that models with both post-Keynesian and neoclassical features are locally stable (for small enough σ_2) spirals or nodes. The root locus uses the Routh–Hurwitz criterion to determine the point of cross-over with the imaginary axis, that is to determine stability, but in addition gives many other qualitative insights as well.

The results of this section are confirmed by a numerical simulation of the system (11.4.2), (11.5.1) and (11.5.5) with plausible parameter values (see Figure 11.3). All simulations are carried out with a version of the Runge–Kutta–Merson routine for numerical integration of nonlinear differential equations [see III, §8.2.] implemented in the library of subroutines compiled by the Numerical Algorithms Group in Oxford. As expected, the simulation yields a stable spiral. Gradual substitution allows firms to industrialize towards a higher capital intensity, although in the process some conflict with workers is inevitable and on average workers are rewarded more than in equilibrium. In the deterministic environments considered so far cycles are damped, but in the real world the class struggle would be maintained by erratic shocks, such as wars, inventions, climate, etc. (cf. Wicksell, 1907; Frisch, 1933). The structural perturbations considered in

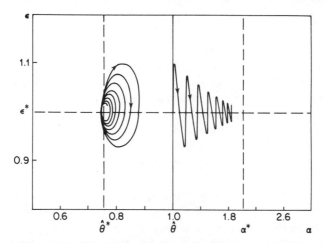

Figure 11.3: Simulation of industrialization and attenuation
of class conflict

section 11.3 may be analysed within the context of the hybrid model by numerical simulation exercises. As before, fear of redundancies, money illusion and adaptive expectations tend to be stabilizing and to remove conflict.

The post-Keynesian and neoclassical approaches considered in sections 11.3–11.5 are concerned with profitability and supply-oriented, since the utilization of capacity is supposed to be fixed over the cycle. The next section considers demand (and utilization) effects in the trade cycle, but ignores changes in the distribution of income. In section 11.7 an economy with supply and demand effects will be considered.

11.6. THE TRADE CYCLE AND KEYNESIAN DEMAND MANAGEMENT

11.6.1. Demand-oriented explanations of the trade cycle

The first model of the trade cycle proposed in this section is the multiplier–accelerator. It consists of a simple consumption and investment specification with a fixed income distribution. It will be shown to generate linear business cycles due to lags in production and induced investment. Let the average time it takes to produce output in response to demand $(C + A + I)$ be τ_q periods, so that the output supply equation is given by $\dot{Q} = 1/\tau_q(C + A + I - Q)$. Hence the new identity for the production account becomes $Q = C + A + I + \dot{F} = Y + D$, where $\dot{Q} = -\dot{F}/\tau_q$, A denotes autonomous demand for goods by the private sector (previously equal to zero) and F denotes the stock of finished goods. Let the average lag for the construction and implementation of new physical assets be τ_i periods, so that

$$\dot{K} = \frac{1}{\tau_i}(\alpha^d Q - K), \tag{11.6.1}$$

where α^d is the desired capital–output ratio. One could interpret α^d as that α which ensures $(\partial Q/\partial E) = W$ or as $(1 - \theta)/\rho$ to capture the deterrent effect of a high interest rate, ρ, on investment. Alternatively, investment in fixed assets depends, with a distributed time lag, on the rate of increase in output. This is known as the *flexible accelerator* and may be written as

$$\dot{K} = \int_0^\infty \omega(s)\alpha^d \dot{Q}(t - s)\,ds, \tag{11.6.1'}$$

where $\omega(s)$ is a nonnegative weighting function, for which $\int_0^\infty \omega(s)\,ds = 1$ holds. When exponential weighting $(\omega(s) = \exp(-s/\tau_i)/\tau_i)$ is used one obtains, after integration, Equation (11.6.1) with an added arbitrary constant of integration. Since $\int_0^{\tau_i} \omega(s)\,ds = 1 - e^{-1} = 0.632$, τ_i is the time required for 63.2% of the induced investment in fixed capital to appear. Yet another interpretation of

(11.6.1) says that net investment increases when the utilization of capacity, defined as $z = \alpha^d Q/K$, is above normal, that is $\dot{K}/K = (z-1)/\tau_i$.

When one assumes either a constant θ, perhaps justified by the 'ability to pay' hypothesis, or $\sigma_1 = \sigma_2$, σ will be a constant and one can use (11.6.1) and the supply equation

$$\dot{Q} = -\frac{1}{\tau_q}\dot{F} = \frac{1}{\tau_q}\left[\frac{1}{\tau_i}(\alpha^d Q - K) + (\gamma + \delta)K - \sigma Q\right] + \frac{A}{\tau_q} \qquad (11.6.2)$$

to describe a trade cycle in terms of Q and K. This system need never be in balanced equilibrium, as long as in the long-run growth in output and the capital stock are below the natural rate of growth ($g \leqslant g^n$). The steady state values of Q and K are, assuming for simplicity that $g^n = 0$, $Q^* = A/(\sigma - (\gamma + \delta)\alpha^d)$ and $K^* = \alpha^d Q^*$. These are easily recognized as a modification of Kahn's multiplier and are compatible with permanent unemployment [cf. Keynes, 1936, and Chapter 4]. An economy can only maintain these steady state levels of output, without violating the labour supply constraints, when the two differential equations (11.6.1)–(11.6.2) are stable. The characteristic polynomial of this system may be found from its (constant) Jacobian and is given by

$$\tau_i \tau_q \lambda^2 + [\tau_i \sigma + \tau_q - \alpha^*]\lambda + [\sigma - (\gamma + \delta)\alpha^*] = 0. \qquad (11.6.3)$$

The solution of the system may be written as $Q(t) = Q^* + c_1 \exp(\lambda_{6t}) + c_2 \exp(\lambda_{7t})$, and similarly for K, where $\lambda_{6,7}$ are the roots of the characteristic polynomial, Q^* denotes the particular integral and the latter two terms [see IV, §7.4.1] denote the complementary solution to the homogeneous system. The general characteristic polynomial $\lambda^2 - \operatorname{tr} \lambda + \det = 0$ gives eigenvalues with only negative real parts when $\operatorname{tr} < 0$ and $\det > 0$. One has oscillations, or non-zero imaginary parts, when the discriminant ($= \operatorname{tr}^2 - 4\det$) is negative. The results follow from these observations. Observing that negative real parts of the roots lead to stability and a pair of complex conjugate roots leads to sine waves, one obtains the following qualitative results for the paths of Q and K in the trade cycle:

$$\alpha^d < [\sqrt{\tau_i \sigma - k} - \sqrt{\tau_q}]^2 + k \quad \text{STEADY DECLINE}$$

$$[\sqrt{\tau_i \sigma - k} - \sqrt{\tau_q}]^2 + k < \alpha^d < \tau_i \sigma + \tau_q \quad \text{DAMPED OSCILLATIONS}$$

$$\tau_i \sigma + \tau_q < \alpha^d < [\sqrt{\tau_i \sigma - k} + \sqrt{\tau_q}]^2 + k \quad \text{EXPLOSIVE OSCILLATIONS}$$

$$\alpha^d > [\sqrt{\tau_i \sigma - k} + \sqrt{\tau_q}]^2 + k \quad \text{MONOTONIC EXPLOSION}$$

where $k = \tau_i(\gamma + \delta)\alpha^d$. Upon setting $k = 0$, these results reduce to the finding of Phillips (1954), correspond to the discrete-time versions of Samuelson (1939) and Hicks (1950) and relate to the mixed differential–difference equation model of Kalecki (1935). When one gradually increases α^d/τ_i, the relative output lag τ_q/τ_i, or σ the economy passes from monotonic decline, to damped oscillations, followed by explosive oscillations and ends up with monotonic explosion. Thus a low savings propensity, perhaps caused by a high share of labour in value added, causes excess demand and may produce explosion. Similarly wages that are too low may cause a lack of effective demand and Keynesian unemployment. Such unemployment is different from the (neo)classical unemployment, owing to too high a cost of labour, discussed in sections 11.3–11.5.

Cycles with highest frequency occur when the length or period of the cycle, defined as $\{2\pi/\mathrm{Im}(\lambda_{6,7})\}$, is a minimum. This occurs when $\alpha^d = \tau_i\sigma + \tau_q$. When one chooses a time unit of a year and plausible bounds on τ_i, τ_q, k and σ, say $\tau_i \leqslant 3$, $\tau_q \leqslant 0.5$, $k \geqslant 0$ and $\sigma \leqslant 0.3$, one obtains $\tau_i\sigma + \tau_q \leqslant 1.4$ and $[\sqrt{\tau_i\sigma - k} + \sqrt{\tau_q}]^2 + k \leqslant 2.74$. Since α^d is unlikely to be less than 2, unstable oscillations or monotonic explosion are the most likely outcomes of the trade cycle (cf. Hicks, 1950). This instability is a disturbing feature, since most economists agree on the existence of a moderately damped 6–8-year trade cycle based on de-stocking and induced investment. Three approaches leading to more realistic cycles have been proposed.

The first approach considers modifications of the trade cycle. For example, to capture adaptive expectations of future income one might introduce a lag in the consumption function which has a stabilizing influence. However, other modifications, such as the introduction of the level of stocks in the supply relationship, say $\dot{Q} = -1/\tau_q\dot{F} + 1/\tau_s(F^* - F)$, to avoid unlimited de-stocking, may well lead to instability (Bergstrom, 1967). The second approach relies on frustration of planned investment and is discussed in section 11.6.2. The third approach relies on the government eliminating unstable trade cycles and is discussed in section 11.6.3.

11.6.2. Frustration of planned investment

This section recognizes that explosive growth in output must eventually be constrained by the productive capacity in the economy. Thus (11.6.2) only holds when there are idle natural resources, $Q < dK^{\omega_2}L^{1-\omega_2}$, otherwise $Q = dK^{\omega_2}L^{1-\omega_2}$ (cf. Hicks, 1950; Malinvaud, 1980). Goodwin (1951) achieves the same objective by introducing a limit to the net capacity of the capital goods trade, say C_c and a maximum scrapping rate for capital equipment, say C_s. Such ceilings to unlimited growth ensure saturation and are often modelled by S-shaped functions (sigmoids [see V, Chapter 3]). This causes severe nonlinearities and transforms the second order system described above into Raleigh's, van der Pol's or Liénard's equation (cf. Gandolfo, 1980). The trade cycle now corresponds to a relaxation mechanism, not unlike a pendulum clock, and causes limit cycles. The existence of such everlasting limit cycles can be established (denied) with the aid of the Poincaré–Bendixon (Bendixon) theorem for second order nonlinear systems [see IV §7.11.4], although one has to resort to the methods of perturbation, averaging, equivalent linearization, singular perturbation or numerical simulation for higher order systems (e.g. Elgerd, 1967). The main advantages of limit

cycles, unlike the linear theory of the trade cycle, are that the result is independent
of initial conditions or particular lag structures, that the oscillations are self-
sustaining and that the dominant limit cycle has constant amplitude and need not
have the symmetrical form of the sine wave. The simplest model, which will
illustrate the above points, is the *threshold oscillator*. Hence ignore lags in supply
or induced investment ($\tau_q = \tau_i = 0$) and consider the investment specification

$$\dot{K} = C_c > 0, \; K^d > K; \; \dot{K} = 0, \; K^d = K; \; \dot{K} = C_s < 0, \; K^d < K, \qquad (11.6.4)$$

where K^d denotes the desired (or utilized) capacity stock. This formulation
ensures that net investment is determined by the capacity of the investment goods
industry and scrapping is limited due to attrition from wear. Since the desired (or
utilized) stock of machinery may be written as a function of $\dot{K}$ only, that is
ignoring depreciation and wealth effects ($\gamma = \delta = 0$)

$$K^d(\dot{K}) = \alpha^d Q = (\dot{K} + A)\alpha^d/\sigma \qquad (11.6.5)$$

one can obtain the phase diagram corresponding to K (see Figure 11.4).

Figure 11.4 allows one to portray the relaxation mechanism for the output
trajectory, since $Q = K^d(\dot{K})/\alpha^d$. When there is insufficient capacity ($K < K^d$) the
economy carries on saving and investing until the utilization of capacity is
normal. At that point investment stops, which causes an immediate drop in
output by the amount C_c and a corresponding under-utilization of capacity. Thus
scrapping starts at the rate C_s and continues until the desired level of capacity is
reached. When this occurs scrapping is discontinued, output is boosted, the
economy becomes over-utilized again and a new cycle sets itself in motion. In
other words the boom ruins itself by fulfilling its being. Observe that the
discontinuity occurs in investment and output rather than in the stock of capital
and that the very instability of the equilibrium maintains a perpetual trade cycle.
Normally $C_c > -C_s$, so that the upswing is shorter than the downswing. When
one introduces lags and relaxes the extreme nature of the investment function, one
must resort to Poincaré–Liénard's method of graphical integration and the tools
referred to above (cf. Goodwin, 1951). From the economic point of view, it is

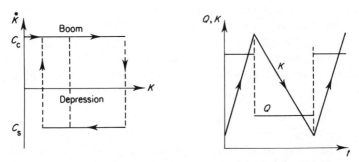

Figure 11.4: Frustration of planned investment in the trade cycle

probably more desirable to model frustration of planned investment in terms of a two-sector economy.

11.6.3. Autonomous demand and reaction functions for economic policy

This section rejects the open-loop nature of (11.6.1)–(11.6.2) and instead introduces a government to pursue a policy of demand management. A public spending term, say G, is added to autonomous private demand (A) in (11.6.2) and together they correspond to the forcing form in a non-homogeneous system of differential equations. When they are not a constant, the particular integral will be different from $Q^* = (A + G)/(\sigma - (\gamma + \delta)\alpha^d)$. For example, when $A + G = (A_0 + G_0)\exp(gt)$ then Q^* is a multiple of $(A + G)$ and when $A + G = (A_0 + G_0)\cos(\omega_{gt})$ then Q^* is a multiple of $(A_0 + G_0)\cos(\omega_{gt} + \theta_g)$. The latter type of passive policy may be caused by a reflationary Labour government followed by a prudent Conservative administration, where the election length equals π/ω_g (cf. section 11.8). Such a policy has the danger of *resonance*, that is as the period of forced oscillations (ω_g) tends towards the period of intrinsic oscillations ($2\pi/\mathrm{Im}(\lambda_{6,7})$ the amplitude of the oscillation in output gets indefinitely large. During resonance the 'electoral cycle' obviously amplifies the trade cycle. None of the above passive policies are directed at stabilizing fluctuations in output. When the government does engage in active demand management, the system (11.6.1)–(11.6.2) becomes a closed-loop system and one enters the domain of normative (rather than positive) economics and feedback control theory. The objective of public policy (G) is to offset a deficiency in private demand, A, while ironing out undesirable fluctuations in output. Following the classic works of Tustin (1953) and Phillips (1954), consider the PID-feedback policy rule for the desired level of public demand

$$G^d = K_p(Q^d - Q) + K_i \int (Q^d - Q)\,dt - K_d \dot{Q}, \qquad (11.6.6)$$

where Q^d denotes the desired (full employment) level of output and K_p, K_i and K_d indicate the intensity of respectively the proportional, integral and derivative components of the policy rule. (This rule implicitly assumes that the productivity of labour and the supply of labour are fixed, so that Q is proportional to the employment rate.) Integral feedback is familiar from the international 'assignment' literature, although derivative and proportional feedback are less known in economics. Actual public demand responds to the desired public demand according to

$$\dot{G} = \frac{1}{\tau_g}(G^d - G), \qquad (11.6.7)$$

where τ_g is the average time taken to implement proposals for government policy. Equations (11.6.6) and (11.6.7) specify a Keynesian feedback policy mechanism

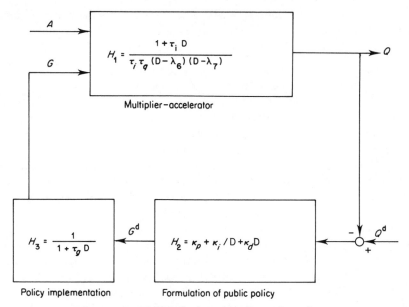

Figure 11.5: Feedback control in the trade cycle

for the system (11.6.1)–(11.6.2) and ensure increases in public works programmes when there is unemployment, a cumulative deficiency from desired output or decline in output and employment. The block diagram for the closed loop system is given in Figure 11.5, where $D = d/dt$ denotes the differential operator. To avoid problems with initial conditions, use the Laplace transform [see IV, §13.4] and analyse deviations from desired rather than actual output. This is best achieved by setting $Q^d = 0, A < 0, Q(0) = \dot{Q}(0) = \ddot{Q}(0) = \ldots 0$, since the Laplace transform of the closed loop system then becomes (e.g. Elgerd, 1967)

$$
\begin{aligned}
q(s) &= \frac{H_1(s)A}{s[1 + H_1(s)H_3(s)H_2(s)]} \\
&= \frac{(1 + \tau_q s)(1 + \tau_i s)A}{(1 + \tau_g s)s[\tau_i \tau_q (s - \lambda_6)(s - \lambda_7)] + [k_d s^2 + k_p s + k_i](1 + \tau_i s)} \\
&= H(s)A,
\end{aligned}
$$

where s denotes the Laplace transform parameter, $q(s)$ denotes the Laplace transform of $Q(t)$, the Laplace transform of the constant A is A/s and the Laplace transform of $d^n Q/dt^n$ reduces to $s^n q(s)$ [see IV, §13.4.3]. (The derivation used the fact that the Laplace transform is a linear operator.) The rational function connecting $q(s)$ and A is referred to as the open loop transfer function ($H_1(s)$) when policy is exogenous and as the closed loop transfer function ($H(s)$) when policy is endogenous [see Engineering §14.10]. Mathematicians might recognize

(11.6.8) as the auxiliary equation ([see IV, §7.4.1]. To analyse the merits of each of the three components of the policy rule, one must consider their implications for the steady state error, given by the Final Value Theorem as $\{Q^d - \lim_{s \to 0} sH(s)\}$, and closed loop stability. No public policy or derivative feedback policy on its own ($K_p = K_i = 0$) gives rise to equilibrium output $Q^* = A/(\sigma - \gamma + \delta)\alpha^d)$. Since $Q^* < Q^d = 0$, private demand is insufficient to maintain full employment in the equilibrium. Under a proportional (and derivative) feedback rule ($K_i = 0$) the steady state output level is a weighted average of Q^* and Q^d, with weights $[\sigma - (\gamma + \delta)\alpha^d]$ and K_p respectively. Equilibrium output is therefore still below full employment output, although as $K_p \to \infty$ the steady state tracking error tends to zero. Integral feedback ($K_i = 0$) does not suffer from steady state error, since it ensures that in the equilibrium full employment is attained ($Q(\infty) = Q^d$) by making the model homogeneous. Open and closed loop stability will be illustrated with a *numerical* example, since analytic results can only be obtained (using the Routh–Hurwitz criterion) when the multiplier–accelerator is drastically simplified. Choose some plausible parameter values, say $\sigma = 0.2$, $\gamma + \delta = 0$, $\alpha^d = 2$, $\tau_i = 3$, $\tau_q = 0.5$, then the open loop eigenvalues are $\lambda_{6,7} = 0.45 \pm 0.31i$. This economy therefore oscillates with a rather long period of $2\pi/0.31 \simeq 20$ years, in an unstable manner around a too low level of equilibrium output. Performance is clearly undesirable, hence consider a proportional and integral feedback policy rule, for example $K_i = K_p = 2$, and assume the policy is implemented on average after 6 months ($\tau_g = 0.5$). In this case the denominator of (11.6.8) is a quartic polynomial given by $q(s) = 0.75 s^4 + 1.05 s^3 + 5.2 s^2 + 8.2 s + 2 = 0$, whose roots may be found from repeatedly solving $\mathrm{Re}\, q(s) = \mathrm{Im}\, q(s) = 0$ for one root at the time with the aid of the Newton–Raphson algorithm [see III, §5.4.1]. The four roots (poles of $H(s)$) are -1.306, -0.297 and $0.101 \pm 2.619i$. Application of partial fractions to these roots [see I, §14.10] enables one to re-write (11.6.8) as

$$q(s) = A \left\{ \frac{0.151}{s + 1.306} + \frac{0.017}{s + 0.297} + \frac{-0.169(s - 0.101) + 0.848(2.619)}{(s - 0.101)^2 + 2.619^2} \right\}.$$

(11.6.9)

and using standard tables for the inverse of the Laplace transform [see IV, §13.4.2] one obtains the general solution for output as

$$Q(t) = A\{0.15 \exp(-1.31t) + 0.02 \exp(-0.30t) - 0.86 \exp(0.10t)$$
$$\cos(2.62t + 1.37)\}.$$

(11.6.10)

As predicted the desired full employment level is reached in the equilibrium, but unfortunately, in contrast with the unregulated cycle, the economy has become more explosive and the period has become much shorter ($2\pi/2.619 = 2.4$ years). To avoid the pathetic dynamic properties of this policy rule, extend the policy rule with a derivative component, say $K_d = 1$, then using the same procedure as above one obtains

$$Q(t) = A\{0.016\exp(-0.299t) - 0.289\exp(-3.968t)$$
$$+ 0.76\exp(-0.566t)\cos(1.388t + 1.21)\}. \tag{11.6.11}$$

The regulated output trajectory consists of harmless (stable) oscillations with a period of 4.5 years, which are actually dominated by a heavily damped, non-oscillatory term.

In summary, integral feedback ensures exact tracking of full employment output in the equilibrium at the expense of increased instability and derivative feedback irons out the undesirable fluctuations caused by the intrinsic dynamics and the other components of the policy rule. Proportional feedback corrects partially for a deficiency in demand, although a too high feedback gain (K_p) may introduce undesirable oscillations. The classical design techniques familiar from the control engineering literature, such as the root locus, Nyquist's and Bode diagrams, and more modern control theory (Aoki, 1976) will confirm the above findings [see Engineering, §14.5]. Recently many of these design techniques have been extended to multi-variable systems, so that the future should hold more applications of control theory to economic policy formulation in store.

The analysis of the trade cycle could have been done in terms of a simultaneous first order state space system in the state variables K and Q. For example, writing the system (11.6.1)–(11.6.2) as $\dot{\mathbf{x}} = \mathbf{Ax} + \mathbf{Bu}$, where $\mathbf{x} = (K, Q)'$, $\mathbf{u} = (A + G)$,

$$\mathbf{A} = \left(\begin{array}{c|c} -\dfrac{1}{\tau_i} & \dfrac{\alpha^d}{\tau_i} \\ \hline \dfrac{\gamma + \delta - \tau_i^{-1}}{\tau_q} & \left(\dfrac{\alpha^d}{\tau_q \tau_i}\right) - \dfrac{\sigma}{\tau_q} \end{array} \right) \text{ and } \mathbf{B} = \left(\begin{array}{c} 0 \\ 1/\tau_q \end{array} \right),$$

one obtains

$$\det(\mathbf{B}|\mathbf{AB}) = \alpha^d \tau_i^{-1} \tau_q^{-2} \neq 0,$$

so that $r(\mathbf{B}|\mathbf{AB}) = \dim \mathbf{x}$ and the system is therefore controllable [see §8.3.2]. This proves the existence of policy rules, which can bring any initial state, $\mathbf{x}(0)$, to an arbitrary desired target state, say $\mathbf{x}^*$, in some finite time. Also, the trade cycle could have been modelled as a set of difference equations and analysed with the aid of the z-transform [see IV, §13.5] or recursive simulation. This is the approach adopted by most of the Keynesian econometric forecasting models and is often used in the discussion of optimal economic policy [see §8.3.3].

11.7. EFFECTIVE DEMAND, THE CLASS STRUGGLE AND ECONOMIC GROWTH

11.7.1. Description of a hybrid economy

In this section the simplest model of an economy with predator–prey, neoclassical and Keynesian features is formulated. The resulting model contains therefore both supply and demand elements, discussed in sections 11.3–11.5 and 11.6 respectively. Such a model allows one to explain why sometimes demand management and at other times a policy for the redistribution of income is required. In particular the conventional 'fine-tuning' of demand, discussed in section 11.6.3, turns out to be inappropriate in situations of unemployment combined with over-utilization of capacity.

To ease the exposition of the synthesis of previous theories the accounting framework and the behavioural equations are re-stated. Consider therefore the system of accounts for both the private and public sector given in Table 11.3 (cf. Table 11.2). The production accounts give production as the sum of total demand (Z) and stockbuilding ($\dot{F}$) or as the sum of the wage-bill, profits and depreciation

$$Q = C + A + G + I + \dot{F} = Z + \dot{F}$$
$$= W{\cdot}E + \Pi + D. \tag{11.7.1}$$

The income and outlay accounts for the private sector define savings as the difference between total income, the sum of wages and profits, and total outlays, the sum of consumption, autonomous demand and direct taxes (T), that is

$$S = W{\cdot}E + \Pi - C - A - T = Y - C - A - T. \tag{11.7.2}$$

The public sector budget deficit equals public spending (G) minus tax revenues (T) and contributes to the accumulation of the public sector debt (R). This must be matched by a corresponding private sector surplus on the capital account, defined as income put aside for replacement of machinery (D) plus savings minus expenditures on investment in machines and inventories, that is the real value of the addition to the public sector debt is defined as

$$\dot{R}/P = G - T = D + S - I - \dot{F}. \tag{11.7.3}$$

By Walras's law the nominal public sector debt (R) equals total holdings of financial assets by the private sector. For simplicity assume that there is only one financial asset, say money, so that the distribution of assets within a portfolio and

Table 11.3 A system of national accounts with the private and public sector distinguished

Incomings \ Outgoings		1	2 Private	2 Public	3 Private	3 Public	Totals
1. Production: private			$C + A$	G	$I + \dot{F}$		Q
2. Income and outlay: private		$W.E + \Pi$					Y
public				T			T
3. Accumulation: private		D	S				$D + S$
public				$T - G$			$T - G$
4. Net acquisition of financial assets					$\dot{R}/P$	$-\dot{R}/P$	0
Totals		Q	Y	T	$D + S$	$T - G$	

interest rates need not be considered and $R = M^s$. The identity $M^s/P = G - T$ is well-known as the public sector budget constraint (e.g. Turnovsky, 1977) and clearly shows that the government is only able to vary two of the three policy variables, G, T and M^s, independently and the third one must follow from the budget constraint. Here it is assumed that the government chooses public demand and taxes and therefore finances the remainder by issuing notes of money. The accumulation of real assets or machinery (K) is due to net investment, that is $\dot{K} = I - D$.

The behavioural assumptions are based on the previous sections and summarized in Table 11.4. To avoid complications wealth effects in the consumption function have been ignored ($\gamma = 0$). The ratio of investment to existing machinery is increased when the expected growth in demand (g^e) or the speed of depreciation is increased. Under-utilization of capacity and high costs of labour dampen animal spirits and retard investment. The first factor represents the Keynesian and the second factor represents the neoclassical (Equation (11.5.1)) or post-Keynesian (Equation (11.5.1')) influence upon investment decisions. Utilization is inversely related to the capital–output ratio, so that explicit bottlenecks are not considered. Expectations of demand are not necessarily fulfilled in the shortrun, but in any case are always fulfilled in the longrun ($g^e = g^n$). No theory of inflation is required in this simple model, since unions compensate themselves for all increases in the costs of living ($p^e = p$, $\mu_4 = 1$). Autonomous private and public demand are specified as a fixed proportion of output, that is $a = (A + G)/Q$.

The above model is complete and has post-Keynesian ($\sigma_1 \neq \sigma_2$, $\phi'' \neq 0$), neoclassical ($\phi' \neq 0$, $\psi' \neq 0$) and Keynesian ($\tau_q \neq 0$, $\tau_i \neq 0$) elements. The model may be written as a system of four ordinary differential equations of the form

$$\dot{\varepsilon} = \{\dot{Q}/Q - \omega - \eta\}\varepsilon = [\{a + (g^e + \gamma + \delta)\alpha + (\alpha^d - \alpha)/\tau_i$$

$$- (1 - \tau)\sigma - \tau\}/\tau_q - \omega(\dot{\alpha}/\alpha) - \eta]\varepsilon \qquad (11.7.4)$$

Table 11.4 Behavioural assumptions of the model of effective demand, the class struggle and economic growth

Consumption	$C = (1 - \sigma)(Q - T)$
Taxation	$T = \tau Q$
Differential savings	$\sigma = \sigma_1(1 - \theta) + \sigma_2\theta, \qquad \theta = WE/Q$
Depreciation	$D = \delta K$
Investment	$I = K\{g^e + \delta + (z - 1)/\tau_i\}$
Utilization	$z = \alpha^d/\alpha, \qquad \alpha = K/Q$
Choice of technique	$\dot{\alpha}^d/\alpha^d = \psi(\theta), \qquad \psi' > 0$
Supply response	$\dot{Q} = (Z - Q)/\tau_q = \{(G - T) + (I - D - S)\}/\tau_q$
Technical progress	$\omega = \dot{Q}/Q - \dot{E}/E = \phi(\dot{K}/K - \dot{E}/E)$
Supply of labour	$\dot{L}/L = \eta$
Wage formation	$\dot{W}/W = \mu_1\varepsilon - \mu_2, \qquad \varepsilon = E/L$

$$\dot\theta = \{\mu_1\varepsilon - \mu_2 - \omega(\dot\alpha/\alpha)\}\theta \tag{11.7.5}$$

$$\dot\alpha = \{g^e + (\alpha^d - \alpha)/\tau_i - \dot\varepsilon/\varepsilon - \omega(\dot\alpha/\alpha) - \eta\}\alpha \tag{11.7.6}$$

$$\dot\alpha^d = \psi(\theta)\alpha^d, \tag{11.7.7}$$

where $\omega' = \phi'/(1 - \phi')$, in terms of the four dimensionless state space variables $\varepsilon, \theta, \alpha$ and α^d.

11.7.2 Structural form systems

Observe that the system (11.7.4)–(11.7.7) is somewhat different from conventional state space systems, because the right-hand side contains the time derivatives of some of the state space variables. More precisely, the system is given by

$$\dot{\mathbf{x}} = \mathbf{f}(\mathbf{x}, \mathbf{u}, \dot{\mathbf{x}}) \tag{11.7.8}$$

rather than by $\dot{\mathbf{x}} = \mathbf{f}(\mathbf{x}, \mathbf{u})$, where the vector of states is defined by $\mathbf{x} = (\varepsilon, \theta, \alpha, \alpha^d)'$ and the vector of controls is defined by $\mathbf{u} = (\alpha, \tau)'$. Such a system of simultaneous differential equations is called a *structural form* rather than a *reduced form* system and occurs in almost all econometric models of realistic size. Before conventional techniques for analysing stability or performing numerical simulation can be applied to systems such as (11.7.8), the system needs to be transformed to its reduced form. This may be done, with the aid of the implicit function theorem [see IV, §5.13], as follows

$$\dot{\mathbf{x}} = \mathbf{g}(\mathbf{x}, \mathbf{u}), (\partial\mathbf{g}/\partial(\mathbf{x}, \mathbf{u})) = \{I - (\partial\mathbf{f}/\dot{\mathbf{x}})\}^{-1}(\partial\mathbf{f}/\partial(\mathbf{x}, \mathbf{y})) \tag{11.7.9}$$

Only when the function $\mathbf{f}(.)$ is linear in $\dot{\mathbf{x}}$, that is when $(\partial^2\mathbf{f}/\partial\mathbf{x}^2) = 0$ (or in the example of Section 11.7.1 $\phi'' = 0$), can the structural form be reduced explicitly to (11.7.9) and be used globally. Otherwise one needs to resort to numerical techniques for solving systems of simultaneous nonlinear equations, such as the Gauss–Seidel method [see III, §3.4] or a Newton-type algorithm [see III, §5.4], to solve for $\dot{\mathbf{x}}$ from the structural form system (11.7.8) given values for $\mathbf{x}$ and $\mathbf{u}$. This implies that in order to simulate the system one uses a hybrid combination of the Gauss–Seidel (or Newton-type) algorithm and the Runge–Kutta method for numerical integration [see III, §8.2]. In discrete-time nonlinear econometric models a similar procedure is required (see Néo-miastchy and Ravelli, 1977/78).

11.7.3. Equilibrium and local stability

The equilibrium or stationary state, say $\mathbf{x}^*$, occurs when $\dot{\mathbf{x}} = \mathbf{0}$ and is given by

$$\mathbf{x}^* = \{\mathbf{x}^*(\mathbf{u})|\mathbf{0} = \mathbf{f}(\mathbf{x}^*, \mathbf{u}, \mathbf{0})\} \tag{11.7.10}$$

The equilibrium of the system (11.7.4)–(11.7.7) is given by $\varepsilon^* = (\omega^* + \mu_2)/\mu_1$,

$\theta^* = 1 - \phi'(\omega^*)$ and $\alpha^* = \alpha^{d*} = \{(1-\tau)\sigma + \tau - a + \tau_q g^n\}/(\gamma + \delta + g^n)$. The equilibrium employment is as always and the equilibrium share of labour in value added is as in sections 11.4 or 11.5.1. The equilibrium capital–output ratio increases with the production lag, τ_q, when there is growth, since then output lags behind demand and this increases the number of machines to be used for the production of one unit of output. When the government operates with a balanced fiscal deficit, that is $\tau = a$, a rise in the size of the public sector depresses the savings ratio and therefore also the equilibrium capital–output ratio.

It may be shown that the Jacobian of the system (11.7.4)–(11.7.9), evaluated by matrix multiplication and inversion from expressing (11.7.9) [see III, §4.5], has eigenvalues with positive real parts when $\phi' = 0$. The system of effective demand and the distribution of income, without substitution, is therefore locally unstable. The intuition underlying this result is the following. Imagine one commences with some under-utilization of capacity ($\alpha > \alpha^*$), but has the distribution of income and the employment rate at their equilibrium values. This situation leads to further under-utilization and higher levels of unemployment; the increasing reserve army of workers is unable to attain the previous growth in real wages and the share of labour therefore diminishes. This causes a decline in effective demand with further loss of jobs and even more under-utilization of capacity. The economy eventually collapses!

This view of a capitalist economy is perhaps too pessimistic, for there are at least three compensating changes elsewhere. Firstly, elements of money illusion or adaptive expectations ($\mu_3 < 1$, $\tau_e > 0$) will secure in a depression, with low rates of cost-push inflation, a shift in the income distribution away from capitalists. This boosts demand and may recover the economy from a depression, especially when one also takes account of increased competition and slashing of prices due to lack of demand. (The inflation rate would then be $\dot{p} = \text{Min}(\dot{p}^c + \dot{p}^d, \dot{p}^m)$, where the component of excess demand inflation is given by $\dot{p}^d = -(1/\tau_d)\dot{F}$.) The above may be re-stated for a situation of excess demand for goods ($I > S/P$): a rise in prices relative to costs, depresses real wages, raises the propensity to save and eventually removes excess demand. Secondly, a more realistic theory models animal spirits of entrepreneurs and has investment depend on (expected) profitability. This may be done by letting the expected return on capital, relative to the interest rate plus some risk premium, influence the desired capital–output ratio ($\eta_2 > 0$). Alternatively, one could relax the strict complementarity between factor inputs by allowing neoclassical substitution possibilities in production ($\phi' > 0$). Thus entrepreneurs will shed machinery (in favour of new jobs) when the share of labour is too low. The relative cheapness of labour therefore induces a neoclassical remedy for lack of effective demand. This effectively complements the theory of effective demand and economic growth, considered so far, with the elements of a class struggle. In this case the economy may recover from effective demand that is too low, since entrepreneurs will take advantage of the relative cheapness of external finance, the high return on equity and the availability of internal finance by investing in new assets. The resulting investment boom may, if strong enough, provide a classical recovery to a Keynesian depression.

Thirdly, the introduction of monetary factors may contribute to stability when the monetary authorities pursue a rule of fixed growth in the money supply (e.g. $m^s = g + \dot{p}^e$). As an illustration imagine an unstable situation with ever-increasing output. This gives rise to an exploding demand for cash for transaction purposes, leaving less and less cash available for speculation purposes and therefore bidding up the real rate of interest. This reduces the desired capital–output ratio and entrepreneurs retard investment. This may return the economy to the dynamic equilibrium (cf. Phillips (1961) for similar results in a model without conflict).

The discussion of this section focused on disequilibrium in the labour and product markets, so that classical and Keynesian unemployment could be distinguished. The approach taken is, however, rather different from recent temporal equilibrium models with rationing (Barro and Grossman, 1976; Malinvaud, 1980), since prices were explained, rather than fixed in the short-term, Keynesian unemployment occurs when $C + I < Q$, rather than when $C + I < \text{Min}(Q^*, Q/(1 - u))$, and classical unemployment occurs when the share of labour in value added is too high, rather than when $Q^* < \text{Min}(C + I, Q/(1 - u))$.

11.8. THE POLITICAL BUSINESS CYCLE

Many empirical studies (e.g. Goodhart and Bhansali, 1970; Kramer, 1971) provide evidence that the popularity of a government depends among other non-economic factors on the inflation rate and the unemployment rate achieved during its term in office. It is clear that one of the main aims of an incumbent political party is survival, so that the probability of winning the next election must be an important objective. This observation suggests that governments are myopic by attempting to reflate an economy just before an election without taking account of the inflationary consequences of such actions. The main objective of this section is to use the framework developed by Nordhaus (1975) to show that such *political* short-sightedness can cause *economic* instability. The first person to suggest such electoral cycles was the Polish economist Kalecki (1943). Such *positive* political explanations of economic policy are in direct contract to the *normative* theories of economic policy discussed in sections 8.3.3 and 11.6.3, since the first theory views the government as a political animal *creating* cycles in order to win votes and the second theory views the government as a benevolent dictator *attempting to avoid* economic instability. Before this type of political decision making can be discussed, an explanation of government popularity is required.

11.8.1. Government popularity and economic performance

Consider the voting intentions of the members of a large nation with a government (1) and an opposition party (2). Let $U_i^k(t)$ denote the utility a voter, i, obtains under the government of party k at time t. It may be decomposed as

$$U_i^k(t) = w^k(t) + b_i^k(t) \qquad (11.8.1)$$

where $w^k(t)$ is a measure of economic performance of party k at time t and $b_i^k(t)$ is a loyalty term specific to voter. i. In other words voters are alike in that they do not differ in their evaluation of a party's economic performance, although they do differ in their attachment (or lack of it) to each political party. The loyalty terms $b_i^k(t)$ vary across voters, since they reflect the influence of a party's non-economic (social, moral, legal, etc.) policies and more generally the (proposed) party platform upon the loyalty of each voter and one would expect such influences to depend on individual tastes. Voter i votes for the party which gives him (her) the highest utility, that is voter i elects party s only if the self-interest postulate

$$U_i^s(t) > U_i^k(t), \quad \text{for all } k \neq s, \qquad (11.8.2)$$

is satisfied. An implicit assumption underlying (11.8.1)–(11.8.2) is that voters hold political parties, at least partially, responsible for economic (mis)management.

Suppose that the bias for the opposition over the ruling party, say $b(t) = b^2(t) - b^1(t)$, is distributed across voters according to the probability density function $f(b(t))$ [see II, §10.1]. It then follows that the proportion of votes going to the ruling party at time t, say $v(t)$, is given by

$$v(t) = \text{Prob}(U_i^1(t) > U_i^2(t)) = \text{prob}(b(t) < w^1(t) - w^2(t)) = F(w(t)),$$
$$\qquad (11.8.3)$$

where $F(\cdot)$ is the cumulative density function of the bias terms at time t [see II, §10.3] and $w(t) = w^1(t) - w^2(t)$ denotes the difference in economic performance between government and opposition. Since this section is mainly concerned with the analysis of one election period and the opposition's performance index, $w^2(t)$, is determined by economic factors which occurred during previous election periods, one can set $w^2(t) = 0$ without loss of generality. It remains to explain the economic performance of the incumbent political party, $w^1(t) = w(t)$.

Suppose this performance is determined by a weighted combination of all present and past successes and failures, say $(W(t - j), j \geqslant 0)$, and assume that the weights diminish as one goes back into time. For example, choose the exponential form with scaling vector $c(t) = \rho/\{1 - \exp(-\rho t)\}$

$$w(t) = c(t) \int_0^t \exp\{-\rho(t-k)\} W(k)\,dk, \quad \rho \geqslant 0, 0 \leqslant t \leqslant T, \qquad (11.8.4)$$

where ρ is the rate of decay of voters' memories and T is the length of the election period. The reader might wish to verify that the weights do add up to unity, that is $\int_0^t c(t) \exp\{-\rho(t-k)\}\,dk = 1$. The parameter ρ is like a backward (rather than a forward) discount rate and in this sense resembles Pigou's 'defective telescopic faculty' (cf. Nordhaus, 1975). Observe that any economic events previous to the current election period are ignored. This assumption is not too serious, since the analysis in the following section is primarily concerned with $v(T) = F(w(T))$ and

$(W(k), k < 0)$ would receive very little weight anyway. A much more important assumption is that $w(t)$ is not affected by $(W(k), k > t)$, so that (rational) expectations of future events by voters are ruled out. This assumption of myopic voting is crucial to the analysis of section 11.8.2.

The measure of current success, W, is assumed to depend negatively on the inflation rate and the unemployment rate say

$$W = W(\dot{p}, u), \qquad W_1 \leqslant 0, \ W_2 \leqslant 0 \qquad (11.8.5)$$

and is an *ordinal* concept and invariant to a linear transformation (cf. Chapter 15). Upon substitution of (11.8.4)–(11.8.5) into (11.8.3), one finally obtains an expression for the proportion of votes going to the ruling party, that is

$$v(t) = F\left\{ c(t) \int_0^t \exp(-\rho(t-k)) W(\dot{p}(k), u(k)) \, dk \right\}. \qquad (11.8.6)$$

When one assumes that the distribution of party biases across voters is time-invariant and follows a uniform density function [see II, §10.2.1], say $f(b(t)) = (q-r)^{-1}, r < b(t) < q$ and $f(b(t)) = 0$, elsewhere, equation (11.8.6) simplifies to the analytically convenient uniform model

$$v(t) = c(t) \int_0^t \left\{ \exp(-\rho(t-k)) V(\dot{p}(k), u(k)) \right\} dk \quad \text{for } r < w(t) < q, \quad (11.8.7)$$

where $V(\cdot) = W(\cdot)/(q-r)$ and $s = r/(q-r)$, $v(t) = 1$, for $w(t) \geqslant q$, and $v(t) = 0$, for $w(t) \leqslant r$. Alternatively, one could assume that the distribution of party biases follows the much more realistic Gaussian density function [see II, §10.4]. This alternative has the advantage that extreme individual biases (reflected in the unobserved attributes of the voters) occur less frequently. It leads to the probit model, familiar from the literature on biological assay (Finney, 1971), which unfortunately cannot be solved explicitly. However, when one chooses a more convenient bell-shaped density function for the terms $b(t)$, say a sequence of independent, identical Weibull variates [see II, §11.9], one obtains the logit model

$$\tilde{v}(t) = \log(v(t)/(1 - v(t))) = c(t) \int_0^t \exp\{-\rho(t-k)\} \, dk \ W\{\dot{p}(k), u(k)\}, \quad (11.8.8)$$

where $\hat{v}(t)$ is the logarithmic lead of the ruling over the opposition party at time t. The logit model may be derived from the axioms of independence of irrelevant alternatives, irrelevance of alternative sets and positivity, for which some support from psychological studies is available (Luce, 1959). The logit model is easily extended to cases with multiple choices (McFadden, 1973), since it assumes that voters make only binary comparisons in deciding for which party to vote. An excellent survey of qualitative choice models and their applications to politics and many other economic fields is provided by Amemiya (1981). Empirical justifications of (11.8.7) and (11.8.8) are given in Fair (1978) and Borooah and van der Ploeg (1983).

11.8.2. Short-sightedness in political decision making

Given that politicians wish to survive, it is not unreasonable to postulate their preferences as wishing to maximize the predicted share of votes (11.8.7) or the logarithmic lead (11.8.8) on election eve. Also assume T is long, so that $c(T) = \rho$. When the government can manipulate public demand to attain any u it desires, u may be interpreted as the decision (or control) variable. In order to maximize the probability of survival the government needs a view of the economy to explain the relationship between $\dot{p}$ and u. The simplest view is, in the terminology of section 11.3, the wage equation (11.3.4$'$) with $\mu_3 = 0$, the cost-push price equation (11.3.17) with $\tau_p = 0$ (to ensure a constant θ or $\dot{p} = \dot{W}/W + \omega$), a fixed capital–output ratio (to ensure $\omega = \omega^*$), $u = 1 - \varepsilon$ and the adaptive expectations mechanism (11.3.20). The above assumptions give rise to the following equation determining the inflation/unemployment trade-off

$$\dot{p} = \hat{\mu}_1(1 - \mu) - \hat{\mu}_2 + \hat{\mu}_4\dot{p}^e - \hat{\mu}_5\omega^* = f(u) + \hat{\mu}_4\dot{p}^e \qquad (11.8.9)$$

with $\mu_5 = 1$, $\hat{\mu}_i = \mu_i/2$ and (11.3.20). The government then chooses u to maximize political welfare subject to (11.8.9) and the state space constraint (11.3.20). The solution proceeds by specifying the Hamiltonian

$$H(u, \dot{p}^e) = \exp(\rho t)V\{f(u) + \hat{\mu}_4\dot{p}^e, u\} + \chi\tau_e^{-1}\{f(u) - (1 - \hat{\mu}_4)\dot{p}^e\}, \quad (11.8.10)$$

where χ is the shadow price (or adjoint variable) corresponding to $\dot{p}^e$ (the cost imputed on the expected rate inflation). The optimal plan $(\dot{u}, \chi)$ maximizes $H(u, \dot{p}^e)$ at all points of time and must satisfy (11.3.20) and the adjoint equation

$$\dot{\chi} = -(\partial H/\partial \dot{p}^e) = -\{\exp(\rho t)V_{\dot{p}^e} - \chi\tau_e^{-1}(1 - \hat{\mu}_4)\} \qquad (11.8.11)$$

or, alternatively, upon substitution of $\hat{\chi} = \chi\exp(-\rho t)$, the adjoint equation

$$\dot{\hat{\chi}} = -V_{\dot{p}^e} + \{\tau_e^{-1}(1 - \hat{\mu}_4) - \rho\}\hat{\chi} \qquad (11.8.11')$$

These optimality conditions follow from Pontryagin's Maximum Principle [see Engineering, §14.11], but may also be derived from Bellman's Dynamic Programming Technique [see IV, §16.3] and use $x = p^e$ and $a = \tau_e^{-1}\{f(u) - (1 - \hat{\mu}_4)p^e\}$ to put the problem into the standard form for calculus of variations). Assuming a specific form for the popularity function, say $V = -u^2 - v\dot{p}$, the stationarity condition for $H(u, \dot{p}^e)$ give

$$\exp(-\rho t)H_u = v\hat{\mu}_1 - 2u - \hat{\chi}\tau_e^{-1}\hat{\mu}_1 = 0 \qquad (11.8.12)$$

or

$$\hat{\chi} = \tau_e(v - 2u/\hat{\mu}_1). \qquad (11.8.13)$$

Differentiate (11.8.13) with respect to time, giving $\dot{\hat{\chi}} = -2\tau_e\dot{u}/\hat{\mu}_1$, and substitute for $\hat{\chi}$ and $\dot{\hat{\chi}}$ into (11.8.11') to obtain

$$\dot{u} = Au + B, \qquad (11.8.14)$$

where $A = (1 - \hat{\mu}_4)/\tau_e - \rho$ and $B = -v\mu_1(\tau_e^{-1} - \rho)/2$. To solve the differential equation (11.8.14), use the fact that as $t \to T$, $\hat{\chi} \to 0$ and $u \to v\hat{\mu}_1/2$. Backward integration of (11.8.14) gives the optimal development of demand management

$$u(t) = (v\hat{\mu}_1/2 + B/A)\exp(A(t - T)) - B/A. \qquad (11.8.15)$$

The solution (11.8.15) allows one to describe the political business cycle. Since $u(T) = -\hat{\mu}_4 u(T)/\tau_e < 0$ and either if $A \geq 0$, $\dot{u} > 0$ then u is always positive, or if $A \leq 0$ and $\dot{u} > 0$ then $\dot{u}(T) > 0$ contradict $\dot{u}(T) < 0$ implies $\dot{u} < 0$ always, so that the unemployment rate must be falling over the entire electoral regime (cf. Nordhaus, 1975). The fall will be relatively faster at the end or beginning depending on whether $A > 0$ or $A < 0$, respectively. Figure 11.6 simulates the outcome of (11.8.15) over a number of election periods. The optimal trajectories for the unemployment and inflation rates are saw-toothed and smoothed respectively. The story is that immediately after an election the new government raises unemployment to a relatively high level in order to combat inflation. As election eve approaches, the unemployment rate is gradually lowered in order to gain

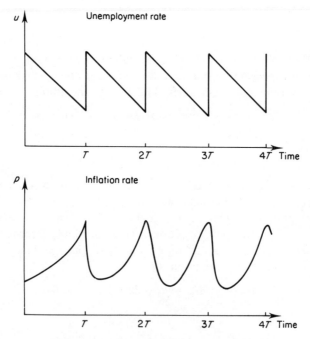

Figure 11.6: The political business cycle

political popularity. This recurring myopic decision making causes the political business cycle.

Further discussion and survey of the literature on political business cycles may be found in Whiteley (1980) and Hibbs and Fassbender (1981).

11.9. CONCLUDING REMARKS

The variety of both positive and normative economic theories discussed in this chapter illustrate the applicability of the theory of ordinary differential equations, stability, feedback and dynamic optimization to the analysis of issues of cyclical growth and economic policy. The reader may wish to refer to the books by Allen (1967), Bergstrom (1967), Aoki (1976) and Gandolfo (1980) for more insight into the mathematical aspects of macro-dynamic economics. For more details on theories of economic growth, one might refer to Wan (1971). A very amusing account of the heated debates on economic growth between the neo-Keynesian and neoclassical schools may be found in Harcourt (1972).

Examples of more recent work are applications of stochastic differential equations [e.g. Chapter 10] or forward and backward z-transforms (e.g. Sargent, 1979) to analyse rational expectations in dynamic models.

Another exciting development is the analysis of chaotic behaviour of certain nonlinear, dynamic *deterministic* systems [see IV, §14.8]. For example, when the predator–prey model of section 11.3.1 or the neo-classical growth model is formulated in discrete time rather than continuous time, the growth cycles will be very irregular and to the eye seem random (Pohjola, 1981, Day, 1982). Furthermore, the *qualitative* behaviour of the system can drastically change owing to a gradual variation in a particular coefficient. Such a drastic change is called a *bifurcation* [see IV, §8.6]. Chaos makes estimation of coefficients very difficult, since apparent randomness may in fact be generated by a deterministic system.

11.10. REFERENCES

Allen, R. G. D. (1967). *Macroeconomic Theory*. Macmillan, London.

Amemiya, T. (1981). Qualitative response models: a survey. *Journal of Economic Literature*, **19**, 1483–1536.

Andronov, A. A., Leontovich, E. A. and Maier, A. G. (1973). *Qualitative Theory of Second-Order Dynamic Systems*. Wiley, New York.

Aoki, M. (1976). *Optimal Control and System Theory in Dynamic Economic Analysis*. North-Holland, New York.

Arrow, K. J. (1962). The economic implications of learning by doing. *Review of Economic Studies*, **80**, 155–173.

Atkinson, A. B. (1969). The time-scale of economic models: how long is the long run?. *Review of Economic Studies*, **106**, 137–152.

Barro, R. J. and Grossman, H. I. (1976). *Money, Employment and Inflation*. Cambridge University Press, Cambridge.

Bergstrom, A. R. (1967). *The Construction and Use of Economic Models*. English Universities Press, London.

Borooah, V. K. and van der Ploeg, F. (1983). *Political Aspects of the Economy*, Cambridge University Press, Cambridge.

Day, R. H. (1982). Irregular growth cycles. *American Economic Review*, **72**, 3, 406–414.

Domar, E. D. (1957). *Essays in the Theory of Economic Growth*. Oxford University Press, New York.

Duesenberry, J. S. (1958). *Business Cycles and Economic Growth*. McGraw-Hill, New York.

Elgerd, O. I. (1967). *Control Systems Theory*. McGraw-Hill, Kogakusha.

Evans, W. R. (1948). Graphical analysis of control systems. *Trans. A.I.E.E.*, **67**, 547–551.

Fair, R. C. (1978). The effects of economic events on votes for President. *Review of Economics and Statistics*, **69**, 159–173.

Finney, D. (1971). *Profit Analysis*, Cambridge University Press, Cambridge.

Freedman, H. I. and Waltman, P. (1975). Perturbations of two-dimensional predator–prey equations. *SIAM Journal of Applied Mathematics*, **28**, 1–10.

Frisch, R. (1933). Propagation problems and impulse problems in dynamic economies. *Essays in honour of Gustav Cassel*, London.

Gandolfo, G. (1980). *Economic Dynamics: Methods and Models*. North-Holland, Amsterdam.

Goodhart, C. A. E. and Bhansali, R. J. (1970). Political economy. *Political Studies*, **18**, 43–106.

Goodwin, R. M. (1951). The nonlinear accelerator and the persistence of business cycles. *Econometrica*, **19**, 1–17.

Goodwin, R. M. (1967). A growth cycle, in C. H. Feinstein (ed.), *Socialism, Capitalism and Growth*. Cambridge University Press, Cambridge.

Harcourt, G. C. (1972). *Some Cambridge Controversies in the Theory of Capital*. Cambridge University Press, Cambridge.

Harrod, R. F. (1948). *Towards a Dynamic Economics*. Macmillan, London.

Hibbs, D. and Fassbender, H. (1981). *Contemporary Political Economy*. North-Holland, Amsterdam.

Hicks, J. R. (1950). *A Contribution to the Theory of the Trade Cycle*. Clarendon Press, Oxford.

Kahn, R. F. (1959). Exercises in the analysis of growth. *Oxford Economic Papers*, **2**, 143–156.

Kaldor, N. (1940). A model of the trade cycle. *Economic Journal*, **50**, 78–92.

Kaldor, N. (1956). Alternative theories of distribution. *Review of Economic Studies*, **23**, 83–100.

Kaldor, N. (1957). A model of economic growth. *Economic Journal*, **67**, 591–624.

Kalecki, M. (1935). A macro-dynamic theory of business cycles. *Econometrica*, **3**, 327–344.

Kalecki, M. (1939). *Essays in the Theory of Economic Fluctuations*. Allen & Unwin, London.

Kalecki, M. (1943). Political aspects of full employment. *Political Quarterly*, October/December, 322–331.

Kennedy, C. (1964). Induced bias in innovation and the theory of distribution. *Economic Journal*, **74**, 541–547.

Keynes, J. M. (1936). *The General Theory of Employment, Interest and Money*. Macmillan, London.

Kramer, G. H. (1971). Short-term fluctuations in U.S. voting behaviour. *American Political Science Review*, **65**, 131–143.

Luce, R. D. (1959). *Individual Choice Behaviour*. Wiley, New York.

Malinvaud, E. (1980). *Profitability and Employment*. Cambridge University Press, Cambridge.

McFadden, D. (1973). Conditional logit analysis of qualitative choice behaviour. in P. Zarembka (ed.), *Frontiers in Econometrics*. Academic Press, New York.

Meade, J. E. (1963). *A Neoclassical Theory of Economic Growth*. Allen & Unwin, London.

Nepomiastchy, P. and Ravelli, A. (1977/78). Adapted methods for solving and optimizing quasi-triangular econometric models. *Annals of Economic and Social Measurement*, **6**, 555–582.

Nordhaus, W. D. (1975). The political business cycle. *Review of Economic Studies*, **42**, 169–190.

Pasinetti, L. (1962). Rate of profit and income distribution in relation to the rate of profit. *Review of Economic Studies*, **29**, 267–279.

Phillips, A. W. (1954). Stabilisation policy in a closed economy. *Economic Journal*, **64**, 290–323.

Phillips, A. W. (1961). A simple model of employment, money and prices in a growing economy. *Economica*, **28**, 360–370.

Pohjola, M. (1981). Stable, cyclic and chaotic growth: the dynamics of a discrete-time version of Goodwin's growth cycle model. *Zeitschrift für Nationalökonomie*, forthcoming.

Robinson, J. (1956). *The Accumulation of Capital*. Macmillan, London.

Rowthorn, R. E. (1977). Conflict, inflation and money. *Cambridge Journal of Economics*, **1**, 215–239.

Samuelson, P. A. (1939). Interactions between the multiplier and the accelerator. *Review of Economics and Statistics*, **21**, 75–78.

Samuelson, P. A. (1965). A theory of induced innovations along Kennedy-Weiszäcker lines. *Review of Economics and Statistics*, **47**, 343–356.

Sargent, T. (1979). *Macroeconomic Theory*. Academic Press, New York.

Solow, R. M. (1956). A contribution to the theory of economic growth. *Quarterly Journal of Economics*, **70**, 65–94.

Swan, T. W. (1956). Economic growth and capital accumulation. *Economic Record*, **32**, 334–361.

Turnovsky, S. J. (1977). *Macroeconomic Analysis and Stabilization Policy*. Cambridge University Press, Cambridge.

Tustin, A. (1953). *The Mechanism of Economic Systems*, Harvard University Press, Cambridge, Mass.

Wan, H. Y. (1971). *Economic Growth*. Harcourt, Brace, Jovanovich, New York.

Whiteley, P. (ed.) (1980). *Models of Political Economy*. Sage, London.

Wicksell, K. (1907). Kris: ernes Gata. *Statsokonomisk Tidsskrift*, **21**, 255–286.

Part IV

Microeconomics

Mathematical Methods in Economics
Edited by F. van der Ploeg
© 1984, John Wiley & Sons, Ltd.

12

Theory of the Firm

VANI K. BOROOAH, *University of Cambridge, Cambridge, UK*

12.1. INTRODUCTION

This chapter is concerned with the activities of producers also called 'firms'. The function of the firm is to transform certain goods (called inputs) into other goods (called outputs) and this chapter deals with the manner in which they do so. We begin with a review of certain basic concepts in production theory. The next few sections discuss the behaviour of a price taking firm—a firm that can buy and sell as much as it wishes at the prevailing price. This consists of examining the nature of its demand for inputs, the supply of its output and the nature of its costs. This is the problem of the 'equilibrium of the firm'. There is then an analysis (using the results of duality theory) of the 'comparative statics of equilibrium' or how the firm's equilibrium position alters in response to exogenous changes in prices. This is followed by a numerical example. The remainder of the chapter is concerned with relaxing the assumption of the firm being a price taker. In this part we look at different sorts of market organization in which the firm cannot buy and sell as much as it wishes and see how this affects the firm's equilibrium position.

12.2. BASIC CONCEPTS IN PRODUCTION THEORY

Without loss of generality assume that the firm (or producer) produces a single commodity as output using as inputs to the production process n commodities,. Let $\mathbf{x} = (x_1, \ldots, x_n)$ be the vector of input quantities used to produce y units of output.

The technology facing a firm is denoted by the *production possibility set Y*. Any point $\mathbf{z} = (y, x_1, \ldots, x_n)$ in Y is technically feasible.

It is assumed that the production possibility set Y satisfies the following properties:

(i) $\mathbf{0} \in Y$ (nothing will produce nothing).
(ii) $(y, \mathbf{0}) \in Y \Rightarrow y = 0$ (nothing will not produce something).

(iii) If $(y, \mathbf{x}) \in Y$ and $\mathbf{x}' \geqslant \mathbf{x}$ then $(y, \mathbf{x}') \in Y$ (at least the same output can be produced with larger inputs, that is free disposal).

(iv) If $(y, \mathbf{x}) \in Y$ and $y' < y$ then there exists $\mathbf{x}' < \mathbf{x}$ such that $(y', \mathbf{x}') \in Y$ (smaller outputs can be produced with smaller inputs).

(v) Y is closed and convex. By closedness, if $\mathbf{z}^1, \mathbf{z}^2, \ldots$ is a sequence of output–input combinations, such that $\lim_{n \to \infty} \mathbf{z}^n = \mathbf{z}$, then $\mathbf{z} \in Y$ [see IV, §11.2]. Convexity implies that if $\mathbf{z}$ and $\mathbf{z}' \in Y$, then for $0 \leqslant \lambda \leqslant 1$ $\{\lambda \mathbf{z} + (1 - \lambda)\mathbf{z}'\} \in Y$, that is any weighted average of feasible output–input vectors is also feasible [see IV, §15.2].

The *production function* associates with every input vector, the maximum output the technology will allow it to produce, i.e. $y = f(x_1, \ldots, x_n)$. The set of input quantities generating the same level of output (via the production function) defines an *isoquant*. It is assumed that the production function is continuously differentiable [see IV, Definition 3.4.1].

In Figure 12.1, the first curve shows all the combinations of the two inputs that can produce y_1 units of output; the second curve shows all the combinations that can produce y_2 units of output. The collection of isoquants for all possible levels of output defines the firm's *isoquant map*.

The point $\mathbf{z} \in Y$ is *efficient* if there does not exist any point in Y which produces the same output using less (of at least one) input or produce more output using the same input quantities.

The production function picks out these efficient points in the production possibility set. Hence it is also referred to as the *efficiency locus*.

Given the production function $y = f(x_1, \ldots, x_n)$, the *technical rate of substitution* between inputs i and j, denoted TRS_{ij}, is the amount by which input j must be increased, following a small decrease in input i, in order to maintain a constant level of output:

$$TRS_{ij} = -\frac{\mathrm{d}x_j}{\mathrm{d}x_i} = \frac{\partial f / \partial x_i}{\partial f / \partial x_j} \tag{12.2.1}$$

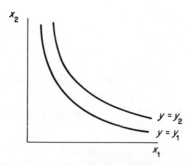

Figure 12.1: The firm's isoquant map

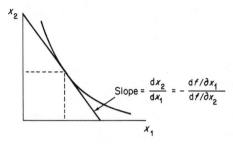

Figure 12.2: The technical rate of substitution

(The minus sign ensures $TRS_{ij} \geqslant 0$). The quantity $\partial f / \partial x_j$, the increase in output consequent upon a small increase in the quantity employed of input j, is called the *marginal product* of input j. Since [see IV, §5.4]

$$dy = \sum_{i=1}^{n} \frac{\partial f}{\partial x_i} dx_i = \frac{\partial f}{\partial x_i} dx_j$$

if $dx_i = 0 \, i \neq j$ and since by property (iv) of the production possibility set Y, $dy/dx_j > 0$ we have

$$\frac{\partial f}{\partial x_j} > 0, \quad j = 1, \dots, n. \tag{12.2.2}$$

Convexity of the production possibility set implies concavity of the production function [see IV, §15.2.6] so that the matrix of second partial derivatives.

$$\mathbf{H} = \left[\frac{\partial^2 f}{\partial x_i \partial x_j} \right], \quad i, j = 1, \dots, n, \tag{12.2.3}$$

is negative definite [see IV, Theorem (5.2.10)].

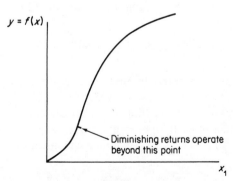

Figure 12.3: The law of diminishing returns

In particular this implies

$$\frac{\partial^2 f}{\partial x_i^2} < 0, \quad i = 1, \ldots, n, \qquad (12.2.4)$$

which is the *law of diminishing returns*. In other words the marginal product of an input diminishes as increasing quantities of it are combined with fixed quantities of other inputs (see Figure 12.3). A well-known example of this law is the Malthusian theory of population based on the application of increasing quantities of labour to a fixed quantity of agricultural land. As a consequence of this, after a point, labour combines less and less efficiently with the fixed factor land and marginal product declines.

On the other hand, *returns to scale* characterize the production function by the behaviour of output when all inputs change by the same proportion. If all inputs quantities are multiplied by the scale factor α, the production function exhibits *constant (increasing, decreasing)* returns to scale if output increases by the same (greater, smaller) proportion.

12.3. HOMOGENEOUS PRODUCTION FUNCTIONS

Homogeneous production functions play an important role in economics because they are intimately connected to the concept of 'returns to scale'.

A production function $f(x_1, \ldots, x_n)$ is said to be *homogeneous of degree k* if

$$f(\lambda x_1, \ldots, \lambda x_n) = \lambda^k f(x_1, \ldots, x_n) \text{ for all } \lambda > 0. \qquad (12.3.1)$$

Correspondingly, returns to scale are increasing if $k > 1$, constant if $k = 1$ and decreasing if $k < 1$. Hence, for example, under constant returns to scale, a doubling of all input quantities, leads to doubling of output produced.

Homogeneous production functions have the following properties:

(i) If $f(x_1, \ldots, x_n)$ is homogeneous of degree k, then $\partial f / \partial x_i$ is homogeneous of degree $k - 1$ $(i = 1, \ldots, n)$.

This is shown by differentiating both sides of (12.3.1) with respect to x_i, yielding

$$\frac{\partial f}{\partial (\lambda x_i)} = \lambda^{k-1} \frac{\partial f}{\partial x_i}, \text{ proving the result.}$$

The marginal product of the ith input, $\partial f / \partial x_i$, depends on the quantities of the other inputs employed, that is $\partial f / \partial x_i = g(x_1, \ldots, x_n)$. Again, under constant returns to scale, if all inputs are changed in the same proportion, the marginal product of each input remains unchanged.

(ii) (Euler's theorem) if $f(x_1, \ldots, x_n)$ is homogeneous of degree k, then

$$\sum_{i=1}^{n} x_i \frac{\partial f}{\partial x_i} = kf(x_1, \ldots, x_n).$$

To establish this, differentiate both sides of (12.3.1) with respect to λ to yield

$$\sum_{i=1}^{n} \frac{\partial f}{\partial(\lambda x_i)} x_i = k\lambda^{k-1} f(x_1, \ldots, x_n)$$

and set $\lambda = 1$.

An important implication of Euler's theorem is that with constant returns to scale, total output will be exactly exhausted if each input is paid its marginal product.

12.4. THE EQUILIBRIUM OF THE COMPETITIVE FIRM

Suppose that a firm operates using the production function $y = f(\mathbf{x})$ and suppose also that the price of the output, p and of the inputs $q_1, \ldots, q_n$ are given to the firm. A firm is in a competitive situation if at exogenously given prices, which are independent of its production decisions, it can buy and sell in any quantities. In other words the competitive firm is a price taker. It is postulated that the objective of the firm, is to choose input quantities so as to maximize profits, π, where profits are the excess of revenue over costs:

$$\pi = py - \sum_{i=1}^{n} q_i x_i$$

$$= pf(\mathbf{x}) - \sum_{i=1}^{n} q_i x_i \tag{12.4.1}$$

In the *long run* when all input quantities can be freely varied (by contrast in the *short run* some input quantities may not be varied), the first order conditions for maximizing (12.4.1) are

$$p\frac{\partial f}{\partial x_i} = q_i, \quad i = 1, \ldots, n, \tag{12.4.2}$$

so that in equilibrium each factor is paid the value of its marginal product.

The second order conditions are that the matrix of second partial derivatives,

$$\mathbf{H} = \left[\frac{\partial^2 f}{\partial x_i \partial x_j} \right], \quad i, j = 1, \ldots, n, \tag{12.4.3}$$

is negative definite [see I, §9.2], that is *marginal products are diminishing* in the neighbourhood of an equilibrium.

The second order conditions reveal another important point: a firm cannot be in competitive equilibrium at a point where *returns to scale* are locally increasing. For suppose, from $x_1, \ldots, x_n$, inputs are increased by $x_1 \cdot d\lambda, \ldots, x_n \cdot d\lambda$ and as a consequence output increases by dy. Then returns to scale are locally increasing if $dy/d\lambda$ is an increasing function of $d\lambda$. However, this contradicts the negative definiteness of $\mathbf{H}$.

From (12.4.2) one can solve for $x_i (i = 1, \ldots, n)$ to obtain:

$$x_i^* = x_i(p, \mathbf{q}), \quad i = 1, \ldots, n, \tag{12.4.4}$$

where $\mathbf{q} = (q_1, \ldots, q_n)$ is a vector of input prices. Equations (12.4.4) define (long-run) *input demand functions* giving optimal input choices, x_i^*, as a function of output and input prices. These functions are homogeneous of degree zero since doubling all prices doubles profits and leaves the marginal conditions unchanged.

Substituting (12.4.4) into the production function yields the optimal level of output as a function of output and input prices

$$y = y(p, \mathbf{q}), \tag{12.4.5}$$

which is the *output supply function.*

Since the input demand functions are homogeneous of degree zero so is the output supply function. This implies that the optimal level of inputs, and therefore by implication the optimal level of output, depend only on relative prices.

In the short run, suppose the quantity of the first input, for example the stock of machinery used, is fixed at $\bar{x}_1$. Then the short-run profit maximization problem is to maximize (12.4.1) subject to the restriction

$$x_1 = \bar{x}_1 \tag{12.4.6}$$

This yields the short run input demand functions

$$x_i^* = x_i(p, \mathbf{q}, \bar{x}_1), \quad i = 2, \ldots, n. \tag{12.4.7}$$

Thus in the short run the decision as to the quantity of the (variable) inputs to employ depends not just on prices but also on the levels at which the non-variable inputs are pegged, since it is with these fixed quantities that the variable inputs will have to combine.

12.5. THE MINIMIZATION OF COSTS

The equilibrium of the firm, analysed in the previous section can be conceptually separated into two parts,

(i) determining the minimum cost of producing each level of output,
(ii) determining the level of output that maximizes profits.

To appreciate why this is possible, consider again the producer's problem. It is to find, with given prices, the profit maximizing levels of inputs (Equation 12.4.1)). Once these optimal levels of inputs are known (Equation (12.4.4)) the optimal level of output follows from the output function (Equation (12.4.5)). The question can now be reversed. Suppose a particular output level was to be produced with a given structure of input prices what input levels would constitute the cheapest way of producing this output and what would be this minimum cost? This question can be answered for all possible levels of output and the minimum cost would depend on the level of output to be produced. Now suppose the producer did not wish to produce an arbitrary level of output but only that level which maximized profits; he would then choose an output level to maximize the difference between revenue and costs. Associated with this output level would be a minimum cost and in turn associated with this minimum cost would be the profit maximizing input levels which is precisely the solution to the producer's problem discussed earlier.

To determine the minimum cost of producing output, say $\bar{y}$, the problem before the firm is to find input quantities $x_1, x_2, \ldots, x_n$ such that

$$\sum_{i=1}^{n} q_i x_i \text{ is minimized subject to the restriction} \qquad (12.5.1)$$

$$\bar{y} = f(x_1, \ldots, x_n). \qquad (12.5.2)$$

The first order conditions for a minimum to this are

$$q_i = \lambda \frac{\partial f}{\partial x_i}, \quad i = 1, \ldots, n, \qquad (12.5.3)$$

and

$$\bar{y} = f(x_1, \ldots, x_n), \qquad (12.5.4)$$

where λ is the Lagrangian multiplier [see IV, §5.15 and §15.1.4].

Condition (12.5.3) yields

$$\frac{q_i}{q_j} = \frac{\partial f / \partial x_i}{\partial f / \partial x_j} = -\frac{dx_j}{dx_i}, \quad i, j = 1, \ldots, n. \qquad (12.5.5)$$

That is, in equilibrium the economic rate of substitution (q_i/q_j)—the rate at which input j can be substituted for input i while maintaining a constant cost— equals the technical rate of substitution $(-dx_j/dx_i)$—the rate at which input j can be substituted for input i while maintaining a constant level of output. Solving (12.5.3) and (12.5.4) yields the optimal input quantities, x_i^* as a function of input prices and the output level:

$$x_i^* = x_i(\mathbf{q}, y), \quad i = 1, \ldots, n. \qquad (12.5.6)$$

These functions are the *conditional* input demand functions that is conditional on the level of output) and are homogeneous of degree zero in input prices. Thus given an output level, a proportionate increase or decrease in all input prices will leave unchanged all input demands and hence only relative prices matter. An illustration of the case with two inputs only is given in Figure 12.4.

It is often convenient to have a measure of how 'substitutable' one input is for another. The *elasticity of substitution* between inputs i and j, denoted δ_{ij}, provides

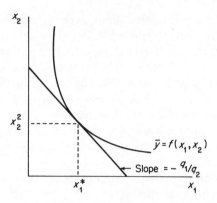

Figure 12.4: The minimization of costs

such a measure and is defined as

$$\delta_{ij} = -\frac{d\log\left[x_i(\mathbf{q}, y)/x_j(\mathbf{q}, y)\right]}{d\log(q_i/q_j)}, \qquad (12.5.7)$$

that is the percentage change in the ratio of inputs, divided by the percentage change in the ratio of input prices (the minus sign ensures that $\delta_{ij} \geqslant 0$) [see IV, §3.2].

The minimum cost of producing output level y, is

$$\sum_{i=1}^{n} q_i x_i^* = \sum_{i=1}^{n} q_i x_i(\mathbf{q}, y) = C(\mathbf{q}, y). \qquad (12.5.8)$$

The function $C(\mathbf{q}, y)$ is called the cost function; it expresses minimum cost as a function of input prices and output level.

The problem embodied in Equations (12.5.1) to (12.5.2) is the _long-run_ cost minimization problem. Suppose, as before, that in the short run the supply of the first input is fixed at $\bar{x}_1$. Then the short-run cost minimization problem is to minimize (12.5.1) subject to (12.5.2) and the additional restriction

$$x_1 = \bar{x}_1. \qquad (12.5.9)$$

This yields short run input demand functions

$$x_i^* = x_i(\mathbf{q}, y, \bar{x}_1), \quad i = 2, \ldots, n, \qquad (12.5.10)$$

and a short-run cost function

$$C(\mathbf{q}, y, \bar{x}_1). \qquad (12.5.11)$$

This means that the short-run costs, in addition to being determined by input prices and the level of output to be produced are also influenced by the level at which the non-variable inputs are pegged.

12.6. PROPERTIES OF THE COST FUNCTION

The cost function, $C(\mathbf{q}, y)$ has the following properties.

(i) If $\mathbf{q}' \geqslant \mathbf{q}$, then $C(\mathbf{q}', y) \geqslant C(\mathbf{q}, y)$, that is costs are non-decreasing in input prices.

(ii) $C(\alpha\mathbf{q}, y) = \alpha C(\mathbf{q}, y)$ for $\alpha > 0$, that is costs are homogeneous of degree 1 in input prices since multiplying all prices by α does not change the cost-minimizing bundle. On the other hand total costs increase by a factor of α.

(iii) $C(\alpha\mathbf{q} + (1 - \alpha)\mathbf{q}', y) \geqslant \alpha C(\mathbf{q}, y) + (1 - \alpha)C(\mathbf{q}', y)$ for $0 \leqslant \alpha \leqslant 1$, that is costs are concave in input prices [see IV, §15.2.6]. The intuition behind the concavity of the cost function is set out in Figure 12.5. $C(\mathbf{q}, y)$ is a concave cost function. Let $\mathbf{x}^*$ be a cost-minimizing bundle at input prices $\mathbf{q}^*$. Suppose the price of factor 1 changes from q_1^* to q_1. If the same quantities of inputs are used as before (that is $\mathbf{x}^*$), costs will be $C = q_1 x_1^* + \Sigma_{i=2}^n q_i^* x_i^*$. However, for cost-minimization, given a change in input price, there will be a change in input quantities used; hence the cost function will lie below the 'no change' line and therefore be concave.

To prove (iii) let $(\mathbf{q}, \mathbf{x})$ and $(\mathbf{q}', \mathbf{x}')$ be two cost-minimizing price-input combinations and let

$$\mathbf{q}'' = \alpha\mathbf{q} + (1 - \alpha)\mathbf{q}' \text{ for } 0 \leqslant \alpha \leqslant 1.$$

Now

$$C(\mathbf{q}'', y) = \mathbf{q}''\mathbf{x}'' = \alpha\mathbf{q}\mathbf{x}'' + (1 - \alpha)\mathbf{q}'\mathbf{x}''$$
$$\geqslant \alpha C(\mathbf{q}, y) + (1 - \alpha)C(\mathbf{q}', y)$$

since $\mathbf{x}''$ is not necessarily the cheapest way of producing y at prices $\mathbf{q}$ or $\mathbf{q}'$.

(iv) If the production function exhibits constant returns to scale, then $C(\mathbf{q}, y) = yC(\mathbf{q}, 1)$ or the least cost of producing y units of output is y times the minimum cost of producing one unit of output.

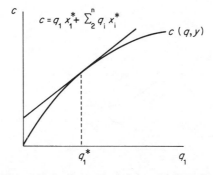

Figure 12.5: Concavity of the cost function

The quantity $\partial C/\partial y$—the change in costs given a small change in output—is called *marginal cost* and the quantity C/y is called *average cost*.

The Lagrangian multiplier λ in (12.5.3) is marginal cost. For differentiating (12.5.8), keeping q_i constant, and using (12.5.3) and (12.5.4):

$$\frac{dC}{d\bar{y}} = \sum_{i=1}^{n} q_i \frac{\partial x_i}{\partial \bar{y}} = \lambda \sum_{i=1}^{n} \frac{\partial f(x)}{\partial x_i} \frac{\partial x_i}{\partial \bar{y}} = \lambda$$

establishing the result.

Depending upon the nature of the cost function, average and marginal costs may be long- or short-term; however, the nature of the time period does not affect the relationship between average and marginal costs, namely

$$\text{if } \frac{d}{dy}\left[\frac{C}{y}\right] \gtreqless 0 \text{ then } \frac{dC}{dy} \gtreqless C/y. \tag{12.6.1}$$

This can easily be shown by noting that $d/dy[C/y] = y{\cdot}dC/dy - C/y^2$. The intuition underlying the proposition is fairly straightforward: when average costs are falling, the additional cost of producing another unit of output must be less than the prevailing average and conversely when average costs are rising. When average costs are neither rising nor falling, that is at a minimum, it follows that they must equal marginal costs (Figure 12.6).

The relationship between short-run and long-run total and average costs is embodied in the *envelope theorem*, which states that the long-run cost curve lies below the short-run cost curve for all levels of output, except one at which they are tangential.

Now by the nature of the short-run and long-run cost minimization problems

$$C(\mathbf{q}, y, \bar{x}_1) \geqslant C(\mathbf{q}, y),$$

where in the short run the quantity of the first factor is fixed at $\bar{x}_1$ whereas it can be freely varied in the long run. This follows because given an output level y and a vector of input prices $\mathbf{q}$, in the long-run optimal quantities of the n inputs, $x_1^*, x_2^*, \ldots, x_n^*$ will be demanded giving rise to a cost. In the short run, however,

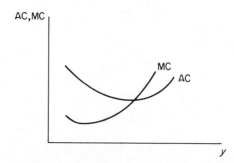

Figure 12.6: Average and marginal costs

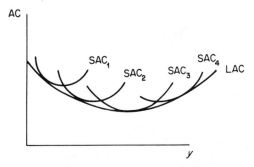

Figure 12.7: Illustration of the envelope theorem

only optimal quantities of the $n - 1$ inputs, $\hat{x}_2, \ldots, \hat{x}_n$, can be chosen, given that the quantity of the first input is fixed at $\bar{x}_1$. It follows therefore that, for every choice of y and $\mathbf{q}$, the short-run costs must be at least greater than long-run costs since the quantity $\bar{x}_1$ of the first factor could have been chosen in the long run.

Given the vector $\mathbf{q}$, since the input demand function for the first factor, $x_1(\mathbf{q}, y)$ is continuous it follows that for some value of y, say $\bar{y}$

$$x_1(\mathbf{q}, \bar{y}) = \bar{x}_1 \text{ and thus } C(\mathbf{q}, \bar{y}, \bar{x}_1) = C(\mathbf{q}, \bar{y}),$$

establishing the envelope theorem.

This is illustrated in Figure 12.7 for average cost curves. The long-run average cost curve is denoted LAC, and the short-run average cost curves corresponding to fixed quantities $\bar{x}_1, \bar{x}_2, \bar{x}_3$ and $\bar{x}_4$ are denoted SAC_1, SAC_2, SAC_3 and SAC_4 respectively.

12.7. THE MAXIMIZATION OF PROFITS

Given the cost function $C(\mathbf{q}, y)$, the second stage of the firm's equilibrium is to find a level of output, y, so as to maximize

$$\pi = py - C(\mathbf{q}, y). \tag{12.7.1}$$

The first order conditions for (12.7.1) are

$$p = \frac{\mathrm{d}C}{\mathrm{d}y}, \tag{12.7.2}$$

that is in equilibrium, the competitive firm equates price to marginal cost and the second order conditions are

$$\frac{\mathrm{d}^2C}{\mathrm{d}y^2} \geq 0, \tag{12.7.3}$$

that is marginal costs should be increasing or constant in a neighbourhood of the profit-maximizing output.

It can be shown that non-increasing marginal returns (condition (12.4.3)) implies (12.7.3) above. Upon total differentiation of (12.5.4) [see IV, (5.10.11)] and (12.5.3) keeping prices constant:

$$d\bar{y} = \sum_{i=1}^{n} \frac{\partial f}{\partial x_i} dx_i \tag{12.7.4}$$

$$d\lambda \frac{\partial f}{\partial x_i} + \lambda \sum_{k=1}^{n} \frac{\partial^2 f}{\partial x_i \partial x_k} dx_k = 0 \quad i = 1, \dots, n. \tag{12.7.5}$$

Multiplying the ith equation of (12.7.5) by dx_i, summing over $i = 1, \dots, n$ and taking account of (12.7.4) one obtains

$$d\lambda \cdot d\bar{y} + \lambda \sum_i \sum_k \frac{\partial^2 f}{\partial x_i \partial x_k} dx_i dx_k = 0.$$

Since λ, the marginal cost is positive, condition (12.4.3) implies

$$d\lambda \cdot d\bar{y} \geqslant 0 \text{ or } \frac{d\lambda}{d\bar{y}} \geqslant 0, \tag{12.7.6}$$

which is the desired result.

Hence a cost curve derived from a production function with non-increasing marginal returns is concave upwards [see IV, §15.2.6].

Substituting the supply function $y(p, \mathbf{q})$ into (12.7.1) one obtains the profit function, $\pi(p, \mathbf{q})$. Analogous to the cost function of the previous section, this has the following properties:

(i) $\pi(p, \mathbf{q})$ is non-decreasing in p and non-increasing in $\mathbf{q}$.
(ii) $\pi(p, \mathbf{q})$ is homogeneous of degree 1 in p and $\mathbf{q}$.
(iii) $\pi(p, \mathbf{q})$ is convex in p and $\mathbf{q}$.

12.8. THE COMPARATIVE STATICS OF THE FIRM

Given the input demand and output supply functions of the firm, the next step is to determine how the equilibrium quantities demanded and supplied alter in response to changes in input and/or output prices. To do so one needs an easy way of deriving these functions. One could, following the steps of the previous section, just solve the profit-maximization problem and express the resulting demands as a function of prices; there is, however, an easier way:

The derivative property : Hotelling's lemma
    Let $y(p, \mathbf{q})$ be the firm's supply function, $x_i(p, \mathbf{q})$ its input demand function, and $\pi(p, \mathbf{q})$ its profit function. Then

$$y(p, \mathbf{q}) = \frac{\partial \pi(p, \mathbf{q})}{\partial p}$$

$$x_i(p, \mathbf{q}) = -\frac{\partial \pi(p, \mathbf{q})}{\partial q_i}, \quad i = 1, \ldots, n,$$

where the derivatives exist [*see* IV, §5.3] *and* $q_i > 0$, $i = 1, \ldots, n$ and $p > 0$.

To demonstrate the lemma suppose $(y^*, \mathbf{x}^*)$ is a profit-maximizing supply–demand plan at prices $(p^*, \mathbf{q}^*)$. Then define

$$g(p, \mathbf{q}) = \pi(p, \mathbf{q}) - (py^* - \sum_{i=1}^{n} q_i x_i^*).$$

Then $g(p, \mathbf{q}) \geq 0$ reaching its minimum value of zero at $p = p^*$ and $\mathbf{q} = \mathbf{q}^*$. The first order conditions for a minimum then imply

$$\frac{\partial g(p^*, \mathbf{q}^*)}{\partial p} = \frac{\partial \pi(p^*, \mathbf{q}^*)}{\partial p} - y^* = 0$$

$$\frac{\partial g(p^*, \mathbf{q}^*)}{\partial q_i} = \frac{\partial \pi(p^*, \mathbf{q}^*)}{\partial q_i} - x_i^* = 0, \quad i = 1, \ldots, n.$$

Since this is true for all $(p^*, \mathbf{q}^*)$ the result is proved. A similar result holds for conditional input demand functions.

The derivative property : Shephard's lemma

Let $C(\mathbf{q}, y)$ and $x_i(\mathbf{q}, y)$, $i = 1, \ldots, n$ be the firm's cost function and conditional input demand functions. Then if C is differentiable at $(\mathbf{q}, y)$

$$x_i(\mathbf{q}, y) = \frac{\partial C(\mathbf{q}, y)}{\partial q_i}, \quad i = 1, \ldots, n.$$

To demonstrate this, let $\mathbf{x}^*$ be the cost minimizing input vector that produces y at $\mathbf{q}^*$. Then define

$$g(\mathbf{q}) = C(\mathbf{q}, y) - \sum_{i=1}^{n} q_i x_i^*.$$

Now $g(\mathbf{q}) \leq 0$ reaching its maximum value of zero at $\mathbf{q} = \mathbf{q}^*$. Therefore the first order conditions imply

$$\frac{\partial g(\mathbf{q}^*)}{\partial q_i} = \frac{\partial C(\mathbf{q}^*, y)}{\partial q_i} - x_i^*, \quad i = 1, \ldots, n.$$

Since this is true for all $\mathbf{q}^*$, the lemma is proved.

The basic economic intuition behind the propositions is this: if one is operating at a cost-minimizing point and the price q_i increases, there will be a direct effect in that the expenditure on the ith input—and hence total costs—will increase. There might be also an indirect effect in that one may wish to change the factor mix. However, since the starting position is a cost-minimizing one, such changes in factor-mix are not profitable for infinitesimal changes in q_i.

From the derivative properties, the questions posed at the beginning of the section are easily answered.

(i) The supply curve slopes upwards since

$$\frac{\partial y(p,\mathbf{q})}{\partial p} = \frac{\partial^2 \pi(p,\mathbf{q})}{\partial p^2},$$

which is nonnegative since π is a convex function.

(ii) The demand functions slope downwards since

$$\frac{\partial x_i(p,\mathbf{q})}{\partial q_i} = -\frac{\partial^2 \pi(p,\mathbf{q})}{\partial q_i^2}, \quad i=1,\dots,n,$$

which is nonpositive since π is a convex function.

(iii) The cross price effects are symmetric since

$$\frac{\partial x_j(p,\mathbf{q})}{\partial q_i} = \frac{\partial}{\partial q_i}\left[-\frac{\partial \pi(p,\mathbf{q})}{\partial q_j} \right] = \frac{\partial x_i(p,\mathbf{q})}{\partial q_j}.$$

12.9. A NUMERICAL EXAMPLE

Consider the technology defined by the production function

$$y = f(x_1, x_2) = A x_1^a x_2^b \tag{12.9.1}$$

Such a production function is called the *Cobb–Douglas* production function with two inputs.

This production function is homogeneous of degree one if $a + b = 1$. It exhibits increasing returns to scale if $a + b > 1$ and decreasing returns to scale if $a + b < 1$ [see §12.3].

The marginal products of the two inputs are respectively

$$\frac{\partial f(x_1, x_2)}{\partial x_1} = A a x_1^{a-1} x_2^b \tag{12.9.2}$$

and

$$\frac{\partial f(x_1, x_2)}{\partial x_2} = A b x_1^a x_2^{b-1} \tag{12.9.3}$$

and the technical rate of substitution between the inputs is therefore [see §12.2]

$$TRS_{12} = \frac{a x_2}{b x_1}. \tag{12.9.4}$$

The input demand functions [see §12.4] are obtained by maximizing

$$\pi = p(A x_1^a x_2^b) - \sum_{i=1}^{2} q_i x_i \tag{12.9.5}$$

which yield the first order conditions

$$\frac{\partial \pi}{\partial x_1} = pAax_1^{a-1}x_2^b - q_1 = 0 \qquad (12.9.6)$$

$$\frac{\partial \pi}{\partial x_2} = pAbx_1^a x_2^{b-1} - q_2 = 0, \qquad (12.9.7)$$

from which it follows that in equilibrium

$$x_1^* = \left[A^{1/(b-1)} p^{1/(b-1)} \left(\frac{b}{q_2}\right)^{b/(b-1)} \frac{q_1}{a} \right]^{(b-1)/(1-a-b)} \qquad (12.9.8)$$

$$x_2^* = \left[A^{1/(a-1)} p^{1/(a-1)} \left(\frac{a}{q_1}\right)^{a/(a-1)} \frac{q_2}{b} \right]^{(1-a)/(1-a-b)}. \qquad (12.9.9)$$

The output supply function is given by

$$y^* = A(x_1^*)^a (x_2^*)^b. \qquad (12.9.10)$$

Note that the input demand functions are well defined only if $a + b < 1$.
   The cost function [see §12.5] is the solution to

$$\text{Minimize } q_1 x_1 + q_2 x_2 \text{ subject to } y = A \cdot x_1^a x_2^b \qquad (12.9.11)$$

or equivalently to

$$\text{Minimize } q_1 x_1 + q_2 (A^{-1} y x_1^{-a})^{1/b} \qquad (12.9.12)$$

Setting the first derivative of (12.9.12) w.r.t. x_1 to zero [see IV, §5.6] one obtains

$$q_1 - \frac{a}{b} q_2 A^{-1/b} y^{1/b} x_1^{-(a+b)/b} = 0, \qquad (12.9.13)$$

which in turn yields the conditional input demand function

$$x_1^* = A^{-1/(a+b)} \left[\frac{aq_2}{bq_1}\right]^{-b/(a+b)} y^{1/(a+b)} \qquad (12.9.14)$$

Similarly

$$x_2^* = A^{-1/(a+b)} \left[\frac{aq_2}{bq_1}\right]^{-a/(a+b)} y^{1/(a+b)} \qquad (12.9.15)$$

and the cost function is given by

$$C(\mathbf{q}, y) = q_1 x_1^* + q_2 x_2^*$$

$$= A^{-1/(a+b)} \left[\left(\frac{a}{b}\right)^{b/(a+b)} + \left(\frac{a}{b}\right)^{-a/(a+b)} \right] (q_1^a q_2^b y)^{1/(a+b)}$$

$$= K(q_1^a q_2^b y)^{1/(a+b)}. \qquad (12.9.16)$$

Under constant returns to scale, that is $a + b = 1$, this becomes

$$C(q,y) = A^{-1}a^{-a}(1-a)^{a-1}q_1^a q_2^{(1-a)}y. \tag{12.9.17}$$

Average and marginal costs are respectively

$$Kq_1^{a/(a+b)}q_2^{b/(a+b)}y^{(1-a-b)/(a+b)} \tag{12.9.18}$$

and

$$\frac{K}{a+b}q_1^{a/(a+b)}q_2^{b/(a+b)}y^{(1-a-b)/(a+b)} \tag{12.9.19}$$

and under constant returns to scale average and marginal costs are equal. The profit-maximizing output, y^*, is given by [see §12.7] maximizing

$$\pi = py - C(\mathbf{q},y), \tag{12.9.20}$$

where $C(\mathbf{q},y)$ is given by (12.9.16). Solving the maximization problem yields

$$y^* = \left[p\frac{(a+b)}{Kq_1^{a/(a+b)}q_2^{b/(a+b)}} \right]^{(a+b)/(1-a-b)}, \tag{12.9.21}$$

which is the output supply function, well defined only with decreasing returns to scale (when $a + b < 1$).

The elasticity of substitution, δ_{12}, (see Equation (12.5.7)) can be easily derived from the Cobb–Douglas production function, $f(x_1,x_2) = x_1^a x_2^{1-a}$, which is obtained by imposing $A = a + b = 1$ on (12.9.1).

$$\delta_{12} = \frac{\partial(x_1(\mathbf{q},y)/x_2(\mathbf{q},y))}{\partial(q_1/q_2)}\frac{(q_1/q_2)}{(x_1/x_2)}. \tag{12.9.22}$$

Now in equilibrium (see Equation (12.5.5))

$$\frac{q_1}{q_2} = \frac{a}{(1-a)}\frac{x_2}{x_1} \quad \text{or} \quad \frac{x_1}{x_2} = \frac{a}{(1-a)}\frac{q_2}{q_1}. \tag{12.9.23}$$

Substituting (12.9.23) into (12.9.22) yields $\delta_{12} = -1$.

Other production functions popular in the literature are the *Constant Elasticity of Substitution (CES)* production function:

$$y = (a_0 + a_1 x_1^\rho + a_2 x_2^\rho)^{1/\rho} \tag{12.9.24}$$

the *Linear production function*:

$$y = a_0 + a_1 x_1 + a_2 x_2 \tag{12.9.25}$$

and the *Leontief (fixed coefficient)* production function:

$$y = \min(ax_1, bx_2). \tag{12.9.26}$$

12.10. PERFECT COMPETITION

In a perfectly competitive market a large number of firms sell a homogeneous product and demand homogeneous inputs with the result that each firm can buy and sell as much as it wishes at the prevailing price. The equilibrium of a competitive firm, that is a firm operating in a perfectly competitive market, has been extensively analysed in the previous sections. In this section we draw together some of these results to bring out the implications for market equilibrium.

The competitive firm chooses its output level so as to equate price with marginal cost since the output level for which this condition is satisfied maximizes its profits (see section 12.7, Equation (12.7.2)). The marginal cost curve of the competitive firm is thus its supply curve, for it tells us what the output supplied would be given a particular price level. This is illustrated in Figure 12.8. The supply curve of the industry is obtained by summing the individual marginal cost curves. The intersection of the industry supply curve and the market demand curve determines the market price which no individual firm is then in a position to influence. This is illustrated in Figure 12.9.

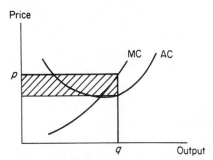

Figure 12.8: The equilibrium of a firm under perfect competition

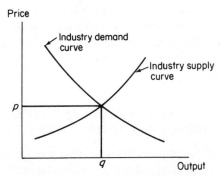

Figure 12.9: Industry equilibrium

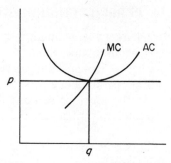

Figure 12.10: Long-run equilibrium of the firm

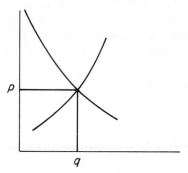

Figure 12.11: Long-run industry equilibrium

Although the market demand curve slopes downwards (reflecting the fact that the industry as a whole can only sell more at a lower price), the demand curves facing the individual firms are horizontal (perfectly elastic) reflecting the fact that at the prevailing price the firm can sell as much as it wishes.

With free entry, in the long run, new firms enter the industry, attracted by the positive profits that existing firms are earning (shaded area in Figure 12.8). This drives the industry supply curve to the right until a price is established at which all firms are earning zero profits and there is no further inducement to entry. This is illustrated in Figures 12.10 and 12.11.

12.11. IMPERFECT COMPETITION: MONOPOLY AND MONOPSONY

So far the theory of the firm has been developed in a competitive framework, the main assumption of which has been the individual firm's inability to influence prices. In this section this assumption is relaxed and the cases of a single seller of a product (*monopoly*) and a single buyer of an input (*monopsony*) are considered. In both cases the analysis extends to situations where the firm, by its actions, exerts an influence on prices.

With monopoly it is assumed that the price of output varies inversely with the quantity sold, that is,

$$p = p(y) \tag{12.11.1}$$

and

$$\frac{dp}{dy} < 0 \tag{12.11.2}$$

To isolate the effects of monopoly it is assumed that the market for inputs is competitive; similarly in discussing monopsony it will be assumed that the output market is competitive. Monopoly profits are now

$$\pi = p(y)y - C(p, y) \tag{12.11.3}$$

and the first order conditions for maximizing (12.11.3) with respect to y are:

$$\frac{dp}{dy}y + p(y) - \frac{d\check{C}}{dy} = 0, \tag{12.11.4}$$

that is *marginal revenue* (the change in revenue consequent upon a small change in output) equals marginal cost.

This is illustrated below in Figure 12.12.

Under competitive conditions, $dp/dy = 0$, and (12.11.4) reduces to (12.7.2).

Defining the *price elasticity of demand*, $\varepsilon(y)$, as the proportionate change in output demanded divided by a proportionate change in price, or

$$\varepsilon(y) = \frac{dy(p)}{dp} \cdot \frac{p}{y(p)} = \frac{d\log y(p)}{d\log p}, \tag{12.11.5}$$

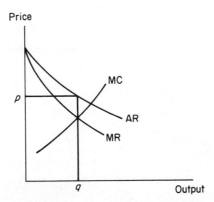

Figure 12.12: Monopoly equilibrium

(12.11.4) can be rewritten as

$$p(y)\left[1 + \frac{1}{\varepsilon(y)}\right] = \frac{dC}{dy},$$ (12.11.6)

that is, the price charged by the monopolist is a mark-up over marginal costs, the level of the mark-up being a function of the price elasticity of demand.

The second order conditions require that

$$\frac{d^2\pi}{dy^2} < 0$$ (12.11.7)

or in equilibrium marginal revenue should not be rising as fast as marginal costs.

Under monospony, it is assumed that the prices of inputs vary directly with the quantity bought, that is,

$$q_h = q_h(x_h), \quad h = 1, \ldots, l,$$ (12.11.8)

where

$$\frac{dq_h}{dx_h} > 0.$$ (12.11.9)

The monopsonist's profits are now:

$$\pi = pf(x) - \sum_{h=1}^{l} q_h(x)x_h$$ (12.11.10)

and the first-order conditions for maximizing (12.11.10) with respect to the x_h's are:

$$p\frac{\partial f}{\partial x_h} = \frac{dq_h}{dx_h}x_h + q_h, \quad h = 1, \ldots, l,$$ (12.11.11)

That is in equilibrium the value of the marginal product of each factor is equal to

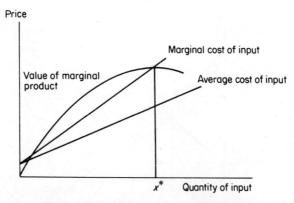

Figure 12.13: Monopsonist's equilibrium

its marginal cost. This is illustrated in Figure 12.13. Under competitive conditions $dq_h/dx_h = 0$ and (12.11.11) reduces to (12.4.2) (12.11.11) can also be given an elasticity interpretation, viz.,

$$p\frac{\partial f}{\partial x_h} = q_h\left[1 + \frac{1}{\varepsilon(x_h)}\right] \tag{12.11.12}$$

where $\varepsilon(x_h)$ is now the price elasticity of supply, $d\log x_h/d\log q_h$.
    The second order conditions require that

$$\frac{d^2\pi}{dx_h^2} < 0 \tag{12.11.13}$$

or in equilibrium the value of each input's marginal product rises less fast than its marginal cost.

12.12. MONOPOLISTIC COMPETITION

The cases of perfect competition and monopoly represent the two extremes of the market structure spectrum. As an intermediate case one might consider a situation in which many firms produce similar, though not identical products. This market structure is called *monopolistic competition*. It is akin to perfect competition in that the number of sellers is sufficiently large so that the actions of an individual firm have no perceptible influence on the actions of its competitors; it is akin to monopoly in that each firm has a downward sloping demand curve for its product.
    The price of the output of the ith firm, p_i, is a function not just of its own output, y_i, but also of the output of other firms

$$p_i = p_i(y_1,\ldots,y_n) = p_i(\mathbf{y}), \quad i = 1,\ldots,n. \tag{12.12.1}$$

Each firm acts so as to maximize its profits, π_i, taking the outputs of other firms as given, where

$$\pi_i = p_i(\mathbf{y})y_i - C_i(y_i), \quad i = 1,\ldots,n. \tag{12.12.2}$$

The large number of firms justifies the assumption that the behaviour of competitors is taken as unchanging.
    The ith firm will be in equilibrium when it is producing an output y_i^* so as to satisfy

$$\frac{\partial \pi_i}{\partial y_i} = \frac{\partial p_i(\mathbf{y})}{\partial y_i}\cdot y_i + p_i(\mathbf{y}) - \frac{\partial C_i(y_i)}{\partial y_i} = 0, \tag{12.12.3}$$

which is the marginal revenue equals marginal cost condition discussed in the previous section. Solving (12.12.3) yields

$$y_i^* = Y_1(y_1,\ldots,y_{i-1}, y_{i+1},\ldots,y_n) \tag{12.12.4}$$

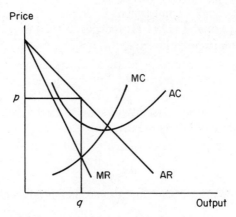

Figure 12.4: Short-run equilibrium of a
firm under monopolistic competition

and corresponding to each level of competitors' output there will be an
equilibrium level of output for the ith firm.

The group will be in equilibrium when each firm is producing its optimal
output $y_i^*(i = 1,\ldots,n)$. In other words the equilibrium vector of outputs,
$y_1^*,\ldots,y_n^*$ must satisfy

$$y_1^* = Y_1(y_2^*,\ldots,y_n^*)$$
$$\vdots \qquad\qquad\qquad (12.12.5)$$
$$y_n^* = Y_n(y_1^*,\ldots,y_{n-1}^*).$$

As will be shown in the next section this represents a Cournot–Nash equilibrium.
An individual firm's equilibrium is illustrated in the Figure 12.14. The firm

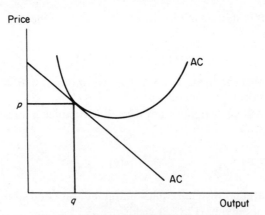

Figure 12.15: Long-run equilibrium of a firm
under monopolistic competition

produces an output at which marginal revenue equals marginal cost and at that output makes positive profits (shaded area).

With free entry, in the long run, new firms will enter the industry attracted by the positive profits that existing firms are making. This process would continue until such profits were competed away. Thus in long-run equilibrium each firm would charge a price, p_i^* and produce an output, y_i^*, such that

$$p_i^* y_i^* = C_i(y_i^*). \qquad (12.12.6)$$

Since this output was also profit-maximizing this would imply that in long-run equilibrium, output levels other than y_i^* would involve losses. Thus the demand curve facing a firm must be tangential to its average cost curve as illustrated in Figure 12.15.

12.13. COMPETITION AMONG THE FEW: OLIGOPOLY

In the market structures that have so far been considered a firm's actions have not been influenced by the actions of its competitors. This has been either because there have been no competitors (monopoly) or because the competitors have been so many that any action on the part of one of them would have a negligible impact on the market. This assumption is relaxed in this section and market structures characterized by there being only a few firms in an industry are considered. Such market structures are called *oligopolistic*. The essence of oligopolistic behaviour is that since the actions of firms affect one another, any given firm, in choosing its action, must make some assumptions about the reaction of its rivals. Different models of oligopoly are generated by making different assumptions about rivals' reactions and some of these models are considered below for the special case of two firms (*duopoly*).

12.13.1 The Cournot–Nash solution

In a market with only two firms producing a homogeneous product, let y_1 and y_2 denote quantities of firm 1 and 2's output respectively. The price consumers are willing to pay depends on aggregate supply, $y_1 + y_2$, that is,

$$p = p(y_1 + y_2). \qquad (12.13.1)$$

The basic assumption in a Cournot–Nash solution is that each firm chooses a profit-maximizing output on the assumption that its choice will leave its rival's output choice unaffected.

Thus the problem before each firm is to choose y_1 and y_2 respectively so as to maximize

$$\pi_1 = p(y_1 + y_2)y_1 - C(y_1) \qquad (12.13.1)$$

$$\pi_2 = p(y_1 + y_2)y_2 - C(y_2). \qquad (12.13.2)$$

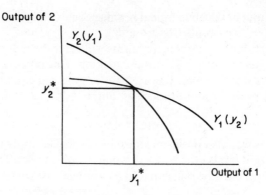

Figure 12.16: Cournot–Nash equilibrium

The solution y_1^* to (12.13.1) must satisfy

$$\frac{\partial p(y_1^* + y_2)}{\partial y_1} y_1^* + p(y_1^* + y_2) = \frac{dC(y_1^*)}{dy_1} \qquad (12.13.3)$$

and an analogous condition holds for y_2^*, the solution to (12.13.2), namely,

$$\frac{\partial p(y_1 + y_2^*)}{\partial y_2} y_2^* + p(y_1 + y_2^*) = \frac{dC(y_2^*)}{dy_2}. \qquad (12.13.4)$$

Solving (12.13.3) and (12.13.4) for y_1^* and y_2^* in terms of y_2 and y_1 respectively yields the *reaction* functions

$$y_1^* = Y_1(y_1) \text{ and } y_2^* = Y_2(y_1) \qquad (12.13.5)$$

and market equilibrium is attained for values of y_1 and y_2 which simultaneously solve both equations of (12.12.5). This is illustrated in Figure 12.16.

12.13.2. The Stackelberg solution

In a Cournot–Nash model each firm takes the other's *actions* as given; in a Stackelberg solution one firm takes the other firm's *reactions* as given. Suppose firm 1's reaction function is $Y_1(y_2)$. Suppose firm 2 believes firm 1 will behave according to its reaction function, i.e. produce $y_1 = Y_1(y_2)$ if firm 2 produces y_2. Then firm 2 should incorporate this information into its profit function so that (12.13.2) becomes

$$\pi_2 = p(Y_1(y_2) + y_2)y_2 - C(y_2). \qquad (12.13.6)$$

Thus firm 2 'leads' by setting its output level y_2 (by maximizing (12.13.6)) and firm 1 'follows' by responding through its reaction function. If both desire to be followers and each assumes the other will be a follower, then a Cournot–Nash solution results. If each desires to be a leader the situation is indeterminate; this situation is called *Stackelberg warfare*.

12.13.3. Collusion

Firms can collude by choosing output levels y_1 and y_2 respectively so as to maximize total industry profits

$$\pi_1 + \pi_2 = p(y_1 + y_2)(y_1 + y_2) - C_1(y_1) - C_2(y_2). \qquad (12.13.7)$$

The first order conditions are

$$\frac{\partial p(y_1 + y_2)}{\partial y_1}(y_1 + y_2) + p(y_1 + y_2) - \frac{dC_1(y_1)}{dy_1} = 0 \qquad (12.13.8)$$

$$\frac{\partial p(y_1 + y_2)}{\partial y_2}(y_1 + y_2) + p(y_1 + y_2) - \frac{dC_2(y_2)}{dy_2} = 0. \qquad (12.13.9)$$

From (12.13.8) and (12.13.9) it is obvious that profit maximization implies

$$\frac{dC_1(y_1^*)}{dy_1} = \frac{dC_2(y_2^*)}{dy_2}.$$

If the cost functions are identical, a symmetric solution, where $y_1^* = y_2^*$ will result. If cost functions differ, the firm with the cost advantage will produce more.

12.14. CONCLUDING REMARKS

This chapter has expounded the neoclassical theory of the firm based upon the twin assumptions of profit-maximizing behaviour and competitive markets. When the latter assumption is relaxed other forms of market structure result in some of which a determinate equilibrium exists (monopoly, monopolistic competition). In other forms of market structure (oligopoly) a determinate solution does not necessarily exist or may exist only under very special assumptions. The assumption that firms maximize profits has also been criticized in the literature. This has taken essentially two forms. The first line suggests that while firms may optimize they may not necessarily regard profits as the target variable. Thus sales or the rate of growth may be alternative and equally plausible target variables. The second line suggests that firms do not and cannot optimize since they are typically faced with a multiplicity of objectives. Therefore, instead, firms 'satisfice' (that is attempt to attain satisfactory levels of performance with respect to their objectives) rather than optimize.

12.15. REFERENCES

Diewert, E. (1974). Applications of duality theory, in *Frontiers of Quantitative Economics*, vol. 2, M. Intriligator and D. Kendrick (eds.). North-Holland, Amsterdam.

McFadden, D. (1978). Cost, revenue and profit functions, in *Production Economics: A Dual Approach to Theory and Applications*, M. Fuss and D. McFadden (eds.). North-Holland, Amsterdam.

Samuelson, P. 1947, *Foundations of Economic Analysis.* Harvard University Press, Cambridge, Mass.

Hicks, J. (1946). *Value and Capital.* Clarendon Press, Oxford.

Shephard, R. (1970). *Theory of Cost and Production Functions.* Princeton University Press, Princeton.

Silberston, A. (1970). Price Behaviour of Firms. *Economic Journal,* **80**, 511–582.

Mathematical Methods in Economics
Edited by F. van der Ploeg
© 1984, John Wiley & Sons, Ltd.

13

Theory of the Household

Vani K. Borooah, *University of Cambridge, Cambridge, UK.*

13.1. INTRODUCTION

This chapter is concerned with the activity of consumers or 'households'. The function of households is to use, for their own needs, certain goods produced by firms. This chapter deals with the manner in which they do so. As before, we begin with a review of basic concepts. Then there is a discussion of the 'equilibrium of the household' (how a household chooses its consumption levels) followed by a discussion of the 'comparative statics' of this equilibrium (how this equilibrium changes in response to economic factors). A discussion of an application using the Linear Expenditure System then concludes the chapter.

13.2. BASIC CONCEPTS IN CONSUMPTION THEORY

The main elements of the theory are as follows: the consumer chooses a vector $\mathbf{x} = (x_1, \ldots, x_n)$ of quantities of the n goods available which, in a sense to be defined, represents his 'best' choice from the set of vectors feasible for him.

Feasibility is defined in terms of the constraints to which the consumer is subject; these constraints are physical and economic:

(i) The vector $\mathbf{x}$ must belong to a set X called the *consumption possibility set* which is given *a priori* and may depend on the individual consumer under consideration. The definition of X takes into account all the physical limitations on the consumer's activity; for example, in defining X, the notion of a subsistence standard, either biological or based on social convention, may be taken into account. One of the goods may be labour, that is the consumer in conjunction with deciding how much of the various goods to buy also decides on the quantity of labour to supply where this supply is also a determinant of his income.

(ii) In addition the consumer has a limited income, I, and must act within a market where each commodity i has a well-defined price p_i. Hence the value of **x** should not exceed I, that is

$$\sum_{i=1}^{n} p_i x_i \leqslant I.$$

For the model of this chapter, I and the p_i are exogenous.

(iii) The consumer's preferences amongst the vectors in X are defined by a real valued function $U(x_1, \ldots, x_n)$, called the *utility function*, whose domain is the set X. Given two vectors $\mathbf{x}^1$ and $\mathbf{x}^2$ in X, $\mathbf{x}^1$ is preferred (indifferent) to $\mathbf{x}^2$ if and only if $U(\mathbf{x}^1) > (=)U(\mathbf{x}^2)$. Given a utility level $\bar{U}$ the set I consisting of all points x which yield the utility level $\bar{U}$, that is $I = \{\mathbf{x}/U(\mathbf{x}) = \bar{U}\}$ defines an *indifference locus or curve*. The set of all indifference curves corresponding to the different possible utility levels defines an *indifference map*.

It is also assumed that

1. The set X is closed, convex, bounded from below and contains the null vector. If it contains a vector $\mathbf{x}^1$, it also contains every vector $\mathbf{x}^2$ such that $x_i^2 \geqslant x_i^1$ for $i = 1, \ldots, n$.

Convexity implies that if X contains $\mathbf{x}^1$ and $\mathbf{x}^2$ it contains the line segment joining them [see IV, §15.2]. This assumption may be violated if certain goods can only be consumed in integral quantities. Suppose this is the case for good 2 when $n = 2$. Then the set X consists of a number of vertical half-lines as in Figure 13.1. It is not convex since $\mathbf{x}^3$ which lies on the line segment connecting $\mathbf{x}^1$ and $\mathbf{x}^2$ does not belong to X. This situation is obviously not serious when one considers quantities of the first good which contain an appreciable number of units; in such cases X may be reasonably approximated by a convex set.

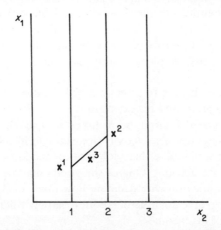

Figure 13.1: Consumption of integral quantities

Closure implies that if a sequence of vectors belonging to X converges to a limit, then the limiting vector also belongs to X. In other words the set X is assumed to contain its boundary [see IV, §11.2].

The boundedness condition (which means that there exists a vector $\bar{\mathbf{x}}$ such that $\mathbf{x} \geqslant \bar{\mathbf{x}}$ for all $\mathbf{x} \in X$) implies that consumption of commodities cannot fall below a prescribed minimum. If the quantity of labour supplied by the consumer is regarded as negative consumption, then the boundedness condition is automatically satisfied if there is an upper limit on the quantity of labour a consumer can supply and if the consumption of other commodities cannot be negative.

The inclusion of the null vector in the feasible set implies—contrary to the notion of a subsistence minimum—that the individual may consume nothing while the last assumption implies that if the consumer has a surplus of commodities over and above what he needs then he can costlessly dispose of the surplus.

2. The utility function $U(\mathbf{x})$ defined on X is continuous, increasing and twice differentiable [see IV, §5.5]. The second property implies that $\partial U(\mathbf{x})/\partial x_i$—the gain in utility following a small increase in the quantity of commodity i, also called the *marginal utility* of i—is positive for all $i = 1, \ldots, n$.

The *marginal rate of substitution* between good i and j, denoted MRS_{ij}, is the amount by which the quantity of good j must be increased following a small decrease in the quantity of good i in order to leave the utility enjoyed by the consumer unchanged, say at the level $\bar{u}$,

$$MRS_{ij} = \left(-\frac{dx_j}{dx_i} \right)_{u=\bar{u}} = \frac{\partial U/\partial x_i}{\partial U/\partial x_j}.$$

For example if from given consumption levels of tea and coffee a consumer requires two ounces of coffee to compensate him for the loss of an ounce of tea then the MRS between tea and coffee is defined as 2.

3. The utility function $U(\mathbf{x})$ is 'strictly quasi-concave' in the sense that if $U(\mathbf{x}^1) \geqslant U(\mathbf{x}^2)$ for two vectors $\mathbf{x}^1$ and $\mathbf{x}^2$, then for every vector $\mathbf{x}$ in the line segment $(\mathbf{x}^1, \mathbf{x}^2)$ (that is $\mathbf{x} = \alpha\mathbf{x}^1 + (1-\alpha)\mathbf{x}^2 0 < \alpha < 1$), $U(\mathbf{x}) > U(\mathbf{x}^1)$ [see V, §4.3.1]. In other words the consumer will prefer an intermediate position to either of two extreme positions although he may be indifferent between these extreme positions.

13.3. THE EQUILIBRIUM OF THE CONSUMER

It is assumed that the objective of the consumer is to choose a consumption vector which, subject to his physical and economic constraints, is 'best'. An equilibrium for a consumer is therefore a vector $\mathbf{x}^* = (x_1^*, \ldots, x_n^*)$ which maximizes $U(\mathbf{x})$ subject to

$$\sum_{i=1}^{n} p_i x_i \leqslant I \tag{13.3.1}$$

and

$$\mathbf{x} \in X. \tag{13.3.2}$$

We now show that, under the assumptions of the previous section, an equilibrium exists, so that the theory provides a consistent explanation of consumer behaviour. Consider the set S of physically and economically feasible vectors $\mathbf{x}$. Then S is the intersection of X and the set R satisfying

$$\left.\begin{array}{c} x_i \geqslant \bar{x}_i \quad i = 1,\dots,n \\[2mm] \sum_{i=1}^{n} p_i x_i \leqslant I \end{array}\right\} \tag{13.3.3}$$

where $\bar{x}_i(i = 1,\dots,n)$ is the lower bound of assumption 1. Since X is closed and since it can be easily shown that R is closed and bounded, it follows that S is closed and bounded (i.e. compact [see V, §5.3]). Also S is not empty since it contains the null vector. Since $U(\mathbf{x})$ is a continuous function defined on a nonempty compact set S, it has a maximum on S, thus establishing the existence of an equilibrium.

Having established the existence of an equilibrium we now turn to its properties. If $\mathbf{x}^*$ is an equilibrium consumption vector then

$$\sum_{i=1}^{n} p_i x_i^* = I.$$

For if

$$\sum_{i=1}^{n} p_i x_i^* < I,$$

there exists a vector $\hat{\mathbf{x}}$, all of whose components are greater than the components of $\mathbf{x}^*$, such that

$$\sum_{i=1}^{n} p_i \hat{x}_i \leqslant I.$$

Then (by assumption 1) $\hat{\mathbf{x}}$ is in X and also in S; but $U(\hat{\mathbf{x}}) \geqslant U(\mathbf{x}^*)$ (by assumption 2) contradicting the fact that $\mathbf{x}^*$ is an equilibrium.

The first order conditions for a solution to the consumer's problem (with, in view of the above remarks, the inequality in (13.3.1) replaced by an equality) are

$$\frac{\partial U(\mathbf{x})}{\partial x_i} = \lambda p_i, \quad i = 1,\dots,n, \tag{13.3.4}$$

$$\sum_{i=1}^{n} p_i x_i = I, \tag{13.3.5}$$

where λ is the Lagrangian multiplier [see IV, §5.15]. Condition (13.3.4) yields

$$MRS_{ij} = \frac{\partial U(\mathbf{x})/\partial x_i}{\partial U(\mathbf{x})/\partial x_j} = \frac{p_i}{p_j}, \quad i, j = 1, \ldots, n, \tag{13.3.6}$$

so that in equilibrium the marginal rate of substitution between goods i and j— the rates at which i and j can be substituted maintaining constant utility—should be equal to the ratio of their prices—the rates at which i and j can be substituted maintaining constant income.

The second order conditions are that the quadratic form

$$\sum_i \sum_j \frac{\partial^2 U(x)}{\partial x_i \partial x_j} dx_i dx_j$$

is negative semi-definite for every vector $d\mathbf{x} = (dx_1, \ldots, dx_n)$ such that [see I, §9.2, and IV, §5.7]

$$\sum_{i=1}^{n} p_i dx_i = 0.$$

In other words, in equilibrium, small variations in quantities will not lead to changes in the level of utility but will lead to a *fall* in the rate of change of utility.

The Lagrangian multiplier, λ, of (13.3.4) can be interpreted as the marginal utility of income since differentiating $U(\mathbf{x})$, applying (13.3.4) and (13.3.5) and keeping prices constant yields

$$dU = \sum_{i=1}^{n} \frac{\partial U(x)}{\partial x_i} dx_i = \lambda \sum_{i=1}^{n} p_i dx_i = \lambda dI.$$

It is easily shown that the marginal properties of equilibrium are not altered if the utility function $U(\mathbf{x})$ is replaced by a monotonic increasing transformation of itself, $F(U(\mathbf{x}))$, $F' > 0$ [see I, §2.7]. In order words a given utility function represents a preference ordering but not uniquely. The function $F(U(\mathbf{x}))$ represents the same preference ordering, since $F(U(\mathbf{x}^1)) \geqslant F(U(\mathbf{x}^2))$ if and only if $U(\mathbf{x}^1) \geqslant U(\mathbf{x}^2)$. This is exactly the same as saying that $U(\mathbf{x})$ is an *ordinal* as opposed to a *cardinal* utility function.

The first order conditions (13.3.4) and (13.3.5) can be solved to yield the *Marshallian demand functions* which express the equilibrium quantities bought, $x_i^*(i = 1, \ldots, n)$ as functions of prices and income:

$$x_i^* = g_i(p_1, \ldots, p_n, I) \quad i = 1, \ldots, n$$
$$= g_i(p, I) \quad \text{where} \quad \mathbf{p} = (p_1, \ldots, p_n).$$

13.4. INDIRECT UTILITY AND THE EXPENDITURE FUNCTION

Consider the consumer's original problem:

$$\text{Maximize } U(\mathbf{x}) \text{ subject to } \sum_{i=1}^{n} p_i x_i = I \tag{13.4.1}$$

and its dual [see I, §11.2]

$$\text{Minimize } I = \sum_{i=1}^{n} p_i x_i \text{ subject to } U(x) = u. \qquad (13.4.2)$$

We can use the same u in both problems, since in the dual we simply use the u which is the maximum attainable in the original problem. Further the outlay in the original is the cost minimum in the dual, since cost minimization and utility maximization must imply the same choice. This is a simple consequence of the saddle point theorem [see IV, §15.3.4]. In both problems the optimal values of $\mathbf{x}$ are being sought. In the original problem the solution is the set of Marshallian demand functions $g_i(\mathbf{p}, I)$. In the dual problem, the optimal quantities, x_i^*, are expressed as a function of prices and utility levels to yield the *Hicksian* or *compensated* demand functions, $x_i^* = f_i(\mathbf{p}, u)$ and since the solutions coincide

$$x_i^* = g_i(\mathbf{p}, I) = f_i(\mathbf{p}, u). \qquad (13.4.3)$$

Each of the solutions in (13.3.3) can be substituted back into their respective problems to yield:

$$U^* = U(x_1^*, \ldots, x_n^*) = V(\mathbf{p}, I) \qquad (13.4.4)$$

$$I^* = \sum_i p_i x_i^* = C(\mathbf{p}, u). \qquad (13.4.5)$$

The function $V(\mathbf{p}, I)$ defined by (13.4.4) represents the maximum utility attainable with given prices and income; it is called the *indirect utility function*. The function $C(\mathbf{p}, u)$, defined by (13.4.5) is the minimum cost of attaining a given utility level with given prices; it is called the *expenditure* or *cost* function.

The expenditure and the indirect utility functions are intimately related since inverting $I = C(\mathbf{p}, u)$ yields $u = V(\mathbf{p}, I)$ and inverting $u = V(\mathbf{p}, I)$ yields $I = C(\mathbf{p}, u)$.

The expenditure function has five main properties:

(i) The expenditure function is homogeneous of degree one in prices, i.e. $C(\theta\mathbf{p}, u) = \theta C(\mathbf{p}, u)$ for any scalar θ. This means that given an utility level a proportionate increase in prices requires an equi-proportionate increase in expenditure to attain that utility level.

(ii) The expenditure function is increasing in u and non-decreasing in $\mathbf{p}$. Thus, given prices, to attain a higher utility level requires higher expenditure. Conversely, a given utility level, with higher prices, cannot be attained with lower expenditure.

(iii) The expenditure function is concave in prices [see IV, §15.2.6].

(iv) The expenditure function is continuous in $\mathbf{p}$ [see IV, §5.3].

(v) The Hicksian demand functions may be obtained by differentiating the expenditure function, that is

$$f_i(\mathbf{p}, u) = \frac{\partial C(\mathbf{p}, u)}{\partial p_i}, \qquad i = 1, \ldots, n.$$

This property is known as the *derivative property* of the expenditure function.

13.5. THE SLUTSKY EQUATION

From the derivative property of the expenditure function, it is evident that from any expenditure function it is possible to derive the corresponding Hicksian demand function. From the Hicksian demand functions it is then possible to derive the Marshallian demand functions as

$$x_i^* = f_i(\mathbf{p}, u) = f_i(\mathbf{p}, V(\mathbf{p}, I)) = g_i(\mathbf{p}, I). \tag{13.5.1}$$

However, one can also derive Marshallian demand functions directly from the indirect utility function. Since the expenditure and indirect utility functions are inverses:

$$V(\mathbf{p}, C(\mathbf{p}, u)) \equiv u. \tag{13.5.2}$$

Differentiating with respect to p_i, when u is held constant, yields [see IV, §5.4]

$$\frac{\partial V}{\partial I} \frac{\partial C}{\partial p_i} + \frac{\partial V}{\partial p_i} = 0 \tag{13.5.3}$$

and, since by (13.4.5) $\partial C / \partial p_i = x_i^*$, this gives *Roy's identity*:

$$x_i^* = g_i(\mathbf{p}, I) = \frac{-\partial V / \partial p_i}{\partial V / \partial I}, \quad i = 1, \ldots, n. \tag{13.5.4}$$

From the above we can derive the *Slutsky equation*:

$$\frac{\partial g_j(\mathbf{p}, I)}{\partial p_i} = \frac{\partial f_j(\mathbf{p}, V(\mathbf{p}, I))}{\partial p_i} - \frac{\partial g_j(\mathbf{p}, I)}{\partial I} x_i^*. \tag{13.5.5}$$

For suppose $\mathbf{x}^*$ maximizes utility at $(\mathbf{p}^*, I^*)$ and let $u^* = U(\mathbf{x}^*)$. Then it is identically true that

$$f_j(\mathbf{p}, u^*) = g_j(\mathbf{p}, C(\mathbf{p}, u^*)). \tag{13.5.6}$$

Differentiating (13.5.6) with respect to p_i and evaluating the derivative at $\mathbf{p}^*$ one obtains:

$$\frac{\partial f_j(\mathbf{p}^*, u^*)}{\partial p_i} = \frac{\partial g_j(\mathbf{p}^*, I^*)}{\partial p_i} + \frac{\partial g_j(\mathbf{p}, I^*)}{\partial I^*} \frac{\partial C(\mathbf{p}, u^*)}{\partial p_i}. \tag{13.5.7}$$

Remembering that $\partial C(\mathbf{p}, u^*) / \partial p_i = x_i$, rearranging (13.5.7) yields (13.5.5).

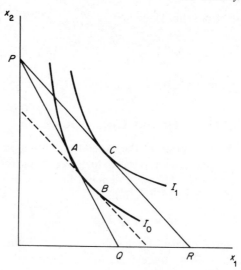

Figure 13.2: Income and substitution effects

The Slutsky equation decomposes the demand change induced by the price change (also called the *uncompensated price effect*) $\partial g_j/\partial p_i$, into two effects:

(i) the *substitution effect* (*or compensated price effect*), $\partial f_j/\partial p_i$, whereby the consumer is 'compensated' for the change in real income induced by the change in price so that he enjoys the same level of utility as before and responds only to the change in relative prices.

(ii) the *income effect*, $(\partial g_j/\partial I)x_i$, whereby the consumer responds to the change in real income induced by the price change but changes in relative prices (to which he has already responded under (i)) are not considered.

This is illustrated in Figure 13.2.

In Figure 13.2 A is the original point of equilibrium where the budget line PQ is tangential to the indifference curve I_0. A fall in the price of good 1 leads to a new budget line PR. If the consumer's income is reduced so that, at the new prices, he obtains the same utility he obtained before the price changes, he is at equilibrium at point B. The movement from A to B is the 'substitution effect'. The movement from B to C, when at unchanged prices, he responds to higher income, is the 'income effect'.

13.6. PROPERTIES OF THE DEMAND FUNCTIONS

(i) *Adding up*

The total value of the Hicksian and Marshallian demand functions is total expenditure, that is,

$$\sum_{i=1}^{n} p_i g_i(\mathbf{p}, I) = \sum_{i=1}^{n} p_i f_i(\mathbf{p}, u) = I. \tag{13.6.1}$$

In other words, the demand functions have the property that the sum of individual expenditures is exactly equal to total expenditure. All expenditure is allocated over the available goods.

(ii) *Homogeneity*

The Hicksian demand functions are homogeneous of degree zero in prices (since they are derivatives of a function which is homogeneous of degree one) and the Marshallian demand functions are homogeneous of degree zero in income and prices (since an equi-proportionate increase in prices and income leaves the constraints (13.3.5) unchanged). This implies that the quantities demanded depend only upon relative prices and real incomes, since a doubling of all prices and income would leave relative prices and real income unchanged leaving quantities demanded unchanged.

(iii) *Symmetry*

The compensated cross price derivatives are symmetric, that is,

$$\frac{\partial f_j(\mathbf{p}, u)}{\partial p_i} = \frac{\partial f_i(\mathbf{p}, u)}{\partial p_j}, \quad i, j = 1, \dots, n. \tag{13.6.2}$$

This means for example, that a compensated penny per pound increase in the price of apples should increase the number of bars of soap bought by a number equal to the number of more pounds of apples bought consequent upon a compensated penny per bar increase in the price of soap. This follows from the derivative property of section 13.3.

(iv) *Negativity*

The matrix of compensated cross price derivatives is negative semi-definite, that is [see I, §9.2]

$$\mathbf{z}'\mathbf{Hz} \leqslant 0, \quad \text{for any vector } \mathbf{z} \tag{13.6.3}$$

where $\mathbf{H} = [\partial f_j / \partial p_i] \quad i, j = 1, \dots, n$.
This follows since, by the derivative property,

$$\frac{\partial f_j}{\partial p_i} = \frac{\partial^2 C}{\partial p_j \partial p_i}$$

and the latter is negative semi-definite since $C(\mathbf{p}, u)$ is a concave function [see IV,

§15.2.6]. In particular property (iv) implies

$$\frac{\partial f_i}{\partial p_i} \leqslant 0 \quad i = 1, \ldots, n, \tag{13.6.4}$$

that is an increase in the price of a commodity with utility held constant leads to its demand falling (or remaining unchanged).

Now define good i as an *inferior* good if its consumption falls as income rises, that is

$$\frac{\partial g_i}{\partial I} < 0. \tag{13.6.5}$$

For example, one might, as income rises, buy less potatoes and more, say, meat, and potatoes in this example would be an inferior good. Then if a good is *not* an inferior good, by (13.5.5) its demand must fall as its price rises, that is its uncompensated own price derivative is negative.

Even if a good is an inferior good the law of demand will hold if the substitution effect outweighs the income effect.

The law of demand will not hold, in which case the relevant good is called a *Giffen* good, only if the good is an inferior good with the income effect outweighing the substitution effect. An example would again be potatoes. If the price of potatoes falls the consumer can buy as many potatoes as before and still have some money left over with which he can buy meat. However, now that he is buying more meat he does not want as many potatoes as before.

13.7. RELATIONSHIPS BETWEEN COMMODITIES

Differentiating the budget constraint (13.3.5) with respect to I and p_i yields

$$\sum_j p_j \frac{\partial g_j(\mathbf{p}, I)}{\partial I} = 1 \tag{13.7.1}$$

and

$$\sum_j p_j \frac{\partial g_j(\mathbf{p}, I)}{\partial p_i} + x_i^* = 0, \quad i = 1, \ldots, n. \tag{13.7.2}$$

Equations (13.7.1) and (13.7.2) have relatively easy interpretations: when all prices are unchanged the change in the value of consumption is equal to the change in income; when only prices alter the change in the value of consumption is zero. The two equations are referred to as *Engel* and *Cournot* aggregation conditions respectively. Combining (13.7.1) and (13.7.2) with the Slutsky equation (13.5.5) yields

$$\sum_j p_j \frac{\partial f_j(\mathbf{p}, u)}{\partial p_i} = 0, \tag{13.7.3}$$

which says that given a change in price the change in the value of the compensated demands will be zero. In other words the budget constraint will continue to be operative with Hicksian demand functions.

Also since $f_j(\mathbf{p}, u)$ is homogeneous of degree zero in prices, applying Euler's theorem yields

$$\sum_{i=1}^{n} p_i \frac{\partial f_j(\mathbf{p}, u)}{\partial p_i} = 0. \tag{13.7.4}$$

Two goods i and j are said to be *substitutes* (*complements*) if $\partial f_j(\mathbf{p}, u)/\partial p_i > 0 \ (< 0)$.

From (13.7.4) it follows (remembering $p_i > 0$ and $\partial f_i/\partial p_i < 0$) that all goods cannot be complements. In particular, when there are only two goods, both must be substitutes. From equation (13.7.1) it follows that all goods cannot be inferior goods.

Multiplying the Slutsky equation (13.5.5) by p_i and summing yields

$$\sum p_i \frac{\partial g_j(\mathbf{p}, I)}{\partial p_i} + \frac{\partial g_j(\mathbf{p}, I)}{\partial I} = 0 \tag{13.7.5}$$

which in turn yields:

$$\sum_i \frac{p_i}{x_j^*} \frac{\partial x_j^*}{\partial p_i} + \frac{\partial x_j^*}{\partial I} \frac{I}{x_j^*} = 0 \tag{13.7.6}$$

or

$$\sum_i e_{ji} + e_{jI} = 0 \tag{13.7.7}$$

or

$$\sum_i e_{ji}^* = 0, \tag{13.7.8}$$

where e_{ji} and e_{ji}^* are the *uncompensated* and *compensated cross price elasticities* of the jth commodity with respect to the ith price and e_{jI} is the *income elasticity* of the jth commodity. Equations (13.7.7) and (13.7.8) imply that a proportionate change in all prices and incomes leaves the consumption levels of every good unaltered.

13.8. MARKET DEMAND

The transition from the microeconomics of consumer behaviour to the analysis of market demand is frequently referred to as the 'aggregation problem'. One role of aggregation theory (and the one considered here) is to provide the conditions under which it is possible to treat aggregate consumer behaviour as if it were the outcome of the decisions of a single utility maximizing consumer.

Let x_i^k be the quantity of good i bought by the kth household so that the demand functions are:

$$x_i^k = g_i^k(\mathbf{p}, I^k), \quad i = 1, \ldots, n, k = 1, \ldots, H. \tag{13.8.1}$$

Equation (13.8.1) implies that total demand, x_i, can be written as

$$x_i = \sum_{k=1}^{H} g_i^k(\mathbf{p}, I^k) = x_i(I^1, \ldots, I^H, \mathbf{p}). \qquad (13.8.2)$$

The aggregation problem has a solution if (13.8.2) can be written as

$$x_i = g_i(\mathbf{p}, I), \quad \text{where} \quad I = \sum_k I^k \qquad (13.8.3)$$

Equation (13.8.3) unlike (13.8.2) does not depend on income distribution. Hence if there is a reallocation of income, total demand must remain unaltered and this will happen if and only if the marginal propensities to spend on i are the same for all consumers, that is

$$\frac{\partial g_i^r}{\partial I^r} = \frac{\partial g_i^s}{\partial I^s} \quad r, s = 1, \ldots, H. \qquad (13.8.4)$$

This implies that the functions (13.8.1) must be linear in I^k, that is

$$x_i^k = \alpha_i^k(\mathbf{p}) + \beta_i(\mathbf{p})I^k, \qquad (13.8.5)$$

where the coefficient on income is not indexed by k.

Therefore if the aggregation problem has a solution then

$$x_i = \alpha_i(\mathbf{p}) + \beta_i(\mathbf{p})I. \qquad (13.8.6)$$

13.9. REVEALED PREFERENCE

Revealed preference is an approach to the theory of the household based on observed choices. If the household buys the bundle $\hat{\mathbf{x}} = (\hat{x}_1, \ldots, \hat{x}_n)$ at prices $\hat{\mathbf{p}} = (\hat{p}_1, \ldots, \hat{p}_n)$ when it could have bought $\tilde{\mathbf{x}} = (\tilde{x}_1, \ldots, \tilde{x}_n)$, then $\hat{\mathbf{x}}$ is revealed preferred to $\tilde{\mathbf{x}}$, written $\hat{\mathbf{x}} R \tilde{\mathbf{x}}$, that is

$$\hat{\mathbf{x}} R \tilde{\mathbf{x}} \text{ if and only if } \sum_{i=1}^{n} \hat{x}_i \hat{p}_i \geqslant \sum_{i=1}^{n} \tilde{x}_i \hat{p}_i \qquad (13.9.1)$$

[see I, §1.3]. The *weak axiom of revealed preference* states that if the bundle $\hat{\mathbf{x}}$ is revealed preferred to $\tilde{\mathbf{x}}$, then $\tilde{\mathbf{x}}$ cannot be revealed preferred to $\hat{\mathbf{x}}$, that is

$$\hat{\mathbf{x}} R \tilde{\mathbf{x}} \text{ implies } \tilde{\mathbf{x}} R \hat{\mathbf{x}}. \qquad (13.9.2)$$

The weak axiom states that when $\tilde{\mathbf{x}}$ was available the household chose $\hat{\mathbf{x}}$, then in a situation where $\tilde{\mathbf{x}}$ was chosen, $\hat{\mathbf{x}}$ should not have been available.

The negativity of the own substitution effect (13.6.4) can be deduced from the weak axiom. For if the bundles $\hat{\mathbf{x}}$ and $\tilde{\mathbf{x}}$ lie on the same indifference curve, then neither is revealed preferred to the other:

$$\sum_i \hat{p}_i \hat{x}_i < \sum_i \hat{p}_i \tilde{x}_i \qquad (13.9.3)$$

$$\sum_i \tilde{p}_i \tilde{x}_i < \sum_i \tilde{p}_i \hat{x}_i. \tag{13.9.4}$$

Defining $\Delta p_i = \tilde{p}_i - \hat{p}_i$ and $\Delta x_i = \tilde{x}_i - \hat{x}_i$, $i = 1,\ldots,n$, (13.9.3) and (13.9.4) imply

$$\sum_i \hat{p}_i \Delta x_i > 0 \quad \text{and} \quad \sum_i (\hat{p}_i + \Delta p_i)\Delta x_i < 0, \tag{13.9.5}$$

which in turn implies

$$\Delta \mathbf{p} \Delta \mathbf{x} < 0, \tag{13.9.6}$$

establishing the negativity of the own price effect.

In fact most of the results of demand theory set out in section 13.6 follow from the weak axiom, but to establish (13.6.2) the *strong axiom of revealed preference* is needed. This states that if bundle $\mathbf{x}^1$ is revealed preferred to $\mathbf{x}^2$ and $\mathbf{x}^2$ is revealed preferred to $\mathbf{x}^3,\ldots,\mathbf{x}^{n-1}$ is revealed preferred to $\mathbf{x}^n$, then $\mathbf{x}^n$ cannot be revealed preferred to $\mathbf{x}^1$, that is $\mathbf{x}^1 R \mathbf{x}^2$, $\mathbf{x}^2 R \mathbf{x}^3,\ldots,\mathbf{x}^{n-1} R \mathbf{x}^n$ implies $\mathbf{x}^n R \mathbf{x}^1$. The strong axiom extends the weak axiom by making preferences transitive.

13.10. THE LINEAR EXPENDITURE SYSTEM

We conclude this chapter by considering an application of the theory of demand developed in the preceding sections to empirical work. The particular application considered is the famous 'linear expenditure system' due to Richard Stone.

Consider the linear equation relating the quantity bought of the ith good, x_i, to prices, p_j ($j = 1,\ldots,n$) and total expenditure, I

$$x_i = \sum_{j=1}^n \alpha_{ij} p_j + \beta_i I, \quad i = 1,\ldots,n. \tag{13.10.1}$$

For (13.10.1) to represent a demand equation it must satisfy the properties set out in section 13.6.

Homogeneity is imposed by dividing the right-hand side of (13.10.1) by the price of one of the goods, say p_i, to yield

$$x_i = \sum \alpha_{ij} \frac{p_j}{p_i} + \beta_i \frac{I}{p_i}. \tag{13.10.2}$$

The *symmetry* of the compensated crossprice derivatives implies that

$$\frac{\partial f_j(\mathbf{p}, u)}{\partial p_i} = \frac{\partial x_j}{\partial p_i} + \frac{\partial x_j}{\partial I} x_i = \frac{\partial x_i}{\partial p_j} + \frac{\partial x_i}{\partial I} x_j = \frac{\partial f_i(\mathbf{p}, u)}{\partial p_j}. \tag{13.10.3}$$

Substituting (13.10.2) into (13.10.3) yields

$$\frac{\alpha_{ji}}{p_j} + x_i \frac{\beta_j}{p_j} = \frac{\alpha_{ij}}{p_i} + x_j \frac{\beta_i}{p_i} \tag{13.10.4}$$

and multiplying both sides of (13.10.4) by $p_i p_j$ in turn gives

$$\alpha_{ji} p_i + \beta_j x_i p_i = \alpha_{ij} p_j + \beta_i x_j p_j. \tag{13.10.5}$$

Substituting (13.10.2) into (13.10.5) yields

$$\alpha_{ji} p_i + \beta_j \left[\sum_{k=1}^{n} \alpha_{ik} p_k + \beta_i I \right] = \alpha_{ij} p_j + \beta_i \left[\sum_{k=1}^{n} \alpha_{jk} p_k + \beta_j I \right]$$

or

$$\alpha_{ji} p_i + \beta_j \sum_{k=1}^{n} \alpha_{ik} p_k = \alpha_{ij} p_j + \beta_i \sum_{k=1}^{n} \alpha_{jk} p_k \quad (i \neq j)$$

or

$$(\alpha_{ji} + \beta_j \alpha_{ii}) p_i + \beta_j \alpha_{ij} p_j + \beta_j \sum_{k} \alpha_{ik} p_k$$

$$= (\alpha_{ij} + \beta_i \alpha_{jj}) p_j + \beta_i \alpha_{ji} p_i + \beta_i \sum_{k} \alpha_{jk} p_k. \tag{13.10.6}$$

Since (13.10.6) holds for all possible price systems, the coefficients on the individual prices must be the same on both sides:

$$\alpha_{ij} = \beta_i [\alpha_{jj}/(\beta_j - 1)]$$
$$\alpha_{ii} = \beta_i (\alpha_{ji}/\beta_j) - (\alpha_{ji}/\beta_j)$$
$$\alpha_{ik} = \beta_i (\alpha_{jk}/\beta_j). \tag{13.10.7}$$

Defining

$$\gamma_k = (\alpha_{jk}/\beta_j) \quad \text{for} \quad k \neq j$$
$$= \alpha_{jk}/(\beta_j - 1) \quad \text{for} \quad k = j,$$

we obtain

$$\alpha_{ik} = \beta_i \gamma_k - \delta_{ik} \gamma_i, \quad i, k = 1, \dots, n, \tag{13.10.8}$$

where [see I, (6.2.7)]

$$\delta_{ik} \begin{aligned} &= 0 \quad \text{for} \quad i \neq k \\ &= 1 \quad \text{for} \quad i = k. \end{aligned}$$

Thus symmetry implies that the price coefficient of $(n - 1)$ equations are expressed in terms of the price and income coefficients of the jth equation and in terms of its own income coefficient.

Re-writing the original Equation (13.10.1) by taking into account homogeneity and symmetry yields

$$p_i x_i = \sum_{j} \alpha_{ij} p_j + \beta_i I$$

$$= \sum_{j} [\beta_i \gamma_j - \delta_{ij} \gamma_i] p_j + \beta_i I$$

$$= \beta_i \sum_{j} p_j \gamma_j - p_i \gamma_i + \beta_i I. \tag{13.10.9}$$

Now the *adding up* property requires that

$$I = \sum_i p_i x_i = \sum_i \beta_i \sum_j p_j \gamma_j - \sum p_i \gamma_i + I \sum \beta_i$$

$$= \sum_j p_j \gamma_j [\sum \beta_i - 1] + I \sum \beta_i = I,$$

which in turn requires $\sum \beta_i = 1$. Hence under homogeneity, symmetry and adding up

$$x_i = \gamma_i + \frac{\beta_i}{p_i} [I - \sum p_j \gamma_j] \quad \text{with} \quad \sum \beta_i = 1. \qquad (13.10.10)$$

Finally the *negativity* of the compensated own price effect implies that

$$\frac{\partial x_i}{\partial p_i} + x_i \frac{\partial x_i}{\partial I} < 0. \qquad (13.10.11)$$

Substituting from (13.10.10) into (13.10.11) we obtain

$$\frac{\partial f_i(\mathbf{p}, u)}{\partial p_i} = \frac{(x_i - \gamma_i)}{p_i} (\beta_i - 1) < 0$$

and given $p_i > 0$ this can only be true if

$$x_i > \gamma_i, \quad 0 < \beta_i < 1. \qquad (13.10.12)$$

Thus by imposing the properties of demand equations on a system of linear equations relating quantities to prices and total expenditures yields

$$p_i x_i = p_i \gamma_i + \beta_i \left[I - \sum_j p_j \gamma_j \right] \qquad (13.10.13)$$

with $0 < \beta_i < 1$, $\sum \beta_i = 1$ and $x_i > \gamma_i$.

A natural interpretation of (13.10.13) is as follows: the total expenditure on good i, $p_i x_i$, can be decomposed into first the minimum 'committed' expenditure, $p_i \gamma_i$, required for a given subsistence level. Having met his subsistence needs the consumer then allocates his 'supernumerary income', $I - \sum_j p_j \gamma_j$, among the n commodities using the proportions $\beta_1, \ldots, \beta_n$.

The linear expenditure system embodied in Equation (13.10.13) can also be derived by the constrained maximization of an appropriate utility function using the techniques of section 13.3.

Define the *Stone–Geary* utility function

$$u = \sum \beta_i \log(x_i - \gamma_i) \qquad (13.10.14)$$

and maximize (13.10.14) subject to the budget constraint

$$\sum p_i x_i = I \qquad (13.10.15)$$

and the normalizing restriction $\sum \beta_i = 1$.

From the first order conditions [see IV, §5.15] we have

$$\beta_i = \lambda p_i(x_i - \gamma_i) \tag{13.10.16}$$

and $\sum \beta_i = 1 = \lambda \sum p_i(x_i - \gamma_i)$ which implies

$$\lambda = \frac{1}{I - \sum p_j \gamma_j} \tag{13.10.17}$$

Substituting (13.10.17) into (13.10.16) yields

$$\beta_i = \frac{p_i(x_i - \gamma_i)}{I - \sum p_j \gamma_j}$$

or

$$p_i x_i = p_i \gamma_i + \beta_i(I - \sum p_j \gamma_j),$$

which is the linear expenditure system.

13.11. REFERENCES

Brown, J. A. C. and Deaton, A. (1972). Surveys in applied economics: models of consumer behaviour. *Economic Journal*, **82**, 1145–1236.

Cook, P. (1972). A one line proof of the Slutsky equation. *American Economic Review*, **42**.

Deaton, A. and Muellbauer, J. (1980). *Economics and Consumer Behaviour*. Cambridge University Press, Cambridge.

Pearce, I. F. (1964). *A Contribution to Demand Analysis*. Oxford University Press, London.

Phlips, L. (1974). *Applied Consumption Analysis*. North-Holland, Amsterdam.

Stone, J. R. N. (1954). Linear expenditure systems and demand analysis: an application to the pattern of British demand. *Economic Journal*, **64**, 511–527.

Mathematical Methods in Economics
Edited by F. van der Ploeg
© 1984, John Wiley & Sons, Ltd.

14

General Equilibrium Theory

CLAUS WEDDEPOHL, *University of Amsterdam, Amsterdam, Netherlands*

14.1. INTRODUCTION

The aim of general equilibrium theory is to describe the behaviour of an economy as a whole, contrary to partial equilibrium theory that deals with the behaviour of individual agents, particularly consumers [see Chapter 13] and producers [see Chapter 12], and also of groups of agents, e.g. all firms in a market of a homogeneous commodity as in oligopoly theory [see §12.13]. Partial equilibrium models are building blocks in general equilibrium models. In a general equilibrium model states of the economy are studied that result from optimizing behaviour of individual agents. The best developed part of general equilibrium theory is the theory of competitive or Walrasian equilibrium and this is the subject of the present chapter. A competitive equilibrium is a state where total demand and supply are equal for all commodities and where demand and supply of individual agents are their 'best choices' when they take the prices prevailing in the market as given, unlike oligopolists or monopolists [see Chapter 12].

Walras (1874) was the first to construct a general equilibrium model and he defined a competitive equilibrium. During the first half of this century the question arose whether the equilibrium as defined by Walras would exist under reasonable conditions. For, without existence of the equilibrium the model could not be accepted as a description of real phenomena. Wald (1936) proved its existence in a very simple model. In the nineteen-fifties Debreu (1952), Arrow and Debreu (1954), McKenzie (1959) and Debreu (1959) proved its existence in more general models. In his *Theory of Value* Debreu (1959) gave a very precise reformulation of the theory and this book was a starting point of a stream of publications in the field and general equilibrium theory became a central topic in mathematical economics. More recently new existence proofs were invented (Gale and Mas-Colell, 1975; Shafer and Sonnenschein, 1975), where particularly assumptions on consumer behaviour were relaxed. In this chapter this new approach is followed. (For a survey on existence, see Debreu (1982).) In section 14.2 an exchange economy is introduced. An exchange economy is a model of a very simple economy with a single type of agents, consumers, and without production. Each consumer owns resources of various commodities, which may be exchanged with other consumers. The origin of the resources is not explained by the model, but it depends on the type of economy described. The resources might be interpreted, for example, as (different kinds of) manna falling from heaven,, as the fruits of the trees, as the results of production activities that do not depend on other variables of the model, etc. If the set of consumers consists of the prisoners in a War camp, the resources are the goods they initially possess. In exchange economies equilibria and related concepts can be defined and most results also hold true in more general models. Therefore a good understanding of an exchange economy is an excellent point of departure for the study of more complex models. This explains that in general equilibrium theory new problems are typically first studied within an exchange economy. In the exchange economy preferences of consumers are an essential part. In section 14.3 preferences are studied and the assumptions that can be made are discussed. In section 14.4 we return to the exchange economy and prove the existence of an equilibrium. Section 14.5 deals with an economy with production: the exchange economy is extended with producers provided with a technology, and with a profit distribution scheme. An existence theorem is given and partially proved, but the last step is postponed to section 14.6, where an abstract economy is studied. It appears that general equilibrium models and games in normal form have basically the same structure, which is modelled as an abstract economy. A solution concept of game theory (there are more solution concepts) is a Nash equilibrium. It is defined in section 14.6.2 and its existence is considered in section 14.6.4 and it is shown that a Walrasian equilibrium is a Nash equilibrium if the economy is suitably reformulated. The idea of using an abstract economy for proving existence was introduced in Debreu (1952) and again applied in Shafer and Sonnenschein (1975). Their theorem is given in section 14.6.4. The proof is different and makes use of Michael's selection theorem (1956), which is also applied in Gale and Mas-Colell (1975).

Some of the mathematics related to set-valued functions is not covered in the handbook, but is instead discussed in the Appendix to this chapter.

14.2. AN EXCHANGE ECONOMY

14.2.1. Allocations

There are n commodities in the economy and $\mathbb{R}^n$ [see I, §5.2] is called the *commodity space*. A vector $\mathbf{x} \in \mathbb{R}^n$ represents a commodity bundle, where $\mathbf{x} = (x_1, x_2, \ldots, x_n)$, x_i being a quantity of the ith commodity. There are m consumers in the economy and $H = \{1, 2, \ldots, m\}$ denotes the *set of consumers*. Each consumer $h \in H$

has a *consumption set* (or consumption possibility set [see §13.2]) $X^h \subset \mathbb{R}^n$, from which he has to obtain one and only one commodity bundle. Each consumer also has a vector of *resources* $\mathbf{w}^h = (w_1^h, w_2^h, \ldots, w_n^h) \in \mathbb{R}^n$. By $\mathbf{w}^H = (\mathbf{w}^1, \mathbf{w}^2, \ldots, \mathbf{w}^m) \in (\mathbb{R}^n)^m$ we denote the *m*-tuple of resource vectors of the *m* consumers in the economy.

DEFINITION 14.2.1. An *allocation* is an *m*-tuple of commodity bundles $\mathbf{x}^H = (\mathbf{x}^1, \mathbf{x}^2, \ldots, \mathbf{x}^m)$ such that

$$\forall h : \mathbf{x}^h \in X^h.$$

A *feasible allocation* is an allocation $\mathbf{x}^H$, such that total consumption exhausts total resources:

$$\sum_{h=1}^m \mathbf{x}^h = \sum_{h=1}^m \mathbf{w}^h.$$

Hence a feasible allocation is a (re)distribution of the total amount of commodities available in the economy, among consumers. If $\mathbf{x}^H$ is a feasible allocation, then $\mathbf{z}^h = (\mathbf{x}^h - \mathbf{w}^h)$ is called consumer h's *net trade*: if $z_i^h > 0$, then he obtained the quantity z_i^h of commodity i, if $z_i^h < 0$, then he gave up the quantity $-z_i^h$.

In an economy with two commodities and two consumers ($n = 2$ and $m = 2$), the set of feasible allocations can be represented by an *Edgeworth box* (Figure 14.1). Let $X^h = \mathbb{R}_+^2$ ($h = 1, 2$) be the space of nonnegative 2-tuples. With respect to O^1, the origin of consumer 1, the point $\mathbf{w} = \mathbf{w}^1$ represents consumer 1's resources, with respect to O^2, $\mathbf{w} = \mathbf{w}^2$ represents consumer 2's resources. The point O^2 equals $\mathbf{w}^1 + \mathbf{w}^2$ w.r.t. O^1. Thus the dimensions of the box show the total amount of resources available in the exchange economy. Each point in the rectangle, e.g. $\mathbf{x}$, is a feasible allocation.

The *price space* is the dual set $\mathbb{R}^n$, to be distinguished from the commodity space $\mathbb{R}^n$; $\mathbf{p} = (p_1, p_2, \ldots, p_n) \in \mathbb{R}_+^n$ is a *vector of prices* (below also called a price), where p_i is the amount that a consumer pays or receives if he obtains or gives up one unit of commodity i. Each price p_i is expressed either in terms of a unit of account (money) that is not a commodity, or in terms of one of the commodities, called the

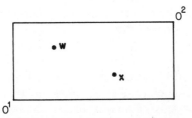

Figure 14.1: The Edgeworth Box

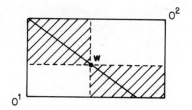

Figure 14.2: Feasible market allocations

numéraire; if commodity 1 is the numéraire, then $p_1 = 1$ always. The *value* of a commodity bundle $\mathbf{x}$ at price $\mathbf{p}$ may be found from the scalar product

$$\mathbf{p} \cdot \mathbf{x} = \sum_{i=1}^{n} p_i \cdot x_i.$$

DEFINITION 14.2.2. A *market allocation* at price $\mathbf{p}$ is a feasible allocation $\mathbf{x}^H$, such that

$$\forall h : \mathbf{p} . \mathbf{x}^h = \mathbf{p} . \mathbf{w}^h.$$

Hence a market allocation is the possible result of exchange at uniform prices. If $\mathbf{z}^h = (\mathbf{x}^h - \mathbf{w}^h)$ is consumer h's net trade and if $\mathbf{x}^H$ is a market allocation, then obviously $\forall h : \mathbf{p} \cdot \mathbf{z}^h = 0$.

In an Edgeworth box the set of market allocations at some price $\mathbf{p}$ consists of all points on a line through $\mathbf{w}$ satisfying $\mathbf{p} \cdot \mathbf{x} = \mathbf{p} \cdot \mathbf{w}$. Minus the slope of the line through $\mathbf{w}$ represents the price of good 2 in terms of the price of good 1. Provided that only positive prices are possible, all points in the shaded area of Figure 14.2 represent possible market allocations for some given price $\mathbf{p}$.

Among the feasible allocations certain allocations are considered by consumers to be optimal in some sense, given their preferences. Therefore we first have to consider preferences.

14.2.2. Preferences and maximal elements

Each consumer $h \in H$ has preferences amongst the commodity bundles in X^h and these are expressed by a correspondence (that is a set valued function) $P^h : X^h \to X^h$ [see I, §1.4]. The set $P^h(\mathbf{x}) \subset X^h$ contains all commodity bundles that h *strictly prefers* to $\mathbf{x} \in X^h$. Hence '$\mathbf{y} \in P^h(\mathbf{x})$' means: '$h$ considers the bundle $\mathbf{y}$ to be better than the bundle $\mathbf{x}$'; '$\mathbf{y} \notin P^h(\mathbf{x})$' means '$\mathbf{y}$ is *not* better than $\mathbf{x}$'. The correspondence P^h is called a strong preference or better-than relation.

In the next section a number of *assumptions* on P^h will be introduced. An assumption that P^h must satisfy if we want to call it a strong preference is that it is *irreflexive*, that is $\forall \mathbf{x} \in X^h : \mathbf{x} \notin P^h(\mathbf{x})$, or, $\mathbf{x}$ is not better than itself.

DEFINITION 14.2.3. Given an irreflexive preference $P^h:X^h \to X^h$ and a set $B \subset X^h$, we call $\mathbf{x} \in B$ a *maximal element* of B if

$$\forall \mathbf{y} \in B: \mathbf{y} \notin P^h(\mathbf{x}).$$

Hence for $\mathbf{x}$ to be a maximal element it is required that the set B (for example the budget set of a consumer) does not contain an element better than $\mathbf{x}$. Obviously $\mathbf{x}$ is a maximal element of B with respect to P^h, if and only if

$$P^h(\mathbf{x}) \cap B = \varnothing.$$

Note that not every set B has a maximal element and that B may contain different maximal elements.

The correspondence P^h only describes preferences between two commodity bundles and thus gives only a direct answer to the question which one of *two* bundles will be chosen. However, a *fundamental hypothesis* in consumer theory is that from an arbitrary set always a maximal element, with respect to P^h, will be chosen (provided that it exists).

14.2.3. Pareto optimality and Walrasian equilibrium

An exchange economy is completely characterized by the set of consumers H, the consumption sets X^h, the resources $\mathbf{w}^h$ and the preferences P^h and it is denoted by

$$\mathscr{E} = \{H, X^h, \mathbf{w}^h, P^h\}.$$

DEFINITION 14.2.4. In $\mathscr{E}$ a feasible allocation $\mathbf{x}^H$ is a *Pareto optimum* if *no other* feasible allocation $\mathbf{y}^H$ exists, such that

$$\forall h \in H: \mathbf{x}^h \notin P^h(\mathbf{y}^h) \text{ and } \exists k \in H: \mathbf{y}^k \in P^k(\mathbf{x}^k).$$

In a Pareto optimum (also called a Pareto efficient allocation) no consumer can be made better off unless another consumer is made worse off. Note that the Pareto optima only depend on $\sum \mathbf{w}^h$ and not on the distribution of resources among consumers. It is assumed that consumers do not mind that other agents become better-off, as long as they do not get worse-off themselves. So jealousy does not feature in the model, nor does the consumption of other agents affect the consumer's well-being for other reasons, or stated differently, external effects are ruled out. In section 14.6.3 a more general case is considered.

DEFINITION 14.2.5. A (Walrasian) *equilibrium* $(\mathbf{x}^H, \mathbf{p})$ in $\mathscr{E}$ is an allocation $\mathbf{x}^H \in \mathbb{R}^{nm}$ and a price vector $\mathbf{p} \in \mathbb{R}^n_+$ such that

(i) $\forall h \in H: \mathbf{x}^h$ is a maximal element from the budget set $\{\mathbf{x} \in X^h | \mathbf{p} \cdot \mathbf{x}^h \leqslant \mathbf{p} \cdot \mathbf{w}^h\}$;
(ii) $\sum_h \mathbf{x}^h = \sum_h \mathbf{w}^h.$

$\mathbf{x}^H$ is called an equilibrium allocation and $\mathbf{p}$ is called an equilibrium price if $(\mathbf{x}^H, \mathbf{p})$ is an equilibrium.

In a Walrasian equilibrium the allocation is feasible and each consumer gets a consumption bundle which is a maximal element from his budget set, the set of commodity bundles he can afford at price $\mathbf{p}$ and with an income equal to the value of his resources [see also §13.3]. By (ii) the value of the net trade is zero that is

$$\mathbf{p} \cdot \mathbf{z}^h = \mathbf{p} \cdot (\mathbf{x}^h - \mathbf{w}^h) = 0$$

and $\mathbf{x}^H$ is a market allocation [Definition 14.2.2]. All trade takes place at uniform prices, and each consumer is a price taker by choosing a maximal element from his budget set. Thus each consumer believes that he could not influence prices favourably for himself, by choosing a different bundle. Each consumer behaves competitively and therefore a Walrasian equilibrium is also called a competitive equilibrium.

Example. In an economy with two commodities and two consumers ($n = 2$ and $m = 2$), with $X^1 = X^2 = \mathbb{R}^2_+$ and $P^h(\mathbf{x}^h) = \{\mathbf{y} \in X^h \mid \mathbf{y} > \mathbf{x}^h\}$, ($h = 1, 2$), we have: if $\mathbf{p} > 0$ and $\mathbf{x}^H$ is a market allocation at $\mathbf{p}$, then $(\mathbf{x}^H, \mathbf{p})$ is an equilibrium.

In an arbitrary exchange economy equilibria and Pareto optima need not exist. In section 14.4 we shall show that under certain *assumptions* on X^h, $\mathbf{w}^h$ and P^h existence is guaranteed.

Hence these assumptions are *sufficient* conditions for existence. Other assumptions will ensure that equilibria and Pareto optima have certain interesting properties.

In the next section we shall discuss preferences and assumptions about preferences that can be made.

14.3. PREFERENCES

14.3.1. Assumptions on preferences

A preference could in principle be defined on any set of alternatives from which an individual has to choose. We first discuss possible properties of preferences that do not depend on the structure of the set of alternatives. Since we consider a single consumer $h \in H$, the index h is suppressed for ease of notation.

Let $S: X \to X$ be a correspondence of an arbitrary set into itself. Then [see I, §1.3]

S is *reflexive* if: $\forall x \in X : x \in S(x)$.

S is *irreflexive* if: $\forall x \in X : x \notin S(x)$.

S is *symmetric* if:	$y \in S(x) \Rightarrow x \in S(y)$.
S is *asymmetric* if:	$y \in S(x) \Rightarrow x \notin S(y)$.
S is *transitive* if:	$x \in S(y)$ and $y \in S(z) \Rightarrow x \in S(z)$.
(or equivalently:	$x \in S(y) \Rightarrow S(x) \subset S(y)$).
S is *negatively transitive* if:	$x \notin S(y)$ and $y \notin S(z) \Rightarrow x \notin S(z)$.
S is *complete* if:	$\forall x, y \in X : x \in S(y)$ or $y \in S(x)$.
(or equivalently:	$\forall x \in X : S(x) \cup S^{-1}(x) = X$).

Each of these properties could be assumed to hold for a preference or for a related correspondence.

If S is complete and transitive, it is called a *complete preordering*; if S is reflexive, symmetric and transitive, it is called an *equivalence*. (Note that completeness implies reflexivity.)

Example. The correspondence $S : \mathbb{R} \to \mathbb{R}$ defined by $S(x) = \{y \in \mathbb{R} | y \geqslant x\}$ is reflexive, transitive, negatively transitive and complete (hence a complete preordering).

For a strong preference, as introduced in 14.2.2, besides irreflexivity, also asymmetry, transitivity and negative transitivity might reasonably be assumed. Asymmetry means that a consumer does not simultaneously prefer x to y and y to x. Transitivity means that a consumer is consistent in his preferences: if he prefers x to y and y to z, he should also prefer x to z. For a chain of preferences, $x^n \in P(x^{n-1}), x^{n-1} \in P(x^{n-2}), \ldots, x^2 \in P(x^1)$, transitivity implies $x^n \in P(x^1)$. Although transitivity of preferences seems to be plausible, it is by no means obvious that each person's preferences always satisfy this assumption (see May (1954) for counter-examples). Negative transitivity means that 'is not better than' is transitive.

THEOREM 14.3.1. *For a preference* $P : X \to X$,
  (i) *asymmetry implies irreflexivity;*
  (ii) *asymmetry and negative transitivity imply transitivity.*

Proof. (i) Suppose $x \in P(x)$; by asymmetry this implies $x \notin P(x)$, a contradiction, (ii) Let $x \in P(y)$ and $y \in P(z)$; suppose $x \notin P(z)$; by asymmetry $z \notin P(y)$; negative transitivity now gives $x \notin P(y)$, a contradiction.

DEFINITION 14.3.1. Given a strong preference $P : X \to X$ the correspondences $R : X \to X$ and $I : X \to X$, defined by

$$R(x) = \{y \in X | x \notin P(y)\}$$
$$I(x) = \{y \in X | y \notin P(x) \text{ and } x \notin P(y)\}$$

are called weak preference and indifference, respectively.

14. General Equilibrium Theory

$y \in R(x)$ means that y is not worse than x, and $y \in I(x)$ means that the consumer is indifferent between y and x. By the irreflexivity of P, I is obviously reflexive and symmetric. It can be expressed in terms of R:

$$I(x) = \{y \in X \,|\, y \in R(x) \text{ and } x \in R(y)\} = R(x) \cap R^{-1}(x). \tag{14.3.1}$$

From R, P can be reconstructed by

$$P(x) = \{y \in X \,|\, x \notin R(y)\} = X \backslash R^{-1}(x). \tag{14.3.2}$$

If R, as defined by Definition 14.3.1, is a complete preordering, it can be consistently interpreted as 'at least as good as' and I, derived by (14.3.1), as 'equivalent'. The following theorem gives assumptions on P that ensure that R is a complete preordering. The proof is straightforward.

THEOREM 14.3.2. *If P is asymmetric and negatively transitive, then*
(i) *R is transitive and complete;*
(ii) *I is reflexive, symmetric and transitive.*

In the literature on consumption and on general equilibrium frequently a weak preference ('at least as good as') is taken as a basic concept instead of a strong preference ('better than'). A strong preference and an indifference can then be derived by (14.3.2) and (14.3.1). In this chapter we use a strong preference as a basic concept, but it should be realized that if P is asymmetric and negatively transitive, we might just as well have started with a weak preference which is a complete preordering.

If there exists a function $u : X \to X$, such that

$$y \in P(x) \Leftrightarrow u(y) > u(x), \tag{14.3.3}$$

then we say that P is *representable* by the *utility function* $u(x)$. Clearly a representable preference P must be negatively transitive and asymmetric, hence R must be a complete preordering. On the converse, see Theorem 3.3 below.

Remark. A preference $P : X \to X$ can be equivalently expressed by its graph [see I, §1.4.1]:

$$\text{Gr } P = \{x, y \,|\, y \in P(x)\} \subset X \times X.$$

It is also frequently expressed by a binary relation: yPx or $y \succ x$ for $y \in P(x)$.

14.3.2. Assumptions on preferences related to the consumption set

On the consumption set $X \subset \mathbb{R}^n$ we shall assume throughout this chapter:

A.1: X is *semi-positive*, that is $X \subset \mathbb{R}^n_+$
A.2: X is *closed* [see IV, §11.2]

A.3: X is *convex* [see IV, §15.2]
A.4: X is *unbounded above*, [see IV, §11.2]

A.1 is equivalent to the assumption that X is bounded below, that is

$$\exists \mathbf{a} \in \mathbb{R}^n, \ \forall \mathbf{x} \in X : \mathbf{x} \geqslant \mathbf{a}. \qquad (14.3.4)$$

Clearly A.1 implies (14.3.4). If (14.3.4) holds with $\mathbf{a} \leqslant 0$, A.1 will hold after the translation: $\hat{X} = X - \mathbf{a}$. Then the preference and the vector of resources should be translated by $\hat{P}(\hat{\mathbf{x}}) = P(\hat{\mathbf{x}} + \mathbf{a}) - \mathbf{a}$ and $\hat{\mathbf{w}} = \mathbf{w} - \mathbf{a}$.

Note that it is not assumed that $0 \in X$, as in Chapter 13.

Given a set X satisfying A.1–A.4, the following assumptions could be made on the preference $P : X \to X$.

Continuity [see V, §5.2.3]. If $\mathbf{x}, \mathbf{y} \in X$ and $\mathbf{y} \in P(x)$, then open neighbourhoods $U_\mathbf{x}$ of $\mathbf{x}$ and $U_\mathbf{y}$ of $\mathbf{y}$ exist, such that

$$(\mathbf{y}' \in U_y \quad \text{and} \quad \mathbf{x}' \in U_x) \Rightarrow \mathbf{y}' \in P(\mathbf{x}').$$

Hence, loosely speaking, if $\mathbf{y}$ is better than $\mathbf{x}$ and $\mathbf{y}'$ and $\mathbf{x}'$ differ only slightly from $\mathbf{y}$ and $\mathbf{x}$ respectively, then $\mathbf{y}'$ is better than $\mathbf{x}'$. Continuity means that P has an *open graph*:

$$\text{Gr } P = \{\mathbf{y}, \mathbf{x} \mid \mathbf{y} \in P(\mathbf{x})\}$$

is an open set in $X \times X$, since for each $\mathbf{x}, \mathbf{y} \in \text{Gr } P$, $U_\mathbf{x} \times U_\mathbf{y}$ is an open set in Gr P, and therefore Gr P is open [see IV, §11.2]. Conversely if U_{yx} is an open neighbourhood in the open set Gr P then neighbourhoods $U_\mathbf{x}$ and $U_\mathbf{y}$ exist, that satisfy the above condition. Note that U_x, U_y, U_{xy} are open *relative to X or $X \times X$* [see V, Chapter 4].

Convexity. $\forall \mathbf{x} \in X : P(\mathbf{x})$ is a convex set [see IV, §15.2 and V, Chapter 4]

If two commodity bundles $\mathbf{y}$ and $\mathbf{z}$ are better than $\mathbf{x}$, then each convex combination $\mathbf{v} = \alpha \mathbf{y} + (1 - \alpha)\mathbf{z}$, for $\alpha \in [0, 1]$ is also better than $\mathbf{x}$. A somewhat stronger version is *strict convexity*: the set $P(\mathbf{x})$ is strictly convex, that is, if $\mathbf{y}, \mathbf{z} \in \text{Cl } P(\mathbf{x})$ then $\mathbf{v} \in \text{Int} P(\mathbf{x})$ if $\mathbf{v} = \alpha \mathbf{x} + (1 - \alpha)\mathbf{z}$ and $\alpha \in (0, 1)$ (Figure 14.3). Now

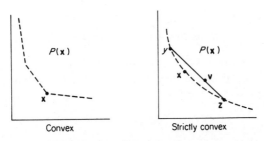

Figure 14.3: Convex preferences

the boundary of $P(\mathbf{x})$ cannot contain linear varieties. Under convexity consumers do not prefer extremes over averages. For example, a consumer who would rather drink either 6 bottles of beer or 2 bottles of wine than 3 bottles of beer and 1 bottle of wine does not have convex preferences.

Monotonicity. Three types can be distinguished:

(i) *strong monotonicity*: $\mathbf{y} \geqslant \mathbf{x}$ and $\mathbf{y} \neq \mathbf{x} \Rightarrow \mathbf{y} \in P(\mathbf{x})$; hence the bundle $\mathbf{y}$ should be strictly greater than $\mathbf{x}$ in at least one component.
(ii) *Monotonicity*: $\mathbf{y} > \mathbf{x} \Rightarrow \mathbf{y} \in P(\mathbf{x})$; a bundle which contains more of all commodities is better than the original bundle.
(iii) *weak monotonicity*: $\mathbf{y} \geqslant \mathbf{x} \Rightarrow \mathbf{x} \notin P(\mathbf{y})$; a bundle $\mathbf{y}$ which is not smaller in any component than a bundle $\mathbf{x}$, is not worse. This holds true particularly if a consumer could dispose freely of any surplus of commodities and is therefore also called *free disposal*.

Local non-satiation.

$$\forall \mathbf{x} \in X, \forall \eta > 0, \exists \mathbf{y} \in X : \mathbf{y} \in P(\mathbf{x}) \text{ and } |\mathbf{y} - \mathbf{x}| < \eta$$

hence for each $\mathbf{x} \in X$ a better bundle can be found which is arbitrarily close to $\mathbf{x}$ (monotonicity implies local non-satiation).

Non-satiation.

$$\forall \mathbf{x} \in X, \exists \mathbf{y} \in X : \mathbf{y} \in P(\mathbf{x}).$$

It is only required that a better bundle can be found but not necessarily close to $\mathbf{x}$.

Example. $X = \mathbb{R}^n_+$, $\mathbf{a} \in \mathbb{R}^n_+$. $P(\mathbf{x}) = \{\mathbf{y} \in X \,|\, \mathbf{y} + \mathbf{a} > \mathbf{x}\}$ satisfies non-satiation, but not local non-satiation.

The following theorem (for a proof, see for example Eilenberg, 1941; Debreu, 1954; gives sufficient conditions for a preference to be representable by a utility function.

THEOREM 14.3.3. *If P is asymmetric, negatively transitive and continuous, then it can be represented by a continuous utility function* [see IV, §5.3].

If a preference is representable by a utility function $u(\mathbf{x})$, strong monotonicity implies that $u(\mathbf{x})$ is increasing in all components and (strict) convexity implies that $u(\mathbf{x})$ is (strictly) quasi-concave [see §13.2]. Since under representability

$$R(\mathbf{x}) = \{\mathbf{y} \in X \,|\, u(\mathbf{y}) \geqslant u(\mathbf{x})\},$$

the following result is easily proved with the help of Theorem 14.3.3.

THEOREM 14.3.4. *If P is asymmetric, negatively transitive, continuous and locally non-satiated, then*

$$R(\mathbf{x}) = \overline{P(\mathbf{x})}$$

where $\overline{P(\mathbf{x})}$ denotes the closure of $P(\mathbf{x})$ [see IV, §11.2].

Theorem 14.3.4 ensures that the indifference curves satisfy

$$I(\mathbf{x}) = \partial R(\mathbf{x}) = \partial P(\mathbf{x})$$

where ∂ denotes the boundary [see IV, Definition 11.2.5], and therefore, by local non-satiation, the indifference curves are thin, that is, there exists no point $\mathbf{x}$, such that a sufficiently small change in *all* directions gives a bundle that is equivalent to $\mathbf{x}$.

14.3.3. Existence of maximal elements

If a preference is negatively transitive, asymmetric and continuous, it can, by Theorem 14.3.3, be represented by a continuous utility function. Since a continuous function always attains its maximum on a compact set [see V, §5.3], a compact set always has a maximal element given such a preference. This implies that under the above assumptions demand is defined for all positive prices. Theorem 14.3.6 below shows that a set has a maximal element also under much weaker assumptions on the preference, provided that it is not only compact, but also convex. For example, demand is also defined if preferences are not transitive, which excludes the existence of a utility function. Note that part (iii) of Theorem 14.3.6 implies that under local non-satiation demand exhausts total wealth. Theorem 14.3.6 is easily proved with the help of Brouwer's fixed point theorem [see V, §5.1] and a selection theorem due to Michael (1956). If F is a correspondence of a set X into a set Y, then a (continuous) function f of X into Y is a (continuous) selection of F, if $f(\mathbf{x}) \in F(\mathbf{x})$ for all $\mathbf{x} \in X$.

THEOREM 14.3.5. *(Michael). If $F : X \rightarrow Y$ is a correspondence, $X \subset \mathbb{R}^n$, $Y \subset \mathbb{R}^m$ and F is lower semi-continuous, and convex valued and nowhere empty, then F has a continuous selection.*

THEOREM 14.3.6. *(Fan, 1961). Given a preference correspondence $P : X \rightarrow X$ and (a budget set) $B \subset X \subset \mathbb{R}^n$; if*
(i) B is compact, convex,
(ii) P is irreflexive, convex and has an open graph,
then a maximal element $\hat{\mathbf{x}} \in B$ exists.
If also
(iii) P is locally non-satiated, then

$$\hat{\mathbf{x}} \in \partial B.$$

Proof. By Definition 14.2.3 a maximal element $\mathbf{x} \in B$ is such that $P(\mathbf{x}) \cap B = \emptyset$. Suppose that no maximal element exists, then $F(\mathbf{x}) = P(\mathbf{x}) \cap B \neq \emptyset$, for all $\mathbf{x} \in B$. Since $P(\mathbf{x})$ and $B(\mathbf{x})$ are convex sets, $F(\mathbf{x})$ is convex. Since P has an open graph, the correspondence $F : B \to B$ has an open graph (relative to B), which implies that it is lower semi-continuous [App. Prop. 1(i)]. By Theorem 14.3.5, F has a continuous selection, that is a continuous function $f : B \to B$ exists such that $f(\mathbf{x}) \in F(\mathbf{x})$. Since B is convex, compact, f has a fixed point $\bar{\mathbf{x}} = f(\bar{\mathbf{x}})$ by Brouwer's fixed point theorem [see V, §5.1], hence $\bar{\mathbf{x}} \in F(\bar{\mathbf{x}}) = P(\bar{\mathbf{x}}) \cap B$, hence $\bar{\mathbf{x}} \in P(\bar{\mathbf{x}})$, but that contradicts irreflexivity. So a point $\hat{\mathbf{x}} \in B$ must exist, such that $P(\hat{\mathbf{x}}) \cap B = \emptyset$. Now let (iii) hold and suppose $\hat{\mathbf{x}} \in \text{Int } B$ (the interior of B [see IV, §11.2]) hence for some $\varepsilon > 0$, $U_x = \{\mathbf{y} \in X \,||\, \hat{\mathbf{x}} - \mathbf{y}| < \varepsilon\} \subset B$. By local non-satiation $\mathbf{y} \in U_x$ exists such that $\mathbf{y} \in P(\hat{\mathbf{x}}) \cap U_x \subset P(\hat{\mathbf{x}}) \cap B \neq \emptyset$. This is a contradiction. $\square$

Examples.
(i) Let $X = \mathbb{R}^2_+$, $P(\mathbf{x}) = \{\mathbf{y} \in X \,|\, \mathbf{y} > \mathbf{x}\}$ and $B = \{\mathbf{x} \in X \,||\,\|\mathbf{x}\| < 1\}$ [see I, §10.1], then the set of maximal elements is $\{\mathbf{x} \in X \,||\,\|\mathbf{x}\| = 1\}$. This preference is not complete.
(ii) Let $B = X = A_1 \cup A_2 \cup A_3$, where A_i are disjoint convex sets in $\mathbb{R}^2$, and $\mathbf{x} \in A_i \Rightarrow P(\mathbf{x}) = A_{i+1}$, with $i = 1, 2, 3$ and $i + 1 = 1$, if $i = 3$. Then B has no maximal element. All assumptions of Theorem 14.3.6 are satisfied, except convexity of X.

The above theorem implies that it is possible to construct a demand curve without requiring the assumption of transitive preferences. When local non-satiation holds, the utility-maximizing bundle will be on the boundary of the budget set.

14.4. EXISTENCE OF EQUILIBRIUM IN AN EXCHANGE ECONOMY

14.4.1. The budget correspondence

We return to the exchange economy $\mathscr{E} = \{H, X^h, P^h, \mathbf{w}^h\}$ as defined in §14.2.3. Each consumer $h \in H$ has a budget correspondence:

DEFINITION 14.4.1. The correspondence $B^h : \mathbb{R}^n_+ \to X^h$, with

$$B^h(\mathbf{p}) = \{\mathbf{x} \in X^h \,|\, \mathbf{p} \cdot \mathbf{x} \leqslant \mathbf{p} \cdot \mathbf{w}^h\}$$

is called h's *budget correspondence.* For given $\mathbf{p}$ $B^h(\mathbf{p})$ is h's budget set.

$B^h(\mathbf{p})$ is the set of all commodity bundles from h's consumption set, that h can afford at price, $\mathbf{p}$, given his resources $\mathbf{w}^h$.

Clearly $B^h(\mathbf{p})$ is *homogeneous of degree zero,* that is

$$B^h(\mathbf{p}) = B^h(\lambda \mathbf{p})$$

for all $\mathbf{p}$ and $\lambda > 0$. A maximal element $\mathbf{x}^h$ from the budget set should satisfy [see

Definition 14.2.3]:

$$P^h(\mathbf{x}^h) \cap B^h(\mathbf{p}) = \varnothing$$

and this is the first condition for an equilibrium [see Definition 14.2.5]. The correspondence $G:\mathbb{R}^n_+$ into $\mathbb{R}^n$, defined by

$$G^h(\mathbf{p}) = \{\mathbf{x} \in X^h \mid P^h(\mathbf{x}) \cap B^h(\mathbf{p}) = \varnothing\}$$

is the *demand correspondence* of consumer h. The demand correspondence is homogeneous of degree zero because the budget correspondence has this property. If the demand correspondence is single-valued it is the Marshallian demand function as defined in §13.3. Note that in the present model demand is written as a function of $\mathbf{p}$ only, income being equal to $\mathbf{p} \cdot \mathbf{w}^h$. Single-valuedness is guaranteed if P^h is representable by a strictly quasi-concave utility function, as assumed in §13.2. Under the assumptions of Theorem 14.3.6 on the preferences, $G^h(\mathbf{p}) \neq \varnothing$, if $\mathbf{p} > 0$, since then $B^h(\mathbf{p})$ is compact, and $\mathbf{p} \cdot \mathbf{x}^h = \mathbf{p} \cdot \mathbf{w}^h$ for $\mathbf{x}^h \in G^h(\mathbf{p})$. This implies

$$\forall h \in H : \mathbf{x}^h \in G^h(\mathbf{p}) \Rightarrow \mathbf{p} \cdot \sum \mathbf{z}^h = \mathbf{p} \cdot \sum (\mathbf{x}^h - \mathbf{w}^h) = 0.$$

This equality is called *Walras' law*, and asserts that the value of total excess demand is always zero. It holds irrespective of whether one has a feasible allocation or not. Note that under strong monotonicity the budget set also has a maximal element if some price is zero, and that Walras' law then also holds.

THEOREM 14.4.1. *If X^h is closed and convex and $\mathbf{w}^h \in X^h$, then the budget correspondence has a closed graph, is convex valued and nowhere empty.*

Proof. We must prove that $\mathrm{Gr}\, B^h = \{\mathbf{x}, \mathbf{p} \mid \mathbf{x} \in B^h(\mathbf{p})\}$ is a closed set. Let $(\mathbf{x}_t, \mathbf{p}_t)$ be a sequence such that $\mathbf{x}_t \to \mathbf{x}$, $\mathbf{p}_t \to \mathbf{p}$ and $(\mathbf{x}_t, \mathbf{p}_t) \in \mathrm{Gr}\, B^h$, for all t. Then for all $t : \mathbf{p}_t \cdot \mathbf{x}_t \leqslant \mathbf{p}_t \cdot \mathbf{w}^h$, hence also $\mathbf{p} \cdot \mathbf{x} \leqslant \mathbf{p} \cdot \mathbf{w}^h$ and since X^h is closed, $\mathbf{x} \in X^h$: therefore $(\mathbf{x}, \mathbf{p}) \in \mathrm{Gr}\, B^h$. Since both X^h and the half space $\{\mathbf{x} \in \mathbb{R}^n \mid \mathbf{p} \cdot \mathbf{x} \leqslant \mathbf{p} \cdot \mathbf{w}\}$ are convex, $B(\mathbf{p})$ is convex, for all $p . B^h(\mathbf{p}) \neq \varnothing$, since $\mathbf{w}^h \in B^h(\mathbf{p})$.

DEFINITION 14.4.2. The set $S = \{\mathbf{p} \in \mathbb{R}^n_+ \mid \Sigma p_i = 1\}$ is called the *price simplex* [see V, §5.3].

Obviously S is closed and compact. Owing to homogeneity of degree zero, an equilibrium price vector may without loss of generality be chosen in the price simplex. Given any $\mathbf{p} > 0$, $\mathbf{p} \notin S$, we have for $\lambda = 1/\Sigma p_i : \lambda \mathbf{p} \in S$ and $\mathbf{B}^h(\mathbf{p}) = B^h(\lambda \mathbf{p})$. Thus prices have been 'normalized'. Another way to normalize prices would be to choose one commodity, e.g. the first, as a 'numéraire' and choose as a set of normalized prices $\{\mathbf{p} \in \mathbb{R}^n_+ \mid p_1 = 1\}$. This set is, however, not compact and it is required that $p_1 > 0$, which excludes the possibility that good 1 is a free good. Under monotonicity not all goods can be free goods simultaneously.

14.4.2. Pareto optimum and equilibrium

Consider first a simple economy in $\mathbb{R}^2$ with two consumers, where $X^1 = X^2 = \mathbb{R}^2_+$, $w^1, w^2 > 0$ and where preferences are represented by continuous *quasiconcave* and *increasing* utility functions $u^h : \mathbb{R}^2_+ \to \mathbb{R}$ [see V, §4.3.1]. Hence

$$P^h(\mathbf{x}) = \{\mathbf{y} \in X^h \mid u^h(\mathbf{y}) > u^h(\mathbf{x})\}$$

is asymmetric and negatively transitive [see §14.3.1], convex [see IV, §15.2.6], continuous [see IV, §5.3] and strongly monotonous [see §14.3.2]. In the Edgeworth box in Figure 14.4 some indifference curves $I^h(\mathbf{x})$ have been drawn of both consumers 1 and 2, with $O^2 = \mathbf{w}^1 + \mathbf{w}^2$ being the origin of consumer 2 (compare Figure 14.1). The *Pareto optima* are represented by all those points where two indifference curves are tangent: in such a point both consumers cannot be made better-off simultaneously. The locus of all Pareto optima is the curve connecting O^1 and O^2. An equilibrium allocation is represented by a point where a line through $\mathbf{w}$ separates two sets of preferred points as the point $\mathbf{e}$ in Figure 14.4. The equilibrium price is the normal of the line through $\mathbf{w}$ and $\mathbf{e}$.

The points $\mathbf{a}$ and $\mathbf{b}$ are equivalent to the resource vector for consumer 1 and 2 respectively. The Pareto optima between $\mathbf{a}$ and $\mathbf{b}$ may be expected to be possible final results from trading, provided that (i) no consumer will accept a trade which makes him worse-off, and (ii) consumers will continue to trade as long as they can both benefit from it. Therefore Edgeworth called the curve $\mathbf{a}, \mathbf{b}$ the *contract curve*. The contract curve has been generalized for exchange economies with n goods and m consumers by the concept of the *core* of the economy (e.g. Hildenbrand, 1982). An equilibrium allocation is always in the core and an interesting result that has been obtained is that the core shrinks, if the number of consumers increases and coincides with the set of Walras equilibrium allocations, if the number of consumers becomes infinite. Figure 14.5 depicts a situation with different equilibria: $\mathbf{c}$ is an equilibrium allocation if the price is the normal of the line through $\mathbf{w}$ and $\mathbf{c}$, whereas if the price vector is perpendicular to the line through $\mathbf{w}$ and $\mathbf{a}$, all convex combinations of $\mathbf{a}$ and $\mathbf{b}$ are equilibrium allocations. The latter multiplicity is due to the fact that both indifference curves have tangent

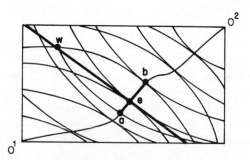

Figure 14.4: Pareto optima

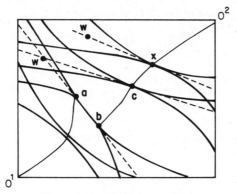

Figure 14.5: Multiple equilibria

flat parts, P^h not being *strictly* convex. The Pareto optima are the points on the curve connecting O^1 and O^2.

In the examples of Figures 14.4 and 14.5 the following properties also hold:

(1) each equilibrium allocation is a Pareto optimum;
(2) each Pareto optimum could be an equilibrium: if the resource vector is on the line separating two sets of preferred points. Consequently each Pareto optimum could be made an equilibrium allocation by redistributing the resources $(\mathbf{w}^1, \mathbf{w}^2)$ among both consumers. Thus in Figure 14.5, $\bar{\mathbf{x}}$ is an equilibrium allocation given the new resource vector $\bar{\mathbf{w}}$.

These two properties, known as the fundamental *welfare theorems* of general equilibrium theory, can be generalized. As Theorem 14.4.2 and 14.4.3 below show, both hold in an exchange economy, under suitable assumptions.

THEOREM 14.4.2. *If in the exchange economy, $\mathscr{E}$, for each $h \in H$:*
(A) X^h is (1) semi-positive, (2) closed, (3) convex and (4) unbounded above,
(B) P^h is (1) asymmetric, (2) negatively transitive and (3) locally not satiated,
then each equilibrium allocation is a Pareto optimum.

Proof. Let $(\mathbf{x}^H, \mathbf{p})$ be an equilibrium. Suppose $\mathbf{x}^H$ is not a Pareto optimum, hence a feasible allocation $\mathbf{y}^H$ exists, such that $\forall h \in H : \mathbf{x}^h \notin P^h(\mathbf{y}^h)$ and $\exists k \in H : \mathbf{y}^k \in P^k(\mathbf{y}^k)$. Since, by the definition of an equilibrium, $P^k(\mathbf{x}^k) \cap B^k(\mathbf{p}) = \varnothing$,

$$\mathbf{p} \cdot \mathbf{y}^k > \mathbf{p} \cdot \mathbf{w}^k.$$

Since $\Sigma \mathbf{p}^h \cdot \mathbf{y}^h = \Sigma \mathbf{p}^h \cdot \mathbf{w}^h$, there must exist $l \in H$, $l \neq k$, such that

$$\mathbf{p} \cdot \mathbf{y}^l < \mathbf{p} \cdot \mathbf{w}^l \qquad \text{(a)}$$

$$\mathbf{x}^l \notin P^l(\mathbf{y}^l). \qquad \text{(b)}$$

By local non-satiation and (b) there exists z^l such that

$$z^l \in P^l(y^l) \tag{c}$$

$$\mathbf{p} \cdot \mathbf{z}^l < \mathbf{p} \cdot \mathbf{w}^l. \tag{d}$$

Since $P^l(\mathbf{x}^l) \cap B^l(\mathbf{p}) = \varnothing$, (d) implies

$$z^l \notin P^l(\mathbf{x}^l). \tag{e}$$

By negative transitivity, (b) and (e) imply $z^l \notin P^l(y^l)$, which contradicts (c) under asymmetry. Hence x^H must be a Pareto optimum.   □

THEOREM 14.4.3. *If in the exchange economy, $\mathscr{E}$, for each $h \in H$:*
(A) X^h *satisfies (A.1)–(A.4) of Theorem 14.4.2,*
(B) P^h *is (1) irreflexive, (2) convex, (3) monotonous, and (4) continuous, and if $\mathbf{x}^H$ is a Pareto optimum such that*
(C) $\forall h \in H : \mathbf{x}^h \in \mathrm{Int}\, X^h$,
then an m-tuple of resources $\bar{\mathbf{w}}^H \in (\mathbb{R}^n)^m$, satisfying $\Sigma \bar{\mathbf{w}}^h = \Sigma \mathbf{w}^h$ and a price $\mathbf{p} \in S$ exist,
such that $(\mathbf{x}^H, \mathbf{p})$ is an equilibrium in the economy $\mathscr{E} = \{H, X^h, P^h, \bar{\mathbf{w}}^h\}$.

We only sketch the proof, since a complete proof is given in Debreu (1959). It can be shown that there exist a price vector $\mathbf{p}$ and numbers α^h, with $\sum \alpha^h = \mathbf{p} \cdot \sum \mathbf{w}^h$, such that, for all h, $\mathbf{x}^h$ is a maximal element of

$$\{\mathbf{z} \in X^h | \mathbf{p} \cdot \mathbf{z} \leqslant \alpha^h\}$$

Now $\bar{\mathbf{w}}^H$ can be found, such that $\mathbf{p} \cdot \bar{\mathbf{w}}^h = \alpha^h$.

This theorem asserts that any Pareto optimal allocation can be attained as a Walrasian equilibrium, after a redistribution of resources. Hence before the equilibrium is established, a new initial distribution is realized by means of transfers of resources from consumers to other consumers. These transfers may be considered as *lump sum* taxes and subventions. They are lump sum, because they do not depend on optimizing behaviour of consumers. Note, however, that some of the required transfers might be impossible in practice, because a resource could be inseparable from the agent, as in the case of labour.

14.4.3. Existence

The theorem below shows that existence of an equilibrium in an exchange economy is ensured under rather weak assumptions on preferences, so that, for example, transitivity is not required. Early existence proofs, particularly those of Arrow and Debreu (1954) and McKenzie (1959) required 'rational' preferences (asymmetry and negative transitivity) but in papers by Gale and Mas-Collell (1975) and Shafer and Sonnenschein (1975) it was shown that weaker assumptions are sufficient. The proof in this section follows a reasoning introduced by Gale and Mas-Colell, using Michael's selection theorem [Theorem 14.3.5].

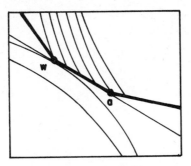

Figure 14.6: No equilibrium

THEOREM 14.4.4. *In the exchange economy $\mathscr{E}$ an equilibrium $(\mathbf{x}^H, \mathbf{p})$ exists if for all $h \in H$:*

(A) $\mathbf{x}^h$ *is* (1) *semi-positive*, (2) *closed*, (3) *convex;* (4) *unbounded above*,
(B) P^h *is* (1) *irreflexive*, (2) *strongly monotone and* (3) *convex, and* (4) *has an open, graph.*
(C) $\mathbf{w}^h \in \text{Int } X^h$.

Assumptions (B) guarantee that the budget sets (for $\mathbf{p} > \mathbf{0}$) have maximal elements, provided that they are not empty [see Theorem 14.3.6]. By (A1) and (C), $\mathbf{w}^h > \mathbf{0}$, hence $\sum \mathbf{w}^h > \mathbf{0}$. If for some h, $\mathbf{w}^h \in X^h$, then his budget set would be empty for some price vector. It is, however, not sufficient to assume that $\mathbf{w}^h$ is in the consumption set, as is shown in the example of Figure 14.6 in an Edgeworth box. $X^2 = \mathbb{R}_+^2$ and X^1 is as indicated in the figure, containing $\mathbf{w}^1$ on its boundary. The indifference curves drawn allow for only one possible equilibrium price, represented by the drawn budget line. However, at this price consumer 1 will choose the point $\mathbf{a}$ and consumer 2 will choose $\mathbf{w}$. Therefore in this example no equilibrium exists.

The proof of Theorem 14.4.4 is in three steps: first we restrict the consumption sets to compact sets, and show that this does not affect the equilibria; this is necessary because we shall appply a fixed point theorem. Secondly we shall construct an *upper-semi-continuous correspondence*, which has a fixed point. Finally it is shown that the fixed point is an equilibrium.

Proof of Theorem 14.4.4.

Step 1: Let $\mathbf{w} = \Sigma \mathbf{w}^h > \mathbf{0}$ and define

$$\hat{X}^h = X^h \cap \{\mathbf{x} \in \mathbb{R}^n \,|\, \mathbf{x} \leqslant 2\mathbf{w}\}$$

$\hat{X}^h$ is compact, convex. Define $\hat{P}^h: \hat{X}^h \to \hat{X}^h$ by (see Figure 14.7)

$$\hat{P}(\mathbf{x}^h) = P(\mathbf{x}^h) \cap \hat{X}^h$$

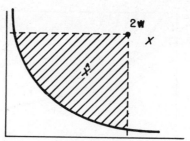

Figure 14.7: Step 1 of theorem 14.4.4

For all $\mathbf{x} < 2\mathbf{w}$, $P^h(\mathbf{x}) \neq \varnothing$ and assumptions (B) hold for $\hat{P}^h$, with the provision that (B3) now requires

$$\mathbf{x} \leqslant \mathbf{y} < 2\mathbf{w} \Rightarrow \mathbf{y} \in \hat{P}^h(\mathbf{x}).$$

By (B4) the graph of $\hat{P}^h$ is open relative to $\hat{X}^h$. It will be proved that an equilibrium exists in

$$\mathscr{E} = \{H, \hat{X}^h, \mathbf{w}^h, \hat{P}^h\}$$

and that is sufficient given

LEMMA 14.4.1. $(\mathbf{x}^H, \mathbf{p})$ *is an equilibrium in* $\mathscr{E}$ *if and only if it is an equilibrium in* $\hat{\mathscr{E}}$, *under the assumptions of Theorem* 14.4.4.

Proof. Sufficiency: $(\mathbf{x}^H, \mathbf{p})$ is an equilibrium in $\mathscr{E}$. Since $\Sigma \mathbf{x}^h = \mathbf{w}$ and $\forall h : \mathbf{x}^h > \mathbf{0}$, $\mathbf{x}^h < 2\mathbf{w}$, hence $\mathbf{x}^h \in X^h$. Since $\forall h : P^h(\mathbf{x}^h) \cap B^h(\mathbf{p}) = \varnothing$, *a fortiori* $\hat{P}^h(\mathbf{x}^h) \cap \hat{B}^h(\mathbf{p}) = \varnothing$, hence $(\mathbf{x}^H, \mathbf{p})$ is an equilibrium in $\hat{\mathscr{E}}$.

Necessity: $(\mathbf{x}^H, \mathbf{p})$ is an equilibrium in $\hat{\mathscr{E}}$, hence $\Sigma \mathbf{x}^h = \mathbf{w}$ and $\mathbf{x}^h \in X^h$. If $(\mathbf{x}^H, \mathbf{p})$ would not be an equilibrium in $\mathscr{E}$, then for some $h \in H$, $\bar{\mathbf{x}}$ would exist with

$$\bar{\mathbf{x}} \in P^h(\mathbf{x}^h) \cap B^h(\mathbf{p}) \neq \varnothing \text{ and } \hat{P}^h(\mathbf{x}^h) \cap \hat{B}^h(\mathbf{p}) = \varnothing.$$

which would imply $\bar{\mathbf{x}} \not< 2\mathbf{w}$. By (B2), (B3) and (B4),

$$\mathbf{x}(\lambda) = \lambda \mathbf{x}^h + (1 - \lambda)\bar{\mathbf{x}} \in P^h(\mathbf{x}^h) \cap B^h(\mathbf{p}) \text{ for } 0 < \lambda < 1.$$

Since $\mathbf{x}^h < 2\mathbf{w}$, for sufficiently large $\lambda < 1 : \mathbf{x}(\lambda) < 2\mathbf{w}$, hence $\mathbf{x}(\lambda) \in \hat{P}^h(\mathbf{x}^h) \cap \hat{B}^h(\mathbf{p})$ and that is a contradiction. □

Step 2. The correspondence $F^0 : \hat{X}^H \to S$, where $\hat{X}^H = \Pi_H X^h$, is defined by

$$F^0(\mathbf{x}^H) = \{\mathbf{p} \in S \mid \mathbf{p} \cdot \Sigma(\mathbf{x}^h - \mathbf{w}^h) > 0\}.$$

F^0 has an *open graph* (if $\mathbf{p} \cdot \Sigma(\mathbf{x}^h - \mathbf{w}^h) > 0$ in $(\mathbf{x}^H, \mathbf{p}) \in \hat{X}^H \times S$, then the inequality is maintained in a neighbourhood of this point) and is convex valued. Therefore the

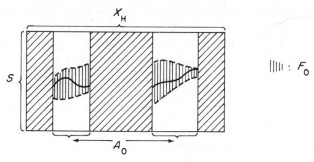

Figure 14.8: Step 2 of theorem 14.4.4

set

$$A^0 = \{\mathbf{x}^H \in \hat{X}^H | F^0(\mathbf{x}^H) \neq \emptyset\} \subseteq \hat{X}^H$$

is *open* relative to $\hat{X}^H$ [see V, Chapter 4]. The restriction of F^0 to A^0, i.e. $F^0 : A^0 \to S$, also has an open graph, hence [App. Prop. 1(ii)] it is lower semi-continuous. By Michael's theorem, F^0 has a continuous selection in A^0, $f^0 : A^0 \to S$, with $f^0(\mathbf{x}^H) \in F^0(\mathbf{x}^H)$. Define a correspondence $G^0 : \hat{X}^H \to S$, by

$$G^0(\mathbf{x}^H) = \begin{cases} f^0(\mathbf{x}^H) & \text{if } \mathbf{x}^H \in A^0 \\ S & \text{if } \mathbf{x}^H \notin A^0. \end{cases}$$

G^0 has a *closed graph* is convex valued and nowhere empty. Since S is compact, this implies [App. Prop. 1(i)] that G^0 is upper semi-continuous. Figure 14.8 gives a schematic representation of G^0.

Define for each $h \in H$ a correspondence $F^h : \hat{X}^h \times S \to \hat{X}^h$

$$F^h(\mathbf{x}^h, \mathbf{p}) = \hat{P}^h(\mathbf{x}^h) \cap \text{Int } \hat{B}^h(\mathbf{p})$$

(where Int $\hat{B}^h(\mathbf{p}) = \{\mathbf{x} \in \hat{X}^h | \mathbf{p} \cdot \mathbf{x} < \mathbf{p} \cdot \mathbf{w}^h\}$). Assumption (C) ensures that Int $\hat{B}^h(\mathbf{p})$ is nowhere empty. F^h has an open graph and is convex valued, since both $\hat{P}^h$ and Int B^h have these properties, hence

$$A^h = \{\mathbf{x}^h, \mathbf{p} | F^h(\mathbf{x}^h, \mathbf{p}) \neq \emptyset\} \subseteq \hat{X}^h \times S$$

is an open set.

The restriction of F^h to A^h is lower semi-continuous and has a continuous selection f^h, with $f^h(\mathbf{x}^h, \mathbf{p}) \in F^h(\mathbf{x}^h, \mathbf{p})$ in A^0. Define $G^h : \hat{X}^h \times : S \to \hat{X}^h$, by

$$G^h(\mathbf{x}^h, \mathbf{p}) = \begin{cases} f^h(\mathbf{x}^h, \mathbf{p}) & \text{if } (\mathbf{x}^h, \mathbf{p}) \in A^h \\ \hat{B}^h(\mathbf{p}) & \text{if } (\mathbf{x}^h, \mathbf{p}) \notin A^h \end{cases}$$

and G^h, is upper semi-continuous since its graph is closed and it is convex valued. The correspondence $G : \hat{X}^H \times S \to \hat{X}^H \times S$ is defined by

$$G(\mathbf{x}^H, \mathbf{p}) = (G^0(\mathbf{x}^H, \mathbf{p}), G^1(\mathbf{x}^1, \mathbf{p}), \dots, G^m(\mathbf{x}^m, \mathbf{p}))$$

and being a cartesian product of upper semi-continuous correspondences it is upper semi-continuous [App. Prop. 2(iii)]. G is convex valued and nowhere empty, whereas $\hat{X}^H \times S$ is compact, hence by Kakutani's fixed point theorem [see V, §5.6] a fixed point $(\hat{\mathbf{x}}^H, \hat{\mathbf{p}})$ with $(\hat{\mathbf{x}}^H, \hat{\mathbf{p}}) \in G(\hat{\mathbf{x}}^H, \hat{\mathbf{p}})$ exists.

Step 3. It remains to prove that $(\hat{\mathbf{x}}^H, \hat{\mathbf{p}})$ is an equilibrium in $\hat{\mathscr{E}}$, that is (i) $\hat{P}^h(\hat{\mathbf{x}}^h) \cap \hat{B}^h(\hat{\mathbf{p}}) \ne \varnothing$ and (ii) $\Sigma \hat{\mathbf{x}}^h = \Sigma \mathbf{w}^h$. Suppose (i) does not hold for some $h \in H$; since $\hat{P}^h(\hat{\mathbf{x}}^h)$ is an open set, this implies

$$F^h(\hat{\mathbf{x}}^h, \hat{\mathbf{p}}) = \hat{P}^h(\hat{\mathbf{x}}^h) \cap \operatorname{Int} \hat{B}^h(\hat{\mathbf{p}}) \ne \varnothing$$

which by definition means that $(\hat{\mathbf{x}}^h, \hat{\mathbf{p}}) \in A^h$ and therefore

$$\hat{\mathbf{x}}^h = f^h(\hat{\mathbf{x}}^h, \hat{\mathbf{p}}) \in G^h(\hat{\mathbf{x}}^h, \hat{\mathbf{p}}) \subset \hat{P}^h(\hat{\mathbf{x}}^h)$$

but by irreflexivity $\hat{\mathbf{x}}^h \notin \hat{P}^h(\hat{\mathbf{x}}^h)$, a contradiction. This proves (i). Suppose that for some commodity $i: \Sigma_H(\hat{x}_i^h - w_i^h) > 0$. If $\bar{\mathbf{p}} \in S$, such that $\bar{p}_i = 1$, $\bar{p}_j = 0$ if $j \ne i$, then $\bar{\mathbf{p}} \cdot \Sigma(\hat{\mathbf{x}}^h - \mathbf{w}^h) > 0$ hence $\bar{\mathbf{p}} \in F^0(\hat{\mathbf{x}}^H)$ and $\hat{\mathbf{x}}^H \in A^0$. This would imply $\hat{\mathbf{p}} = f^0(\hat{\mathbf{x}}^H)$ and $\hat{\mathbf{p}} \cdot \Sigma(\hat{\mathbf{x}}^h - \mathbf{w}^h) > 0$. But that contradicts that $\forall h: \hat{\mathbf{p}} \cdot (\hat{\mathbf{x}}^h - \mathbf{w}^h) \le 0$. Suppose finally that for some commodity $i: \Sigma_H(\hat{x}_i^h - w_i^h) < 0$. Since by strong monotonicity, $\forall h: \hat{\mathbf{p}} \cdot (\hat{\mathbf{x}}^h - \mathbf{w}^h) = 0$, this would imply $\hat{p}_i = 0$ [see Theorem 13.3.6]. However, by strong monotonicity

$$(\hat{x}_1^h, \hat{x}_2^h, \ldots, \hat{x}_i^h + \varepsilon, \ldots, \hat{x}_n^h) \in \hat{P}^h(\hat{\mathbf{x}}^h) \cap \hat{B}^h(\hat{\mathbf{p}}) \ne \varnothing$$

and that is a contradiction. This proves (ii).

14.5. AN ECONOMY WITH PRODUCTION

14.5.1. The economy

In the economy with production studied in this section, there are two types of agents, consumers and producers. As in the exchange economy, consumers sell part of their resources and buy consumption goods, and producers sell outputs to consumers and other firms, and buy inputs from consumers and other firms. The commodity space is $\mathbb{R}^n$ and among the commodities typically figure different types of labour. $H = \{1, 2, \ldots, m\}$ in the set of consumers, as in the exchange economy. Consumers have consumption sets X^h, preferences P^h and resources $\mathbf{w}^h$ [see §14.2.1], some of the resources being quantities of labour. Further they receive profits from firms in the way defined below. $F = \{1, 2, \ldots, l\}$ is the set of producers in the economy. The technology of firm $f \in F$ is given by a *production (possibility) set* $Y^f \subset \mathbb{R}^n$, specifying all input–output combinations that are available to the firm [compare §12.2]. In a production vector $\mathbf{y}^f = (y_1^f, y_2^f, \ldots, y_n^f) \in Y^f$, *positive* components $y_i^f > 0$ are *outputs* and *negative* components $y_j^f < 0$ are *inputs* of the production process (hence unlike the case considered in Chapter 12, there are multiple outputs possible). Given a price

$\mathbf{p} \in \mathbb{R}^n_+$ and $\mathbf{y}^f \in Y^f$, $\mathbf{p} \cdot \mathbf{y}^f = \Sigma p_i y_i^f$ is the profit obtained if the price $\mathbf{p}$ prevails and firm f chooses to produce $\mathbf{y}^f$. ($\mathbf{p} \cdot \mathbf{y}$ = value of outputs − value of inputs given our sign convention).

Without loss of generality we may choose $\mathbf{p} \in S$ [see Definition 14.4.2]. Each firm is assumed to behave competitively, that is maximize profits at *given prices* [see §12.4] and therefore chooses a profit-maximizing vector $\mathbf{y} \in Y^f$. The positive components of $\mathbf{y}^f$ are his supply and the negative components are his demand for inputs. We shall, however, call this vector $\mathbf{y}^f$ the supply vector.

DEFINITION 14.5.1. The function $\pi^f : S \to \mathbb{R}$, defined by [see I, §2.6.3]

$$\pi^f(\mathbf{p}) = \sup \{ \mathbf{p} \cdot \mathbf{y}^f \,|\, \mathbf{y}^f \in Y^f \} \equiv \sup \mathbf{p} \, Y^f$$

is firm f's *profit function* and

$$A^f(\mathbf{p}) = \{ \mathbf{y}^f \in Y^f \,|\, \mathbf{p} \cdot \mathbf{y}^f = \pi^f(\mathbf{p}) \}$$

is firm f's *supply correspondence*.

Clearly

$$A^f(\mathbf{p}) \neq \varnothing \Leftrightarrow \pi^f(\mathbf{p}) = \max \mathbf{p} \, Y^f$$

that is supply is defined if and only if the supremum is attained. Obviously the profit function is homogeneous of degree zero.

There are ml parameters $\theta^{hf} \in [0, 1]$, θ^{hf} being the share of consumer h in the profit of firm f, and they satisfy

$$\Sigma_H \theta^{hf} = 1 \quad \text{for} \quad f \in F.$$

Hence profits are completely distributed among consumers. If firm f's production vector is $\mathbf{y}^f \in Y$, then consumer h obtains the amount $\theta^{hf} \mathbf{p} \cdot \mathbf{y}^f$ from firm f. Under profit maximization by all firms, h's total income will be

$$\mathbf{p} \cdot \mathbf{w}^h + \sum_F \theta^{hf} \pi^f(\mathbf{p}).$$

The shares can be interpreted as the result of property rights of consumers on firms.

The economy with production denoted by $\mathscr{E}_P$ is completely characterized by the concepts introduced above, i.e.

$$\mathscr{E}_P = \{ H, F, X^h, P^h, \mathbf{w}^h, \theta^{hf}, Y^f \}.$$

By adding the production sets of all firms $f \in F$ we obtain the total production set Y:

$$Y = \Sigma \, Y^f = \{ \mathbf{y} \in \mathbb{R}^n \,|\, \mathbf{y} = \Sigma \mathbf{y}^f, \forall f : \mathbf{y}^f \in Y^f \}.$$

Total profits are defined by

$$\pi(\mathbf{p}) = \Sigma \pi^f(\mathbf{p}) \quad \mathbf{p} \in S$$

and total supply equals

$$A(\mathbf{p}) = \Sigma A^f(\mathbf{p}) \quad \mathbf{p} \in S.$$

The following theorem shows that profit maximization by each individual firm amounts to the same as profit maximization on the total production set, which implies that production decisions can be decentralized under perfect competition (for a proof see e.g. Debreu, 1959):

THEOREM 14.5.2.
(1) $\pi(\mathbf{p}) = \sup \mathbf{p} Y$
(2) $A(\mathbf{p}) = \{\mathbf{y} \in Y | \mathbf{p} \cdot \mathbf{y} = \sup \mathbf{p} Y\}.$

THEOREM 14.5.3. *Let* $T^f = \{\mathbf{p} \in S | \pi^f(\mathbf{p}) < \infty\}$. *Then* T^f *is a convex set and* $\pi^f : T^f \to \mathbb{R}$ *is a convex function which is continuous in the interior of T.*

Proof: If $\mathbf{p}, \bar{\mathbf{p}} \in T^f$, then for $0 \leqslant \lambda \leqslant 1$,

$$\sup(\lambda \mathbf{p} + (1 - \lambda)\bar{\mathbf{p}}) Y^f \leqslant \lambda \sup \mathbf{p} Y^f + (1 - \lambda) \sup \bar{\mathbf{p}} Y^f$$

hence $\lambda \mathbf{p} + (1 - \lambda)\bar{\mathbf{p}} \in T^f$ and T^f is convex. Since

$$\pi^f(\lambda \mathbf{p} + (1 - \lambda)\bar{\mathbf{p}}) \leqslant \lambda \pi^f(\mathbf{p}) + (1 - \lambda)\pi^f(\bar{\mathbf{p}}),$$

π is a convex function and a convex function is continuous on the interior of its domain [see IV, Theorem 15.2.11].

On the production sets Y^f the following *assumptions* will be made, for all $f \in F$:

(D1) $\mathbf{0} \in Y^f$ (possibility of inaction);
(D2) $\mathbf{y} \in Y$ and $\mathbf{y}' < \mathbf{y} \Rightarrow \mathbf{y}' \in Y^f$ (free disposal);
(D3) Y^f is closed;
(D4) Y^f is convex;

and on the total production set $Y = \Sigma Y^f$

(D5) $Y \cap (-Y) \subseteq \{\mathbf{0}\}$ (irreversibility).

(D1) ensures that $\pi^f(\mathbf{p}) \geqslant 0$, for all $\mathbf{p} \in S$. By (D5) it is excluded that both $\mathbf{y}$ and $-\mathbf{y}$ are in Y, so that it is not possible that one firm uses the output of another firm as an input, to produce exactly the input needed by the other firm, as in Figure 14.9. (D5) and (D1) imply

$$\mathbf{y} > \mathbf{0} \Rightarrow \mathbf{y} \notin Y$$

that is no output without input, excluding the case of Figure 14.10. (D4) excludes increasing returns to scale.

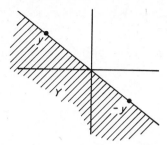

Figure 14.9: Reversibility of production

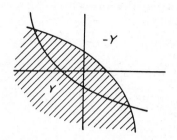

Figure 14.10: Output without input

These assumptions are equivalent to the ones given in §12.2 for the single output model: (D1) corresponds to (i), (D2) to (ii), (D3) and (D4) to (v), whereas (iv) is implied by (D1) and (D3) and (ii) is implied by (D5).

14.5.2. Allocations and equilibria

Feasible allocations, Pareto optima and equilibria in the economy with production are analogous to those concepts in the exchange economy [see Definitions 14.2.1, 14.2.4 and 14.2.5].

DEFINITION 14.5.4. An *allocation* in $\mathscr{E}_P$ is an $(m+l)n$-tuple $(\mathbf{x}^H, \mathbf{y}^F)$, where $\mathbf{x}^H = (\mathbf{x}^1, \mathbf{x}^2, \dots, \mathbf{x}^m)$ and $\mathbf{y}^F = \{\mathbf{y}^1, \mathbf{y}^2, \dots, \mathbf{y}^l\}$, such that $\forall h \in H : \mathbf{x}^h \in X^h$ and $\forall f \in F : \mathbf{y}^f \in Y^f$.

A *feasible allocation* is $(\mathbf{x}^H, \mathbf{y}^F)$ such that

$$\sum_H \mathbf{x}^h = \sum_F \mathbf{y}^f + \sum_H \mathbf{w}^h.$$

So in a feasible allocation the consumption of each commodity equals net production plus the initial holdings by consumers.

DEFINITION 14.5.5. A feasible allocation $(\mathbf{x}^H, \mathbf{y}^F)$ in $\mathscr{E}_P$ is a Pareto optimum if *no other* feasible allocation $(\hat{\mathbf{x}}^H, \hat{\mathbf{y}}^F)$ exists, such that

$$\forall h \in H : \mathbf{x}^h \notin P^h(\hat{\mathbf{x}}^h) \text{ and } \exists k \in H : \hat{\mathbf{x}}^h \in P^h(\mathbf{x}^h).$$

Note that the level of profit does not appear in this definition: the Pareto optimum only takes into account consumer's preferences.

If producers maximize profits, the total supply vector $\Sigma_F \mathbf{y}^f$ satisfies $\mathbf{p} \cdot \Sigma_F \mathbf{y}^f = \Sigma_F \pi^f(\mathbf{p})$, whereas the demand vector of a consumer, provided that he exhausts income, satisfies $\mathbf{p} \cdot (\mathbf{x}^h - \mathbf{w}^h) = \Sigma_F \theta^{hf} \pi^f(\mathbf{p})$, hence $\mathbf{p} \cdot \Sigma_H (\mathbf{x}^h - \mathbf{w}^h) = \Sigma_F \pi^f(\mathbf{p})$ and this implies that *Walras' law* [see §14.4.1] holds:

$$\mathbf{p} \cdot [\Sigma_H (\mathbf{x}^h - \mathbf{w}^h) - \Sigma_F \mathbf{y}^f] = 0,$$

asserting that the value of total excess demand equals 0, at a given price. In an equilibrium the excess demand vector is zero.

DEFINITION 14.5.6. A (Walrasian) equilibrium $(\mathbf{x}^H, \mathbf{y}^F, \mathbf{p})$ in $\mathscr{E}_p$ is an allocation $(\mathbf{x}^H, \mathbf{y}^F)$ and a price vector $\mathbf{p} \in S$, such that
  (i) $\forall h \in H : \mathbf{x}^h$ is a maximal element from
       $\{\mathbf{x} \in X^h | \mathbf{p} \cdot \mathbf{x}^h \leqslant \mathbf{p} \cdot \mathbf{w}^h + \Sigma_F \theta^{hf} \mathbf{p} \cdot \mathbf{y}^f\}$,
  (ii) $\forall f \in F : \mathbf{p} \cdot \mathbf{y}^f = \sup \mathbf{p} Y^f$,
  (iii) $\Sigma_F \mathbf{y}^f + \Sigma_H \mathbf{w}^h = \Sigma_H \mathbf{x}^h$.

Clearly condition (ii) of this definition implies that in the equilibrium $\mathbf{p} \cdot \mathbf{y}^f = \pi^f(\mathbf{p})$, and h's income is $\mathbf{p} \cdot \mathbf{w}^h + \Sigma_F \theta^{hf} \pi^f(\mathbf{p})$ and his budget correspondence [compare §14.4.1] is

$$B^h(\mathbf{p}) = \{\mathbf{x} \in X^h | \mathbf{p} \cdot \mathbf{x} \leqslant \mathbf{p} \cdot \mathbf{w}^h + \sum \theta^{hf} \pi^f(\mathbf{p})\},$$

hence condition (i) of Definition 14.5.6 is equivalent to

$$\forall h : \mathbf{x}^h \in B^h(\mathbf{p}) \text{ and } P^h(\mathbf{x}^h) \cap B^h(\mathbf{p}) = \varnothing.$$

In the economy $\mathscr{E}_p$ two *welfare theorems* hold, similar to the ones expressed by Theorems 14.4.2 and 14.4.3 for the exchange economy. To the assumptions on the consumption set and the preferences must be added assumptions on production. The first welfare theorem, asserting that each equilibrium allocation is a Pareto optimum, holds under assumptions (D1), (D2) and (D3). For the second, asserting that any Pareto optimum is an equilibrium after a redistribution of resources and profits, assumptions (D1)–(D5) are sufficient.

14.5.3. Interpretations of the commodity space

In section 14.2.1 we introduced the commodity space $\mathbb{R}^n$. It was only required that n commodities exist in the economy and consumption and production bundles were defined as vectors in the commodity space. Nothing has been said as yet on what commodities are. We have postponed a discussion on the interpretation of the commodity space, because it seems desirable that the reader should first become familiar with the way in which the concept is used. Actually different interpretations are possible.

A first, but not very satisfactory interpretation would be to assume that the models just deal with a single period (month, year), hence the commodities are bought and sold, produced and consumed, during this single period, without any explicit relation with future periods. This is not very satisfactory, because decisions on production and consumption in the real world also take account of (expected) future developments, so that consumption and production in one period are related to production and consumption in subsequent periods, and therefore an equilibrium should rather be defined as an intertemporal phenomenon.

An alternative interpretation therefore is to distinguish commodities with respect to *type*, *location* and *time*. Suppose that there are $\bar{s}$ types of commodities, with $s = 1, 2, \ldots, \bar{s}$, $\bar{u}$ locations, with $u = 1, 2, \ldots, \bar{u}$, and $\bar{t}$ time periods, with $t = 1, 2, \ldots, \bar{t}$, while $\bar{s}.\bar{u}.\bar{t} = n$. If $\mathbf{z} \in \mathbb{R}^n$, then the component z_{sut} of $\mathbf{z}$ is a quantity of the commodity of type s, available at location n in (i.e. at the end of) period t. The economy is assumed to end with period $\bar{t}$.

In this framework a consumption vector $\mathbf{x} \in X^h$ is a *consumption plan* of consumer h, drawn up at the beginning of period 1 (moment 0), which prescribes where and when the consumption of the different types of commodities will occur, and X^h contains all possible consumption plans. Similarly a resource vector $\mathbf{w}^h$ consists of quantities w_{sut}^h that will become available. A vector $\mathbf{y} \in Y^f$ is a *production plan* of firm f, where inputs and outputs may be needed or become available respectively in different places and in different periods: thus inputs (investments) in one period may cause outputs in a subsequent period and a particular technology in Y^f (transportation) may require inputs in one and give outputs in another place.

The price p_{sut} of the commodity indexed sut is the price to be paid at moment 0, for future delivery at t of type s commodity, at location u. The maximal profit $\pi^f(\mathbf{p})$ is the net result of the optimal production plan, computed and distributed at moment 0, which permits consumer h to spend his total wealth $\Sigma_H \mathbf{p} \cdot \mathbf{w}^h + \Sigma_F \theta^{hf} \pi^f(\mathbf{p})$.

Markets are assumed to exist for all $n = sut$ commodities hence all commodities, or rather claims on all commodities are traded. In an equilibrium all markets are cleared. Consumers are able to distribute their wealth over all periods. Thus it is possible to spend in period t income originating from resources in period $t' \neq t$, which permits implicitly (dis)saving by consumers.

The above interpretation of the commodity space subsumes a *certain* future. It is, however, also possible to allow for uncertainty by introducing trade in *contingent claims*. Suppose that there are only two periods, $t = 1$ (present) and $t = \bar{t} = 2$ (future). The state of the world in period 1 is known, but there are $\bar{e}$ *events* or possible states of the world in period 2, with $e = 1, 2, \ldots, \bar{e}$. If there are $\bar{s}$ types of commodities (and only a single location) then there are $n = \bar{s}(1 + \bar{e})$ commodities, namely $\bar{s}$ first period commodities and $\bar{s}\bar{e}$ future commodities. Now if $\mathbf{z} \in \mathbb{R}^n$, z_{s2e} is a quantity of the commodity of type s, to be delivered or received in period 2, provided that event e obtains. It is traded and paid at moment 0 at price p_{s2e}, but delivery only takes place if event e will be the state of the world in period 2 and therefore z_{s2e} is a claim, contingent on the state of the world. This can be generalized for $\bar{t} > 2$ (e.g. Debreu, 1959; Arrow, 1971).

If in an economy markets for all future periods and all possible events exist it is said that the system of markets is *complete*. If markets are not complete, then allocation over time is not possible without restriction. Clearly in the real world there do not exist markets for all future commodities or for all uncertain events. Therefore it seems worthwhile to consider economies with incomplete markets.

To study such economies new equilibrium concepts are to be defined. This is done in the theory of *temporary equilibrium* (e.g. Grandmont, 1977), where it is assumed that only trade in present commodities is possible and that there exists some (monetary) commodity which can be transferred to the next period.

14.5.4. Existence of an equilibrium

This section proves the existence of a Walrasian equilibrium in an economy with production.

THEOREM 14.5.7. *In the economy $\mathcal{E}_P$ an equilibrium $(\mathbf{x}^H, \mathbf{y}^F, \mathbf{p})$ exists if*

(A) X^h *is* (1) *semi-positive,* (2) *closed,* (3) *convex and* (4) *unbounded above, for all $h \in H$;*

(B) P^h *is* (1) *irreflexive,* (2) *continuous,* (3) *convex and* (4) *locally non-satiated, for all $h \in H$;*

(C) (1) $\mathbf{0} \in Y^f$, (2) $-\mathbb{R}^n_+ \subset Y^f$ *and* Y^f *is* (3) *closed* (4) *convex, for all $f \in F$ and* (5) $Y \cap (-Y) \subset \{\mathbf{0}\}$;

(D) *If $\mathbf{p} \in S$ and $\forall f \in F : \pi^f(\mathbf{p}) < \infty$, then for all $h \in H$, $\exists \mathbf{x}^h \in X^h : \mathbf{p} \cdot \mathbf{x}^h < \mathbf{p} \cdot \mathbf{w}^h + \sum_F \theta^{hf} \pi^f(\mathbf{p})$.*

The assumptions (A) and (B) are the same as those of Theorem 14.4.4 on the exchange economy, with the exception of (B4): strong monotonicity has been replaced by local non-satiation, which is possible because of the assumptions on production, particularly (C2). The assumptions (C) were discussed in §14.5.1. Assumption (D) plays the same role as assumption (C) in Theorem 14.4.4; clearly it is a bit weaker than the assumption that $\mathbf{w}^h \in \text{Int } X^h$.

The proof of Theorem 14.5.7 is similar to that of Theorem 14.4.4. The economy $\mathcal{E}_P$ is reduced to a 'compact' economy $\hat{\mathcal{E}}_P$ by defining compact sets $\hat{X}^h$ and a single compact production set $\hat{Y}$, applying Theorem 14.5.2. Next the equilibrium is reformulated in such a way that it fits into the definition of a Nash equilibrium in an *abstract economy*. Abstract economies, Nash equilibria and their existence are discussed in the next section, and it appears that the reformulated Walras equilibrium is a particular case of a Nash equilibrium.

Given the economy $\mathcal{E}_P$ as defined in §14.5.1 and a vector $\mathbf{a} \in \mathbb{R}^n, \mathbf{a} > \Sigma \mathbf{w}^h$, the economy

$$\hat{\mathcal{E}}_P = \{H, 1, \hat{X}^h, \mathbf{w}^h, \hat{P}^h, \rho^h, \hat{Y}\}$$

with a single firm and profit distribution $\rho^h : S \to \mathbb{R}$, is defined by

$$\hat{X}^h = X^h \cap (Y + \mathbf{a}) \qquad \text{(see Figure 14.11)}$$
$$\hat{Y} = Y \cap \{\mathbf{y} \in \mathbb{R}^n | \mathbf{y} \geq -\mathbf{a}\} \qquad \text{(see Figure 14.11)}$$
$$\hat{P}^h(\mathbf{x}) = P^h(\mathbf{x}) \cap \hat{X}^h$$
$$\rho^h(\mathbf{p}) = \Sigma_F \theta^{hf} \pi^f(\mathbf{p}).$$

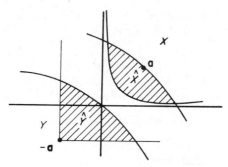

Figure 14.11: Compact consumption and production sets

Now $\rho^h(\mathbf{p})$ is the total profit obtained by consumer h under profit maximization, hence $\hat{B}^h(\mathbf{p}) = \{\mathbf{x} \in \hat{X}^h \,|\, \mathbf{p} \cdot \mathbf{x}^h \leqslant \mathbf{p} \cdot \mathbf{w}^h + \rho^h(\mathbf{p})\}$. Define $\hat{T} \subset (\cap T^j)$ by

$$\hat{T} = \{\mathbf{p} \in S) \,|\, \pi(\mathbf{p}) \leqslant \alpha\}$$

for

$$\alpha = \sup \{\mathbf{p}\,\hat{Y} | \mathbf{p} \in S\}$$

Lemma 14.5.1 the proof of which is omitted, summarizes the properties of the compact economy, that are needed in the existence proof and that are similar to the assumptions made for the original economy. (5) of the lemma ensures that the profit function does not change by the truncation of the production set for allocations that might be an equilibrium in the original economy. Lemma 14.5.2, also given without proof, shows that the equilibria in the two economies are essentially the same. They are not identical, because there is only an aggregate production set in the compact economy.

LEMMA 14.5.1. *Under the assumptions of Theorem 14.5.7,*
(1) *$\hat{X}^h$, $\hat{Y}$ and $\hat{T}$ are compact, convex,*
(2) *$\rho^h : S \to \mathbb{R}$ are continuous functions for all h,*
(3) *$\hat{B}^h$ has a closed graph and Int $\hat{B}^h$ has an open graph: $\hat{B}^h$ is convex valued and not empty for $\mathbf{p} \in \hat{T}$,*
(4) *$\hat{P}^h$ has an open graph, is convex valued and if $\mathbf{x} \in \text{Int } \hat{X}^h$, then $\hat{P}^h(\mathbf{x}^h)$ is locally non-satiated at $\mathbf{x}$.*
(5) *if $\mathbf{y} > -\mathbf{a}$ and $\mathbf{p} \cdot \mathbf{y} = \sup \mathbf{p}\hat{Y}$ then $\hat{\pi}(\mathbf{p}) = \sup \mathbf{p}\hat{Y} = \sup \mathbf{p}\,Y$ and $\mathbf{p} \in \hat{T}$.*

LEMMA 14.5.2. *Under the assumptions of Theorem 14.5.7,*
(1) *If $(\mathbf{x}^H, \mathbf{y}^F, \mathbf{p})$ is an equilibrium in $\mathscr{E}_P$, $(\mathbf{x}^H, \Sigma_F \mathbf{y}^f, \mathbf{p})$ is an equilibrium in $\hat{\mathscr{E}}_P$,*
(2) *If $(\mathbf{x}^H, \mathbf{y}, \mathbf{p})$ is an equilibrium in $\hat{\mathscr{E}}_P$, there exists $\mathbf{y}^F$ such that $\forall f \in F : \mathbf{y}^f \in Y^f$ and $\Sigma \mathbf{y}^f = \mathbf{y}$ and $(\mathbf{x}^H, \mathbf{y}^F, \mathbf{p})$ is an equilibrium in $\mathscr{E}_P$.*

Profit maximization by the aggregate producers (as well as by individual producers) can be expressed with the help of a preference correspondence of the producer $P : \hat{Y} \times S \rightarrow \hat{Y}$, defined by

$$P(\mathbf{y}, \mathbf{p}) = \{\tilde{\mathbf{y}} \in \hat{Y} | \mathbf{p} \cdot \tilde{\mathbf{y}} > \mathbf{p} \cdot \mathbf{y}\}. \tag{14.5.1}$$

Note that this preference also depends on $\mathbf{p}$. $P(\mathbf{y}, \mathbf{p})$ contains the points of $\hat{Y}$ that are more profitable than $\mathbf{y}$. A profit-maximizing vector $\mathbf{y}$ at $\mathbf{p}$ is a maximal element of $\hat{Y}$ with respect to P [see Definition 14.2.3] that is

$$P(\mathbf{y}, \mathbf{p}) = P(\mathbf{y}, \mathbf{p}) \cap \hat{Y} = \varnothing.$$

P has an open graph (relative to $\hat{Y}$), is compact, convex valued and $\mathbf{y} \notin P(\mathbf{y}, \mathbf{p})$.

We introduce an artificial agent, a 'market manager', who 'chooses' prices so as to maximize the value of excess demand $\sum(\mathbf{x}^h - \mathbf{w}^h) - \mathbf{y}$. He has a preference $P^0 : X^H \times \hat{Y} \times \hat{T} \rightarrow \hat{T}$, defined by

$$P^0(\mathbf{x}^H, \mathbf{y}, \mathbf{p}) = \{\tilde{\mathbf{p}} \in \hat{T} | \tilde{\mathbf{p}} \cdot (\sum(\mathbf{x}^h - \mathbf{w}^h) - \mathbf{y}) > \mathbf{p} \cdot (\sum(\mathbf{x}^h - \mathbf{w}^h) - \mathbf{y})\} \tag{14.5.2}$$

and the value of excess demand is maximum if

$$P^0(\mathbf{x}^H, \mathbf{y}, \mathbf{p}) = P^0(\mathbf{x}^H, \mathbf{y}, \mathbf{p}) \cap \hat{T} = \varnothing.$$

Clearly this holds true in an equilibrium, where excess demand must be zero. P^0 has an open graph, is compact convex valued and $\mathbf{p} \notin P^0(\mathbf{x}^H, \mathbf{y}, \mathbf{p})$.

LEMMA 14.5.3. *Under the assumptions of Theorem* 14.5.7:
(1) *If* $(\mathbf{x}^H, \mathbf{y}, \mathbf{p})$ *satisfies*
    (a) $\forall h \in H : \hat{P}^h(\mathbf{x}^h) \cap \hat{B}^h(\mathbf{p}) = \varnothing$ *and* $\mathbf{x}^h \in \hat{B}^h(\mathbf{p})$,
    (b) $P(\mathbf{y}, \mathbf{p}) \cap \hat{Y} = \varnothing$ *and* $\mathbf{y} \in \hat{Y}$,
    (c) $P^0(\mathbf{x}^H, \mathbf{y}, \mathbf{p}) \cap \hat{T} = \varnothing$ *and* $\mathbf{p} \in \hat{T}$,
then $(\mathbf{x}^H, \sum(\mathbf{x}^h - \mathbf{w}^h), \mathbf{p})$ *is an equilibrium in* $\mathscr{E}_P$.
(2) *There exists* $(\mathbf{x}^H, \mathbf{y}, \mathbf{p})$ *satisfying* (a), (b) *and* (c).

Proof: (1) Let $\mathbf{z} = \sum(\mathbf{x}^h - \mathbf{w}^h)$. Since $\mathbf{p} \cdot \mathbf{z} = \mathbf{p} \cdot \mathbf{y}$ by (a) and (b), $P(\mathbf{z}, \mathbf{p}) = P(\mathbf{y}, \mathbf{p})$ (see (14.5.1)), hence $P(\mathbf{z}, \mathbf{p}) \cap \hat{Y} = \varnothing$. Therefore if $\mathbf{z} \in \hat{Y}$, $(\mathbf{x}^H, \mathbf{z}, \mathbf{p})$ satisfies (i), (ii) and (iii) of Definition 14.5.6 by (a) and (b) and by the definition of $\mathbf{z}$. So suppose $\mathbf{z} \notin \hat{Y}$. We have $\hat{\pi}(\mathbf{p}) = \mathbf{p} \cdot \mathbf{z} = \sum \rho^h(\mathbf{p})$. Let

$$\lambda = \max \{\mu | \mu \mathbf{z} + (1 - \mu)(-\mathbf{a}) \in \hat{Y}\}.$$

This maximum exists, since $-\mathbf{a} \in \hat{Y}$ and $\mathbf{z} \notin \hat{Y}$. Choose

$$\bar{\mathbf{y}} = \lambda \mathbf{z} + (1 - \lambda)(-\mathbf{a})$$

$\bar{\mathbf{y}}$ is a boundary point of $\hat{Y}$. Since $\hat{Y}$ is a closed and convex set, there exists, by the theorem of supporting hyperplanes [see IV, §15.2.3], a hyperplane supporting $\hat{Y}$ in $\mathbf{y}$, i.e. $\mathbf{q} \in \mathbb{R}^n$ exists such that $\mathbf{q} \cdot \bar{\mathbf{y}} = \gamma$ and $\forall \mathbf{y} \in \hat{Y} : \mathbf{q} \cdot \mathbf{y} \leqslant \gamma$ and $\mathbf{q} \cdot \mathbf{z} > \gamma$ (see Figure 14.12). By (C2) $\mathbf{q} \geqslant 0$. Since $\sup \mathbf{q} \hat{Y} = \gamma = \mathbf{q} \cdot \bar{\mathbf{y}}$ and $\bar{\mathbf{y}} \in \hat{Y}$, $(1/\sum q_i)\mathbf{q} = \bar{\mathbf{q}} \in \hat{T}$. Hence

$$\bar{\mathbf{q}} \cdot (\mathbf{z} - \mathbf{y}) > \mathbf{p} \cdot (\mathbf{z} - \mathbf{y}) = 0$$

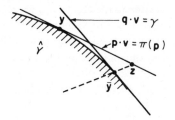

Figure 14.12: Supporting hyperplane

which implies $\bar{\mathbf{q}} \in P^0(\mathbf{x}^H, \mathbf{y}, \mathbf{p}) \cap \hat{T}$ and this contradicts (c) of the lemma, hence $\mathbf{z} \in \hat{Y}$.

(2) will be proved at the end of §14.6.4: it will appear that $(\mathbf{x}^H, \mathbf{y}, \mathbf{p})$ is a Nash equilibrium, to be defined below. $\qquad\qquad\qquad\qquad\qquad\qquad\qquad\qquad$ □

14.6. AN ABSTRACT ECONOMY

14.6.1. The model

An abstract economy, also called a generalized game (in the sense of game theory), is defined by a set of agents, a set of possible actions of each agent, restrictions on the actions and preferences of the agents on combinations of actions of agents (see Shafer and Sonnenschein, 1975). In this economy a Nash equilibrium is a combination of actions of each agent, such that no agent prefers another action, provided that the other agents stick to their actions. It appears that more specific economic models fit into the model of an abstract economy. This holds true for the exchange economy and the economy with production, where Walrasian equilibria can be modelled as Nash equilibria, and also for economies with (non-Walrasian) fixed price equilibria (Greenberg and Muller, 1979) and for economies with public goods (e.g. Ruys and Weddepohl, 1979). Some partial equilibrium models on oligopoly have the same structure [see §14.6.2].

There are $\bar{a}$ agents, $A = \{1, 2, \ldots, \bar{a}\}$ being the set of agents. Each agent $a \in A$ has a set of actions $X^{\bar{a}}$, from which he has to choose one and only one action. In this choice he has to take into account external restrictions which limit this choice. Let X^A be the cartesian product of the sets of actions of the agents, that is $X^A = \prod_A X^a = (X^1, X^2, \ldots, X^a)$ [see I, §1.2.6]. Then $x^A \in X^A$ is an $\bar{a}$-tuple of actions, one for each agent. Further X^{-a} is defined by

$$X^{-a} = (X^1, X^2, \ldots, X^{a-1}, X^{a+1}, \ldots, X^{\bar{a}}),$$

hence if $x^{-a} \in X^{-a}$, then $x^A = (x^a, x^{-a})$, for each $a \in A$.

Each $a \in A$ has a *preference* P^a, $X^A \to X^a$. If $y^a \in P(x^A)$, then a prefers the $\bar{a}$-tuple (y^a, x^{-a}) over (x^a, x^{-a}), that is he will rather choose y^a than x^a if the other agents choose x^{-a}. Hence an agent's preferences depend (in principle) also on the actions of other agents. This may be due to the fact that the agents directly evaluate other agent's actions, but it could also be caused by effects from the combined actions of other agents on the consequences of one's own action. For example in the economy with production the action of the 'market agent' (price setting) acts upon the 'preference' of the producer, but not on the preferences of the consumers. For each $a \in A$ a *restriction* correspondence $B^a : X^{-a} \to X^a$ determines the set of actions from which the agent a might choose, given the actions of the other agents: if $x^a \in B^a(x^{-a}) \subset X^a$, then a can choose x^a, hence (in principle) the restriction set depends on actions chosen by other agents; for example, the budget set of consumers depends on prices and thus on the action of the 'market agent'. For ease of notation we shall write $B^a(x^A)$, with the convention that x^a acts as a dummy.

The abstract economy is completely characterized by the above concepts, that is

$$\mathscr{E}_A = \{A, X^a, P^a, B^a\}$$

14.6.2. Nash equilibrium

DEFINITION 14.6.1. In the abstract economy $\mathscr{E}_A$, a *solution* is an $\bar{a}$-tuple of actions $x^A \in X^A$ and a *feasible solution* is a solution such that

$$\forall a \in A : x^a \in B^a(x^A)$$

DEFINITION 14.6.2. A *Nash equilibrium* in $\mathscr{E}_A$ is a solution x^A such that
(i) $\forall a \in A : x^a \in B^a(x^A)$,
(ii) $\forall a \in A : P^a(x^A) \cap B^a(x^A) = \varnothing$.

In other words, in a Nash equilibrium each agent chooses an action from his restriction set which is a maximal element, *given* the actions chosen by the other agents. Definition 14.6.1 is similar to Definitions 14.2.1 and 14.5.4 of feasible allocations, whereas Definition 14.6.2 is similar to Definitions 14.2.5 and 14.5.6 of Walras equilibria. By (ii) of Definition 14.6.2 no agent has a better choice, given the actions of the other agents, which occur in the preference as well as in the restriction.

The preferences P^a only allow for comparison of pairs of $\bar{a}$-tuples of the type (y^a, x^{-a}) and (x^a, x^{-a}), but (y^a, y^{-a}) and (x^a, x^{-a}) cannot be compared. For this we need an extended preference $Q^a : X^A \to X^A$ and from this preference P^a can be derived by

$$(y^a, x^{-a}) \in Q^a(x^a, x^{-a}) \Leftrightarrow y^a \in P^a(x^a, x^{-a}).$$

In the preceding sections consumer preferences were assumed to depend only on each agent's own action (consumption). In that case Q^a could be trivially derived from P^a. Note however, that if Q^a satisfies

$$(y^a, x^{-a}) \in Q^a(x^a, x^{-a}) \Rightarrow \forall y^{-a} \in X^{-a} : (y^a, y^{-a}) \in Q^a(x^a, y^{-a}),$$

this does not exclude that $(x^a, x^{-a}) \in Q^a(y^a, y^{-a})$. That is, if agent a prefers y^a over x^a if the other agents stick to the same action, then he may prefer the pair (x^a, x^{-a}) over the pair (y^a, y^{-a}).

The extended preference Q^a permits the definition of a Pareto optimum in the abstract economy [see Definitions 14.2.4 and 14.5.5]:

DEFINITION 14.6.3. In the abstract economy $\{A, X^a, Q^a, B^a\}$ a Pareto optimum is a feasible solution $\hat{x}^A$ such that no other feasible solution x^A exists such that

$$\forall a \in A : \hat{x}^A \notin Q^a(x^A) \text{ and } \exists b \in A : x^A \in Q^b(\hat{x}^A).$$

Pareto optimality could also be defined relative to some subset $B \subseteq A$, by requiring that the condition of the definition only holds for agents in B. If the economy with production is formulated as an abstract economy, as in §14.5.4 [see particularly Lemma 14.5.3], then the Pareto optima satisfying Definition 14.5.5 are relative to the set H of consumers only.

14.6.3. Examples of abstract economies

Games in normal form have the structure of an abstract economy. Note that in game theory, besides Nash equilibria, many solution concepts are studied [see I, §13.3]. General equilibrium models fit into the model of an abstract economy, after addition of one or more artificial agents, as done in §14.5.4.

In the famous prisoner's dilemma game [see I, Example 13.4.2], each of two criminals a and b $(A = \{a, b\})$ have to choose between two actions: not confess the crime they committed together, or confess it: $X^a = \{n^a, c^a\}$, $X^b = \{n^b, c^b\}$. Their preferences can be derived from the table below, which gives the imprisonment in years that will result from each combination of actions, assuming that the preferences only depend on each agent's own sentence.

	n^b	c^b
n^a	$a : 1$ $b : 1$	$a : 10$ $b : \frac{1}{3}$
c^a	$a : \frac{1}{3}$ $b : 10$	$a : 3$ $b : 3$

hence

$$P^a(n^a, n^b) = c^a \qquad P^b(n^a, n^b) = c^b \qquad Q^a(n^a, n^b) = (c^a, n^b)$$
$$P^a(n^a, c^b) = c^a \qquad P^b(n^a, c^b) = \varnothing$$
$$P^a(c^a, n^b) = \varnothing \qquad P^b(n^a, n^b) = c^b$$
$$P^a(c^a, c^b) = \varnothing \qquad P^b(c^a, c^b) = \varnothing \qquad Q^a(c^a, c^b) = \{(n^a, n^b), (c^a, n^b)\}.$$

(n^a, n^b), (n^a, c^b) and (c^a, n^b) are *Pareto optima* and (c^a, c^b) is the unique *Nash equilibrium*, which is not a Pareto optimum. Clearly the Nash equilibrium is a reasonable outcome of this game if the prisoners cannot communicate and cannot make binding agreements.

Another example of an abstract economy is the duopoly model, studied in §12.13.1. Each firm has to choose an action y_1 and y_2 respectively, y_j being quantities of output, hence the sets of actions are the nonnegative real numbers or some interval. The preferences follow from the profit functions (cf. (12.4.1)) for agent 1,

$$\tilde{y}_1 \in P^1(y_1, y_2) \Leftrightarrow \pi^1(\tilde{y}_1, y_2) > \pi^1(y_1, y_2).$$

The restriction is constant and coincides with the set of actions, that is $B^1(y_1, y_2) = X^1 = \mathbb{R}_+^1$. The Nash equilibrium is the 'Nash–Cournot solution' of Chapter 12 where each firm maximizes profit, taking the output of its competitor as given. This Nash equilibrium is not a Pareto optimum: the firms could do better by coordinating their actions.

These two examples show that a Nash equilibrium is not a Pareto optimum in general. That the Walras equilibrium is Pareto optimal (in the formulation as a Nash equilibrium, only with respect to consumers) is due to the necessary assumption that preferences do not depend on the consumption of other consumers.

14.6.4. Existence of a Nash equilibrium

The abstract economy was defined in §14.6.1 for arbitrary sets of actions. The following theorem proves the existence of a Nash equilibrium if the sets of actions are subsets of $\mathbb{R}^n$, under assumptions similar to the assumptions we met in §§14.3, 14.4 and 14.5 above on consumption sets, production sets, budget correspondences and preferences. This theorem is applied to prove (2) of Lemma 14.5.3.

THEOREM 14.6.4 (*Shafer and Sonnenschein*, 1975). *If in $\mathscr{E}_A = \{A, X^a, P^a, B^a\}$, for each $a \in A$:*
(A) $X^a \subset \mathbb{R}^n$ *is compact, convex, non-empty;*
(B) B^a *is a continuous correspondence (upper semi-continuous and lower semi continuous);*

(C) B^a is convex, compact valued and nowhere empty;
(D) P^a has an open graph in $X^a \times X^A$;
(E) $\forall \mathbf{x}^a \in X^a : \mathbf{x}^a \notin \text{Conv } P^a(\mathbf{x}^a, \mathbf{x}^{-a})$ (where Conv denotes the convex hull [see IV, §15.2.2];)
then a Nash equilibrium $\hat{\mathbf{x}}^A$ exists in $\mathscr{E}_A$. If also in $\hat{\mathbf{x}}_A$
(F) P^a is locally non-satiated in $\hat{\mathbf{x}}^A$, then $\hat{\mathbf{x}}^a \in \partial B^a(\hat{\mathbf{x}}^A)$.

Proof: Let $F^a : X^A \to X^a$ be the correspondence

$$F^a(\mathbf{x}^A) = \text{Conv } P^a(\mathbf{x}^A) \cap B^a(\mathbf{x}^A)$$

and

$$W^a = \{\mathbf{x}^A \in X^A | F^a(\mathbf{x}^A) \neq \varnothing\}.$$

Conv P^a has an open graph, since P^a has, by (D [from App. Prop, 1(i) and Prop. 2(ii)]), and therefore it is lower semi-continuous. By (B), B^a is lower semi-continuous. Both P^a and B^a are convex valued. In W^a their intersection is non-empty and therefore [App. Prop. 2(iii)] the restriction of F^a to W^a is lower semi-continuous. Hence by Michael's theorem [Theorem 14.3.5], there exists a continuous selection, $f^a : W^a \to X^a$, with $f^a(\mathbf{x}^A) \in F^a(\mathbf{x}^A)$. Define $G^a : X^A \to X^a$ (compare §14.4.3 and Figure 14.8) by

$$G^a(\mathbf{x}^A) = \begin{cases} f^a(\mathbf{x}^A) & \text{if } \mathbf{x}^A \in W^a. \\ B^a(\mathbf{x}^A) & \text{if } \mathbf{x}^A \notin W^a. \end{cases}$$

G^a is upper semi-continuous since B^a is, by (B) and $f^a(\mathbf{x}^A) \in B^a(\mathbf{x}^A)$ in W^a. G^a is compact and convex valued and nowhere empty, by (B) and (C). Define $G : X^A \to X^A$ by

$$G(\mathbf{x}^A) = \prod_A G^a(\mathbf{x}^A).$$

Being a cartesian product of upper semi-continuous correspondences, G is upper semi-continuous, it is compact and convex valued and nowhere empty, hence, by Kakutani's theorem [see V, §5.6] it has a fixed point $\hat{\mathbf{x}}^A \in G(\hat{\mathbf{x}}^A)$.

It remains to prove that this fixed point is a Nash equilibrium. Since $\hat{\mathbf{x}}^a \in G^a(\hat{\mathbf{x}}^A) \subset B^a(\hat{\mathbf{x}}^A)$, for all $a \in A$, (i) of Definition 14.6.2 is satisfied. For all $a \in A$, $\hat{\mathbf{x}}^A \notin W^a$, since in $W^a, f^a(\hat{\mathbf{x}}^A) = G^a(\hat{\mathbf{x}}^A) \subset \text{Conv } P^a(\hat{\mathbf{x}}^A)$ and by (E), $\hat{\mathbf{x}}^a \notin \text{Conv } P^a(\hat{\mathbf{x}}^A)$, and for $\hat{\mathbf{x}}^A \in X^A \setminus W^a$, by the definition of W^a,

$$\text{Conv } P^a(\hat{\mathbf{x}}^A) \cap B^a(\hat{\mathbf{x}}^A) = \varnothing,$$

which proves (ii) of Definition 14.6.2.

Finally, if (F) holds and $P^a(\hat{\mathbf{x}}^A) \neq \varnothing$, then it is not possible that $\hat{\mathbf{x}}^a$ is in the interior of $B^a(\hat{\mathbf{x}}^A)$.   □

Now we can prove part (2) of Lemma 14.5.3. In the economy $\mathscr{E}_P$ the set of agents is $\{H, 1, 0\}$, with sets of possible actions $\hat{X}^h, \hat{Y}$ and $\hat{T}$, preferences $\hat{P}^h, P$ and P^0 [see (14.5.1) and (14.5.2)]; the restrictions are the budget correspondences $\hat{B}^h$

and the (fixed) sets $\hat{Y}$ and $\hat{T}$. For these sets and correspondences the assumptions of Theorem 14.6.4 holds, so that the Nash equilibrium exists, which by (1) of Lemma 14.5.3 is an equilibrium.

14.7. CONCLUDING REMARKS

In the preceding sections, we only studied the basic models of general equilibrium theory and we proved the existence of a Walrasian equilibrium. Many topics in general equilibrium theory were left out of consideration. Some of these topics are briefly discussed below.

In section 14.4.2 we showed, by means of an example, that a Walrasian equilibrium need not be unique. No plausible assumptions are known that guarantee uniqueness. The problem has been analysed particularly in exchange economies. It was shown (Debreu, 1972) that, if preferences can be represented by a differentiable utility function, the number of equilibria is *finite* and the equilibria consist of a set of discrete points. A related question is, what happens to the equilibria if the data of the exchange economy, that is the initial resources and the preferences of the agents (the agents characteristics), change continuously (for some well-defined concept of a continuous change of preferences). Does the equilibrium then also change continuously? It can be shown that equilibria exist such that a slight change in the data will entail a discontinuous jump. Such equilibria are called critical (versus regular equilibria) and cannot be considered as pathological cases. A regular economy (see Dierker, 1982) is an economy without critical points. It has been shown that critical economies (with critical points) are *rare*, in the sense that the set of parameters representing critical economies, is small in the set of all parameters (more precisely, the set of critical economies has measure zero, in terms of a well-defined measure on the set of agents characteristics).

In Walrasian equilibria agents are assumed to behave competitively, that is act as price takers. Even in an exchange economy it is possible that some agents, or groups of agents, could do better by a different type of behaviour. The set of allocations that might occur if cooperation between agents is possible and that are Pareto optimal is called the *core*. The core is a generalization of the contract curve [see §14.4.2] and it consists of all allocations such that no group of consumers (coalition) could improve their position by distributing among themselves the resources they possess. In a finite economy the core contains all Walrasian allocations, but also other allocations. However, if the number of agents increases, the core becomes smaller. If the number of agents becomes infinite, then each consumer becomes 'negligible' and in that case the core and the set of Walras allocations coincide. Hence in this limit case no agent can do better by not behaving competitively (see Hildenbrand, 1982.) In economies with production collusive behaviour of firms cannot be excluded *a priori* and non-cooperative behaviour will not necessarily result in competitive equilibria if the number of firms is small. Typically the Nash–Cournot equilibrium of the second example in section 14.6.3 models behaviour of a small number of firms. The following questions arise: under what assumptions does collusive behaviour become improbable and under what assumptions do coomperative equilibria of the Nash–Cournot type get very close to competitive equilibria. For these questions the reader is referred to Mas-Colell (1980) and to the references in that paper.

A major weakness of the general equilibrium model discussed in this chapter, seems to be that a Walrasian equilibrium excludes ever-increasing returns in production. These, however, are not consistent with perfect competition. Taking into account increasing returns requires in any case the definition of (non-Walrasian) equilibria that allow for monopolistic competition (e.g. Negishi, 1961; Arrow and Hahn, 1971). Note, however, that the case that increasing returns obtain up to a level which is low relative to the market (the case of so-called U-shaped cost curves) can be dealt with in a competitive framework (compare Novshek and Sonnenschein, 1980).

Another important problem is the *stability* of Walrasian equilibria: how are equilibrium prices obtained. This requires an adjustment process that generates equilibrium prices when prevailing prices are not equilibrium prices; e.g. after some disturbance or after a change of parameters (in preferences or technologies) or because expectations change. An equilibrium established by such a process is called *stable* (with respect to that process). Traditionally the price mechanism is believed to produce equilibrium prices: if there is excess demand of some commodity (that is demand is larger than supply), the price of that commodity increases. If there is excess supply, the price decreases. This does, however, not guarantee that an equilibrium price vector is attained and even less that it is attained quickly enough. If we want to study the question if the price mechanism generates equilibrium prices, we have to construct a model of that mechanism that fits within the equilibrium model.

The *tâtonnement process* as a model of price adjustments was proposed by Walras. It is quite remarkable that this is a centralized process, since the price mechanism is generally considered to be decentralized. In the *tâtonnement* process, there is a central agent, an auctioneer, who is informed about demand and supply of each agent in the economy at the prevailing prices. The auctioneer computes excess demands and supplies for each commodity and he adjusts the prices on the basis of these results. The new prices are communicated to the agents and they report their new demands and supplies to the auctioneer. This is repeated until all excesses have become zero, which, by definition, can only happen in an equilibrium. Only after equilibrium prices have been established transactions are concluded, hence no transactions occur at non-equilibrium prices. Arrow, Block and Hurwicz (1959) proved the stability of the *tâtonnement* process in an exchange economy under the assumption of gross substitutability. This assumption represents a rather severe restriction, since gross substitutability requires that the increase of the prices of one commodity entails an increase of the demand for *all* other commodities. Apart from this assumption, however, the *tâtonnement* process does not seem to be a good description of the price mechanism, firstly because contracts may only be concluded at the end, and secondly because it is centralized. In the real world an auctioneer can hardly be observed but price adjustments rather are realized when excesses appear while the trading goes on. For that reason *non-tâtonnement processes* have been proposed (Hahn, 1962; Negishi, 1964). At an initial set of (non-Walrasian) prices, contracts are concluded. Not all agents can realize the trade they desire and excesses on the markets appear, which generate price adjustments. At the new prices agents can again trade and again excesses will come out, generating new price adjustments. Hence during the process not only the prices change, but also the quantities of commodities in the hands of the traders. These quantities, however, only change through trade and not by consumption or production. Production and consumption are assumed to take place only when the equilibrium prices have been established. The process ends if all excesses have disappeared. These processes do not generate equilibrium prices: the last price is not an equilibrium price and the final allocation is not an equilibrium allocation, but is a Pareto optimal allocation. A satisfactory model of the prices mechanism has, however, not been found as yet (Hahn, 1982).

Various extensions of the basic general equilibrium models are possible: the introduction of a government that raises taxes gives rise to theories of (optimal) taxation, money can be explicitly introduced in the model, economies with incomplete markets and temporary equilibrium models [compare §14.4.3] can be studied. For these problems the reader is referred to Arrow and Hahn (1971). Another extension is the theory of fixed price equilibria, where prices are assumed to be fixed or sticky in the short run, which entails that agents cannot realize the transaction that they desire and have to be rationed (Benassy, 1975; Dreze, 1975; Grandmont, 1977).

14.8. APPENDIX: MATHEMATICAL CONCEPTS

A *correspondence* F of a set X into a set Y, denoted $F : X \to Y$, is a mapping of X into the *subsets* of Y, hence $F(\mathbf{x}) \subset Y$. A correspondence is also called a set valued function, a multivalued function or a point to set mapping [see I, §1.4]. It is not excluded that for some $\mathbf{x} \in X$, $F(\mathbf{x}) = \varnothing$, the empty set. A correspondence is said to be convex (compact, etc.) *valued* if $F(\mathbf{x})$ is convex (compact, etc.) for each $\mathbf{x} \in X$. If such a property holds particularly in some point $\mathbf{x}_0$, then we say, for example, that F is compact valued in $\mathbf{x}_0$ [see IV, §15.2.6 and V, §5.2].

The *inverse* of a correspondence $F : X \to Y$ is denoted $F^{-1} : Y \to X$ with $F^{-1}(\mathbf{y}) = \{\mathbf{x} \in X / \mathbf{y} \in F(\mathbf{x})\}$, and its *graph* by Gr F [see I, §1.4.1].

In the remainder of this appendix we only consider correspondences such that X and Y are subsets of Euclidean spaces, that is, $X \subset \mathbb{R}^n$ and $Y \subset \mathbb{R}^m$ [see I, §5.2].

For such correspondences two types of continuity can be defined, *upper* and *lower* semi-continuity. The first type of continuity is important in economics, because the upper semi-continuity of a correspondence of a convex compact set X into itself, which is non-empty, convex, compact valued, ensures the existence of a fixed point by Kakutani's fixed point theorem [see V., §5.6]. Lower semi-continuity of a convex valued correspondence ensures the existence of a continuous selection, by Michael's theorem [see 14.3.6].

DEFINITIONS. Let $F: X \to Y$ be a correspondence. F is *upper semi-continuous* (u.s.c.) *at a point* x_0 if for each open set $A \subset Y$, such that $F(x_0) \subset A$, there exists an open enighbourhood $U(x_0)$ of x_0, such that

$$x \in U(x_0) \Rightarrow F(x) \subset A.$$

F is *lower semi-continuous* (l.s.c.) *at a point* x_0 if for each open set $A \subset Y$, such that $F(x_0) \cap A \neq \varnothing$, there exists an open neighbourhood $U(x_0)$ of x_0 such that

$$x \in U(x_0) \Rightarrow F(x) \cap A \neq \varnothing.$$

F is continuous at x_0 if it is both u.s.c. and l.s.c. in x_0. F is u.s.c. (l.s.c.) if it is u.s.c. (l.s.c.) in all points $x \in X$.

Both types of continuity are related to properties of the graph of the correspondence, particularly

PROPOSITION 1.
(i) *If F has an open graph (relative to $X \times Y$), that is, if* Gr F *is an open set* [*see IV,* §11.2], *then F is l.s.c.*
(ii) *If F has a closed graph (relative to $X \times Y$) and if Y is compact* [*see V,* §5.2], *then F is u.s.c.*

The following properties are applied in Chapter 14:

PROPOSITION 2.
(i) *If F is a l.s.c. correspondence then the correspondence* Conv F, *defined by* (Conv F) $(x) = $ Conv$(F(x))$ *is also l.s.c.*
(ii) *If $F: X \to Y$ and $G: X \to Y$ are l.s.c. correspondences that are convex valued and if for all $x \in X$,* Int$(F(x) \cap G(x)) \neq \varnothing$, *then the correspondence $H: X \to Y$, defined by $H(x) = F(x) \cap G(x)$, is also l.s.c.*
(iii) *If $F: X \to Y$ and $G: X \to Z$ are u.s.c. correspondences, then the cartesian product $H: X \to Y \times Z$, defined by $H(x) = F(x) \times G(x)$ is also u.s.c.*
(iv) *If $f: X \to Y$ is a continuous function, then the correspondence $F: X \to Y$, defined by $F(x) = \{f(x)\}$ is a continuous correspondence (that is, both u.s.c. and l.s.c.).*

Proofs of these propositions can be found in Berge (1966), Hildenbrand (1974) and Nikaido (1968).

14.9. REFERENCES

Arrow, K. J. (1971). *Essays in the theory of risk-bearing.* North-Holland, Amsterdam.

Arrow, K. J., Block, H. D. and Hurwicz, L. (1959). On the stability of the competitive equilibrium II: *Econometrica,* **27**, 82–109.

Arrow, K. J. and Hahn, F. H. (1971). *General competitive analysis.* Holden Day, San Francisco.

Arrow, K. J. and Debreu, G. (1954). Existence of an equilibrium for a competitive economy. *Econometrica,* **22**, 265–290.

Arrow, K. J. and Intriligator, M. (eds) (1982). *Handbook of mathematical economics.* North-Holland, Amsterdam.

Benassy, J. P. (1975). Neo-Keynesian disequilibrium in a monetary economy. *Review of Economic Studies,* **42**, 502–523.

Berge, C. (1966). *Espaces topologiques.* Dunod, Paris.

Debreu, G. (1952). A social equilibrium existence theorem. *Proceedings of the National Academy of Sciences,* **38**, no. 10, 886–893.

Debreu, G. (1954). Representation of a preference ordering by a numerical function, in R. M. Thrall, C. H. Coombs, R. L. Davis (eds.), *Decision Processes.* Wiley, New York, pp. 159–165.

Debreu, G. (1959). *Theory of Value.* Wiley, New York.

Debreu, G. (1972). Smooth preferences. *Econometrica,* **40**, 603–615.

Debreu, G. (1982), Existence of competitive equilibrium, Chapter 15 in Arrow and Intriligator (1982).

Dierker, E. (1982). Regular economies, Chapter 17 in Arrow and Intriligator (1982).

Drèze, J. H. (1975). Existence of an exchange equilibrium under price rigidities. *International Economic Review,* **16**, 301–320.

Eilenberg, S. (1941). Ordered topological spaces. *American Journal of Mathematics,* LXIII, 39–45.

Fan, K. (1961). A generalization of Tychynoff's fixed point theorem. *Math. Annals,* **142**, 305–310.

Gale, D. and Mas-Colell A. (1975). An equilibrium existence theorem for a general model without ordered preferences. *Journal of Mathematical Economics,* **2**, 19–25.

Grandmont, J. M. (1977). Temporary general equilibrium theory. *Econometrica,* **45**, 535–572.

Greenberg, J. and Muller, H. (1979). Equilibrium under price rigidities and externalities, in O. Moeschlin and D. Palaschske (eds.), *Game theory and related topics.*, North-Holland, Amsterdam.

Hahn, F. H. (1962). On the stability of pure exchange equilibrium. *International Economic Review,* **3**, 206–213.

Hahn, F. H. (1982), Stability, Chapter 16 in Arrow and Intriligator (1982).

Hildenbrand, W. (1974). *Core and equilibria of a large economy.* Princeton university Press, Princeton.

Hildenbrand, W. (1982). Core of an economy, Chapter 18, in Arrow and Intriligator (1982).

Mas-Colell, A. (1980), Noncooperative approaches to the theory of perfect competition: presentation. *Journal of Economic Theory,* **22**, 121–135.

May, K. O. (1954). Transitivity, utility and aggregation in preference patterns. *Econometrica,* **22**.

McKenzie, L. W. (1959). On the existence of general equilibrium for a competitive market. *Econometrica,* **27**, 54–71.

Michael, E. (1956). Continuous selections I. *Annals of Mathematics,* **63**, 361–382.

Negishi, T. (1961). Monopolistic competition and general equilibrium theory. *Review of Economic Studies,* **28**, 196–201.

Negishi, T. (1964). The stability of a competitive economy. *Econometrica*, **30**, 635–669.

Nikaido, H. (1968). *Convex structures and economic Theory.* Academic Press, London, New York.

Novshek, W. and Sonnenschein, H. (1980). Small efficient scale as a foundation for Walrasian equilibrium. *Journal of Economic Theory*, **22**, 243–255.

Rapoport, A. (1974). *Game theory as a theory of conflict resolution.* Reidel, Dordrecht.

Ruys, P. H. M. and Weddepohl, H. N. (1979). Economic theory and duality, in J. Kriens (ed.), *Convex analysis and mathematical economics.* Springer, Berlin, pp. 1–72.

Shafer, W. and Sonnenschein, H. (1975). Equilibrium without ordered preferences in abstract economies. *Journal of Mathematical Economics*, **2**, 345–348.

Wald, A. (1936). Uber einige Gleichungssysteme der mathematischen Ökonomie. *Zeitschrift für Nationalökonomie*, **7**, 637–670.

Walras, L. (1874). *Elements d'économie politique pure.* Corbez, Lausanne, Paris and Basle.

Mathematical Methods in Economics
Edited by F. van der Ploeg
© 1984, John Wiley & Sons, Ltd.

15

Social Choice, Interpersonal Comparability and Welfare Economics

BEN LOCKWOOD, *Birckbeck College, University of London, U.K.*

15.1. INTRODUCTION

This chapter is concerned with the relationship between welfare economics and the more general question of the possibility of rational collective choice. Before considering the connection between the two, it is useful to make a distinction between two sub-problems, or aspects of 'the' collective choice problem.

The first is the problem of collective *decision*, where a best element or elements must be chosen from a feasible set. A typical example would be a committee which must choose one of a number of different courses of action, upon which the members hold opposing views.

The second, which is the one relevant to welfare economics, is where the judgements, or rankings, of individuals in society over pairs of elements in the feasible set of alternatives are to be *aggregated* into a single social ranking of pairs of alternatives.

One feature which these two approaches have in common is the 'data' of the problem. It is usually assumed that individuals in society are rational in the sense that they can rank every pair of alternatives, and that if anybody judges **x** to be at least as good as **y**, and **y** to be at least as good as **z**, then he/she will also judge **x** to be at least as good as **z**. In other words, it is assumed that all individuals have *preference orderings* over X the set of alternatives, or that each individuals preference relation is complete, transitive, and reflexive [see §15.2.1 for definitions]. They differ in that the objective of the aggregation problem is to arrive at a *social* preference ordering, whereas the objective of the decision problem is to formulate a choice function, $C(.)$ which associates with each non-empty subset Z of X (an "agenda") a choice, **x**. In general the existence of a complete ordering on X does not imply the existence of a choice function. Conversely, although a choice function can always generate a binary relation, R, on X it need not be an ordering.

371

Both problems, however, are not even well-defined unless some kind of restriction relating the data to the objective is chosen. An important example of such a restriction is one originally due to the economist V. Pareto, which states that if all individual rank x at least as good as y then so should the social ranking.

Unfortunately, in most choice situations the Pareto principle does not give a ranking of all pairs in X. In particular, if a change from state x to state y is contemplated where some individuals gain and some lose, the Pareto principle cannot be used. This strongly suggests that if a *complete* social ranking is to be arrived at, some kind of interpersonal comparisons must be made in the process of aggregating individual orderings. It is the purpose of this chapter to make this intuition precise, by constructing a framework in which an exact definition of interpersonal comparability, and also an exact statement of the conditions under which some type of interpersonal comparability is *necessary* for successful aggregation of individual preference orderings can be made.

The motivation for such an investigation is provided by Arrow's famous Impossibility Theorem (Arrow, 1963). He showed that if the aggregation process satisfied three 'reasonable' conditions (one of which was the Pareto principle [see §§15.2.3 and 15.3.1 for a full statement], there was no process which would aggregate *all* possible configurations of individual preference orderings.

There are four possible responses to this. The first three are that *either* one or more of the three 'reasonable' conditions can be relaxed, *or* the aggregation process can be required to work for a strict subset of all possible individual preference configurations, *or* the requirement that aggregation lead to a social ordering be relaxed. Each of these options has generated a vast literature (see Sen, 1970) but none of them is really interesting from the point of view of welfare economics [see Sen (1977) and §15.3.2].

The fourth response, which is the one taken in this chapter, is to take a broader view of Arrow's framework of analysis and note that the data, or 'information' used in the aggregation process is simply a list of individual preference orderings on X. Given a technical assumption [§15.2.1], these individual preferences can always be represented by utility functions so that the 'information' is summarized by a list of n functions from X to $\mathbb{R}$. However, if $U_i(.)$ is a representation of individual i's preference ordering then so is $\phi_i(U_i(.))$, where ϕ_i. $\mathbb{R} \to \mathbb{R}$ is strictly increasing, so $(U_1(.),\ U_2(.)...U_n(.))$ and $\phi_1(U_1(.))$. $\phi_2(U_2(.)),...\phi_n(U_n(.)))$ are equivalent pieces of information in Arrow's framework.

The point is that in such a framework, interpersonal comparability of any kind, such as the statement that 'i is better off in state y than j is' has no meaning since transforms, ϕ_i, $i = 1,...,n$ of any particular representation of the preference orderings can be found that make both that statement and its negation true.

However, by placing restrictions on the 'allowable' transforms ϕ_i one can introduce interpersonal comparability assumptions into the Arrow framework; this is done in section 15.2.4. Then, with such comparability, aggregation of individual preferences *is* possible, even if Arrow's reasonable conditions are retained. In fact, one can characterize the class of possible social orderings on X by the type of comparability assumption, and obtain Arrow's Impossibility Theorem as a by-product. For example the classical Utilitarian principle of 'greatest welfare of the greatest number' or maximization of the sum of utilities can be derived as the consequence of a certain type of comparability. Sections 15.3, 15.4 and 15.5 below are concerned with this. An important critique of Arrow's 'reasonable' conditions is considered in section 15.6.

Finally, a historical note. The first economist to explicitly suggest the idea of a complete social ordering of X as the basis for welfare economics was Bergson (1938), although he talked in terms of a social welfare function. For this reason, these terms, when used in the text are prefaced by his name.

15.2. A FRAMEWORK FOR ANALYSIS

15.2.1. Some useful technicalities

In this section, some terms and concepts to be used in the sequel are briefly reviewed. This is not a systematic introduction to these topics. For such an introduction, the reader is referred to Vol. I, Chapter 1.

Suppose X is a set of feasible alternatives.

A binary relation, R, on a set X is a subset of $(X \times X)$, the Cartesian product of X and X [see I, §1.3].

For example, suppose X is $\mathbb{R}^m$ [see I, Example 5.2.2]. Then the relation '$=$' is given by the subset of $\mathbb{R}^m \times \mathbb{R}^m$ defined as

$$R = \{(\mathbf{x}, \mathbf{y}) \in \mathbb{R}^m \times \mathbb{R}^m \mid \mathbf{x} = \mathbf{y}\}.$$

Rather than write $(\mathbf{x}, \mathbf{y}) \in R$, however, it is more convenient to write $\mathbf{x} R \mathbf{y}$, and this notation will be adopted in what follows.

The binary relations used in this chapter satisfy some combination of:

Reflexivity:	$\mathbf{x} R \mathbf{x}$, all $\mathbf{x}$ in X
Transitivity:	$\mathbf{x} R \mathbf{y}, \mathbf{y} R \mathbf{z} \rightarrow \mathbf{x} R \mathbf{z}$ all $\mathbf{x}, \mathbf{y}, \mathbf{z}$ in X
Completeness:	either $\mathbf{x} R \mathbf{y}$ or $\mathbf{y} R \mathbf{x}$ for all $\mathbf{x}, \mathbf{y} \in X$
Symmetry:	$\mathbf{x} R \mathbf{y} \rightarrow \mathbf{y} R \mathbf{x}$ all $\mathbf{x}, \mathbf{y} \in X$.

Here an arrow '$\rightarrow$' denotes logical implication, whereas '$\leftrightarrow$' will be used interchangeably with the phrase 'if and only if'.

By far the most familiar type of relation to the economist is the weak preference relation, say R, meaning 'at least as good as'.

Here it is assumed to be *reflexive*, *transitive* and *complete*, and is called a preference ordering.

The usual justification for requiring these properties of the 'at least as good as' relation is that rational choice is impossible without them. This is as true if R is to be a *social* preference relation on X as it is if R is an individual preference relation.

Associated with R are the equally familiar strict preference relation, P, and the indifference relation I:

$$x\,I\,y \leftrightarrow x\,R\,y \quad \text{and} \quad y\,R\,x \quad \text{all} \quad x, y \in X$$
$$x\,P\,y \leftrightarrow x\,R\,y \quad \text{and not} \quad y\,R\,x \quad \text{all} \quad x, y \in X.$$

It is easily checked that I is *reflexive, symmetric,* and *transitive*. Any relation that satisfies these conditions is called an *equivalence relation* [see I, §1.3.3].

(Another example of an equivalence relation is the relation $x = y$ for $x, y \in \mathbb{R}^m$.) Furthermore, an equivalence relation I on $X \times X$ partitions X into a set of equivalence classes, such that x, y are in the same class if and only if $x\,I\,y$.

It is often more convenient to work with a numerical representation of a preference ordering, a utility or welfare function, than with the preference ordering itself.

A preference ordering, R, is representable (by a utility function) if there exists a utility function, $U : X \rightarrow \mathbb{R}$ such that

$$x\,R\,y \leftrightarrow U(x) \geqslant U(y)$$

[see I, §1.4.1].

If X is a finite set, it is obvious that any R on X is representable. However, if X is a subset of $\mathbb{R}^m$, m-dimensional Euclidean space, as is often the case in economic applications, then *not all* preference orderings on X are representable. A theorem, for a proof see Debreu (1959), states that a preference ordering R defined on a connected subset of $\mathbb{R}^m$ [V, §5.2.4] is *representable* if and only if R is *continuous*, that is the sets

$$\{x \mid x\,R\,y\} \quad \text{and} \quad \{x \mid y\,R\,x\}$$

are closed [V, §5.2.1]. In other words if x_n is a sequence in $\mathbb{R}^m$ converging to $\bar{x}$, and $x_n\,R\,y$ for all n, it is required that $\bar{x}\,R\,y$. This theorem is in fact more general: it is also true if X is a topological space with a countable base of open sets [V, §5.2.1].

The classic example of a preference ordering that is not continuous, and hence not representable, is the lexicographic ordering. A rather trite textbook example is that of a dedicated spirits drinker who is choosing between bundles (vectors in $\mathbb{R}^2_+$) consisting of (infinitely divisible) bottles of whiskey and wine. If any bundle contains more whiskey than another, it is strictly preferred; if two bundles contain the same amount of whiskey then the drinker's subsidiary preference for wine implies that the bundle with the strictly larger wine component will be preferred.

Such a preference ordering is clearly not continuous. The bundle $(1 + 1/n, 1)$ is weakly preferred to $(1, 2)$ but $(1, 2)$ is strictly preferred to the limiting bundle as $n \rightarrow \infty$, $(1, 1)$.

Another property of a preference ordering referred to below is convexity [see IV, §15.2]; R is convex if for every $y \in X$ (X a subset of $\mathbb{R}^m$) the set

$$\{x \mid x\,R\,y\}$$

is convex.

Finally, the *cardinality* of a set X refers to the number of elements in X.

15.2.2. A statement of the social choice problem

The formulation of 'the' social choice problem presented here is originally due to Arrow (1963), as modified by Sen (1970). The intention is to formulate the problem in as general a way as possible.

It can then be interpreted either as an aggregation problem, or in a more 'political' sense, e.g. the problem of designing a 'reasonable' constitution.

Suppose that there is a finite set of individuals $N = \{1, 2, \ldots, n\}$ in society. Also, let the set of possible social states be X. Depending on the interpretation, this may range from a set of political candidates to a set of feasible economic allocations. Accordingly, no restrictions are placed on X, as long as it contains at least three elements. Next let $R(X)$ be the set of all possible preference orderings on X. Call an element $R \in R(X)$ a social welfare ordering (SWO). A SWO captures the idea of Bergson's social welfare function, although it is a little more general in that it does not require R to be continuous.

Finally, moving from definitions to an assumption, it is supposed that all individuals have representable preference orderings on X. The strength of this assumption depends on the particular social choice problem under consideration. It is, however, essential to what follows. Thus, let U be the set of real-valued functions on $X \times N$, continuous in the first argument [see IV, §2.3]. Therefore, for a fixed $i \in N$, $u(\cdot, i)$ is a representation of i's preferences over X. (Also, $u(x, \cdot) \in \mathbb{R}^n$ is an n-dimensional vector of utility levels associated with any state.)

Now the social choice problem is to associate with each u in D, some subset of U, an ordering over X. Sen formalised this idea by defining a social welfare functional (SWFL), f, mapping from DCU to $R(X)$.

The logical distinction between a SWO, or a social welfare function as it is used in economics, and a social welfare functional should now be clear. In particular the 'reasonable conditions' imposed by Arrow are conditions on the SWFL and *not* the SWO.

This then is the formal framework. Within this framework, it is possible to distinguish sharply between (i) the informational basis of social choice, which refers to the implications various degrees of interpersonal comparability have for the relationship between U and f and (ii) aggregation conditions which impose 'desirable' restrictions on f, such as the Pareto principle involving both U and $R(X)$. These two topics will be taken up in sections 15.2.3 and 15.2.4, but before this is done some remarks on the formal framework are in order.

First, it seems that the Arrow framework is strongly welfaristic, in the sense that the domain of f includes only welfare information. In other words, if u, u' in U are the same, then $f(u) = f(u')$; if two societies have the same utility profiles over the set of alternatives, then these alternatives must be ordered in the same way for each society. However, for a given $u \in U$, the social choice between $\mathbf{x}$ and $\mathbf{y}$ in X need not depend just upon welfare information. For example, consider two societies $\mathbf{x}$ and $\mathbf{y}$ which are alike in all respects except that in $\mathbf{y}$ there is a law forbidding individuals to sell themselves into slavery, whereas in both $\mathbf{x}$ and $\mathbf{y}$ nobody finds it advantageous to do so. Suppose further that all individuals in this society are Utilitarians so that their preferences between legal systems depend only upon the end results of these systems, which in this example are indistinguishable. However, there are strong grounds for preferring $\mathbf{y}$ to $\mathbf{x}$ on non-welfare grounds and there is nothing in the Arrow–Sen framework that rules out such a social choice—it is just a formal model. The degree to which non-welfare information is excluded depends on the specification of the feasible set, and what is assumed about the ethical views of members of society (see Hahn, 1981).

A rather different problem is that the economist may find the framework rather abstract. The answer to that is that it is always possible to specialize the framework and then one can apply the theorems proved below to the case in point.

For example, let $X = \{\mathbf{x} \in \mathbb{R}^n \mid x_i \geqslant 0, \sum_i x_i = \bar{X}, i = 1, \ldots, n\}$ be the set of social

states and choose a u in U such that

$$u(\mathbf{x}, i) = x_i.$$

This is the problem of dividing a cake of fixed size among n individuals, each of whom has 'selfish' preferences linear in income. Many of the results obtained apply to this case [see §15.6.1 below].

15.2.3. Aggregation conditions

As pointed out above, the social choice problem can equally well be viewed either as a problem of constructing a social welfare ordering from a given amount of utility information, or as a problem of designing an ideal constitution. It is that latter interpretation that provides the motivation for the conditions here. They are to be understood as conditions which any reasonable constitution should satisfy.

The first such condition is that social choice should respect unanimous individual strict preference; if all individuals prefer $\mathbf{x}$ to $\mathbf{y}$, then the social ordering should reflect this.

(WP): Weak Pareto Principle
   Let $\mathbf{x}$, $\mathbf{y} \in X$, $u \in U$, and $R = f(u)$.

If $U(\mathbf{x}, i) > U(\mathbf{y}, i)$ all i in N then $\mathbf{x}\,P\,\mathbf{y}$.

A rather stronger condition is respect of unanimous indifference:

(PI): Pareto Indifference

Let $\mathbf{x}, \mathbf{y} \in X$, $u \in U$ and $R = f(u)$.

If $U(\mathbf{x}, i) = U(\mathbf{y}, i)$ all i in N then $\mathbf{x}\,I\,\mathbf{y}$.

This is restrictive in the sense that it rules out the use of non-welfare information in ordering states when welfare information gives no grounds for choosing between them (e.g. the example in §15.2.2.) In what follows, the conjunction of conditions (WP) and (PI) will usually be assumed, and will be denoted (P).

The idea behind the next condition is that preferences over nonfeasible alternatives should not affect the social ordering over the feasible set.

(IIA): Independence of Irrelevant Alternatives

For any u^0, $u^1 \in U$ and $A \subseteq X$ if

(i) $u^0(\mathbf{x}, i) = u^1(\mathbf{x}, i)$ all $\mathbf{x}$ in A, all i in N, and

(ii) $R^0 = f(u^0)$, $R^1 = f(u^1)$, then $R^0 = R^1$ on A, or in other words,

$$\mathbf{x}\,R^0\,\mathbf{y} \leftrightarrow \mathbf{x}\,R^1\,\mathbf{y} \text{ for all } \mathbf{x},\,\mathbf{y} \text{ in } A.$$

More precisely if A is some strict subset of X, and welfare information coincides over A, then the SWOs should coincide over that subset, no matter how welfare information may vary over the complement of A.

There are SWFLs, such as the rank order voting method, which do not satisfy (IIA); for details, the reader is referred to Sen (1970).

Usually this condition is stated as a binary one, with $A = \{\mathbf{x}, \mathbf{y}\}$ but it is also true that apparently weaker conditions, with the cardinality of A larger than two imply binary independence, as well as vice versa.

The final condition is that the SWFL can map every element of U into $R(X)$.

(U): Unrestricted Domain

$D = U$.

To clarify the meaning of this condition, consider a celebrated example of a SWFL that does not satisfy (U), the majority voting SWFL. Define this to be '$\mathbf{x}\,R\,\mathbf{y}$ if and only if the number of individuals who strictly prefer $\mathbf{x}$ to $\mathbf{y}$ is at least as great as the number who prefer $\mathbf{y}$ to $\mathbf{x}$'.

Then consider $X = \{\mathbf{x}, \mathbf{y}, \mathbf{z}\}$ and $u \in U$ such that:

$$U(\mathbf{x}, 1) > U(\mathbf{y}, 1) > U(\mathbf{z}, 1)$$
$$U(\mathbf{y}, 2) > U(\mathbf{z}, 2) > U(\mathbf{x}, 2)$$
$$U(\mathbf{z}, 3) > U(\mathbf{x}, 3) > U(\mathbf{y}, 3).$$

This is Condorcet's famous voting paradox, so called because a majority prefers $\mathbf{x}$ to $\mathbf{y}$, $\mathbf{y}$ to $\mathbf{z}$, and $\mathbf{z}$ to $\mathbf{x}$ and therefore violates transitivity. For this utility profile the majority voting rule would generate a binary relation on X, which is not transitive. In other words, majority rule does not map all of U into $R(X)$.

Now (PI), (IIA) and (U) taken together are very effective in ruling out the use of non-welfare information. Jointly they imply the following condition:

(*N*) *Neutrality*

If for any $\mathbf{x}$, $\mathbf{y}$, $\mathbf{w}$, $\mathbf{z} \in X$, u^0, $u^1 \in U$

(i) $U^0(\mathbf{x}, i) = u^1(\mathbf{w}, i)$ all i in N,

(ii) $u^0(\mathbf{y}, i) = u^1(\mathbf{z}, i)$ all i in N, and

(iii) $R^0 = f(u^0)$, $R^1 = f(u^1)$ then $\mathbf{x} R^0 \mathbf{y} \leftrightarrow \mathbf{w} R^1 \mathbf{z}$.

This says that if welfare information relating to two pairs of states $\{\mathbf{x}, \mathbf{y}\}$ and $\{\mathbf{w}, \mathbf{z}\}$ is the same for two utility profiles, then the two associated SWOs should agree over these two pairs. Any non-welfare information contained in the descriptions of these states is ignored.

(N) is clearly stronger than (IIA). For example, if $\mathbf{x} = \mathbf{w}$ and $\mathbf{y} = \mathbf{z}$ then (N) reduces to the latter. It also has the following important implication that when f satisfies (N) and (U) all of the orderings $f(u)$ of $Xu \in U$, can be represented by a single ordering of $\mathbb{R}^n$, the space of n-tuples of utility levels [see I, Example 5.2.2].

LEMMA 15.2.1. *A SWL f satisfies (PI), (IIA) and (U) if and only if there exists an ordering R^* of $\mathbb{R}^n$ such that for all $\mathbf{x}$, $\mathbf{y} \in X$, $u \in U$, $\mathbf{a}$, $\mathbf{b} \in \mathbb{R}^n$*

$$\mathbf{x} R \mathbf{y} \leftrightarrow \mathbf{a} R^* \mathbf{b} \quad \text{where} \quad R = f(u),$$

$$\mathbf{a} = u(\mathbf{x}, \cdot), \quad \mathbf{b} = u(\mathbf{y}, \cdot).$$

Proof. To show sufficiency of (PI), (IIA) and (U) a unique R^* is constructed as follows. Choose arbitrary $\mathbf{a}$, $\mathbf{b} \in \mathbb{R}^n$. By (U), there exists $u \in U$, $\mathbf{x}$, $\mathbf{y} \in X$ such that

$$u(\mathbf{x}, \cdot) = \mathbf{a}, \quad u(\mathbf{y}, \cdot) = \mathbf{b}.$$

Then define R^* by $\mathbf{a} R^* \mathbf{b} \leftrightarrow \mathbf{x} R \mathbf{y}$, $\mathbf{b} R^* \mathbf{a} \leftrightarrow \mathbf{y} R \mathbf{x}$, $R = f(u)$. In general, (U) implies that there will be other $u' \in U$, $\mathbf{w}$, $\mathbf{z} \in X$ with

$$u'(\mathbf{w}, \cdot) = \mathbf{a}, \quad u'(\mathbf{z}, \cdot) = \mathbf{b}$$

but neutrality guarantees that the same ordering R^* will be generated by $\mathbf{a} R^* \mathbf{b} \leftrightarrow \mathbf{w} R' \mathbf{z}$ $\mathbf{b} R^* \mathbf{a} \leftrightarrow \mathbf{z} R' \mathbf{w}$, $R' = f(u')$. The reflexivity, completeness, and transitivity of R follows from the fact that R satisfies these, and (U) and (N). The details are left to the reader.

Necessity involves showing that if an ordering on $\mathbb{R}^n$ exists, defined as above, then the SWFL must satisfy the stated properties.

For example, to prove (U) it must be shown that for any $u \in U$, the binary relation, R, generated by R^* on X is an ordering. Choose *any* $\mathbf{x}$, $\mathbf{y} \in X$; then $u(\mathbf{x}, \cdot) = \mathbf{a}$, $u(\mathbf{y}, \cdot) = \mathbf{b}$, and as R^* is complete, either $\mathbf{x} R \mathbf{y}$ or $\mathbf{y} R \mathbf{x}$ so R is complete.

Similarly, R can be shown to be reflexive and transitive. The proof of the necessity of (PI) and (IIA) is left to the reader. $\qquad\qquad \square$

This is a result of key importance as it reduces the analysis of possible SWFLs satisfying (PI) (IIA) and (U) and particular comparability/measurability conditions to the analysis of an ordering R^* satisfying the corresponding conditions on $\mathbb{R}^n$, and the latter is usually a much simpler task.

Finally, a condition similar in spirit to neutrality is given. It says that if a $u \in U$ is thought of as a list of utility functions and that list is permuted then both the original list and the permutation give rise to the same SWO. What really matters is the list of utility functions, not the names attached to them. Accordingly this condition is called

(*A*) *Anonymity*

Let ∂ be a permutation of N, that is a bijection from N to N [see I, §8.1]. Then if $u^0, u^1 \in U$, $R^0 = f(u^0)$, $R^1 = f(u^1)$ and

$$u^0(i) = u^1(\partial(i))$$

then $R^0 = R^1$.

This has an analogue for R^*:

(*A**) For every $\mathbf{a}, \mathbf{b} \in \mathbb{R}^n$, $\mathbf{a}\, I^*\, \mathbf{b}$ if there exists a permutation ∂ of N such that for all i in N,

$$a_{\partial(i)} = b_i$$

that is $(b_1, \ldots, b_n)$ is a rearrangement of elements $(a_1, \ldots, a_n)$.

There is also a natural analogue of (P) for R^*:

(*P**) For every $\mathbf{a}, \mathbf{b} \in \mathbb{R}^n$, if $a_i \geq b_i$ all $i \in N$, then $\mathbf{a}\, R^*\, \mathbf{b}$, and if $a_i > b_i$ all $i \in N$ then $\mathbf{a}\, P^*\, \mathbf{b}$.

It is straightforward, using similar arguments to those in the proof of Lemma 15.2.1, to show the following.

LEMMA 15.2.2. *Suppose the SWFL satisfies (PI) and (IIA). Then*
  the SWFL satisfies (WP) if and only if R^* satisfies (P*); and
  the SWFL satisfies (A) if and only if R^* satisfies (A*).

This result can be found in D'Aspremont and Gevers (1977), and is used extensively in sections 15.3, 15.4 and 15.5 below.

15.2.4. Comparing individuals

In modern consumer theory the utility function only has ordinal significance, in the sense that it merely conveys information about the consumers' preference ordering; in that statements of the type 'x yields i twice as much utility as y' are not taken to be meaningful.

Mathematically, if $u(\cdot, i)$ is one representation of the ith individual's preference ordering on X then $u'(\cdot, i) = \phi(u \cdot, i))$ (where $\phi: \mathbb{R} \to \mathbb{R}$ is strictly increasing) is also a representation of the same preference ordering, and thus conveys the same information. This is expressed concisely by saying that if $u'(\cdot, i)$ can be arrived at from $u(\cdot, i)$ by a strictly increasing transformation then the two are equivalent, or $u(\cdot, i) \sim u'(\cdot, i)$.

If, on the other hand, statements involving differences in utility levels are taken to be meaningful, (as well as ordinal statements) then $u(\cdot, i) \sim u'(\cdot, i)$ if and only if $u'(\mathbf{x}, i) = \alpha + \beta u(\mathbf{x}, i)$, $\beta > 0$ all $\mathbf{x} \in X$. That is ϕ must be an affine (linear) transformation, since a nonlinear transformation of $u(\cdot i)$ will not, in general, preserve utility difference [see I, §5.13].

In the former case, utility is said to be *ordinally* measurable; in the latter, it is said to be *cardinally* measurable. Thus, formally a measurability condition is an equivalence relation on the set of all possible utility functions on X. In the framework presented in 15.2.2, a particular *interpersonal* comparability assumption can be formalized in exactly the same way.

Consider for example, the assumption made by Arrow (1963) that individual preference orderings are ordinally measurable and that no comparability between individuals is allowed. Suppose $u \in U$ is a utility profile. Then analogously to the case of the single individual, any $u' \in U$ such that

$$u'(\cdot, i) = \phi_i(u(\cdot, i)) \text{ all } i \in N$$

with $\phi_i: \mathbb{R} \to \mathbb{R}$ strictly increasing, embodies the same information as u. Therefore, one could say that u is equivalent to u' under Arrow's assumption.

Thus, an interpersonal comparability/measurability assumption can be expressed by Φ, a set of n-tuples of functions from the reals into the reals. Any element of this set induces a relation upon $U \times U$:

$$u' \sim u \leftrightarrow u' = \phi(u), \quad \text{for some } \phi \in \Phi,$$

where $u' = \phi(u)$ is shorthand for $u'(\cdot, i) = \phi_i(u(\cdot, i))$ all $i \in N$. To ensure that this relation is indeed an equivalence relation, Φ must satisfy three conditions. In particular, it must contain the n-tuple of identity transforms (reflexivity); if $\phi \in \Phi$, then ϕ^{-1} must be in Φ (symmetry); and if $\phi_1, \phi_2 \in \Phi$ then $\phi_1 \cdot \phi_2 \in \Phi$ (transitivity).

Not all seemingly reasonable sets Φ qualify. Consider $\Phi = \times_{i=1}^{n} \Phi_i$,

$$\Phi_i = \{\phi_i | \phi_i(z) = \alpha + \beta_i z, \beta_i > 0 \quad z \in \mathbb{R}\}.$$

Then $\phi_i^{-1}(z) = 1/\beta_i \cdot z - \alpha/\beta_i$ so that the constant terms differ across individuals if not all the β_i are equal, so in this case $\phi^{-1} \notin \Phi$. If Φ does satisfy these conditions then the induced equivalence relation induces a partition of U, and all three ways of defining a comparability/measurability condition are equivalent (Φ, an equivalence relation on $U \times U$, a partition of U).

Next, say that a SWFL *satisfies* a particular comparability/measurability condition if for all $u, u' \in U$ such that $u' \sim u, f(u') = f(u)$. The meaning of this is that if $u' \sim u$, the two utility profiles yield identical information and thus imply the same choice of social welfare ordering.

As with the aggregation conditions discussed in section 15.2.3, this definition for the SWFL has an analogue in terms of R^*. Say that R^* *satisfies* a particular measurability/comparability condition* if $\mathbf{a} \; R^* \; \mathbf{b} \leftrightarrow \phi(\mathbf{a}) \; R^* \; \phi(\mathbf{b})$ all $\mathbf{a}, \; \mathbf{b} \in \mathbb{R}^n$ and $\phi \in \Phi$.

It is easy to show, along the lines of Lemma 15.2.1 above, that if the (SWFL) satisfies (U), (PI) and (IIA), the two definitions are equivalent; the SWFL satisfies any condition if and only if R^* satisfies any condition*. The proof of this is left to the reader.

These definitions may be clarified by means of an example. The majority voting SWFL satisfies ordinal non-comparability as independent monotonic transformations of the utility functions do not affect the number of individuals preferring one alternative to another. However, the Utilitarian SWFL defined as

$$\sum_i u(\mathbf{x}, i) \geq \sum u(\mathbf{y}, i) \to \mathbf{x} \, R \, \mathbf{y}$$

does not satisfy this condition. This is most easily seen by considering the corresponding Utilitarian SWO on utility space:

$$\sum_i a_i \geq \sum_i b_i \to \mathbf{a} \, R^* \, \mathbf{b}.$$

Then there always exist strictly increasing transformations ϕ_i, and a pair $\mathbf{a}, \mathbf{b} \in \mathbb{R}^n$ such that $\sum_i a_i \geq \sum_i b_i$, but $\sum_i \phi_i(a_i) < \sum_i \phi_i(b_i)$, which violates the definition above.

It remains to list the particular measurability/comparability conditions to be used in this chapter, and discuss the relations between them.

First, the condition used by Arrow:

(*ONC*) *Ordinal Non-Comparability*
Here Φ consists of the set of *n*-tuples of functions

$$\phi_i(z), \; z \in \mathbb{R}$$

with ϕ_i strictly increasing [see IV, §2.7].

Next, individual utilities may be cardinally measurable:

(*CNC*) *Cardinal Non-Comparability*

$$\phi_i(z) = \alpha_i + \beta_i z \quad z \in \mathbb{R}$$

Comparison of welfare *levels* across individuals is possible under:

(*OLC*) *Ordinal Level Comparability*

$$\phi_i(z) = \phi(z), \quad z \in \mathbb{R}$$

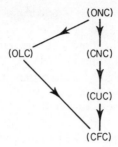

Figure 15.1: Comparing individuals

$\phi(z)$ strictly increasing. Alternatively, welfare gains across individuals are made comparable by

(CUC) Cardinal Unit Comparability

$$\phi_i(z) = \alpha_i + \beta z \quad \beta > 0, z \in \mathbb{R}$$

Finally, both gains and levels are comparable under

(CFC) Cardinal Full Comparability

$$\phi_i(z) = \alpha + \beta z \quad \beta > 0, z \in \mathbb{R}$$

Note that all these sets Φ of functions satisfy the three conditions above, so that their associated equivalence relations are well-defined. Finally, say that one condition is stronger than another if the set of invariance transforms for the first is contained in the set for the second. The relationships between the various conditions are depicted in Figure 15.1, where an arrow denotes increasing strength.

15.3. NON-COMPARABILITY AND DICTATORSHIP

15.3.1. Arrow's impossibility theorem

In this section, the framework developed in sections 15.2.2 to 15.2.4 is put to use in proving Arrow's Impossibility Theorem. This is the fundamental result that provided the original motivation for the axiomatic approach to the study of interpersonal comparability and aggregation that is surveyed in this chapter.

Arrow (1963) demonstrated that any SWFL that satisfies unrestricted domain, the Pareto principle, the irrelevance of independent alternatives, and does not allow any form of comparability between individuals (that is satisfies either (CNC) or (ONC)) must be a dictatorship. By a dictatorship Arrow meant that there must exist an individual whose strict preference between any pair of alternatives must also be society's preference no matter what others' preferences are, for all possible utility profiles, and for all pairs of states in X. This is clearly an undesirable feature of any constitution, and so Arrow imposed the additional condition of non-dictatorship on the SWFL thus obtaining his celebrated Impossibility Theorem; there exists no SWFL satisfying (U), (P), (IIA), (ONC) or (CNC) and non-dictatorship.

In the remainder of this subsection, a version of Arrow's Theorem is proved. The proof essentially consists of showing that if R^* satisfies (P*) and (ONC*) or (CNC*) then there is an $i \in N$ such that for any $\mathbf{a}$, $\mathbf{b} \in \mathbb{R}^n$, $a_i > b_i \rightarrow \mathbf{a} \, P^* \, \mathbf{b}$. It then follows from Lemmas 15.2.1 and 15.2.2 and the discussion in section 15.2.4 that if the SWFL satisfies Arrow's conditions there is an $i \in N$ such that $U(\mathbf{x}, i) > U(\mathbf{y}, i) \rightarrow \mathbf{x} \, P \, \mathbf{y}$ all $\mathbf{x}$, $\mathbf{y} \in X$ all $u \in U$.

The first step in the proof, which is the crucial one, is to show that if the strict preference of some individual $i \in N$ is reflected in the social ordering over *some* pair $\mathbf{a}$, $\mathbf{b} \in \mathbb{R}^n$, where $a_i > b_i$, $b_j > a_j \, j \neq i$ (that is where the other individuals' preferences are strongly opposed to i's) then i's strict preference prevails over *all* pairs $\mathbf{a}$, $\mathbf{b} \in \mathbb{R}^n$. Loosely speaking, if any individual has dictatorial power over one pair of alternatives, this power is infectious—he or she is then a dictator.

From this result, it is a short step to show that with unrestricted domain, *some* individual must have dictatorial power over *some* pair, and the existence of a dictator follows from these two facts.

To begin with, a formal statement of this definition is needed. An individual $i \in N$ is *weakly decisive* if there exists a pair $\mathbf{a}$, $\mathbf{b} \in \mathbb{R}^n$, $a_i > b_i$, $b_j > a_j \, j \neq i$ and $\mathbf{a} \, P^* \, \mathbf{b}$. Note that by this definition, weak decisiveness is a property of the ordering R^*, *not* a condition on the SWFL. Its purpose is merely to aid proof of Arrow's Theorem. Clearly if $i \in N$ is a dictator, then he or she is weakly decisive. However, with no comparability between individuals, the converse is also true:

LEMMA 15.3.1. *If R^* satisfies (P*) and (CNC*) or (ONC*) then if $i \in N$ is weakly decisive, then i is a dictator.*

This result is true only if no comparability between individuals is possible, although a weakened form of it holds with ordinal level comparability [see §15.4.1 below). It is straightforward to prove, but the proof for $n = 2$ is particularly simple and intuitive, and is given below.

Proof. Suppose individual 1 is weakly decisive. Then for any $\mathbf{c}$, $\mathbf{d} \in \mathbb{R}^2$ with $c_1 > d_1$, it must be shown that $\mathbf{c} \, P^* \, \mathbf{d}$. There are three possibilities: either (i) $c_2 > d_2$, or (ii) $c_2 < d_2$, or (iii) $c_2 = d_2$. If $c_2 > d_2$, then $\mathbf{c} \, P^* \, \mathbf{d}$ by the Pareto principle. In case (ii), as 1 is weakly decisive there exist $\mathbf{a}$, $\mathbf{b} \in \mathbb{R}^2$ with $a_1 > b_1$, $a_2 < b_2$ and $\mathbf{a} \, P^* \, \mathbf{b}$. As $\phi_i(z) = z - b_i$, $i = 1$, 2, are (CNC) transforms, $\phi(\mathbf{a}) \, P^* \, \phi(\mathbf{b})$ or $(\mathbf{a} - \mathbf{b}) \, P^* \, \mathbf{0}$. Now consider the transforms

$$\phi_i(z) = \frac{(c_i - d_i)}{(a_i - b_i)} \cdot z = \lambda_i \cdot z.$$

Note $\lambda_i > 0$, $i = 1$, 2, by definition so these are (CNC) transforms the $\phi(\mathbf{a} - \mathbf{b}) P^* \phi(\mathbf{0})$ or $(\mathbf{c} - \mathbf{d}) P^* \mathbf{0}$. Finally as $\phi_i(z) = z + d_i$, $i = 1$, 2, are (CNC) transforms, $\mathbf{c} P^* \mathbf{d}$.

In case (iii) define $\mathbf{e} \in \mathbb{R}^2$ by $e_1 = c_1$, $e_2 = c_2 - \varepsilon$, $\varepsilon > 0$. Then $\mathbf{c} R^* \mathbf{e}$ and $e_1 > d_1$, $e_2 < d_2$ so by the argument for case (ii), $\mathbf{e} P^* \mathbf{d}$. By transitivity of R^*, $\mathbf{c} P^* \mathbf{d}$.

Therefore, 1 is a dictator. An exactly similar argument applies if 2 is weakly decisive. □

Lemma 15.3.1 can now be used to show that with no comparability the only SWFL must be dictatorial.

THEOREM 15.3.1 (*Arrow's Impossibility Theorem*). *If the SWFL satisfies* (U), (IIA), (P) *and* (CNC) *or* (ONC) *then there is an* $i \in N$ *such that for all* $u \in U$, $x, y \in X$

$$u(\mathbf{x}, i) > u(\mathbf{y}, i) \rightarrow \mathbf{x} P \mathbf{y}.$$

Proof. As remarked above it must be shown that for some $i \in N$, all $\mathbf{a}$, $\mathbf{b} \in \mathbb{R}^n$, $a_i > b_i \rightarrow \mathbf{a} P^* \mathbf{b}$. Suppose, to the contrary, such a dictator does not exist. Define the following vectors:

$$\mathbf{a}^0 = (1, 1, \ldots, 1)$$
$$\mathbf{a}^1 = (2, 1 - \varepsilon, 1 - \varepsilon \ldots 1 - \varepsilon), \frac{1}{n-1} > \varepsilon > 0$$

Now $a_1^1 > a_1^0$, $a_i^0 > a_i^1 i \neq 1$. Therefore, if $\mathbf{a}^1 P^* \mathbf{a}^0$, individual 1 would be weakly decisive and thus a dictator by Lemma 15.3.1. Thus, $\mathbf{a}^0 R^* \mathbf{a}^1$.

In general, a sequence of vectors with this property can be defined. For $k = 2, 3, \ldots, n$ let

$$\mathbf{a}^k = \begin{cases} a_j^k = a_j^{k-1} - \varepsilon, j \neq k \\ a_k^k = 2 \end{cases}.$$

Then if $\mathbf{a}^k P^* \mathbf{a}^{k-1}$, individual k is weakly decisive, and thus a dictator. This is impossible by assumption, so $\mathbf{a}^{k-1} R^* \mathbf{a}^k k = 2, 3, \ldots, n$. Then $\mathbf{a}^0 R^* \mathbf{a}^n$ by transitivity. But $\mathbf{a}^n = (2 - (n-1)\varepsilon, 2 - (n-2)\varepsilon, \ldots 2)$ so as $\varepsilon < 1/(n-1)$, $\mathbf{a}^n > \mathbf{a}^0$, so $\mathbf{a}^n P^* \mathbf{a}^0$ by the Pareto principle, a contradiction. So a dictator exists after all. □

Note that Arrow's Theorem holds irrespectively of whether utilities are measured cardinally or ordinally. However, the Theorem says nothing about social choice when $i \in N$ is indifferent between two alternatives. One way of resolving this indeterminacy is to assume that the ordering R^* is continuous. Then it it representable by a Bergson social welfare function $W: \mathbb{R}^n \rightarrow \mathbb{R}$ and the corresponding result to Arrow's Theorem is that $W(\mathbf{a}) = a_i$ (that is W is a projection onto one of its coordinates). Then if $a_i = b_i$, $W(\mathbf{a}) = W(\mathbf{b})$ or $\mathbf{a} I^* \mathbf{b}$ so the dictator dictates even when he or she is indifferent.

15.3.2. Relaxing Arrow's conditions

A great deal of effort and ingenuity has been expended in trying to find out just how robust Arrow's theorem is to relaxation of the conditions. Until recently, most work was devoted to two avenues of approach. The first was to restrict 'unrestricted domain' so that certain types of preferences were ruled out of the domain of the SWFL. This approach was largely inspired by an attempt to find conditions under which the majority decision SWFL would produce a transitive social preference ordering [recall the example in §15.2.3.] This approach is not discussed partly for reasons of space, and partly because in the context of 'economic' models of social choice (that is where X is a subset of Euclidean space and individual utility functions are quasi-concave [see V, §4.3.1] and differentiable [see IV, §5.3]) necessary and sufficient conditions for transitive majority rule are very restrictive (see Kramer, 1973).

A second approach is to relax the condition that the SWF be an *ordering*, that is complete, reflexive and transitive. For example, the requirement may be relaxed to quasi-transitivity (transitivity of the strict preference relation). However, similar impossibility theorems to Arrow's exist for all such relaxations of transitivity (see Kelly, 1978).

From the point of view of the economist, by far the most interesting escape from Arrow's theorem has been fully developed only recently by D'Aspremont and Gevers (1977) and Roberts (1980a) among others using the framework developed here, and proceeds by relaxing the stringent conditions excluding interpersonal comparability that are necessary for Arrow's Theorem.

The next three sections are in one way or another, devoted to this development.

15.4. POSITIONAL DICTATORSHIP AND THE MAXIMIN SOCIAL WELFARE FUNCTION

15.4.1. A possibility theorem

The precise definition of interpersonal comparability developed at some length in section 15.2.4 now has its reward. By weakening the invariance requirement on the SWFL bit by bit it is possible to show how larger and larger classes of non-dictatorial SWFLs become possible. In addition, such classes are *characterized* by the relevant invariance transformation; a SWFL belongs to the stated class if and only if it satisfies (U), (IIA), (P) and the appropriate invariance requirement.

In this section, ordinal level comparability (OLC), a simple and appealing relaxation of (ONC) is considered. The idea is that judgements of the form 'person i is better off in state **x** than person j is in state **y**' are considered meaningful. For example, different states may refer to redistributions of income; then, as Arrow (1973) has remarked, ordinal level comparability 'is probably the standard way in which people make judgements about appropriate income distributions: if I am richer than you, I may find it easy to make the judgement that it is better for you to have the marginal dollar than for me!'

If (OLC) comparisons are allowed, it is possible to rank individuals from worst-off to best-off in any given state. Therefore, individuals can now be identified both by their 'names' and by their place in the utility ranking in each state. If the former means of identification is ruled out by imposing anonymity (A) then it can be shown that if any *rank* or position (e.g. the worst-off) has dictatorial power over *some* pair of alternatives, it has power over all pairs, or more concisely, there is a *positional dictatorship*. One then obtains a result similar to Arrow's Theorem; if the SWFL satisfies (U), (IIA) (P), (A) and (OLC) it must be a positional dictatorship. To state the result precisely and clearly, however, one bit of additional notation is needed.

For any $x \in X$, there is an associated set of n real numbers, the utility ranks of the n individuals (the number 1 denotes best-off, 2 next best-off etc.). Let this set be M. Also, let S_x be a permutation function (bijection) from M to N, (N the set of individuals) such that if $i \in N$ has rank $r \in M$ in state $\mathbf{x}$, $S_x(r) = i$. For example, if the utility vector in state $\mathbf{x}$ is $\mathbf{u}(\mathbf{x}, \cdot) = (1, 7, 3)$ then $S_x(1) = 2$ (as individual 2 is best-off), $S_x(2) = 3$ and $S_x(3) = 1$. If there are two or more individuals with equal utilities in some state $\mathbf{x}$, S_x is not unique. For example if $u(\mathbf{x}, \cdot) = (7, 1, 1)$ then both $(S_x(1) = 1, \ S_x(2) = 2, \ S_x(3) = 3)$ *and* $(S_x(1) = 1, \ S_x(2) = 3, \ S_x(3) = 2)$ fulfil the requirements.

Then a *positional dictator* exists if for all $u \in U$, $\mathbf{x}, \mathbf{y} \in X$ there is a rank $r \in M$ such that

$$u(\mathbf{x}, S_x(r)) > u(\mathbf{y}, S_y(r)) \to \mathbf{x} \, P \, \mathbf{y}.$$

As in the case of the Arrow dictator, there is an indeterminacy in the definition of positional dictatorship. If the positional dictator is indifferent between $\mathbf{x}$ and $\mathbf{y}$, then a choice can be made arbitrarily. By imposing the requirement that R^* be continuous, this indeterminancy can be eliminated—for example, the dictatorship of the worst-off, or nth position, along with continuity is the maximum SWF, familiar to economists. Formally the SWFL is maximin if $\min_i u(\mathbf{x}, i) \geqslant \min_i u(\mathbf{y}, i) \to \mathbf{x} \, R \, \mathbf{y}$. The corresponding Bergson SWF is of the form $W(\mathbf{a}) = \min_{i \in N} a_i$. The possibility theorem referred to above, originally due to Gevers (1979) and Roberts (1980a, b) can now be stated.

THEOREM 15.4.10. *If the SWFL satisfies* (U), (IIA), (P), (OLC) *and* (A) *then there is a positional dictator.*

As with Arrow's Theorem, this is most easily proved by first proving the corresponding theorem stated in terms of the ordering R^*. To do this requires a restatement of the concept of a positional dictator.

For any $\mathbf{a} \in \mathbb{R}^n$, let $\mathbf{a}^0$ be any permutation of $\mathbf{a}$ such that $a_1^0 \geqslant a_2^0 \ldots \geqslant a_n^0$. Then a rank $r \in M$ is a *positional dictator* if for any pair of vectors $\mathbf{a}, \mathbf{b} \in \mathbb{R}^n$, $a_r^0 > b_r^0 \rightarrow$ $\mathbf{a} \, P^* \, \mathbf{b}$. This is just a restatement of the definition above. Also, say that a rank $r \in M$ is weakly decisive if there is a pair of vectors $\mathbf{a}, \mathbf{b} \in \mathbb{R}^n$ such that $a_r^0 > b_r^0$, $a_j^0 < b_j^0 \; j \neq r$, and $\mathbf{a} \, P^* \, \mathbf{b}$.

As noted above, there is a direct analogue of Lemma 15.3.1 in the proof of Arrow's Theorem:

LEMMA 15.4.1. *If R^* satisfies (P^*), (A^*) and (OLC^*) then if a rank $r \in M$ is weakly decisive, then r is a positional dictator.*

The proof of this in the general case is rather complicated, but it can be proved much more simply and intuitively if $n = 2$.

Proof. Let the two ranks in M be 1 and 2. Suppose rank 1 is weakly decisive, and choose any $\mathbf{c}, \mathbf{d} \in \mathbb{R}^2$ with $c_1^0 > d_1^0$; it must be shown that $\mathbf{c} \, P^* \, \mathbf{d}$. There are three possibilities: either (i) $c_2^0 > d_2^0$, or (ii) $c_2^0 = d_2^0$ or (iii) $c_2^0 < d_2^0$. In (i) $\mathbf{c} \, P^* \, \mathbf{d}$ by the Pareto principle. In case (iii), as 1 is weakly decisive there exist $\mathbf{a}, \mathbf{b} \in \mathbb{R}^2$ such that $a_2^0 < b_2^0 < b_1^0 < a_1^0$ and $\mathbf{a} \, P^* \, \mathbf{b}$. Thus, as $c_2^0 < d_2^0 < d_1^0 < c_1^0$ there exists a strictly increasing function $\phi : \mathbb{R} \rightarrow \mathbb{R}$ such that $\phi(a_i^0) = c_i^0$, $\phi(b_i^0) = d_i^0$, $i = 1, 2$, as in Figure 15.2.

By definition, ϕ is an admissible (OLC^*) transform. Also by definition $\mathbf{a} \, P^* \, \mathbf{b}$. By (A^*), $\mathbf{a}^0 \, P^* \, \mathbf{b}^0$ so $\phi(\mathbf{a}^0) \, P^* \, \phi(\mathbf{b}^0)$ or $\mathbf{c}^0 \, P^* \, \mathbf{d}^0$ or by (A^*) again $\mathbf{c} \, P^* \, \mathbf{d}$.

In case (ii) define $\mathbf{e} \in \mathbb{R}^2$, $e_1 = c_1^0 e_2 = c_2^0 - \varepsilon$, $\varepsilon > 0$. Then by the argument for case (iii), $\mathbf{e} \, P^* \, \mathbf{d}^0$ and by the Pareto principle $\mathbf{c}^0 \, R^* \, \mathbf{e}$ so $\mathbf{c}^0 \, P^* \, \mathbf{d}^0$, or $\mathbf{c} \, P^* \, \mathbf{d}$.

Therefore, if rank 1 is weakly decisive, it is a positional dictator. An identical argument applies to rank 2 so the Lemma is proved for $n = 2$. $\qquad \square$

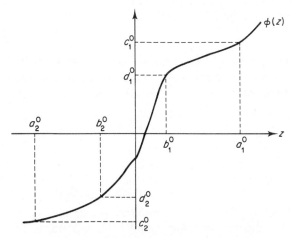

Figure 15.2: Illustration of Lemma 15.4.10

Given Lemma 15.4.1, the existence of a positional dictator is easily proved.

Proof of Theorem 15.4.1. Suppose a positional dictator does not exist. Choose a vector of utilities

$$\mathbf{a}^0 = (1, 1,\ldots, 1)$$

and let individual 1 occupy the top rank (recall ties can be broken arbitrarily if two or more components of a utility vector are equal). Then consider

$$\mathbf{a}^1 = (2, 1 - \varepsilon, 1 - \varepsilon\ldots 1 - \varepsilon), \quad 0 < \varepsilon < \frac{1}{2n - 1}.$$

If $\mathbf{a}^1 P^* \mathbf{a}^0$, then the top rank would be weakly decisive, and thus a dictator. Thus, $\mathbf{a}^0 R^* \mathbf{a}^1$. Next, choose

$$\mathbf{a}^2 = (2 - \varepsilon, 2 - 2\varepsilon, 1 - 2\varepsilon\ldots 1 - 2\varepsilon).$$

Comparing $\mathbf{a}^1$ and $\mathbf{a}^2$ and letting individual 2 occupy the second rank in $\mathbf{a}^1$, exactly the same argument applies if the second rank is not to be a dictator, so $\mathbf{a}^1 R^* \mathbf{a}^2$.

In general, one can construct a sequence of vectors of this type inductively:

$$\mathbf{a}^k = \begin{cases} a_k^k = a_{k-1}^{k-1} - 2\varepsilon, \\ a_l^k = a_l^{k-1} - \varepsilon, \quad l \ne k. \end{cases} \quad k = 2, 3,\ldots, n.$$

At each point comparing $\mathbf{a}^k$ and $\mathbf{a}^{k-1}$ shows that the kth rank is weakly decisive and thus a dictator if $\mathbf{a}^k P^* \mathbf{a}^{k-1}$. By hypothesis, this is ruled out, so $\mathbf{a}^{k-1} R^* \mathbf{a}^k$. Then $\mathbf{a}^0 R^* \mathbf{a}^n$ by transitivity. But

$$\mathbf{a}^n = (2 - \varepsilon(n - 1), 2 - \varepsilon \cdot n,\ldots, 2 - \varepsilon(2n - 1))$$

so as $\varepsilon < (1/2n - 1)\mathbf{a}^n > \mathbf{a}^0$ so $\mathbf{a}^n P^* \mathbf{a}^0$, by Pareto a contradiction. Therefore, *some* rank must be weakly decisive. By Lemma 15.4.1, there must be a positional dictator. □

To illustrate Theorem 15.4.1, suppose again that $n = 2$ and the SWO is continuous. Then there are exactly two possible social welfare functions: $W(\mathbf{a}) = \max_{i=1,2} a_i$ dictatorship of the best-off, or $W(\mathbf{a}) = \min_{i=1,2} a_i$ dictatorship of the worst-off. The former possibility may strike the reader as highly inegalitarian. For example, if the social choice problem were to divide a cake of fixed size, and individual utilities were increasing functions of one's own share of the cake, the solution would be to give all the cake to one person.

In contrast, the other possibility, the maximin SWF involves allocating equal utility levels to both individuals in almost all conceivable allocation problems.

This shows clearly that the assumption that a certain type of interpersonal comparability is valid does not embody any value judgements relating to equity. With the axiomatic approach surveyed in this chapter if one wants possible SWFs to be 'inequality-averse' or quasi-concave, then it is necessary to impose an additional equity axiom on the aggregation process. This is taken up in the next section.

15.4.2. Equity and the maximin social welfare function

In this section a condition, first suggested by Sen (1973) and developed by Hammond (1976), is discussed which if imposed on the SWFL in conjunction with the other conditions in Theorem 15.4.1, is sufficient to eliminate all the positional dictators except the worst-off. However, it is also powerful enough to eliminate all other possibilities for social choice even when stronger comparability conditions such as cardinal full comparability are allowed. Indeed, if the SWFL satisfies (U), (IIA), (A), (P) and the 'equity axiom' then maximin is the only possibility no matter how strong the comparability condition, e.g. even if the only allowable transform is the identity transform, so *all u, u′ ∈ U* can be distinguished. (In this case without the 'equity axiom' *all* orderings R^* on $\mathbb{R}^n$ are possible.)

Hammond's condition appeals to intuition by specifying a rule for resolving conflicts in preference between *two* individuals only. Specifically, Hammond calls any $u \in U$, x, $y \in X$ such that for all but two individuals, $u(x, k) = u(y, k)$ a two-person situation.

Then the Hammond–Sen equity axiom is:

(E) For any pair x, $y \in X$, $u \in U$ such that $u(x, i) < u(x, j)$ and $u(y, i) < u(y, j)$ while $u(y, k) = u(x, k)$ for all $k \neq i, j$ then x P y provided $u(y, i) < u(x, i)$ irrespective of $u(x, j) \lesssim u(y, j)$.

The idea is that in a two-person situation, if one individual is worse-off than another in both states, then the former's wishes should prevail, no matter what the utility levels of those indifferent between x and y.

If the preference aggregation problem is conceived of as one of designing the 'idea' constitution, (E) can be thought of as a just method of resolving conflicts by means of positive discrimination in favour of the worse-off.

Alternatively, in the special case of the income distribution problem [recall §15.2.2] then (E) is simply a variant of the Pigou–Dalton condition on income inequality measures that transferring income from a richer person to a poorer person should raise welfare (see Sen, 1973, Chapter 2).

It should be noted at this point that the SWFL must satisfy ordinal level comparability, or stronger measurability/comparability conditions, in order for the equity axiom (E) even to be well-defined. For example, let $n = 2$ and $u(y, 1) = 2$, $u(x, 1) = 3$, $u(x, 2) = 4$, $u(y, 2) = 5$. Then by (E), x P y. However, the (CNC) transform $(\phi_1(z) = 3.z, \phi_2(z) = z)$ reverses the utility rankings so y P x by (E). Therefore, no SWFL satisfying the (CNC) or (ONC) invariance requirement could also satisfy (E).

Denote the class of conditions at least as strong as (OLC) by $(OLC)^+$. Then

THEOREM 15.4.2. *If the SWFL satisfies* $(U), (IIA), (P), (A), (E)$ *and* $(OLC)^+$, *then*

$$\min_i U(\mathbf{x}, i) > \min_i U(\mathbf{y}, i) \to \mathbf{x} P \mathbf{y}.$$

Before proving this result, it is convenient to state the analogue of (E) for R^*:

(E^*) for every $\mathbf{a}, \mathbf{b} \in \mathbb{R}^n$, such that

$$b_i < a_i < a_j < b_j$$

and

$$a_k = b_k, k \neq i, j, \mathbf{a} P^* \mathbf{b}.$$

Proof. As above, the result is proved for the ordering R^*.

For any $\mathbf{a}, \mathbf{b} \in \mathbb{R}^n$ define $\mathbf{a} P^M \mathbf{b} \leftrightarrow \min a_i > \min b_i$. It must be shown that $\mathbf{a} P^M \mathbf{b}$ implies $\mathbf{a} P^* \mathbf{b}$ all $\mathbf{a}, \mathbf{b} \in \mathbb{R}^n$ if R^* satisfies $(P^*), (A^*)$ (E^*) and $(OLC^*)^+$.

Suppose first at $a_i > b_i$ for *all* $i \in N$. Then certainly $\mathbf{a} P^M \mathbf{b}$, and $\mathbf{a} P^* \mathbf{b}$ by (P^*), the Pareto principle. Now the proof proceeds by induction. It will be assumed that for any $\mathbf{a}, \mathbf{b} \in \mathbb{R}^n$ such that $\mathbf{a} P^M \mathbf{b}$ and $a_i > b_i$ for exactly $m \leqslant n$ individuals, $\mathbf{a} P^* \mathbf{b}$. Suppose $\mathbf{a} P^M \mathbf{b}$ and $a_i > b_i$ for exactly $m - 1$ individuals. It must be shown that $\mathbf{a} P^* \mathbf{b}$. Define $\mathbf{a}^0$, a permutation of $\mathbf{a}$ such that $a_n^0 \leqslant a_{n-1}^0 \ldots \leqslant a_1^0$ as above, and $\mathbf{b}^0$ similarly [see I, §8.1].

It will be shown that $\mathbf{a}^0 P^* \mathbf{b}^0$. Then as R^* satisfies (A^*), $\mathbf{a}^0 I^* \mathbf{a}$, $\mathbf{b}^0 I^* \mathbf{b}$, so $\mathbf{a} P^* \mathbf{b}$ and the theorem will be proved.

Define the non-empty set $J = \{i \in N \mid a_i^0 \leqslant b_i^0\}$, and the vector $\mathbf{c}$ as follows.

$$\begin{cases} a_n^0 > c_n > b_n^0 \\ a_j^0 > c_j > c_n & \text{some} \quad j \in J \\ c_k = b_k & k \neq n, j \end{cases}$$

As $a_n^0 > c_n$, $\mathbf{a}^0 P^M \mathbf{c}$. Also, as $a_i > c_i$ for exactly m individuals, by the induction hypothesis, $\mathbf{a}^0 P^* \mathbf{c}$. Next, define a vector $\mathbf{d}$, as follows.

$$\begin{cases} c_n > d_n > b_n^0 \\ d_j = b_j^0 \\ d_k = c_k, \quad k \neq n, j. \end{cases}$$

By the definitions, $d_n < c_n < c_j < d_j$, and $d_k = c_k$ for $k \neq n, j$, so that by (E^*), $\mathbf{c} P^* \mathbf{d}$. Finally, $d_i \geqslant b_i^0$ all $i \in N$, so $\mathbf{d} R^* \mathbf{b}^0$ by Pareto. Thus $\mathbf{a}^0 P^* \mathbf{c}$, $\mathbf{c} P^* \mathbf{d}$, and $\mathbf{d} R^* \mathbf{b}^0$ so $\mathbf{a}^0 P^* \mathbf{b}^0$, as was to be shown.   □

This result shows that Hammond's axiom, in allowing the worse-off individual to win in all cases, is really very strong. However, if the SWFL satisfies (OLC), D'Aspremont and Gevers (1977) have shown that (E) is implied by two milder conditions. These two apparently unobjectionable conditions are; (i) that the best-off individual is not a positional dictator, and (ii) that the utility levels of individuals who are indifferent between all **x** in X should not affect social choice (separability).

An alternative approach is of course to impose conditions on the social welfare function itself, such as concavity [see IV, §15.2.6], which would rule out inegalitarian rankings of utility or income distributions. This is common practice in the literature on the measurement of income inequality for example [see Sen (1972) and Chapter 16 in this volume]. Just because there is no axiomatic basis for such concavity assumptions, it does not follow that income inequality measures based on them (e.g. Atkinson's measure) are not normatively based. Rather, the problem is that it is rather hard to tell exactly what ethical judgement is being made when a particular degree of concavity is decided upon.

15.5. UTILITARIANISM AND BEYOND

15.5.1. Intensity of preference and utilitarianism

Here, the implications of another strenghtening of non-comparability, cardinal unit comparability, are considered. As with (OLC) in Section 4.1, it is useful to have an intuitive motivation for considering this type of interpersonal comparability. To this end, consider the social choice problem where $N = (1, 2)$ $X = (\mathbf{x}, \mathbf{y}, \mathbf{z})$ and for some $u \in U$, utility levels are as below:

	x	**y**	**z**
1	1	0.9	0
2	0	0.9	1

Clearly 1 has a much stronger preference for **y** over **z** than 2 has for **z** over **y**, and similarly 2 has a stronger preference for **y** over **x** than 1 has for **x** over **y**. If this information is to be used in deriving a social ordering over X then one would want to choose a comparability condition which would 'preserve' this information.

Why, however, should this information be relevant? One reason is that in many choice problems a small minority suffers (or gains) a great deal to the marginal benefit (or loss) of the majority. For example, the sitting of a new airport may lead to a large reduction in the quality of life for local inhabitants, but only slightly improve the service offered to the air-traveller. In such a case, there are no good arguments for ignoring the welfare change of either the minority or the majority. Intuition indicates that these changes should be weighed against each other, or that comparison of differences should be attempted.

The relevant information, then, is, in this framework, vectors of differences in utilities between pairs of social states in X. Say that u and $u' \in U$ are equivalent if the corresponding vectors of utility differences between any pair $\mathbf{x}$, $\mathbf{y} \in X$ are the same up to multiplication by a scalar multiple. As the reader can verify, this definition of equivalence is indeed an equivalence relation, and thus induces a partition of u. Furthermore, this partition is exactly the one induced by the (CUC) invariance transforms: u is equivalent to u' by the above definition if and only if $u'(\cdot, i) = \alpha_i + \beta \cdot u(\cdot, i)$, $\beta > 0$, $i = 1, \ldots, n$.

Thus, (CUC) captures precisely the idea of comparing intensities of preference. (It is of course possible to have weaker comparisons of utility differences. For example, by invariance transforms 'between' (CUC) and (CNC) where $\phi_i(z) = \alpha_i + \beta_i \cdot z$ with the β_i satisfying some interpersonal restrictions. This is examined by Sen (1970).)

As defined in section 15.2.4, the Utilitarian SWFL satisfies (CUC). More surprisingly, it is the *only* SWFL to satisfy (U), (IIA), (P), (CUC) and anonymity.

THEOREM 15.5.1. *If the SWFL satisfies* (U), (IIA), (P), (CUC) *and* (A) *then*

$$\sum_i u(\mathbf{x}, i) \geqslant \sum_i u(\mathbf{y}, i) \rightarrow \mathbf{x} \, R \, \mathbf{y}.$$

Proof. To prove Theorem 15.5.1, all we have to show is that if R^* satisfies (P*), (A*) and (CUC*) then

$$\sum a_i \geqslant \sum b_i \rightarrow \mathbf{a} \, R^* \, \mathbf{b}.$$

Thus, we assume $\sum a_i \geqslant \sum b_i$ but $\mathbf{b} \, P^* \, \mathbf{a}$ and obtain a contradiction. As $\phi_i(z) = z - b_i$ is a (CUC*) transform, assuming this is clearly equivalent to assuming

$$c_i = a_i - b_i, \sum c_i \geqslant 0 \quad \text{but } \mathbf{0} \, P^* \, \mathbf{c},$$

Now, define the set $\{\mathbf{c} \mid \mathbf{0} \, P^* \, \mathbf{c}\}$. Using (CUC*) transforms, it is easily verified that $\{\mathbf{c} \mid \mathbf{0} \, P^* \, \mathbf{c}\}$ is convex [see IV, §15.2].

(A*) implies that if $\mathbf{0} \, P^* \, \mathbf{c}$, then $\mathbf{0} \, P^* \, \mathbf{c}^0$, where $\mathbf{c}^0$ is any permutation of $\mathbf{c}$ [see I, §8.1]. Define $\bar{\mathbf{c}} = (1/n \sum_i c_i, 1/n \sum_i c_i, \ldots)$, vector of average utilities. Now a well-known result of Hardy, Littlewood and Polya says that $\bar{\mathbf{c}}$ is equal to the convex combination of a finite number of permutations of $\mathbf{c}$ (see Sen, 1973, p. 54). Putting these two facts together, $\mathbf{0} \, P^* \, \bar{\mathbf{c}}$. But as $\bar{\mathbf{c}} \geqslant 0$ by assumption, $\bar{\mathbf{c}} \, R^* \, \mathbf{0}$, by (P*) which is a contradiction.   □

The idea is illustrated in Figure 15.3 for the case $n = 2$. This result is due to D'Aspremont and Gevers (1977). So far then, two natural modifications of non-comparability, (OLC) and (CUC) have been considered. The former allows comparisons of utility levels but not differences and leads to positional dictatorship; the latter allows comparisons of differences but not levels, and implies classical Utilitarianism. In the next section, a condition that is stronger than both of these conditions (see Figure 15.1), cardinal full comparability is

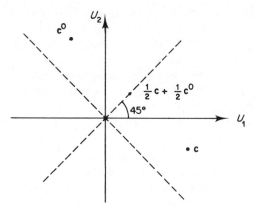

Figure 15.3: Illustration of theorem 15.5.1

analysed. As is shown below, a kind of synthesis is achieved. Admissible SWFLs can now depend both on the sum of utilities and the distribution of that sum.

15.5.2. Levels and differences

Cardinal full comparability allows both comparison of levels of utility between individuals in any state in X, *and* comparison of differences in utility between any two states across individuals.

To examine the possibilities for social choice, a slightly different method than the one used so far is adopted. It is supposed that R^* is continuous [see IV, §2.3] and thus representable by a Bergson SWF, $W(\cdot)$. Given this assumption, it is straightforward to characterize the possible functional forms for $W(\cdot)$.

Choose $\mathbf{b} \in \mathbb{R}^n$ so that $b_1 = b_2 = \cdots b_n = b$, that is $\mathbf{b}$ lies on the diagonal in $\mathbb{R}^n$. Then consider the transformation

$$\phi_i(z) = (1 - \lambda)b + \lambda \cdot z, \quad \lambda > 0,$$

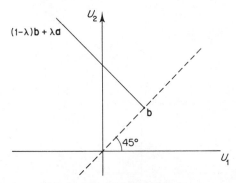

Figure 15.4: Indifference curves

which clearly belongs to the (CFC) class. Now it is possible to construct the indifference map for $W(\cdot)$. Suppose that $W(\mathbf{a}) = W(\mathbf{b})$. Then applying the above transform, $W(\phi(\mathbf{a})) = W(\phi(\mathbf{b}))$ or $W((1 - \lambda)\mathbf{b} + \lambda\mathbf{a}) = W(\mathbf{a})$ all $\lambda > 0$. Diagrammatically, as λ goes from zero to infinity it traces out an indifference curve on one side of the 45° degree line as in Figure 15.4.

Second, note that such indifference curves (in fact half-lines) are parallel. If they were not, then being straight lines, (or planes in $\mathbb{R}^n$) two indifference curves would cross, violating the transitivity of R^* (the reader should verify this).

Finally, the arguments just given apply independently to each side of the diagonal, so, in general, indifference surfaces are 'kinked'. To be mathematically precise, they are cones with vertices lying along the diagonal, as in Figure 15.5.

It is also possible to obtain an explicit expression for the functional form of $W(\cdot)$. To do this, note that if any continuous ordering R^* on $\mathbb{R}^n$ is represented by $W(\cdot)$, then it is also represented by $V(W(\cdot))$ where $V : \mathbb{R} \to \mathbb{R}$ is strictly increasing [see IV, §2.7]. In other words there is a degree of freedom in choosing $W(\cdot)$ and thus, without loss of generality, it is possible to normalize by setting

$$W(\mathbf{b}) = b \quad \text{if} \quad b_1 = b_2 = \cdots b_n = b.$$

Then it is possible to show that $W(\cdot)$ is homogeneous of degree one [see I, (14.15.3)]. For any $\mathbf{a} \in \mathbb{R}^n$, $W(\mathbf{a}) = b$, for some $b \in \mathbb{R}$. As $\phi_i(z) = \lambda.z$ is admissible under (CFC),

$$W(\mathbf{a}) = b \to W(\lambda\mathbf{a}) = \lambda.b$$

or $W(\lambda\mathbf{a}) = \lambda W(\mathbf{a})$. This proves homogeneity. Next, define $\bar{\mathbf{a}} = (1/n\sum a_i, 1/n\sum a_i \ldots)$. Then $\phi_i(z) = z - 1/n\sum a_i$ is admissible, so

$$W(\mathbf{a}) = b \to W(\mathbf{a} - \bar{\mathbf{a}}) = W(\mathbf{b} - \bar{\mathbf{a}}) = b - \frac{1}{n}\sum a_i,$$

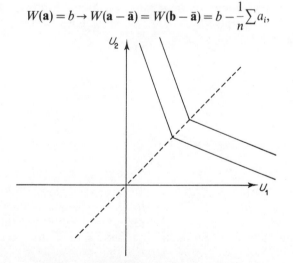

Figure 15.5: Kinked indifference surfaces

where the last equality follows from the fact that $\mathbf{b} - \bar{\mathbf{a}}$ lies on the diagonal. Then $W(\mathbf{a} - \bar{\mathbf{a}}) = b - 1/n\sum a_i$ or $W(\mathbf{a}) = 1/n\sum a_i + W(\mathbf{a} - \bar{\mathbf{a}})$ for any $\mathbf{a} \in \mathbb{R}^n$. In other words:

THEOREM 15.5.2. *If the SWFL satisfies (U), (IIA), (P) and (CFC) and is continuous then there exists a homogeneous of degree one function $g(\cdot)$, $\mathbb{R}^n \to \mathbb{R}$, such that for all $u \in U$, $\mathbf{x} \in X$*

$$\bar{u}(\mathbf{x}) + g(u(\mathbf{x}, \cdot) - \bar{u}(\mathbf{x})) \geqslant \bar{u}(\mathbf{y}) + g(u(\mathbf{y}, \cdot) - \bar{u}(\mathbf{y})) \to \mathbf{x}\, R\, \mathbf{y}$$

where

$$\bar{u}(\mathbf{x}) = \frac{1}{n}\sum_i u(\mathbf{x}, i) \text{ and similarly for } \bar{u}(\mathbf{y}).$$

This result can be found in Roberts (1980a). One example of such a SWF is

$$W(\mathbf{a}) = \frac{1}{n}\sum a_i + \gamma \min_i \left(a_i - \frac{1}{n}\sum a_i \right).$$

For $\gamma = 0$, it is Utilitarian; for $\gamma = 1$ it is the maximin rule. Therefore, a larger γ corresponds to greater concavity of the SWF.

A perhaps more interesting example of a SWF in the (CFC) class is the one underlying the Gini coefficient [see §16.2]. For any $\mathbf{a} \in \mathbb{R}^n$, take, as in section 15.4, the permutation $\mathbf{a}^0$ of $\mathbf{a}$ with $a_1^0 \geqslant a_2^0 \geqslant \ldots a_n^0$. Then the welfare function underlying the Gini coefficient is [see Sen (1973) or §16.4]

$$W(\mathbf{a}) = \sum_{i=1}^n i \cdot a_i^0$$

or, rewriting, using the fact that $\sum_{i=1}^n i = \dfrac{n(n+1)}{2}$ [see I, (1.7.2)],

$$W(\mathbf{a}) = \bar{a} + \frac{2}{n(n+1)} \sum_{i=1}^n i(a_i^0 - \bar{a}),$$

where $\bar{a} = 1/n\sum_{i=1}^n a_i^0$.

Finally, it is worth discussing briefly an obvious modification of (CFC) obtained by setting the constant term equal to zero, or in other words, only admitting transformations of the type $\phi_i(z) = \beta \cdot z$. Such a strengthening of (CFC) is sometimes called ratio-scale comparability. Clearly, under this latter invariance requirement, the SWF is still homogenous of degree one—the proof is exactly the same as above for (CFC). However, ratio-scale comparability (RSC) differs from all others considered so far, in that the functional form of $W(\cdot)$ may differ on each orthant of $\mathbb{R}^n$. The reason for this is clear. If any non-zero constant term is allowable in the transformation then, for any $\mathbf{a}, \mathbf{b} \in \mathbb{R}^n$, $W(\mathbf{a}) \geqslant W(\mathbf{b})$ if and only if $W(\mathbf{a} + \lambda) \geqslant W(\mathbf{b} + \lambda)$, where λ can be chosen so that $\mathbf{a} + \lambda, \mathbf{b} + \lambda \in \mathbb{R}_+^n$; that

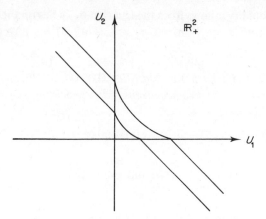

Figure 15.6: A possible SWFL under (RSC)

is, the functional form of W is constrained to be the same on the whole of $\mathbb{R}^n$. (This fact is of course implicit in Theorem 15.5.2.) Without the non-zero term, this constraint no longer holds. All that is required for continuity of $W(\cdot)$ is that the social indifference maps on each orthant of $\mathbb{R}^n$ 'match up' with the other indifference maps at their common boundaries.

(As an illustration, consider a possible SWFL for $n = 2$,

$$W(a_1, a_2) = \begin{cases} (a_1^{1/2} + a_2^{1/2})^2 & a \in \mathbb{R}^2_+ \\ a_1 + a_2 & a \in \mathbb{R}^2/\mathbb{R}^2_+. \end{cases}$$

This is illustrated in Figure 15.6. For a detailed analysis of the possibilities under (RSC), the reader is referred to Blackorby and Donaldson (1982).

15.6. SINGLE-PROFILE SOCIAL CHOICE

One of the first objections to Arrow's Theorem, voiced mainly by Samuelson and by Little (1952) was that it had no direct bearing on the possibility of a non-dictatorial Bergson SWF, since the latter was defined for *fixed* tastes and not subject to conditions based on hypothetical comparisons of changing tastes. As Little says 'First, tastes are given. If tastes change, we may expect a new ordering of all the conceivable states; but we do not require that the difference between the new and the old ordering should have any particular relation to changes of taste which have occurred'.

Little's criticism is very clear here. In this framework, he is objecting to the aggregation conditions on the SWFL which involves hypothetical comparisons of several utility profile in U. Two of these, (IIA) and (A) were present in section 15.2.3 above. To meet Little's objections, it is necessary to reformulate the social choice problem somewhat.

Suppose that tastes are fixed, so that the utility information is a single profile $\bar{u}$

in U. Then, in contrast to the multi-profile case, the problem is no longer to impose certain conditions on the social welfare functional f in order to restrict its functional form, but rather to impose certain conditions on the ordering $\bar{R} = f(\bar{u})$.

The two analogous conditions to those found in section 15.2.3 are single-profile neutrality and the single-profile weak Pareto condition. Before these can be defined, however, it is necessary to define the set of u in U which are equivalent to $\bar{u}$ according to the particular measurability/comparability assumption made.

$$D = \{u \in U \mid u = \phi(\bar{u}), \phi \in \Phi\}$$

Then it is possible to define a single-profile version of neutrality

(SPN) Single-Profile Neutrality
$\bar{R}$ satisfies single-profile neutrality if for any **x, y, w, z** $\in X$, and $u, v \in C$
(i) $u(\mathbf{x}, \cdot) = v(\mathbf{w}, \cdot)$
(ii) $u(\mathbf{y}, \cdot) = v(\mathbf{z}, \cdot)$
then $\mathbf{x} \bar{R} \mathbf{y}$ if and only if $\mathbf{w} \bar{R} \mathbf{z}$.

The meaning of (SPN) is that if utility information coincides over two pairs of states then they should be socially ordered in the same way. The difference between (SPN) and (N) is that in the former there is only one $\bar{u}$ and one $\bar{R}$ involved in the definition.

Next,

(SPWP) Single-Profile Weak Pareto
$\bar{R}$ satisfies single-profile weak Pareto if

$$u(\mathbf{x}, i) > u(\mathbf{y}, i) \quad \text{all} \quad i \in N$$

implies

$$\mathbf{x} \bar{R} \mathbf{y} \quad \text{for all} \quad \mathbf{x}, \mathbf{y} \in X, u \in C.$$

Given that $\bar{R}$ satisfies these conditions, and no interpersonal comparability is allowed, then the Samuelson–Little critique of Arrow is not valid. An important result, established by Parks (1976) and Kemp and Ng (1976) and others is that if $\bar{R}$ satisfies (SPN) and (SPWP), either (ONC) or (CNC) *are* assumed, then, given a technical assumption, there exists a single profile dictator. That is, there exists some i in N such that if $\bar{u}(\mathbf{x}, i) > \bar{u}(\mathbf{y}, i)$ then $\mathbf{x} \bar{R} \mathbf{y}$.

In other words it is possible to transpose Arrow's 'reasonable' conditions into a single-profile framework and obtain an analogue of his Impossibility Theorem.

The technical assumption is a joint condition on C and X which in effect, requires both that X be 'large enough', and preferences be 'diverse enough'. The version given here is due to Roberts (1980b).

(D) Diversity
C and X satisfy diversity if for any $\mathbf{a}, \mathbf{b}, \mathbf{c} \in \mathbb{R}^n$, all being different, there exist **x, y,** $\mathbf{z} \in X$, and $u \in C$ such that $u(\mathbf{x}, \cdot) = \mathbf{a}$, $u(\mathbf{y}, \cdot) = \mathbf{b}$, and $u(\mathbf{z}, \cdot) = \mathbf{c}$.

One can see intuitively from the statement of (D) that in some sense, the 'larger' X is, for a given C the more likely (D) is to be satisfied. This can in fact be made rigorous. For example, if the (ONC) condition is assumed, X must contain at least 3^n elements if (D) is to be satisfied. (This is not, however, sufficient; if $\bar{u} \in U$ is such that all individuals have identical preferences over X, for all $i, j \in N$ then (D) will be violated, no matter how large X is. In other words, one also requires sufficient diversity of preferences.) Furthermore, the stronger the comparability/measurability condition, the 'larger' the minimum size for X. For example, if (CNC) is assumed, X must be at least uncountable. This contrasts starkly with the minimum size assumption (sometimes called a domain restriction) for the multiprofile case, which just requires that X contain at least three elements. (The reader may verify that if $\# X = 2$, the assumptions of (IIA) and the transitivity of R lose their force, so that the assumption $\# X \geqslant 3$ is an integral part of the Arrow framework.)

One example of a social choice problem where X is uncountable and preferences are diverse is the problem of finding a social ranking of income distributions presented at the end of section 15.2.2. Recall that the choice set is the set of all possible distributions of a cake of fixed size, $X = \{\mathbf{x} \in \mathbb{R}^n \mid x_i \geqslant 0, \sum x_i = k\}$ and utilities are linear in income, $u(\mathbf{x}, i) = x_i$. It is easily verified that with (ONC) or (CNC), diversity is satisfied for this particular preference profile. This is because preferences are 'selfish'; each individual cares only about his or her own income level.

Therefore, we have the result that if ranking of income distributions satisfies neutrality, the Pareto principle and either ordinal or cardinal non-comparability, it must be dictatorial.

Using the results of Roberts (1980b) it is in fact possible to show that if the technical assumption of diversity is satisfied, then all the possibility results of this chapter [i.e. Theorems 15.3.1, 15.4.1, 15.4.2, 15.5.1, 15.5.2] go through for the single profile case. The problem, as discussed above, is to ensure that (D) is satisfied. For the income distribution problem, slightly modified, to allow for 'free disposal' (i.e. $X = \{\mathbf{x} \in \mathbb{R}^n \mid x_i \geqslant 0, \sum x_i \leqslant \bar{x}\}$), X does satisfy (D) under ordinal level comparability. Therefore, if one requires that $\bar{R}$ satisfy Hammon's equity axiom, then the only possible social ranking of income distributions is $\mathbf{x} P \mathbf{y}$ if and only if $\min_i x_i \geqslant \min_i y_i$.

For this income distribution problem, the Equity Axiom is simply the Pigou-Dalton condition that a transfer of income from richer to poorer must increase welfare, so within this framework this apparently reasonable condition, combined with limited comparability between individuals, rules out almost all social rankings of income distributions. The reader should contrast this conclusion with the discussion of the axiomatic approach to income inequality measures in Chapter 16.

15.7. CONCLUSIONS

In this chapter a general has been constructed which allows various axioms and conditions on the aggregation of preferences to be compared in terms of their 'end products' (i.e. classes of allowable social preference orderings).

However, this framework is restrictive in the sense that some non-welfare information cannot be used when the Pareto indifference principle is imposed. Recall the example of the two societies in section 15.2.2—Pareto indifference requires that these be ranked socially indifferent.

Roberts (1980a) shows that it is possible to drop Pareto indifference and obtain essentially the same results as those in sections 15.3, 15.4 and 15.5.

Another limitation of the analysis in this chapter, and indeed the whole axiomatic literature on social choice is that it excludes any consideration of how the utility information is to be obtained in order to calculate the social ordering. The problem is that individuals may have an incentive to reveal incorrect information about their preferences in order to manipulate the social choice of an element in X to their advantage. There is in fact a strong connection between this problem, properly formulated, and Arrow's Impossibility Theorem; the reader is referred to Dasgupta, Hammond and Maskin (1979) for an elegant and complete survey of this literature.

15.8. REFERENCES

Arrow, K. J. (1963). *Social Choice and Individual Values*, Cowles Foundation Monograph.

Arrow, K. J. (1973). Values and collective decision-making, in E. S. Phelps (ed.), *Economic Justice*. Penguin, Harmondsworth.

Bergson, A. (1938). A reformulation of certain aspects of welfare economics. *Quarterly Journal of Economics*, **52**.

Blackorby, C. and Donaldson, D. (1982). Ratio-scale and translation-scale full interpersonal comparability without domain restrictions: admissible social welfare functions. *International Economic Review*, **23**.

Dasgupta, P. S., Hammond, P. J. and Maskin, E. S. (1979). The implementation of social choice rules: some general results on incentive compatibility. *Review of Economic Studies*, **46**.

D'Aspremont, C. and Gevers, L. (1977). Equity and the informational basis of collective choice. *Review of Economic Studies*, **44**.

Debreu, G. (1959). *Theory of Value: An Axiomatic Analysis of Economic Equilibrium*, Wiley, New York.

Fishburn, P. C. (1973). *The Theory of Social Choice*. Princeton University Press, Princeton, Mass.

Gevers, L. (1979). On interpersonal comparability and social welfare orderings. *Econometrica*, **47**.

Hahn, F. H. (1981). On some difficulties of the utilitarian economist. *Mimeo.*

Hammond, P. J. (1976). Equity, Arrow's conditions, and Rawls' difference principle. *Econometrica*, **44**.

Kelly, J. S. (1978). *Arrow Impossibility Theorems*, Academic Press, London.

Kemp, M. C. and Ng Y.-K. (1976). On the existence of social welfare functions, social orderings, and social decision functions. *Economica*, **43**.

Kramer, G. H. (1973). On a class of equilibrium conditions for majority rule. *Econometrica*, **41**.

Little, I. M. D. (1952). Social choice and individual values. *Journal of Political Economy*, **60**.

Parks, R. P. (1976). An impossibility theorem for fixed preferences: a dictatorial Bergson–Samuelson social welfare functions. *Review of Economic Studies*, **43**.

Roberts, K. W. S. (1980a). Interpersonal comparability and social choice theory. *Review of Economic Studies*, **47**.

Roberts, K. W. S. (1980b). Social choice theory; the single-profile and multi-profile approaches. *Review of Economic Studies*, **47**.

Sen, A. K. (1970). *Collective Choice and Social Welfare*. North-Holland, Amsterdam.

Sen, A. K. (1973). *On Economic Inequality*. Clarendon Press, Oxford.

Sen, A. K. (1977). Social choice theory: a re-examination. *Econometrica*, **45**.

Part V

Economic Methodology

Mathematical Methods in Economics
Edited by F. van der Ploeg
© 1984, John Wiley & Sons, Ltd.

16

The Measurement and Decomposition of Inequality and Poverty

S. M. Ravi Kanbur, *University of Essex*

16.1. INTRODUCTION

Interest in the measurement of inequality is related to interest in inequality itself. The efficiency–equity trade-off is something all undergraduates are taught about, but the emergence of a specific literature dealing exclusively with the measurement of inequality can be dated to the 1960s[1], an emergence that is not wholly unrelated to the social and political factors of that time. Whatever the future of these factors, and of inequality measurement towards the end of this century, the developments of the last two decades have constituted a significant advance which it is our intention to survey here.

We shall be interested in measuring the inequality of an income distribution represented by a vector of incomes [see I, §5.2]

$$(y_1 y_2, \ldots, y_n) \tag{16.1.1}$$

where y_i is the income of the ith income receiving unit, $i = 1, 2, \ldots, n$. In an empirical context we would be interested in the detail of such data—the definition of income, the definition of income receiving unit, the sampling and questionnaire frame used in deriving the data in (16.1.1), etc. But here we assume that these problems have been solved, or at any rate adequately discussed, noting only that the measurement exercises we will engage in (particularly in their normative aspects) will not necessarily be independent of answers to such questions. Since our sole interest is in the measurement of inequality, we shall assume that the 'size of the cake'

$$Y = \sum_{i=1}^{n} y_i \tag{16.1.2}$$

is fixed. We will also assume that the size of population is fixed at n, but we will comment on this in due course.

Two approaches can be discerned in the literature on the measurement of inequality. The first approach is *positive*, seeking only to describe the pattern of income distribution and in fact to summarize it in a single statistic. The second approach is *normative*, and this bases the measurement of inequality on value judgements which are sometimes too strong but nevertheless have the advantage of being made explicit. Considerable confusion exists in the applied and policy literature on these two types of inequality measurement. It is our task here to provide, from a theoretical point of view, an exposition of these two types of inequality measurement and, most importantly, the links between them. In section 16.2 below we begin the exercise by characterizing the positive measurement of inequality and providing some illustrations. Section 16.3 considers measures of inequality that are based entirely and explicitly on value judgements embodied in a social welfare function. Section 16.4, as a 'half-way house' between the two approaches of sections 16.2 and 16.3, considers the approach of specifying criteria for inequality measures.

There has always been considerable interest in the 'causes' of inequality. Section 16.5 discusses a technique of analysis which may help in decomposing, in an accounting fashion, the sources of inequality into broad factors. The positive and normative implications of such decomposition analysis, a technique which has developed at great pace during the last few years, are discussed in section 16.5.

Section 16.6 of this survey focuses on the lower end of the income distribution and asks the question: What are the normative properties of commonly used poverty measures, and what would be the properties of an ideal poverty index? Once again, the literature here has developed rapidly over the last few years—we will survey the state of the art and suggest directions for further research.

Section 16.7 of this survey makes the link between the largely theoretical discussion of the earlier sections and the main body of empirical work, which must perforce rely on grouped data in many cases. Section 16.8 concludes the survey with a discussion of possibilities for research in the future.

16.2. POSITIVE MEASUREMENT: INEQUALITY AS STATISTICAL DISPERSION

Let the vector of incomes in 16.1.1 be written in ordered form as

$$y_1 \leqslant y_2 \leqslant \ldots \leqslant y_n, \tag{16.2.1}$$

where ties are broken arbitrarily. The exercise of positive measurement of inequality can be specified as the calculation of an *index of dispersion* of the numbers in (16.2.1). This can be characterized in terms of a number of steps:

(i) Choose a reference level of income.
(ii) Calculate the 'gap' between every income and this reference level of income, on the basis of a chosen metric for distance (see IV, §11.1].
(iii) Sum these gaps and calculate the average gap.
(iv) Express the average gap as a fraction of the average income.

This is, of course, a very general procedure which can apply to any collection of numbers, not just a distribution of income. As we shall see, many measures of income inequality fall into this category, differing only in their choice of the reference level of income and in their definition of the 'gap'.

The most common reference level of income is of course the mean of the distribution [see II, §8.1]

$$\mu = \frac{Y}{n} = \frac{\sum\limits_{i=1}^{n} y_i}{n} \qquad (16.2.2)$$

although it would be interesting to study the consequences of using other measures of central tendency [see II, §10.4] for step (i) of the procedure. Taking the absolute difference between each y_i and μ as the definition of the gap [see I, (2.6.5)], we get as the inequality measure the relative mean deviation:

$$r = \frac{\sum\limits_{i=1}^{n} |\mu - y_i|}{n\mu}. \qquad (16.2.3)$$

If we allow a more general concept of averaging then we can state a generalized relative mean deviation measure as

$$r(\theta) = \frac{1}{\mu} \left\{ \frac{1}{n} \sum_{i=1}^{n} \{|\mu - y_i|\}^\theta \right\}^{1/\theta}. \qquad (16.2.4)$$

It is seen that for $\theta = 2$, $r(\theta)$ becomes the coefficient of variation [see II, §9.2.6], a commonly used measure of inequality. Using the most general concept of averaging we get an even more general family of indices than (16.2.4):

$$r = r(\phi\{\cdot\}) = \frac{1}{\mu} \phi^{-1} \left\{ \frac{1}{n} \sum_{i=1}^{n} \phi\{|\mu - y_i|\} \right\}. \qquad (16.2.5)$$

The positive and normative properties of this family of indices would be interesting to investigate in an empirical and theoretical context.

It is also possible to derive measures of inequality by applying the steps discussed above not to the distribution of the y_is but to the distribution of some transform of the y_is. A common measure of equality is derived by applying steps (i)–(iii) of the procedure outlined above to the distribution of the logarithms of income:

$$V = \frac{1}{n} \sum_{i=1}^{n} (\tilde{\mu} - \tilde{y}_i)^2, \qquad (16.2.6)$$

where $\tilde{y}_i = \log y_i$ [see IV, §2.11] and $\tilde{\mu} = 1/n \sum_{i=1}^{n} \tilde{y}_i$. The 'variance of logs' measure is one of the most frequently used measures of inequality, partly because of its 'decomposition' properties, which we will discuss in section 16.5. The normative properties of this essentially statistical measure of inequality will be discussed in section 16.4.

The crucial feature of the above measures is that in step (i) of the procedure they use as the reference level of income a measure of central tendency (the mean) of the distribution. However, an alternative point of view is to use each income level in the distribution in turn as the reference income, and to calculate and average the gaps for each of the n^2 comparisons that result. Applying steps (ii), (iii) and (iv), and using the absolute difference definition of a gap leads to a measure known as the relative mean difference:

$$R = \frac{\frac{1}{n^2} \sum_{j=1}^{n} \sum_{i=1}^{n} |y_i - y_j|}{\mu}. \qquad (16.2.7)$$

Now (16.2.7) can be generalized in the manner of (16.2.4) or (16.2.5), but we shall see presently that as stated in turns out to be closely related to another measure of inequality, derived from a quite different perspective, and it is to this perspective that we now turn.

An alternative approach to the representation of the dispersion of an income distribution (16.1.1) is to use the ordering (16.2.1) to work out the relationship between cumulative population share and cumulative income share. Clearly, the bottom 0% get 0% of the total cake while the bottom 100% get 100% of the cake. In between is a curve which can be traced out by the points [see V, Chapter 3]

$$(0,0); \left(\frac{1}{n}, \frac{y_1}{Y}\right); \left(\frac{2}{n}, \frac{y_1 + y_2}{Y}\right); \dots ; (1,1). \qquad (16.2.8)$$

This is the well-known *Lorenz curve*, and is plotted as curve L_1 on the $\{(1,0); (1,0)\}$ plane as shown in Figure 16.1. In Figure 16.1 the curve is shown as composed of a number of linear pieces—clearly as n becomes large we approach a smooth curve.[2] Also drawn in Figure 16.1 is the 45° line, which is known as the diagonal of perfect equality since this is what the Lorenz curve would look like if $y_1 = y_2 = \cdots = y_n$. Otherwise the Lorenz curve must lie below the 45° line and must increase at an increasing rate, i.e. have a convex shape. This is because given the (ascending) order in which income is cumulated, each additional person increases population share by a constant amount $1/n$, but since he is the richest person so far he adds more to the income share than the previous person. Notice also that the slope of the line between the points

$$\left(\frac{k}{n}, \frac{\sum_{i=1}^{k} y_i}{Y}\right) \quad \text{and} \quad \left(\frac{k+1}{n}, \frac{\sum_{i=1}^{k+1} y_i}{Y}\right)$$

is simply equal to $(y_k/Y)/(1/n) = y_k/\mu$. The implication of this for the continuous case is that the slope of the tangent to the Lorenz curve at any point is simply the

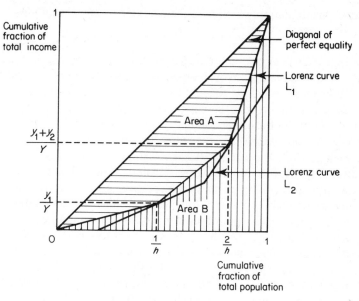

Figure 16.1: The Lorenz curve

income level at that point of cumulation divided by the overall mean income. This property will be put to good use in subsequent sections.

'Perfect inequality' in the Lorenz diagram is represented by a Lorenz curve which lies along $(0, 0)$ and $(0, 1)$ followed by the vertical section from $(0, 1)$ to $(1, 1)$. This happens when all of the income is owned by just one person. In between such perfect inequality and the diagonal of perfect equality are Lorenz curves representing varying degrees of inequality. How is this inequality to be measured? One suggestion is to use the 'closeness' of the actual Lorenz curve to the Lorenz curve of perfect equality. The area between two curves [see IV, §4.2] is one measure of closeness between two curves, and for L_1 the areas A and B in Figure 16.1 are used to define:

$$G = \frac{A}{A + B} = 2A \qquad (16.2.9)$$

the *Gini coefficient*, one of the best known and most commonly used measures of inequality. It is easy to see that the measure lies between 0 and 1. It is less obvious, but nevertheless true, (see Anand, 1982, Annex), that the Gini coefficient is exactly one half the relative mean difference R, defined in (16.2.7):

$$G = \frac{R}{2} = \frac{\sum_{j=1}^{n} \sum_{i=1}^{n} |y_i - y_j|}{2n^2 \mu} = 1 + \frac{1}{n} - \frac{2}{n^2 \mu} \sum_{i=1}^{n} y_i(n + 1 - i) \qquad (16.2.10)$$

after some manipulation which uses the fact [see I, §2.6.2] that

$$|y_i - y_j| = y_i + y_j - 2\min(y_i, y_j).$$

Expression (16.2.10) also reveals another feature of the Gini coefficient, that it is related to a *rank weighted* sum of incomes. This property will be discussed further in the following sections.

We can see, therefore, that the income distribution analyst can appeal to the statistical analysis of the dispersion of distributions to derive inequality indices. These measures of dispersion can of course be applied to the distribution of any variable whatsoever. The fact that this is so should worry us, and this is precisely the subject of the next section. However, it cannot be denied that appealing to the statistical literature in order to derive positive or descriptive measures of inequality is extremely convenient for the income distribution analyst. Another example of a measure which has been derived from an established field is Theil's (1967) entropy measure, which is drawn from the post-war literature on information theory (cf. Shannon, 1948). If there are n events possible with probabilities $p_1, p_2, \ldots p_n$, consider the 'information content' of an event occurring. It is postulated that, firstly, this information content should be a decreasing function of the probability of the event [see IV, §2.7] and, secondly, that the information content of the simultaneous occurrence of independent events be the sum of the information contents of each event. Thus if $h(p)$ is the 'information content function', we require that $\partial h/\partial p < 0$ [see IV, §5.2] and $h(p_1 p_2) = h(p_1) + h(p_2)$. These properties are satisfied by

$$h(p) = \log\frac{1}{p}$$

[see IV, §2.11]. The expected or average information content of $p_1, p_2, \ldots, p_n$ is then [see II, §8.1]

$$\sum_{i=1}^{n} p_i \log\frac{1}{p_i}$$

and this is also known as the *entropy* of the system. An inequality measure is generated if we replace p_i by s_i, the income share of the ith individual, and subtract the actual value of entropy given above from its maximum possible value, which occurs when $s_i = 1/n$. This gives us

$$T = \sum_{i=1}^{n} s_i \log ns_i \qquad (16.2.11)$$

as the *Theil index of inequality*.

The Theil index is a very commonly used measure of inequality. It has convenient 'decomposition' properties, which will be discussed in Section 16.5, and its normative properties have also been found to be appealing (see Section 16.4). However, the 'information theoretic' motivation for it is perhaps not as intuitive as one would like it to be. In fact, the Theil index can be better motivated by considering directly the *entropy* of a distribution of incomes over individuals, using a development common in statistical mechanics and thermodynamics (cf. Alonso and Finn, 1968). Suppose, then, that we have Y dollars to distribute between n individuals who are identical in every respect. Each dollar is given to one of the individuals at random; the probability of any one individual getting it is thus $1/n$. We then consider the probabilities of different distributions of dollars among the individuals—in particular, the probability of the observed configuration—under the random process described above. If the observed distribution is

$$(y_1, y_2, \ldots, y_n),$$

then it can be shown (see Alonso and Finn, 1968) that the probability of this configuration is [see I, (3.7.1)]

$$P = \prod_{i=1}^{n} \frac{\left(\frac{1}{n}\right)^{y_i}}{y_i!}. \tag{16.2.12}$$

Physicists would recognize (16.2.12) as being related to the Maxwell–Boltzmann distribution law for Y particles distributed between n equi-probable energy levels. The concept of entropy or disorder in a distribution is related to the probability of its occurrence under the specified process. In fact entropy in the thermodynamics literature is defined as being proportional to

$$\log P = Y \log \frac{1}{n} - \sum_{i=1}^{n} \log y_i.$$

Using Stirling's approximation for the factorial of a very large number [see IV, (10.2.15)]

$$\log x! \sim x \log x - x$$

we get

$$\log P \sim Y \log \frac{1}{n} + Y - \sum_{i=1}^{n} y_i \log y_i$$

A measure of inequality can be derived by comparing the probability of the observed distribution with the probability of the most likely distribution under the process. It can be shown that the latter occurs when $y_i = Y/n$, so that the maximum entropy is given by

$$\log P^* = Y - Y \log Y$$

hence

$$\log P^* - \log P$$

$$= \sum_{i=1}^{n} y_i \log y_i - Y \log \frac{1}{n} - Y \log Y$$

$$= \sum_{i} y_i \log \frac{n y_i}{Y}.$$

Normalizing by Y, we get the Theil index of inequality

$$T = \sum_i \frac{y_i}{Y} \log n \frac{y_i}{Y} = \sum_i s_i \log ns_i. \tag{16.2.13}$$

We have now covered, among others, three of the most commonly used measures of inequality—the Gini coefficient, the variance of logs and the Theil index. We see that each of these has a motivation in another context but has nevertheless been found to be useful in the positive measurement of inequality. However, the *normative* content of such measurement is as yet unclear, and it is to an examination of the normative measurement of inequality that we now turn our attention.

16.3. NORMATIVE MEASUREMENT: THE SOCIAL WELFARE FUNCTION APPROACH

Discussions of inequality always have some normative content, be it explicit or, more likely, implicit. In comparing a 'positive' measure of inequality such as the Gini coefficient at two points in time, say, the statement 'the Gini has increased' is rarely made in purely descriptive spirit. More often the statement has a persuasive element, asking for government intervention or implying that the society is in some sense worse-off. The normative approach to the measurement of inequality takes the view that it is best to make the exact nature of egalitarian value judgements explicit, and to derive inequality measures based on these judgements, rather than to rely on implicit persuasion based on descriptive measures.

The major analytical vehicle for deriving normative measures of inequality is the Social Welfare Function (SWF) [see Chapter 15]. We postulate that social welfare W is a function of the vector of incomes in society:

$$W = W(y_1, y_2, \ldots, y_n). \tag{16.3.1}$$

We are still restricting ourselves to the distributional problem, so that the size of the cake Y is assumed to be given—our task is to evaluate alternative distributions of this fixed total. The SWF in (16.3.1) is meant to capture all of society's value judgements—specific properties of W will model specific judgements. The task is made easier if we assume (16.3.1) to be twice continuously differentiable in its arguments [see IV, §5.5]. One restriction which is usually imposed is that

$$\frac{\partial W}{\partial y_i} > 0; \quad i = 1, 2, \ldots, n. \tag{16.3.2}$$

In other words the marginal impact on social welfare of a higher income for one individual, given all other incomes, is always positive. We say that a SWF is *income egalitarian* if this marginal impact decreases as the individual's income increases, i.e.,

$$\frac{\partial^2 W}{\partial y_i^2} < 0, i = 1, 2, \ldots, n. \tag{16.3.3}$$

There are many ways of restating condition (16.3.3). An intuitive interpretation is that a unit of income taken from a rich man and given to a poor man (so long as the transfer does not reverse their ranks) will increase welfare. A further mathematical link can be established by noting that for differentiable functions a necessary and sufficient condition for strict concavity is that the Hessian of the function [see IV, §5.7] be negative definite [see I, §9.2], which in turn implies (16.3.3). The property of *concavity* can be stated as

$$\alpha W(\mathbf{x}) + (1 - \alpha) W(\mathbf{y}) \leqslant W(\alpha \mathbf{x} + (1 - \alpha)\mathbf{y}) \text{ for } 0 \leqslant \alpha \leqslant 1, \tag{16.3.4}$$

where $\mathbf{x} = (x_1, \ldots, x_n)$ is another distribution of income [see IV, §15.2.6]. Note that when $0 \leqslant \alpha \leqslant 1$,

$$\text{Min}\{W(\mathbf{x}), W(\mathbf{y})] \leqslant \alpha W(\mathbf{x}) + (1 - \alpha)W(\mathbf{y}) \leqslant W(\alpha \mathbf{x} + (1 - \alpha)\mathbf{y})$$

The inequality

$$\text{Min}[W(\mathbf{x}), W(\mathbf{y})] \leqslant W(\alpha \mathbf{x} + (1 - \alpha)\mathbf{y}), \quad 0 \leqslant \alpha \leqslant 1, \tag{16.3.5}$$

defines *quasi-concavity*. Thus concavity implies quasi-concavity. Essentially quasi-concavity states that social indifference curves must be convex to the origin. It turns out that for many of our results on inequality measurement we can make do with the weaker requirement of strict quasi-concavity. There is another reason why quasi-concavity may be a better mathematical tool for expressing egalitarian sentiments that concavity. This is that while concavity is only invariant under cardinal (that is positive linear) transformations of the social welfare function, quasi-concavity is invariant under ordinal (that is monotonic increasing [see IV, §2.7]) transformations as well, as can be readily verified from (16.3.4) and (16.3.5). Thus if we are only willing to impose ordinality on W, then we should work with quasi-concavity to represent egalitarianism.

We will return to some other properties of W presently. For now let us consider how one might construct an index of inequality based upon W. One way of doing this is to consider the 'price' that society (that is the SWF) would be willing to pay to achieve perfect equality. In order to arrive at this price we proceed via the *equally distributed equivalent level* of income, a concept defined by Atkinson (1970) as that level of mean income which, if distributed equally, would provide the same level of social welfare as the current distribution of income. Denoting this equally distributed equivalent as $\bar{y}$, we see that $\bar{y}$ is defined as the solution to

$$W(y_1, y_2, \ldots, y_n) = W(\bar{y}, \bar{y}, \ldots, \bar{y}). \tag{16.3.6}$$

The gap between this and mean income is $\mu - \bar{y}$, which is always positive by virtue of strict quasi-concavity. Applying the procedure of taking this gap as a fraction of mean income we get

$$I = 1 - \frac{\bar{y}}{\mu} \qquad (16.3.7)$$

as the *Atkinson index of inequality.*

Notice that since $\bar{y}$ is given as a solution to (16.3.6), it depends both on the current pattern of income distribution $y_1, y_2, \ldots, y_n$ and on the value judgements implicit in the exact form of $W(\cdot)$. Hence the inequality index (16.3.7) is inextricably tied to the SWF $W(\cdot)$—the ultimate in an explicitly normative approach to inequality measurement. Notice also from (16.3.6) that $\bar{y}$ and hence I depend only on the ordinal properties of $W(\cdot)$.

Thus given a $W(\cdot)$, (16.3.7) provides us with a normative measure of inequality. But two questions immediately arise:

(i) What is the specific form of $W(\cdot)$ used to calculate $\bar{y}$ and I in any given situation?
(ii) How does the measure (16.3.7) relate to the positive measures of inequality discussed in the previous section?

In a remarkable result of Atkinson's (1970), later generalized by Dasgupta, Sen and Starrett (1973), a partial answer was simultaneously provided to the above two questions in the following theorem:

> *Consider two distributions of income* **x** *and* **y**, *of the same total size,* $Y = \sum_i x_i = \sum_i y_i$. *Let* **x** L **y** *denote a binary relation [see I, §1.3.1] such that the Lorenz curve of* **x** *lies nowhere below the Lorenz curve of* **y**. *Further, let* $W(\cdot)$ *be quasi-concave and symmetric [cf. I, §14.16]. Then*
>
> **x** L **y** *if and only if* $W(\mathbf{x}) \geqslant W(\mathbf{y})$ *for all* $W(\cdot)$. $\qquad (16.3.8)$

What this theorem says is that there is an intimate link between the Lorenz curve method of measuring inequality and the explicitly normative measurement of inequality. If two Lorenz curves do not intersect, then from the point of view of descriptive measurement the one uniformly closer to the line of perfect equality represents greater equality. The result (16.3.8) says that in this case the Lorenz curve closer to the line of equality will also have associated with its higher social welfare for *any* SWF provided it is quasi-concave[3] (that is, egalitarian) and symmetric. Thus the normative measure of inequality I as defined in (16.3.7) will be lower for this Lorenz curve and there is no conflict between these positive and normative measures of inequality. However, the theorem also warns that if two Lorenz curves intersect then the normative measures of inequality for the two distributions will depend upon the exact functional form postulated for $W(\cdot)$ and that there will also, in general, be potential conflict between positive and normative measures of inequality.

Before sketching out a proof of this theorem let us consider for the moment the requirement that $W(\cdot)$ be symmetric, that is, any permutation of the indices $1,\ldots,n$ leaves the value of $W(\cdot)$ unchanged. This requirement imposes a sort of anonimity on individuals—the only thing relevant about them to the SWF is their income, not who they are or how they came by their income. This is by no means a non-controversial value judgement. Later critics, e.g. Sen (1979) have commented on the *consequentialist* view implicit in this assumption—the *process* of income generation is not credited with any welfare significance. It is clear that one can both defend and attack the symmetry (or anonymity) assumption, the defence being of course that we are interested solely in the *ex post* distribution of rewards—bygones are bygones. But whether we defend it or not, the fact of the matter is that it is required for Theorem (16.3.8), as the proof sketched below indicates.

The proof proceeds by using certain well-known results of Hardy, Littlewood and Polya (1934) on mathematical inequalities. Given $x_1 \leqslant x_2 \leqslant \ldots \leqslant x_n$ and $y_1 \leqslant y_2 \leqslant \ldots \leqslant y_n$, they show that the following two conditions are equivalent

(i)
$$\sum_{i=1}^{n} x_i = \sum_{i=1}^{n} y_i \text{ and for all } k \leqslant n, \ \sum_{i=1}^{k} x_i \geqslant \sum_{i=1}^{k} y_i,$$

with at least one $k < n$ such that

$$\sum_{i=1}^{k} x_i > \sum_{i=1}^{k} y_i.$$

(ii) If **y** is not **x** nor a permutation of **x**, there exists a bistochastic matrix (i.e. a matrix with nonnegative elements each of whose rows and columns sum to unity [see I, §7.11]) **Q** such that

$$\mathbf{x} = \mathbf{Q}\mathbf{y}.$$

The first condition is of course the condition that the Lorenz curve of **x** be closer to the line of equality than the Lorenz curve of **y**. The second condition can be used to prove the necessary part of (16.3.8) by using a well-known result that a bistochastic matrix can be written as a convex combination of a set of permutation matrices $\mathbf{P}_s$ [see I, §6.7(xi)]:

$$\mathbf{Q} = \sum_{s} a_s \mathbf{P}_s; \sum_{s} a_s = 1, \quad a_s \geqslant 0 \text{ for all } s$$

Now by symmetry permutations do not alter social welfare. Thus **x** can be written as a convex combination of distributions each of which has the same level of social welfare as **y**. By quasi-concavity it follows that social welfare in **x** must be no lower than that in **y**.

The details of this proof can be found in Dasgupta, Sen and Starrett (1973). Let us turn, however, to the case when Lorenz curves *do* intersect. The above theorem tells us that generality will now have to be abandoned and that we will have to specify a functional form for the SWF from which to derive the measure of inequality (16.3.7). Atkinson (1970) has suggested the following functional form:

$$W(y_1,\ldots,y_n) = \begin{cases} \sum_{i=1}^{n} \dfrac{y_i^{1-\varepsilon}}{1-\varepsilon}, & \varepsilon \neq 1, \\ \sum_{i=1}^{n} \log y_i, & \varepsilon = 1, \end{cases} \tag{16.3.9}$$

which can be interpreted as the sum of utility functions

$$U(y_i) = \frac{y_i^{1-\varepsilon}}{1-\varepsilon}, \quad \varepsilon \neq 1; \; U(y_i) = \log y_i, \quad \varepsilon = 1, \tag{16.3.10}$$

which have 'constant elasticity of marginal utility', $\partial(\log \partial U/\partial y)/\partial \log y$, equal to $-\varepsilon$. The parameter ε can be interpreted as the degree of inequality aversion, and can range from zero for the linear case to infinity for the Rawlsian Maximin (Rawls, 1971)—where Social Welfare is the welfare of the least-well-off individual. Using the functions (16.3.9), we can write the inequality measure in (16.3.8) as follows:

$$I_\varepsilon = \begin{cases} 1 - \left\{ \dfrac{1}{n} \sum_{i=1}^{n} \left(\dfrac{y_i}{\mu} \right)^{1-\varepsilon} \right\}^{1/1-\varepsilon}, & \varepsilon \neq 1. \\ 1 - \exp\left\{ \dfrac{1}{n} \sum_{i=1}^{n} \log\left(\dfrac{y_i}{\mu} \right) \right\}, & \varepsilon = 1. \end{cases} \tag{16.3.11}$$

This specific index suggested by Atkinson (1970) has now become the major workhorse for normative measurement of inequality. It has the advantage that it is convenient to handle and easy to manipulate, and that the consequences of different degrees of inequality aversion can be traced out by varying a single parameter ε. Indeed, one of Atkinson's (1970) contributions was to show how inequality rankings could be radically altered by choosing different values of ε. However, it should also be noted that by tying ourselves to (16.3.11) we are committing ourselves to a highly specialized functional form of the social welfare function, with a specific view on the welfare effects of income transfers. One feature of the I_ε measure which has caused some comment is the fact that it is scale independent. Doubling everybody's income would leave the inequality index unaffected. Whether this feature is problematic is yet to be clarified—should we be more inequality averse at low average levels of income or not? But it is worth noting that this is a key feature of the I_ε measure, as indeed it will be a feature of every measure based on a SWF which is homogeneous of degree one [see IV, §5.1][4].

This brings us to the end of our section on the explicitly normative measurement of inequality. Provided we can specify our social welfare function, we can measure inequality from a normative perspective. The debate then switches to the issue of which specific SWF to use—each will imply a different judgement on inequality and, except in the special class of cases identified by the theorem discussed in this section, each will in general give a different answer. With this background, we can now investigate some normative properties of positive measures of inequality.

16.4. CRITERIA FOR INEQUALITY MEASURES

Rather than nail our colours to the mast of a particular SWF, which we will be required to do in the extreme version of the normative measurement of inequality, we may prefer to specify certain properties which inequality measures ought to satisfy. This is clearly a weaker requirement than specifying the SWF, and we will be left with possibly a large number of measures all of which satisfy these criteria. But that is the way it has to be—if we are not prepared to specify a given SWF then we must at the same time be prepared to admit the validity of a number of measures of inequality. An alternative view of this exercise, however, is to see it simply as evaluating various properties of standard positive measures of inequality.

One of the most common criteria discussed in the literature is that of *income scale independence*. Thus, if we write the inequality index as

$$I = I(y_1, y_2, \ldots, y_n), \tag{16.4.1}$$

this requirement comes down to the mathematical condition that the function $I(\cdot)$ be homogeneous of degree zero:

$$I = I(\lambda y_1, \lambda y_2, \ldots \lambda y_n), \quad \lambda > 0. \tag{16.4.2}$$

The argument here is that since we are considering the *distribution* of income, a proportionate increase in everybody's income should make no difference at all to inequality. While this may be appealing as a requirement in the positive measurement of inequality, it should be emphasized that in the normative context (16.4.2) embodies a value judgement that inequality valuations should be independent of proportionate changes in income. With the measure (16.3.7), for example, this implies that the social welfare function $W(\cdot)$ be homogeneous of degree one: $W(\lambda \mathbf{y}) = \lambda W(\mathbf{y})$ [see IV, §5.1]. However, requirement (16.4.2) has now become standard in the literature. It can be easily checked that all of the positive measures of inequality discussed in section 16.2 satisfy this property.

The second major criterion in the literature for evaluating inequality indices is the *Pigou–Dalton Principle of Transfers*. This requires that whenever a unit of income is transferred from a rich man to a poor man, and such a transfer does not reverse the ranking of the two individuals, then the measure of inequality should decrease. This is an expression of egalitarianism, which we require inequality measures to satisfy.

Of the positive measures discussed in section 16.2 it is seen that the relative mean deviation, defined in (16.2.3) is completely insensitive to transfers of the above type if neither income crosses the mean owing to the transfer—the reduction in the rich man's distance from the mean is compensated completely by the increase for the poorer man and the measure is unaltered. If either income does cross the mean in the transfer then the measure will respond to the transfer and in the right way. However, since it does not respond to *all* transfers, we have to pronounce that the measure fails to satisfy the Pigou–Dalton principle of transfers. The coefficient of variation, the Gini coefficient and the Theil index all satisfy the principle, but the variance of logarithms, defined in (16.2.6), does not. As is shown by Creedy (1977), if the two incomes involved in the transfer are either less than the geometric mean or on either side of the geometric mean [see IV, §21.2.3], then the transfer will reduce inequality. But for incomes considerably higher than the geometric mean, a transfer from rich to poor may well increase inequality. Creedy (1977) has analysed the income levels at which this happens and has also calculated what he terms 'the probability of a violating transfer' for empirical distributions. He argues that this is rather low. However, it has to be said that from a theoretical point of view it is a crucial weakness of the variance of logs that it does not satisfy the principle of transfers.

A number of other criteria have been suggested for evaluating inequality indices, and we will treat them briefly here. One criterion develops further the principle of transfers. In its purest form the principle requires only that the measure of inequality be sensitive to transfers in the appropriate way—the *extent* of the sensitivity is left undiscussed. As Sen (1973) notes 'It is possible to argue that the impact should be greater if the transfer takes place at a lower income level...'.[5] But he continues that 'by now we are dealing with areas in which our intuitive ideas of inequality are relatively vague and checking the measures in terms of some commonly accepted notions of inequality is no longer altogether easy'. In fact it is not clear what exactly might be meant by 'the transfer takes place at a lower income level'. What is this income level? Is it one of the two incomes between which the transfer is taking place, or is it some average of the two incomes? One approach to the formalization of the above discussion might be as follows. Choose two income levels, $y_i < y_j$(i.e. $i < j$) between which the transfer is taking place. The transfer is parametrized by a marginal change in y_j with a compensating change in y_i which leaves total income Y constant so that

$$\left.\frac{dy_i}{dy_j}\right|_{y=\text{constant}} = -1.$$

From now on the notation $Y=$ constant will be taken as understood and will be dropped for convenience. From (16.4.1)

$$\frac{dI}{dy_j} = \frac{\partial I}{\partial y_j} + \frac{\partial I}{\partial y_i}\frac{dy_i}{dy_j} = \frac{\partial I}{\partial y_j} - \frac{\partial I}{\partial y_i}.$$

The Pigou–Dalton Principle of Transfers requires, of course, that the above expression be positive. We can stipulate the requirement of *increased sensitivity to transfers at lower income levels* by the condition

$$\frac{\partial\left[\dfrac{dI}{dy_j}\right]}{\partial y_j} = \frac{\partial\left[\dfrac{\partial I}{\partial y_j} - \dfrac{\partial I}{\partial y_i}\right]}{\partial y_j} > 0. \tag{16.4.3}$$

How do the various positive measures of inequality discussed in section 16.6.2 fare with regard to the 'sensitivity to transfers' requirement in (16.4.3)? For the Gini coefficient, it is clear from (16.2.10) that

$$\frac{dG}{dy_j} = \frac{2}{n^2\mu}[j - i] \tag{16.4.4}$$

so that (16.4.3) is not satisfied—the sensitivity of the Gini to a transfer between two incomes depends solely on the ranks of these two incomes and not on their levels. For the Theil index in (16.2.13),

$$\frac{dT}{dy_j} = \frac{1}{Y}\log\frac{y_j}{y_i} \tag{16.4.5}$$

Hence (16.4.3) is indeed satisfied for the Theil index. Consider now the normative measure of inequality defined in (16.3.6) and (16.3.7). From these it is seen that

$$\frac{dI}{dy_j} = -\frac{1}{\mu}\frac{d\bar{y}}{dy_j} = -\frac{1}{\mu}\left[\frac{\partial\bar{y}}{\partial y_j} - \frac{\partial\bar{y}}{\partial y_i}\right] = -\frac{1}{\mu}\frac{\dfrac{\partial W(y_1,y_2,\ldots,y_n)}{\partial y_j} - \dfrac{\partial W(y_1,y_2,\ldots,y_n)}{\partial y_i}}{\sum\limits_k\dfrac{\partial W(\bar{y},\bar{y},\ldots,\bar{y})}{\partial y_k}}$$

$$\tag{16.4.6}$$

Now from (16.3.4), (16.4.6) is of course positive—with an egalitarian social welfare function inequality must decrease when a transfer is made from rich to poor. But what of the sensitivity of this inequality change to the income level from which the transfer is made? For this we calculate

$$\left\{\sum_k\frac{\partial W(\bar{y},\bar{y},\ldots,\bar{y})}{\partial y_k}\right\}^2\frac{\partial\left(\dfrac{d\bar{y}}{dy_j}\right)}{\partial y_j}$$

$$= \left\{\sum_k\frac{\partial W(\bar{y},\bar{y},\ldots,\bar{y})}{\partial y_k}\right\}\left\{\frac{\partial^2 W(y_1,y_2,\ldots,y_n)}{\partial y_j^2} - \frac{\partial^2 W(y_1,y_2,\ldots,y_n)}{\partial y_i\partial y_j}\right\}$$

$$- \frac{\left\{\dfrac{\partial W(y_1,y_2,\ldots,y_n)}{\partial y_j}\right\}\left\{\sum\limits_k\sum\limits_l\dfrac{\partial^2 W(\bar{y},\bar{y},\ldots,\bar{y})}{\partial y_k\partial y_l}\right\}}{\sum\limits_k\dfrac{\partial W(\bar{y},\bar{y},\ldots,\bar{y})}{\partial y_k}}\left\{\frac{\partial W}{\partial y_j} - \frac{\partial W}{\partial y_i}\right\}. \tag{16.4.7}$$

As can be seen, the requirement of a particular pattern of sensitivity of transfers (e.g. (16.4.7) > 0) is stronger than simply requiring that the SWF be egalitarian. The SWF can be eagalitarian and yet in general not satisfy the requirement that

$$\frac{\partial\left(\dfrac{dI}{dy_j}\right)}{\partial y_j} > 0.$$

However, in the case of the *additively separable* SWF in (16.3.9) leading to the Atkinson index (16.3.11), the cross derivative terms in (16.4.7) are zero, and it can be shown that

$$\frac{\partial\left[\dfrac{dI_\varepsilon}{dy_j}\right]}{\partial y_j} = \frac{\varepsilon}{n^2\mu^{2(1-\varepsilon)}}\left\{\frac{1}{n}\sum_k\left(\frac{y_k}{\mu}\right)^{1-\varepsilon}\right\}^{2\varepsilon-1/1-\varepsilon}\{y_i^{-\varepsilon}-y_j^{-\varepsilon}\}y_j^{-\varepsilon}$$

$$+\frac{\varepsilon}{n\mu^{1-\varepsilon}}\left\{\frac{1}{n}\sum_k\left(\frac{y_k}{\mu}\right)^{1-\varepsilon}\right\}^{\varepsilon/1-\varepsilon}\{y_j^{-\varepsilon-1}\} > 0 \qquad (16.4.8)$$

Finally in this section, we note a property referred to as the *principle of population* by Cowell (1977) and as the *principle of population replication* by Shorrocks (1980). This states that combining *r* societies, each with identical income distributions, should not alter the measure of inequality. Letting **y** be the vector of incomes and *n* the total number in each society,

$$I(\mathbf{y},\mathbf{y},\ldots,\mathbf{y};rn) = I(\mathbf{y};n). \qquad (16.4.9)$$

Cowell (1977) argues 'it is not self-evident that this property is desirable', giving the example of combining two two-person societies, in each of which one person has all the income and the other none. It is not clear that the four-person society has the same degree of inequality as each of the two-person societies. For explicitly normative measurement of inequality, this property can be generated by what Dasgupta, Sen and Starrett (1973) call 'The Symmetry Axiom for population'. The motivation here is that if two societies with identical populations and identical income distributions are combined, then *per capita* welfare of the whole should equal *per capita* welfare of each constituent society. Mathematically, we require

$$W(\mathbf{y},\mathbf{y},\ldots,\mathbf{y};rn) = rW(\mathbf{y};n) \qquad (16.4.10)$$

Then it is clear that the measure of inequality in (16.3.7) is unchanged, since both the mean income μ and the equally distributed equivalent level of income $\bar{y}$ are unchanged.

16.5. DECOMPOSITION OF INEQUALITY

Having meticulously collected good data on income distribution, having made all the adjustment necessary to make data consistent and comparable, and having selected an inequality index with due regard to normative issues, the income distribution analyst may further wish to examine the *structure* of inequality rather more closely. There are many factors which are associated with the income of an individual, and the pattern of these influences will determine the pattern of income distribution. In delineating these factors, care must be taken before any causality is attributed from factors to income—all we may be able to assert, given the context, is mere association. However, there are some variables which may reasonably be taken to be exogenous—those which an individual cannot change or can only change relatively slowly. Demographic characteristics are of this type—sex, race and age are the ones that come readily to mind. Region of residence could be taken as exogenous for many purposes, but in a highly mobile society this is no longer true—the processes which affect income also affect migration simultaneously.

Whether the characteristics chosen to identify individuals are exogenous or not, and we shall see that exogeneity will be a key issue in policy discussions, it is a common enough exercise in income distribution analysis to group individuals according to given characteristics—say different age groups or different racial groups—and ask how the pattern of inequality is accounted for by these groupings. Particular interest attaches to the extent of overall inequality which is accounted for by inequality *within* these groups and inequality *between* these groups. It is over the precise definition of these components, and their consistency with overall inequality, that there is debate in the literature on *decomposability* of inequality measures.

Let us start in an ad hoc way, by noticing that some common measures of inequality can be rewritten in a way which takes account of group differences. Thus for example, the variance of logs can be written as

$$V = xV_1 + (1 - x)V_2 + x[\tilde{\mu}_1 - \tilde{\mu}]^2 + (1 - x)[\tilde{\mu}_2 - \tilde{\mu}]^2 \qquad (16.5.1)$$

when there are two groups of interest, 1 and 2, where V stands for variance of logs, $\tilde{\mu}$ for mean of logs, subscripts refer to the two groups and x is the population share of group 1. The Theil index can be written in similar fashion as

$$T = \frac{x\mu_1}{\mu} T_1 + \frac{(1 - x)\mu_2}{\mu} T_2 + \frac{x\mu_1}{\mu} \log \frac{\mu_1}{\mu} + \frac{(1 - x)\mu_2}{\mu} \log \frac{\mu_2}{\mu}. \qquad (16.5.2)$$

Here T is the Theil index while μ is the arithmetic mean. A similar 'decomposition' can be presented for a number of other indices.

In expressions (16.5.1) and (16.5.2), the first two terms on the right-hand side can in each case be thought of as the 'within group' component of inequality— being a weighted average of the inequality indices within each group. The second two terms are constructed as follows: equalize incomes in each group at some level and then calculate the index on the resulting overall distribution. For V the incomes in each group are equalized to the mean of logs in that group, while for T they are equalized to the arithmetic mean in each group. The last two terms in (16.5.1) and (16.5.2) can thus be thought of as representing 'between group' inequality. The square of the coefficient of variation can be decomposed as follows

$$C^2 = x\left(\frac{\mu_1}{\mu}\right)^2 C_1^2 + (1-x)\left(\frac{\mu_2}{\mu}\right)^2 C_2^2 + x\frac{(\mu_1-\mu)^2}{\mu^2} + \frac{(1-x)(\mu_2-\mu)^2}{\mu^2}. \quad (16.5.3)$$

Here again the first two and last two terms can be interpreted respectively as within-group and between-group components of inequality. But notice now that the weights on C_1^2 and C_2^2 do not sum to one.

It should be clear, of course, that the application of (16.5.1), (16.5.2), (16.5.3) and to specific data on, for example, inter-racial or intra-racial inequality will give different answers as to the contribution of race to overall inequality. These indices are different and will naturally decompose in different ways. But what is striking from the theoretical point of view is the lack of any sort of consistency of principle in the decompositions. In some cases group incomes are equalized to the group mean in order to compute the between group component, in other cases they are not. In some cases the weights on sectoral inequalities used in calculating the within group component sum to unity, in other cases they do not. It is the mathematical properties of the index which give us the exact decomposition. However, there are sufficient similarities in the decompositions that we may turn the question around and ask—what decomposability properties should we require from an index? Having specified these requirements, we can then see which indices satisfy them.

Bringing together the different features of the decompositions in (16.5.1), (16.5.2) and (16.5.3), we can, perhaps, state a common definition of decomposability. The 'between group' component should be the value of the inequality index when incomes in each group have been equalized. The question of what level each group's income should be equalized at is still an open one, though we might perhaps restrict ourselves to feasibility—the income level at which a group's income is equalized should be less than or equal to the mean income in that group. Let us in fact make this reference level of income exactly the mean income of each group. So far as the 'within group' component is concerned, we may specify that this should be a weighted sum of the inequality index for each group. Finally, we require *additive decomposability* if we impose the condition that the sum of the within group and between group components add up to the overall index for any grouping.

Let us now introduce some notation in order to provide a mathematical statement of decomposability. Following Shorrocks (1980), Let the inequality index be given by

$$I = I(\mathbf{y}; n), \quad (16.5.4)$$

where $\mathbf{y} = (y_1, y_2, \ldots, y_n)$ are the n incomes. Divide these incomes into G mutually exclusive and exhaustive subgroups, indexed by $g = 1, 2, \ldots, G$. Let n_g be the number in group g and let $\mathbf{y}^g = (y_1, y_2, \ldots, y_{n_g})$ be the incomes in the gth group.

Then the condition for *additive decomposability* as developed above can be written as

$$I(\mathbf{y}^1, \mathbf{y}^2, \ldots, \mathbf{y}^G; n) = \sum_g w_g^G(\mathbf{u}, n) I(\mathbf{y}^g; n_g) + I(\mu_1 \mathbf{e}_{n_1}, \ldots, \mu_G \mathbf{e}_{n_G}; n) \quad (16.5.5)$$

where $\mathbf{e}_{n_g} = (1, 1, 1, \ldots, 1)$ is the vector of n_g ones and w_g^G is the weight on the inequality of the gth group, shown to depend on G, on $\mu = (\mu_1, \mu_2, \ldots, \mu_G)$ on $\mathbf{n} = (n_1, n_2, \ldots, n_G)$.

Let us now impose some commonly used restrictions on I. In particular, assume [see IV, §5.1 and §5.2]

$I(\mathbf{y}, n)$ is continuous and symmetric in $\mathbf{y}$ (16.5.6)

$I(\mathbf{y}; n) \geqslant 0$ with equality iff $\mathbf{y} = \mu \mathbf{e}_n$ (16.5.7)

$I(\mathbf{y}; n)$ has continuous partial derivatives $\dfrac{\partial I}{\partial y}$.   (16.5.8)

Then Shorrocks (1980) has shown that a function $I(y:n)$ satisfies (16.5.6)–(16.5.8) *if and only if*

$$I(\mathbf{y}:n) = \frac{1}{\theta(\mu, n)} \sum_i [\phi(y_i) - \phi(\mu)], \quad (16.5.9)$$

where $\theta(\mu, n)$ is positive and $\phi(\cdot)$ is strictly convex [see V, §4.3.1]

We can ask whether the family of indices give in (16.5.9) satisfies a property like the Pigou–Dalton Principle of Transfers. The answer is that it does, and this fact is easy to establish via the convexity of the $\phi(\cdot)$ function. What about the principle of population replication, as stated in (16.4.9), and income scale independence, as stated in (16.4.2)? Shorrocks (1980) shows that the entire class of indices which satisfy these properties as well as (16.5.9) are given by the one parameter family:

$$I_c(\mathbf{y}) = \frac{1}{n} \frac{1}{c(c-1)} \sum_i \left[\left(\frac{y_i}{\mu} \right)^c - 1 \right], \quad c \neq 0, 1.$$

$$I_0(\mathbf{y}) = \frac{1}{n} \sum_i \log \frac{\mu}{y_i}, \quad c = 0. \quad (16.5.10)$$

$$I_1(\mathbf{y}) = \frac{1}{n} \sum_i \frac{y_i}{\mu} \log \frac{y_i}{\mu}, \quad c = 1.$$

The only two cases where the weights $w_g^G(\mu, \mathbf{n})$ sum to one are in fact $c = 0$ and $c = 1$. $I_1(\mathbf{y})$ is easily recognizable as Theil's entropy index. $I_0(\mathbf{y})$, however, is less well known but is just the logarithm of the ratio of the arithmetic mean to the geometric mean. It was suggested by Theil (1967), as an alternative measure of inequality.

In the above discussion of decomposition, all our requirements of additive decomposability are captured in the mathematical formulation (16.5.5), which in turn was distilled from the mathematical features of decomposition for standard measures such as (16.5.1), (16.5.2) and (16.5.3). However, we may state explicitly what we mean by decomposability as follows. For the between group inequality, eliminate all inequality in each group by equalizing incomes at the mean for each group. Calculate the inequality for this hypothetical distribution:

$$I_B = I(\mu_1 \mathbf{e}_{n_1}, \mu_2 \mathbf{e}_{n_2}, \ldots, \mu_G \mathbf{e}_{n_G}; n). \tag{16.5.11}$$

For the within group component, equalize all group means to the overall mean by proportionate scaling of incomes in each group. If the inequality index is mean independent, then inequality within each group is unchanged but the inequality between groups has been eliminated. Calculate the inequality index for this hypothetical distribution:

$$I_W = I\left(\frac{\mu}{\mu_1}\mathbf{y}^2, \frac{\mu}{\mu_2}\mathbf{y}^2, \ldots, \frac{\mu}{\mu_g}\mathbf{y}^g; n\right). \tag{16.5.12}$$

Following Anand (1982), we can say that a measure is additively decomposable if

$$I = I_W + I_B = I\left(\frac{\mu}{\mu_1}\mathbf{y}^1, \frac{\mu}{\mu_2}\mathbf{y}^2, \ldots, \frac{\mu}{\mu_g}\mathbf{y}^g; n\right) + I(\mu_1 \mathbf{e}_{n_2}, \mu_2 \mathbf{e}_n, \ldots, \mu_G \mathbf{e}_{n_G}; n) \tag{16.5.13}$$

for all partitions $\mathbf{y}^1, \mathbf{y}^2, \ldots, \mathbf{y}^G$ [see I, §7.6].

Let us see whether the well known Theil index, which belongs to the I_c family in (16.5.10), satisfies (16.5.13). From the formula for the Theil index it can be verified that

$$\left.\begin{array}{l} I_B = \sum_g \frac{n_g \mu_g}{n\mu} \log \frac{\mu_g}{\mu} \\[2mm] I_W = \sum_g \frac{n_g}{n} T(\mathbf{y}^g; n_g) \end{array}\right\} \tag{16.5.14}$$

where $T(y^g; n_g)$ is the Theil index for group g. But

$$T(\mathbf{y}; n) = \sum_g \frac{n_g \mu_g}{n\mu} T(\mathbf{y}^g; n_g) + \sum_g \frac{n_g \mu_g}{n\mu} \log \frac{\mu_g}{\mu} \neq I_W + I_B. \tag{16.5.15}$$

Thus although the Theil index is decomposable according to the definition (16.5.5), it is *not* decomposable according to the definition (16.5.13). In fact it can be shown that of the family (16.5.10), only the $c = 0$ case satisfies (16.5.13). Let us denote $I_0(\mathbf{y})$ by L. This measure is decomposable in the strict sense of (16.5.13) and decomposes as follows:

$$L(\mathbf{y}; n) = L_W + L_B = \sum_g \frac{n_g}{n} L(\mathbf{y}^g; n_g) + \sum_g \frac{n_g}{n} \log \frac{\mu}{\mu_g}. \tag{16.5.16}$$

Finally in this section, let us consider some of the uses of decomposition analysis. Its commonest use is in the descriptive presentation of the facts of inequality in an 'accounting for inequality' framework. For example, Theil (1967) presented a decomposition of the Theil index for the United States in terms of inequality between and within the states, and in terms of inequality between and within racial groupings. Anand (1982) presents the Theil decomposition for inequality between and within the three main racial groupings (Indians, Malays and Chinese) in Malaysia. Anand (1982) also draws specific policy conclusions from his calculations, in the context of the socio-economic concerns in Malaysia. The Malaysian government has put forward the narrowing of differences between mean incomes of the three races (by a policy of 'Malaysianization', for example) as one method of reducing overall inequality. We may quantify the impact of this as the elimination of the between group component I_B as given in (16.5.14). However, while I_B measures the inequality that would remain if all within-group inequality were eliminated (leaving only between-group inequality) the direct measure of the impact of the policy of equalizing means is in fact $I - I_W$, where I_W is given by (16.5.12). But from (16.5.15) it is seen that

$$I_B \neq I - I_W$$

so that these two measures of the impact of policy will in general give different answers. The difficulty arises precisely because the Theil index is not *strictly* additively decomposable as in the definition (16.5.13), although it is additively decomposable according to the definition in (16.5.5). The only measure of the I_c family which gives the same answer to the two questions asked above is Theil's second index L, as is clear from (16.5.16).

Another use of decomposition analysis for policy purposes is that of Paglin (1975). Paglin's contention is that standard measurement of inequality leads to an overstatement of inequality because some of the income variation is due purely to mean income variations over the life cycle. What is important from a normative point of view, according to Paglin, is the intra-cohort inequality—the 'within-group' component according to our terminology. Here again, this effect can be quantified as the answer to two distinct questions: (i) 'How much inequality would remain if mean incomes were equalised across cohorts? and (ii) 'How much do intra-cohort variations contribute to overall inequality?' Whatever the ethical arguments for ignoring the inter-cohort component of inequality for policy purposes, it is important to note that except for the L index in (16.5.16) all common indices will in general give different answers to these two questions (Paglin (1975) uses the Gini coefficient, which is not decomposable according to *either* of the definitions in (16.5.5) or (16.5.13)).

Strict additive decomposability as in (16.5.13) is thus a necessary requirement if two different ways of quantifying between and within group components of inequality are to give the same answer. However, if one of these quantifications is dictated by the policy measure under consideration—for example, in the case of the 'Malaysianization' policy $I - I_W$ is an appropriate quantification—then the measure does not have to be strictly decomposable as in (16.5.13), it being noted that such strict decomposability restricts us to the single index as given in (16.5.16). Decomposability as in (16.5.5) can still be useful in answering specific questions. For example, in his discussion of equity goals for the United States, Thurow (1980) argues as follows:

> Let me start by suggesting a possible specification of economic equity. In the United States there is a strong allegiance to the principle that everybody should fairly compete for a distribution of market prizes. At the same time, there is the recognition that the market has not given everyone an equal chance to win. The group that comes closest to our ideal vision of the natural lottery is composed of fully employed white males. They do not suffer from the handicap of discrimination, lack of skills, or unemployment.... Let me suggest that our general equity goal should be to establish a distribution of earnings for everyone that is no more unequal than that which *now* exists for fully employed white males.

Now Thurow's (1980) position is by no means uncontroversial. However, if we were to accept his view, then decomposition analysis could be useful in giving us the limits to inequality in groups other than the reference group of 'white males'. To illustrate, consider (16.5.2) and let index 1 refer to the reference group and index 2 to the other group in society (let us say 'blacks'). Thurow's (1980) requirement is that matters be organized such that $T = T_1$, or

$$T = T_1 = T_2 + \frac{x\mu_1}{(1-x)\mu_2} \log\frac{\mu_1}{\mu} + \log\frac{\mu_2}{\mu}. \qquad (16.5.17)$$

Now T_1 is given by what it is currently, and Thurow (1980) accepts this as the appropriate national level of inequality. The population shares x and $(1 - x)$ are also given (if the groupings are on a racial basis). Thus (16.5.17) gives the ranges of T_2 and μ_1/μ_2 which are consistent with the Thurow level of inequality. An empirical application of decomposition analysis of the Theil index and other indices would be of considerable interest.

To end this section we note another use of inequality decomposition, this time in the comparative static analysis of the impact of tax policy on inequality, as conducted in Kanbur (1982). Rewrite the expression (16.5.1) for the variance of logs as

$$V = xV_1 + (1-x)V_2 + x(1-x)[\tilde{\mu}_1 - \tilde{\mu}_2]^2. \qquad (16.5.18)$$

Let ρ denote a policy parameter, such as the progressivity of taxation, and let the two groups 1 and 2 be two occupations, say. Differentiating (16.5.18) yields a taxonomy of the total impact of tax change on inequality as follows [see IV, §3.2]

$$\frac{\partial V}{\partial \rho} = x\frac{\partial V_1}{\partial \rho} + (1-x)\frac{\partial V_2}{\partial \rho}$$

$$+ \frac{\partial x}{\partial \rho}(V_1 - V_2)$$

$$+ x(1-x)\frac{\partial\{(\tilde{\mu}_1 - \tilde{\mu}_2)^2\}}{\partial \rho}$$

$$+ \frac{\partial x}{\partial \rho}(1-2x)(\tilde{\mu}_1 - \tilde{\mu}_2)^2. \tag{16.5.19}$$

Let group 1 be an 'entrepreneurial' occupation. Then $\partial x/\partial \rho$ is of interest as the impact of policy on the fraction of people engaged in the entrepreneurial activity. However, this is only one of the influences on inequality. Broadly speaking, we can classify the influence of the policy parameter into three effects:

(i) The change in inequalities within each class ($\partial V_1/\partial \rho$ and $\partial V_2/\partial \rho$).
(ii) The change in the difference between the log geometric means of the two groups ($\partial\{[\tilde{\mu}_1 - \tilde{\mu}_2]\}^2/\partial \rho$).
(iii) The change in the relative numbers in the two groups ($\partial x/\partial \rho$).

Given a specific model of individual occupational choice in the face of risk, decomposition analysis can be used to follow through the impact of a policy change component by component, as is done in Kanbur (1982).

16.6. MEASUREMENT OF POVERTY

Poverty can be defined as the extent to which individuals in society fall below a minimum acceptable standard of living. However, such a definition is still some way from being an operational tool for measuring poverty and comparing it across different societies. For a start there is the problem of how we are to specify a minimum acceptable standard of living. Is it to be a basic nutritional minimum, or is it to be related to the average standard of living in the society? Is the standard to be specified in terms of a consumption bundle and then translated to an income level through appropriate prices? These are difficult questions, which are much debated in the literature (see, for example, Atkinson (1975) and Townsend (1979)). But the problem we will consider in this section is the construction of an index of poverty from an income distribution *given* the poverty level. Let this poverty line be denoted by z and let

$$y_1 \leqslant y_2 \leqslant \ldots \leqslant y_h \leqslant z < y_{h+1} \leqslant \ldots \leqslant y_n \tag{16.6.1}$$

so that h out of the total population of n are found to be below the poverty line. One straightforward index of poverty is

$$P_1 = \frac{h}{n},$$

which is known as the *headcount ratio* and is one of the most frequently used indices of poverty. However, popular as it is this index does have some problems. Consider, for example, an income distribution identical to (16.6.1) except that y_1 is replaced by $y_1 - \Delta$. The poverty index P_1 is unaffected—yet the poorest person has been made even poorer! In fact, suppose y_1 is replaced by $y_1 - \Delta$ and y_n by $y_n + \Delta$, so that richest of rich is made better-off by a direct transfer from the poorest of the poor: P_1 is still unaffected.

One index which overcomes these problems is the *income gap ratio*, defined as

$$P_2 = \frac{1}{z} \left\{ \frac{1}{h} \sum_{i=1}^{h} (z - y_i) \right\} \tag{16.6.2}$$

which is the average gap of poor people from the poverty line, taken as a ratio of the poverty line itself. The 'distance' between the poor and the poverty line is here being taken as the simple difference between the poverty line and the relevant income level. However, following the discussion in section 16.2, we might consider a generalized average gap and hence generate an index

$$P_2(\theta) = \frac{1}{z} \left\{ \frac{1}{h} \sum_{i=1}^{h} (z - y_i)^\theta \right\}^{1/\theta} \tag{16.6.3}$$

or, more generally,

$$P_2(\phi) = \frac{1}{z} \phi^{-1} \left\{ \frac{1}{h} \sum_{i=1}^{h} \phi(z - y_i) \right\}. \tag{16.6.4}$$

It is seen that the index (16.6.2) goes up if income is taken from any of the poor, as does the generalized index (16.6.4) so long as $\phi(\cdot)$ is an increasing function [see IV, §2.7]. But what if income is taken from the poorest person and transferred to the next person up? If the transfer is small enough, the headcount ratio will be unchanged, as will the income gap ratio. The reason why the latter remains unchanged is of course because we have simply restricted ourselves to the average distance of the poor from the poverty line, with no regard to the *distribution* of these distances. Another problem with the income gap ratio (16.6.2) can be highlighted by considering the distribution where every individual *below* the poverty line in the distribution (16.6.1) is replaced by two individuals with the same income:

$$y_1 = y_2 \leqslant y_3 = y_4 \leqslant y_5 = y_6 \leqslant \ldots \leqslant y_{2h-1} = y_{2h} \leqslant z < y_{2h+1} \leqslant y_{2h+2} \leqslant \ldots \leqslant y_{h+n}.$$
$$\tag{16.6.5}$$

The head count ratio changes from h/n to $2h/(h+n)$, which is an increase since $h < n$, but it is easy to check that the income gap ratio (16.6.2) remains unchanged, as indeed does the general class of indices in (16.6.4).

Sen (1976) has suggested an index which seems to overcome the shortcomings of both the headcount ratio and the income gap ratio. The *Sen poverty index* is

$$P_3 = P_1[P_2 + (1 - P_2)G_P], \qquad (16.6.6)$$

where G_P is the Gini coefficient of the income distribution *among the poor*. This measure responds positively to a transfer of income from a poor individual to any individual (whether poor or not) who has a higher income, and to a replication of the poor as in (16.6.5). This index has now become the workhorse of the literature on poverty measurement (e.g. Anand, 1977); Kakwani, 1980), but there is debate as to its exact normative content. Sen (1976) presented an axiomatization of his index and alternative axiomatizations produce alternative indices (e.g. Takayama, 1979). We may benefit, however, by considering the explicitly normative approach of Blackorby and Donaldson (1980), who start by defining

$$\mathbf{y}^p = (y_1, y_2, \ldots, y_h)$$

as the income distribution vector of the poor and

$$W^p(\mathbf{y}^p)$$

as the social evaluation function for this vector. Then, following the discussion in section 16.4,

$$W^p(\bar{y}^p, \bar{y}^p, \ldots, \bar{y}^p) = W^p(y_1, y_2, \ldots, y_h) \qquad (16.6.7)$$

defines the 'representative' income of the poor, $\bar{y}^p$. The 'representative income gap ratio' can thus be defined as

$$\frac{z - \bar{y}^p}{z}$$

and a poverty index can be written as

$$P(\bar{y}^p) = f\left(\frac{h}{n}, \frac{z - \bar{y}^p}{z}\right). \qquad (16.6.8)$$

What properties might we require of an index such as (16.6.8)? Firstly, we might require that doubling all incomes and doubling the poverty line should leave the index unaltered. The index would then be a 'relative poverty index'. Such a requirement is equivalent to $\bar{y}^p$ being homogeneous of degree zero, which in turn is equivalent to $W^p(\mathbf{y}^p)$ being homogeneous of degree one (see the discussion relating to homogeneity of SWFs in section 16.3 and 16.4). Secondly, we might require that the index be homogeneous of degree one in h/n and in $(z - \bar{y}^p)/z$. With a further normalization.

$$f(1, 1) = 1$$

this specifies (16.6.8) as

$$P_4 = \frac{h}{n}\left[\frac{z - \bar{y}_p}{z}\right].$$
(16.6.9)

Thus to every social welfare function for the incomes of the poor, there corresponds an appropriate poverty index (16.6.9). It would be interesting to see empirical applications of this index for parametrized social welfare functions like the family in (16.3.9).

16.7. SOME PROBLEMS OF GROUPED DATA

Finally in this survey, let us consider some problems of measurement of inequality and poverty when data are in grouped form. In other words, instead of individual observations on income y_i, $i = 1, 2, \ldots, n$, we may have data for k income ranges as given in Table 16.1.

Although income distribution data are now available in some advanced countries in individual form, in most countries the analyst has access only to tabulated data. How are we to calculate the indices of inequality and poverty, discussed in previous sections, for such data? A straightforward approach is to construct the income distribution with proportions

$$\left(\frac{N_1}{N}, \frac{N_2}{N}, \ldots, \frac{N_k}{N}\right) \text{ at incomes}$$

$$y_1^* \leqslant y_2^* \leqslant \ldots \leqslant y_k^*, \quad y_i^* = \frac{Y_i}{N_i}$$
(16.7.1)

All the measures of inequality and poverty discussed in the earlier sections of this paper can now be calculated for this new distribution. However, it is clear that the new distribution suppresses inequality within each income range and as such tends to *understate* inequality.

Let us consider the Lorenz curve of the income distribution in the above table.

Table 16.1

Income range	Numbers	Total income
$y_1 - y_2$	N_1	Y_1
$y_2 - y_3$	N_2	Y_2
$y_i - y_{i+1}$	N_i	Y_i
$y_k - y_{k+1}$	N_k	Y_k
Total	N	Y

Of course we cannot know the *true* Lorenz curve since we do not have information on distribution within income ranges. However, using the properties of the Lorenz curve discussed in section 16.2, we may put *bounds* on the true Lorenz curve as follows. Notice first of all that the true Lorenz curve must go through the points

$$(0,0), \left(\frac{N_1}{N}, \frac{Y_1}{Y}\right), \left(\frac{N_1+N_2}{N}, \frac{Y_1+Y_2}{Y}\right), \ldots, (1,1). \qquad (16.7.2)$$

This is clear from Table 16.1. What is the Lorenz curve closest to the line of perfect equality, consistent with the requirement that the curve be increasing and convex? The answer is that it is the Lorenz curve obtained by joining the points in (16.7.2), L_1 in the Figure 16.1. Of course, this is the Lorenz curve of the distribution (16.7.1). This provides us with an inner bound on the true Lorenz curve. What of the outer bound? We use the fact, discussed in section 16.2, that the tangent at any point on the Lorenz curve has slope given by the income of the individual at that point divided by the mean. Thus, for example, a line of slope y_3/μ drawn through the point $[(N_1+N_2)/N, (Y_1+Y_2)/Y]$ is the tangent to the true Lorenz curve. Appealing once again to the convexity of the true Lorenz curve, it must lie-above the curve obtained by joining the intersections of these tangents, shown as L_2 in Figure 16.1. Defining Π_i as the cumulative population share of incomes below y_{i+1}, and s_i as their cumulative income share, these points are given as:

$$(0,0), \ldots, \left\{ \frac{\mu(s_{i+1}-s_i)+(\Pi_i y_{i+1}-\Pi_{i+1}y_{i+2})}{y_{i+1}-y_{i+2}}, \right.$$

$$\left. \frac{\mu(y_{i+2}s_i-y_{i+1}s_{i+1})-(\Pi_i-\Pi_{i+1})y_{i+1}y_{i+2}}{\mu(y_{i+2}-y_{i+1})} \right\}, \ldots, (1,1) \qquad (16.7.3)$$

Implicit in *this* Lorenz curve is a distribution with proportions

$$\left\{ \frac{y_i-\mu(s_i-s_{i-1})}{y_i-y_{i+1}}[\Pi_i-\Pi_{i-1}] + \frac{\mu(s_{i+1}-s_i)-y_{i+2}}{y_{i+1}-y_{i+2}}[\Pi_{i+1}-\Pi_i] \right\} \qquad (16.7.4)$$

at incomes y_{i+1}, $i=1,2,\ldots k$.

The measures of inequality discussed in sections 16.2, 16.3 and 16.4 can now be calculated for this distribution. Comparison with values calculated for the distribution (16.7.1) then indicates the range of possibilities with grouped data — see, for example, Gastwirth (1972).

Consider now the problem of measuring poverty with grouped data when the poverty line falls *within* an income range, say

$$y_i < z < y_{i+1}.$$

For the headcount ratio and income gap ratio measures, what matters is how people and total income are allocated between the two sub-ranges (y_i, z) and

(z, y_{i+1}). Let N_i^L and Y_i^L be the population and income allocations respectively, for the lower range and let $N_i^U (= N_i - N_i^L)$ and $Y_i^U (= Y_i - Y_i^L)$ be the corresponding allocations for the upper range. These allocations can be arbitrary except for the constraints that

$$y_i \leqslant \frac{Y_i^L}{N_i^L} \leqslant z \leqslant \frac{Y_i^u}{N_i^u} \leqslant y_{i+1}. \tag{16.7.5}$$

Each allocation satisfying the above restriction will generate alternative values of the headcount ratio and the income gap ratio. Straightforward as they may seem, failure to take account of these restrictions has led to considerable debate in the empirical literature (see Fields, 1977; Ahluwalia *et al.*, 1980).

For the Sen index of poverty we need to have the distribution *within* the group of the poor. There is thus a further range of 'sensitivity analysis' that can be carried out. As is clear from the formula in (16.6.6), given the headcount ratio and the income gap ratio, the minimum value of the index P_3 occurs when G_P is minimum and the maximum value occurs when G_p is maximum. Given the allocations consistent with (16.7.5), therefore, we can work out the maximum and minimum possible values of the Sen index (for some calculations of the Sen index with grouped data for developing countries, see Parker (1981) and Foncerrada and Thompson (1981)).

16.8. CONCLUDING REMARKS

This has been a highly selective, and perhaps idiosyncratic, survey of a large literature which is growing rapidly. We have not touched on much detailed work that has been done and is being done. Similarly, space constraints have prevented me from surveying important recent advances (cf. Shorrocks's (1982) work on extending decomposability to income factor components). Such a detailed survey is being undertaken elsewhere (Kanbur, 1983). However, it is to be hoped that the present survey has given a flavour of research in this area, and acquainted newcomers with the mathematical techniques that are found useful in income distribution analysis. We would like to end with a selection of three areas in which future research would be useful. Firstly, we have to formulate links between processes of income generation and the measurement of inequality. In section 16.2, for example, the Theil index was motivated in terms of the likelihood of the current unequal distribution relative to the most likely distribution under what might be termed an egalitarian process (random allocation of dollars to individuals). Such a motivation may appeal more to intuition than the Social Welfare Function approach discussed in section 16.3. Secondly, decomposition analysis should be put to greater use in analytical models, to trace out the effects of policy change on the different components of inequality. Finally, a fruitful area of research must be the empirical applications of the results surveyed here to data from many countries and at different points in time, in particular the sensitivity analysis discussed in section 16.7, in order to give analysts a better 'feel' for how our mathematical constructs behave when confronted with the facts of life.

16.9. NOTES

1. There are exceptions to this generalization, of course. Kuznets (1955) had discussed the relationship between inequality and growth a decade earlier.
2. When income is a continuous variable with density function $f(y)$ in the population [see II, §10.1], the Lorenz curve is the graph $\{\int_0^x f(\theta)d\theta, \int_0^x \theta f(\theta)d\theta\}$.
3. In fact, we can make do with the even weaker property of 'S-concavity'. See Dasgupta, Sen and Starrett (1973).
4. Other problems are apparent in the additivity implied by the form of the SWF in (16.3.9). It is not clear why such additivity should necessarily be imposed. It would follow from a strict Utilitarian view of social welfare, but Utilitarianism has itself been criticized—see Sen (1979). Others, e.g. Harsany i (1955), have attempted to derive an additive social welfare function from individual decision making under uncertainty but this approach has also not been without its critics (see Diamond, 1967).
5. Cowell (1977) develops the notion of the 'Strong Principle of Transfers' in order to capture this property.

16.10. REFERENCES

Ahluwalia, M. S., J. H. Duloy, G. Pyatt and T. R. Srinivasan (1980). Who benefits from economic development?: comment. *American Economic Review*, 242–245.

Alonso, M. and Finn, E. J. (1968). *Fundamental University Physics*, Vol. III. *Quantum and Statistical Physics*. Addison Wesley, New York.

Anand, S. (1977). Aspects of poverty in Malaysia. *Review of Income and Wealth*.

Anand, S. (1982). *Inequality and Poverty in Malaysia : Measurement and Decomposition*. Oxford university Press, Oxford.

Atkinson, A. B. (1970). On the measurement of inequality. *Journal of Economic Theory*, **2**, 242–263.

Atkinson, A. B. (1975). *The Economics of Inequality*. Oxford University Press, Oxford.

Blackorby, C. and Donaldson, D. (1980). Ethical indices for the measurement of poverty. *Econometrica*, **48**, 4, 1053–1060.

Cowell, F. (1977). *Measuring Inequality*. Philip Allen, Deddington, Oxon.

Creedy, J. (1977). The variance of logs and the principle of transfers. *Oxford Bulletin of Economics and Statistics*.

Dasgupta, P., Sen, A. K., and Starrett, D. (1973). Notes on the measurement of inequality. *Journal of Economic Theory*.

Diamond, P. (1967). Cardinal welfare, individualistic ethics and interpersonal comparisons: a comment. *Journal of Political Economy*.

Fields, G. S. (1977). Who benefits from economic development?—A reexamination of Brazilian growth in the 1960s. *American Economic Review*.

Foncerrada, L., and Thompson, B. (1981). Poverty in Mexico: 1968 and 1977. Woodrow Wilson School, Princeton University (mimeo).

Gastwirth, J. (1972). The estimation of the Lorenz curve and the Gini index. *Review of Economics and Statistics*.

Hardy, G. H., Littlewood, J. E. and Polya, G. (1934). *Inequalities*, Cambridge University Press, London.

Harsanyi, J. C. (1955). Cardinal welfare, individualistic ethics, and interpersonal comparisons of utility. *Journal of Political Economy*.

Kakwani, N. C. (1980). *Income Inequality and Poverty.* Oxford University Press, Oxford.

Kanbur, S. M. (1982). Entrepreneurial risk taking, inequality and public policy: an application of inequality decomposition analysis to the general equilibrium effects of progressive taxation. *Journal of Political Economy.*

Kanbur, S. M. (1983). *Income Distribution: Theory, Measurement and Policy* (in preparation).

Kuznets, S. (1955). Economic growth and income inequality. *American Economic Review.*

Paglin, M. (1975). The measurement and trend of inequality: a basic revision. *American Economic Review.*

Parker, D. (1981). Rural Poverty in India 1960/61 to 1968/69: an application of Sen's poverty index. Woodrow Wilson School, Princeton university (mimeo).

Rawls, J. (1971). *A Theory of Justice.* Oxford University Press, London.

Sen, A. K. (1973). *On Economic Inequality.* Oxford University Press, London.

Sen, A. K. (1976). The measurement of poverty: an axiomatic approach. *Econometrica,* **44**, 219–232.

Sen, A. K. (1979). Personal utilities and public judgements: or what's wrong with welfare economics? *Economic Journal.*

Shannon, C. E. (1948). A mathematical theory of communication. *Bell System Technical Journal.*

Shorrocks, A. F. (1980). The class of additively decomposable inequality measures. *Econometrica,* **48**, 3, 613–626.

Shorrocks, A. F. (1982). Inequality decomposition by factor components, *Econometrica.* **50**, 1, 193–212.

Takayama, N. (1979). Poverty, income inequality, and their measures: Professor Sen's axiomatic approach reconsidered. *Econometrica,* **47**, 3, 747–760.

Townsend, P. (1979). *Poverty in the United Kingdom.* Penguin, Harmondsworth

Theil, H. (1967). *Economics and Information Theory.* North-Holland, Amsterdam.

Thurow, L. (1980). *The Zero-Sum Game: Distribution and the Possibilities for Economic Change.* Basic Books, New York.

17

Decision Under Uncertainty

JOHN D. HEY, *University of York, York, UK*

17.1. INTRODUCTION

Although much of mainstream economic theorizing adopts the simplifying assumption that economic decisions are made under conditions of certainty, the past two decades have witnessed increasing recognition of the potential importance of uncertainty for the behaviour of economic agents. Indeed, there is now a formidable body of literature devoted to the analysis of economic behaviour under uncertainty; and it is clear that this literature has contributed significantly to the explanatory and descriptive power of economic theories. With the benefit of hindsight, it is now apparent that, in certain areas, only an uncertainty-based explanation can make sense—previous attempts at certainty-based explanations being inevitably doomed to failure.

A crucial stimulus to the incorporation of uncertainty into economic theory was the development of a general framework of analysis for decision-making under uncertainty. This development was pioneered by the mathematician John von Neumann and the economist Oskar Morgenstern whose names remain linked with the subject through the use of the term 'Neumann–Morgenstern utility theory' for this general framework. More recently, particularly with the further refinement of those aspects of the framework dealing with probabilities, the more general term 'Subjective Expected Utility theory' (or SEU theory) has increasingly replaced the earlier term.

The major and primary purpose of this chapter is to describe and discuss Subjective Expected Utility theory, and to give examples of how it can be used to model economic behaviour under conditions of uncertainty. Clearly it is impossible in the space of one short chapter to explore, or even to hint at, all potential applications of the theory; nevertheless, it is to be hoped that, after completing this chapter, the reader will be in a position to tackle the voluminous literature on the Economics of Uncertainty by him- or her-self.

As the above discussion suggests, most the literature in this area is based on the general apparatus of Subjective Expected Utility theory. However, this theory is not without its critics. Indeed, the very recent past has witnessed a number of significant theoretical developments which threaten the supremacy of the prevailing SEU paradigm. While these developments have not yet come to fruition, it would be misleading to present a chapter on 'decision under uncertainty' without some mention of them; this we do briefly at the end of the chapter, before our concluding remarks.

We begin with the prevailing paradigm, Subjective Expected Utility theory.

17.2. SUBJECTIVE EXPECTED UTILITY THEORY

17.2.1. A framework for analysis

Subjective Expected Utility theory provides a method for describing, and hence predicting, decision-making under conditions of uncertainty. The general type of problem under consideration is one in which the decision-maker must choose one of several courses of action, the precise consequences of which are not certain at the time the decision is made. We use the letter C (with an appropriate subscript) to denote a *Choice* or a course of action. To capture the idea that the consequences of a particular C are not certain at the same time the decision is made, we suppose that the ultimate consequence depends not only on C but also on what *state of the world* ultimately prevails. We use the letter S (with an appropriate subscript) to denote a State of the World, and we note that this terminology is deliberately chosen to convey the notion that the individual (or the individual's choice) has no influence on which state of the world ultimately prevails. Corresponding to each (choice, state of the world) pair, (C, S), there is some ultimate *outcome* or consequence as far as the individual is concerned. We use the letter O to denote a final Outcome, and add subscripts so that, for example, O_{ij} is the final consequence of the pair (C_i, S_j).

SEU theory assumes that the individual can list the set of all possible C, the set of all possible S, and the associated set of all possible O. Moreover, the theory assumes that all the elements of these sets are certain and known; that is, that there is no residual uncertainty with respect to them. These assumptions are by no means innocent, and it may be worthwhile pausing briefly to examine their implications. The assumption that the set of all possible C is certain and known is probably the most innocent: even though in practice, people sometimes overlook possible courses of action (or realize them only when it is too late), the economic theorist need hardly worry about whether a decision-maker will choose a course of action he or she has overlooked! The parallel assumption about the set of all possible S is considerably harder to shallow: indeed, it is rather difficult to envisage real-life situations in which one felt one could list all possible eventualities (of relevance to the choice problem). But the counter argument here is quite strong: how can a decision-maker take into account eventualities which he or she cannot even imagine? Finally, the parallel assumption about the set of all possible O; this is justified either by arguing that, if there is some residual uncertainty about the consequences, then the set of states of the world is not sufficiently detailed, and hence must be expanded; or (though this is essentially the same argument re-presented by) arguing that the method of backward induction [see IV, §16.4] will provide 'certainty equivalents' of any residual uncertainties. (This is not an argument we can pursue here; the interested reader could consult Hey (1981), especially pages 48 to 51.)

While there is assumed to be no uncertainty with respect to the sets of all possible C, S and O, the decision-maker *is* faced with uncertainty in that he or she does not know which particular S will occur, and thus does not know which will be the final O corresponding to any C. At a first glance, it would appear that there is a variety of forms that this uncertainty may take: at one extreme, there may be well-defined 'objective' *probabilities* attached to the various possible states of the world [see II, Chapter 2]; at the other extreme, the individual may feel so uncertain about the various possibilities that he or she feels totally unable to assign probabilities to the states of the world; in the 'middle', there might be a situation in which the individual may feel able to *rank* the states of the world in terms of their relative likelihoods, yet feel unable to attach precise probabilities to them.

Perhaps contrary to intuition, SEU theory denies the existence of this 'spectrum of uncertainty'. As we will discuss, if our decision-maker obeys some apparently innocent axioms (which appear to be the embodiment of 'rational' behaviour), then it can be shown that the decision-maker always acts as if he or she is assigning probabilities to the various states of the world. Naturally, these probabilities are subjective; hence the first word in the name of the theory.

For expository reasons, we will approach the full version of SEU theory somewhat obliquely. Rather than explain both the 'subjective probability' part and the 'expected utility' part simultaneously, we shall begin with the rather more modest task of explaining the 'expected utility' part in the context of a decision-problem in which 'objective' probabilities can be invoked.

First, we need to state what we mean by 'objective' probability; after we have done this, we will be in a position to sketch out the distinction between this and 'subjective' probability. Consider an urn containing a large number of small balls, which are identical except insofar as a proportion p are white while the remainder are black; consider the experiment of shaking the urn and drawing out one ball at random; call event E_p the event of drawing out a white ball [see II, §3.2]. We say that event E_p has 'objective' probability p of occurring; this is what we mean by 'objective' probability in this context. Furthermore, if some individual regards some other event S (unconnected with the above experiment) as being equally likely as event E_p (in a sense to be made precise in due course), we will say that this individual's subjective probability of event S is p. Thus 'objective' probability serves as a benchmark by which to interpret 'subjective' probability. The distinction will become clearer as we proceed.

We now turn to the task of explaining SEU theory in the context of a decision-problem in which 'objective' probabilities can be invoked; in deference to its originators, we label this subsection by its earlier name.

17.2.2. Von Neumann–Morgenstern utility theory

The purpose of this subsection is to construct a framework which enables us to describe and hence predict choice in situations in which 'objective' probabilities are assigned to the various states of the world. In essence, the framework enables an indicator of preference to be attached to each choice; following standard economic terminology this indicator is called the *utility* of the choice. For choice C, this utility is denoted by $U(C)$. The purpose of this subsection is to show how $U(C)$ can be expressed in terms of the characteristics of the choice C.

We begin by introducing some notation to describe the characteristics of some choice. Recall that the final consequences of any choice depend partly on that choice but also on which state of the world ultimately prevails: for choice C_j, the final consequence will be one of the set $\{O_{jk}; j, k = 1, 2, \ldots\}$. To reduce notational complexity, we will introduce the set $\{A_i; i = 1, 2, \ldots, I\}$ defined by

$$\{A_i; i = 1, 2, \ldots, I\} \equiv \{O_{jk}; j = 1, 2, \ldots; k = 1, 2, \ldots\}.$$

Thus, all the final consequences belong to the (single-subscripted) set $\{A_i; i = 1, 2, \ldots, I\}$. In practice, I may be finite or infinite; for expositional purposes we will assume that I is finite—the theory can readily be extended to include the infinite case (see, for example, Arrow, 1971).

For any given choice, the final consequence will be one of the elements of the set A. Since we are assuming, in this subsection, that probabilities can be attached to the various possible states of the world, it follows that probabilities can also be attached to the elements of the set A as possible consequences of any given choice. Thus, we can express the characteristics of a choice C in the following general form:

$$C = [(p_i, A_i), i = 1, \ldots, I]. \tag{17.2.1}$$

By this is meant that choice C leads to consequence A_1 with probability p_1, to consequence A_2 with probability $p_2, \ldots$, and to consequence A_I with probability p_I. Since ultimately one and only one of the consequences will be realized, it follows that

$$\sum_{i=1}^{I} p_i = 1. \tag{17.2.2}$$

Of course, it may well be the case that for some choice, some final consequences are impossible; in this case the corresponding p_i would be zero. If some choice leads to just one or two possible consequences, we will simplify our notation further by expressing the choice as

$$A_i \tag{17.2.3}$$

or

$$[p_i, A_i, A_j] \tag{17.2.4}$$

as appropriate. In (17.2.3), the choice yields A_i with certainty; in (17.2.4) the choice yields A_i with probability p_i and A_j with the residual probability $1 - p_i$.

We are now in a position to describe the procedure by which the 'utility' of choice C, $U(C)$, is expressed in terms of the characteristics of the choice. There are two stages: in the first stage, utility indicators $u_i \equiv u(A_i)$ are assigned to each of the final consequences; in the second stage, the utility of choice C is expressed in terms of the probabilities and the utilities of the possible final consequences. To be specific, if C is as given in (17.2.1), then $U(C)$ is given by

$$U(C) = \sum_{i=1}^{I} p_i u_i \equiv \sum_{i=1}^{I} p_i u(A_i). \tag{17.2.5}$$

Thus, $U(C)$ is simply the expected value of the utility of the final consequences (where the expectation is taken in the normal fashion using the probabilities as weights [see II, §8.1]).

Of these two stages, the first is the *descriptive* stage, the second the *predictive* stage. The essence of von Neumann–Morgenstern utility theory is to show that, under certain assumptions, the descriptive stage can actually be carried out, and that the predictive stage does produce valid predictions. Let us now turn to a proof of the theory; we will introduce the necessary assumptions as and when we need them.

We begin with an assumption which is of a type familiar to economists: we assume that the individual whose choice we are describing and predicting can rank the (certain) elements of the set A in order of preference. This is Assumption One. We will use it to renumber the elements of the set in decreasing order of preference; that is, we chose the subscripts $i = 1, 2, \ldots, I$ so that

$$A_1 \succcurlyeq A_2 \succcurlyeq A_3 \succcurlyeq \ldots \succcurlyeq A_I, \tag{17.2.6}$$

where $\succcurlyeq$ denotes 'preferred or indifferent to'. We will also assume that the choice problem is non-trivial in that

$$A_1 \succ A_I, \tag{17.2.7}$$

where $\succ$ denotes 'strictly preferred to'. (Indifference will be denoted by $\sim$).

We now turn to the descriptive stage, that is, the assigning of utility indicators $u_i \equiv u(A_i)$ to each of the final consequences. This we do by considering pairwise choices of the following form. Consider choices C_1 and C_2 defined by

$$C_1 \equiv A_i \quad C_2 \equiv [p_i, A_1, A_I]. \tag{17.2.8}$$

Thus C_1 yields A_i with certainty; while C_2 implies a gamble between 'the best' $(A_1,$

the most preferred final consequence) and 'the worst' (A_I, the least preferred final consequence) with respective probabilities p_i and $1 - p_i$.

Assume for the moment that $A_1 \succ A_i \succ A_I$ (a parallel argument, which we leave to the reader, goes through in either of the special cases $A_1 \sim A_i$ or $A_i \sim A_I$). Then, if $p_i = 0$ (that is, C_2 yields A_I with certainty) the individual would prefer C_1 to C_2, whereas if $p_i = 1$ (that is, C_2 yields A_1 with certainty) the individual would prefer C_2 to C_1. It would, therefore, be reasonable to assume that for a value of p_i somewhere between 0 and 1 the individual is *indifferent* between C_1 and C_2. We denote this point of indifference by u_i; thus when $p_i = u_i$ the individual is indifferent between C_1 and C_2 as defined in (17.2.8). This is Assumption Two, and we formalize it as follows:

$$\text{For each } i, \text{ there exists } u_i \text{ such that } A_i \sim [u_i, A_1, A_I]. \qquad (17.2.9)$$

Moreover, we assume that if $p_i < u_i$ then $C_1 \succ C_2$ and if $p_i > u_i$ then $C_2 \succ C_1$.

Assumption Two simply asserts that for each 'intermediate' consequence, there is some gamble involving the best and the worst consequence that the individual regards as being equally preferred. This appears intuitively acceptable. The u_i so defined will be termed the utility of the consequence A_i, and we will write $u_i \equiv u(A_i)$. It is clear that $u_1 = 1$ and $u_I = 0$. This completes the descriptive stage.

We now turn to the predictive stage. In this, we show that preference over risky choices can be represented by the expression in Equation (17.2.5). Consider a general choice of the form

$$C = [(p_i, A_i), i = 1, \ldots, I]. \qquad (17.2.10)$$

Moreover, define a_i by

$$a_i \equiv [u_i, A_1, A_I]. \qquad (17.2.11)$$

Recall that, from (17.2.9)

$$A_i \sim a_i; \qquad (17.2.12)$$

that is, the individual is indifferent between (the certainty) A_i and (the gamble) a_i. Now we make a key assumption: that not only is the individual indifferent between A_i and a_i when faced with a pairwise choice between them, but the individual is also indifferent between them in any other context. In other words, the context is irrelevant. This is Assumption Three, otherwise known as the assumption of the *independence of irrelevant alternatives*. It enables us to write

$$C \sim [(p_i, a_i), i = 1, \ldots, I]. \qquad (17.2.13)$$

The move from (17.2.10) to (17.2.13) appears innocent, but in fact it is quite significant. In particular, note that (17.2.10) is a single-stage risk while (17.2.13) represents a two-stage risk: the 'consequences' in the original gamble being themselves gambles. Note also that the *ultimate* consequence in (17.2.13) must be either A_1 or A_I—all the other A_i having been 'substituted out'. We assume that the individual can perceive this, and indeed can work out the relevant probabilities of ultimately ending up with A_1 or A_I. This is Assumption Four. As the reader can verify, the probability of ending up with A_1 in (17.2.13) is

$$\sum_{i=1}^{I} p_i u_i. \tag{17.2.14}$$

(Since, for each i, there is a probability p_i of 'getting' a_i, from which there is a conditional probability of u_i of ending up with A_1 [see II, Theorem 16.2.1]). Obviously the probability of ending up with A_I is 1 minus the expression in (17.2.14).

If one focuses attention on the final outcomes and their probabilities (and ignores any intermediate considerations, such as the route travelled), then it is clear that the two-stage risk in (17.2.13) is the same as the single-stage risk:

$$\left[\sum_{i=1}^{I} p_i u_i, A_1, A_I \right]. \tag{17.2.15}$$

Our individual should, therefore, be indifferent between (17.2.15) and the risk on the right-hand side of (17.2.13). If we further assume that the individual's preference ordering over risky choices is transitive (Assumption Five), it follows that

$$C \sim \left[\sum_{i=1}^{I} p_i u_i, A_1, A_I \right]. \tag{17.2.16}$$

Finally, we make the apparently innocent assumption that, when faced with pairwise choices amongst gambles involving only the best and worst as possible final consequences, the individual will always prefer the choice for which the probability of getting the best is the higher. This is Assumption Six; formally:

$$[p, A_1, A_I] \succcurlyeq [q, A_1, A_I] \quad \text{if and only if } p \geqslant q. \tag{17.2.17}$$

It follows immediately from this combined with (17.2.16) that the expression

$$\sum_{i=1}^{I} p_i u_i$$

is an indicator of preference: the higher it is, the more preferred is the choice. We can, therefore, conclude that preference over choices can be represented by the utility function:

$$U(C) = \sum_{i=1}^{I} p_i u_i = \sum_{i=1}^{I} p_i u(A_i). \tag{17.2.18}$$

This is what we set out to demonstrate.

Before proceeding, we must clarify one important point: while we have shown that (17.2.18) reflects preference, we have not shown that it is the *only possible* representation of preferences. On reflection, it is clear that there are other representations; for example, consider the v_i defined by

$$v_i = a + bu_i \quad (i = 1, 2, \ldots, I) \quad \text{where} \quad b > 0, \tag{17.2.19}$$

and let $V(\cdot)$, with choice as the argument, be defined by

$$V(C) = \sum_{i=1}^{I} p_i v_i. \tag{17.2.20}$$

From (17.2.18), (17.2.19) and (17.2.20) it is clear that

$$V(C) = a + bU(C), \tag{17.2.21}$$

and hence (since $b > 0$), that

$$V(C_1) \geqslant V(C_2) \quad \text{if and only if} \quad U(C_1) \geqslant U(C_2).$$

Thus, $V(\cdot)$, which is a linear transformation of $U(\cdot)$ [see I, §5.13], is also an indicator of preference. However, by a parallel argument, it can be shown that *only* linear transformations of our original representation can indicate preference: a nonlinear transformation would introduce higher moments of the set $\{u_i; i = 1, 2, \ldots, I\}$ [see II, §9.11], and, as we have already shown, only the first moment of this set is needed to determine preference. Thus the utility function we have derived is *unique up to a linear transformation*.

Let us give a very brief illustration. Suppose there are just $(I =)$ 5 possible final consequences: $A_i = W + 25(5 - i)$ $(i = 1, 2, \ldots, 5)$. Each of these are denominated in money, with W representing the individual's initial wealth. We assume that increasing i represents decreasing preference. First, we find the u_i $(i = 1, 2, \ldots, 5)$. You should determine your own u_i by introspection; here we assume that the appropriate value for our individual are found to be:

$$u_1 = 1 \quad u_2 = 0.9 \quad u_3 = 0.7 \quad u_4 = 0.4 \quad u_5 = 0.$$

(For example, $u_3 = 0.7$ indicates that the individual is indifferent between $W + 50$ with certainty and a gamble in which there is an 0.7 chance of getting $W + 100$ and an 0.3 chance of getting $W + 0$.) This completes the descriptive stage. Now, consider the simple example of predicting the individual's decision when confronted with the choice between

$$[0.5, A_1, A_5] \quad \text{and} \quad [0.5, A_2, A_4].$$

Using (17.2.18), it follows that the utility of the first of these is

$$0.5u_1 + 0.5u_5 = 0.5 \times 1 + 0.5 \times 0 = 0.5,$$

while the utility of the second is

$$0.5u_2 + 0.5u_4 = 0.5 \times 0.9 + 0.5 \times 0.4 = 0.65.$$

Thus (if the individual behaves in accordance with our six assumptions), the individual will choose the second. A further example (which you should verify yourself) shows that this individual, if confronted with a choice between

$$[1/3, A_1, A_4] \quad \text{and} \quad [2/3, A_2, A_5],$$

will be indifferent between them (since both have utility, calculated according to (17.2.18), of 0.6).

Incidentally, before we conclude this subsection, it may be of interest to point out that von Neumann–Morgenstern utility theory can be used to resolve the famous 'St. Petersburg's paradox'. In essence, this paradox is that no-one will offer more than a finite amount (and usually only a relatively small amount) to enter a game in which the reward to the player is £2^i with probability $1/2^i$ ($i = 1, 2, \ldots$), despite the fact that this game has infinite expected reward. The paradox is resolved if, for example, utility is bounded above; for further details, see Samuelson (1977).

17.2.3. Subjective probabilities

The utility of a risky choice is the expected utility of the final consequences. There are thus two key ingredients: the $u_i \equiv u(A_i)$, the utilities attached to the final consequences; and the p_i, the probabilities implied by the probabilities attached to the various states of the world. In the previous subsection we showed how the u_i could be derived, but we took for granted the 'objective' existence of the p_i. In this subsection we show how, in the absence of generally agreed objective probabilities, subjective probabilities may be inferred from the individual's preference structure. We continue to assume that the set $\{A_i; i = 1, 2, \ldots, I\}$ contains all the possible final consequences; moreover, we suppose that the individual's $u_i = u(A_i)$ have already been obtained by the process described above. Our discussion will be relatively informal; we leave it to the interested reader to fill in the gaps in the formal logic. Consider a particular state of the world S_j, and suppose our individual is confronted with the following choice problem:

states of the world

		S_j	$\bar{S}_j$
choices	C_1	1	0
	C_2	w_j	w_j

Here $\bar{S}_j$ denotes the event that the state of the world S_j does not occur, and the table entries denote the *utilities* of the final consequences implied by the various (C, S) combinations: thus C_1 leads to utility 1 if S_j occurs and 0 otherwise, while C_2 always leads to utility w_j. Assuming that the individual neither regards S_j as certain to occur nor as certain not to occur (in either case, the subjective probability being therefore immediately apparent), the individual will prefer C_1 to C_2 if $w_j = 0$

and C_2 to C_1 if $w_j = 1$. Following a similar argument to that used in the previous subsection, it would appear reasonable to suppose that there exists some value of w_j, call it p_j, at which the individual is indifferent between C_1 and C_2. (Moreover, if $w_j < p_j$ then $C_1 \succ C_2$ while if $w_j > p_j$ then $C_2 \succ C_1$). Then the individual's subjective probability for state of the world S_j is p_j, since this probability equates the expected utilities of C_1 and C_2. Obviously we require that this inferred probability be independent of the context in which it was inferred. Thus, for example, if the entries in the C_1 row were linearly transformed to $a + b$ and a respectively ($b > 0$), then the value of w_j at which indifference occurred would have to become $a + bp_j$. We could then consider the individual as viewing S_j as equally likely as event E_{p_j} (defined with respect to the 'urn experiment' in the previous subsection). If S_j is so regarded, *irrespective of the context*, then we can simply replace each S_j by the corresponding E_{p_j}, and the problem reduces to that examined in detail in the previous subsection. We note that not only are the u_i subjective, but the p_j are also. Hence the name—Subjective Expected Utility theory.

To summarize: we first find the individual's $u_i \equiv u(A_i)$ in the manner described above; we then find the individual's $p_j \equiv P(S_j)$ in the manner described above. Then, to predict choice, we calculate the expected utility of each choice using the utilities and probabilities so obtained.

17.2.4. Measuring risk aversion and measuring risk

As we have repeatedly emphasized, the u_i are *subjective*; they may well differ from individual to individual. Given their definition (see Equation (17.2.9)) in the context of choices involving risky prospects, it is clear that the magnitude of the u_i reflect, in some way, the individual's attitude towards risk. The first purpose of this subsection is to explore the precise way in which aversion to, or preference for, risk is encapsulated in the individual's utility function. The second purpose is to examine a 'conjugate' problem: the circumstances under which we can say that some choice is 'riskier' than some other choice. (These are conjugate problems in the sense that of two individuals, the less risk averse of the two will tend to opt for the riskier choices.)

We begin with the problem of defining and measuring attitudes to risk. Although the general theory discussed above allows for the elements of the set A to be perfectly general, we shall, in this subsection invoke an enormous simplification to our problem by considering the special case in which the elements of A are all denominated in terms of a single variable. This variable, which we denote by X, can for convenience be thought of as money. This restriction to the univariate case is the restriction adopted by the vast majority of the literature in the Economics of Uncertainty; some flavour of the difficulties involved with the multivariate extension can be obtained from Rusell and Seo (1978), one of the few articles on the subject.

Thus the u_i are expressible in terms of the utility function $u(\cdot)$, the argument of which is X. The individual's attitude to risk will, therefore, be embodied in the form of the function $u(\cdot)$. Let us begin our analysis with the intuitive notion that a *risk-averse* person is one who always prefers a certainty to a risky prospect with the same expected return. In contrast, a *risk-loving* person always prefers the risky prospect, while a *risk-neutral* person is always indifferent between them. Formally, this notion can be written.

$$\text{a risk-}\begin{Bmatrix}\text{averse}\\\text{neutral}\\\text{loving}\end{Bmatrix}\text{ individual is one for whom } Eu(X) \lesseqgtr u(EX) \text{ always.}$$

$$(17.2.22)$$

In (17.2.22), E denotes the Expectation operator [see II, §8.1]; thus, if X is discrete, $Eg(X) = \Sigma g(x)f(x)$, where $f(x)$ denotes the probability that X equals x and the summation is over all values of X. More generally [see II, §10.4.1], we can write

$$Eg(X) = \int g(x)\mathrm{d}F(x) \qquad (17.2.23)$$

where the (Riemann–Stieltjes) integration is carried out over all values for X, and where $F(\cdot)$ denotes the *distribution function* of X; that is

$$F(x) = P(X \leqslant x) \qquad (17.2.24)$$

[see II, §10.3.1]. (Before proceeding we note that we should make a distinction between these individuals who are *strictly*, and those who are *weakly*, risk-averse and risk-loving. For the former the inequalities in (17.2.22) are strict; for the latter they are weak. To maintain this distinction throughout the subsequent discussion would be rather tedious; we accordingly leave it to the reader to make the appropriate distinctions where necessary.)

The reader who is familiar with Jensen's inequality [see IV, §21.3] will realize that it can be used to deduce the following from the definition (17.2.22):

$$\text{a risk-}\begin{Bmatrix}\text{averse}\\\text{neutral}\\\text{loving}\end{Bmatrix}\text{ individual is one for whom } u(\cdot) \text{ is }\begin{Bmatrix}\text{concave}\\\text{linear}\\\text{convex}\end{Bmatrix}. \qquad (17.2.25)$$

Alternatively, (17.2.25) can be obtained by the following simple argument: since a risk-averter will always prefer a certainty of a to a gamble yielding $(a - b)$ and $(a + b)$ each with probability $\frac{1}{2}$, (where $b > 0$), then for a risk-averter.

$$u(a) \geqslant \tfrac{1}{2}u(a - b) + \tfrac{1}{2}u(a + b).$$

It follows from this that

$$u(a) - u(a - b) \geqslant u(a + b) - u(a),$$

and hence that the gradient of u between $(a - b)$ and a is not less than the gradient of u between a and $(a + b)$. Thus, the gradient of u must be non-increasing, and since this must hold for all a and $b(> 0)$, then $u''(x) \leqslant 0$ everywhere, and so $u(\cdot)$ is concave [see IV, §15.2.6]. The remaining parts of (17.2.25) follow by parallel arguments.

An alternative approach is through the notion of the *risk-premium*. This is denoted by r and is defined by:

$$Eu(X) = u(EX - r). \qquad (17.2.26)$$

Comparison of (17.2.22) and (17.2.26) shows immediately that:

$$\text{a risk-}\begin{cases}\text{averse} \\ \text{neutral} \\ \text{loving}\end{cases}\text{individual is one for whom } r \gtreqless 0. \qquad (17.2.27)$$

Thus, for example, a risk-averse person would always be willing to pay some (nonnegative) amount to replace a risky prospect by its expected value.

The risk-premium can also be used to determine whether one individual is *more* risk-averse than some other individual. Intuition suggests that, if one individual's risk-premium is always larger than a second individual's, then the first is more risk-averse than the second. Jensen's inequality can be used to show that this implies that the first individual's utility function can be expressed as a *concave transformation* of the second's utility function. (The reader may like to verify this result.) Alternatively, one can construct an index of risk-aversion in order to check whether the first person's index is everywhere greater than the first person's. Clearly, the *degree* of concavity of the utility function is critical in determining the *strength* of risk-aversion, and, at a first glance one might be tempted to use $-u''(x)$ as an index of risk-aversion. (Note that $u'' < 0$ for a risk-averter, so if one wants an index of risk-*aversion*, it is natural to take the negative of u''.) However, when it is remembered that the utility function is unique only up to a linear transformation, it is clear that $-u''(x)$ suffers from the disadvantage that its value changes when linear transformations are made. An alternative (whose value is invariant under such transformations) is the *absolute risk-aversion index*, $R^A(x)$, defined by:

$$R^A(x) = -u''(x)/u'(x). \qquad (17.2.28)$$

It can indeed be shown that this is a useful index of risk aversion in the sense that if one individual's $R^A(x)$ is greater than a second individual's $R^A(x)$, for all values of x, then the first individual will always be willing to pay a larger risk premium than the second.

To summarize: the shape of an individual's utility function encapsulates the individual's attitude to risk. Risk-aversion is indicated by concavity, risk-neutrality by linearity and risk-loving by convexity. One individual is more risk-averse than a second if the utility function of the first is a concave transformation of that of the second; two exactly equivalent conditions for this are that the first individual is always willing to pay a higher risk premium than the second, and that the risk-aversion index $R^A(x)$ is everywhere larger for the first individual.

We now turn to the 'conjugate' problem: that of measuring the riskiness of prospects. We continue to restrict attention to the univariate case, and ask the specific question: when is one distribution (of X) riskier than a second? On reflection, it is clear that, to make the question meaningful, we must first restrict attention to pairs of distributions that have the same mean (that is, same expected return): riskiness is meaningful only relative to a given return [see II, §10.4].

We describe distributions in terms of their distribution functions: let $F(\cdot)$ and $G(\cdot)$ be the distribution functions of two prospects whose riskiness we wish to compare [see II, §10.3.1]. For notational and mathematical simplicity we will assume that all distributions are defined over a finite range, which we shall take, without loss of generality, to be the closed interval $[0,1]$. The requirement that the two distributions have equal means implies that

$$\int_0^1 x \, dF(x) = \int_0^1 x \, dG(x).$$

This implies (using integration by parts [see IV, §4.3]) that

$$\int_0^1 [G(x) - F(x)] \, dx = 0. \tag{17.2.29}$$

Now consider what might be meant by the statement that 'G is riskier than F'. One obvious interpretation is that F (the less risky) is preferred by all risk-averters to G (the more risky). In mathematical terms, this means that, for all concave $u(\cdot)$,

$$\int_0^1 u(x) \, dF(x) > \int_0^1 u(x) \, dG(x).$$

This implies (again using integration by parts) that, for all concave $u(\cdot)$,

$$\int_0^1 [G(x) - F(x)] u'(x) \, dx > 0. \tag{17.2.30}$$

Now it can be shown, using the second mean value theorem of the integral calculus [see IV, Theorem 4.5.2], that for $u''(x) \leqslant 0$, there must exist a value $y \in [0,1]$ such that the integral on the left-hand side of (17.2.30) is equal to

$$u'(0) \int_0^y [G(x) - F(x)] \, dx.$$

Thus (given that $u' > 0$), it follows that a *sufficient* condition for (17.2.30) to be true for all concave $u(\cdot)$ is that

$$\int_0^y [G(x) - F(x)] \, dx \geqslant 0 \quad \text{for all} \quad y \in [0,1]. \tag{17.2.31}$$

In fact, it can be shown that (17.2.31) is also a necessary condition. (The proof, which we omit, can be found in Hey (1981). Thus (given (17.2.29), of course), all risk-averters prefer F to G if and only if (17.2.31) holds. Actually, it also follows that (17.2.29) and (17.2.31) are similarly necessary and sufficient conditions for all risk-lovers to prefer G to F. (Obviously (17.2.29) by itself implies that all risk-neutrals are indifferent between F and G.) It seems perfectly natural to conclude that G is riskier than F if (17.2.31) (and (17.2.29)) hold. This is known as the *Rothschild–Stiglitz* definition.

One using should be immediately apparent about this definition: it leads to a *partial* (rather than a *complete*) ordering [see I, §1.3.2] of distributions (by riskiness). This is apparent from a study of (17.2.31): clearly one can imagine many pairs of distributions for which neither (17.2.31) or its 'converse' (with F and G interchanged) hold. In such cases, some risk-averters prefer F while others prefer G; it therefore seems perfectly sensible to conclude that neither distribution is riskier than the other. In contrast, an ordering of distributions (with equal means) in terms of their variance is *complete*: this suggests that one should be rather careful about using the variance as a measure of risk.

The Rothschild–Stiglitz approach gains further support from the fact that it is identical to definitions based on other alternative approaches: first, one that regards a distribution as being riskier if it has more 'weight in its tails'; second, one that regards a distribution as being riskier if it is equivalent to the other 'plus noise'. Further details can be found in Hey (1981).

The Rothschild–Stiglitz approach is widely used in the Economics of Uncertainty. Another popular approach is that proposed by Sandmo, and defined as follows. Let X be some random variable with mean EX; define a new random variable Y by

$$Y = \alpha(X - EX) + EX, \quad \text{where} \quad \alpha > 0. \tag{17.2.32}$$

Clearly $EY = EX$ [see II, §8.4]. An increase in α can thus be regarded as a stretching of the distribution around a constant mean. It can be shown that any such Sandmo increase in risk is also a Rothschild–Stiglitz increase in risk, though the converse is not always true. The Sandmo approach thus yields an even more partial ordering than the Rothschild–Stiglitz approach.

17.2.5. A simple illustration

A number of important concepts have been introduced in this section. It may prove useful to illustrate some of them through a simple example. Suppose an individual has a utility function

$$u(x) = a - b \exp(-Rx). \tag{17.2.33}$$

Elementary differentiation [see IV, §3.2] shows that this individual's absolute risk-aversion index, $R^A(x)$, is given by (see (17.2.28)):

$$R^A(x) = R \quad \text{for all } x.$$

Thus, in this special case, the index is constant at all values of x, and so the individual displays the same attitude to risk at all levels of x. One implication of this is that the individual's risk premium for risks of the form $x_0 + X$, where x_0 is fixed and X is risky, is the same irrespective of the value of x_0.

Envisage, as an interesting special case, this individual being confronted with a random variable which is normally distributed [see II, §11.4]. Specifically, suppose X is $N(\mu, \sigma^2)$. Standard statistical results show that in this case expected utility is a linear transformation of the moment generating function of the normal distribution and given by

$$Eu(X) = a - b \exp(-R\mu + \tfrac{1}{2}R^2\sigma^2) \qquad (17.2.34)$$

The individual's risk premium r, for such a prospect is given by (see (17.2.26))

$$a - b \exp(-R\mu + \tfrac{1}{2}R^2\sigma^2) = a - b \exp[-R(\mu - r)].$$

This solves to give:

$$r = \tfrac{1}{2}R\sigma^2. \qquad (17.2.35)$$

Thus, in this special case, we get the rather neat result that the risk premium is directly proportional to the risk-aversion index R, and to the variance of the random variable. Of course, r is independent of μ, for reasons we have already discussed.

Note that in this case [cf. (17.2.35)] the variance is clearly a meaningful measure of riskiness. Indeed, it can be shown that this result applies generally to any class of utility functions, not merely those of the form (17.2.33): consider the set of distributions which are normal with a given mean; then it follows that one member of this set is riskier than another according to the Rothschild–Stiglitz approach (and according to the Sandmo approach) if and only if the first has a larger variance than the second. (But note that this result does not necessarily generalise to distributions other than the normal.)

17.3. SOME ECONOMIC APPLICATIONS

17.3.1. Insurance

Our first application is a simple problem in insurance. Consider a risk-averse individual who owns two assets, one of which is risky. The value of the safe asset is A, and that of the risky asset B. There is a known probability p that the risky asset will be destroyed (and hence become worthless) in a given period, and correspondingly a probability $1 - p$ that the asset will not be destroyed (and thus continue to be worth B). The individual may insure the risky asset during the period for a given insurance premium [see I, §15.2]. Let us ask the question: what is the *maximum* premium P that the individual will be willing to pay?

Clearly, P is defined by indifference between the individual's utility insured and uninsured; that is, P is given by

$$u(A + B - P) = pu(A) + (1 - p)u(A + B),$$ (17.3.1)

where $u(\cdot)$ is the individual's utility (of wealth) function. Using Jensen's inequality [see IV, §21.3] (or, equivalently, by using the fact that for a risk-averter $Eu(X) \leqslant u(EX)$), it follows that the right-hand-side of (17.3.1) is less than or equal to

$$u[pA + (1 - p)(A + B)] = u(A + B - pB).$$

It follows, therefore, that $A + B - P$ is less than or equal to $A + B - pB$, and hence that

$$P \geqslant pB.$$ (17.3.2)

The expression pB measures the expected loss (or the actuarial loss); thus (17.3.2) states that a risk-averse individual may be willing to pay more than the actuarially fair price for the insurance. This is an eminently sensible result: if it were not true, the existence of insurance companies could be in some doubt!

Using (17.3.1) we can also explore the effects of parameter changes (in A, B and p) on the maximum premium P. For example, consider a change in p with A and B held constant. Differentiating (17.3.1), and re-arranging, yields:

$$dP/dp = [u(A + B) - u(A)]/u'(A + B - P).$$

This is clearly positive, as is:

$$dP/dB = 1 - (1 - p)u'(A + B)/u'(A + B - P)$$

(since, for a risk-averter marginal utility is decreasing in wealth). Both these results are straightforward: they state that the maximum premium is an increasing function of both the probability and the magnitude of the loss. Rather more interesting is the effect of a change in A, the value of the riskless asset. From (17.3.1) we get

$$dP/dA = 1 - [pu'(A) + (1 - p)u'(A + B)]/u'(A + B - P).$$

Using the fact that $p = [u(A + B - P) - u(A + B)]/[u(A) - u(A + B)]$ from (17.3.1), this 'simplifies' to

$$dP/dA = N(P)/u'(A + B - P),$$ (17.3.3)

where

$$N(P) \equiv u'(A + B - P) - u'(A + B)$$
$$- [u'(A) - u'(A + B)] \frac{[u(A + B - P) - u(A + B)]}{u(A) - u(A + B)}.$$

It is clear from this that $N(0) = N(B) = 0$, and that

$$N'(P) = u'(A + B - P)\left[R^A(A + B - P) + \frac{u'(A) - u'(A + B)}{u(A) - u(A + B)} \right] \quad (17.3.4)$$

where $R^A(\cdot)$ is given by (17.2.28).

From (17.3.4) it can be seen that *if the absolute risk-aversion index R^A is a decreasing function of wealth*, then $N'(P)$ is an increasing function of P. Given that $N(0) = N(B) = 0$, it follows that $N(P)$ is everywhere negative for $0 < P < B$. Thus, from (17.3.3), $dP/dA < 0$, that is, the maximum premium is a decreasing function of riskless wealth, if the individual displays decreasing absolute risk-aversion. On reflection, this is clearly a sensible result.

17.3.2. The competitive firm and output price uncertainty

Our second application explores the impact of an uncertain output price on the output decision of the otherwise perfectly competitive firm [see Chapter 12]. Here, let x denote output, p output price, $C(\cdot)$ the cost function, and π the firm's profit. Suppose that the firm obeys the axioms of SEU theory, and that the (single) argument of the firm's utility function is π. Finally, suppose that the firm has a subjective probability distribution over P, but the firm must choose x before the realized value of p is known.

The firm's problem is to choose x so as to maximize

$$Eu(\pi) = Eu[px - C(x)],$$

where the expectation is taken with respect to the (subjective) distribution of p. The first- and second-order conditions for this maximization are respectively:

$$E\{u'(\pi)[p - C'(x)]\} = 0 \quad (17.3.5)$$

and

$$D \equiv E\{u''(\pi)[p - C'(x)]^2 - u'(\pi)C''(x)\} < 0 \quad (17.3.6)$$

[see IV, §3.5]. From (17.3.6) it can be seen that a pair of sufficient (though not necessary) conditions for the second-order condition to be satisfied are that the firm be risk-averse and marginal cost be non-decreasing. We will assume for the remainder of this subsection that (17.3.6) is satisfied.

Since x is a constant, the first-order condition (17.3.5) can be written:

$$E\{u'(\pi)p\} = C'(x)E\{u'(\pi)\}.$$

Subtracting $(Ep)E\{u'(\pi)\}$ from both sides, we get

$$E\{u'(\pi)(p - Ep)\} = [C'(x) - Ep]E\{u'(\pi)\}. \quad (17.3.7)$$

We now note that the left-hand side of (17.3.7) is simply the covariance between $u'(\pi)$ and p [see II, §9.6]. This covariance can be easily signed: as p increases, so does π; if the firm is risk-averse this implies a decrease in $u'(\pi)$. Thus, for the risk-averse firm this covariance is negative. A parallel argument shows that the covariance is zero for a risk-neutral firm and positive for a risk-loving firm. It follows, therefore from (17.3.7) that

$$C'(x) \lesseqgtr Ep \text{ according as the firm is risk-} \begin{cases} \text{averse} \\ \text{neutral} \\ \text{loving} \end{cases}. \qquad (17.3.8)$$

This immediately implies (assuming marginal cost is increasing) that the risk-averse firm will produce a smaller output when the output price is random with a given mean than when the output price is constant and equal to the given mean. In contrast, a risk-loving firm will produce more under uncertainty, while the output of a risk-neutral firm will be unchanged.

Equation (17.3.5) can also be used to generate some comparative static propositions. As might be anticipated, these propositions depend crucially on the attitude to risk of the firm. For instance, it can be shown that, if the firm displays decreasing absolute risk-aversion, then optimal output will (a) increase with a bodily rightward shift of the price distribution, (b) decrease with a Sandmo increase in risk of the price distribution, (c) decrease with an increase in fixed costs (an upward shift of the cost function) and (d) decrease with a multiplicative increase in the cost function. Proofs of these and other propositions can be obtained from (17.3.5), with a little help from Hey (1979, 1981) if necessary.

A special case, which the reader should be able to verify, is when the utility function displays constant absolute risk-aversion (that is, is of the form (17.2.33)), and when p is normally distributed (with mean μ and variance σ^2 [see II, §11.4]). In this case, Equation (17.3.5) reduces to [cf. (17.3.8)].

$$C'(x) = \mu - x R \sigma^2. \qquad (17.3.9)$$

Thus optimal output is a decreasing function of both the firm's index of risk-aversion (R) and the variance of the price distribution. The reader may like to compare Equations (17.2.35) and (17.3.9).

17.3.3. Consumer search

Our final application is somewhat different from the first two in that an *active*, rather than a *passive*, response by the economic agent is required. By this we mean that, whereas in the first two applications the agent simply 'accepted' whatever value of the random variable was realized, in this final application the agent can observe as many realizations as he or she wants before accepting one of them. Obviously there must be a cost to this extra freedom, otherwise the agent would simply go on observing forever: the problem, therefore, becomes one of choosing the optimal trade-off between the benefits and costs of further observations.

We examine, in this subsection, the simplest possible model of *consumer search*. The assumptions of the model are as follows: we suppose that the consumer has decided to buy one unit of some good, this good being sold at an infinitely large number of shops. The price varies from shop to shop, however, and, although it is assumed that the consumer-searcher knows the distribution of prices across shops (as given by the distribution function $F(\cdot)$), the searcher does not know, *ex ante*, the actual price charged by any particular shop. To ascertain this, he must pay a *search cost*, which is presumed to be the same $c > 0$ for each shop. Thus, each price quote costs c. Moreover, before search commences, all shops appear identical (that is there is no particular reason to search some shops before others). Penultimately, it is assumed that the searcher has full recall—that is, when a decision to buy is made, the searcher can buy at any of the shops whose prices have been ascertained. Finally, it is assumed that the searcher is risk-neutral, and that the objective is to choose a strategy which minimizes expected total costs (that is, purchase cost plus search costs).

The crucial problem is to decide when to stop searching. Suppose that at some stage in the search process, the searcher's lowest price quote is p. Should search continue? Consider the following two choices:

(1) accept p—that is, buy at price p;
(2) search one more shop and then buy at the lowest price by then encountered.

Ignoring the cost already incurred in any previous searches (which is irrelevant to the choice between (1) and (2)), the expected costs, $C_1(p)$ and $C_2(p)$ respectively of the two choices are given by:

$$
\left. \begin{aligned}
C_1(p) &= p. \\
C_2(p) &= c + p[1 - F(p)] + \int_0^p q\,dF(q).
\end{aligned} \right\} \tag{17.3.10}
$$

(The first term in C_2 is the search cost; the second term is the cost of buying at price p times the probability that p will still be the lowest price even after one more search; the third term is the expected price, given that it is lower than p, and hence that it is the new minimum, times the probability that the new quote will be less than p.) Denote by $G(p)$ the expected gain in choosing (2) rather than (1)—that is, $G(p)$ is the expected reduction in cost if one more search is made before purchasing. From (17.3.10), using integration by parts [see IV, §4.3] to simplify, we get:

$$
G(p) = C_1(p) - C_2(p) = \int_0^p F(q)dq - c. \tag{17.3.11}
$$

Now define p^* by $G(p^*) = 0$ or

$$
\int_0^{p^*} F(q)\,dq = c. \tag{17.3.12}
$$

Examination of (17.3.11) and (17.3.12) shows that

$$G(p) \gtreqless 0 \text{ according as } p \gtreqless p^*. \tag{17.3.13}$$

Equation (17.3.13) states that if the lowest price so far encountered is greater than p^*, then it is worth searching (at least) once more before buying, while if the lowest price is less than p^*, it is best to stop and buy at that price. Indifference exists if p equals p^*. The price p^* is called the optimal *reservation price*, and the optimal strategy, given our assumptions, is simply to keep on searching until a price less than, or equal to, p^* is found, and then to stop and buy at that price. This is an intuitively satisfying result.

The optimal strategy is defined by (17.3.12). From this, comparative static propositions can be obtainable. For example, it is immediate that $dp^*/dc = 1/F(p^*) > 0$, and thus an increase in search costs leads to a higher reservation price (and no less search). Less immediate (though obtainable from an examination of (17.2.31) and (17.3.12)) is the result that a Rothschild–Stiglitz increase in the riskiness of the price distribution leads to a *decrease* in p^*: search is more intense with a more dispersed distribution.

17.4. ALTERNATIVE APPROACHES

17.4.1. Objections to SEU theory

Despite the fact that SEU theory appears to be the embodiment of 'rational' behaviour, and despite the voluminous body of literature in the Economics of Uncertainty built upon the foundation of SEU theory, the theory is not without its critics. The purpose of this section is to outline briefly the thrust, and implications, of some objections raised by these critics. We do not have the space here to go into any detail; the interested reader could turn to Hey (1982) and the references therein.

The majority of the objections to SEU theory arise out of the findings of simple 'laboratory-type' experiments investigating whether subjects behave according to the axioms of the theory (as discussed in section 17.2.2 above). These experiments typically confront subjects with sequences of (hypothetical) pairwise choices, and ask them which they *would* choose. For example, subjects might first be asked to choose between

$$C_1 = £3000 \quad \text{and} \quad C_2 = [0.8, £4000, £0];$$

and then to choose between

$$C_3 = [0.25, £3000, £0] \quad \text{and} \quad C_4 = [0.20, £4000, £0].$$

To be consistent with SEU theory, subjects should choose C_1 (in preference to C_2) if and only if they choose C_3 (in preference to C_4). (Note that $C_3 = [0.25, C_1, £0]$ and $C_4 = [0.25, C_2, £0]$.) However, experimental evidence suggests many subjects' behaviour violates this and other consistency checks. (This is referred to as Allais's paradox; see Allais and Hagen (1979).)

17.4.2. Some alternatives

What response does such 'evidence' necessitate. One extreme response would simply be to ignore the evidence as not being really indicative of what people would *actually* do when faced with real decisions in the real world. The opposite extreme response would be to scrap SEU theory. A more balanced response than either of this two extremes would recognize that, whereas SEU theory may be appropriate for some individuals, it may require modification or adaption (or even scrapping) for other individuals.

The very recent past has seen some important developments in this direction. Of particular significance is 'Prospect Theory' as developed by Kahneman and Tversky (1979), 'expected utility theory without the independence axiom' as initiated by Machina (1981), and a 'new theory of rational choice under uncertainty' pioneered by Loomes and Sugden (1982).

In essence, the Machina approach drops Assumption Three (the independence of irrelevant alternatves), but retains the other assumptions. Machina shows that this implies a utility of choice given by

$$U(C) = \sum_{i=1}^{I} p_i u(A_i; \mathbf{p})$$
(17.4.1)

instead of by (17.2.5). The difference between (17.2.5) and (17.4.1) is that the vector $\mathbf{p} \equiv (p_1, p_2, \ldots, p_I)$ enters the latter but not the former: this implies the existence of *local*, rather than *global*, utility functions of the final consequences.

The Loomes and Sugden approach focuses attention on the choice context, and argues that the utility of a choice depends not only on the choice itself, but on the other choices forgone. Specifically, if a choice is to be made between C_1 and C_2, then preference is determined by the larger of $U(C_1)$ and $U(C_2)$ as given by (using an obvious notation):

$$U(C_1) = \sum_{i=1}^{I} p_i [u(A_{i1}) + r(A_{i1}, A_{i2})].$$

and
(17.4.2)

$$U(C_2) = \sum_{i=1}^{I} p_i [u(A_{i2}) + r(A_{i2}, A_{i1})].$$

Here, the additional term $r(\cdot, \cdot)$ is a 'regret/rejoicing' function defined over the consequences of the choice selected and the consequences of the choice forgone.

The distinguishing feature of *Prospect Theory* is the notion that decision-making consists of two separate phases: an editing phase and an evaluation phase, carried out in that order. The evaluation phase proceeds along relatively familiar lines, with the edited prospects being evaluated by a function of the form:

$$U(C) = \sum_{i=1}^{I} w(p_i)v(A_i').$$ (17.4.3)

In this, $w(\cdot)$ is a weighting function applied to the probabilities while $v(\cdot)$ is a utility function applied to the edited prospects (denoted by A_i').

It is clear from a comparison of (17.2.5) with (17.4.1), (17.4.2) and (17.4.3) that the latter three each contain (17.2.5) as a special case. As such the three new approaches constitute generalizations of SEU theory. Which, if any, will supersede SEU theory remains to be seen.

17.5. CONCLUSIONS

Despite some rumblings of discontent, Subjective Expected Utility theory continues to reign supreme in the Economics of Uncertainty. As is clear from the detailed discussion of section 17.2, the theory appears to be the embodiment of 'rational' behaviour under uncertainty. Certainly, a large body of literature has been erected on the foundations laid by SEU theory. Moreoever, this literature has produced some important insights into economic behaviour in conditions of uncertainty, and has produced explanations of economic phenomena hitherto unexplained. But in an uncertain world, it would be a foolish man indeed who would state that this was the end of the story.

We conclude with some suggestions for further reading. The classic text for von Neumann–Morgenstern utility theory is obviously von Neumann and Morgenstern (1947), though the notation and style now appear somewhat dated. A useful contemporary discussion is provided by Friedman and Savage (1948).

Arrow (1971) is an important collection of seminal works in the Economics of Uncertainty, while more recent surveys of developments, techniques and applications can be found in Hey (1979, 1981), Hirshleifer and Riley (1979) and Lippman and McCall (1981). A collection of important articles is contained in Diamond and Rothschild (1978). Degroot (1970) and Luce and Raiffa (1957) provide useful background material.

Recent criticisms of SEU theory can be found in Allais and Hagen (1979), Kahneman and Tversky (1979), Machina (1981) and Loomes and Sugden (1982). A summary and survey of these criticisms is given in Hey (1982).

17.6. REFERENCES

Allais, M. and Hagen, O. (1979). *Expected Utility Hypothesis and the Allais Paradox.* Reidel, Dordrecht.
Arrow, K. J. (1971). *Essays in the Theory of Risk Bearing.* Markham, Chicago.
Degroot, M. H. (1970). *Optimal Statistical Decisions.* McGraw-Hill, New York.

Diamond, P. A. and Rothschild, M. (1978). *Uncertainty in Economics*. Academic Press, New York.

Friedman, M. and Savage, L. J. (1948). The utility analysis of choices involving risk. *Journal of Political Economy*, **56**, 279–304.

Hey, J. D. (1979). *Uncertainty in Microeconomics*. Martin Robertson, Oxford.

Hey, J. D. (1981). *Economics in Disequilibrium*. Martin Robertson, Oxford.

Hey, J. D. (1982). Towards double negative economics, in Wiseman, J. (ed.), *Beyond Positive Economics*. Macmillan, London.

Hirshleifer, J. and Riley, J. G. (1979). The analysis of uncertainty and information: an expository survey. *Journal of Economic Literature*, **17**, 1375–1421.

Kahneman, D. and Tversky, A. (1979). Prospect theory: an analysis of decision under risk. *Econometrica*, **47**, 263–291.

Lippman, S. A. and McCall, J. J. (1981). The economics of uncertainty: selected topics and probabilistic methods, in Arrow, K. J. and Intriligator, M. (eds.), *Handbook of Mathematical Economics*, Vol. 1. North-Holland, Amsterdam.

Loomes, G. and R. Sugden (1982). Regret theory: an alternative theory of rational choice under uncertainty. *Economic Journal*, **92**, 805–824.

Luce, R. D. and Raiffa, H. (1957). *Games and Decisions*. Wiley, New York.

Machina, M. J. (1981). 'Expected utility' analysis without the independence axiom. *Econometrica*, **49**.

Russell, W. R. and Seo, T. K. (1978). Ordering uncertain prospects: the multivariate utility functions case. *Review of Economic Studies*, **45**, 605–610.

Samuelson, P. A. (1977). St. Petersburg paradoxes: defanged, dissected and historically described. *Journal of Economic Literature*, **15**, 24–55.

von Neumann, J. and Morgenstern, O. (1947). *Theory of Games and Economic Behavior*. Princeton University Press, Princeton, Mass.

Mathematical Methods in Economics
Edited by F. van der Ploeg
© 1984, John Wiley & Sons, Ltd.

18

Actuarial Mathematics

S. Vajda (Hon. Member, Institute of Actuaries) *University of Sussex, Brighton, UK*

> The task of a modern actuary is above all to find the right formulation of his problem. The mathematical tools he needs are almost certain to be available.
>
> (K. Borch, 1967, p. 443)

18.1. INTRODUCTION

In 1845 the professors of the University of Göttingen in the state of Hanover were worried about the solvency of their widows' and orphans' fund. Previous forecasts of the numbers of wives becoming widows had proved incorrect, and the more pessimistic members proposed drastic measures. However, other forecasts were also subject to doubts, and it was not clear which of the proposed measures were sufficient, or which were perhaps unnecessary. The professors turned to one of their esteemed colleagues, who was known to be well-versed in financial matters, though not more than other members of the University. But he was also one of the greatest mathematicians of all times: C. F. Gauss (1777–1855).

In a minute dated 9.1.1845 Gauss said that 'those gentlemen who thought that I could complete my report within four weeks have a very mistaken idea about the length of such calculations', and that 'the calculations cannot be carried out thoroughly without the necessary data of which nothing exists at present'. He produced his valuation on 1.10.1845 and was asked to submit another valuation six years later (Gauss, 1889–1912).

We shall not describe here Gauss's actuarial endeavours in detail. Actually, little is known about how he went about his task. But it is worth noting that he was quite clear about the necessity of having adequate data available for actuarial calculations.

To stress the relationship between the work of actuaries and mathematics, we might mention that the Royal Charter of the Institute of Actuaries in London (founded 1848) of 1884 defined as one of its objects the 'extension and improvement of the methods of science which has its origin in the application of the doctrine of probabilities to the affairs of life'.

The early history of actuarial ideas mentions the names of a number of Fellows of the Royel Society of London, for instance John Graunt (1620–1674), Edmund Halley (1656–1742), and others. Nor must we forget Leonhard Euler (1707–1783), who published in 1767 in Berlin an essay on life annuities and in 1776 in St. Petersburg formulas for other types of insurance, including an assurance of payments to the survivor of two lives.

In this chapter we shall not try to write a textbook account of actuarial mathematics. We shall, rather, mention those aspects of an actuary's work where he needs mathematical tools, and we shall mention some of these against the appropriate background, referring where convenient to the chapters of the Handbook where a more detailed mathematical explanation can be found.

We do not pretend that all actuaries use all these tools all the time, or even frequently, but we feel that they might be interested to know what tools are available for their use, if required.

The actuary's main duties concern the identification of hazards and the construction and administration of insurance schemes to meet their consequences. However, their training enables them to deal with other aspects of a risk business as well, such as with problems of investment and portfolio management. Techniques of quadratic programming have been applied in this context (Markowitz, 1959).

18.2. COLLECTION OF DATA

The efficient performance of an insurance business depends on reasonable predictions of future events from past observations. We shall now describe how the actuary processes his observations to make them the basis for his forecasts, and hence for his computations.

Starting with life insurance, we deal with the derivation of *mortality rates*, q_x, defined as the ratio

$$q_x = \frac{l_x - l_{x+1}}{l_x},$$

where l_x is the number of lives observed at age x, and l_{x+1} the number of those still observed one year later.

We shall group the lives which we have observed at a given age into homogeneous groups, as concerns some characteristic which we think might influence mortality, for instance sex, racial origin, occupation, type of insurance (we might assume that applications for annuities will be made by healthy lives), perhaps also according to the time elapsed since the last medical examination, etc. We shall then determine the ratio of those members of a group who died at the age considered.

The individuals of the same age might have been observed at different times. Therefore, we may have to take into account past and anticipated future trends of mortality. This leads to some computational intricacies, but it does not raise any problems of mathematical interest.

At this stage one will want to see whether the mortality rates are, in fact, different in the various groups which have been chosen by different characteristics. The groups may be considered to be samples from large populations of the same characteristics, and observed differences may be due to chance. Whether this is so, or whether those differences are systematic, can be decided by an application of the statistical techniques of Analysis of Variance (Vajda, 1944–6) [see VI, Chapter 8] and significance tests [see VI, Chapter 5].

Having determined the crude mortality rates for homogeneous groups, we shall often find inconsistencies. For instance, it might be found that the succession of rates for increasing ages do not follow a smooth curve, or that they contradict the natural assumption that, at mature ages, mortality increases with age. Such inconsistencies might again be due to chance fluctuations in the samples, and to put the crude values into an acceptable form, methods of graduation, or smoothing, will be used [see III, Chapter 6].

The mortality values will be adjusted to follow a smooth curve graphically, mechanically, or analytically.

A graphical graduation is a matter of common sense. Joshua Milne's life tables were based on the numbers of deaths in the city of Carlisle during 1779–1787, and the numbers of exposed to risk as well as those of the deaths were graduated graphically.

Most mechanical methods use linear combinations of equidistant crude rates, and the computation involves successive summations.

Analytical methods depend on the assumption of an analytical formula which connects the true mortality rates of successive ages, it being assumed that the deviations between the 'true' and observed mortalities are Normally distributed with constant variance [see II, §11.4]. The graduation will be carried out by the Method of Least Squares [see VI, §3.5.2], or by the Method of Moments [see VI, §3.5.3]. In 1725, De Moivre suggested $l_x = l_0(1 - x/86)$ $(x = 0, 1, \ldots, 86)$. A more sophisticated formula was that of Gompertz and Makeham

$$\log(1 - q_x) = a + bc^x$$

for age x, where a, b, and c are suitable constants. This gives

$$l_x = ks^x g^{c^x}$$

where $a = \log s$, $b = (c - 1)\log g$, and k is a constant, dependent on the choice of l_0.

More recently, the general formula

$$q_x = e^{f(x)}/(1 + e^{f(x)})$$

has been suggested (Continuous Mortality Investigation, 1976) where $f(x)$ is a polynomial of appropriate degree. We have then

$$f(x) = \log [q_x/(1 - q_x)].$$

(Here, and everywhere in what follows, logarithms have base e.)

The coefficients of the polynomial are chosen to maximize the log-likelihood function [see VI, §6.2]. When $f(x)$ is linear, then the result is the same as that obtained by the Method of Moments.

Our description was concerned with mortality rates. Similar techniques apply to the determination of other rates which are relevant to insurance schemes, for instance disability rates, sickness rates, and in particular, for social insurance schemes, to fertility rates, marriage and re-marriage rates, etc.

We turn now to *non-life* branches. Here no succession of ages need concern us, and this is in a way a simplification. On the other hand, non-life insurance is faced with other complications.

More than one claim can arise in any given time interval, and the amount of any claim can only be determined after the event.

In many non-life branches, for instance in fire insurance, it has been found satisfactory to use for the probability of n claims arising during time t from an individual contract the Poisson formula [see II, §5.4]

$$e^{-\lambda t}(\lambda t)^n/n! = p_n(\lambda, t),$$

say, where λ is the expected (average) number of claims in unit time ('proneness').

If the amount of each claim is C, then $p_n(\lambda, t)$ is the probability of a total claim amount of nC.

If the amount of a claim is itself a random variable, with cumulative distribution function $P(x)$ [see II, §§4.3.2, 10.1.1], then the probability of the total of two claims not exceeding x will be given by the convolution P^{2*} of the function P with itself, viz.

$$\int_0^x P(x - y)\,dP(y) = P^{2*}(x),$$

say, and in general the probability of the total amount from n claims not exceeding x will be

$$\int_0^x P^{(n-1)*}(x - y)\,dP(y) = P^{n*}(x),$$

the nth convolution of $P(x)$ [see II, §7.8].

The integrals above have the form of Stieltjes integrals [see IV, §4.8], because the individual claim amount can vary both continuously and discretely [see II, § §4.3, 10.1]. In practice they will, of course, be integral multiples of some monetary unit.

We remark that for computing convolutions the concepts of the Laplace transform and its inverse are often relevant [see II, §12.3 and IV, §13.4].

The probability of precisely n claims arising, with total amount not exceeding x, is now

$$p_n(\lambda, t)P^{n*}(x)$$

and the total claim x from an individual contract during time t has the distribution

$$\sum_{n=0}^{\infty} \frac{e^{-\lambda t}(\lambda t)^n}{n!} P^{n*}(x) = F(x, \lambda, t),$$

say. This distribution has been variously called a generalized, a convolution mixed, or a compound Poisson distribution [see II, §14.3].

The mean of $F(x, \lambda, t)$ is

$$\int_0^\infty x \, dF(x, \lambda, t) = \lambda t m_1$$

and its variance is $\lambda t m_2$, where m_1 is the mean, and m_2 is the second moment of $P(x)$, that is,

$$\int_0^\infty x \, dP(x) \quad \text{and} \quad \int_0^\infty x^2 \, dP(x).$$

respectively [see II, §§10.4, 9.11].

Only a few explicit forms, suitable for computation, have been suggested for the function $P(x)$. We mention the following:

if

$$P(x) = 1 - e^{-x}, \quad \text{then} \quad P^{n*} = 1 - e^{-x} \sum_{i=0}^{n-1} x^i / i!,$$

and for $\lambda = 1$, which we may assume without loss of generality,

$$F(x, 1, t) = 1 - e^{-x} \int_0^t e^{-s} I_0(2\sqrt{xs}) \, ds$$

where

$$I_0(x) = \sum_{i=0}^{\infty} (\tfrac{1}{2}x)^{2i} / (i!)^2,$$

a modified Bessel function [see II, §12.1.7 and IV, §10.4.3]. (Seal, 1969a, p. 33, quoting a paper of 1939 by W. G. Ackermann.)

Other forms of $P(x)$ were the log-normal [see II, §11.5], the Pareto distribution $1 - (x/x_0)^{-a}(x_0 \leqslant x < \infty)$ [see II, §11.8], the Weibull distribution $1 - e^{-(1/a)(bx)^a}$ [see II, §11.9], and a mixture of negative exponentials [see II, §§11.4, 14.2].

As an approximation to $F(x, \lambda, t)$ an expansion into a series has been used, in terms of the normal distribution and its derivatives [see II, §11.4].

For these and other computational aspects consult Seal (1969a), or Beard, Pentikäinen and Pesonen, 1969.

The function $P(x)$ has been introduced above as the distribution of an individual claim amount. The same mathematical model applies in sickness insurance, where $P(x)$ may be the distribution of the length of an illness.

The very same model appears also in the theory of telephone communication, where the number of calls has a Poisson distribution, and the length of a call is a random variable, for instance a negative exponential [see II, §11.2]. It follows that the extensive literature of that theory can be made use of in the theory of non-life insurance as well.

The validity of the Poisson formula depends on the assumption that the probability of a claim, divided by the time interval, tends to a non-zero constant, that the probability of more than one claim arising tends to zero when the time interval tends to zero, and that claims are independent of one another.

If the ratio of the probability to the time interval does not tend to a constant, but is a function of m, the number of claims that have already occurred (*contagion* [see II, §20.1.6]), then we get a different result. If λ in $p_n(\lambda, t)$ is a linear function of n, say $a + bn$, then the probability $p_n(\lambda, t)$ of n claims in time t is obtained as a solution of

$$\frac{\partial p_n}{\partial t} = (a + bn - b)p_{n-1} - (a + bn)p_n \quad (n = 1, 2, \ldots)$$

[cf. II, §20.4], that is,

$$p_n(t) = e^{-at} \binom{\frac{a}{b} + n - 1}{n} (1 - e^{-bt})^n.$$

These values are terms of a negative binomial distribution [see II, §5.2.4]. The mean of this distribution is $(a/b)(e^{bt} - 1)$, and its variance is

$$\frac{a}{b}(e^{bt} - 1)e^{bt}.$$

The difference between mean and variance makes this formula often more appropriate than the Poisson formula, which has its mean equal to its variance, and therefore produces frequently an awkward fit.

We have just mentioned contagion. If a different form of contagion is assumed, whereby the probability of having n claims in a given time interval depends on the number of claims in the preceding interval of the same length under the same contract, then an application of Markov chain theory would be indicated [see II, Chapters 19 and 20].

Now assume that the probability of n claims during time t from an individual contract equals

$$p_n(\lambda, t) = e^{-\lambda t}(\lambda t)^n/n!$$

as before, but that λ is itself a random variable, with distribution function $U(\lambda)$.

The probability that an individual contract chosen at random will have n claims within time t is then

$$\int_0^\infty \frac{e^{-\lambda t}(\lambda t)^n}{n!} dU(\lambda) = p_n(t),$$

say. This has been called a mixed, and (again) a compound Poisson distribution, or process.

The total claim for an individual contract during time t has distribution

$$\sum_{n=0}^\infty p_n(t)P^{n*}(x) = F(x, t),$$

say. Various forms have been suggested for $U(\lambda)$. For instance, if

$$dU(\lambda) = \frac{c^m}{\Gamma(m)} e^{-\lambda c} \lambda^{m-1} d\lambda$$

a Gamma density function [see II, §11.3], then

$$p_n(t) = \binom{n+m-1}{n} \left(\frac{c}{t+c}\right)^m \left(\frac{t}{t+c}\right)^n$$

a negative binomial [see II, §5.2.4].

If information is available about the number of claims during a previous period, then an application of Bayes' theorem [see II, §16.4] to an initial estimate of the distribution function $U(\lambda)$ leads, in the case of a gamma density function, once more to a negative binomial.

If $U(\lambda) = 1 - e^{-\lambda}$ (the above case with $c = m = 1$) and $P(x) = 1 - e^{-x}$, then $p_n(t)$ reduces to

$$t^n(t+1)^{n+1}$$

and

$$F(x, t) = 1 - \frac{t}{t+1} \exp[-x/(1+t)]$$

(Lundberg, 1940, p. 115.)

So far, we have been dealing with individual contracts. If we turn now to a whole portfolio, we find that attempts have been made to fit distributions to a series of annual claim ratios, that is, to the ratio of the total of claims of a year to the aggregate sums insured. This has been done mainly in fire insurance, but also in hail and in automobile accident insurance.

The distributions which have been satisfactory in different cases show various forms. Pearson-type I, III (Gamma), and IV distributions [see II, §11.2] have been fitted by the method of moments [see VI, §3.5.3], though it has also been found sometimes that the moments had features which were incompatible with Pearson curves. This has happened, for instance, in automobile insurance.

In life insurance, where not more than one claim can arise from a single contract in any one time period, the situation is simpler. If there are N policies, all of unit sum assured, and if the mortality rate is q, then the expected total claim from mortality is Nq. The probability of n claims has the binomial form

$$\binom{N}{n} q^n (1-q)^{N-n} = C(n),$$

say, [see II, §5.2.2]. According to the central limit theorem of probability theory [see II, §17.3] this converges, with increasing N, to the normal distribution, in the sense that the probability of

$$\frac{C(n) - nq}{\sqrt{nq(1-q)}}$$

being in the interval (t_1, t_2) converges to

$$\frac{1}{\sqrt{2\pi}} \int_{t_1}^{t_2} \exp\left(-\tfrac{1}{2}x^2\right) \mathrm{d}x.$$

If q decreases while N increases, in such a way that $Nq = \lambda$ remains constant, then $C(n)$ converges to the Poisson law $e^{-\lambda}\lambda^n/n!$ [see II, §5.4]

18.3. COMPUTATION OF ACTUARIAL FUNCTIONS

When we consider computations, it is again necessary to distinguish the two types of insurance business: life insurance, and non-life insurance.

In life insurance payments of both parties depend on the survival of an insured life to given dates, or on earlier death. For instance, in whole-life assurance the sum assured is due when the insured dies, in endowment assurance at death before a given term, or on survival to that term. In annuity business periodical payments are made at given intervals, as long as the insured is alive. There exist more complicated arrangements, but we are not here concerned with the intricacies of life insurance contracts.

In general, the amounts payable in life insurance business are fixed in advance (apart from special clauses, such as double indemnity if death is due to specified causes, or when the sum assured is linked to the price of gold).

In non-life insurance business the situation is different. Consider, as an example, fire insurance, or sickness insurance. The amount of damage due to a single fire, or the length of a sickness, cannot be determined in advance. However, it is assumed in all branches of insurance that the facts which determine payments are governed by known probabilities.

We deal first with life insurance. The fundamental rule for the computation of premiums to be paid by the policy-holder is the 'principle of equivalence', which demands that the present expected value of the net premiums payable during the term of the contract should be equal to the present value of the expected claims covered by the contract, both discounted at a given rate of interest.

To the net premium a loading is added to cover administrative costs, possible fluctuations, and in some cases the policy-holder will pay an addition to the net premium, to entitle him to participation in a bonus.

We shall ignore such loadings in the sequel, and assume that the administrative loading covers precisely the cost of administration and overheads.

On the lowest level of sophistication it is assumed that all payments are made at the beginning or end of discrete time intervals, say one year.

Using the set of mortality rates q_x, which we have chosen as our basis, we introduce the *Life Table*, a set of values l_x for $x \geqslant 0$ (or some other lowest age), for integer x. These values are related by

$$l_{x+1} = l_x(1 - q_x),$$

where l_0 is some chosen value, and q_x is the rate of mortality at age x. We consider these l_x to be the expected numbers of lives left after $1, 2, \ldots$ years from a 'cohort' of l_0 original lives, assuming that the rates of mortality are those prevailing at the times when the lives reach ages $1, 2, \ldots$etc. We also assume l_∞ to be zero.

The probability of a life aged x to survive to age $x + n$ is l_{x+n}/l_x. It follows that the present value of a unit payment to a life now aged x, due after n years provided the person is then alive, and discounted at a rate of interest i p.a., is

$$\frac{l_{x+n}}{l_x} \frac{1}{(1 + i)^n}.$$

Take, as an example, the computation of an annual net premium P_x for a whole-life assurance on a life aged x, with sum assured 1. The total expected value of the payments by the policy-holder, discounted to the start of the insurance, is

$$P_x \left[\sum_{s=0}^{\infty} \frac{l_{x+s}}{l_x} \frac{1}{(1 + i)^s} \right] = P_x \ddot{a}_x,$$

say and that of the company is, say

$$\sum_{t=0}^{\infty} \frac{l_{x+t} q_{x+t}}{l_x} \bigg/ (1 + i)^{t+1} = \sum_{t=0}^{\infty} \frac{l_{x+t} - l_{x+t+1}}{l_x} \bigg/ (1 + i)^{t+1} = A_x.$$

By the principle of equivalence P_x is found by equating the two expressions

$$P_x = A_x/\ddot{a}_x.$$

Now consider the discounted losses (positive or negative) of the company from such a whole-life contract. If the insured dies during the tth year of insurance, and the sum assured is being paid at the end of that year, then the loss L_t equals

$$v^t - P_x \sum_{s=0}^{t-1} v^s, \quad \text{where we have written } v \text{ for } (1 + i)^{-1}.$$

The probability of this loss is

$$\frac{l_{x+t-1} - l_{x+t}}{l_x}$$

so that the expected value of the loss from the contract, discounted to the beginning of the insurance, is

$$L = \sum_{t=0}^{\infty} \frac{l_{x+t} - l_{x+t+1}}{l_x} L_{t+1}$$

$$= \sum_{t=0}^{\infty} \frac{l_{x+t} - l_{x+t+1}}{l_x} \left(v^{t+1} - P_x \sum_{s=0}^{t} v^s \right).$$

If we invert the order of the double summation in the last term, then we have, because of $l_{\infty} = 0$,

$$P_x \sum_{s=0}^{\infty} v^s \sum_{t=s}^{\infty} \frac{l_{x+t} - l_{x+t+1}}{l_x} = P_x \sum_{s=0}^{\infty} \frac{l_{x+s}}{l_x} v^s.$$

Thus

$$L = \sum_{t=0}^{\infty} \frac{l_{x+t} - l_{x+t+1}}{l_x} v^{t+1} - P_x \sum_{s=0}^{\infty} \frac{l_{x+s}}{l_x} v^s$$

$$= A_x - P_x \ddot{a}_x.$$

If P_x satisfies the principle of equivalence, then $L = 0$. No loss or gain arises from the expected mutual net payments. This may be taken as another formulation of that principle.

In section 18.5 we shall be interested in the variance of losses.

In non-life assurance, although clearly the claims are paid later (and frequently much later) than the premiums, interest yield is traditionally, though illogically, treated as not affecting 'underwriting' profit.

The assumption that all payments are made at the beginning or at the end of a year is clearly incorrect in practice. In life insurance, payments of the company are, in general, made soon after the claim arises. (In non-life assurance, the settlement of claims takes occasionally an inordinately long time.) Also, the payments of the policy-holder may be made half-yearly, or at shorter intervals.

It is convenient mathematically to let the time interval converge to zero and to consider payments at any time on a continuous scale. Then instead of probabilities, we shall have to consider probability densities.

De Moivre (1667–1754) used Newton's fluxions in his essay on annuities in 1743. The Institute of Actuaries made 'higher mathematics' compulsory for all candidates of its examinations in 1891, though George King had already introduced calculus in his *Institute of Actuaries' Text Book* of 1887.

We introduce the *yield intensity*, or *force of discount*,

$$\delta = \log(1 + i)$$

and the *force of mortality*, defined as

$$\mu_x = -\frac{1}{l_x}\frac{\mathrm{d}l_x}{\mathrm{d}x}$$

so that

$$l_x = l_0 \exp\left(-\int_0^x \mu_z \, \mathrm{d}z\right).$$

If l_{x-t} and l_{x+t} are developed by Taylor's series [see IV, §3.6], then we obtain to a first approximation

$$\mu_x = (l_{x-t} - l_{x+t})/2l_x t.$$

If μ_x has the form $a + bc^x$, then $l_x = ks^x g^{c^x}$, where $a = -\log s$, and $b = -\log c \cdot \log g$. (This may be compared with the relationship between l_x and $\log(1 - q_x)$, rather than μ_x, mentioned on page 459.)

The payment of a unit amount after time t, if a person now aged x is then still alive, has present discounted value

$$\exp\left[-\int_x^{x+t}(\mu_t + \delta)\,\mathrm{d}t\right] = \exp\left[-\int_0^t(\mu_{x+t} + \delta)\,\mathrm{d}t\right].$$

We introduce the notation

$$\bar{D}_x = \exp\left[-\int_0^x(\mu_t + \delta)\,\mathrm{d}t\right].$$

Then the present value, at age x, of a whole-life assurance with sum assured 1 is

$$\int_0^\infty \mu_{x+t}\frac{\bar{D}_{x+t}}{\bar{D}_x}\,\mathrm{d}t,$$

while a continuously payable annuity of unit density of payments to a person now aged x has present value

$$\bar{a}_x = \int_0^\infty \frac{\bar{D}_{x+t}}{\bar{D}_x}\,\mathrm{d}t.$$

If $l_x = ks^x g^{c^x}$, then $\bar{a}_x$ can be transformed into

$$\frac{e^\lambda}{\lambda^m \log c}\int_\lambda^\infty u^{m-1}e^{-u}\,\mathrm{d}u$$

(a Gamma integral), where $m = \log s + \log v)/\log c$, and $\lambda = -\log g^{c^x}$ [see IV, §10.2].

If the annuity is payable in instalments of $1/h$ at the beginning of each $1/h$th of a year, then its present value is

$$\sum_{t=0}^\infty \bar{D}_{x+t/h}/\bar{D}_x.$$

In our formula above the value of a whole-life assurance was written in the form of a product integral, and so are many other actuarial formulae. For the computation of such integrals Gaussian quadrature formulae are available [see III, §7.3].

In the most usual life-insurance contracts, such as whole-life or endowment assurance, the policy-holder pays a constant premium p.a., though the mortality rate increases with age. This has the effect that in the early years of the contract he pays more than is required to cover the current risk, and the difference is reserved, to make up, with its interests, for his later paying less than covers the then current risk. The insurer accumulates a fund throughout the term of the contract.

The portion of the fund, after k years, referring to an individual policy, is called its *policy value*, denoted by $_kV_x$ for an assurance on a life aged x at the start of the insurance.

If we use continuous notation, then $_kV_x$ satisfies the differential equation (called after Thiele)

$$\frac{d(_kV_x)}{dk} = _kV_x(\delta + \mu_{x+k}) + \bar{p} - \mu_{x+k},$$

where $\bar{p}$ is the intensity of premium payments.

In order to reduce the volume of work for determining the total policy value for a complete portfolio, at least to an acceptable approximation, methods of linear programming [see I, Chapter 11] have been applied to ascertain the largest and the smallest amount compatible with easily ascertainable characteristics of the portfolio, such as the sum assured (Benjamin and Bennett, 1958).

If an actuarial function has been computed for a number of interest rates and the result is required for an intermediate rate, then interpolation formulae [see III, §2.3] may be employed, e.g. that of Lagrange

$$f(x) = \sum_{k=0}^{n} f(x_k)g_k(x),$$

where $g_k(x)$ equals

$$\frac{(x - x_0)\ldots(x - x_{k-1})(x - x_{k+1})\ldots(x - x_n)}{(x_k - x_0)\ldots(x_k - x_{k-1})(x_k - x_{k+1})\ldots(x_k - x_n)}.$$

With the advent of electronic data processing equipment Monte Carlo methods [see VI, §20.6] are being progressively used to determine values whose mathematical form is complicated, or not established. Seal (1969, p. 34) mentions the evaluation of convolutions. Actually one of the earliest applications of simulation methods was the use of Model Offices in actuarial literature, in connection with valuation. (Cf. H. W. Manly in *J.I.A.* 1868, and G. King who first used this term in 1877, and again in *J.I.A.* 1903).

18.4. REINSURANCE

The extent of deviations from expected values in an insurance portfolio depends critically on the distribution of the claim amounts. Possibly large claims will make the yearly results uneven and widely fluctuating. This may endanger the stability of the business. Another reason for wishing to avoid large fluctuations in the yearly results is the desirability of keeping to a policy of stable bonus schemes for policy-holders, and of stable dividend yields for shareholders.

The amplitude of fluctuations can be reduced if the company makes arrangements with other companies to cede a portion of the risk, for an appropriate reinsurance premium.

Various types of reinsurance contracts have been devised. The arrangements can be based on individual contracts, or on the complete portfolio.

An arrangement of the former type is the quota reinsurance, whereby a fixed proportion of every risk is ceded. (This is sometimes due to the fact that the ceding company is affiliated to the reinsurance company, which thereby participates proportionately in the former's business.) Another type frequently used is the *excess contract*, whereby only the excess of the sum assured over a given amount is ceded.

A reinsurance form based on the total portfolio is the *stop-loss* reinsurance, which obliges the reinsurer to indemnify the first insurer for any total claim amount in a given period in excess of a specified limit. In the earlier literature this type used to be called an *excess-loss* contract.

If the distribution of claim amounts x is known to have the form $P(x, \theta)$, with unknown parameter θ, then the net reinsurance premium for the excess, if any, over c, will be

$$\int_c^\infty (x - c)\, \mathrm{d}P(x, \theta).$$

If x is observed, then 0 or $(x - c)$ (whichever is larger) is an unbiased estimator [see VI, §3.3.2], but the standard error of this estimator [see VI, §3.1] is often large (dependent on the relation between c and the expected value of x) and it would frequently lead to a zero premium.

One might be tempted to use the observations on x to find an estimate of the parameter θ. However, it has been shown that in general the integral above is not an unbiased estimator of the expected value of the excess claim amount if θ is an unbiased estimate of the true parameter value (Vajda, 1951). An unbiased estimator of the integral can be found, though, and in particular one with minimum standard error, when P is the normal distribution. [see II, §11.4]. In its theory, the concepts of sufficient and of complete statistics [see VI, §3.4] are used (Vajda, 1955).

Various modifications of the straightforward stop-loss reinsurance method have been suggested. In the so-called *ecomor* (excédent du cout moyen relatif) treaty the reinsurer undertakes to pay the excess of each of the n largest individual claims in a given period over the amount of the nth claim. The reinsurance premium is paid when the actual size of the nth largest claim has become known. Only the rate is fixed in advance, assuming a Pareto distribution of the upper tail of the claim amounts [see II, §11.8]. (Actually A. Thépaud, who suggested this type of reinsurance in 1950, added the stipulation that if any of the n largest claims exceeded a given ceiling, the payment of the reinsurer is restricted to that ceiling).

Formally, if $y(j)$ is the amount of the jth largest claim, then the reinsurer pays

$$\sum_{j=1}^{n} y(j) - ny(n) = r_n,$$

say. If $P(y)$ is the distribution of claim amounts, and the probability of n claims in time t is Poisson [see II, §5.4], with average claim amount unity in unit time, then the density function of the nth largest claim size in time t is

$$\sum_{k=n}^{\infty} e^{-t} \frac{t^k}{k!} \binom{k}{k-n} P(y)^{k-n}(1 - P(y))^{n-1} n \, dP(y)$$

$$= e^{-t[1 - P(y)]} \frac{t^n}{(n-1)!} [1 - P(y)]^{n-1} \, dP(y)$$

and in particular, when $P(y)$ has the Pareto form $1 - y^{-a}$, then the expected jth largest value will be

$$\frac{t^{1/a}}{(j-1)!} \int_0^t e^{-x} x^{j-1-1/a} \, dx = E(y(j)),$$

say (the integral is an incomplete Gamma function [see II, §11.3]) and the expected value of r_n is then approximately

$$(n-1)E(y(n))/(a-1)$$

(see Seal (1969) pp. 149ff, quoting a paper of 1964 by H. Ammeter).

By reinsuring, the ceding company relinquishes the prospect of a portion of its expected profits, in order to avoid the risk of high fluctuations in its results, that is, in order to increase its stability. If the stability is measured by the variance of the results, then it can be proved that, for a given reinsurance premium, the retained risk is minimized by a stop-loss contract (Kahn, 1961), and in fact the sum of the risks of both parties is also reduced. On the other hand, with the additional condition that the ratio of the reimbursement to the total claim be a non-decreasing function of the latter, the risk of the reinsurer is minimized when the reinsurance arrangement is a quota treaty (Vajda, 1963).

Insurance practice also knows reciprocal reinsurance contracts between two or more companies. The attractiveness of such contracts, for any of the parties to it, depends on an evaluation by the companies. The determination of the optimal amounts to be reinsured respectively can be viewed from the point of view of partial opposition of interests, and this is the subject of game theory, in particular that of non-zero-sum games [see I, §13.4].

18.5. THEORY OF RISK

The purpose of the mathematical theory of risk is the study of the effect of random fluctuations of claims, and hence of the business results, and to suggest steps that counteract any harmful effects. It should be distinguished from the economic theory of risk discussed in Chapter 17, especially section 3.1.

Because this time the deviations from the expected values are decisive, we need more assumptions than those we made when we computed premiums. We need to know the probability distribution of claims.

In the formal development of the individual risk theory in life assurance we assume that the mutual payments of the contracting parties have known probabilities, and lead to gains or losses arising from the single policies. In section 18.3 we have quoted the formula for the loss L_t to the company from a whole-life assurance, if the insured dies during the tth year of duration, and the total expected loss

$$L = \sum_{t=0}^{\infty} \frac{l_{x+t} - l_{x+t+1}}{l_x} L_{t+1} = 0.$$

The variance of the losses equals

$$M^2 = \sum_{t=0}^{\infty} \frac{l_{x+t} - l_{x+t+1}}{l_x} L_{t+1}^2$$

because $L = 0$.

We call M the *mean risk*.

According to the central limit theorem of probability [see II, §17.3] the sum of random variables will be approximated, under fairly general conditions, by the Normal distribution. This approximation will be the better, the larger the number of single policies. The error of the approximation, when the number of policies is finite, is in many practical cases large, and therefore other asymptotic formulae have been suggested, for instance of the type

$$a e^{-bx}/x^{1/2}.$$

The collective theory of risk deals with the portfolio as a whole, and makes certain assumptions regarding its development.

The business is regarded as a continuous set of games of chance. During time dt the policy-holders pay a total amount of dP (the net premium plus risk loading) into a risk reserve, while the company pays the claims arising out of this risk reserve.

In discrete time intervals the development of the risk reserve may be considered as a random walk [see II, §18.3]. The walk starts with an initial capital S and finishes when the capital reaches 0 (an absorbing barrier). When the risk capital exceeds Z, the surplus is paid out as a dividend, or in taxes (a reflecting barrier). The expected length of life $D(S)$ of the company, given S and P, satisfies the Fredholm integral equation for $S \geqslant 0$ [see III, §10.2]

$$D(S) = 1 + \int_0^{S+P} D(S+P-x)\,dF(x) = 1 - \int_0^{S+P} D(x)\,dF(S+P-x),$$

where P is the premium in one period, and $F(x)$ is the claim distribution. If $F(x) = 1 - e^{-x}$ for $x \geqslant 0$, then the integral equation can be reduced, by differentiation with respect to S [cf. III, §10.1.2], to the differential–difference equation

$$D(S) + D'(S) = 1 + D(S+P)$$

(Borch, 1967, pp. 445–446).

It is also possible to establish a relation between risk theory and queueing theory [see II, §20.5]. For instance, the equation describing the probability of the risk reserve becoming exhausted (probability of ruin) is equivalent to that expressing the time of a new customer having to wait for service.

As founded by F. Lundberg (see Cramér (1930) and the Swedish literature mentioned there) the collective theory of risk assumes that the successive games of chance are independent and ignores the number and distribution of the individual sums assured. Also, and this is fundamental, instead of time t, the accumulated risk premium P is taken as the independent variable.

The main problem dealt with is that of the probability distribution of the amount of the risk reserve, and in particular the question of the probability of its becoming zero at some time in a given interval. The time interval considered may be finite, or infinite.

Let the risk reserve at time $P = 0$ have value u, and consider the probability that it will be negative at some time in the future. This is equivalent to the case of starting with a risk reserve zero, and asking for the probability that the minimum value of the risk reserve is less than $-u$, as P increases without limit. Denote this probability by $\psi(u)$.

If we introduce $\chi(u, v)$ to denote the probability density that the risk reserve will at some time be less than $-u$, and that the first time this happens it will lie between $-(u+v)$ and $-(u+v+dv)$, then for positive u

$$\psi(u) = \int_0^{\infty} \chi(u, v)\,dv.$$

The function $\chi(u, v)$ satisfies the differential equation

$$\frac{\partial \chi}{\partial u} - \frac{\partial \chi}{\partial v} = \chi(0, v)\chi(u, 0)$$

and also the equation

$$\chi(0, v) = \frac{1}{1 + \alpha} \int_v^\infty p(z)\, \mathrm{d}z$$

(Cramér, 1930), where α is the loading factor in the premium and $p(z)$ is the probability density of a claim of amount z.

If we normalize by

$$\int_0^\infty z p(z)\, \mathrm{d}z = \int_0^\infty p(z)\, \mathrm{d}z = 1,$$

then it follows that

$$\psi(0) = \int_0^\infty \chi(0, v)\, \mathrm{d}v = \frac{1}{1 + \alpha} \int_0^\infty \int_v^\infty p(z)\, \mathrm{d}z\, \mathrm{d}v$$

$$= \frac{1}{1 + \alpha} \int_0^\infty \int_0^z \mathrm{d}v p(z)\, \mathrm{d}z = \frac{1}{1 + \alpha}.$$

Whatever the initial value of the risk reserve, the probability that it will at some time fall below this value is independent of $p(z)$ and depends only on the loading factor α.

Moreover,

$$\psi(u) = \int_0^u \psi(u - v)\chi(0, v)\, \mathrm{d}v + \int_u^\infty \chi(0, v)\, \mathrm{d}v$$

which is an integral equation of Volterra type [see III, §10.3], a renewal equation [see II, Chapter 21]. If, in particular, $p(z) = e^{-z}$, then

$$\chi(0, v) = e^{-v}/(1 + \alpha), \quad \psi(u) = \exp\left[-\alpha u/(1 + \alpha)\right]/(1 + \alpha).$$

We have defined $\psi(u)$ as the probability that, starting from a risk reserve u, it will fall below zero at some future time. We might be interested only in a finite length of time T, and ask for the probability that during this time the risk reserve becomes negative. The analysis proceeds on lines similar to those for $\psi(u)$, but is more complicated. It leads to a Fokker–Planck equation for that probability [see II, §18.4].

For the numerical computation of probabilities relating to the risk reserve, once more Monte Carlo methods have proved to be useful (Seal, 1969b).

18.6. POPULATION MATHEMATICS

The device and cooperation of actuaries is also required, outside the confines of an insurance office, for instance regarding problems of social insurance. One of these problems is that of the analysis of the development of a population.

The population of a country, or of a region, is affected by entries and exits. Entries arise from birth, immigration etc., and exits are due to death, emigration, and other causes.

In general, entries and exits are in some way linked. If their effect is such that the total as well as the age distribution remains unchanged, then we call the population *stationary*. If only the total remains unchanged, the population is *constant*, if only the age distribution is unaffected, then the population is *stable*.

The *Life Table*, which we have mentioned in section 18.3, is an example of a stationary population, when exits are due to deaths only, and if entries are constant at the lowest age. In continuous notation,

$$l_0 = \int_0^\infty l_x \mu_x \, dx$$

keeps the total constant, and

$$\mu_x = -\frac{1}{l_x} \frac{dl_x}{dx}$$

(as on p. 467) preserves the age distribution. (This force of mortality is assumed to be independent of time.)

Let the density of those living at time t of age x be $l_x(t)$, and let deaths at time t be replaced at once by $l_0(t)$ entrants of age 0. These deaths have occurred amongst those who were already members of the given initial population, in number, say

$$\int_0^\infty l_x(0) \exp\left[-\int_x^{x+t} \mu_\tau \, d\tau \right] \mu_{x+t} \, dx = H(t).$$

Deaths have also occurred amongst those who have entered since, replacing earlier deaths. These number

$$\int_0^t l_0(t-x) \exp\left[-\int_0^x \mu_\tau \, d\tau \right] \mu_x \, dx.$$

Thus

$$l_0(t) = H(t) + \int_0^t l_0(t-x) f(x) \, dx, \qquad (*)$$

where we have written $f(x)$ for $\exp\left[-\int_0^x \mu_\tau \, d\tau \right] \mu_x$.

This is again a renewal equation, an integral equation of the second type [see III, §10.3]. It can be solved by an application of Laplace transforms [see IV, §13.14]. If $f(x)$ has certain specified analytical forms—perhaps found by curve fitting—then the integral equation reduces to a differential equation.

The solution of the integral equation for $l_0(t)$ gives the number of entrants at time t, and the age distribution at time t is computed by

$$l_x(t) = l_0(t-x) e^{-\int_0^x \mu_\tau \, d\tau} \quad \text{for } x \leqslant t$$

and

$$= l_{x-t}(0)\, e^{-\int_{x-t}^{t} \mu_\tau \mathrm{d}\tau} \quad \text{for } x \geqslant t.$$

we could also have started from

$$\int_0^\infty l_x(t)\,\mathrm{d}t = \int_0^\infty l_x(0)\,\mathrm{d}x, \text{ (a constant)} \qquad (**)$$

an integral equation of the first type [see III, §10.4]. Differentiation with respect to t shows that (*) and (**) are equivalent.

The function $l_x(t)$ will be independent of t, if the initial population is given by

$$l_x(0) = l_0(0)\, e^{-\int_0^x \mu_\tau \mathrm{d}\tau}.$$

Under general conditions which are known (Feller, 1941) any initial population will tend towards a stable one, dependent on the properties of $f(x)$. If the population remains constant, then Markov theory [see II, Chapters 19 and 20] proves in the discontinuous case, that it converges to a stationary population, unless it repeats itself periodically. What happens depends on the eigenvalues [see I, Chapter 7] of the transition matrix [see II, §19.3].

18.7. CONCLUDING REMARKS

It will have been seen that actuaries use—sometimes—fairly sophisticated mathematical techniques. This has not always been so, of course. In the early days of life insurance those responsible for calculating premiums used rather primitive statistics—in the sense of collecting observations. Actuaries were then content to compute expected values and relied on some theorem of large numbers to trust that these values formed an acceptable basis for their forecasts.

It was with the start of the Theory of Risk, created mainly by Scandinavian statisticians, that concepts of mathematical statistics entered, not surprisingly, since risk is precisely due to possible deviations from expected values.

What could, perhaps, not been foreseen was the application of mathematics to non-life branches, although by hindsight it must be recognized that the great variety of non-life contracts—fire, accident, transport, third party liability, etc.— offers a great opportunity for applicable, and applied, mathematics. Although there are still managers who (pretend to) work out the level of premiums 'on the back of an envelope', the competition between powerful companies has forced management in many cases to accept the services of mathematical statisticians.

We were careful to point out that the way of computing premiums which we have described concerned net premiums. In practice additions are made for administrative expenses and for a flow into safety reserves. A further addition is made in the case of with-profit policies, where the policy-holder is entitled to participation in 'profits'. We cannot describe here the many forms of such contractual participation, and the various ways in which the relevant profit is being ascertained and distributed. In passing we mention the so-called bonus–

malus system, in motor insurance, where not only is a claim-free record rewarded by a reduction of the premium, but where an unfavourable experience attracts a surcharge.

18.8. REFERENCES

Beard, R. E., Pentikäinen, T. and Pesonen, E. (1969). *Risk Theory*. Methuen, London.

Benjamin, S. and Bennett, C. W. (1958). The application of elementary linear programming to approximate valuation. *Journal of the Institute of Actuaries*, **84**, 1–37.

Borch, K. (1967). The theory of risk. *Journal of the Royal Statistical Society* (B), **29**, 432–467.

Continuous Mortality Investigation Report, no. 2 (1976). Institute of Actuaries and Faculty of Actuaries, p. 58.

Cramér, H. (1930). *On the mathematical theory of risk*. Skandia Jubilee Volume, Stockholm.

Cramér, H. (1955). *Collective risk theory*. Skandia Jubilee Volume, Stockholm.

Feller, W. (1941). On the integral equation of renewal theory. *Annals of Mathematical Statistics*, **12**, 243–267.

Gauss, C. F. (1889–1912), *Gesammelte Werke*, Nachlass Band 4, p. 119, Königliche Akademie der Wissenschaften, Göttingen.

Kahn, P. M. (1961). Some remarks on a recent paper by Borch. *Astin Bulletin*, **1**, 265–272.

Lundberg, F. (1930). Ueber die Wahrscheinlichkeitsfunktion einer Risikenmasse. *Skandinavisk Aktuarietidskrift*, **13**, 1–83.

Lundberg, O. (1940). *On random Processes and their application to Sickness and Accident Statistics*. Almqvist and Wicksells, Uppsala.

Markowitz, H. M. (1959). *Portfolio Selection : Efficient Diversification of Investments*. Wiley, New York.

Seal, H. L. (1969a). *Stochastic Theory of a Risk Business*. Wiley, New York.

Seal, H. L. (1969b). Simulation of the ruin potential of non-life insurance companies. *Trans. Soc. Actu.*, **21**, 563–590.

Vajda, S. (1944–6). The analysis of variance of mortality rates. *Journal of the Institute of Actuaries*, **72**, 240–245.

Vajda, S. (1951). Analytical studies in stop-loss reinsurance. *Skandinavisk Aktuarietidskrift*, **34**, 158–175.

Vajda, S. (1955). Analytical studies in stop-loss reinsurance, II. *Skandinavisk Aktuarietidskrift*, **38**, 180–191.

Vajda, S. (1963). Minimum variance reinsurance. *Astin Bulletin*, **2**, 257–260.

See also papers in the *Bulletin of the Institute of Mathematics and its Applications*, **8**, January, 1972. Special issue: Mathematics in Actuarial Work.

Part VI

Optimization Over Space and Time

Mathematical Methods in Economics
Edited by F. van der Ploeg
© 1984, John Wiley & Sons, Ltd.

19

Aspects of the New Urban Economics

DAVID LIVESEY, *University of Cambridge, Cambridge, UK*

19.1. INTRODUCTION

Richardson (1977) defined the new urban economics as 'urban economic theories based upon deriving general equilibrium from the principle of utility maximization in a one-dimensional city'. He recognized that this was a narrow definition but it suffices to describe a large number of papers published in the 1970s. These papers used mathematical techniques which several of their authors, for example Dixit (1973), Mirrlees (1972), Sheshinski (1973), Solow (1972) and Stern (1972), had previously deployed in studies of macroeconomic growth theory. In the new urban economics the variation of economic behaviour over time was replaced by variation over space. The subject has its origins in papers and books written in the 1960s, Alonso (1960, 1964), Muth (1961, 1969) and Wingo (1961), which dealt with location and land use, cities and housing and transportation and urban land. Most influential of all were the papers by Beckmann (1969) and Mills (1967). An example of that influence is the volume of conference papers edited by Papageorgiou (1976) in which a majority of the authors discussed variations of the original Mills (1967) model as extended in the paper by Mills and de Ferranti (1971). This chapter also uses this model as a convenient framework for a discussion of mathematical analyses of land use, housing, industrial location and transportation theory.

To set the new urban economics in its proper context the chapter begins with an account of the origins of urban location theory. The focus then moves to simple models of agricultural, residential and industrial land markets. These models not only illustrate the original foundations of land rent theory but also prepare the ground for the more detailed analysis which follows. Starting with a suburban residential location model and then moving on to a Central Business District (CBD) workplace model, the central sections of the chapter focus upon the optimal allocation of land between transportation and other uses. More detailed models of particular urban markets are examined in the final sections.

19.2. THE URBAN STAGE

Before embarking upon the narrow range of topics treated by this chapter, it is only proper to give a brief summary of the breadth of issues and ideas encompassed by urban economics. A starting point for the presentation is the question: Why do cities exist?

The standard general equilibrium model of an economic system [cf. Chapter 14], in which land is a homogeneous non-produced input of production processes, leads to a world without cities. Economic activity is spread uniformly over the globe since, under the standard assumption that unit costs do not vary with the level of production, transportation costs can be eliminated if all products are produced at the locations at which they are consumed. There are no benefits to be reaped from the agglomeration of economic activity. To adopt any one of the three following assumptions is to ensure the existence of cities since each guarantees a spatial variation of land rents:

—regional variations in the endowment of natural resources;
—the existence of an industry in which there are increasing returns to scale, that is per unit costs of production decrease as the volume of production increases; or
—regional variations in amenity resources, that is climate, ports, mountains etc.

Whilst these assumptions will all lead to the existence of cities, not all, but some, will help to explain where cities locate, and it is doubtful whether they will explain why cities engage in trade.

The three classic works on location theory are by von Thünen (1826), Weber (1909), and Lösch (1940). The most recent general theory of location is Isard (1956). Von Thünen considered the pattern of agricultural production around a single town in the middle of an isolated plain. In his model transportation costs were proportional to the weight of the commodity and the distance which it was carried. He found that a series of concentric zones would develop around the town each devoted to a single crop. In recent years von Thünen's work has been applied to the analysis of cities. This is done by translating the town in the middle of a plain into a central business district (CBD) surrounded by suburbs in which the consumers and workers live. An example of zone formation in the suburbs is Varaiya and Artle (1972). Von Thünen type models are discussed in section 19.3.1, which deals with agricultural rents, section 19.3.2, which covers residential rents, and in section 19.3.3, which discusses industrial rents.

Weber was the first person to pose the question of why several plants, each producing a homogeneous commodity, tended to locate near one another. He provided precise answers to this and related questions but, unfortunately, relaxing some of Weber's assumptions invalidates his conclusions. An account of his work and a game theoretic extension of his ideas is given in Isard and Smith, (1967).

Lösch developed the concept of a demand funnel which surrounds the supplier of a commodity. This funnel is a transposition of the demand curve (assumed identical for all consumers) into the spatial distribution of demand which results from transportation costs being added to the factory price. Out of this analysis Lösch evolved the concept of hexagonal market areas, with a different size for different commodities. The most striking conclusion of the work was that six meshes of differently sized hexagons can be arranged to form a 'cogwheel' pattern which closely resembles empirically observed spatial structure. Valavanis (1955), is a short and readable account of Lösch's work.

Hotelling (1929), was one of the first explicitly to explore spatial structure in terms of the competition which a firm faces. In particular he considered a duopolistic model and was able to demonstrate that a competitive equilibrium maximized the transport costs which consumers had to pay. His results depended upon the assumption of a completely inelastic demand curve and also that one firm does not expect its rival to react to its decisions both about price and location. More recently the analysis has been extended to three dimensions by Devletoglou (1965), and to the case of three firms by Lerner and Singer (1939).

Urban economics has not only to explain where cities locate but how and why they grow. Jane Jacobs (1969), illustrated the export multiplier theory of urban growth by describing the evolution of Detroit. In 1820 its principal export was flour, but by the 1840s locally built ships for carrying the flour were themselves exported. By 1860, the marine engines for steam ships were the leading export commodity, only to be replaced a few years later by refined copper. Thus locally manufactured inputs into export commodities, often grow into export commodities themselves.

Since the vast literature on national growth depends to a large extent upon the assumption of linear homogeneous production functions, it is clear that urban growth models cannot simply rely upon a 'nation city' approach, not only because increasing returns to scale are an important feature of the urban economy, but also because in cities external trade is a higher proportion of economic activity than it is for a nation. There is also the problem of deciding how one measures urban growth.

Since data are very scarce, population growth inevitably becomes the prime measure of urban growth. If alternatively one examines the social welfare of a city, there is not only the problem of determining an appropriate functional form, but also, the problem of defining the spatial domain of the function. The difficulties are most acute if a city is able to exercise a degree of exclusion, that is if like a private club it can deter or even prohibit the admission of new members. Although the physical changes in a city are an important indicator of urban growth, it is necessary to distinguish between the evolution of a city, as a result of changing tastes and technology, and its growth. Thompson (1965) postulated that there are five stages in the growth of a city: (1) export specialization, when the local economy is very dependent upon one industry; (2) export complex, where there is a broadening of local industry; (3) economic maturation, as imports are replaced by local products; (4) regional metropolis, with the city the hub of a series of neighbouring cities; (5) technical and professional virtuosity, gives the city national eminence in some specialized industrial or financial skill.

Central place theory is one of the demand oriented models of urban growth. It assumes that the city grows as a result of supplying goods and services to the surrounding region. Bos (1965) tested empirically some of the conclusions of central place theory. Objections to the theory focus on the fact that cities grow for reasons other than their provision of goods and services to the hinterland. A more general demand approach, which assumes that a city's goods may be demanded from anywhere outside its boundaries, is urban base theory. This is the model which Jane Jacobs (1969) had in mind, it is essentially a theory of export-led growth. An unresolved problem is whether the existence of exporting industries encourages the necessary investment in service industries or whether the existence of good service industries in a city attracts the fast-growing firm to locate there.

Supply oriented models rest on the belief that the growth potential of a city depends upon its ability to create and attract from outside the productive resources needed for growth. To grow fast a city must act as a magnet for migrants, outside capital, and non-local managerial and technical talent, since there is a limit to the ability of a city to generate all its demands internally when it is undergoing a fast rate of growth.

There are also other constraints which a city may not find as easy to overcome: (1) space constraints—mainly short-run imposed by the capacity of existing buildings; (2) construction constraints—there is a limit to the output of the local construction industry; (3) labour market constraint—this reflects the rate of natural population increase, the rate of migration and variations in the labour participation rates; (4) planning constraints—local planners, if they so wish, can halt completely the growth of a city.

There are also those who hold that the larger a city the faster it grows; this is known as the scale effect. Thompson (1965), postulated the existence of a ratchet effect. He advances several reasons why there might be a critical city size short of which growth is not inevitable but beyond which absolute contraction is highly unlikely.

The divergencies between private and social costs, the indivisibilities of urban investments, the potential conflict between individual preferences and planning requirements and the inter-relatedness of everything in the city: all of these are problems which crop up when one considers the economics of urban transportation. Congestion is the most intractable problem in this area. It arises because of the limited size of the road network which cannot cope with the peak load of journeys from home to work. Since the load factor (ratio of average load to peak load) is as low as 35% it is uneconomic to provide for peak demand, as is done in the electricity supply industry which has a load factor of 80%. If working hours were to be staggered, or if firms were to be more spatially dispersed, congestion would be reduced but at the cost of more expensive communications between firms and their employees. These advantages arising from close proximity must be significant since they account for the agglomeration of economic activity in the first place.

Congestion can be seen as a form of rationing and also as a progressive taxation scheme. But it is primarily a pricing problem, in which the need is for a method of imposing the full social cost on the motorist. Provided that one is not beset by second-best considerations, the objective should be to charge each journey at its marginal social cost. Social cost because congestion results from the externalities which arise from a car trip. There is of course a severe measurement problem when it comes to estimating these social costs. Sections 19.4, 19.5 and 19.6 are devoted to a variety of models which examine the social costs of congestion and optimum deployment of resources.

There are three broad pricing strategies which could be employed. Taxes on suburban and dispersed living, the object of which is to make residents in the suburbs pay the full cost of low density living. Subsidies to public transportation can be justified on several grounds and there are various ways of paying the subsidy. Of the three the most effective way of tackling the problem is clearly some form of direct road pricing. Other forms of taxing the motorist, such as differential petrol taxes, or road fund licences are too indirect and may not meet their target. Not only would road pricing reduce externalities but also it would provide a more reliable data base for future urban investment decisions. The cost of implementation need not be large compared with the social benefits which would result. Walters (1961), and Meyer, Kain and Wohl (1965), provided a full discussion of these issues.

There is of course a fundamental link between transportation problems and the spatial structure of the city. Indeed many theories of residential location assume that people trade housing costs against the cost of the journey from home to work. Muth (1969) and Wingo (1961) are the best examples of this approach. Congestion has been seen by some authors as the major source of social costs in the city and they have attempted to find the optimum city size which would minimize these costs for a given population size—Solow (1972) and Livesey (1973). Section 19.4.1 introduces these ideas in greater detail.

The discussion so far shows that city size is an important parameter in many aspects of urban economic theory. It is therefore natural to ask what determines city size, indeed whether there is an optimal city size. Richardson (1973) is a book solely devoted to answering the latter question. Since there is no such thing as an unambiguous optimum, one has to define the measure by which different city sizes are judged.

The principal source of benefits conferred by an urban area are the economies of agglomeration. But it is important to remember that higher incomes and a stable, diversified and progressive economic structure may both prove to be a source of considerable benefits. Many of the economies of large cities accrue to business firms. It has been shown that the ratio of internal to external trade rises markedly with the logarithm of city size. Thus, large cities are more self-contained and hence more efficient in the sense that this saves transport costs to and from other places. In sections 19.5.3 to 19.5.6 economies of scale in production are incorporated into an urban model.

Other external economies are enjoyed by households, such as the opportunities for earning higher incomes and a wider choice in jobs, shopping facilities and variety in housing. Also there are threshold city sizes for the efficient provision of educational facilities, transportation, hospitals, leisure and entertainment opportunities. On the other hand, the benefits do not necessarily increase continuously with city size, and there may be some levelling off in the medium size range.

Richardson (1973) felt that 'the search for an optimal city size is almost as idle as the quest for the philosopher's stone'. Optimality in the urban economy may have meaning if it relates size to form and structure, but the crude measures of size in the literature have lacked a spatial dimension. He conceded that there might be a minimum threshold size and even an upper bound on city size above which efficient growth is not possible. 'But these modifications destroy the concept of a unique optimum.' However, as was started earlier, no-one ever thought that there was.

It is impossible, in this chapter, to cover all aspects of urban economics. The subject is as broad as economics itself and perhaps more difficult, since, as the remarks above have sought to demonstrate, the structure of cities and their populations renders some standard techniques of economic analysis, if not invalid, at least of doubtful value. We have only to remember the question of why cities exist to illustrate the point. If the world were a large flat plain with resources evenly distributed throughout and all economic activity exhibited constant returns to scale—that is, output increases by the same proportion as all the inputs are increased—then there would be no cities. Whether the world is flat or round is not relevant. What is crucial is that, either there has to be uneven resource endowment or increasing returns to scale, if cities are to exist. Geographical factors are important and can provide a satisfactory framework for explaining and recounting the historical evolution of particular places. Jane Jacobs proved that 'young Detroit is as good a place as any to observe the beginning of a city economy' (Jacobs, 1969). For the economist accidents of geography are secondary considerations and economic agglomeration is the key variable. Nevertheless, it remains true that urban economists are better at explaining the growth and structure of cities rather than their physical location.

19.3. URBAN LAND RENTS

19.3.1. Agricultural rents

In the new urban economics, the standard model of urban land use is derived from von Thünen (1826). Suppose the land around a city is a fertile plain with soil of uniform quality. If potatoes can be grown at a cost, excluding land rent, of c_p per tonne and they cost t_p per tonne per mile to transport to the city where they are sold for a price of p_p per tonne, then the profit per tonne of potatoes, π_p, is given by

$$\pi_p = p_p - c_p - t_p u - r(u),$$

where $r(u)$ is the rent paid for sufficient land, at a distance u from the city centre, to grow a tonne of potatoes. Since there is a finite supply of land at u and many potential potato growers, one may assume that the landlord fixes the rent, $r(u)$, so that the profit, π_p, is zero. Hence

$$r(x)_p = p_p - c_p - t_p u$$

is the bid rent for potatoes. The terminology becomes clear when the possibilities available to wheat growers are considered, these imply that

$$r(u)_w = p_w - c_w - t_w u,$$

where the variables refer to the same costs and prices but the subscript 'w' denotes that they are for wheat. Since [see IV, §3.2]

$$\frac{dr(u)_p}{du} = -t_p \quad \text{and} \quad \frac{dr(u)_w}{du} = -t_w,$$

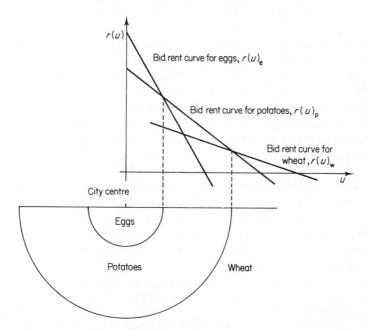

Figure 19.1: Bid-rent curves and their relationship to concentric zones around city centre

then, if $t_p > t_w$, potatoes will, if grown at all, only be grown nearer to the city than wheat. Similarly if the cost of transporting eggs is greater than that for potatoes, eggs will be reared nearer the city than either potatoes or wheat. This analysis gives rise to von Thünen's concentric rings and is illustrated in Figure 19.1, which shows that the slope of the bid rent curve determines the order of the crops.

Whereas relative transportation costs determine the relative distances from the city centre at which products are farmed, whether a crop is actually grown depends upon its profitability. If $p_w - c_w > p_p - c_p$ then $r(u)_w > r(u)_p$ for all u and potatoes will not be grown at all since it is reasonable to assume that landlords will always exact the highest rent.

19.3.2. Residential rents

Alonso (1964) extended the concept of a bid rent to the location decisions of households and firms in a monocentric city. This model which underlies much of the new urban economics is a modern interpretation of von Thünen's world. The city is located on a featureless plain and transportation is possible in every direction. All employment and all goods and services are only available in the city centre known as the CBD (central business district). The market for land is perfectly competitive so that to farmers one field is only distinguishable from another by its distance from the city centre. Since one is dealing mainly with the urban economy, it is more a matter of one location only being distinguishable by firms or households from another location by its distance from the city centre.

The standard utility maximizing approach to consumer demand theory can be used to illustrate some of the origins of a household's bid-rent function. A household is assumed to want to maximize its welfare or utility subject to the possibilities available to it. In the simplest urban model, a household purchases two goods: housing services, h, and a consumption good, c. The latter can be thought of as a composite good which represents all the other household expenditures apart from housing. Since c is like a basket of goods it can be treated as a numeraire and the price of housing services, $r(u)$, can be expressed relative to it. $r(u)$, denotes that the pricing of housing is a function of the distance from the city centre whereas the model assumes that the consumption good has the same price wherever it is purchased. Household income is derived from the sale of labour services in the CBD. In other words, everyone works in the city centre and receives an income y in exchange. Commuting costs $t/2$ per mile. The variables y and t are measured relative to the cost of the consumption good c.

Household utility, $U(h, c)$, is a function of the level of housing services and other consumption which can be obtained subject to the budget constraint [cf. Chapter 13],

$$y = r(u)h + c + tu.$$

Utility maximization subject to the budget constraint is equivalent to the unconstrained maximization of the Lagrangian,

$$L = U(h,c) + \lambda(y - tu - r(u)h - c)$$

[see IV, §5.15 and §15.1]. The first order conditions for optimality [see IV, §3.5] imply that

$$\frac{dU}{dh} \bigg/ \frac{dU}{dc} = r(u). \tag{19.3.1}$$

This is a standard result in consumer demand theory: the ratio of the marginal utilities of two expenditures are equal to the ratio of their relative price [see §13.3].

If the utility function is given an explicit functional form then a rent gradient can be derived from this model. Suppose that $U(h,c) = c^{\alpha}h^{(1-\alpha)}$, where $0 < \alpha < 1$ then Equation (19.3.1) becomes

$$\frac{(1-\alpha)c}{\alpha h} = r(u).$$

Incorporating this result into the budget constrain leads to the demand functions for housing services and consumption goods:

$$c = \alpha(y - tu) \qquad \text{and} \qquad h = \frac{(1-\alpha)}{r(u)}(y - tu),$$

so that consumption of housing and other consumption goods is an increasing function of household income and an increasing function of the cost of commuting. It therefore follows that the utility of a household located u miles from the city centre is given by

$$\bar{U}(y, t, r(u), u) = \alpha^{\alpha}(1 - \alpha)^{1-\alpha}(y - tu)r(u)^{\alpha-1}.$$

The level of household utility achieved obviously depends upon the level of household income, the commuting costs and the level of housing rents but its dependence upon location can cause problems since it implies that a household has an optimum location. If a city consists of many identical households they cannot all live in the same place. Clearly competition for the preferred housing locations will alter the rent, $r(u)$, until identical households (that is with the same utility function and budget constraint) are indifferent to their location. In other words

$$\frac{d\bar{U}(y, t, r(u), u)}{du} = \left[\frac{-t}{y - tu} + \frac{(\alpha - 1)r'(u)}{r(u)} \right] \bar{U} = 0$$

and the bid rent is given by the differential equation

$$\frac{r'(u)}{r(u)} = \frac{t}{(\alpha - 1)(y - tu)}. \tag{19.3.2}$$

The solution of which is the function $r(u) = r(0)(y - tu)^{1/(1-\alpha)}$ [see IV, §7.2], so that rents decline as one moves away from the CBD.

Once again the analysis yields a statement about relative rents: the absolute levels have to be determined using further assumptions. Suppose that the alternative use for land is agriculture with a constant bid rent of R_A, then the city boundary $\bar{u}$ will be given by

$$\bar{u} = \frac{1}{t}[y - (R_A/r(0))^{1-\alpha}]$$

Even this does not completely solve the urban system. A full solution needs an assumption about the size of the city population either an explicit one or an implicit figure derived from the demand for the goods it manufactures in the CBD. This will be examined further in later sections.

19.3.3. Industrial rents

Having examined agriculture and residential rents, leaves industrial location to be considered. Most (urban) economic analysis leans heavily upon models in which many of the structures of commerce are neglected or grossly simplified so that the sparse framework which remains highlights the important features under examination. Hence elementary models of industrial location assume that only land and labour are used for production and that constant returns to scale prevail. The starting point for the analysis is the ith industry's unit cost function $C_i(w, r)$ which is the minimum cost of producing one unit of output as a function of the wage rate, w, and the land rent r. Competition ensures that the cost of production equals the product price p_i minus the unit transport cost q_i.

In chapter 12 the properties of cost functions have been discussed where it was shown that the partial derivatives of C_i with respect to r_i and w are equal to industry i's demand for land and labour per unit of output. One can apply the implicit function theorem [see IV, §5.13] to the equality

$$C_i(w, r_i) = p_i - q_i(u)$$

to derive

$$r_i(u) = r_i(u, w), \tag{19.3.3}$$

with the partial derivatives [see IV, §5.1]

$$r_{iu}(u) \equiv \partial r_i(u)/\partial u = -q_i'(u)/C_{ir}(u) = -q_i'(u)/h_i(u), \tag{19.3.4}$$

$$r_{iw}(u) \equiv \partial r_i(u)/\partial w = -C_{iw}(u)/C_{ir}(u) = -n_i(u), \tag{19.3.5}$$

where h_i is industry i's demand for land per unit of output and n_i is industry i's demand for labour per unit of land. For each industry equation (19.3.3) gives the bid rent and once again we have a city of concentric zones, as in Figure 19.1. In this case, however, the zones are for different industries rather than different agricultural crops. The order in which they occur depends upon the slope of the bid rent curve, $r_{iu}(u)$, given by Equation (19.3.4). Whether or not an industry exists in the city depends upon its profitability, a point which is discussed below.

Following Miyao (1981) we can turn to the labour market and use the full employment condition as a way of deriving the city size. Suppose that at each distance, u, a fraction, g, of the total area of a thin ring with inner radius u and outer radius $u + du$ is available for production. Then industry i's demand for labour in the thin ring is equal to $n_i(u)g(u)2\pi u\,du$. n_i is as defined above and is the ith industry's labour–land ratio and is a function of r_i and w. If the total amount of labour available in the city is given as N, then to fully employ the labour force requires the equation [see IV, §4.2]

$$2\pi \sum_{i=1}^{m} \int_{u_{i-1}}^{u_i} n_i(u)g(u)u\,du = N$$

to be satisfied.

It may appear that there is sufficient information above to enable one to completely identify the city's size. This is not the case since the analysis is a partial rather than a general equilibrium analysis. Consider the ith industry its total revenue is given by

$$\int_{u_{i-1}}^{u_i} \frac{(p_i - q_i(u))g(u)u\,du}{h_i(u)}$$

and for it to remain in business must be equal to consumer's total expenditure on its product. If the city exports most of the output, then one needs to know the volume in order to decide on the city size. If one were analysing an isolated city state which did not trade then the demand for the ith good could be derived from a generalization of section 19.3.2

A conclusion to be drawn from this analysis is that some of the features of urban life neglected in the inevitably simple models, presented above, have an important impact on city size and geography. For instance, the analysis of industrial rents makes no provision for the transportation of goods or workers to and from the factories. This particular aspect will be discussed in section 19.5 below when we look at the CBD city.

The monocentric city model, which dominates the literature on the new urban economics, assumes that a city has a CBD to and from which workers travel daily from the surrounding suburbs. It has been shown above how mathematical analysis of land rents and travel costs provide an explanation for the decline of rents with distance from the city centre. In the following sections in which traffic congestion is taken into account, important differences arise between the structure and size of a city in which resources are allocated by market forces and a city with the socially optimum structure which a planner might seek to impose. The differences result from the way in which the economic activity of an individual or group within a city has important effects on others. These externalities can be nuisances like noise, smoke or congestion or else they can be public goods like information or uncongested roads. Urban economics seeks to analyse the relationship between spatial structure and these externalities without which there would be no cities and which cities wish to be without.

19.4. THE OPTIMAL ALLOCATION OF SUBURBAN LAND FOR TRANSPORT AND RESIDENTIAL USE

Here the calculus of variations in the form of Pontryagin's Maximum Principle is used to analyse the problem of allocating land in a city so as to minimize the social costs which arise from a congested transportation system [see IV, §12 and Engineering, Chapter 14]. A simple urban model is used in which suburban land can either be used for housing or roads and land in the CBD can either be used for roads or business purposes. Later sections will discuss ways in which the urban model can be extended to caputre other crucial features of city life. The object of this section is to illustrate the way in which the mathematical techniques are used to extract the properties of the optimal city.

The simple model of spatial structue in a city is based on a series of concentric zones. In this hypothetical city the central point offers maximum accessibility, a factor which is regarded as a major determinant of urban land rent. Accessibility declines with distance from the city centre and, empirically, one knows that land rent does as well. In most cities, even if they are not circular, one can distinguish concentric zones, the biggest distinction being between the central business district and the suburbs. People work in the former and live in the latter with the result that severe congestion arises during journeys to and from work. There are social costs associated with these 'rush-hour jams' which could be reduced by using more land for roads. If each inhabitant occupies a fixed amount of land, only an increase in the physical size of a city will provide the land for the extra roads, assuming the population remains unchanged. A larger city means not only increased land costs but also a longer journey to the CBD for those living on the city boundary. These are some of the issues which are explored in the problem below.

19.4.1. The Mills–de Ferranti problem

The questions to which Mills and de Ferranti (1971) provided an answer was: given that N people work in the CBD of a circular city and live in the suburbs which lie beyond the CBD, how should the land available be allocated between transportation use and residential use in the suburbs so as to minimize the social costs arising from congestion when these N people travel to and from work? Since the land used for the city has social value how large should the city be?

Although the city is assumed to be circular the analysis is generalized slightly by assuming that only $\theta(\leqslant 2\pi)$ radians of land is available, see Figure 19.2. For the reasons discussed in section 19.3.2, each location in the city is identified solely

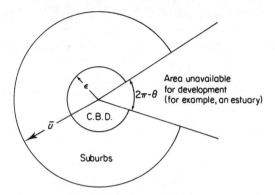

Figure 19.2: The circular city

by its distance from the city centre, u. The number of travellers at a point is denoted by $T(u)$; the amount of land used for transportation by $L_2(u)$; and $L_1(u)$ denotes land used for residence in the suburbs. All available land at any radius, θu, is allocated for one purpose or another; hence

$$L_1(u) + L_2(u) = \theta u. \qquad (19.4.1)$$

Also no more than all the available land can be allocated for a single use, i.e.

$$L_1(u) \geqslant 0 \qquad \text{and} \qquad L_2(u) \geqslant 0. \qquad (19.4.2)$$

The boundary of the CBD with the suburbs occurs at a fixed radius, E, from the city centre and the boundary of the city at a radius $\bar{u}$. Since all the N workers in the CBD live in the suburbs it follows that the boundary conditions are

$$T(0) = 0 = T(\bar{u}) \qquad \text{and} \qquad T(\varepsilon) = N. \qquad (19.4.3)$$

The residential density in the suburbs, a_s, is assumed constant and can be adjusted to cover the case where each worker has a family which stays at home and does not travel to work in the CBD. (Section 19.3.2 discusses an alternative model in which residential density varies with location.) The number of workers residing in the suburbs at a radius u from the city centre, $N_s(u)$ is therefore given by

$$N_s(u) = a_s L_1(u) = a_s(\theta u - L_2(u)). \qquad (19.4.4)$$

The land on which the city is to be built is assumed to have a rental value of R_A. This valuation can either be thought of as the market rent for an alternative non-urban use or as the social valuation of open space and parks. The congestion costs per traveller, $p(u)$, increase with the number of travellers per unit of land, that is the traffic flow, and are given by the function

$$p(u) = \rho_1 \left[\frac{T(u)}{L_2(u)} \right]^{\rho_2}, \qquad (19.4.5)$$

which is the form suggested by Vickrey (1969). Empirical evidence suggests that the average delay per vehicle is proportional to traffic volume raised to a power of at least three if not five. In this analysis $T(u)/L_2(u)$ is the appropriate measure of traffic flow. Hence total social costs are given by the integral

$$\int_\varepsilon^u [\rho_1 T(u)C(u)^{\rho_2} + R_A \theta u] \, du, \qquad (19.4.6)$$

where $C(u) = T(u)/L_2(u)$. The limits of the integral indicate that we are only interested in the suburbs.

This then is the city with which Mills and de Ferranti (1971) worked and it had a CBD of given radius, ε, all the residents of the city worked in the CBD and lived in the suburbs. The route to work is assumed to be along the radius of the city passing through the place of residence. Social costs arise from these journeys to work and from the use of land for the city. Given that N people work in the CBD how big should the suburbs be and what is the optimal allocation of land between residential and transportation uses which minimizes social costs?

Given the assumption of the route to work above, it follows that the number of travellers at a point u, within the suburbs, is given by

$$T(u) = \int_u^u N_s(v) \, dv. \qquad (19.4.7)$$

Equation (19.4.7) can be differentiated, using the definition of $N_s(v)$ given by (19.4.4) yielding the differential equation [see IV, §7.2]

$$T'(u) = C'(u)L_2(u) + C(u)L_2'(u) = a_s L_2(u) - a_s \theta u. \qquad (19.4.8)$$

The Mills–de Ferranti problem is to minimize the costs given by (19.4.6) subject to the differential equation (19.4.8) and the inequalities (19.4.2) on the decision variable $L_2(u)$.

$$L_2(u) \geqslant 0, \; L_2(u) \leqslant \theta u. \qquad (19.4.9)$$

Since $C(u)$ becomes infinite when $L_2(u) = 0$ and $T_2(u) \neq 0$, clearly no part of the optimally planned city can have zero land allocated for transportation as it would imply infinite social costs and therefore the first inequality will not hold with equality at the optimum.

The Hamiltonian, H^s, for the Mills–de Ferranti problem is [see IV, §17.4.6]

$$H^s = \rho_1 T(u)C(u)^{\rho_2} + R_A \theta u + [-a_s \lambda(u) + \mu(u)][\theta u - L_2(u)], \quad (19.4.10)$$

where $\mu(u)$ is the multiplier applying to the constraint $L_2(u) \leqslant \theta u$ and $\lambda(u)$ is the Lagrangian multiplier for the differential equation (19.4.8) $\mu(u) \leqslant 0$ if $L_2(u) = \theta u$ and $\mu(u) = 0$ if $L_2(u) < \theta u$. (19.4.10) represents the total social costs of the city. The multipliers λ and μ are shadow prices, that is they value respectively the cost, in terms of congestion and alternative land use costs of commuters travelling through a particular location and the scarcity value of land when all available land is devoted to transportation.

The usual first order conditions [see IV, §3.5] follow immediately from (19.4.10):

$$\frac{dH^s}{dT} = -\frac{d}{du}\lambda(u) = \rho_1(\rho_2 + 1)C(u)^{\rho_2} \tag{19.4.11}$$

and

$$\frac{dH^s}{dL_2} = -\rho_1\rho_2 C^{\rho_2 + 1} + a_s\lambda - \mu = 0. \tag{19.4.12}$$

At the edge of the city, $u = \bar{u}$, there is a transversality condition, that is $H^s(\bar{u}) = 0$, which gives the following condition:

$$R_A\theta\bar{u} + [-a_s\lambda(\bar{u}) + \mu(\bar{u})][\theta\bar{u} - L_2(\bar{u})] = 0, \tag{19.4.13}$$

since $T(\bar{u}) = 0$. The economic interpretation of the transversality condition is that at the city boundary the cost of increasing the amount of land taken by the city, $R_A\theta\bar{u}$, is just balanced by the reduction in congestion costs that the extra land would make possible.

If the problem is to have a meaningful solution, that is the city boundary is further out than the CBD suburban border, then $\bar{u} > \varepsilon > 0$, so (19.4.13) implies that $L_2(\bar{u}) \neq \theta\bar{u}$ and therefore $\mu(\bar{u}) = 0$. Assuming that $L_2(u) = 0$, then (19.4.13) becomes

$$\lambda(\bar{u}) = \frac{R_A}{a_s}. \tag{19.4.14}$$

This implies that at the city boundary with the non-urban area, the social cost of a traveller is equal to the alternative non-urban use value of the land taken up by his house.

Since $u(u) = 0$, Equation (19.4.12) can be solved for λ. When substituted into Equation (19.4.12) one obtains a first-order differential equation in terms of C, $\dot{C} = -a_s/P_2$ which may be solved [see IV, §7.2] to yield

$$C(u) - C(\bar{u}) = \frac{a_s}{\rho_2}[\bar{u} - u], \tag{19.4.15}$$

that is congestion is a decreasing linear function of the radius u.

Equations (19.4.15) together with (19.4.8) can be combined to derive a relation describing the optimal allocation of land for those parts of the suburbs beyond the last point at which all land is used for transportation. More precisely one obtains a first-order differential equation for the amount of land used for transportation purposes, $L_2(u)$:

$$L_2'(u) = \frac{d}{du}L_2(u) = \frac{\rho_2 + 1}{Q(u)}\left[L_2(u) - \frac{\rho_2\theta u}{\rho_2 + 1}\right], \tag{19.4.16}$$

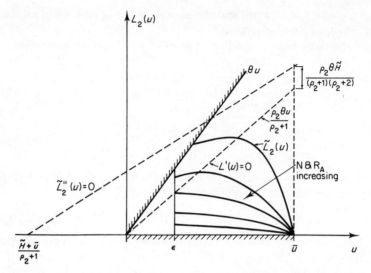

Figure 19.3: Optimal allocation of land for transportation in the suburbs

where

$$Q(u) = \frac{\rho_2 C(u)}{a_s} = \bar{u} - u + H; \quad H = \frac{\rho_2 C(\bar{u})}{a_s}$$

and

$$L_2''(u) = \frac{d^2}{du^2} L_2(u) = \frac{(\rho_2 + 1)(\rho_2 + 2)}{Q(u)^2} \left[L_2(u) - \frac{\rho_2 \theta u}{\rho_2 + 2} - \frac{\rho_2 \theta(\bar{u} + H)}{(\rho_2 + 1)(\rho_2 + 2)} \right].$$

$$(19.4.17)$$

Using (19.4.16) and (19.4.17) one can sketch the form of the optimal solution for $L_2(u)$, see Figure 19.3. For each pair (N, R_A) there is a unique $\bar{u}$ solution and Figure 19.3. shows the optimal allocation of land for transportation associated with a particular u and varying values of N and R_A.

Thus for some values of N and R_A the allocation of land for transportation, $L_2(u)$, increases monotonically [see IV, §2.7] as one moves in from the city boundary, for lower values of (N, R_A), $L_2(u)$ reaches a maximum value and then falls for the rest of the distance to the CBD boundary. The rental value of land R_A may be sufficiently low that at some point $L_2(u)$ reaches its constrained value of θu; from this point inwards Equation (19.4.16) is no longer valid and perhaps nearer the city centre $L_2(u)$ again becomes less than θu. This is what is considered next.

Before considering the constrained portion of the optimal land allocation, in particular the conditions under which one would exist, it is worth pausing to consider the way in which the mathematical analysis above has been used to derive urban economic theory. The primary concern has been with the qualitative nature of the solution. Although an exact solution to the differential equation (19.4.16) can easily be obtained, it is given in (19.4.19) below, the solution shown in Figure 19.3 derived using Equations (19.4.16) and (19.4.17) gives all the information that is needed, in particular that the land allocated to transportation uses commands a decreasing proportion of the total land available as one moves onwards from the CBD boundary. It is interesting to note that it is more appropriate to present the solutions in terms of $L_2(u)$ itself rather than as one might have intuitively expected in terms of the proportion of land at a given radius used for transportation, $L_2(u)/(\theta u)$.

When the constraint on the absolute amount of land available for transportation is binding, $L_2(u) = \theta u$, and $\mu \neq 0$. If one differentiates (19.4.12) and uses the value of $\lambda'(u)$ given by (19.4.11) the following differential equation in $\mu(u)$ is obtained:

$$\frac{d}{du}\mu(u) = -\rho_1(\rho_2 + 1)C^{\rho_2}\left[a_s + \rho_2\frac{dC}{du}\right]. \tag{19.4.18}$$

Along the constraint $L_2(u) = \theta u$, since there is no housing the number of travellers, $T(u)$, remains constant at some value, say $\bar{T}$, and therefore $C(u) = \bar{T}/(\theta u)$ whenever (19.4.18) is valid. Since

$$\frac{d}{du}C(u) = -\frac{\bar{T}}{\theta u^2} = -\frac{C}{u}$$

along the constraint, from (19.4.18) it follows that $d\mu/du > 0$ for all u such that $[\rho_2 C(u)]/a_s = Q(u) > u$. Hence, as is shown below, the constraint remains binding as $u \to \varepsilon$.

From Equations (19.4.18) and (19.4.15) can be derived an expression for $L_2(u)$, which is valid from $\bar{u}$ inwards until the constraint $L_2(u) = \theta u$ is reached, it may be written as,

$$L_2(u) = \frac{\rho_2\theta u}{\rho_2 + 2} + \frac{\rho_2\theta(H + \bar{u})}{(\rho_2 + 1)(\rho_2 + 2)} - \frac{\rho_2\theta}{(\rho_2 + 1)(\rho_2 + 2)}\left[\frac{H}{Q}\right]^{\rho_2 + 1}(H + (\rho_2 + 2)\bar{u}). \tag{19.4.19}$$

Noting that the third term on the right-hand side of (19.4.19) is always positive and referring to (19.4.17) it shows that $L_2(u)$ always lies below the $L_2''(u)$ line. If u^* is the point at which $L_2(u)$ reaches the constraint then

$$\theta u^* < \frac{\rho_2\theta u^*}{\rho_2 + 2} + \frac{\rho_2\theta(H + \bar{u})}{(\rho_2 + 1)(\rho_2 + 2)}$$

or

$$u^* < \frac{\rho_2}{\rho_2 + 2}[H + \bar{u} - u^*] = \frac{\rho_2 Q(u^*)}{\rho_2 + 2} < Q(u^*). \tag{19.4.20}$$

For $u < u^*$, one has $L_2(u) = \theta u$ and as was shown earlier $Q(u) = (\rho_2\bar{T})/(a_s\theta u)$, hence $Q(u) > Q(u^*)$. Using condition (19.4.20) gives $Q(u) > Q(u^*) > u^* > u$ for all $u < u^*$ which is the necessary and sufficient condition that $\mu(u)$ is a monotonic function for $u > 0$ [see IV, §2.7]. Therefore it has been shown that once $L_2(u)$ reaches its constrained maximum value, u, it remains constrained from that point inwards to the CBD boundary.

Figure 19.3 illustrates possible solutions to the Mills–de Ferranti problem. One case which remains to be discussed is the form of the solution when there is no land rent, that is $R_A = 0$. This is quite simply derived from (19.4.19) remembering that $H = 0$ when $R_A = 0$. As Figure 19.3 shows, under these circumstances the $L_2''(u) = 0$ line intersects the $L_2'(u) = 0$ line at $\bar{u}$. $L_2(u)$ is a linear function of u; made up of two segments, the $L_2''(u) = 0$ line when $L_2(u) < \theta u$ and $L_2(u) = \theta u$ for the rest of the distance to the CBD boundary. The optimum value of $\bar{u}$ is in this case given by

$$\bar{u}^2 = \frac{2(\rho_2 + 1)N}{a_s \theta (\rho_2 + 2)},$$

and may be regarded as an upper bound city size if we accept the *a priori* assumption that $R_A > 0$. It is to be expected that the optimum city size would always be finite since an increase in city size means not only an increase in total land rent cost but also that congestion occurs over a wider area. At any point, where there is a non-zero number of travellers, congestion costs cannot be reduced below the level associated with all available land being used for transportation. The sum of these minimum congestion costs over an infinite area are clearly infinite and since there exist solutions to the problem with finite costs such a solution cannot be optimal.

In touching on the topic of existence, the previous paragraph also serves as a reminder that nothing has been said so far about the sufficiency conditions. The first order conditions and the transversality conditions given in Equations (19.4.11), (19.4.12) and (19.4.13) are both necessary and sufficient for a global solution to the problem. Necessity follows from the maximum principle. Sufficiency follows from the differentiability and convexity of the integrand in (19.4.6), from the linearity of the differential equation (19.4.8), and the linearity of the inequality constraints (see Mangasarian, 1966). The measure of congestion costs at a point in the city $\rho_1 T(u)C(u)\rho_2$ is a convex function for all nonnegative values of ρ_2 [see IV, §15.2.6] which, as the earlier discussion of the measure established, is a reasonable *a priori* assumption.

19.4.2. Extensions of the Mills–de Ferranti problem

Roads and houses not only represent an investment in land but also in capital and this is one of the ways in which the preceding analysis has been extended by Legey, Ripper and Variaya (1973). Again the size of the CBD remains fixed and one is only interested in the distribution of resources in the suburbs, $a_s(u)$

households at u, each occupying one unit area of living space, take up only one unit area of land as a result of $\alpha_s(a_s(u))^{\beta_s}$ capital invested in housing. Similarly the effective surface available for transportation at u is $a_2(u)L_2(u)$, at a capital cost of $\alpha_2(a_2(u))^{\beta_2}$, where $a_2, a_s > 0$ and $\beta_2, \beta_s > 1$. Hence a_s, in Equation (19.4.8), is now a function of u and the definition of congestion, $c(u)$, becomes

$$c(u) = \frac{T(u)}{a_2(u)L_2(u)}. \qquad (19.2.1)$$

Social costs as defined in (19.4.6) have to be supplemented by the total annual cost of capital, given an interest rate of r per annum,

$$r \int_{\varepsilon}^{\bar{u}} \{\alpha_s(a_s(u))^{\beta_s}L_1(u) + \alpha_2(a_2(u))^{\beta_2}L_2(u)\}\, du \qquad (19.4.22)$$

In the modified problem one is seeking to minimize total social costs, equal to the sum of (19.4.16) and (19.4.22) subject to the state equation (19.4.8), the inequality constraints (19.4.9) and the additional constraints

$$a_s(u) > 0, \; a_2(u) > 0. \qquad (19.4.23)$$

The Hamiltonian [see IV, §17.4.6] becomes

$$H^s = \rho_1 T(u)c(u)^{\rho_2} + r(\alpha_s + \pi_s)a_s^{\beta_s}(\theta u - L_2(u)) + r(\alpha_2 + \pi_2)a_2^{\beta_2}L_2(u) + R_A\theta u$$
$$+ [-a_s\lambda(u) + \mu(u)][\theta u - L_2(u)], \qquad (19.4.24)$$

where $\pi_s = 0$ if $a_s > 0$, $\pi_s \leqslant 0$ if $a_s = 0$ and similarly for a_2 and π_2. (19.4.11) remains unchanged as the equation for the shadow price (cost) of a traveller $\lambda(u)$. a_s and a_2 have to be chosen to minimize the Hamiltonian and therefore [see IV, §3.5]

$$r(\alpha_s + \pi_s)\beta_s a_s^{\beta_s - 1} = \lambda(u) \qquad (19.4.25)$$

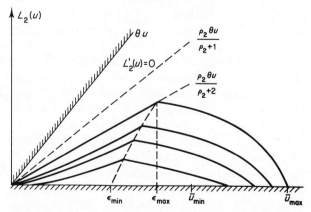

Figure 19.4: Optimal allocation of land for transportation in both the CBD and the suburbs for a fixed working population

and

$$r(\alpha_2 + \pi_2)\beta_2 a_2^{\beta_2 - 1} = \rho_1 \rho_2 c(u)^{\rho_2 + 1}. \tag{19.4.26}$$

$L_2(u)$ is given by

$$\frac{\partial H^s}{L_2(u)} = -\rho_1 \rho_2 a_2 C^{\rho_2 + 1} + r\alpha_2 a_2^{\beta_2} - r\alpha_s a_s^{\beta_s} + a_s \lambda(u) = 0. \tag{19.4.27}$$

Finally, the transversity condition is

$$\lambda(\bar{u}) = \frac{R_A + r\alpha_s (a_s(\bar{u}))^{\beta_s}}{a_s(\bar{u})}. \tag{19.4.28}$$

An interpretation of the first-order conditions and a comparison with those in (19.4.12) and (19.4.13) is most easily achieved if we assume that $\alpha_s = \alpha_2 = 0$, i.e. $\alpha_s > 0$ and $a_2 > 0$. $\lambda(u)$ is the marginal social benefit of an extra household at u whereas the left-hand side of (19.4.25) is the marginal capital cost of a household. Similarly the left-hand side of (19.4.26) is the marginal capital cost of investment in road capacity and at the social optimum it equals the benefits derived from lower congestion costs. The allocation of land to transportation in (19.4.12) ignoring the $L_2(u) \leqslant \theta u$ constraint, is such that $a_s \lambda(u)$ the social value of land devoted to housing equals the congestion costs generated by the households living on it. In (19.4.6) the extra terms reflect the capital costs of substituting land for capital in transportation and housing respectively. In other words less land devoted to transportation means that more capital will be needed whereas the housing sector can use the land instead of capital. At the city boundary the soical value of land devoted to housing is equal to the opportunity cost of land R_A plus the cost of substituting capital for land as Equation (19.4.28) shows.

As is to be expected, the form of the solution obtained from these necessary conditions closely parallels, the results for the simpler Mills–de Ferranti problem. There are three possible cases: (i) is the normal one where the entire city outside the CBD is unsaturated (i.e. at no point is all the available land used for transportation), (ii) a ring immediately surrounding the CBD is entirely devoted to transportation and beyond this the city is unsaturated, and (iii) is bizarre with alternating rings of saturated and unsaturated regions. Legey, Ripper and Variaya derive a sufficient condition which rules out case (iii) as a possible solution.

Although their analysis is a little more complex than that in section 19.4.1 and their problem a little more realistic, the most interesting feature of the work by Legey, Ripper and Variaya is their exploration of the market solution to their problem. Since this is in marked contrast to any of the material in section 19.4.1, it is worth examining in some detail. Section 19.4.1 took the viewpoint of a central authority which determines the allocation of resources which minimized total social costs. An alternative approach would be to decentralize allocative power so that on the one hand landlords, taking the rent profile as given, determine the amount of capital devoted to housing which maximizes their profit. On the other hand city government, taking the rent as given, determines the amount of land and capital devoted to transportation which maximizes net benefit.

Differences in transport cost give rise to the only locational advantage in the model, so that the competitive rent paid by identical households located at u, $\Lambda(u)$, which gives rise to household equilibrium is given by

$$\Lambda'(u) = -\rho_1 C(u)^{\rho_2}; \qquad (19.4.29)$$

in contrast with (19.4.11), the shadow rental equation, if (19.4.29) did not hold then household income would vary with location. The state equation (19.4.8) remains unchanged.

The value of a unit area of land at a distance u is

$$A_s(u)\Lambda(u) - r\alpha_s(A_s(u))^{\beta_s}, \qquad (19.4.30)$$

where the first term is the number of households times the rent per household and the second term is the rental cost of the capital invested. Thus profit maximizing landlords relate the rent and their capital, $A_s(u)$, by the usual marginal profitability relationship:

$$r\alpha_s\beta_s(A_s(u))^{\beta_s-1} = \Lambda(u). \qquad (19.4.31)$$

In the contrasting shadow equation, (19.4.25) are the multipliers associated with the constraint $a_s \le 0$. However, since $\lambda(u) \le 0$ always it follows that a nonnegative a_s will always be found to satisfy (19.4.25) and so $\pi_s = 0$ and similarly for π_2.

At the edge of the city the value of land, (19.4.30) evaluated at $\bar{u}$, must equal the alternative rental value of land R_A: this is equivalent to the transversatility condition (19.4.28). The city government buys land, $L_2(u)$, and invests in transportation, $A_2(u)$, so as to minimize the sum of transportation plus capital costs and the value of the land. To achieve this they ensure that

$$r\alpha_2\beta_2 A_2^{\beta_2-1} = \rho_1\rho_2 C(u)^{\rho_2+1}, \qquad (19.4.32)$$

and

$$-\rho_1\rho_2 A_2 C(u)^{\rho_2+1} + r\alpha_2 A_2^{\beta_2} - r\alpha_s A_s^{\beta_s} + A_s\Lambda(u) = 0. \qquad (19.4.33)$$

(19.4.32) is equivalent to (19.4.26) and differs from it because the latter incorporates the $a_2(u) > 0$ constraint and (19.4.33) is similarly equivalent to (19.4.27) and holds only if it implies $L_2(u) < \theta u$ otherwise $L_2(u) = \theta u$.

The only major difference between the market solution and centrally planned city is in the determination of rental values. Legey, Ripper and Variaya establish that, provided the condition which rules out case (iii) holds, the size of the optimal city is smaller than the size of the market city with the same population. It also follows, from the similarity of the two solutions, that were the city authorities to impose a tax on rents which brought market rents into line with the shadow rents then once could achieve the optimal allocation of land through the market mechanism. Unfortunately as they point out 'no realistic adjustment process can be achieved which can bring about this solution. The reason for this is that capital is residences and transportation is "sunk" capital, with little or no *ex post* substitutability. Hence it is impossible that the allocation of capital in city structures is in static equilibrium'.

This analysis is not only of interest for the contrast that it provides between a market and an optimal solution but also for the way in which the market solution gives us an economic interpretation of the necessary conditions for optimality. Differences arise in the rental equations because the individual in the market economy only considers his own costs arising from congestion whereas the central planner takes into account the additional cost which the individual imposes on everybody else. In this example, however, the divergences between social and private costs are not as numerous as they could be because the transportation system is run by a public authority which maximizes social benefit, rather than profit, using market prices. Hence the maximand used is little different from the Hamiltonian. In the next section there is a market city with no government intervention.

19.5. INDUSTRIAL AND BUSINESS LOCATION

19.5.1. The CBD city

Many of the early articles on mathematical theories of optimal city size concentrated upon those aspects of the urban economy that determine the lands use pattern in the suburbs. Suburban problems were studied to the almost total exclusion of those economic activities that take place within the CBD. It is almost as though the new urban economists believed that urban problems can conveniently be compartmentalized into suburban problems and city-centre problems which are individually solvable. In order to consider the validity of this compartmentalization, it is necessary to consider both the suburbs and the city centre before determining the extent to which urban problems can be decomposed.

Livesey (1973) and Sheshinski (1973) both used this approach to test the validity of the suburban land use pattern derived by mills and de Ferranti (1971). A necessary step in their solution was to consider CBD land use when suburban costs are neglected: a complementary problem, which Livesey (1976) called the CBD city, to that considered in section 19.4.1. The CBD city is considered to be made up entirely of a CBD with all the workers living outside the city limits. Land must be allocated between transportation and business uses so that for a given number of workers, N, social costs are minimized and an optimum radius for the city, ε, is determined. All the workers are assumed to travel to and from the city boundary along the radius passing through their place of work.

The CBD city is assumed to be circular with only $\theta(< 2\pi)$ radians of land suitable for either business or transportation purposes. Every point in the city is identified by its distance from the city centre, u. This implicitly assumes that one is indifferent between points equidistant from the city centre. The number of travellers at a point is denoted by $T(u)$; the amount of land used for transportation by $L_2(u)$; and $L_1(u)$ denotes the land used for business purposes. Since the land on which the city is to be built is assumed to have a social rental value of R_A, when used for some other economic activity such as agriculture, we can argue on efficiency grounds that all available land at any radius u is allocated for either business or transportation purposes. Hence, as in section 19.4.1, Equation (19.4.1) is satisfied and the same inequality constraints apply namely (19.4.2) and (19.4.9).

Since all the N workers in the CBD live in the suburbs, it follows that the boundary conditions [see IV, §7.1] are given by

$$T(0) = 0 \text{ and } T(\varepsilon) = N. \tag{19.5.1}$$

The density of workers on business land in the CBD, $a_c(u)$, is initially assumed to be a constant value, a_c. Armed with this assumption which later sections will reconsider, one can derive an expression for the number of people working in the CBD at a radius u from the city centre.

$$N_c(u) = a_c L_1(u) = a_c(\theta u - L_2(u)). \tag{19.5.2}$$

From our earlier assumption about people's route to work, a differential equation can be derived which differs from (19.4.8) only in that the parameter a_s is replaced by a_c. Hence the CBD city is an identical problem to the Mills–de Ferranti one as far as the mathematics is concerned.

19.5.2. The optimum CBD city

This section is completely analogous to section 19.4.1 and explores the optimum land use pattern but within the CBD rather than in the suburbs. The analysis rests on the same assumption that in the CBD, social costs arise from congestion and from the alternative use of value of the land and that total social costs can be represented by the cost function (19.4.6) except that the integration is taken over the CBD rather than the suburbs. The problem is to choose a city size, ε, that will minimize (19.4.6) but still employ N workers. Full details of the solution are given in Livesey (1973, pp. 151–156).

One can establish that at no point in the CBD city, whatever the value of N and R_A, are the inequality constraints binding. In other words, land is always used for both industrial and transportation purposes. Below it is shown that there is, for a given working population N, a minimum city size ε_{min}, given by

$$a_c \theta \varepsilon_{min}^2 = 2N$$

and a maximum city size, ε_{max}, given by

$$a_c \theta \varepsilon_{max}^2 = (\rho_2 + 2)N.$$

Both of these city sizes are independent of the alternative and rental value R_A. The minimum city size is the limiting case in which no land is used for transportation. The optimum city size tends to the limit ε_{min} as the alternative use value of land, R_A, rises forcing up the amount of congestion since less land is used for transportation. In the CBD city the transversality condition, similar to Equation (19.4.13), requires that at the CBD boundary the shadow price of land must equal the alternative land use costs of expanding the city's size. The shadow price of land is proportional to congestion costs. Hence as alternative land use costs rise so too must the amount of congestion in the city. The derivation of the maximum city size follows from the allocation of land to transportation purposes which is given by

$$L_2(u) = \frac{\rho_2 \theta u}{\rho_2 + 2} - \frac{\rho_2 \theta (G - \varepsilon)}{(\rho_2 + 1)(\rho_2 + 2)} \left[1 - \left[\frac{G - \varepsilon}{G - \varepsilon + u} \right]^{\rho_2 + 1} \right]. \qquad (19.5.3)$$

$G = p_2 N / a_c L_2(\varepsilon) \geqslant \varepsilon > 0$. Hence

$$L_2(u) \leqslant \frac{\rho_2 \theta u}{\rho_2 + 2}, \qquad (19.5.4)$$

since the second term on the right side of (19.5.3) is always negative. The largest CBD city is therefore when $G = \varepsilon$ and the allocation of land to transportation is a constant fraction $\rho_2/(\rho_2 + 2)$ of the available land. Another feature of this particular solution is that the ratio of travellers to land is a linear function of distance from the city centre. There is, for a given city population, only one value of land rent for which the optimal solution is ε_{max}. For land rents above and below this value the city is of a smaller size.

The implication of these results is that if, as is often assumed, $\rho_2 = 4$, then the ratio of maximum city size to minimum city size is $\sqrt{3}$ to 1. Also the land devoted to transportation is, at every point in the city, less than two-thirds of the total land available.

19.5.3. Mills's market model of the CBD

Here market models of the CBD city are described and the section begins with the model, outlined by Mills (1967), in which the city exists because there are increasing returns arising from production on a contiguous site. Hence, like Dixit (1973), Mills assumes that the CBD consists mainly of one factory that can be described by the Cobb–Douglas production function:

$$x_1 = AL^\alpha N^\beta K^\gamma, \qquad (19.5.5)$$

where A is the scale parameter and $\alpha + \beta + \gamma = H$, the returns to scale. Unless the quality and quantities of the services provided by land are dependent upon its location, one needs increasing returns to scale for our CBD city to exist. X_1 is the total output of goods in the CBD and L, N, and K are the total inputs of land, labour, and capital goods used in the production process. All these variables refer, as does the production function itself, to the total inputs and outputs. It follows from the earlier definitions that the total input of land is given by

$$L = \int_0^{\varepsilon} L_1(u) \, du. \tag{19.5.6}$$

The second economic activity in the CBD city is transportation which, as Mills recognized, is a sector where a great deal of factor substitution is possible. Clearly, the output of transportation services X_2 could be made to be dependent upon the number of people employed in that sector and the capital investment in transportation equipment. Instead, it is assumed that there is a constant ratio between the amount of land devoted to transportation and the output, measured in the number of passenger miles, that is, there are fixed technological coefficients and no factor substitution, so

$$L_2(u) = b X_2(u). \tag{19.5.7}$$

Next, one needs to consider the market conditions. Since the city's size is endogenous to our analysis, it is reasonable to assume that workers and investment have to be bid away from alternative uses represented by the exogenously given wage rate w and the rental rate on capital r. The demand for the output X_1 must depend upon its price, p_1, since it is produced under conditions of increasing returns to scale. Therefore the assumption is that the demand curve is given by

$$X_1 = a_1 p_1^{-\lambda_1}, \tag{19.5.8}$$

where λ_1 is the price elasticity of demand and is assumed to be greater than 1 [see Chapter 12]. Hence, the profit arising from production in the CBD is

$$p_1 X_1 - R_A L - wN - rK = a_1^{\lambda_1}(AL^{\alpha} N^{\beta} K^{\gamma})(\lambda_1 - 1)/\lambda_1 - R_A L - wN - rK, \tag{19.5.9}$$

where the rental value of the land used by the CBD is the exogenously given rate R_A. If the urban entrepreneur is a profit maximizer, then the marginal productivity conditions imply that the partial differentials of (19.5.9) with respect fo L, N and K are zero (see IV, §5.6] and hence

$$\frac{\alpha_1(1 - 1/\lambda_1)}{R_A L} = \frac{\beta(1 - 1/\lambda_1)}{wN} = \frac{\gamma(1 - 1/\lambda_1)}{rK} = \frac{1}{p_1 X_1}; \tag{19.5.10}$$

or in other words, the returns from extra units of land, labour and capital are equated to their cost. The total profit, (19.5.9) becomes, after substituting (19.5.10) into (19.5.9)

$$p_1 X_1 [1 - (1 - 1/\lambda_1)H], \tag{19.5.11}$$

which is only nonnegative if

$$H \leqslant \frac{\lambda_1}{\lambda_1 - 1}. \tag{19.5.12}$$

Proceeding as though (19.5.12) were true means that the demand for a good produced under conditions of large increasing returns to scale has a low price elasticity.

To solve this market model of the CBD, one begins with the relationship between the amount of land and the number of people employed, given in (19.5.10) which can be written as

$$\alpha w \int_0^\varepsilon N(v) \, dv = \beta R_A \int_0^\varepsilon L_1(v) \, dv. \tag{19.5.13}$$

The transportation sector services the total number of workers passing a point, hence (19.5.7) is

$$L_2(u) = bX_2(u) = b \int_0^u N(v) \, dv, \tag{19.5.14}$$

which (19.5.13) allows to be rewritten as

$$L_2(u) = b \frac{\beta R_A}{\alpha w} \int_0^u L_1(v) \, dv. \tag{19.5.15}$$

Substituting for $L_2(u)$, from (19.5.15), into Equation (19.4.1) and differentiating with respect to u yields the first order differential equation

$$L_1'(u) + \frac{b\beta R}{\alpha w} L_1(u) = \theta, \tag{19.5.16}$$

in terms of the land used for business purposes, $L_1(u)$. At the city centre there is no land, that is, $L_1(0) = 0$, so the solution of (19.5.16) may be expressed as

$$L_1(u) = \frac{\theta \alpha w}{b \beta R_A} \left[1 - \exp\left(\frac{-b\beta R_A u}{\alpha w} \right) \right]. \tag{19.5.17}$$

From these results, Mills (1967) draws some fairly strong conclusions about CBD traffic congestion. Before examining these in any detail, one needs to compare the results with those obtained in section 19.5.2 for the optimum CBD.

19.5.4. A comparison of market and social solutions for the CBD

Here the results of the previous two sections are critically contrasted and they are found to be unsatisfactory in some aspects. It would not normally be unusual to find some discrepancies between socially optimum and market solutions, since one might reasonably hope to reconcile the differences through a system of taxes and subsidies. But here it is shown that the two models have a few fundamental differences that stem from their specifications. These differences are fairly obvious. In considering the optimum CBD city, the productive side of the CBD was not discussed at all and, instead, one concentrated exclusively upon the choice of transportation land use pattern that minimized social costs. The market model, on the other hand, assumed a fixed land-to-travellers ratio in transportation and concentrated upon the economics of production.

As far as the market model of transportation is concerned, the key assumption is (19.5.7). When one identifies the output of the transportation system as the number of travellers, it implies that

$$C(u) = \frac{T(u)}{L_2(u)} = \frac{1}{b}. \tag{19.5.18}$$

The effect of this assumption is to reduce the social planning problem to the minimization of (19.4.6), which can be written as,

$$\int_0^\varepsilon [\rho_1 L_2(u)b^{-(\rho_2 + 1)} + R_A \theta u]\, du \tag{19.5.19}$$

subject to (19.5.1) and (19.5.2). There is no choice about the level of congestion at different points in the city; it is effectively assumed to be a constant. Hence

$$T(u) = \frac{\theta}{b}\left[u - \frac{1 - e^{-a_c bu}}{a_c b}\right] \tag{19.5.20}$$

assuming that $T(0) = 0$. Given that $T(\varepsilon)$ must equal N, (19.5.20) will determine ε, the size of the CBD city. The land use pattern is also now known since (19.5.18) and (19.5.20) yield an expression for $L_2(u)$, which in its turn dictates, using the assumption (19.4.1), that

$$L_1(u) = \frac{\theta}{a_c b}(1 - e^{-a_c bu}). \tag{19.5.21}$$

Even though nothing has yet been said about production, except that it employs N workers, an equation that is identical to (19.5.17), when

$$a_c = \beta R_A/\alpha w, \tag{19.5.22}$$

has been derived. However, this has reduced the problems to their lowest common denominator and, thereby, dictated the level of social costs, as is now shown.

From the marginal productivity conditions can be derived N, L, and K, while using (19.5.20), the social costs, (19.5.19), become

$$\int_0^\varepsilon [\rho_1 b^{-(\rho_2 + 1)} bT(u) + R_A \theta u]\, du$$

$$= \tfrac{1}{2}[R_A + \rho_1 b^{-(\rho_2 + 1)}]\theta\varepsilon^2 - \rho_1 N/a_c b^{\rho_2 + 1}.$$

Since, as previously established, ε is solely a function of N determined by (19.5.20), the social costs in this version of the CBD city are solely a function of the fixed linear relations between the outputs of production and transportation and their relative inputs of land.

The time has come to take stock of the comparison of the two models. It is obvious from the foregoing discussion that both the optimum and the market models make restrictive assumptions which rob their subsequent analysis of more general conclusions. To assume, as is done for the market model, that congestion (the ratio of travellers to land devoted to transportation) is a constant means that the plans for the optimum CBD city are so constrained that the level of total social costs cannot be varied. On the other hand, the assumption for the optimum model, that the land–labour ratio is constant in the production sector regardless of its location, is also restrictive, even though it appears to follow from our market analysis. Some of these difficulties stem from the specification of the production function (19.5.5) in terms of total land devoted to production and the total number of workers employed. This yields marginal productivity conditions relating the exogenously given wage rate and land rental rate to the total number of people employed and the total amount of land used in production. A certain amount of hand waving is required to get from Equation (19.5.14) to Equation (19.5.15). It does not necessarily follow, as is there implicitly assumed, that the land–labour ratio is constant throughout the CBD and equal to the aggregate value.

The market analysis neglected to discuss the costs of congestion in the CBD. Even if it is argued that a separate calculation has been done for the transport sector, which has resulted in the fixed congestion parameter approach of Equation (19.5.7), it is not explained who bears these costs. If they are paid by the workers, then the labour force will not be indifferent between the various locations possible for their employment in the CBD. Effectively, each man is paid less the nearer the city centre he works. This is of course inconsistent with the assumption of an exogenously determined wage rate. That assumption can only be sustained if the firm pays for each worker's congestion costs. Any payments made by the firm will reduce profits and should appear in the definition of profits, (19.5.9). One has now arrived at a situation in which the wage rate depends upon the location and hence, since it is cheaper to produce at the edge of the city, land rents will also depend upon location. It is by no means certain therefore that the labour–land ratio will be constant throughout the CBD.

The optimum analysis failed to consider the social profit of production, and concentrated instead upon the social costs of congestion. The next section extends the earlier analysis to include the production section; and, in particular, the land–labour ratio will be allowed to vary. What this section has shown is how each approach to urban economics is focused on one small part of the urban stage at the expense of simplifying assumptions about the rest of the scene.

19.5.5. The optimum factory town

Here, the allocation of land within the CBD of, what Dixit (1973) has called, the optimum factory town is considered. There is one firm producing a single commodity under increasing returns to scale with the production function specified in (19.5.5). The problem is to maximize the social benefits of production when weighed against the social costs of congestion. We therefore wish to minimize

$$\int_0^\varepsilon [\rho_1 T(u)C(u)^{\rho_2} + R_A \theta u + wN + rK - p_1 X_1] \, du \qquad (19.5.23)$$

subject to the constraints (19.4.1) and (19.4.2) on the allocation of land, the definition (19.5.1) of N, and the demand function (19.5.8). In (19.5.23), the social cost function (19.4.6) has effectively been combined with the profit function (19.5.9), except that the $R_A L$ term is omitted. The social cost of land is now covered by the $R_A \theta u$ term, which costs not only land used for production but also the land used for transportation. It was yet another unsatisfactory feature of the market model that no-one paid for the transportation system's use of land.

For every point in the CBD the planner must choose the amount of land to devote to transportation, $L_2(u)$, and this will determine the amount of land available for productive uses. He also needs to decide how many men will work at a particular location—or, to put it another way, the optimum land–labour ratio, $a_c(u)$, where

$$N_c(u) = a_c(u)L_1(u). \qquad (19.5.24)$$

At the edge of the CBD city, there has to have been accumulated sufficient land and labour for the aggregate marginal social efficiency conditions to hold. One says 'the edge of the city' because the analysis specified an aggregate production function. This has rather drastic consequences unless further assumptions are provided.

Consider the following solution, which is optimal for the problem set out above. The CBD is entirely devoted to productive activity, there is no land used for transportation, and so

$$L = \int_0^\varepsilon L_1(u) = \tfrac{1}{2}\theta\varepsilon^2. \qquad (19.5.25)$$

At every point, except the edge of the city ($u = \varepsilon$), no workers are employed and hence

$$a_c(u) = 0 \text{ for all } u \in [0, \varepsilon]. \qquad (19.5.26)$$

But at the edge of the city,

$$a_c(\varepsilon) = N/\theta\varepsilon \qquad (19.5.27)$$

so that

$$T(\varepsilon) = \int_0^\varepsilon a_c(u)L_1(u)\,\mathrm{d}u = N. \qquad (19.5.28)$$

No-one travels within the CBD; but, at the edge, the factory town employs N workers. This may be the optimum solution but it is a very limiting world. It implies that N men working on the periphery of a large plant are just as efficient as the same number of people spread around the site. If one is interested in the distribution of workers throughout the CBD, then there are two alternatives available.

The first approach is to assume an aggregate technology which determines the input ratios and these land–labour, and land–capital relations must hold at every point in the city. This is very like the earlier analysis. Once again, a_c is a constant, but it is no longer defined as in Equation (19.4.6)—the formula takes into account the costs of congestion. One can now formally specify the problem as:

$$\text{minimize } wN + rK - p_1 X_1 + \int_0^\varepsilon [\rho_1 T(U)C(u)^{\rho_2} + R_A\theta u]\,\mathrm{d}u \qquad (19.5.29)$$

subject to (19.4.9), (19.5.1), (19.5.2), (19.5.5), (19.5.6) and (19.5.9). Since $C(u)$ becomes infinite when $L_s(u) = 0$, and $T(u) \neq 0$, no part of the optimally planned CBD city can have zero land allocated for transportation since it would imply infinite social costs. The Hamiltonian, H, for the problem is [see IV, §17.4.6]

$$H = \rho_1 T(u)C(u)^{\rho_2} + R_A\theta u + [a_c\lambda(u) + \mu(u)][\theta u - L_2(u)], \qquad (19.5.30)$$

where $\mu(u)$ is the multiplier applying to the remaining part of constraint (19.4.9), and $\lambda(u)$ is the Lagrangian multiplier for the differential equation derived from (19.5.2) [see IV, §15.1.4]. Given the close similarity with the results in section 19.5.2 we can assume that $\mu(u) = 0$ for all μ.

In fact the whole problem defined in (19.5.29), can be solved by using the results of the optimum-city model. The principal difference is that the working population of the CBD is endogenous. It can be derived by substituting for K, in Equation 19.5.5), the marginal productivity of capital condition, which is identical to the appropriate part of (19.5.10). The other marginal conditions are, however, different since at the CBD boundary the shadow price a worker, $\lambda(\varepsilon)$, reflecting as it does the increase in social costs that would arise from extra people travelling to work in the city, must be equal to the extra rental, $R_A\theta\varepsilon$. This is the same transversality condition as in section 19.5.2's solution. An extra degree of freedom is introduced by the condition that

$$\lambda(\varepsilon) = w - \frac{(1 - 1/\lambda_1)p_1 X_1}{T(\varepsilon)}, \qquad (19.5.31)$$

in other words the shadow price of labour at the CBD boundary is the wage rate less the marginal productivity of an extra man.

This is therefore a model of the CBD city which can be solved completely and the results contrasted with those of Mill's market model. One conclusion Mills (1967) draws from Equation (19.5.17) is that 'in a sufficiently large city, transportation will require nearly all the land near the edge of the CBD'. This result is not true for the model here since, from Equation (19.5.4), there is an upper bound on the land used for transportation. To note that this result arises in a model in which there is a constant land–labour ratio throughout the CBD is to imply that one needs to examine the implications of relaxing this assumption by taking a more disaggregated approach.

19.5.6. A disaggregated faculty town

The second approach to the optimum CBD city problem is to disaggregate the technology so that the production function is location specific, that is,

$$X_1(u) = AL_1(u)^\alpha N_c(u)^\beta K(u)^\gamma \tag{19.5.32}$$

but price is still determined by total production

$$Y(\varepsilon) = \int_0^\varepsilon X_1(u)\,du = a_1 p_1^{-\lambda_1}.$$

The problem is now to minimize

$$-a_1^{1/\lambda_1} Y(\varepsilon)^{1-1/\lambda_1} + wT(\varepsilon) + rZ + \int_0^\varepsilon [\rho_1 T(u)C(u)^{\rho_2} + R_A \theta u]\,du$$

by choosing $L_2(u)$, $N_c(u)$ and $K(u)$, with the following differential equations as constraints:

$$T'(u) = N_c(u); \quad Y'(u) = X_1(u); \quad \text{and} \quad Z'(u) = K(u).$$

The costs at the CBD boundary, $S(\varepsilon) = -a_1^{1/\lambda_1} Y(\varepsilon)^{1-1/\lambda_1} + WT(\varepsilon) + rZ$, are in fact the aggregate costs of labour and capital for the whole city less the sales revenue from the city's total production.

The Hamiltonian is, using $T(u)C(u)^{\rho_2} = T(u)^{\rho_2+1}L(u)^{-\rho_2}$ or $T(u) = L(u)C(u)$

$$H = \rho_1 T(u)C(u)^{\rho_2} + R_A \theta u + \lambda(u)N_c(u) + \phi(u)X_1(u) + \psi(u)K(u),$$

where $\lambda(u)$, $\phi(u)$ and $\psi(u)$ denote the adjoint variables or shadow prices. Hence, in the optimal CBD, the following marginal conditions must hold:

$$\frac{\partial H}{\partial L_1(u)} = -\rho_1\rho_2 C(u)^{\rho_2+1} + \frac{\phi(u)\alpha X_1(u)}{L_1(u)} = 0 \tag{19.5.33}$$

$$\frac{\partial H}{\partial N_c(u)} = \lambda(u) + \frac{\phi(u)\beta X_1(u)}{N_c(u)} = 0 \tag{19.5.34}$$

$$\frac{\partial H}{\partial K(u)} = \frac{\phi(u)\gamma X_1(u)}{K(u)} + \psi(u) = 0 \tag{19.5.35}$$

$$- \lambda'(u) = \frac{\partial H}{\partial T} = \rho_1(\rho_2 + 1)C^{\rho_2} \tag{19.5.36}$$

$$- \phi'(u) = \frac{\partial H}{\partial Y} = 0 \tag{19.5.37}$$

$$- \psi'(u) = \frac{\partial H}{\partial Z} = 0. \tag{19.5.38}$$

The first condition (19.5.33) implies that the marginal social productivity of land is its marginal productivity revalued using the shadow price of total output, $\phi(u)$. It also implies that the marginal reduction in congestion costs resulting from more land being devoted to transportation has to equal the marginal social productivity of land. Similarly the shadow price of travellers $\lambda(u)$, is equal to the marginal social product of labour in (19.5.34) and in (19.5.35) $\psi(u)$, the shadow price of capital is equal to its marginal social product. The shadow price of labour varies with location as (19.5.36) shows. Whereas, (19.5.37) and (19.5.38) state that the shadow prices of output and capital are constant. At the edge of the CBD city the shadow prices have to be equal to those ruling in outside markets, which follows straightforwardly from the terminal boundary conditions

$$\frac{dS(\varepsilon)}{dT(\varepsilon)} = \lambda(\varepsilon) = w, \frac{-dS(\varepsilon)}{dY(\varepsilon)} = -\phi(\varepsilon)$$

$$= \left[1 - \frac{1}{\lambda_1}\right]\left[\frac{Y(\varepsilon)}{a_1}\right]^{-1/\lambda_1} \text{ and } \frac{dS(\varepsilon)}{dZ(\varepsilon)} = \psi(u) = r.$$

An alternative way of writing the marginal productivity conditions (19.5.33)–(19.5.38) is:

$$\frac{\alpha}{\rho_1\rho_2 C(u)^{\rho_2+1}L_1(u)} = \frac{\beta}{\lambda(u)N_c(u)} = \frac{\gamma}{rK(u)} = \frac{-1}{\phi(u)X_1(u)},$$

which enables them to be contrasted with those given in (19.5.10). The Hamiltonian along the optimal path is

$$H = \rho_1 C(u)^{\rho_2} T(u) + R_A \theta u + \phi(u)X_1(u)[1 - \beta - \gamma]$$

and must be zero when $u = \varepsilon$. Hence

$$- R_A \theta\varepsilon = \phi(\varepsilon)X_1(\varepsilon)\left[1 - \beta - \gamma - \frac{\alpha}{\rho_2}\frac{L_2(\varepsilon)}{L_1(\varepsilon)}\right],$$

which is a transversality conditon. It implies that

$$L_2(\varepsilon) < \frac{\rho_2\theta\varepsilon}{\rho_2 + \alpha/(1 - \beta - \gamma)}$$

For a positive solution to exist.

Alao (1976) works with constant returns to scale in the production sector and does not consider the revenue from the sales of the product. Instead he assumes that capital is used to maintain labour productivity at a predetermined rate. He is thus able to eliminate a factor of production from the model. Using the marginal condition relating to capital in Equation (19.5.35), (19.5.32) can be written as

$$x_1(u) = BL_1(u)^{\alpha/(1-\gamma)}N_c(u)^{\beta/(1-\gamma)},$$

where B depends not only on the constants of the model but also on $Y(\varepsilon)$. There is therefore a constant capital–output ratio in the CBD city. It is the one possibility which Alao does not discuss although it arises naturally for this problem. If one also assumes a constant land–labour ratio then the marginal condition for land becomes

$$\frac{-\phi(u)x_1(u)}{L_1(u)} = \frac{\rho_1\rho_2 C^{\rho_2+1} + a_c\lambda(u)}{\alpha+\beta}. \qquad (19.5.39)$$

When there are assumed to be constant returns to scale, as in Alao (1976), then the left side is a constant. Hence differentiating (19.5.39) with respect to u yields a differential equation in $C(u)$ for which (19.5.3) is the optimum allocation of land. On the other hand, the most general solution to the disaggregated factory town is more difficult to derive by analytical techniques.

Little has been said in the later sections of this chapter about the divergence between the optimum and the market solutions. This is because when there is a single producer who pays the commuting costs of his workers within the CBD there is no difference between the two solutions. The adoption of a model with an increasing returns to scale production function has explained why the city exists but it has not completely captured other important aspects of the CBD.

19.6. EXTENSIONS AND OTHER URBAN THEMES

19.6.1. Congestion in a unified CBD and suburban plan

The analysis in section 19.4 of this chapter has shown that, under certain circumstances, both in the simple allocation of land problem studied by Mills and de Ferranti (1971) and in the allocation of land and capital considered by Legey *et al.* (1973), a zone in the suburbs adjacent to the CBD boundary may have all available land devoted to transportation. Such an optimal city does not sound very pleasant and one possibility which springs to mind is to alter the CBD boundary so that it takes in this zone devoted entirely to transportation. It is also appropriate to wonder how great the congestion costs must be in the CBD, where offices and roads have to be fitted in, if nearby the optimal allocation is to have all roads. Hence it is obviously sensible to consider the optimality of the whole city defined by the CBD and suburbs. This problem was considered by Livesey (1973) and Sheshinski (1973) who have shown that the solution to the Mills–de Ferranti problem together with the solution for the CBD city of section 19.5 can be fitted together to provide a solution for the whole city.

Whilst in section 19.4.1 the social costs arising within the CBD were ignored and in the CBD problem in section 19.5.2 the social costs arising in the suburbs were neglected, they are both considered below.

In this unified problem the Hamiltonian has two functional forms, that applicable in the suburbs, H^s, is given by (19.4.10) and that for the CBD is

$$H^c = R_A \theta u - \rho_1 C(u)^{\rho_2 + 1}[\rho_2 \theta u - (\rho_2 + 1)L_2(u)]. \tag{19.6.1}$$

(19.6.1) is the form which the Hamiltonian takes after the values of the multipliers given by the first order condition have been substituted in. Since the number of travellers crossing the CBD boundary into the suburbs is equal to those leaving the CBD, one natural boundary condition is that

$$T(\varepsilon^-) = T(\varepsilon^+) = N, \tag{19.6.2}$$

where ε^- denotes 'on the CBD side of the boundary' and ε^+ 'on the suburban side of the boundary'. A further boundary condition is that $H^c(\varepsilon^-) = H^s(\varepsilon^+)$ and this implies that

$$\left[\frac{L_2(\varepsilon^-)^{\rho_2 + 1}}{L_2(\varepsilon^+)} - \frac{(\rho_2 + 1)L_2(\varepsilon^-) - \rho_2 \theta \varepsilon}{(\rho_2 + 1)L_2(\varepsilon^+) - \rho_2 \theta \varepsilon} \right] = 0 \tag{19.6.3}$$

since

$$C(\varepsilon^+)/C(\varepsilon^-) = T(\varepsilon^+)/L_2(\varepsilon^+) \cdot l_2(\varepsilon^-)/T(\varepsilon^-) = L_2(\varepsilon^-)/L_2(\varepsilon^+).$$

One solution to (19.6.3) is that there is continuity in the allocation of land across the CBD boundary, i.e. $L_2(\varepsilon^-) = L_2(\varepsilon^+)$. That this is the only feasible solution for the boundary conditions follows from the monotonicity of (19.6.3) as a function of $L_2(\varepsilon^-)$. Since the Hamiltonians (19.4.10) and (19.6.1) hold whether or not the inequality constraints are binding, and since for the CBD problem it has already been established that $L_2(\varepsilon) \leqslant \rho_2 \theta \varepsilon/(\rho_2 + 2)$, then it follows from the results of section 19.4.1 that the optimal allocation of land for transportation in the CBD and the suburbs never consumes all the available land.

The solution to the unified problem for a given urban working population can easily be constructed by combining the solutions to the CBD and Mills–de Ferranti problems and is shown in Figure 19.4. The optimal allocation of land for transportation as one moves out from the city centre is a monotonically concave function until the boundary of the CBD is reached after which it becomes a monotonically decreasing convex function until the boundary of the city is reached when it is zero [see IV, §§2.7 and 15.2.6].

Livesey (1973) establishes that

$$\left[\frac{\bar{U}_{max}}{\bar{U}_{min}} \right]^2 \simeq \frac{(\rho_2 + 2)(1 + (a_s/a_c))}{2(\rho_2 + 1)^2}$$

for all values of R_A and N except $R_A = 0$. When the social cost of land is zero the city's size is unbounded with all firms and households located on either side of the boundary, of infinite radius, between the CBD and the suburbs.

In this section it has been shown that by extending the Mills–de Ferranti problem to deal with the optimal allocation of land for transportation both in the suburbs and the CBD, the conclusion of Mills that at some point in the city all land may be used for transportation is no longer valid. Indeed it has been proved that there exists an upper limit on the amount of land used for transportation and on the maximum city size for a given working population, except in the case of the alternative rental value of land being zero. It is comforting to find that the Mills– de Ferranti vision of a city consisting entirely of roads at some points is false when a wider view of the problem is adopted. This is a far more appealing result, than that obtained for the Mills–de Ferranti problem and follows from the more logical approach of considering congesting costs in the CBD as well as in the suburbs.

19.6.2. Square cities

All the analysis in this chapter has been presented in terms of a monocentric city in which travellers use radial roads. Whilst this might be a reasonable approximation for European cities, the grid pattern of most US towns seems difficult to accommodate in this framework. Miyao (1978, 1981) is one of the authors who has tackled this problem by abandoning the monocentric assumption as well as the radial routes. Traffic is generated by commerce between business areas and travels along vertical and horizontal routes. He concludes that it is analytically impossible to characterize equilibrium traffic patterns for all conceivable road configurations in the two-dimensional rectangular city. However, in the case that the road width is constant and identical horizontally as well as vertically, there is an equilibrium traffic pattern such that between any pair of traffic origin and destination the two routes along the boundaries of the smallest rectangle that includes the points of origin and destination at its corners are exclusively and equally used by individual road users. Armed with this result it can then be established that in the two-dimensional city square city with $\rho_2 \geq 1/2$, land use decisions based on market rents tend to create too many roads everywhere in the city. The tendency towards excessive road building is stronger near the city boundaries than the city centre. Miyao (1981) also considers the case when the city size is determined so as to maximize the net social product which arises from production, with economies of scale, less the costs of congestion. In other words, his analysis is equivalent to that in section 19.5 for the circular city. He concludes that for the square city with economies of scale and traffic congestion, an optimal city size is uniquely determined. The free entry of competitive firms yields a city size which is greater than optimal, provided that the size of the economies of scale, measured by the elasticity of land productivity with respect to city size does not exceed unity, that is $\alpha \geq 1$ in Equation (19.5.5).

An alternative approach to the grid pattern of urban roads has been taken by several authors including Capozza (1976). This is to retain the monocentric city with all trade taking place through the CBD but to replace the radial road pattern by a grid of streets. Transport cost is then linear in distance and under certain assumptions the relevant distance is proportional to the distance from the city centre so that all the usual circular city results apply.

19.6.3. Non-malleable cities

All of the new urban economics presented above has assumed that the structure of a city can costlessly be re-ordered to accommodate changing economic circumstances. Investment in both housing offices is fixed and location specific. Both relocation decisions and changes in the density of occupation involve costs which are not independent of the current use and physical structure of a site. Vousden (1980) and Büttler and Beckmann (1980) both considered models of housing which assumed that the stock of housing was not perfectly malleable and divisible. Vousden showed that the assumption of a malleable housing stock cannot be assumed to provide a valid description of a city even in the long run. Urban phenomena such as slums and the demolition of older housing can only be explained in the context of a non-malleable model.

Büttler and Beckmann (1980) considered not only the design parameters of a residential building but also the attributes of the acommodation provided. By means of structural analysis an engineering cost function was obtained in terms of design parameters. This function was then used to simultaneously derive the demand for and supply of housing attributes. Their equilibrium analysis was for the housing market rather than the land market. They were able to show that in equilibrium housing rent, land rent, design parameters for the building and population density all depended on distance from the city centre and on the parameters of the problem: income, city population, diameter of the city and technical coefficients.

19.6.4. Market power

Markusen and Scheffman (1978) examined the effects of urban land ownership being concentrated in the hands of a few owners. They were particularly interested in the impact that the pattern of ownership had on the equilibrium land use pattern in a circular city. At the heart of their approach was the observation that the natural limit on the supply of land at a fixed location from the city centre constituted a monopolistic market. In particular any owner of land holding a significant proportion of the available land at a particular distance from the city centre has market power to the extent that he can affect the rent profile for the city by withholding some or all of his land. They showed that the existence of such a large landowner may imply the existence of vacant land at points inside the city boundary since withholding some land increases rents and gices a higher profit on the rest which the landowners lets out.

Vousden (1981) relaxed the malleability assumption and showed that even when the Markusen and Scheffman model is extended to allow for non-malleable, indivisible housing their results carry over. In particular he shows that the large landowner will act in a way which pushes up the rent profile for the city and thereby increases the radius of the city. Vousden's analysis considers a wide range of tactics which might be used by the large landowner. These include not only withholding vacant land but also supplying land at a lower density than would be supplied by competitive developers, delaying the redevelopment of a particular location and leaving existing structures unoccupied. His analysis results in a control problem that is linear in the tactics available to the large landowner. This implies that the optimal solution involves either employing or not employing a particular tactic for all the land owned at a particular distance from the city centre.

19.6.5. Other themes

A detailed list and bibliography of the urban themes which have not been covered in this chapter would occupy many pages. The material presented above has given a flavour of the literature on the new urban economics and a reasonable number of signposts to the literature on the subject. A substantial portion of the discussion has been taken up with the costs of congestion. Kanemoto (1980) covers much of this material in greater detail although he does not consider the CBD city. In particular he considers the case when traffic congestion is not properly priced. Then prices no longer reflect the marginal social values of goods and the market rent does not equal the social marginal value of residential land. The naive use of cost–benefit analysis by policy makers therefore gives rise to an inefficient use of land.

Much of the literature cited above is concerned with static equilibrium in a city although many important issues particularly urban economic growth have important dynamic aspects. Miyao (1981) tackled a dynamic analysis of the urban economy. He considered growth not only in residential areas but also industrial growth and rural–urban migration.

19.7. REFERENCES

Alao, N. (1976). On some determinants of the optimum geography of an urban place, in *Mathematical Land Use Theory* (ed. G. J. Papageorgiou), pp. 199–214. Lexington Books, Lexington, Mass.

Alonso, W. (1960). A theory of the urban land market. *Papers and Proceedings of the Regional Science Association*, **6**, 147–157.

Alonso, W. (1964). *Location and Land Use*. Harvard University Press, Cambridge, Mass.

Beckmann, M. J. (1969). On the distribution of urban rent and residential density. *Journal of Economic Theory*, **1**, 60–67.

Bos, H. C. (1965). *The Spatial Dispersion of Economic Activity*. North-Holland, Amsterdam.

Büttler, H. J., and Beckmann, M. J. (1980). Design parameters in housing construction and the market for urban housing. *Econometrica*, **48**, 201–225.

Capozza, D. R. (1976). Employment/population ratios in urban areas: a model of the urban land, labour and goods markets, in *Mathematical Land Use Theory* (ed. G. J. Papageorgiou), pp. 127–143. Lexington Books, Lexington, Mass.

Devletoglou, N. E. (1965). A dissenting view of duopoly and spatial competition. *Economica*, **32**, 140–160.

Dixit, A. K. (1973). The optimum factory town. *Bell Journal of Economics and Management Science*, **4**, 637–651.

Hall, P. G. (1966). *Von Thünen's Isolated State*. Pergamon Press, Oxford.

Hotelling, H. (1929). Stability in competition. *Economic Journal*, **39**, 41–57.

Friedrich, C. J. (1929). *Alfred Weber's Theory of the Location of Industries*. University of Chicago Press, Chicago.

Isard, W. (1956). *Location and Space-Economy*. M.I.T. Press, Cambridge, Mass.

Isard, W., and Smith, T. W. (1967). Location games: with applications to classic location problems. *Papers of the Regional Science Association*, **19**, 45–80.

Jacob, J. (1969). *The Economy of Cities*. Random House, New York.

Kanemoto, Y. (1980). *Theories of Urban Externalities*. North-Holland, Amsterdam.

Legey, L. M. Ripper and Varaiya, P. (1973). Effects of congestion on the shapes of a city. *Journal of Economic Theory*, **6**, 2, 162–179.

Lerner, A. P., and Singer, H. W. (1939). Some notes on duopoly and spatial competition. *Journal of Political Economy*, **45**, 145–186.

Livesey, D. A. (1973). Optimum city size: a minimum congestion cost approach. *Journal of Economic Theory*, **6**, 144–161.

Livesey, D. A. (1976). Optimum and market land rents in the CBD city, in *Mathematical Land Use Theory* (ed. G. J. Papageorgiou), pp. 215–227. Lexington Books, Lexington, Mass.

Lösch, A. (1940). *Die Räumliche Ordnung der Wirtschaft*. G. Fischer, Jena. (For translation see Lösch (1954).)

Lösch, A. (1954). *The Economics of Location*. Yale University Press, New Haven, Conn.

Mangasarian, D. L. (1966). Sufficient conditions for the optimal control of nonlinear systems. *S.I.A.M. Journal of Control*, **4**, 139–152.

Markusen, J. R., and Scheffman, D. T. (1978). Ownership concentration and market power in urban land markets. *Review of Economic Studies*, **45**, 519–526.

Meyer, J. R., Kain, J. F., and Wohl, M. (1965). *The Urban Transportation Problem*. Harvard University Press, Cambridge, Mass.

Mills, E. S. (1967). An aggregative model of resource allocation in a metropolitan area. *American Economic Review., Papers and Proceedings*, **57**, 197–210.

Mills, E. S., and de Ferranti, D. M. (1971). Market choices and optimum city size. *American Economic Review*, **61**, 340–345.

Mirrless, J. A. (1972). The optimum town. *Swedish Journal of Economics*, **74**, 114–135.

Miyao, T. (1978). A note on land use in a square city. *Regional Science and Urban Economics*, **8**, 371–379.

Miyao, T. (1981). *Dynamic Analysis of the Urban Economy*. Academic Press, New York.

Muth, R. F. (1961). The spatial structure of the housing market. *Papers and Proceedings of the Regional Science Association*, **7**, 207–220.

Muth, R. F. (1969). *Cities and Housing*. Chicago University Press, Chicago.

Papageorgiou, G. J. (ed.) (1976). *Mathematical Land Use Theory*. Lexington Books, Lexington, Mass.

Richardson, H. W. (1973). *The Economics of Urban Size.* Saxon Houese, Farnborough, England.

Richardson, H. W. (1977). *The New Urban Economics: and Alternatives.* Pion, London.

Sheshinski, E. (1973). Congestion and the optimum city size. *American Economic Review Papers and Proceedings,* **63**, 61–66.

Solow, R. M. (1972). Congestion, Density and the Use of Land in Transportation. *Swedish Journal of Economics,* **74**, 161–173.

Stern, N. H. (1972). The optimal size of market areas J. *Journal of Economic Theory,* **4**, 154–173.

Thompson, W. R. (1965). *A Preface to Urban Economics.* Johns Hopkins Press, Baltimore, Maryland.

Thünen, J. H. von (1826). *Der Isolierte Staat in Beziehung auf Nationalökonomie und Landwirtschaft.* Gustav Fischer, Stuttgart. (Reprint 1966; for translation see Hall (1961).)

Valavanis, S. (1955). Lösch on Location. *American Economic Review,* **65**, 637–644.

Varaiya, P., and Artle, R. (1972). Locational implications of transaction costs. *Swedish Journal of Economics,* **74**, 174–183.

Vickrey, W. S. (1969). Congestion theory and transport investment, *American Economic Review,* Papers, **59**, 251–260.

Vousden, N. (1980). An open city model with non-malleable housing. *Journal of Urban Economics,* **7**, 227–248.

Vousden, N. (1981). Market power in a non-malleable city. *Review of Economic studies,* **48**, 3–19.

Walters, A. A. (1961). The theory and measurement of private and social cost of highway congestion. *Econometrica,* **39**, 676–699.

Weber, A. (1909). *Über den Standort der Industrien.* Tübingen. (For translation see Friedrich (1929).)

Wingo, L. (1961). *Transportation and Urban Land.* Resources for the Future, Washington, D.C.

Mathematical Methods in Economics
Edited by F. van der Ploeg
© 1984, John Wiley & Sons, Ltd.

20

The Economics of Oil

DAVID M. NEWBERY, *Churchill College, Cambridge, UK*

20.1. INTRODUCTION

Oil, like phosphate, copper ore, coal and other minerals, is an exhaustible natural resource, available in finite, if uncertain, total amount. It differs from conventional produced goods in an essential way—if more oil is consumed today, then that much less is available for consumption in the future. In contrast, if one more loaf of bread is consumed today, it will have no effect on the available supply of bread next year or thereafter. Renewable resources, such as timber, ocean-dwelling fish and the like, occupy an intermediate position, in which current consumption does affect the current stock (as for exhaustible resources) but this stock is able to regenerate (unlike barren metal) and, given time, the future sustainable yield of the resource will be unaffected by current consumption (unless the stock is driven to extinction).

The theory of exhaustible resources was developed, largely by Hotelling (1931), to take account of the depletable nature of the given stock of resource. It can be readily extended to deal with the more complex case of renewable resources in which the stock is augmented by reproduction. The key result of this theory is that the price of the exhaustible resource is made up of two components—the (marginal) extraction cost, and the (marginal) rent. The first element is, of course, common to all produced private goods, whilst the rental component measures the opportunity cost of using up the stock of resource, for once used, it vanishes. The theory of exhaustible resources is largely the theory of the determinants and behaviour of this rental component. In a way which will be made precise below, the size of the rent depends on the value of the exhaustible resource and the scarcity of the remaining stock, measured, for example, by the number of years at which current rates of consumption can be enjoyed before exhaustion. The larger the rental component of price (that is the fraction of the price accounted for by rent) the more important is its behaviour, and the more the exhaustibility of the resource manifests itself. In contrast, exhaustible resources whose stocks are large (several hundred years at current extraction rates) or which are easily substituted for by alternatives (and whose value or essentiality is thus limited) have prices close to production costs, and behave more like produced goods.

When resource rents are large relative to production costs, two important consequences follow. The first, trivial point is that we need a theory to account for its level and behaviour. The second, and less trivial consequence is that a host of political economic issues become important. Rents are an attractive source of costless income, and their ownership may be of significant value. It will be worth spending substantial resources to capture these rents, either by market or extra market methods. Governments will almost inevitably become embroiled in the pursuit or defence of these rent-yielding resources, and will in turn be attracted by their taxable capacity, particularly as a properly designed tax will have no distortionary impact, and thus will yield costless revenue to the State. It is therefore most unlikely that high rent resources will be produced under perfectly competitive conditions. At best, if the tax system really is neutral—that is, if it has no effect on the allocation of the resource, the final sales will be competitive. However, implementing a neutral tax, though theoretically possible in certain cases, is in practice almost impossible, and hence the theory of exhaustible resources must necessarily address issues of market power if it is to be relevant.

The quintessential example of an exhaustible resource with a high ratio of rent to cost is, of course, oil. In 1981, the price of Gulf crude was about $US35 per barrel whilst its production cost was probably less than $1. Importing countries levied additional taxes which in some cases nearly doubled the retail price of gasoline and motor diesel, and these taxes can be considered in part as appropriable rents (in this case, at the expense of consumer rents, or consumer surplus). Clearly, oil exhibits these rent-seeking activities by companies, and subsequently governments with a vengeance, as many fascinating accounts of the activities of the 'majors' (the large oil companies) or OPEC testify. It is hard to think of other examples where the rental component of price is so marked, except perhaps for diamonds. It has been argued that phosphate deposits may become comparably rent-dominated since they are essential (not easily substituted) and in limited remaining supply, but after a dramatic price rise in 1973, recent history does not yet confirm this prediction. Most metals, minerals, and coal appear to have cost-dominated prices, and hence exhibit less dramatic market behaviour. It is therefore tempting to conclude that the main application of the theory of exhaustible resources is to oil, a temptation to which this chapter freely succumbs. It is often useful to have a concrete example in mind against which to test theoretical predictions to see if they make sense.

There is another important characteristic of exhaustible resources which is in danger of being overlooked if they are analysed within a conventional economic framework. Commodities sold on markets are typically assumed to be produced under conditions of well-defined property rights. In the case of oil, this means that the oil field is usually assumed to be owned by someone or somebody (a corporation, or government) with clearly defined title to the oil. Moreover, the key question facing such an owner is whether to sell the oil now or later, and for this decision to be made within the same framework of property rights, he is assumed to have clear title to the future oil. However, taxes alter these property rights in a fundamental way. A 50% rent tax is in effect a diluted title—a claim on half the rents generated. If the tax rate at all future dates were known with certainty, then not much would be altered. But future tax rates have nothing like the same immutability that conventional property rights have, and, as we shall see below, this may have profound implications for the marketing and pricing of oil.

20.1.1. The problem of dynamic consistency

The essence of the theory of rent determination for an exhaustible resource is that the time pattern of rents should be such as to persuade resource owners to release the resource over time at the right rate. In the competitive case where each owner has no perceptible influence on price, this means that the time pattern of prices (and hence, after deducting extraction costs, of rents), is such that owners are willing to sell some of the resource now and keep some for future sale. To do this they compare the value of rent from current sales and compare it with the present discounted value of future rent. Only if they are equal will they be willing to sell now and in the future—otherwise they will either flood the market now if current rents are high, or hold off for future profits. (As we shall show in the next section, this arbitrage condition essentially determines the time path of rents and hence prices, but for the moment the important conclusion to draw from this is that current supply decisions depend not only on current prices, but also on *future* prices, since the resource owner must compare present and future rents to decide when to extract the resource.) Consequently, in principle the resource owner needs to forecast the whole time path of future prices in order to make his current supply decision, and once he has made this forecast, he can plan this entire future supply. We can now describe the notion of intertemporal equilibrium in a resource market, at least, in a world of no uncertainty. (The equilibrium concept can be extended to deal with uncertainty without much difficulty, but solving for the equilibrium becomes sufficiently complicated that it would distract us from our main objective of characterizing the essential features of exhaustible resource theory.) A full intertemporal binding contract equilibrium, or a *perfect foresight* binding contract equilibrium (a *binding contract equilibrium* for brevity) is a time path of resource prices, $p(t)$, from the present date ($t = 0$) to the date of exhaustion (or the last date on which the resource is actually sold) ($t = T$) and a production *plan* for each producer i of sales $q^i(t)$ at each date from $t = 0$ to $t = T$ such that:

(i) For each producer his plan maximizes total profits discounted to date $t = 0$.
(ii) The plan is *feasible* for each producer; that is, production is nonnegative, and cumulative extraction does not exceed total stocks owned by i.

(iii) Total demand at price $p(t)$ is equal to total supply at each date:

$$Q(p(t), t) = \sum q^i(t), \quad 0 \leqslant t \leqslant T.$$

(iv) Producers will follow this plan over time.

Condition (iv) is rarely stated explicitly, though it is normally implicitly assumed, and makes clear the sense in which the equilibrium involves binding contracts—the producers are to be imagined as signing long-term supply contracts to which they will be bound. But why is it necessary to be so explicit on this point, since it is usually implicit in the notion of equilibrium—producers will surely supply what it is in their best interest to supply? But consider Figure 20.1.

Suppose that the profit-maximizing binding contract plan at date 0 when the plan is devised involves selling amounts over time along ABC. Suppose that at some later date t the producer recomputes his best plan from date t onwards, given his stocks at date t, and the remaining stocks held by all other producers. Suppose also that nothing unexpected has happened, and that if he continued on his old plan, then the prices would follow their predicted course just as had been foreseen at date 0. If his newly computed plan differs from his old plan, as, for example, it does if his new plan is DEF, then the original plan is *dynamically inconsistent*. To be dynamically consistent the best plan recomputed at each subsequent date must coincide with the remainder of the original plan.

It is interesting to ask when the binding contract equilibrium might be dynamically inconsistent. Necessary (but not sufficient) conditions for dynamic inconsistency are:

(i) the future affects the present, and
(ii) at least one agent has market power, whilst others are affected by it.

It is very easy to see why in the present context, which, for concreteness, we shall from now on describe as the oil market. If a producer has market power,

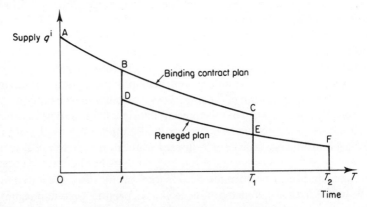

Figure 20.1: Supply plans for producer i

then his future sales will affect the future price. But future prices influence other producers in deciding their current level of sales, which in turn affects the current price, which affects the original producer's current profits. Hence, it may be in the dominant producer's interest to announce high future sales in order to drive down the future price, and induce his rivals to sell early. After they have sold their stocks, however, the dominant producer has increased market power, which he may now find advantageous to exploit. Hence, he would wish to reduce his supplies.

If an equilibrium is dynamically inconsistent, then it is crucial to enquire whether indeed agents can be bound to their original plan. If they can, then there is no problem with the equilibrium concept, but if not, then the equilibrium is not credible—agents would not expect rational maximizing rivals to follow their stated plans. Instead, an alternative equilibrium must be computed. The *rational expectations* equilibrium is a price trajectory and set of supply plans such that

(i) the plans are feasible,
(ii) total supply equals total demand at $p(t)$ at each t,
(iii) the plans are present profit maximizing for each agent from each date, given the stocks on hand at that date, and given that the future plans must be profit maximizing from the future dates, given the future levels of stocks implied by current and future extraction plans.

The distinction between binding contract and rational expectations equilibrium coincides with the distinction between *open loop* and *feedback* strategies in dynamic game theory. An open loop strategy is a time path of a control variable $u(t)$ as a function of time and the initial state of the game only. A feedback strategy allows the control at date t to be a function of the state of the game at that date. In the present case the state of the system is described by the stocks held by the different producers. A feedback strategy is by construction dynamically consistent.

An alternative formulation is that a plan is dynamically consistent if it satisfies the *Principle of Optimality* (Bellman, 1957), that is if, when the initial stages of the plan have been implemented, the economy or system evolves to a position for which the remaining stages of the plan continue to be the best choice from the new position.

For the moment the important lesson to draw is that many of the standard techniques for solving for the optimal plan (e.g. the use of the Maximum Principle or dynamic programming [see IV, Chapter 16]) implicitly solve for the binding contract equilibrium, since they solve for the best time path of the control from the initial date. It may still be possible to use the Maximum Principle if the conditions for dynamic consistency can be formulated as additional constraints to be satisfied. The solution must be checked for dynamic consistency. If the solution is dynamically inconsistent, and if there is no mechanism to enforce binding contracts, then a different solution technique must be employed. The problem is that for a wide class of exhaustible resource problems, whilst it is easy to characterize and solve for the open loop solution, it is very difficult to solve for the feedback solution. Moreover, the problem is clearly important in the oil market for oil is traded between sovereign nation states who are not subject to a supranational legislative body with powers to impose sanctions for breach of contract, and hence contracts are not enforceable. Likewise, democratic governments may find it difficult to bind their successors to continue to honour tax agreements, and hence even within countries suppliers face a similar lack of commitment on the part of the Government. The evidence of past experience suggests that in fact contracts and agreements are frequently renegotiated (i.e. broken), whilst tax regimes in, for example, the North Sea, change almost every year. There is thus little confidence on the part of oil-producing companies that they will face stable tax regimes.

This same problem of dynamic inconsistency may also arise in the context of choosing optimal macroeconomic policies for an economy in which agents make their current decisions (for investment, employment, etc.) on rational expectations about the future course of the economy, including the future levels of macroeconomic policies. (The key paper here is Kydland and Prescott (1977), but see Calvo (1978) and the survey by Buiter (1980). The problem of dynamic inconsistency was originally studied by Strotz (1955) in his study of optimal intertemporal planning.) Although the problem of the inconsistency of conventionally derived 'optimal' policies is now widely recognized in the macroeconomic policy debate, a satisfactory solution to be problem is still awaited. The fact that the same problem of dynamic inconsistency can arise for exhaustible resources is less widely appreciated, and, in contrast to the macroeconomic analysis, a satisfactory solution to the problem has been found in certain special cases by Maskin and Newbery (1978) and Newbery (1980).

20.1.2. Chapter plan

The thrust of the introduction was that the mechanical application of standard optimization techniques might be seriously misleading as a method of finding market equilibrium in the absence of enforceable contracts. Nevertheless, these techniques are very powerful, and will give the right solutions under certain circumstances—namely, when the binding contract solution is dynamically consistent. The next section will therefore show how to apply these techniques to a variety of exhaustible resource problems, and how these techniques give very simple rules which can then be applied constructively in certain cases. The reason for deriving simple techniques is that it is then much easier to understand the solution, and hence to check to see if it is consistent. The aim is thus to show that simple intuition can be applied systematically to these problems, and if so applied, may avoid some of the errors which the mechanical application of complex mathematics may occasion.

As section 20.2 confines itself to models of perfect competition or pure monopoly, the binding contract solution is dynamically consistent, but the remainder of the chapter is devoted to the analysis of cases where one, dominant, agent has market power, and the remaining agents act competitively. In these cases the binding contract equilibrium may well be dynamically inconsistent.

In section 20.3, the dominant agent is the government of a closed economy setting taxes on oil. Simple non-distortionary tax rules can be derived under certain conditions, and the question of their credibility, which is this context is essentially equivalent to their dynamic consistency, is discussed. The following section shows how crucial the assumption of a closed economy is, and demonstrates that the binding contract import tariff on oil is necessarily dynamically inconsistent where the importer is the dominant agent. The consistent solution can be computed for a very simple example, and has surprising properties.

Section 20.5 looks at market power on the production side and argues that the binding contract equilibrium will probably, but not necessarily, be dynamically inconsistent. The final sections consider various qualifications and draw conclusions.

20.2. PARTIAL EQUILIBRIUM FORMULATION FOR A SINGLE PRODUCER

20.2.1. Hotelling's arbitrage principle

In this section we shall demonstrate how to solve for the binding contract extraction plan for a single producer using the Maximum Principle. (Other dynamic optimization techniques such as Dynamic Programming [see IV, Chapter 16] or the Calculus of Variations [see IV, Chapter 12] would work just as well.) Then we shall show that the conclusions have a very simple economic interpretation, and hence can be readily grasped by those unfamiliar with these dynamic optimization techniques. Let

$R(q,t)$ be the revenue from sales of oil q at date t
$C(q,t)$ be the total cost of extracting q at t
r be the rate of discount
$S(t)$ be the stock of oil remaining at t.

Then the producer's problem [see IV, §15.1] is to maximize present discounted profits [see IV, §4.1 and I, §15.1.1]:

$$V = \int_0^T \{R(q,t) - C(q,t)\} e^{-rt} dt, \qquad (20.2.1)$$

subject to the constraint that cumulative extraction not exceed remaining reserves:

$$\int_t^T q(\tau)\,d\tau \leqslant S(t), \quad 0 \leqslant t \leqslant T. \tag{20.2.2}$$

Here T is the time horizon, which may be infinite.

In general, there will be additional constraints, for example that extraction rates are limited by reservoir pressure and installed well capacity. In the interests of simplicity, we shall ignore these for the moment, and deal with them briefly in section 20.6 below. We shall also ignore the possibility that extraction costs depend on the size of remaining reserves, and all issues of uncertainty, exploration, etc. Again, some of these are mentioned in section 20.6.

In order to apply the Maximum Principle, Equation (20.2.2) can be written in its differential form:

$$q(t) = -\frac{dS}{dt} \equiv -\dot{S}, \quad 0 \leqslant t \leqslant T. \tag{20.2.3}$$

$$S(t) \geqslant 0.$$

The standard Hamiltonian [see IV, §17.4.6] can be written

$$H^* = \{R(q,t) - C(q,t)\}e^{-rt} + \mu\dot{S},$$

where μ denotes the adjoint variable corresponding to the state variable S of Equation (20.2.3). It is convenient to multiply H^* by e^{rt} to give, after substituting from (20.2.3):

$$H \equiv H^*e^{rt} = R(q,t) - C(q,t) - \lambda q, \quad \lambda = \mu e^{rt}.$$

Then $q(t)$ is chosen to maximize H subject to any constraints on q. If these constraints do not bind, then q solves [see IV, §5.6]

$$\frac{\partial H}{\partial q} = 0 \quad \text{or} \quad \frac{\partial}{\partial q}(R - C) = \lambda. \tag{20.2.4}$$

Now, $R - C$ is the *rent* accruing to the resource (i.e. the profits attributable to the scarcity of the exhaustable resource) and $(\partial/\partial q)(R - C)$ is the *marginal rent*. Equation (20.2.4) states that whilst the resource is being extracted and providing it is not constrained by any production limits (so that the solution is interior), the marginal rent is equated to the shadow price of the resource, λ. This shadow price, or, more precisely, the original shadow price μ in turn satisfies the arbitrage equation (the adjoint equation):

$$\frac{d\mu}{dt} = \frac{-\partial H^*}{\partial S} = 0 \tag{20.2.5}$$

or

$$\lambda = \lambda_0 e^{rt}. \tag{20.2.6}$$

Thus the shadow price, λ, must rise at the rate of interest. This fundamental result can be summarised as:

Hotelling's arbitrage principle. Over a time interval during which a producer freely chooses a positive production level, then, providing the rate of extraction at any date does not affect extraction costs at any other date, his marginal rent must be rising at the rate of interest. More generally, at any date at which he chooses an unconstrained positive supply, the present discounted marginal rent must be the same, that is

$$e^{-rt} \frac{\partial}{\partial q} \{R(q, t) - C(q, t)\} = \lambda_0, \text{ constant.} \qquad (20.2.7)$$

Hotelling (1931) derived this as a condition for flow equilibrium in the resource market, since it leaves resource holders indifferent between extracting and holding at each instant, whilst Solow (1974), in his Ely lecture, deduces it as a condition for stock equilibrium in the asset market: all assets of the same risk class must earn the same total rate of return, allowing for capital gains.

The qualification that extraction costs do not depend on remaining reserves is important, for otherwise if total extraction costs are $C(q, S, t)$ the arbitrage equation would be:

$$\frac{d}{dt}(\lambda e^{-rt}) = \frac{-\partial H^*}{\partial S} = \frac{\partial C}{\partial S} e^{-rt},$$

$$\dot{\lambda} - r\lambda = \frac{\partial C}{\partial S},$$

[see IV, §3.2] and marginal rent as defined would no longer rise at the rate of interest. Put another way, the full marginal cost of extraction when current extraction affects future extraction costs is more complex than $\partial C/\partial q$, as Solow and Wan (1976) and Heal (1976) demonstrate.

20.2.2. Special case: constant marginal cost, perfect competition or pure monopoly

A perfectly competitive producer cannot affect the price [see §12.10], and if his marginal costs are constant at c_i, then

$$\frac{\partial R}{\partial q} = p(t), \quad \frac{\partial C^i}{\partial q} = c_i$$

and producer i will be willing to supply between t_{i-1} and t_i along the price path $p(t)$:

$$p(t) - c_i = e^{r(t - t_{i-1})}\{p(t_{i-1}) - c_i\}, \quad t_{i-1} \leqslant t \leqslant t_i. \qquad (20.2.8)$$

For a pure monopolist [see §12.11]

$$m = \frac{\partial R}{\partial q} = p(t)\left(1 - \frac{1}{\varepsilon}\right) \tag{20.2.9}$$

is the marginal revenue at date t when the price is p and the demand schedule has elasticity ε (defined to be positive) greater than 1:

$$\varepsilon = \frac{-p(t)\partial q(t)}{q(t)\partial p(t)} > 1.$$

(If the elasticity is less than unity, other considerations discussed below must be invoked.)

During the period in which he is selling, if his unit costs are c, then the price must satisfy

$$p(t)\left\{1 - \frac{1}{\varepsilon(p)}\right\} - c = \left[p_0\left\{1 - \frac{1}{\varepsilon(p_0)}\right\} - c\right]e^{r(t - t_0)}, \tag{20.2.10}$$

where $p_0 = p(t_0)$, and t_0 is the date at which sales begin.

20.2.3. Terminal conditions

So far, we have remained silent on what determines the period of sale, or the date of final sale, and what determines the price level (that is the value of p_{i-1} or p_0 in Equations (20.2.8) and (20.2.10)). The short answer is that, since rent rises over time, the price will in general also rise (abstracting from very rapid technical progress lowering costs over time) and eventually will reach a level at which demand falls to zero. (There are models for which demand remains positive at all finite prices, but, given the substitutes for oil, this seems empirically implausible.) It makes no sense to hold profitably extracted oil after that date, and so the initial price should be at a level which ensures that all such oil is sold by the time the price reaches this 'choke' level. The higher the initial price, the sooner this will be and the less oil will cumulatively be demanded. Lowering the initial price gradually increases cumulative demand until it is equal to available stocks, and this then fixes the level of the price path and the date of exhaustion (or final sale). It is convenient to summarize this argument in two steps.

The terminal price principle

The first principle in locating the price trajectory was the Hotelling principle, which can be interpreted as determining the present level of rent by discounting the future level of achievable rent. If there is some price above which the resource cannot be sold, then this price will limit the future rent and hence anchor the present rent and price. It is convenient to assume that there is a ceiling price, or backstop price, $\bar{p}$, which may arise for two different reasons:

(i) Demand falls to zero at $\bar{p}$, most easily captured by the linear demand schedule for consumption q [see Chapters 12 and 13]:

$$q = b(\bar{p} - p). \tag{20.2.11}$$

The linear demand schedule has the attractive feature that the elasticity of demand tends to infinity at $\bar{p}$, so that marginal revenue is there equal to the price.

(ii) There is a 'backstop technology', to use the terminology of Nordhaus (1973), which provides a perfect and inexhaustible substitute elastically at $\bar{p}$ (such as the breeder reactor for energy). In this case the marginal revenue is also equal to the price at $\bar{p}$.

The importance of this principle that there is a terminal price is that it allows the price trajectory to be derived by working backwards from the backstop price using the Hotelling principle. For example, if $\bar{p}$ is reached at date T, and the industry is competitive with constant marginal extraction costs c, then at date t, the price must satisfy Equation (20.2.8)

$$\begin{aligned}
\bar{p} - c &= (p_t - c)e^{r(T-t)}, \quad t \leqslant T, \\
p_t &= c + (\bar{p} - c)e^{r(t-T)}, \quad t \leqslant T.
\end{aligned} \tag{20.2.12}$$

and as $\bar{p} > c$ the price rises over time.

If, however, the 'backstop technology' is not elastically available at a constant price, because, for example, it is very capital intensive and hence is capacity constrained, then much of the simplicity of this principle must be sacrificed.

The exhaustion principle

If extraction costs from any field do not vary with time, then there is a well-defined stock of oil which it is profitable to extract at prices up to the terminal price. (Otherwise the volume of oil which can be sold will depend on the time path of prices and can only be found simultaneously with solving for the price path.) The exhaustion principle states that all this oil must be consumed by the date at which the price reaches $\bar{p}$.

If, in addition, the demand schedule does not shift over time, and if marginal extraction costs from any field are constant, then the *date* of exhaustion, T, can be very simply computed as follows. Let us run time backwards, setting the clock to zero at the date of exhaustion. If the demand shifts over time, then the consumption rate x years before exhaustion will depend on the date of exhaustion, T, and the proposed method will require a series of iterative approximations to locate T. The price trajectory can be found from the first two principles (i.e. the Hotelling principle and the terminal price principle) and prices now fall as we move backwards through time towards the present. The price at each date fixes the amount consumed and hence the total amount consumed from the time we started the clock. When the total stock available runs out, stop the clock, and time shown is T, the required date of exhaustion.

Consider the simple competitive case with the linear demand schedule of Equation (20.2.11), and let x be the date shown on the backward-running clock, that is the time remaining before exhaustion.

From Equation (20.2.12), since $x = T - t$:

$$p_x = c + (\bar{p} - c)e^{-rx}. \tag{20.2.13}$$

Consumption is from Equation (20.2.11)

$$q_x = b(\bar{p} - c)(1 - e^{-rx}), \tag{20.2.14}$$

and cumulative consumption is [see IV, §4.1]

$$Q_x = \int_0^x q_z \, dz = b(\bar{p} - c)\psi(r, x), \tag{20.2.15}$$

where ψ is the integral [see IV, §4.2]

$$\psi(r, x) \equiv \int_0^x (1 - e^{-rz}) \, dz = \frac{rx + e^{-rx} - 1}{r}.$$

Since Q_x is obviously monotonically increasing in x [see IV, §2.7], the value of x at which $Q_x = S_0$, the actual stock of oil, is uniquely determined (and can be easily found on a pocket calculator, given S_0, $\bar{p}$, c, and r). Diagrammatically, this is shown in Figure 20.2.

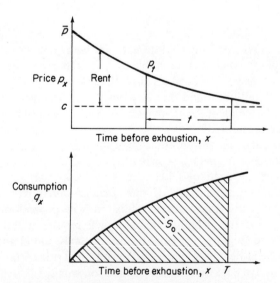

Figure 20.2: Locating the competitive price trajectory

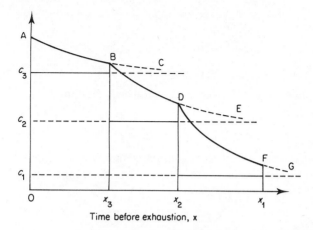

Figure 20.3: The competitive price path with different fields

Implicitly, we have been assuming that there are a large number of essentially identical producers competing, all with the same costs. If there are several categories of producers, classified by extraction cost, who behave competitively (so, presumably, there are sufficiently many producers within each cost category), then the price path is found by solving a sequence of such problems, as shown in Figure 20.3.

ABC is the competitive price path for cost c_3, the highest cost field, and this field is exhausted over Ox_3. BDE is the competitive price path for cost c_2, starting from B, and exhausts over $x_3 x_2$, and so on. Notice that low cost fields are exhausted first, and that this provides no incentive for high cost producers to produce early, as even if their rents are positive (as for c_3 producers for some period between B and D), they are rising faster than the rate of interest, and are hence best delayed.

The same principles apply for a pure monopolist, except now the price trajectory is derived from the marginal revenue trajectory.

If marginal cost is constant at c and demand isoelastic, the Hotelling principle of Equation (20.2.7) gives the marginal revenue x years before exhaustion as:

$$m_x = c + (m_T - c)e^{-rx}, \quad m_x \equiv \frac{\partial R}{\partial q_x}.$$

Since demand is a function of price, which is functionally related to marginal revenue, cumulative consumption in the last x years of extraction can be written as

$$Q_x = \int_0^x q(m_z)\,dz.$$

For example, in the case of the linear demand schedule of Equation (20.2.11) where $m_T = \bar{p}$:

$$m_t = 2p_t - \bar{p},$$

whence

$$p_t = \tfrac{1}{2}(m_t + \bar{p}). \qquad (20.2.16)$$

Consumption x years before exhaustion can be found from the demand schedule:

$$q_x = \tfrac{1}{2}b(\bar{p} - c)(1 - e^{-rx}), \qquad (20.2.17)$$

which is half the rate at which a competitive economy would then consume, given by Equation (20.2.14). The exhaustion date under monopoly, T^m, would be determined by the solution to

$$S_0 = \tfrac{1}{2}b(\bar{p} - c)\psi(r, T^m).$$

Figure 20.4 illustrates the difference between competitive and monopoly oil price and supply paths for the case of linear demand, and demonstrates the delay in the date of exhaustion under monopoly compared with the competitive date, T^c, which solves:

$$S_0 = b(\bar{p} - c)\psi(r, T^c).$$

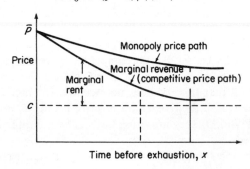

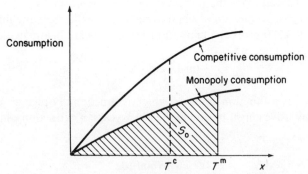

Figure 20.4: Monopolistic and competitive trajectories compared

20.2.4. More on the backstop technology

There is a slight complication in dealing with the backstop technology as specified above for the case of the pure monopolist, and that is that the relationship between marginal revenue and price is slightly more complicated than Equation (20.2.9) suggests, for marginal revenue is discontinuous at the backstop price, $\bar{p}$, as there is a kink in the demand schedule facing the monopolist, shown in Figure 20.5.

It might appear that the marginal revenue is not well-defined at $q(\bar{p})$, but this is to look at the problem from the wrong perspective. In fact the marginal revenue is determined by the Hotelling principle, and if it lies anywhere between A and B, then the market price is set equal to $\bar{p}$, which is well defined. This is demonstrated in Figure 20.6, where again the monopolist has constant extraction costs, c^m.

As in Figure 20.4, the marginal revenue falls as the time before exhaustion increases so that the marginal rent declines at the rate of interest. Between the date of exhaustion, 0, and x_1 years before exhaustion, the marginal revenue lies between A and B in Figure 20.5, so that the price stays at $\bar{p}$, but at x_1, the limit

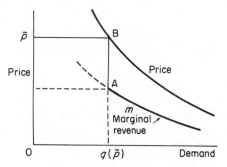

Figure 20.5: Marginal revenue with limit pricing by backstop

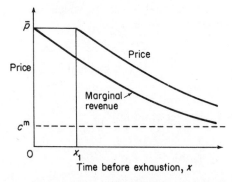

Figure 20.6: Price trajectory for a monopolist with a backstop technology

price $\bar{p}$ ceases to constrain the monopolist, and between the present and that future date x_1 years before exhaustion, the price will be changing as shown in Figure 20.6.

If the elasticity of demand is below unity at $\bar{p}$, then the monopolist will sell all his oil at $\bar{p}$ (unless faced with competition—a case we consider below.)

Within the formal framework of the Maximum Principle, the last argument can be applied as follows. The revenue function $R(q)$ is continuous [see IV, §2.3] but only piecewise differentiable [see IV, §20.2]:

$$R^1(q) = qp(q), \quad p < \bar{p}, q > q(\bar{p}),$$
$$R^2(q) = q\bar{p}, \qquad p = \bar{p}, q < q(\bar{p}).$$

Depending which part of the function R is relevant, the choice of q now has to allow for the possibility of a corner solution. Substituting these alternatives with the (transformed) Hamiltonian, Equation (22.2.4) now becomes

$$\left.\begin{array}{l} \dfrac{\partial R^1}{\partial q} - \dfrac{\partial C}{\partial q} - \lambda \leqslant 0 \\[2mm] q \geqslant \bar{q} \end{array}\right\} \text{ complementary inequalities.} \qquad (20.2.18)$$

Marginal rent $((\partial/\partial q)(R^1 - C))$ increases as q decreases, and given λ_0, Equation (20.2.18) and (20.2.6) can be satisfied with equality for $0 \leqslant t \leqslant t_1$:

$$\frac{\partial R^1}{\partial q} - \frac{\partial C}{\partial q} = \lambda_0 e^{rt}, \quad 0 \leqslant t \leqslant t_1. \qquad (20.2.19)$$

At some date t_1 the right-hand side first equals marginal rent evaluated at $\bar{p}$, and for $t > t_1$ Equation (20.2.18) cannot be satisfied with an equality, implying that the solution is $q = \bar{q}$:

$$\frac{\partial R^1(\bar{q})}{\partial q} - \frac{\partial C(\bar{q})}{\partial q} < \lambda_0 e^{rt}, \quad t > t_1.$$

However, there is an additional constraint which now becomes relevant, for Equation (20.2.4) can also be written

$$\left.\begin{array}{l} \dfrac{\partial R^2}{\partial q} - \dfrac{\partial C}{\partial q} - \lambda \geqslant 0, \\[2mm] q \leqslant \bar{q}, \end{array}\right\} \text{ complementary inequalities.}$$

Since $\partial R^2/\partial q = \bar{p}$, sales are set at $\bar{q}$ until

$$\bar{p} - \frac{\partial C(\bar{q})}{\partial q} = \lambda_0 e^{rt_2},$$

at which date q must fall below $\bar{q}$, and, since there is no advantage in selling at any rate between zero and $\bar{q}$, the monopolist should arrange to exhaust his stock at date t_2. This rather tortuous argument is all summarized in Figure 20.5 and the verbal argument given above.

There is one other form of backstop technology which is easy to analyse in the present frameork, but which has potentially rather different implications for the terminal price of oil (that is the price at the date of exhaustion). Suppose that the backstop becomes available at, and not before, date M, and is then elastically available at price $\bar{p}$. (For example, the technology is still under development and will not be available until some predicted future date.) There are then two possibilities. Either the date of introduction is before the date of exhaustion computed by ignoring the constraint on availability, or it is not. If so, then the previous solution remains valid, if not, then logically, oil should be depleted by date M, and the terminal price, $p(M)$, will exceed $\bar{p}$, and will be chosen to exhaust stocks at date M. The price will then drop suddenly upon the introduction of the backstop, in contrast to the earlier continuous price paths.

20.2.5. The effect of market structure on dynamic inconsistency

All the examples considered so far in which the market is perfectly competitive or one of pure monopoly, are dynamically consistent, as can be checked by noting that the paths were constructed by working back from the terminal price. The location of this path does not depend on the size of reserves, only its duration; hence as reserves are used up, producers move to positions (prices) which are optimal given their remaining reserves. This confirms the intuitive explanation of the conditions necessary for dynamic inconsistency given in section 20.1.1 above. If producers are competitive, they cannot manipulate the future to benefit the present, and hence only predict the future, not bind themselves to any future actions. A pure monopolist, on the other hand, is only playing against himself in the simple models described so far, for no other agents make intertemporal decisions which depend on his actions. Providing the monopolist's objective remains consistent or unchanged, he therefore has no reason to change his plans. Dynamic inconsistency requires one agent to have market power which affects the intertemporal decisions of other agents, which in turn affect the dominant agent. The simplest market structure in which this condition is satisfied is one in which a dominant agent (or *leader*) confronts a large number of individually insignificant and hence price taking competitive agents, who *follow* or respond to the actions of the leader [see §12.3.2]. The leader takes account of this response when choosing his actions. The appropriate equilibrium concept for such a market is the *Stackelberg* equilibrium named after von Stackelberg (1952). In the general form of this equilibrium, there is no requirement that the followers be competitive, merely that they ignore the effect their actions have on the leaders' choice of action (which then affects them). The leader, in contrast, operates at a higher level of sophistication, choosing his actions taking into account the predicted response of the followers. Unless the leader has some first mover advantage, it is difficult to justify such asymmetric behaviour unless the followers lack market power. In the present case in which we assume followers are competitive, this objection does not arise, and the equilibrium concept appears quite appropriate. In what follows we shall apply it to three problems. Within a country of competitive producers, the Government has market power and, in choosing its tax policy, can act as a leader [see §20.3]. In the world economy a large oil importer, such as the US, can in principle act as a leader if suppliers are competitive [see §20.4]. Finally, in the world oil market, OPEC, if it acts as a cohesive cartel, could act as a leader whilst the remaining small countries act as a competitive fringe of followers [see §20.5]. Clearly, in the oil market, there is an inconsistency between the second and third cases, where a model of bilateral oligopoly may be more appropriate, but the analysis of such a model would take us too far from the main theme of this chapter. The next few sections work through this catalogue of models and study the derivation and nature of the *binding contract Stackelberg equilibrium*, and examine its dynamic consistency.

20.3. THE TAXATION OF OIL PRODUCED IN A CLOSED ECONOMY

In the introduction it was remarked that the significant rents currently enjoyed by oil are very tempting objects of taxation. However, since tax rates will affect current supply decisions, it becomes important to see if currently announced tax plans are dynamically consistent, for it is difficult to bind future governments to adhere to the tax programs of their predecessors. In this and the next section, we illustrate the importance of this problem.

It is a familiar proposition of conventional tax theory that a tax on rent (or pure profits correctly defined) is non-distortionary. This is also true for exhaustible resources using the natural definition of rent, providing the future is predictable.

Suppose the cost of extracting q units of oil at date t is $C(q, S, t)$. Suppose also that there is a perfect substitute which can be produced indefinitely from a backstop technology at a cost $B(z, t)$ for supply z. Let the dollar value of consumption be $U(q + z, t)$ so that the efficient path solves

$$\text{Max} \int_0^\infty [U(q + z, t) - C(q, S, t) - B(z, t)]e^{-rt}\,dt, \qquad (20.3.1)$$

subject to $q = -\dot{S}$ where r is the rate of discount.

This problem can be solved using the Maximum Principle as in section 20.2. Define the transformed Hamiltonian H as before

$$H = U(q + z, t) - C(q, S, t) - B(z, t) - \lambda q.$$

Maximizing with respect to q, z gives:

$$\left.\begin{array}{c} \dfrac{\partial U}{\partial q} - \dfrac{\partial C}{\partial q} \leqslant \lambda \\ q \geqslant 0 \end{array}\right\} \text{ complementarily,}$$

$$\left.\begin{array}{c} \dfrac{\partial U}{\partial z} \leqslant \dfrac{\partial B}{\partial z} \\ z \geqslant 0 \end{array}\right\} \text{ complementarily.}$$

These equations have the following interpretation. The demand price of energy, $p = \partial U/\partial q$ or $\partial U/\partial z$, is initially equal to marginal cost plus rent, until it is exhausted at date T, say, after which it is determined by the marginal cost of the substitute (that is $p = \partial B/\partial z$ for $t \geqslant T$). The date of exhaustion, T, is the first date at which the price of oil, p, has risen to the marginal cost of replacing oil by the backstop, and the initial price is set to exhaust oil by that date. The time path of rent is given by the arbitrage equation (20.2.5).

$$\frac{d\lambda}{dt} - r\lambda = -\frac{\partial H}{\partial S} = \frac{\partial C}{\partial S}$$

which, substituting for λ, and replacing $\partial C/\partial q$ by c, gives

$$\frac{dp}{dt} = \frac{dc}{dt} + \frac{\partial C}{\partial S} + r(p - c), \quad 0 < t \leqslant T. \tag{20.3.2}$$

Note that in (20.3.2) and also (20.3.5), dc/dt is the total derivative [see IV, §5.4]:

$$\frac{dc}{dt} = \frac{\partial c}{\partial q}\frac{dq}{dt} + \frac{\partial c}{\partial S}\frac{dS}{dt} + \frac{\partial c}{\partial t}.$$

Now consider the effect of taxing rents, defined as $pq - C$, at a constant rate τ, so that competitive oil producers choose q to maximize

$$\int_0^\infty (1 - \tau)(pq - C)e^{-rt}\,dt,$$

subject to the same depletion condition as before. This time the (transformed) Hamiltonian is

$$H = (1 - \tau)\{pq - C(q, S, t)\} - \lambda q, \tag{20.3.3}$$

and, when q is positive

$$\frac{\partial H}{\partial q} = 0 \Rightarrow (1 - \tau)(p - c) = \lambda, \tag{20.3.4}$$

$$-\frac{\partial H}{\partial S} = \dot{\lambda} - r\lambda = (1 - \tau)\frac{\partial C}{\partial S},$$

whence

$$\frac{dp}{dt} = \frac{dc}{dt} + \frac{\partial C}{\partial S} + r(p - c), \tag{20.3.5}$$

exactly as for the efficient solution. Since the same terminal conditions on exhaustion apply, it follows that

PROPOSITION 20.3.1. *Any constant* ad valorem *tax on rent defined as revenue less current extraction costs imposed on a competitive exhaustible resource industry leaves extraction Pareto efficient.*

An excise tax on the output of a normal competitive industry is distortionary unless supply is completely inelastic, just as monopoly control of such an industry is distortionary. In the case of an exhaustible resource, provided that the marginal cost of extraction of the final unit is (sufficiently) below the terminal price, the total (cumulative) supply will be inelastic and hence a well chosen excise tax might be non-distortionary. This is true, and, indeed, in special cases an excise tax will be identical to a pure rent tax, allowing all the surplus to be taxed away.

Let p be the consumer (after tax) price, and p_n be the net producer price, so that the excise tax τ_e is $p - p_n$. Efficiency requires equation (20.3.2) to hold for p, whilst in equilibrium, during positive production the producer price facing competitive resource holders must satisfy (20.3.5), replacing p by p_n.

Excise taxes will be efficient, if, subtracting equation (20.3.5) from (20.3.2)

$$\frac{d\tau_e}{dt} = r\tau_e, \tag{20.3.6}$$

and

$$p_n - c \geqslant 0, \quad 0 \leqslant t \leqslant T.$$

The requirement that net rent remains positive is non-trivial, since it may severely limit the degree of excise taxation. In particular, if some oil is left in the ground because it is too expensive to extract, then the rent on this marginal oil will be zero, and there is no non-distortionary excise tax. Summarizing, we have

PROPOSITION 20.3.2. *An excise tax which rises at the rate of interest is non-distortionary provided that it does not drive producer rents below zero.*

It is interesting to note that although both excise taxes and rent taxes are non-distortionary, the time profile of tax payments will differ if costs are stock-dependent for the rent tax payments per unit of oil $T = \tau(p - C)$ will behave as

$$\frac{dT}{dt} = rT + \tau\frac{\partial C}{\partial S}, \tag{20.3.7}$$

from Equation (20.3.5), whilst the excise tax rises at the rate of interest. If costs are independent of stocks the two taxes are exactly equivalent.

The intuitive explanation of these results is that an excise tax rising at the rate of interest has constant present value, so that it acts as a lump sum tax provided it does not affect the amount of oil sold; that is, provided marginal oil is still worth extracting. It is equivalent to the static problem of an excise tax on an inelastically supplied commodity. If, in addition, marginal costs are constant and stock independent, the excise tax is exactly the same as the non-distortionary rent tax.

The next question to ask is whether these taxes are dynamically consistent. The difficulty in answering this question is that it is not obvious why the rent tax is set at one level rather than any other, so it is difficult to predict how future tax agencies might wish to alter it. As modelled, there is nothing to prevent the authorities from setting the tax rate at 99.9% with no adverse consequences, though in practice this seems implausible, for several reasons not captured in the model. The first is that the higher the rent tax (or profit taxes in general), the less the managerial incentive to reduce production costs and raise productivity. In short, some of the profits are reward for managerial effort and higher taxes will presumably have an adverse effect on this. This argument does not suggest that the optimum rate of tax will be changed over time, and hence does not introduce any potential inconsistency.

The main argument for non-confiscatory rent or profit tax for national resources is that the tax agency does not have a clear idea of the total stock of resources awaiting discovery and has to induce companies to explore and possibly waste resources in unproductive search, by the prospect of future profits. The problem with this argument is, as all oil companies are well aware, that after the oil has been proven and no more remains to be discovered, there is no reason why the tax agency should not increase the tax rate, as has happened in the North Sea, in Alaska, and in many other instances. Consequently, a low rent tax rate is dynamically inconsistent, and potentially highly distortionary, since the companies will expend considerable resources attempting to extract the oil under the currently favourable tax regime, rather than waiting and risking a more severe tax rate.

If taxes on domestically produced oil can in principle be efficient and dynamically consistent (though in practice there may be problems) the situation is quite different for oil import tariffs, as the next section shows.

20.4. OPTIMUM TARIFFS ON COMPETITIVELY SUPPLIED OIL

Whilst it is plausible that long-term supply contracts within a country can be legally enforced, the same is not true for international trade between sovereign nation states, as we remarked in the introduction. This can have profound consequences for the choice of import tariff policy for large countries like the US which import a large enough fraction of traded oil to be able to influence its price.

If we were to apply standard optimization techniques to derive the optimum tariff, we would implicitly and quite inappropriately be assuming that the tariff plan resulting would be adhered to, or the importing country could be bound to it. To demonstrate the implausibility of this, we shall calculate the optimum tariff on this assumption for a simple example. We suppose that all producers are competitive to avoid problems of bilateral monopoly.

To make the argument more transparent, assume that extraction costs are independent of stocks and flows and that every country has access to the backstop technology. The backstop can provide unlimited supplies of energy at a constant cost $\bar{p}(t)$. Our country derives dollar benefits $U(x)$ from the import and consumption of x units of oil, and the demand by the rest of the world for oil of price p is $y(p)$. The problem is to choose a level of imports x, a production level z from the backstop technology, and a price trajectory p to maximize

$$W = \int_0^\infty \{U(x+z) - px - \bar{p}z\}e^{-rt}dt, \tag{20.4.1}$$

subject to

$$-\dot{S} = x + y(p), \tag{20.4.2}$$

and the arbitrage equation which must be satisfied if competitive producers are to be willing to supply oil (cf. (20.2.12)):

$$\dot{p} = \dot{c} + r(p - c). \tag{20.4.3}$$

At some date T stocks of oil $S(T)$ will be exhausted and $p(T) = \bar{p}$, with the rest of the world switching to the backstop technology. The Hamiltonian is

$$H = (U - px - \bar{p}z)e^{-rt} - \mu\{x + y(p)\} + \lambda\{\dot{c} + r(p - c)\}. \tag{20.4.4}$$

Maximizing with respect to x, z:

$$\left.\begin{array}{c} U' \leqslant p + \mu e^{rt} \\ x \geqslant 0 \end{array}\right\} \text{ complementarily,} \tag{20.4.5}$$

$$\left.\begin{array}{c} U' \leqslant \bar{p} \\ z \geqslant 0 \end{array}\right\} \text{ complementarily,} \tag{20.4.6}$$

$$-\partial H/\partial S = \dot{\mu} = 0. \tag{20.4.7}$$

Since $U'(z)$ is the domestic price of oil, p^d, (or its perfect substitute), μe^{rt} is the import duty per unit of oil, and it rises at the rate of interest, just as did the efficient excise tax of the previous section. As soon as the domestic price reaches $\bar{p}$, the country stops importing and switches to the backstop.

The logic of the tariff is as follows. It is the least distortionary way of lowering the importer's total demand for oil, since the present value of the tariff is constant, and hence does not introduce any unnecessary rescheduling of supply and demand. The importer announces that he will switch to the backstop 'early' and thus plan to consume less oil in total, and this reduced claim on world oil drives down its price, to the advantage of the importer. An alternative way of looking at the tariff is that at date $t = 0$, oil reserves are auctioned off, on the understanding that there will be no future trade in oil. Consumers buy whatever quantity of reserves they plan to cumulatively consume, and then set domestic prices to use the reserves efficiently. The dominant importer buys fewer wells than if he behaved competitively, and hence has a higher domestic price which reaches the backstop price earlier. Notice that he still wants rent to rise at the rate of interest, hence the excess of his price over the competitive price (the tariff) must also rise at the rate of interest.

However, this tariff policy is clearly inconsistent for consider the position of the dominant importer just before the domestic price reaches the backstop. The reason he announced his willingness to switch to the backstop before other consumers was to drive the price of oil down, and he has by now exhausted all the benefits of that strategy, and merely faces the costs of continuing to follow his stated plan, namely, the cost of more expensive backstop instead of cheaper imported oil. Hence the temptation to change his plan. In terms of the oil well auction story, the dominant importer would announce that he has bought enough oil not to need to buy later in the world market, but, of course, having exhausted his own oil early he would in fact like to buy more later. If the dominant importer cannot bind himself to his import tariff policy (and we would argue that in practice he cannot) then suppliers will predict that he will depart from this stated tariff policy, and hence drive up the price of oil in the future. Anticipating this, they will delay early oil sales and drive up the price. The inability to bind himself to future actions harms the importer.

Thus the binding contract tariff is not a credible plan—rational producers will not believe that the dominant importer will follow it. How does one find a credible plan, that is a plan which it will be in the interest of the dominant importer to follow when the time comes, or equivalently, how can the Stackelberg feedback strategy be computed? The idea is straightforward but in general solving the problem is very difficult. The first step is to solve for the last period, just before exhaustion, when there remains no further future to be inconsistent. Then, given the final period actions, one can compute the penultimate set of actions, assuming that in the final period choices will be as already solved, and so on, recursively, back to the present. The following example will illustrate this, and is taken from Maskin and Newbery (1978), where a fuller discussion is provided.

20.4.1. Simple two-period model of oil tariffs

Competitive oil producers must exhaust a stock of oil, S, in periods 1 and 2 before a cheap substitute becomes available in period 3. Extraction is costless, hence producers only supply in both periods if they expect the price at i, p_i, to satisfy

$$p_1 = \beta p_2, \qquad (20.4.8)$$

where β is the discount factor. The dominant importer derives net \$ utility

$$U' = a' \log x_1 + \beta \log x_2 - (p_1 x_1 + \beta p_2 x_2), \qquad (20.4.9)$$

from imports and consumption x_i in period i, and the rest of the world has demand

$$y_1 = \frac{b'}{p_1}, \quad y_2 = \frac{1}{p_2}. \qquad (20.4.10)$$

Define new variables $a' = a\beta$, $b = b'\beta$, $p = p_2$, so $p_1 = \beta p$, and the dominant importer's utility function can be written

$$U = U'/\beta = a \log x_1 + \log x_2 - px_1 - px_2. \qquad (20.4.11)$$

The *competitive equilibrium* forms a useful benchmark, and is easily computed. The dominant importer, or monopsonist, chooses x_i, given p as parametric, to maximize U:

$$x_1 = \frac{a}{p}, \ x_2 = \frac{1}{p}, \ x_1 + x_2 + y_1 + y_2 = S = \frac{a+b+2}{p}. \qquad (20.4.12)$$

Hence

$$p = (a+b+2)/S.$$

In the *binding contract* equilibrium the monopsonist allows for the effect his demand has on price. Since p only depends on his total demand, $X = x_1 + x_2$, the problem is best broken into two stages: maximizing

$$a \log x_1 + \log x_2 - p(x_1 + x_2),$$

gives [see IV, §5.6]

$$x_1 = \frac{aX}{1+a}, \quad x_2 = \frac{X}{1+a}. \qquad (20.4.13)$$

But total demand equals total supply or

$$X = S - y_1 - y_2 = S - \frac{1+b}{p} = X(p). \qquad (20.4.14)$$

The monoponist's utility is now a function of p:

$$U(p) = a \log \frac{X(p)}{1+a} + \log \frac{X(p)}{1+a} - pX(p), \qquad (20.4.15)$$

and, choosing X, or equivalently, choosing p, yields

$$\frac{dU}{dp} = 0 : p = \frac{1+b+\sqrt{(1+b)^2 + 4(1+a)(1+b)}}{2S}. \qquad (20.4.16)$$

To interested reader can check that this equilibrium can be sustained by a constant *ad valorem* tariff, as has been computed above. (Note that prices rise at the rate of interest with zero extraction costs.)

Finally, the *rational expectations Stackelberg equilibrium*, or the feedback Stackelberg equilibrium, is found recursively [cf. IV, Chapter 16], solving first for the final period. Let S_1 be stock at the start of the second period, then the monopsonist chooses x_2 to maximize

$$\log x_2 - px_2 \text{ subject to } x_2 = S_1 - 1/p, \tag{20.4.17}$$

Thus

$$x_2 = \frac{g-1}{p}, \ p = \frac{g}{S_1}, \tag{20.4.18}$$

where $g \equiv \frac{1}{2}(1 + \sqrt{5}) = 1.618$, the golden mean [see IV, §15.9.4].

In the first period demand equals supply: $x_1 + y_1 = S - S_1$, or

$$x_1 = S - \frac{b}{p} - \frac{g}{p} = S - \frac{G}{p}, \ G \equiv g + b. \tag{20.4.19}$$

Again, x_1 and x_2 are functions of p, and the monopsonist's problem is to choose x_i, or, equivalently, p, to maximize

$$U(p) = a\log\left(S - \frac{G}{p}\right) + \log\left(\frac{g-1}{p}\right) - p\left(S - \frac{1+b}{p}\right), \tag{20.4.20}$$

whence

$$p = \frac{G - 1 + \sqrt{(G+1)^2 + 4aG}}{2S}. \tag{20.4.21}$$

Given numerical values, p, x_i, and hence U, can be computed. For example, if $a = 0.2, b = 5, S = 1$ (this is just a normalization), then the various equilibria are as shown in Table 20.1. It will be seen that $U_2 > U_1 > U_3$, subscripts referring to equilibria. The monopsonist is disadvantaged by his market power if the suppliers correctly forecast his future actions, and is worse-off than as a competitive importer. The producers are also worse-off in the Stackelberg equilibrium than with binding contracts (their profits are $p_1 S = \beta p S$).

In this example the monopsonist is disadvantaged because he places a relatively high premium on second period imports, and has relatively greater monopsony power then. (In competitive equilibrium he counts for only 4% of the first period demand, but 50% of the second period's.) His incentive to renege on the initial tariff plan is thus great, and can only be eliminated by reducing

Table 20.1 Comparison of equilibria

	Competitive (1)	Binding Contract (2)	Stackelberg (3)
p	7.2	7.025	6.788
x_1	0.028	0.024	0.025
x_2	0.139	0.122	0.091
U	-3.891	-3.875	-3.921

second period supplies to the point where his great need for consumption offsets his monopsony power. This is done by producers, who fear a low second period price selling more in the first period, and driving the price below the binding contract price. The example is thus rather extreme, but bears an unpleasant similarity to the US position, itself derived from past profligacy in consuming domestic oil stocks. The boundary values for a, b, such that the Stackelberg equilibrium is no worse then the competitive equilibrium roughly satisfy $b^* = 2 + 4.6a^*$, for $0 < a < 1$. For $b < b^*$ or $a > a^*$ the monopsonist is advantaged by his market power.

This example is interesting for several reasons. It demonstrates rather dramatically the consequences of the dynamic inconsistency of the binding contract equilibrium when there are in fact no binding contracts. It therefore is a sharp reminder that a mechanical application of the Maximum Principle which derives the binding contract equilibrium may give the wrong solution. And it shows that the correct solution can, in principle, be computed. The next section looks at the last class of Stackelberg problem to be discussed, and takes up another of the themes of the introduction, namely that relatively simple principles allow a diagrammatic or algebraic solution for the binding contract equilibrium if demand is static and costs constant. The section follows Newbery (1981) closely.

20.5. MODELLING THE WORLD OIL MARKET

The world oil market consists of a variety of producers differing in their power, extraction costs, and discount rates. The problem is to forecast the equilibrium time path or trajectory of the price of oil, where a trajectory is an equilibrium if no agent wishes to alter his extraction plan given the forecast, and these extraction plans together generate the forecast price trajectory. The equilibrium must, therefore, be consistent with each producer's perceptions of his market power, and this requires selecting an appropriate equilibrium concept for the industry. One of the more attractive simple possibilities is to distinguish between a cartel, who act as a cohesive and dominant supplier, and the rest, who act as a competitive fringe. The advantage of this characterization is that it avoids the implausible extremes of perfect competition and pure monopoly, without running into the difficulties of characterizing an oligopolistic equilibrium. It seems, therefore, a useful benchmark, and has been defended as a first approximation to the oil market by Pindyck (1978) on the grounds that the gains to OPEC from forming the cartel are large relative to the profits which would otherwise accrue to the suppliers. On this view there is considerable incentive for maintaining the cartel intact.

Thus again we can use the Stackelberg equilibrium concept, which is characterized as follows. The dominant producer acts as the leader who announces a supply strategy. The fringe producers are each individually incapable of influencing the price at any date, and therefore take the price as given when determining their supply plans. The leader chooses his best supply plan taking into account the effect it will have on the market price and hence on the supply decisions of the fringe producers. One of the most interesting questions to ask is how far the presence of a competitive fringe reduces the market power of the cartel compared to the pure monopoly equilibrium, where the benchmark is the competitive equilibrium.

We shall first show how to calculate the Binding Contract Stackelberg equilibrium for the static demand, constant cost case and then enquire whether the equilibrium is dynamically consistent. To do so we appeal to the principles stated in section 20.2, namely *Hotelling's arbitrage* principle, the *terminal price* principal and the *exhaustion* principle. To these must be added a further principle to deal with the presence of a competitive fringe limiting the power of the dominant producers.

The *limit pricing principle* calculates the monopoly price associated with a given marginal revenue, as discussed above in section 20.2.4. There we showed how to solve for a monopolist's price and sales given a limit price set by a backstop technology, but the same principle can be applied if the limit price is set by the willingness of a competitive fringe to sell at any price at or above $p(t)$. However, it is important to distinguish between two possibilities.

(*i*) *Prices Facing Fringe Unaffected by Cartel Reallocations.* The presence of a competitive fringe will typically set a limit price which constrains the cartel over some part of its extraction plan. In general, if it reallocates oil from the period when it is unconstrained to the period when it is constrained, this will affect the date and the price at which the fringe sells its oil. As a result of this change, the whole price path facing the cartel will be shifted, and the change in cartel profits will not just equal the instantaneous marginal revenue of Equation (20.2.9), but will be the (discounted) change in revenue at each date at which the price changes. If, however, the reallocation of cartel oil leaves the fringe unaffected, then the marginal revenue is given by the conventional static formula of Equation (20.2.9). An example may help to clarify this distinction. Consider first the case in which the cartel faces a backstop technology and a competitive fringe whose (constant) extraction cost c^f are significantly higher than those of the cartel, c^m. (We adopt the superscripts f for fringe, m for both monopoly and a cohesive cartel.) The price path, shown again measuring the time *before* exhaustion, is shown in Figure 20.7.

In the absence of the fringe, the monopoly price trajectory would be ABCDE, as in Figure 20.6 located by the marginal revenue which is asymptotic to the extraction cost, c^m. If the fringe has high extraction costs, c^f, then the competitive price path would have the same form as BD, asymptotic to c^f, and therefore less steep than the monopoly price path. Confronted with such a limit price path, the cartel would prefer to advance its sales and sell at the lower end of the competitive price path. Thus, the different phases are readily pieced together. The fringe is the

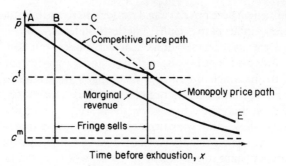

Figure 20.7: Cartel facing high cost fringe

sole supplier along DB, along which $p - c^f$ rises at the rate of interest. The length of the bite BD taken out of the unconstrained monopoly path ABCDE is determined by the condition that the fringe exhaust along DB. The leader is then the sole supplier along ED and BA.

Why can the presence of the fringe be essentially ignored in computing the price path (except for the bite which the fringe takes out along DB)? The reason is that the competitive trajectory is fixed at B (at the backstop price) and has a length BD determined solely by the condition that the fringe stock be cumulatively exhausted along DB. The position of D does not therefore depend on the actions of the cartel. Moreover, the cartel is free to transfer oil from A to any point along DE without affecting the location of the competitive price path BD, and hence without affecting the location of the monopoly path DE.

(*ii*) *Prices facing fringe affected by cartel allocations.* Contrast this with the case in which the fringe has only a slight cost disadvantage over the cartel, so that the competitive price path is steeper than the monopoly price path, as shown in Figure 20.8.

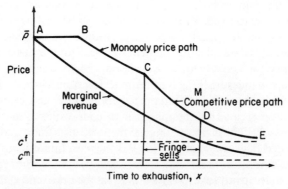

Figure 20.8: Cartel constrained by competitive fringe

The monopoly price path is ABCM, asymptotic to some price above c^f, and the steeper competitive price path is CDE. As Ulph and Folie (1981) show, the cartel will split its sales into two phases: ED, during which time it is constrained by the limit pricing competitive fringe, and CBA, during which time the cartel is unconstrained by the fringe. It is easy to show that it would not pay the cartel to confine its sales to the later unconstrained period CBA, for the following reason. Suppose its sales were confined to CBA, with the fringe selling first from D to C. Consider a transfer of one unit of oil from date C to the initial date D. It would sell at a price D, above the marginal revenue trajectory at the point, F, and hence would be attractive. Since it sold at a lower price than C, it would be sold faster, and hence the date at which the monopoly phase would be reached would be sooner, which is also attractive. Hence both factors make it attractive to advance sales. Notice, however, that transfers from ABC to DE *shift the location of the competitive phase* CD, and hence alter the timing of the monopoly phase, and the price at each point at which the cartel sells. There is no longer any simple way to measure the marginal revenue of selling more along the phase DE, and hence no simple way of computing the location of the two phases. Ulph and Folie (1981) suggest that this is best done by finding the location of each phase ABC, CD, DE, as a function of cumulative sales along each segment, and then allocating the cartel total stock between ABC and DE to maximize its profits. This will typically require a (very simple) computer search since profits are a complex implicit function of the allocation of stocks.

Whether the first or second case applies depends on the relation between the extraction costs, and is considered further in the Appendix.

20.5.1. Solving for the price trajectory

We wish to find the rational expectations Stackelberg equilibrium in which the cartel acts as a single cohesive dominant producer whilst the remaining oil producers act as a competitive fringe, and contrast this with the binding contract equilibrium. We shall assume that marginal extraction costs are constant, but differ between the cartel and the fringe. There are four cases to consider, and only in the first case is the binding contract equilibrium dynamically consistent. Except for the third case all suppliers face the same rate of discount. In the first case the fringe has sufficiently higher extraction costs than the cartel that it wishes to defer extraction until the cartel is exhausted. Since the fringe does not enter the market until after the cartel has exhausted its presence causes no problems of dynamic inconsistency and the equilibrium price trajectory is easy to derive. In the second case the cartel has higher extraction costs than the fringe. In fact OPEC (the cartel) has lower extraction costs than the fringe, but the second case raises the problem of dynamic inconsistency in a simple form and is a useful introduction to the third case, in which the cartel faces a lower rate of discount than the fringe, and also has lower extraction costs.

The final case is in some ways the most interesting, and is also empirically plausible. Here the fringe has extraction costs which are greater than the cartel's, but not sufficiently great to cause it to delay extraction until after the cartel is exhausted. In his case Ulph (1980) demonstrated that the binding contract equilibrium was dynamically inconsistent, though the inconsistency is of a more subtle kind than in the other cases. It therefore provides a searching test of our proposed solution.

20.5.2. Fringe delay extraction until end of monopoly phase

Again let c denote marginal cost, and use superscript m to refer to the dominant producer or cartel, f to refer to the fringe, then the fringe will delay extraction until the end of the monopoly phase provided the competitive price path is less steep than the monopoly price path, as shown in Figure 20.7. The Appendix shows that this requires the fringe extraction costs to be sufficiently greater than the cartel's costs. In Figure 20.7, the competitive phase comes after the monopoly phase, but is itself followed by a limit pricing phase in which the cartel sells at the backstop price. Instead of solving explicitly for this case, let us consider the case in which there is a linear demand schedule, given by Equation (20.2.11), and no backstop technology. (This case is explicitly solved in Ulph and Folie (1981) by computational, rather than graphical methods, and is thus of some interest in demonstrating the power of the graphical method.) The Appendix shows that the required condition on the extraction costs for this case is $c^f > \frac{1}{2}(c^m + \bar{p})$.

The price path with a competitive fringe is shown in Figure 20.9, again plotted as a function of the time *before* exhaustion, x. The price trajectory is BCE, with exhaustion taking a period T and occurring at price $\bar{p}$. During BC the cartel is unconstrained by the fringe, during CD the cartel is constrained by the competitive price path CDE, but is the sole supplier. The cartel exhausts at D, and the fringe then supplies along DE. The location of these points is found as follows. The point E is fixed at the choke price, $\bar{p}$, and the price at date x years before exhaustion is, from Equation (20.2.13):

$$p_x^f = c^f + (\bar{p} - c^f)e^{-rx}. \tag{20.5.1}$$

Demand at each point along DE is thus determined by Equation (20.2.14) replacing c by c^f, and the length of the phase DE is such that total consumption is equal to total fringe stocks, Q^f. If the length of this phase is τ years, then τ solves Equation (20.2.15):

$$b(\bar{p} - c^f)\psi(r, \tau) = Q^f. \tag{20.5.2}$$

At the point D the cartel's marginal rent (marginal revenue less marginal cost) must be equal to the competitive price (since the fringe imposes a limit price path CDE on the cartel), and along AD the marginal rent rises at the rate of interest. Along BC the unconstrained monopoly price implied by the marginal rent is below the competitive price path, but between C and D the cartel must limit price. The length of the phase BCD is again determined by the condition that cumulative consumption is equal to the cartel's stock of oil.

Notice that the cartel is free to reallocate oil along BC and to D without affecting the location of the competitive price path (or, to be precise, without affecting the transition price D, and hence without affecting the location of the cartel's trajectory BCD). We can therefore invoke the *limit pricing principle* of section 20.5, case (i), and establish a simple relationship between price and marginal revenue. If p_τ is the price at D, fixed by Equations (20.5.1) and (20.5.2), then the marginal revenue trajectory ADG satisfies

$$m_x = c^m + (p_\tau - c^m)e^{r(\tau - x)},$$

again measuring x from the date of exhaustion, whilst the monopoly path BCHG satisfies equation (20.2.16):

$$p_x^m = \tfrac{1}{2}(m_x + \bar{p}).$$

Notice also that there is no problem of dynamic inconsistency, as the cartel exhausts first, and is compelled to adhere to its plan because the fringe retains oil which it would be willing and able to sell if ever the price rose above CDE.

Ulph and Folie (1981) conjecture that if the fringe joins the cartel in this case then it will *lower* the initial price and hence possibly reduce the inefficiency of resource allocation—an interesting example of a second-best policy where apparently reducing competitiveness may increase efficiency. The advantage of the graphical approach is that it is easy to prove that the initial price *must* be reduced if the fringe joins the cartel. Fix the terminal price at E, in Figure 20.9, and, since the marginal revenue is equal to the price at the choke price $\bar{p}$(or E), once the fringe joins the cartel its *marginal revenue* must now follow the path

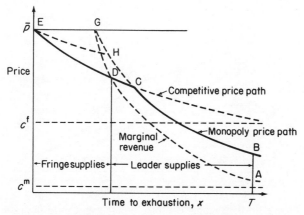

Figure 20.9: Dominant producer price trajectory

CDE up to the point E. The price associated with this marginal revenue is the path HE. As shown, at H the fringe's (monopoly) price meets the cartel's price path BCHG, so that BCHE is a possible price trajectory for the unified cartel—except that it lies above the previous trajectory BCDE. There is thus less consumption along the new price path, which means that the time taken to exhaust the stock must be longer, and hence the initial price lower.

20.5.3. Cartel's costs above fringe costs

Though empirically implausible, this case illustrates the general point established by Maskin and Newbery (1978) that in the absence of binding contracts the rational expectations equilibrium differs from and is inferior to the equilibrium which would emerge if binding contracts could be enforced. It is also the case which has been fully analysed in the special case of unit elastic demand by Newbery (1980). The problem is simply stated. If

$$c^f < c^m$$

then the competitive phase will come before the monopoly phase if the elasticity of demand is constant or increasing with price. The cartel will wish to sell some oil during the competitive phase, when it will face a limit price set by the ability of fringe producers to reallocate sales along the competitive phase. However, since the cartel has higher costs than the fringe it will wish to sell at the end of the competitive phase rather than at the beginning (in contrast to the cases shown in Figure 20.7 and 20.8.) This requires the fringe to exhaust its stocks before the price reaches the unconstrained monopoly level, but if this happens, the cartel will no longer be constrained by the ability of the fringe to limit price, and so will raise the price. Anticipating this, the fringe will hold back oil, forcing the cartel to supply earlier than it would like.

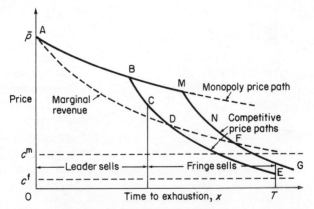

Figure 20.10: Binding contract and Nash–Cournot price trajectories

This can be seen by examining the binding contract Stackelberg equilibrium which is shown in Figure 20.10.

ADF is the marginal revenue trajectory, asymptotic to the cartel's cost, c^m, ABM is the implied monopoly price trajectory on the assumption that the cartel is unconstrained, and BCD is a competitive price trajectory steeper than the monopoly price path.

The binding contract equilibrium is again found as in Figure 20.8. The leader (cartel) allocates his sales between the monopoly path AB and the competitive path BC to maximize his profit. The shorter is AB, the lower will be the price along the phase CE when the fringe sells, and the more rapidly will it be exhausted, to the advantage of the leader. This must be balanced against the disadvantage of selling at a price along BC below the monopoly level.

It is easy to demonstrate that this solution is dynamically inconsistent. The length of the competitive phase BC is an increasing function of the size of the fringe stock—if this were negligible there would be little advantage in accelerating fringe sales and C would be close to B. As time proceeds and fringe stocks are depleted, so the leader would like to shorten the period of competitive sales, BC—in other words, having derived some advantage from keeping down the competitive price in the shape of rapid depletion of the fringe, he would now like to draw up a plan more advantageous to himself.

It is thus clear that this solution is not a rational expectations equilibrium in the absence of binding contracts, for, running time in the correct direction, it requires the fringe to sell all its oil along EDC. At C, the leader no longer has to face any further competition from the fringe, and he is free to raise the price to the unconstrained monopoly trajectory ABM. The fringe will therefore hold back oil in the expectation of a capital gain, and the proposed solution will break down.

What, then, is the rational expectations equilibrium without binding contracts? It must satisfy two conditions: the fringe must not exhaust before reaching the unconstrained monopoly price trajectory if it is to remove the risk of a price jump, and the leader must have no incentive to deviate from the price path before it reaches the unconstrained monopoly path—after this the monopolist will not wish to deviate from the predicted trajectory. This was the solution strategy followed in solving for the simple version of the optimum oil import tariff above, and the new technique can be applied in a correspondingly simplified version of the present model (see Newbery, 1981). In general, however, it is exceedingly difficult to solve for the Rational Expectations Stackelberg equilibrium (or feedback Stackelberg equilibrium) and it is interesting to ask whether there are other equilibrium concepts which are dynamically consistent, and which reflect the market power of the producer (or producers, if OPEC is viewed as a collection of rival oligopolists). Fortunately, there is such an equilibrium concept, which is both familiar in oligopoly theory [see §12.13], and easy to compute. It is the (open loop) Nash–Cournot equilibrium in which each producer chooses his supply plan on the assumption that he will have no effect on other producers' supply plans. Its derivation and application are described in the next section.

20.5.4. The Nash–Cournot equilibrium

The terminology describes the equilibrium—a Nash equilibrium is one in which agents make plans simultaneously, and thus assume that they cannot affect the plans of others. They then choose the best plan given the predicted choices of others, who are likewise assumed to follow the same rule in choosing their plans. A Cournot equilibrium is one in which the choices are about levels of supply. Thus producer i at date τ chooses a production level $q^i(t)$ for $\tau \leq t \leq T$ to maximize

$$\int_\tau^T e^{-r(t-\tau)}[p\{q^i(t) + Q^{-i}(t)\}q^i(t) - C(q^i)]\,dt, \qquad (20.5.3)$$

subject to

$$q^i(t) = -\dot{S}^i(t), \quad \tau \leq t \leq T,$$

and

$$Q^{-i}(t) = \sum_{j \neq i} q^j(t), \quad \text{given.}$$

Rather than solving this (straightforward) problem using the Maximum Principle, we shall derive the intuitive solution for the present simple problem in which the fringe is competitive, costs are constant, and demand static.

Suppose at some date that the fringe sells q^* regardless of the amount sold by the dominant producer. His (static) marginal revenue from selling q is then

$$m \equiv \frac{d}{dq}[qp(q^* + q)] = p\left(1 - \frac{\alpha}{\varepsilon}\right) \qquad (20.5.4)$$

where

$$\alpha = \frac{q}{q + q^*}$$

is the producer's share of total supply, and ε is the elasticity of total demand (cf. Equation (20.2.9)). The fringe, predicting that this will be the dominant producer's choice, will choose $q^*(t)$ to arbitrage their competitive rent over the period in which they plan to sell, and hence, during this period, the price will be set at the competitive level. The dominant producer's marginal revenue, if he is willing to supply, is set by the usual intertemporal conditions, and hence, if p and m are fixed functions of time, and since ε, the elasticity of demand, is a function of p, the only unknown in Equation (20.5.4) is the market share, α:

$$\alpha = \varepsilon\left(\frac{p - m}{p}\right). \qquad (20.5.5)$$

It is now straightforward to solve for the Nash–Cournot equilibrium for the problem just considered. In Figure 20.10 the Nash–Cournot equilibrium has the form ABMFG. Along ABM the leader is the unconstrained sole supplier. Along MNF (until the competitive price path cuts the marginal revenue path ADF) both the fringe and the leader simultaneously supply, and the market share of the leader is given by the Nash–Cournot solution of Equation (20.5.5) for both the price and marginal revenue are already fixed.

At point F (where $m = p$) the leader ceases to supply and the remainder of the phase FG is solely supplied by the competitor. The transition point M is found from the requirement that consumption of the leader over ABMF is equal to his stock, and the point G is found from the requirement that consumption of the fringe over MFG is equal to the fringe stock. The difference between the Nash–Cournot equilibrium and the binding contract equilibrium is that the leader has no choice over the point of transition, since his sales over MF are completely fixed by Equation (20.5.5), leaving a fixed amount to sell on the monopoly phase ABM. The relative location of MFG and BCDE will depend on the size of the initial fringe stocks, and it is possible that they could concide. If, however, the Nash–Cournot path lies to the right of the binding contract path in Figure 20.10, then the time taken to exhaust all the oil is longer and the initial price higher, and conversely if the Nash–Cournot path is to the left. This can be readily seen if we transfer the information from Figure 20.10 to Figure 20.11, which has time running in the conventional direction. In this case the initial price must be higher under Nash–Cournot, because one price trajectory cannot lie entirely above the other and still have the same total consumption. The lower part of the figure shows how the market gradually passes from the fringe to the leader along F'M'. The lower part of Figure 20.11 is shown for the linear demand function of Equation (20.2.11). For other demand functions, the dominant producer's sales can be discontinuous at M, though this makes no difference to the analysis. For the two cases of constant demand elasticity or linear demand it is simple to solve for the Nash–Cournot path. Thus if elasticity of demand is constant:

$$q = ap^{-\varepsilon}$$

then Equation (20.5.4) or (20.5.5) gives

$$q^m = a\varepsilon(p - m)p^{-(1+\varepsilon)}.$$

Since p and m are simple functions of the time to exhaustion, x, cumulative extraction can be readily found and the location of points G and E fixed. If, on the other hand, the demand schedule is linear, and given by Equation (20.2.11), then q^m can be found directly:

$$q^m = b(p - m). \tag{20.5.6}$$

Again, since p and m are known, q^m can be found.

Is the Nash–Cournot equilibrium (NCE) then the rational expectations

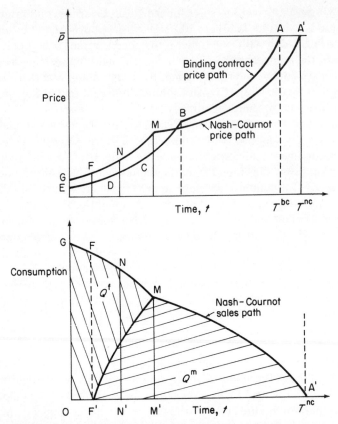

Figure 20.11: Price and consumption trajectories compared

Stackelberg equilibrium (RESE)? Notice first that it is dynamically consistent, for the following reason. Suppose, in Figure 20.11, that the phase GN has already elapsed, with the associated consumption of fringe and leader's stocks implied by the area OGNN' in the lower part of Figure 20.11. The Nash–Cournot path starting from point N would coincide with the original path, since the transition point M is fixed not by the leader's choice, but by the requirement that the fringe be exhausted by M whilst satisfying the market share condition of Equation (20.5.5). Next, suppose that the competitive fringe is following the proposed trajectory GFNM in Figure 20.11, then once it reaches F it has a fixed residual stock which it must, over the remaining time, inelastically supply. Moreoever, along the equilibrium price path FNM the fringe will inelastically supply the required amount at each date to induce the leader to keep the price on the predicted trajectory. If the leader undersupplies, and the fringe expanded to make up the short fall, then the fringe would run out before M, and the leader would be free to raise the price. In this case the fringe would do better by not expanding its supply and waiting to make a capital gain. Consequently it would seem that the leader is unable to force the fringe to deviate from its supply plan, in which case the best it can achieve is the Nash–Cournot equilibrium of Equation (20.5.4). The fringe is content to exhaust at M because the leader then has no incentive to deviate from MBA, as it has on the unconstrained monopoly path.

However, persuasive though this argument is, it is not strong enough to prove that the rational expectations Stackelberg equilibrium is the Nash–Cournot equilibrium in cases where the binding contract equilibrium is dynamically inconsistent. The reason is that the Nash–Cournot equilibrium attributes too little power to the leader, who does have some influence over the supply plans of the fringe. In particular, the leader is assumed to have no choice in the allocation of his sales between the monopoly phase ABM of Figure 20.11 and the competitive phase MNF, since his sales along MNF are fixed by Equation (20.5.5). If the leader were to change his allocation between these two phases he would alter the supply response of the fringe, and so he must be presumed to optimize against this instead of ignoring it, as in Nash–Cournot.

Newbery (1980) shows how this is done for the special case of a leader facing a unit elastic demand, a fixed terminal date after which oil is valueless (because replaced by a cheap substitute) and a fringe whose extraction costs are zero. Given these very strong assumptions it is possible to solve for the RESE and show that it differs from the Nash–Cournot equilibrium but has the form of a perturbation from this equilibrium, whose magnitude decreases with the time remaining on the competitive phase. In this sense the Nash–Cournot equilibrium is an approximation to the correct equilibrium, with the advantage that it can be easily computed. Indeed, except in highly special cases, it appears that the RESE is almost insuperably difficult to solve.

However, whilst it is not possible to give a general solution for the present case, it is possible to draw on the insights of Newbery (1980) to investigate its relation to the NCE. First, in Figure 20.10, it is clear that the RESE and NCE must coincide at their intersection with the monopoly price path at M, for in that last period the sale of the fringe really are fixed. The question is then what happens before this date, along the competitive phase GFNM? Certainly the price path must still be GFNM if it is to be a rational expectations equilibrium for otherwise the fringe would retain profitable arbitrage opportunities. The only question is then the level of sales by the leader. The lower is the price and the further away from the transition point M, the larger will be the unexhausted fringe stocks, and the greater will be the attraction to the leader of accelerating their sales and advancing the date of reaching the monopoly price path. This suggests that the leader sells progressively less than the Nash–Cournot level as the distance from M and the size of fringe stocks increase, in order to induce the fringe to sell at a faster rate. Certainly this is the case in the example solved in Newbery (1980). If so, then this suggests that the monopoly phase will be longer in the RESE than in the NCE, as the leader will sell less during the competitive phase, and the difference between the RESE and the NCE will increase with the size of the competitive fringe stocks.

To summarize, if the intuition gained from the analysis by Newbery (1980) is applicable in the present case, the rational expectations Stackelberg equilibrium price path will have the same form as the Nash–Cournot equilibrium, except that the monopoly phase will be longer. The total time taken to exhaust will also be longer, and the initial price will be higher

20.5.5. Different discount rates

One of the main sources of inefficiency in the world energy market is the inability of the 'Low Absorbing' OPEC producers to earn a satisfactory real rate of return on their overseas assets. A simple model of this capital market imperfection would have the cartel discounting at a lower rate of interest, r^m, than the fringe, r^f, whilst enjoying lower extraction costs:

$$r^m < r^f, c^m < c^f.$$

A wide variety of possible trajectories is possible, depending on the parameters of the model, but it is clear that the problem of dynamic inconsistency must arise if the cartel wishes (*ex ante*) to sell oil at the competitive price after the fringe has exhausted its stock. Figure 20.12 illustrates one possibility. The cartel faces a backstop technology which sets a limit price at $\bar{p}$. Immediately below this price demand is elastic and the unconstrained monopoly price path is BCM, the point B being fixed by the limit pricing rule as in Figure 12.5. CDEF is a competitive price path, asymptotic to the fringe extraction cost, c^f. HDEG is a path along which the present value of the cartel's rent, $p - c^m$, discounted at the lower rate of discount, r^m, is constant. HDEG is asymptotic to the lower cartel extraction cost, c^m, but because $r^m < r^f$, it may cut CDEF at a point where it is less steep, at D, as shown.

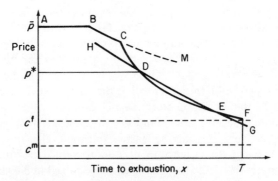

Figure 20.12: Dynamic inconsistency because of lower discount rates

In this case, the binding contract equilibrium has the cartel selling in two separate phases: initially, along FE, and finally, along DCBA. The fringe exhausts between E and D, and its stock determines the length of this phase and hence the location of the constant present value path HDEG. The only remaining choice open to the cartel is the position of the transition from the monopoly path to the competitive path at C. The lower this is set, the more rapidly the fringe is exhausted, but the more oil will be sold at the competitive rather than the monopoly price. As with Figure 20.8, the optimum is found by balancing those costs and benefits, and cannot, unfortunately, be found by simple graphical methods.

Clearly, the binding contract equilibrium is dynamically inconsistent, as the cartel will wish to raise its price at D, once the fringe is exhausted. For this configuration to be possible the competitive price path must be steeper at D (and price p^*) than the constant present value path, HDEG, or

$$r^f(p^* - c^f) > r^m(p^* - c^m),$$

whilst p^* must be below the monopoly price path BCM. A sufficient condition for this is for

$$\frac{r^f}{r^m} > \frac{\hat{p} - c^m}{\hat{p} - c^f} > 1,$$

where $\hat{p}$ is the minimum price at which the monopolist would be willing to sell if unconstrained, that is where marginal rent is zero. If the elasticity of demand at $\hat{p}$ is ε, then

$$\hat{p} = \frac{c^m}{1 - 1/\varepsilon},$$

whilst for the linear demand case

$$\hat{p} = \tfrac{1}{2}(\bar{p} + c^m).$$

Notice that if the fringe has sufficient stocks, the competitive price path will eventually cut the constant present value (at E, yielding two phases during which the cartel sells, but if the fringe stocks are small, the initial price will be above E and the cartel will withhold all sales until D. Notice also that if demand in inelastic, but there is a backstop technology, then the problem of dynamic inconsistency *always* arises if

$$\frac{r^m}{r^f} < \frac{\bar{p} - c^f}{\bar{p} - c^m},$$

(cf. the special cases considered by Gilbert (1978) in which the problem does not arise because $r^m = r^f$, $c^m = c^f = 0$). Most estimates and predictions agree that oil demand is price inelastic, and not implausible numbers would be (in US$ 1980)

$\bar{p} > \$30$, $c^f > \$10$, $c^m < \$5$, suggesting that if $r^m < (4/5)r^f$ the problem of dynamic inconsistency will arise. This *could* explain why OPEC is currently selling oil despite the inelastic demand (though capacity constraints on depletion rates are also potentially important determinants of extraction rates and have been ignored in this analysis. See Gilbert (1978) for a discussion of their importance.)

Since the present oil market is probably best described by an inelastic demand up to a backstop price it is of some interest to explore this case further. Suppose the demand schedule is piecewise linear:

$$q = b(a - p), \quad p \le \bar{p} < 2a,$$
$$= 0, \qquad\quad p > \bar{p},$$

which has an elasticity at price p of

$$\varepsilon = \frac{p}{a - p} < 1 \quad \text{for} \quad p \le \bar{p} < 2a.$$

Figure 20.13 illustrates one possible configuration, again with the direction of time reversed to exploit the fact that the price paths are anchored by the exhaustion date. AFM is the marginal revenue trajectory, decreasing slowly becasue of the low cartel discount rate, r^m, and asymptotic to the cartel's costs, c^m.

BCD, EFG are competitive price paths, steeper because of the high fringe discount rate r^f, asymptotic to the higher fringe costs, c^f. Fringe stocks are assumed small enough for only one intersection with the marginal revenue, as at F.

ABCD is the binding contract price trajectory, with the fringe as sole supplier over DC, and the cartel being the sole supplier over CBA. Since the cartel is no longer constrained by the fringe at C it will wish to raise the price to the monopoly level, which, since demand is inelastic below $\bar{p}$, is at (strictly, infinitesimally below) the backstop price, $\bar{p}$, and so the binding contract

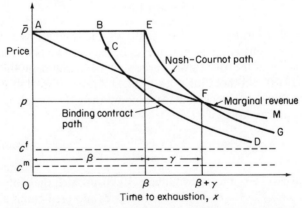

Figure 20.13: Dynamic inconsistency with inelastic demand

equilibrium is dynamically inconsistent. The duration of the competitively constrained monopoly phase, CB, affects the rate of extraction of the fringe, and hence cannot be found by graphical methods, using the limit pricing principle of section 20.5, case (i). Instead, it must be found as in Figure 20.8 by optimally allocating monopoly sales between the two phases.

The arguments advanced in the previous section suggest that the RESE will be better approximated by the NCE in the absence of binding contracts. In Figure 20.13 the NCE is the price path ABEFG. The fringe are initially the sole suppliers along GF, until the marginal revenue cuts the competitive price path at F. Along FE the market is increasingly transferred to the cartel, with the cartel as sole supplier along EBA only when the price has risen to the monopoly level. The location of the NCE is readily found, for if the duration of AE is β years, and of FE is γ years, then at F marginal revenue is equal to price, p^*, say. At a date t years later than F

$$m_t = (p^* - c^m)e^{\delta t} + c^m, \quad \delta = r^m,$$
$$p_t = (p^* - c^f)e^{rt} + c^f, \quad r = r^f,$$

whilst from Equation (20.5.6), the cartel's sales are

$$q_t^m = b(p_t - m_t), \quad 0 \leqslant t \leqslant \gamma. \tag{20.5.7}$$

This can be expressed as a function of time and p^*, but p^* itself must be such that marginal revenue is there equal price, or

$$p^* = (\bar{p} - c^f)e^{-r\gamma} + c^f = (\bar{p} - c^m)e^{-\delta(\gamma + \beta)} + c^m. \tag{20.5.8}$$

Substituting for p^* in Equation (20.5.7) allows us to compute total cartel sales during FE, whose duration is γ years, Q^c:

$$Q^c = b\left[\gamma(c^f - c^m) + (\bar{p} - c^f)\left(\frac{1 - e^{-r\gamma}}{r}\right) - (\bar{p} - c^m)e^{-\delta\beta}\left(\frac{1 - e^{-\delta\gamma}}{\delta}\right)\right].$$

Cartel sales during the backstop phase, whose duration is β years, are thus Q^b:

$$Q^b = b\beta(a - \bar{p}).$$

This gives two equations to determine the two unknown durations, β and γ: Equation (20.5.8) and the exhaustion condition that total cartel stocks Q^m be sold over the two phases:

$$Q^m = Q^b(\beta) + Q^c(\beta, \gamma). \tag{20.5.9}$$

For example, suppose that the parameters take the following values

$a = 100$	$b = 1$	
$\bar{p} = 45$	$c^f = 15$	$c^m = 5$
$r^f = r = 8\%$	$r^m = \delta = 2\%$	
$Q^m = 1000$	$Q^f = 2000.$	

Table 20.2 Comparison of equilibria

	Binding contract	Nash–Cournot
Backstop phase, β years	16.30	17.27
Constrained monopoly phase, γ years	1.80	10.50
Competitive phase, years	26.90	17.56
Time to exhaustion, years	45.00	45.34
Initial price, p_0	18.02	18.18
Present value of monopoly profits at $t = 0$	19,481	19,351
Present value of fringe profits at $t = 0$	6,040	6,357
Present value of total profits	25,520	25,708
Present cost to consumers (at $r^f = 8\%$, $t = 0$)	21,650	21,883

(These cost and price figures are not implausible in US$ 1980, and the elasticity of demand is assumed to rise from 0.25 at $20 to 0.82 at the backstop price of $45. What is, of course, more implausible, is the assumption of a stationary, linear, demand schedule.) Table 20.2 compares the two equilibria. (The calculations were derived from a simple computer program which finds the binding contract equilibrium by a simple search.)

In this example, and for all other chosen parameter values, the backstop phase is longer under the Nash–Cournot equilibrium than in the binding contract equilibrium, as shown in Figure 20.13. In such cases and for the same reasons given for Figure 20.11 the initial price will be higher in the absence of binding contracts, at G, than in their presence, at D. The sole beneficiaries of the contract failure will be the fringe producers. Countries which have domestic producers but are net importers will therefore find it doubly difficult to devise solutions to the contract failure, for the politically powerful domestic producer lobby will have an interest in reducing the credibility of any long-term agreements between the cartel and the importing country. The case of the United States provides an illuminating example of this difficulty.

Parenthetically, for this set of parameter values we can compute various other equilibria. Clearly the fringe benefits from the market power of the cartel, and would benefit even more if it joined the cartel, then increasing its profits to 19,500. However, the cartel would suffer if the fringe joined, with its profits falling to 16,204. Consumers would suffer even more.

It is also interesting that in the present example the cartel is not seriously inconvenienced by the absence of binding contracts, for in some of the calculations reported in Newbery (1980), the cartel lost nearly half its profits, and finished up worse-off than in competitive equilibrium.

20.5.6. Dynamic inconsistency by price shading

The final case is in some ways the most interesting type of dynamic inconsistency, and was discovered by Ulph (1980). Here all producers discount at

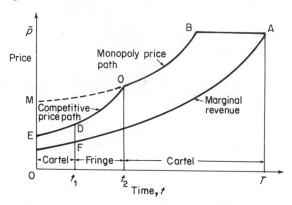

Figure 20.14: Price paths from figure 20.8

the same rate of interest, r, and the cartel enjoys a cost advantage over the fringe, as one would expect. If, however, the cost disadvantage of the fringe is not too great, the monopoly phase will occur later than the competitive phase, as shown in Figure 20.8, and reproduced below in Figure 20.14 with time running in the normal direction.

It was argued above that in Figure 20.8 it would not pay the cartel to confine its sales to the later unconstrained monopoly phase ABC for it could always profitably transfer oil to the start of the competitive phase, at D. Indeed, it is possible that the cartel will wish to sell its entire stock along the competitive price path before the fringe sells, in which case there is no problem of dynamic inconsistency. The conditions for this are given in the Appendix, but are ruled out if the cartel has sufficiently large stocks. Suppose this to be the case, then the binding contract solution balances the advantages of selling oil earlier at the limit competitive price against the disadvantage of selling at a lower than monopoly price. However, consider what happens as time passes, and the early constrained monopoly sales along ED take place, in Figure 20.14. At date t, the price is still above the marginal revenue trajectory, so it is still profitable for the cartel to reallocate oil from later dates, such as C or A, to this early date. The cartel then has an incentive to undercut the fringe continuously, and the binding contract equilibrium is dynamically inconsistent. The Appendix shows that this form of dynamic inconsistency can occur for a wide range of plausible parameter values, and always occurs if demand is inelastic at the backstop price and the fringe's costs exceed the cartel's costs.

The case is particularly interesting as there are three candidates for the rational expectations equilibrium. Given the incentive for the cartel to advance the date of its oil sales continuously, one obvious candidate is for the cartel to sell its entire stock of oil at the start of the competitive phase, along DC in Figure 20.15 with the fringe selling at the end, along CA. This is certainly dynamically consistent, and is indeed the binding contract solution if the cartel has a small stock of oil, as

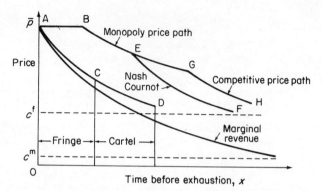

Figure 20.15: Alternative resolutions of dynamic inconsistency

the Appendix shows. If, as assumed, the cartel has large stocks, it will be unattractive as it makes minimal use of the cartel's monopoly power. The second possibility is for the cartel to refrain from any sales at the competitive price, and retain its oil until the price has risen to the unconstrained monopoly level. In Figure 20.15 the fringe exhausts along HG, leaving the cartel to sell along GEBA, the location of the paths being fixed as usual by the stocks of the cartel and the fringe. Again, this solution is dynamically consistent, and it certainly exhibits the market power of the cartel, but it makes too little use of the ability of the cartel to accelerate the sales of the fringe.

The final possibility, which appears to overcome these objections, is the Nash–Cournot equilibrium price path, FEBA in Figure 20.15. Both fringe and cartel sell along FE, whose length is fixed by the condition that the fringe exhaust by E, leaving the cartel free to follow the monopoly price path EBA. Sample computer calculations suggest that of the three paths this is the preferred solution for the cartel.

Once again, the Nash–Cournot equilibrium appears to be the best approximation to the rational expectations Stackelberg equilibrium. One would expect the initial price to be higher than in the binding contract equilibrium as the cartel will shift oil from the now relatively less attractive competitive phase to the later monpoly phase. Again, this harms consumers and benefits the fringe.

20.5.7. Conclusions for modelling the world oil market

This section has shown how to analyse the world oil market on the assumption that OPEC (or some subset of OPEC) acts as a cohesive cartel facing a competitive fringe. All the agents are assumed to have full information about extraction costs, discount rates, demand conditions and remaining reserves, and can calculate the rational expectations equilibrium price and depletion path. In some cases the Stackelberg equilibrium is dynamically consistent, hence it remains in the interests of all parties to follow the initial plan. However, we have argued that in most practically important cases the solution calculated by conventional dynamic programming methods is dynamically inconsistent, and although it describes the best solution for the cartel, it is not credible unless the cartel can bind itself to fulfil the plan. In the absence of binding contracts the cartel will have an incentive to depart from the initial plan at some future date. Anticipating this, the fringe producers are forced to impute an equilibrium which reflects the cartel's market power and options at each successive moment. In one special case it is possible to solve for this equilibrium and in this case the equilibrium is structurally similar to the Nash–Cournot equilibrium. We argued that for this and other reasons the Nash–Cournot equilibrium, which is dynamically consistent, is the best simple approximation to the rational expectations Stackelberg equilibrium. This is necessarily less advantageous to the cartel than the binding contract equilibrium, and in certain cases can be inferior to the (non-credible) competitive equilibrium. However, for plausible parameter values the cartel still enjoys substantial monopoly rents, and the absence of credible contracts benefits the fringe producers whilst harming consumers. The political economic implications of dynamic inconsistency are profound, for producers within importing countries have an incentive to undermine international negotiations. Whilst there is an incentive for both consumers and the cartel to negotiate international supply agreements, there remains the incentive for producers to break their agreements subsequently, causing mistrust and potential conflict.

20.6. PRACTICAL PROBLEMS

The previous two sections argued that dynamic inconsistency was likely to be a pervasive problem in the oil market, providing both the incentive for international co-operation and reasons for mistrust. suspicion and conflict. Given the importance of these issues, one should ask whether there are features of the oil market which would tend to limit the scope for dynamic inconsistency.

20.6.1. Enforcement of international contracts

One method by which an oil exporter might bind himself to honour a supply contract is to deposit assets abroad which become forfeit if the contract is broken. There are several problems with this remedy. If the cartel wishes to delay sales, then it may not have accumulated initial assets to pledge, although it might work for the last type of dynamic inconsistency discussed. There would be a problem of writing a sufficiently flexible contract which adequately covered all contingencies—given the incentive to conceal these. *Force majeure* has been invoked too often recently to be credible. The underlying problem is that exporters and importers wish to make an intertemporal trade, and there are no obvious mechanisms to prevent contract failure.

20.6.2. Supply constraints

In practice oil supply cannot be varied costlessly since it is typically capacity constrained, with additional capacity costly to install. This effectively locks producers into a production pattern with reduced freedom for subsequent change, and allows a certain amount of precommitment. However, the producers with most flexibility are the larger Middle Eastern states who constitute the core of OPEC, and it is these who are required to be able to precommit.

20.6.3. Incomplete rationality

It might be argued that the model assumes an unreasonable measure of sophistication in calculating supply plans. Surely the Sheikhs are neither so subtle nor so single-minded in their quest for profit? But in the model it is the fringe producers who need to be skilled forecasters anticipating future changes in cartel plans. The cartel can pursue its self-interest rather myopically—indeed, it is the fear that they will in the future change their plans that causes our problem. And the fringe producers do use sophisticated forecasting models such as those here.

20.6.4. Uncertainty

A more serious objection is that we have ignored uncertainty [see Chapter 17], which typically tends to blunt fine calculations and favour more robust rules of behaviour. To the extent that this is true, it adds weight to the Nash–Cournot equilibrium concept, which is the best strategy to play if other suppliers choose strategies by relatively insensitive rules of thumb. To that extent the problem of dynamic inconsistency will be overcome, and the only question is at what cost. On this question it is difficult to be dogmatic, though it is clearly very inefficient to be simultaneously extracting from the North Sea, Alaska and the Middle East.

20.6.5. Cohesiveness of OPEC

Finally, one might reasonably ask how plausible it is to model OPEC (or some subset of OPEC) as a cohesive cartel. On this it is difficult to be dogmatic, except to note that the events of 1979 suggests that even a relatively small producer like Iran can exercise considerable influence on the price. Together, Saudi Arabia, Kuwait, UAE and Qatar clearly do have substantial market power, and might reasonably be expected to develop behavioural rules which ensured implicit cartel collusion. Other alternatives such as oligopoly are also possible, though it is worth noting that the Nash–Cournot equilibrium is fairly robust to such a change in market power—the level of prices might change, but the form of the solution remains the same. See, for example, Salant *et al.* (1979).

20.7. CONCLUSIONS

This chapter has set out the standard theory of exhaustible resources and demonstrates how to solve for market equilibrium using dynamic optimization techniques such as the Maximum Principle. If costs are constant and demand is static, then many of the problems can be solved graphically and algebraically, thus avoiding the 'curse of dimensionality' of standard dynamic optimization techniques. These simpler techniques allow intuition more scope and are thus less prone to error.

The main difference between the treatment of exhaustible resources advanced here, and other standard treatments available (e.g. Dasgupta and Heal, 1979) is that we have concentrated on oil, as the main example to which the theory applies, and hence recognized the importance of market power, and hence, the potential dynamic inconsistency of the standard solutions. This chapter has therefore stressed the distinction between the binding contract equilibrium, or open-loop solution, and the rational expectations equilibrium, or feedback solution. In imperfectly competitive markets, the two solutions will in general differ. If, in addition, long-term contracts cannot be enforced, then the binding contract equilibrium is an inappropriate solution and may be dramatically different from the correct equilibrium. Again, the strength of the graphical solution techniques advocated here is that they are easy to inspect for dynamic inconsistency.

20.8. APPENDIX: SEQUENCING OF MONOPOLY AND COMPETITIVE PHASES

In Figure 20.5 (and in Figure 20.7) the competitive price path was less steep than the monopoly price path at their point of intersection, implying that the competitive phase would come later, whilst in Figure 20.6 the converse was true. If discount rates are the same, and fringe costs are above monopoly costs, the order of the phases is entirely determined by the relative slopes of the two paths at the point of intersection, p^*, provided that the elasticity of demand is constant or increases with price. If the elasticity varies non-monotonically with price it is possible that there could be several alterations between the dominant supplier and the fringe. We ignore this complication. The competitive phase comes later if

$$\frac{\mathrm{d}}{\mathrm{d}t}[c^f + (p^* - c^f)e^{rt}]_{t=0} < \frac{\mathrm{d}}{\mathrm{d}t}p^m(p^*). \qquad (20.A.1)$$

If demand is linear, given by Equation (20.2.11), the monopoly price is given by Equation (20.2.16):

$$p^m = \tfrac{1}{2}[\bar{p} + c^m + (m^* - c^m)e^{rt}], \quad m^* = 2p^* - \bar{p}$$

So (20.A.1) is satisfied if

$$(p^* - c^f) < p^* - \tfrac{1}{2}(\bar{p} + c^m) \qquad (20.A.2)$$

or

$$c^f > \tfrac{1}{2}(\bar{p} + c^m).\tag{20.A.2}$$

If demand has constant elasticity, ε, then (20.A.1) is satisfied if

$$c^f > \frac{\varepsilon c^m}{\varepsilon - 1}.\tag{20.A.3}$$

In both cases the static marginal revenue pricing condition is satisfied.

If the competitive phase comes earlier, the condition for the cartel to hold back oil to sell at the later monopoly price is readily found. Let V be the present discounted value of cartel oil if it is sold only during the competitive phase, and let p^* again be the transition price. Let T be the total time to exhaustion, and M the duration of cartel sales, then [see I, §15.1.1]

$$V = e^{-rM} \int_0^M q(p_x)(p_x - c^m)e^{rx}\,dx,\tag{20.A.4}$$
$$p_x = (p^* - c^f)e^{-rx} + c^f.$$

A unit of oil transferred from the start of the cartel's sales to sell at the monopoly price when that is the backstop price $\bar{p}$ raises total profit by

$$(\bar{p} - c^m)e^{-rT} - \frac{dV}{dM}\frac{dM}{dQ},$$

where Q is total cartel stock, and $dQ/dM = q_0$, the initial rate of sales. Profit is raised and hence retaining oil for later sale is profitable if

$$\frac{rV}{q_0} > (p_0 - c^m) - e^{-rT}(\bar{p} - c^m),\tag{20.A.5}$$

where the right-hand side of Equation (20.A.5) is the initial difference between the competitive price and the marginal revenue trajectory. Since V is increasing in cartel stock, provided the cartel has large enough stocks, delay is profitable.

20.9. REFERENCES

Bellman, R. (1957). *Dynamic Programming*. Princeton University Press, Princeton, N.J.
Buiter, W. H. (1980). The macroeconomics of Dr. Pangloss: a critical survey of the new classical macroeconomics. *Economic Journal*, **90** (1), 34–50.
Calvo, G. A. (1978). On the time inconsistency of optimal policy in a monetary economy. *Econometrica*, November, **46** (6), 411–28.
Dasgupta, P. and Heal, G. M. (1979). *Economic Theory and Exhaustible Resources*. Cambridge University Press, Cambridge.
Gilbert, R. J. (1978). Dominant firm pricing in a market for an exhaustible resource. *Bell Journal of Economics*, **9** (2), 385–395.
Heal, G. (1976). The relationship between price and extraction cost for a resource with a backstop technology. *Bell Journal of Economics*, **7** (2), 371–378.

Hotelling, H. (1931). The economics of exhaustible resources. *Journal of Political Economy*, **39**, 137–175.

Kydland, F. E. and Prescott, E. C. (1977). Rules rather than discretion: the inconsistency of optimal plans. *Journal of Political Economy*, **85** (3), 473–491.

Maskin, E. and Newbery, D. M. G. (1978). Rational expectations with market power— the paradox of the disadvantageous tariff on oil. *Warwick Economic Research Paper*, No. 129.

Newbery, D. M. G. (1980). Credible oil supply contracts. Mimeo, Cambridge.

Newbery, D. M. G. (1981). Oil prices, cartels, and the problems of dynamic inconsistency. *Economic Journal*, **91**, 617–646.

Nordhaus, W. D. (1973). The allocation of energy resources. *Brookings Papers in Economic Activity*, 3.

Pindyck, R. S. (1978). Gains to producers from cartelization of exhaustible resources. *Review of Economics and Statistics*, **60**, 238–251.

Salant, *et al.* (1979). Imperfect competition in the international energy market: A computerised Nash–Cournot model, ICF, Inc.

Solow, R. M. (1974). The economics of resources or the resources of economics. *American Economic Review*, **64** (2), (May), 1–14.

Solow, R. M. and Wan, F. Y. (1976). Extraction costs in the theory of exhaustible resources. *Bell Journal of Economics*, **7** (2), 359–370.

Strotz R. H. (1955). Myopia and inconsistency in dynamic utility maximisation. *Review of Economic Studies*, **33**, 165–180.

Sweeney, J. L. (1977). Economics of depletable resources: market forces and intertemporal bias. *Review of Economic Studies*, **44**, 125–142.

Ulph, A. (1980). Modelling partially cartelised markets for exhaustible resources. Mimeo, Southampton.

Ulph, A. and Folie, G. M. (1980). Dominant firm models of resource depletion. Paper presented to A.U.T.E. Conference, Durham.

von Stackelberg, H. (1952). *The Theory of the Market Economy*. Oxford University Press, London.

Index